ADVISORY EDITOR IN HISTORY

George E. Mowry

UNIVERSITY OF CALIFORNIA, LOS ANGELES

THE

Colonial Experience

READINGS IN EARLY AMERICAN HISTORY

EDITED AND WITH AN INTRODUCTION BY

H. Trevor Colbourn

INDIANA UNIVERSITY

HOUGHTON MIFFLIN COMPANY

Boston

FOR CHARLES AND LOUISE

Printed in the U.S.A.

PREFACE

For all the proliferation of readings books in American history during recent years surprisingly few such collections have been devoted solely to the colonial period. This paucity of interesting and convenient sources of collateral reading is all the more perplexing in view of the healthy condition of American colonial studies today. It is almost twenty years since Carl Bridenbaugh uttered his complaint that almost no one was studying colonial history.[1] He would not now repeat this charge. The past two decades have witnessed a near-revolution in colonial scholarship, a transformation to which Professor Bridenbaugh himself has contributed powerfully.

This reinvigoration of scholarship has been happily reflected in the curricula of American colleges and universities. Where courses in colonial history once were rare they are now commonplace, and appear to be attracting more than their share of the burgeoning student enrollments. The new scholarship is moving from the study to the classroom: the colonists' absorption with their past is now becoming better understood by their twentieth-century beneficiaries.

This volume is something like a sampler for the study of early American history. It incorporates primary and secondary materials from which both instructor and student can draw at will for illumination, and, it is hoped, stimulation. The emphasis is on new writing, rather than the more familiar classics of historical literature; primary materials are included, less for their own sake than for their contribution to the particular subject under consideration.[2] If there is an emphasis upon secondary materials, there is also a preference for selections of meaningful length; this, inevitably, at the cost of a more complete coverage of the colonial field that would otherwise have been possible.

The organization of this book, like the selections it presents, is necessarily arbitrary. It is *not* meant to dictate the form of a course in colonial history. There are ten sections, each one focusing upon an important facet of the colonial period of American history, each amplifying a vital chapter in the colonial experience, each reflecting the convictions of this particular editor. There are, it seems to me, certain verities: colonial America was the product of a protracted imperial rivalry, the product of English energy and success, the product of religious (and intellectual) friction. Colonial society in turn reflected these origins and circumstances as it adapted itself to American conditions. Particularism was a theme upon which the colonists played many variations throughout their history: the reasons for their departure from the mother country often inform on their later behavior. When Americans declared their independence they did so, paradoxically, as Englishmen who demanded their rights as Englishmen — and yet shied away from the degree of union their plight seemed to require. In short the plan of this book is thematic and topical rather than chronological, although the sequence of colonial development is properly respected.

[1] Carl Bridenbaugh, "The Neglected First Half of American History," *American Historical Review*, LII (1947–48), 506–517.

[2] Readers seeking a compilation of documents should look to Merrill Jensen's excellent *American Colonial Documents to 1776* (New York, 1955), or volume one of Henry Steele Commager's *Documents of American History* (seventh edition, New York, 1963).

Any historian, compiling a volume of this kind, is likely to indulge some of his own scholarly proclivities. For example, the eighteenth century emerges in more detail than the seventeenth. But the eighteenth century saw the cultural and political flowering of the American colonies; and the period following the War for the Empire justly receives close attention in the classroom. The sixteenth and seventeenth centuries have hardly been ignored, but neither have they attracted the attention of contemporary scholars as has the Era of the American Revolution.[3]

The principal criteria for choosing the selections which follow have been their readability and their relevance to their subjects. The quest has been for information and ideas. The introductory essays are deliberately abbreviated, partly to afford the maximum space for the readings which follow and partly to reduce the amount of overlapping with material furnished by the textbooks this volume is designed to supplement. For similar reasons the suggestions for additional reading have been kept short. In some instances, footnotes have been deleted — again in the interest of conserving space.

Finally, I wish to thank those colleagues who, asked and unasked, have been so generous with their advice and counsel. I am particularly grateful for the suggestions afforded me by Professors Winthrop Jordan, of the University of California, Berkeley, Hugh Rankin, Tulane University, Mack Thompson, University of California, and my former colleague, Rena Vassar, now at San Fernando State College.

H.T.C.

[3] One of the more notable efforts to illuminate seventeenth-century colonial history is *Seventeenth-Century America,* ed. James Morton Smith (Chapel Hill, 1959).

CONTENTS

PART ONE

England and Her Rivals

"Before the establishment of the American states," Thomas Jefferson once reminded John Adams, "nothing was known to History but the Man of the Old World." The European explorers did indeed confront a "tabula rasa," a virgin and uncharted continent, when they first ventured into the New World. Their experiences there can best be understood, however, in terms of the conflicts and achievements of European civilization. To understand fully the American colonial experience, one must first consider the factors which permitted colonization and the motives which stimulated it. The decline of feudalism, the accelerating growth of commercial capitalism (influenced by the Crusades which had stimulated the Western demand for Eastern goods), the role of the Renaissance and the new scientific aids to navigation, the rise of the nation-state, and the religious climate that led to the Protestant Reformation — all were factors in promoting the expansion of the Old World into the New.

England's eventual supremacy in North America was far from predictable in the sixteenth century. Spain, united by the marriage of Isabella of Castile to Ferdinand of Aragon, took an early lead in exploration, conquest and colonization. At the time of Columbus' death in 1504, Spain's achievements were still modest, but the knowledge she had gained through early explorations was successfully exploited in the succeeding half-century. The resultant empire was highly centralized, its trade tightly controlled, and the Roman Catholic faith vigorously propagated. Spanish power was centered in South and Central America. With the exception of settlements established in Florida and exploratory expeditions sent into the southern and southwestern regions of the present United States, the Spaniards demonstrated little interest in North America. Bullion — gold and silver — had been found in abundance in Mexico and Peru, and it was to these areas that Spain directed her energies.

While the first century of American colonization was dominated by Spain, there were also signs of English and French interest and activity in the New World. Both nations embarked on empire hesitatingly, and moved only slowly into the vacuum created by Spanish disinterest in the North. In both England and France domestic distractions caused delay and ultimately affected the character of later and more serious colonization endeavor. But definite patterns had emerged by the end of the sixteenth century. The limitations of the Spanish empire had been defined; Spain's new-found wealth had excited envy among the other European nations; the opportunities for expansion into North America had been recognized by France and England; religious quarrels were creating dissension and Dissenters in France and England that would affect the colonial movement; and particularly notable, England's economic growth had proceeded apace during the reign of Elizabeth I.

1

England and Colonial Enterprise

The New Wealth: Economic Advance

Why did England, a small island nation, emerge as the victorious colonizer of North America? How was England able to challenge and surpass the authority and power of Spain in the New World? The answer lies partly in England's economic strength and partly in the religious and political unity which permitted England to concentrate her attention upon other matters. The first of the Tudors, Henry VII, had devoted his energies to repairing the ravages of the War of the Roses and to tightening his hold on the English throne; Henry VIII continued his father's work so effectively that neither the uncertainties of Edward VI's reign (1547–1554), nor the religious obsessions of Queen Mary (1553–1558), could reverse England's progress. By the accession of Anne Boleyn's daughter in 1558, the base of England's prosperity had been laid.

Dr. A. L. Rowse, *a Cornishman and an Englishman in that order (and also a Fellow of All Souls College, Oxford), writes with authority on the economic origins of England's first empire. In a highly personal style — he cannot resist comparing the age of Elizabeth I with that of Elizabeth II — he communicates to the reader his own sense of excitement over England's awareness of her economic and national purpose in the late sixteenth century. Citing the accumulation of capital, so necessary to the colonization effort, and the growth of industry in a society unusually free from crippling feudal restrictions, Dr. Rowse concludes that these "dynamic forces" made possible the English adventure in empire.*

Reprinted with permission of The Macmillan Co. from *The England of Elizabeth* by A. L. Rowse. Copyright 1950 by The Macmillan Co. And with permission of The Macmillan Company of Canada, Limited.

During the sixteenth century the medieval world was unfixed from its foundations and lost the security of its ancient limitations. It underwent a revolution more far-reaching, a series of experiences more disturbing, than those of which we are so conscious in our time. In this particular sense, among others: it initiated that expansion of Europe which made the modern world as we know it. The discovery of a new and unsuspected continent in America was only one part, though the most spectacular, in the process of expansion. In that process the lead was taken — mainly by reason of geographical position, partly accidentally — by Portugal and Spain. For them, especially for Castile, it was a golden age of miraculous achievement: "Within three generations Spaniards discovered, subdued and colonised the most extensive territorial empire the world has ever seen."[1]

> Este mar que de Atlante se apellida,
> en immensas llanuras extendido,
> que a la tierra amenaza embravecido,
> y ella tiembla a sus olas impelida . . .[2]

Part of this profound process, with its pulls hidden and overt, that was changing the world as the medievals knew it, was the shift of gravity from the Mediterranean to the Atlantic, westward to Spain, and ultimately northwest to the English Channel. All this is more important than the Reformation, profound as the effect of that was: indeed it may profitably be viewed as part of the larger process, the pull of the northern peoples away from the apron-strings of their ancient mother, Rome. It is the shift of gravity north-west that interests us. Its full

[1] C. H. Haring, *The Spanish Empire in America*, p. 4.

[2] Francisco de Rioja, in *Poetas de los siglos XVI y XVII*, p. 337.

development takes up long beyond our present period and occupies the centuries that follow, until with the eighteenth and nineteenth the island power emerges as the leading power in the modern world. That nineteenth-century perspective has made it difficult for us to appreciate the full greatness of the Spanish achievement. (Our Elizabethan ancestors made no such mistake, for they were up against it.) For, indeed, the Spanish achievement in the outer world has its lasting character, and there remains an interesting dichotomy between it and the English: the two great systems of colonisation and empire overseas.

We have to see the Elizabethan effort against this background. It was a couple of generations later that the impulse which had excited Castile reached the English and touched them to fire and fever:

> Avid of life, with dream and fever of mind
> possessed.

The Elizabethans awoke to the new world to find the Spaniards and Portuguese already entrenched in it. All the more striking that they caught up with them, in a rush of energy and enterprise. It is rewarding to investigate how the shift of power came to rest with England, when Spain had had such a lead; how the lasting advantages of the new economic trends, in trade and treasure, came to this country, leaving Spain, their initiator, impoverished and discouraged. The contrast between the economies of the two countries, the policies followed in one and the other and their subsequent fortunes, is exceedingly instructive. By the end of the Elizabethan Age people were already reflecting on it.

The most striking of these new economic forces, by its very newness, was the rise in prices throughout Western Europe consequent upon the immense import of treasure from the American mines into Spain from the middle of the century. The amounts went on increasing with each decade until 1600, when they reached their apogee — Spanish power was already showing symptoms of over-strain. The stream of silver pouring into Europe had consequences unsettling, stimulating, uncontrollable: upsetting old ties and established relationships of value, stimulating new enterprise, reinforcing pressures creative of a new order. The rise in prices differed from one country to another; there was a different time-sequence. In Andalusia prices increased five-fold during the century; in France two and a half times; in England the threefold rise did not culminate until 1650. That gives us an under-swell of a slower, more gradual duration, a long wave of profit inflation and capital accumulation which bore up the expansive achievements of the age in every sphere. "Never in the annals of the modern world has there existed so prolonged and so rich an opportunity for the business man, the speculator and the profiteer." So thought Lord Keynes: one may wonder whether the nineteenth century was not as good a time for them. Some people have thought that the earlier period saw the birth of modern capitalism. Lord Keynes lent the authority of his name to this fancy; but capitalism goes much further back into the Middle Ages. Still the rise in prices greatly strengthened the forces transforming the old economic order.

It is a mistake to over-estimate the purely monetary factor — or any one other for that matter. Historic movements of this kind are so complex that one despairs of capturing the subtleties of life and rendering them on paper. We can only do our best to suggest them. Equally important, even on the economic plane, was the aggressive nationalism of the time — of which no people had a larger share than the English — which drove men to break into preserves of trade hitherto monopolised by others, to open up new routes and markets in the outer world. There was the drive — consistently encouraged by government and carried out by a new class of entrepreneurs, nowhere more effectively than in this country — to open up and exploit its own natural resources. There were the striking improvements in industrial and financial technique; the increased mobility of labour, particularly in the iron, coal and glass industries, special fields for the new capitalist; the growth of investment in new enterprises, the opening up of markets in America, Asia, Africa. In all these things England, at length, caught up and went ahead. This may be concretely brought home in the contrast between this country and Spain, which may be taken as an illustration of the argument. We went in for the real things of substance: building up the nation's resources, not consuming them profitlessly; accumulating capital; a healthy balance of trade. The facts of economic life are more important than their monetary symbols.

One effect of the rise in prices was that wages lagged behind. We must not exaggerate the effect of this either, for those who lived mainly by wages, though a growing element with the growth of capitalism, were a minority of the nation. In so far as they were producers, as the bulk of them were, they share to some extent in the increasing prosperity. But not proportionately: the greater proportion of the surpluses made went into the pockets of the richer classes. The Elizabethan Age was a period of increasing class disparity, of subtler class differentiation, of more marked contrasts and greater ostentation. Some people with a contemporary prejudice may regard this as a defect. We may reflect that upon this rested the many achievements of the age — the voyages, the colonial experiments, the building, the arts, the conspicuous consumption of the time which has left us such permanent memorials as against the evanescent ephemera of our own; the interesting extravagance upon luxuries that have lasted, jewels, stuffs, fabrics, music; the demand for books, literature, the drama: those unforgettable responses to the demand for a richer, more varied life of the mind. It is open to us to prefer the consumption of what the society produces on one dead level, a shared and equalised mediocrity, offering no excitements, no inducements, no interest even — dreary tenements in place of Elizabethan palaces, the ability of all to go to the cinema instead of an elect society that made the music and drama of that age. Though this may have its easy satisfactions for the mass of a population of fifty millions it offers no hope of the glittering achievements of their population of five.

The increased rate of accumulation of capital came not so much from this source as from the growth of wealth out of returns from land and commerce. Improved methods of farming, we saw, produced larger yields. The Dissolution gave an invaluable incentive to more efficient cultivation all over the country: men will do for and with their own property what they will not do for others. Then, too, there was a notable influx of investment from abroad. There was the capital that useful religious refugees from Flanders and France brought with them, not only fixed capital and money, but their industrial skill. Italians, like Spinola and Palavicino, invested in English enterprises; the Augsburg mining firm of Haug put money into starting the copper mines and mineral works of Cumberland — not all of which they saw back. There was the part played by the bullion brought into the country in the course of the duel with Spain by the capture of rich prizes and exploits of which the most resounding example was Drake's raid upon the treasure-route off the coast of Peru. Much of that money went to support Elizabeth's policy in the Netherlands. A small portion of it was enough to float the Levant Company. Members of the Levant Company in turn fostered the East India Company, from which grew an Empire. It is an interesting concatentation. Even so, it was not so much the absolute value of the bullion brought in that mattered as the indirect effect upon profit and enterprise, the increment of the country's wealth in buildings, equipment, improvements. Individuals gained and lost; but they had every incentive to be up and doing; they were not left without the incentive to achieve anything. Drake made a fortune; the family he established lasted right up to our own less fortunate time. Raleigh spent £40,000 on his voyages of discovery and gained nothing from them. Humphrey Gilbert ruined himself, spent his own patrimony and his wife's in pursuit of his mirage. The Earl of Cumberland, a man of vast estates, pledged himself heavily over his privateering enterprises: sometimes he caught a prize, more often he saw no return on his outlay. No doubt he enjoyed himself. The adoption of the joint-stock technique enabled the unavoidable losses in establishing new enterprises to be borne.

This method of collecting and regulating capital — more important in itself than the new mechanical inventions — enabled the necessary outlay to be more for industrial development at home and opening up trades abroad. Economic life under the early Tudors proceeded on a simple medieval basis; shortage of capital was its chronic limiting factor. Elizabeth's reign saw an expansion of credit and an extension of credit facilities along with the growth of capital. The popular outcry against usurers was constant — and sometimes justified. *The Merchant of*

Venice was written, as usual with that author, on a theme that much appealed to its audience. The disputes about the rate of interest played the part in that age which disputes about wages play in ours: interest or "usury" was a more acute matter for a community with a need for more capital for its growing concerns and in which wages were a secondary consideration. Lenders came in for much mud-slinging, though they performed an invaluable function, in the absence of banks, in enabling trade to extend its basis. Proposals were made for establishing a bank; but Elizabethan England got no further forward than to throw up a number of interesting financiers, speculators and entrepreneurs: such men as Sir Thomas Gresham, Sir Horatio Palavicino, Thomas Sutton, Customer Smythe and his son Sir Thomas. Among these the Countess of Shrewsbury, Bess of Hardwick, makes an unexpected figure with her four great coffers of money and evidences in her bedchamber at Hardwick. The rustic mind of the parson of Radwinter, inured to hard and simple pleasures, noted about the middle of the reign "the great store and plenty of treasure which is walking in these parts of the world, far more in these our days than ever our forefathers have seen in times past." We may observe the more forceful fixation of Drake's mind on treasure: he told his faltering men at Nombre de Dios in 1572 that he had "brought them to the mouth of the Treasure house of the World."

The industrial development of the country was equally remarkable — and has only recently come to be appreciated. Professor Nef, who has made it his subject, thinks that it amounted to a sort of 'Industrial Revolution.'[3] He thinks that England achieved the position of leadership in industrial technology and heavy industry she held till the late nineteenth century largely during the century between the Dissolution and the Civil War; that Elizabeth's reign saw a shift in the centre of progress in both science and technology from the Continent here, where more fresh industries were started and more new kinds of machinery and furnaces were developed than in any other country. The Renaissance impulse signalised itself in a host of new inventions: the printing press, the blast furnace, furnaces for separating silver from copper ore, for using coal in glass-making, steel and brick-making, for drying malt in brewing; boring rods for exploring underground strata, horse and water driven engines for draining mines — an immense field of development here as new mines were opened up and old workings deepened; the stocking knitting frame, the Dutch loom for knitting small wares, besides more specialised scientific devices and inventions.

Here there was a time-lag: naturally the impulse took longer to reach the island. But when it eventually arrived it found a peculiarly propitious soil. The discoveries, the experiences of a century were for the English crowded into those last decades of Elizabeth's reign. What must it have been like to have been alive then, sentient and intelligent? — alas, the mirage the historian pursues! One is tempted to say that England was the New Country were it not liable to be misinterpreted, for indeed she was even then an old one with a long and hardy history behind her. But she was a new field for investment, of the most rapid development and of the greatest promise for the future in Europe. She had some great advantages favouring her, which all the writers of the time cried up and made the nation conscious of. The island had an abundance of natural products, corn, wood, coal, timber, iron. Here was the basis of industry. In the woollen industry it had a long-standing tradition of manufacturing skill and commercial experience. The traditional skill of the many hundreds of smiths and nailers, scythe-makers and cutlers of the Black Country and Sheffield formed the basis for the later expansion of industry in those areas. The makings were already there. What was necessary was that the wind of the spirit of creative enterprise should blow upon them.

The circumstances of English society were propitious: a social flexibility that was always greater here than anywhere else, save possibly the Netherlands — our nearest likeness. Then, too, there was the natural energy, inventiveness, enterprise of the people, that was elicited, encouraged and rewarded by the arrangements of society and the policies of government, not discouraged, thwarted and stifled by over-regulation. One of the clues to the early industrial

[3] J. U. Nef, "War and Economic Progress, 1540–1640," *Econ. Hist. Rev.*, 1942.

success of this country is that there was far less regulation here than abroad; the rivers and internal communications were free of the crippling tolls that cramped navigation on the Rhine and the Loire. Still freer was the sea — and much of English traffic was coastwise. The country presented in short a large free-trade area, where abroad innumerable tolls interfered with domestic trade. This already suggests — a factor that we must allow for — the good sense of the English, who kept their internal jars and broils at a minimum. The American Professor says, perhaps too kindly, of us: "In a variety of ways the industrial losses of the warring countries were peaceful England's gains."[4] Too kindly, for it was our insularity, then as now, that gave us our comparative immunity from invasion. We took advantage of it; we made the most of it — as long as Elizabeth lived, and until Stuart incompetence brought down the Civil War upon us. By then the new forces were so strong that it did not do much harm. But when one thinks of what the Netherlands — the most highly industrialised area in Europe — lost by the religious wars, the ruin of Antwerp, the commercial and financial capital of Northern Europe, the destruction of her trade and the gain to London — one realises something of what we owed to insularity and good sense. Whole areas of the Continent were overrun, and so much of its energy taken up, by wars, while there were no battles on English soil till the Civil War. One remembers how proud of it the Queen was, and how she wept to the French Ambassador at the record being even slightly soiled by the flurry of the Northern Earls in 1569. (No doubt her tears were political or even financial, for she counted the cost; on the other hand, they may equally well have been genuine.) We must lastly take into account the fortunate geographical situation of the country in relation to the outer world and for the strategy of commerce: a country, naturally rich and skilled, athwart the main ocean-routes at the entry to Northern Europe.

German scholars, particularly the gross Sombart, have attached the greatest importance in the development of the new industrial capitalism to the factor of war. So like a German! In fact we do not find this to be so in the Elizabethan experience. Peace was more propitious for the development of large-scale industry. The striking increase in coal output taking place was due to the shortage of timber and charcoal, and the profitability of mining, not to war. In the early years of the reign London got its refined sugar from Antwerp. After it was sacked, the sugar refining was moved to London. Several large refineries were built, haberdashers, grocers, merchant tailors, ironmongers combined with Dutch refiners to invest in the new industry here. Richard Carmarden, "perhaps the best informed and most reliable of Queen Elizabeth's customs officials," wrote with some satisfaction: "Now the English can supply Germany and the Low Countries better cheap than they can supply us." The right spirit: a clear economic gain. Such were the rewards of political security and good sense. The textile industry of the Spanish Netherlands was permanently hit by war. By the end of the century the output of copper and metals in Central Europe, the production of iron in Burgundy, had declined. Only in England (and perhaps Sweden) was the production of iron, copper, brass increasing rapidly. The foundries of Sussex and Kent were able to supply guns to the Continent. The manufacture of woollens and cottons in Lancashire spread on such a scale that the changes brought about were scarcely less important than those of the Industrial Revolution of the late eighteenth century. The coal trade from Newcastle to London saw an astonishing growth: coal shipments from the North multiplied tenfold between 1545 and 1625. In the same period the tonnage of the Navy doubled, while the number of the country's merchantmen, perhaps the tonnage also, increased fivefold. Peace, at any rate internal peace, stimulated the growth of the population, which was more marked in England than anywhere. And nowhere more than in London, which grew from some 60,000 at the time of the Reformation to over 300,000 before the Civil War. By then it had succeeded to something of Antwerp's position as the commercial capital of Northern Europe.

From about the middle of the century, after the English had worked out their characteristic compromise in settlement of the Reformation conflict, the new industries began to be introduced from abroad or set on foot. The discovery

[4] *Ibid.*, p. 25.

of calamine, the ore of zinc, with the first effective mining of copper made brass-making possible and battery works were set up in London and elsewhere. By the end of the reign the soap-building industry of the capital, which was carried on in factories, supplied most of the kingdom. The new salt-making industry was mainly concentrated on the Tyne and the Wear, the older brine-pans of Cheshire and Staffordshire were extended. The first papermill was set up at Dartford by a German immigrant: its operation was characteristically described in a long poem by Thomas Churchyard. Steel works were set on foot, with German workmen, in Sussex; the glass manufacture was started there by Huguenot immigrants, later it was carried to the Black Country. The wire works of Tintern were employing a hundred "hands" by 1581. There was a constant search to solve the problem of smelting ores with coal: its solution takes us long beyond our period, but the preliminary steps were taken in it. Before 1612 coal had been successfully substituted for charcoal in making glass: an English invention which was introduced on the Continent. Largest and most important of all industries, the woollen manufacture was expanding rapidly: the increase of the population gave it greater markets, above all in London, and a stronger basis still for its exports.

Professor Nef tells us that not till the later eighteenth century was the rate of expansion as fast again as it had been during Shakespeare's lifetime. "The rise of industrialism in Great Britain can be more properly regarded as a long process stretching back to the middle of the sixteenth century . . . than as a sudden phenomenon associated with the 18th and early 19th centuries."[5] The expansion was more continuous than in any other country: that gave it its naturalness and strength. We must, however, remember its small scale, its localisation: the land was vastly more important than any other interest, indeed than all the others together. We can hardly expect to get the right perspective from Camden, who was old-fashioned and antiquarian-minded, fired even more by Roman Britain than Elizabethan England. If we judged by him, industry occupied a small space on the map. But even though the larger space it was beginning to occupy was small enough in relation to the roomy countryside of those days, it was the cloud no larger than a man's hand that portended a tremendous future. Here were the dynamic forces that were to transform the whole.

[5] Cf. J. U. Nef, "The Progress of Technology and the Growth of Large-Scale Industry in Great Britain, 1540–1640," *Econ. Hist. Rev.*, 1934, p. 22.

2

The Inactive Colonizers

Elizabethan Politics and Colonial Enterprise

Although England was equipped economically for adventure abroad, for political reasons she was slow to exploit her advantages. The Age of Elizabeth was a remarkably peaceful one — considering the intrigues and rivalries which existed in all the courts of Europe — and the Queen had no desire to precipitate her as yet not fully united nation into open warfare. Well aware of the political tightrope upon which she walked, she avoided conflict whenever possible and husbanded her resources with a miserly skill reminiscent of her grandfather, Henry VII.

Dr. Louis B. Wright, *the distinguished and prolific historian who is Director of the Folger Library in Washington, D.C., argues that England's hesitation to undertake colonial ventures stemmed mainly from the political climate of Elizabeth I's reign. He contends that England's resources and leadership were yet limited, that there were major handicaps restraining England's ambition for empire which were not overcome*

Louis B. Wright, "Elizabethan Politics and Colonial Enterprise," from *The North Carolina Historical Review*, XXXII (1955), 254–269.

until after Elizabeth's death in 1603. Certainly among such handicaps were the conflicting political purposes of Elizabeth's counsellors.

England was late in claiming a place in the sun of the New World. Indeed, she almost lost her opportunity. For nearly a century before England gained a foothold, Spain had been creating a vast empire that stretched from Tierra del Fuego to Texas and beyond. She was comfortably settled in Florida and was reaching north, with an outpost on the coast of Georgia. Her explorers had ventured into Chesapeake Bay and other inlets of the North Atlantic seaboard. Her fishermen, along with those of France, had long frequented the cod fisheries around Newfoundland and Labrador. It seemed only a question of time before Spain would envelop most of the New World. However, Jacques Cartier, it must not be forgotten, had explored the St. Lawrence in 1536 and claimed it for the King of France, but France had been as slow as England in proving her claim.

A faint hint of eventual opposition to Spain lay in the almost forgotten voyage of John Cabot, a Genoese, naturalized in Venice. He had entered the employ of the first Tudor king, Henry VII, and in 1497 had explored the northern coasts of America, probably the shores of Newfoundland and Nova Scotia, and had reported to his royal master that he had claimed the country in his name. Upon the slender claims of Cabot's discovery, England later based her right to territory in the North Atlantic. Why had England, for nearly a century, done so little to assert these claims and to take such a rich possession? To us who have been steeped in the intricacies of geopolitics and the belief in the necessity of access to essential natural resources, it seems incredible that a nation as shrewd — and acquisitive — as the English would have been so negligent of its opportunities.

The answer lies of course in the tangled skein of Tudor politics and England's slow realization of her place in the international scene. We may see a similar parallel in the United States' own groping toward political maturity, and her slowness to grasp the implications of international power and responsibility. For a long time England's destinies were controlled by doctrines that our own isolationists would understand and approve. But there were many complicating factors.

The first was the instability of the Tudor throne. Looking backward from our point of vantage in time, we remember the long reign of the first Elizabeth and think that few monarchs could have felt more secure in the affections of their countrymen. But we forget that Henry VII had a very shaky title to the crown which he snatched from Richard III, and that Henry VIII in his efforts to establish a male line of succession, stirred up a hornet's nest at home and abroad, alienated Spain and Mother Church, sowed the seeds of rebellion, and left only a sickly minor son and two uncertain daughters, whose partisans were ready time after time to plunge the country into civil war. Edward VI's brief reign saw a Protestant regime, followed by Mary Tudor's reversal of the state religion and marriage with Philip II of Spain, chief protagonist of Catholic power in Europe. Mary in turn was followed by Elizabeth in 1558, who cast her lot with the new religion, though it is doubtful whether she had much enthusiasm for religion of any kind. But as the daughter of Anne Boleyn she was regarded by the Catholic Church as illegitimate and therefore without claim to the throne. Her religious position was forced upon her.

On her accession, Elizabeth was faced with the internal rebellion of powerful Catholic subjects like the Howards in the North and with the threat of invasion from the Continent if she offended her late half brother-in-law, Philip II. Few young girls have had more problems to perplex them. But few girls possessed such natural cunning and shrewdness, and few have ever had so wise and adroit a counsellor as William Cecil, later Lord Burghley, whom she inherited from her sister Mary. For most of her reign — until his death in 1598 — Elizabeth kept Burghley by her side. She was often angry with him, frequently deceived him, and was not above engaging in political intrigues behind his back, but she never felt comfortable when she went against Cecil's advice, and she always stood a bit in awe of him. No other man ever succeeded in awing Elizabeth. And yet Elizabeth never let Cecil become dictator over her mind. She kept other politicians in her service and she played them against each other on the constantly shifting chess board of national policy. As Lord Treasurer, Burghley occupied a paramount position.

Her other great statesman and counsellor was Francis Walsingham, about ten years younger than Burghley, whose appointment as ambassador to France, Burghley procured in 1570. Less than a year after the Massacre of St. Bartholomew's Day, August 24, 1572, Walsingham returned to become Principal Secretary of the Queen. The slaughter of the Huguenots had helped to confirm an ardent Protestantism which influenced his political point of view until his dying day in 1590. Though Walsingham and Burghley began as friends, they soon found themselves on opposite sides of the political fence, particularly in matters of foreign policy. Much Elizabethan history must be interpreted with a knowledge of the personalities and attitudes of Walsingham and Burghley in mind. Remote as all this may seem, it had much to do with the planning that preceded the attempt to colonize North Carolina.

Walsingham became the leader of the Protestant cause, or more particularly, the wing of the Protestant faction that eventually became known as the Puritan group. Burghley, on the other hand, became the architect of Elizabeth's *via media* in religion, a state church that would not be too hard for former Catholics to accept and yet not so ritualistic as to alienate moderate Protestants. The brilliant biographer of both of these men, Professor Conyers Read, thus states their differences: "I think Cecil was a good Protestant, but he subordinated religion to material considerations, and while Walsingham looked upon Puritans as crusaders, Cecil, as he grew older, came to regard them as a nuisance. Clapham says of him [Cecil] that he disliked Catholics because of their superstition and the Puritans because of their singularity." Villainous as Cecil may have regarded such acts as the St. Bartholomew's Massacre or the cruelties perpetrated by the Spaniards on the Dutch Calvinists, he never let his emotions sway his judgment. He did not intend for England to lead a Protestant crusade on the Continent. Though he placed no great trust in Spaniards, he believed that co-existence of a sort was possible with them, and he was opposed to any policy that would bring open conflict.

Walsingham, though a man of prudence, also became convinced as early as the "seventies" that appeasement of Spain could go too far. In 1576, he was supporting secret aid to the Dutch rebels and Burghley was opposing it. The Spanish Ambassador in London, Bernardino de Mendoza, reported in 1578, that Walsingham and the Earl of Leicester were pleading the Dutch cause under the color of religion which made it hard for Burghley to oppose them, particularly since Leicester, "despite his bad character," was in high favor with the Queen.

The Queen's relations with Leicester remain one of the mysteries of history. Whether Leicester was ever actually her lover may be doubted, but she was emotionally stirred by this ambitious man whose influence was greater than his abilities as a soldier or statesman. Yet better men than Leicester used him as a "front" and thereby gained a favorable hearing from the Queen. One of these men was Walsingham.

Walsingham's personal sympathies lay with the extreme Protestant or Puritan wing of the church, and he and Leicester are sometimes described as leaders of the "Puritan party." That is an over-simplification of their activities. Walsingham was too shrewd a statesman to become a narrow partisan, but both he and Leicester were irrevocably committed to opposition to Spain. After the Sea Beggars seized Brill and Flushing in 1572, and the revolt of the Netherlands excited the hopes of Protestants throughout Europe, Walsingham and Leicester argued earnestly in the Privy Council that England should recognize Philip II as an enemy and go to the aid of the rebels. Henceforth, they were the recognized leaders of the anti-Spanish faction in the Privy Council and of what Corbett has called the "war party."[1] Elizabeth was so upset on one occasion in 1576 by the constant pressure to aid the Dutch that she ran into her bedroom, locked the door, and refused to come out until members of her household threatened to batter down the door to retrieve her. As one observer reported, "Her Majesty is troubled with

[1] Julian S. Corbett, *Drake and the Tudor Navy.* (London, 1899), I, 190 *ff*. Hereafter cited as Corbett, *Drake and the Tudor Navy.*

these causes, which maketh her very melancholy and [she] seemeth greatly to be out of quiet." Everybody else was "out of quiet." Cautious, prudent William Cecil, now Lord Burghley, was beside himself. He and the conservative members of the Privy Council did not want to see Spain — or France either — supreme in the Low Countries, yet Burghley, like the Queen, feared open war. The result, for the time being, was another effort by the Queen to mediate between Philip and the Dutch. She ended by lending the Dutch money and allowing English "volunteers" to serve in the Low Countries; eventually she sent her favorite Leicester to command English troops fighting with the Dutch.

The decade from 1578 to 1588 was a period of cold war with hot intervals, an era in some respects like our own unhappy age. Throughout these years Burghley continued to hope for a peaceful solution with Spain.

Around Walsingham, however, another group collected, a group intent upon harassing Spain in every way. Their strategy was to unleash as many commerce raiders as they could muster and let them prey on Spanish shipping and Spanish treasure ships. They even contemplated establishing operational bases in the New World, and of raiding Spain's life lines from such bases. These were the earliest plans for English settlements overseas. These bold spirits included John Hawkins, Francis Drake, Humphrey Gilbert, Walter Raleigh, and Richard Hakluyt, the dedicated propagandist of English expansion overseas. It was not mere whim that made Hakluyt dedicate the 1589 edition of the *Principal Navigations* to Walsingham. In addition to the immediate purpose of crippling the Spanish capacity to make war — and of enriching themselves — by capturing Spanish treasure ships, these men were coming to believe that England's future strength and prosperity demanded outposts in the New World. Seizure of American bases would mean a frontal attack on Spanish interests and would incur the risk of a counterattack on England and the loss of English commerce with Spain and the Spanish dominions.

Burghley was opposed to such bold measures on several counts. First, he did not believe that England was equipped to wage a war with Spain, the colossus of Europe. Spanish armies were the mightiest Europe had ever seen. The Spanish infantryman had proved himself invincible on many a field and Spain's reservoir of manpower seemed inexhaustible. Burghley's natural caution made him loath to offend so dangerous an enemy. Furthermore, he believed that the national interest lay in preserving peace and encouraging trade. Despite religious and political suspicion and hatred of Spain, England had a profitable trade with the Iberian peninsula and with Flanders. Burghley had been constantly negotiating to expand that trade. War, Burghley believed, would certainly bring on financial disaster. The best interests of England would be served if the nation should content itself with trade, keep the peace, and grow prosperous. Some way would be found to circumvent the political and military threats from Spain. In short, Burghley was a "little Englander" — at least for the time being — and wanted no part of overseas expansion, if that expansion meant war with the greatest military power in Europe.

Between Burghley and the conservatives on one side and the adventurers who looked to Walsingham for leadership, there was a constant struggle, often not open, but always persistent. Where did the Queen stand in the midst of the great debate? Precisely where it suited her at the moment. With characteristic Tudor cunning, she played both sides against the middle. She would not outwardly oppose Burghley and favor the irreparable affront to Spain; yet she secretly encouraged her corsairs and sometimes invested in their privateering expeditions. Always she demanded and got a royal share of the booty. But she took care that she could disavow any particularly embarrassing foray by her seamen.

The political background of Drake's famous circumnavigation of the world in 1577–1580 illustrates the duplicity of the Queen with her own ministers. In the summer of 1576, Walsingham was in despair over the Queen's consideration of a plan to make friends with Philip, and he was eager to take advantage of any change of mood that would harden her against the Spanish king. In the spring of 1577 the Queen became suspicious that Philip was nurturing a plot to aid Mary Stuart and Walsingham lost no time in encouraging that mood. He advised her that she should secretly encourage some of her sea-captains to strike a blow at Spanish shipping that would prove to Philip that England was a power that he might not trifle with. At this moment Walsingham sought out Drake. "Secretary Walsingham did come to confer with him and declared unto him that Her Majesty had received divers injuries of the King of Spain, for the which she desired to have some revenge," a contemporary report giving Drake's account of the proceeding states. Whereupon, Walsingham whipped out a map and asked Drake to write down in his own hand the places on the map where the King of Spain "might be most annoyed." This Drake refused to do, pointing out "that Her Majesty was mortal, and that if it should please God to take Her Majesty away, it might be that some prince might reign that might be in league with the King of Spain, and then will my own hand be a witness against myself." Nevertheless, Drake agreed to tell the Queen in person of a plan to attack the Spaniards from the South Sea and to raid the west coast of Spanish America. This Drake did, and he reported that "Her Majesty did swear by her Crown that if any within her realm did give the King of Spain to understand hereof (as she suspected too well) they should lose their heads therefor." And lastly Drake said, "Her Majesty gave me special commandment that of all men my Lord Treasurer should not know it." So Burghley, the Lord Treasurer, must be kept in the dark. Was he completely fooled by the secrecy surrounding the feverish preparations for the impending voyage? That is doubtful. It was hard to keep secrets from so knowing a man as Burghley. It was given out that this was to be a voyage of discovery in search of Terra Australis Incognita, and it was hinted for Burghley's benefit, in case he heard of the project, that nothing was farther from Drake's intent than injury to the King of Spain.

Clearly Burghley knew something about the projected voyage, for among the gentlemen-officers whom Drake found it expedient to take along was a mysterious person named Thomas Doughty, who had long cultivated Drake's friendship. Doughty's precise role has been a subject of speculation, but it is certain that he was Burghley's agent. Perhaps Burghley placed upon him responsibility for frustrating any belligerent move against Spain. Perhaps he was there merely to report to Burghley what happened.

At any rate, Doughty proved a troublemaker from the start, and when Drake reached the Straits of Magellan late in June 1578, he anchored in Santa Cruz Bay and brought Doughty to trial for mutiny and other crimes. With characteristic English regard for the forms of law, Drake gave Doughty a jury trial; he was found guilty and sentenced by Drake, who served as presiding judge, to death. Again with characteristic English regard for decorum, Drake took communion with the prisoner, sat with him at his last dinner, and had him beheaded as a traitor. Whatever the formal charges were, Doughty's fatal crime in Drake's eyes was being the agent to betray him to Burghley, the Lord Treasurer. Drake was realist enough to know that he himself was caught in the web of Elizabethan politics, that, in Corbett's words, "he was being used as an instrument to upset Burghley's policy of peace."[2]

The story of Drake's epoch-making voyage has been often told and does not need repeating, but its political aspects and its relation to other anti-Spanish ventures are frequently overlooked. Drake's raids on the defenceless towns of Chile and Peru were enough to precipitate war, it would seem. But when Mendoza, the Spanish ambassador, complained of the "master thief" as he called Drake, Elizabeth blandly retorted that she had no proof of his guilt. Elizabeth, of course, was ready to repudiate a liability, but Drake's safety lay in the extraordinary wealth brought back from the pillage of Spanish ships and towns. To repudiate Drake now would mean restitution of the stolen goods to Spain, and Elizabeth, once she had glimpsed the gold and jewels in the "Golden Hind's" cargo had no mind to send them to Spain and hang Drake merely to please the Spanish ambassador and his royal master. Instead, on April 4, 1581, she went down to Deptford where the "Golden Hind" lay at anchor and knighted Drake on his own deck. Surely this was an open affront to Philip and proof of the success of Walsingham's scheme.

Burghley and the peace party, however, continued to work for a rapprochement with Philip. The London merchants trading with Spain and

[2] Corbett, *Drake and the Tudor Navy,* I, 244.

Portugal were fearful of the loss of their business and their ships in case of open war and they also exerted all their influence to prevent a conflict. Burghley even counselled the Queen to restore the stolen treasure to Spain. Drake was by now a popular hero and the Queen had added to her treasury too much of his gold to permit restitution. The precise amount of wealth brought home in the "Golden Hind" will never be known but it is estimated at the least to have equalled "nearly twice a year's normal revenue of the English crown, and yielding [to the investors in the voyage] a profit said to have worked out at 4,700 percent." Even after the Queen had taken her full share, Drake was wealthy and the lowliest cabin boy in his crew had a rich reward. Small wonder that he was a hero.

Though Burghley might stave off open war for a while longer, Drake's success whetted the appetite of corsairs and expansionists who would continue to harass Spain until peace would be impossible. Drake had shown that the Spanish Empire was vulnerable, and Walsingham's group became more importunate for overseas expansion. By now they can be described as incipient imperialists. They were beginning to think in terms of territorial expansion overseas.

The man who did more than any other to rationalize this point of view was the preacher, Richard Hakluyt, who became the greatest propagandist of his age for overseas expansion. His compilations of voyages were intended for something other than romantic reading. They were to inspire his countrymen to further explorations and to provide practical information which they might use. In dedications and introductions, Hakluyt argued cogently that the destiny of England required her to settle strategic areas in the New World. Walsingham early recognized the importance of Hakluyt's work and encouraged him in it. Hakluyt indeed became an influential cosmographer and advocate in the Walsingham group of expansionists.

As early as 1580 Hakluyt prepared a paper, probably for Walsingham, entitled "A Discourse of the Commodity of the Taking of the Straight of Magellanus" in which he argued that without "great charge and without open war" England might cripple Spain by fortifying the passage to the Pacific. He also suggested the seizure of Cape St. Vincent in Brazil as a subsidiary base and the continued search for a Northeast passage to Asia. In order not to antagonize the King of Spain he suggested that "To the Str. of Magellanus may be sent Clerke [Thomas Clarke] the pirate upon promise of pardon, and to color the matter he may go as of himself and not with the countenance of the English state, or some such man may be sent." He further suggested that the fort at the Straits might be garrisoned with slaves and half-breeds rescued from the Spanish colonies. A few English convicts, male and female, might also win their freedom by going to the Straits. Thus the fortification of this area would serve a Christian and humanitarian purpose and benefit the nation. Though there is no record that Hakluyt's memorandum had any immediate effect, it is evidence of the growing realization of the expansionists that England must checkmate Spain in the New World.

Hakluyt's first compilation, the *Divers Voyages* of 1582, dedicated to Walsingham's son-in-law, Sir Philip Sidney, contained further arguments of the value of English bases overseas. The dedication rebukes his countrymen for their negligence of duty and for putting privateering ahead of colonization out of what he calls "a preposterous desire of seeking rather gain than God's glory." These beliefs Hakluyt set forth in a long and closely-reasoned state paper, presented in person to the Queen in 1584; this paper, generally known today as the *Discourse of Western Planting,* shows the handiwork, not only of Hakluyt but of Raleigh and possibly of Walsingham. It is a sort of platform of the expansionists and makes a convincing argument for state support of colonization.

Adroitly Hakluyt wrapped his argument in a medley of religious and practical reasons which even a hostile critic would find hard to controvert. The princes of the reformed religion, of whom Queen Elizabeth is the leader, he asserts, have a responsibility to see that the heathen of the New World are not allowed to become a solid Catholic block. It is not sufficient just to send a few Protestant missionaries to the heathen, Hakluyt points out. Salvation must be a concomitant of colonization. He then paints a gorgeous picture of the profits to English merchants and the enrichment of the English crown from the commodities of the New World which Spain at present monopolizes. The power of Spain, he insists, is much inflated, and he prophesies that King Philip's pride will be brought low when Englishmen launch a determined attack on the outposts of his empire.

All of this reasoning, all of this argument for governmental support of colonial enterprises of course is propaganda for Raleigh's own projects to settle the coast of North Carolina. In the political alignment of the 1580's Raleigh held an interesting position. Walsingham undoubtedly sympathized with many of his views on expansion and helped to promote them. Yet Walsingham never liked or trusted Raleigh and frequently opposed him. Neither did Burghley like or trust Raleigh. "Seek not to be Essex; shun to be Raleigh," was Burghley's advice to his own son Robert. Yet Raleigh tried on numerous occasions to cultivate Burghley's good will and Burghley was not above using Raleigh's influence with the Queen when Raleigh was in favor and it suited Burghley's purposes. The truth was that Raleigh, brilliant and versatile, was also grasping and arrogant and had few friends. Before the Queen he was a charming and gracious courtier and for a time he stood high in her favor. It was during a period of royal favor that he won Walsingham's approval of his colonial ventures and managed to avoid Burghley's veto. From the Queen he obtained a favorable charter, and the settlement of North Carolina was theoretically possible.

Raleigh had another advantage: the experience of his half-brother, Sir Humphrey Gilbert, fifteen years his senior, a respected soldier in Ireland and the Low Countries, at one time an advocate for explorations in search of the Northwest passage, and the would-be colonizer of Newfoundland. Gilbert had been knighted for his services in Ireland in the 'sixties and had the respect even of Burghley, who, along with other conservatives like the Earl of Sussex, subscribed to his project for the settlement of Newfoundland in 1580–1584.

Yet Gilbert had been one of the most ardent supporters of the policy of attacking Spain in the New World. Indeed, in November 1577, he had prepared two papers with similar titles: "A Discourse How Her Majesty May Meet with and Annoy the King of Spain." Just at the time when Drake was preparing to sail on his expedition around the world, Gilbert proposed that he should lead an expedition to seize the Spanish, Portuguese, and French fishing fleets off Newfoundland and then combine forces with other privateers to take Cuba and Santo Domingo in the West Indies. This action undoubtedly would have "annoyed" the King of Spain, not to mention the King of France, but combined with Drake's attack on the west coast, it might have broken the back of the Spanish Empire. Such measures, however, were too strong for Elizabeth, and she contented herself with surreptitious aid to Drake. Thereafter, Gilbert busied himself with less provocative ventures in Newfoundland. A staunch Protestant, he was convinced that God had especially reserved certain portions of the New World for a Protestant empire, and Newfoundland looked like the promised land. Nevertheless, he was ready to admit English Catholic refugees as colonists, because that would drain a troublesome element out of England and put them to constructive work in a country where they could do no harm. Since Gilbert's Newfoundland colony did not appear to contravene Spanish interests sufficiently to arouse violent reactions from that quarter, even Burghley smiled upon it. Perhaps he thought of the benefits to the cod fishery, his own pet project for improving the economic state of England. At any rate, the efforts to establish a colony in Newfoundland helped to get the Queen and Burghley used to the idea and made it easier for Raleigh to obtain his charter.

The story of Raleigh's efforts to establish a colony in North Carolina is known to all. With the growing zeal for colonial enterprise, we may wonder why these efforts failed. A study of the reasons for the failures and mishaps of Raleigh's ventures — and of the first years at Jamestown — would be a profitable undertaking, but it would take more than the hour alloted for this paper. A few factors, however, are worth mentioning. The principal reasons lay in inexperience, poor organization, lack of strong administrative control, insufficient capital, and greed for quick profits.

Some of the promoters of colonial enterprises overseas, notably Gilbert and Raleigh, had served in Ireland and had observed the efforts to found English colonies there. In some respects the Irish plantations presented problems not unlike those encountered in the New World. Certainly the wild Irish were as fierce as any Indians on the coast of North Carolina. One would think that the Irish experience would have been helpful in the New World, but it appears to have taught the promoters very little. All of the early colonial ventures were inadequately equipped, poorly manned, and poorly led. Even when a capable leader emerged, he was handicapped by a divided command, jealousy among the "gentlemen" in the group, and the lack of firm authority. Because the government in the initial period refused to take any responsibility for colonies, the administration of the ventures was a private affair without any well-tried plan or procedure.

Not one of the early colonial efforts had sufficient financial backing to insure its success. The Elizabethans — and the Jacobeans too, for that matter — were slow to learn how expensive colonies can be in their first stages of development.

One prime reason why the Elizabethans failed to establish colonies was their obsession with privateering — or simple piracy — as the Spaniards called it. Raleigh's colonial undertakings were expected to pay the investors a profit out of Spanish prizes captured by the prowling ship-captains. Both Gilbert and Raleigh had difficulty keeping their skippers headed for Newfoundland or North Carolina when there was a prospect of prizes in the West Indies. The lure of Spanish galleons to be taken in American waters rather than the national preoccupation with defense against the Spanish Armada accounts for the long delay in attempting to succor the colony on Roanoke Island. A privateering syndicate organized by a merchant named John Watts in 1591 had as an incidental objective the rescue of the Roanoke colony. Raleigh was one of the investors and John White went along in the ship "Hopewell." The other vessel was the "Moonshine." They coasted along the shores of North Carolina, blew trumpets, and sang English songs, but could get no response, and finally headed for home. Nevertheless, the voyage showed a profit from prizes taken of eighty-five per cent on the investment of the shareholders. Yet this handsome return was regarded by Raleigh as so trifling that he complained to Burghley that "we might have gotten more to have sent them a-fishing." When the profits from piracy were so great, speculators were not interested in the slow returns on money invested in colonies.

The eventual war with Spain and the victory over the Armada removed the fear of offending Spain as a political reason against colonial undertakings. Gradually, as English capital built up, and as the moneyed men in the City, the merchants of London, began to realize that sources of raw materials and eventual markets could be found in North America, a new and healthier basis for colonization developed. When King James made peace with Spain, the old zest for piracy disappeared. No longer would the sovereign and some of the principal ministers in the government take stock in piratical voyages. Profits had to be sought in another type of adventure. The initiative for colonization passed from sea-captains and courtiers to the directors of stock companies. Though colonial ventures were still subject to much trial and error, a sounder colonial procedure was in sight.

3

Weakness in Strength: Spain's Early Glory

Dirge for the Conquistadors

Spanish colonial policy in the first half of the sixteenth century was less concerned with colonization than with conquest. The military

From *The Conquistadors* by Jean Descola. Copyright 1957 by Jean Descola. Reprinted by permission of The Viking Press, Inc.

adventurers and explorers of Catholic Spain — known as the Conquistadors — have long been debated and often denounced — especially by Protestant writers. Ironically, it was a Spanish bishop, Bartolomeo de Las Casas, who supplied much of the substance for such criticism in his Brevisima Relación de la Destrucción de las Indias, *a scathing indictment of the inhumanity of his fellow countrymen in America. The English welcomed Las Casas' book, translated it and published it in London just five years before the Anglo-Spanish crisis of 1588.*

Not all historians judge the Conquistadors as did Las Casas. According to Jean Descola, *whose* Les Conquistadors *won Le Grand Prix d'Histoire on publication in France, they deserve more sympathy and respect than they usually receive. As a Frenchman, Descola is less influenced by national prejudice than have been Dutch, English, and Spanish historians. He admires the Conquistadors, and he is ready to judge them by the standards of the age in which they lived. The Spanish conquerors of America belonged to an age of cruelty and intolerance, and their actions reflected the temper of their times. They succeeded, in large part, because they were prepared to be ruthless. The Conquistadors, concludes Descola, were patriots, heroes, and, by their lights, dedicated Christians.*

"There will come a time when the ocean will loosen the bonds by which things are encircled, when the immense earth will be revealed, when Tethys will discover the universe anew and Thule will no longer be the end of the world." Seneca's mysterious prophecy was fulfilled fifteen centuries later with Bermejo's cry of "Land!" in the night of October 11–12, 1492. Two Spaniards greeted each other through time and space.

Not only was Thule surpassed, but a whole world emerged from the shadows into the light of dawn. What a world it was! It stretched from California to Chile, from the West Indies to Patagonia, and covered all Central America; it was more than 6000 miles from north to south, through 67 degrees of latitude, and covered nearly 10,000,000 square miles. This was the Spanish Empire, thirty times larger than Spain itself. Brazil was left for Portugal, thanks to the pen of a Borgia, and humid Guiana and the frozen far north were for those who were to come later. Spain had taken the largest share, which was just, for she had been the first to reach the young land of America.

The first Europeans in the New World were Spaniards, and no one has dreamed of contesting their priority. But from the second quarter of the sixteenth century, other Europeans followed in their wake, the first of whom were the French.

In 1534 Cabeza de Vaca crossed North America on foot from the shores of Texas to the western coast of Mexico. In the same year a Frenchman, Jacques Cartier, having set out from Brittany, reached Newfoundland and the gulf of the St. Lawrence; he had discovered Canada. In the years that followed, the colony of Canada gradually acquired the Great Lakes and the valley of the Mississippi. Hernando de Soto went up the Mississippi at the same time that Frenchmen came down it, and it was only by a narrow margin that the subjects of Charles V and Francis I avoided spreading to the Mississippi region the war which was then in progress between Nice and Perpignan, for the two parties failed to meet. Other Frenchmen, cruising along the American coasts, strove to plant the fleur-de-lis banner of the Capetians. Jean Ribaut founded Charlefort, now Fort Royal, South Carolina, and went as far as Florida. René Laudonnière built Fort Caroline in Florida.

South America also received a visit from the French: Jean Duperot, sailing on the *La Pèlerine,* touched land at Pernambuco, which is now Recife. The Sire de Villegaignon, following difficulties with the king, went into exile and founded a Protestant colony on an island in the bay of Rio. Eldorado did not fail to draw the French, and they, too, searched for it in Guiana and Amazonia. It is noteworthy that their passage through these territories left an excellent impression in the minds of the Indians. The courtesy and civility of certain gentlemen surprised natives who were used to Spanish arrogance and German stiffness, and sometimes French officers even took up arms by the side of the local people against the Spanish or Portuguese occupiers. It has always been the privilege of European minorities in a territory dominated by another European power to feel sympathy for the conquered populations, provoked for the most part by dislike for the conqueror. Later, France was also to have its piece of Eldorado: Guiana and its sordid towns: Cayene, Saint Laurent du Maroni, and Oyapock — a sinister Eldorado which, after having been the poor relation of French colonies, in 1947 became the most backward of French *départements.*

The Germans were even less successful than the French, since the latter, by securing Guiana — desolate though this equatorial land might be — could count that they had their hands on part of the New World; but the bank clerks from Augsburg left Venezuela empty-handed and without hope of returning. As for the Dutch, only a part of Guiana and few names elsewhere on the map of South America — Cape Orange on the northern coast of Brazil, Waterhuys, Roohoeck, at the mouth of the Amazon — record their passing. The future founders of New Amsterdam — New York — touched the southern continent only lightly. The English had to wait for Cromwell before becoming aware of their imperial mission. The incursions of Fenton, Withrington, and Cavendish on the Brazilian littoral, Raleigh's trip along the Orinoco — yet another! — in search of Eldorado, the descent of the famous corsair Drake on Santo Domingo and Cartagena were nothing but profitable raids or single engagements. Easily last in the conquest, the English were the first in the share-out. But, like the French, in South America they secured only a scrap of Guiana — though the best piece to be sure.

But all these were only isolated endeavors, like nets cast haphazardly into the Dark Sea. They had nothing in common with the Spaniards' ventures, which were carefully prepared, and part of a vast hegemonical plan sketched by an emperor under the benevolent eye of a Pope. Frenchmen, Germans, Dutch, Englishmen — contemporaries of the Spaniards of the conquest, sailing in similar caravels and having the same means, steered for the same shores. To what end but to conquer?

Here we face a problem of definition: were these conquerors of other races conquistadors too? Farther back in time the question applies also to Genghis Khan and Kublai, the conquerors of Cathay, or, nearer the present time, to Galliani, Savorgnan de Brazza, and Lyautey, the founders of the French Empire, and to Ferdinand de Lesseps, who thought of the canal that cut the isthmus. Could they, too, be called conquistadors? When Captain Gouraud captured the Sudanese chief Samory in the heart of his camp, was he so very different from Francisco Pizarro when he captured Atahualpa? These are attractive analogies, but in truth the Conquistador resembles no one but himself. He is a Spaniard, the product of the conquering and mystical Spain of the sixteenth century, made in its image, and reflecting the somber glory of its contradictory passions. He carries in himself, with a sort of terrible ingenuity, the whole of Spain. He *is* Spain. And just as we cannot define in one word, or reduce to a single formula, the historic face of Charles V's Spain, so we must consider successively the various aspects of the Conquistador, so that a true portrait may emerge, one removed both from the "black legend" and from the romantic image.

Neither Saints nor Bandits

Here are a few judgments on the Conquistadors. Heinrich Heine was categorical: "They were bandits," he said. Angel Ganivet claims that they conquered "by spontaneous necessity, by virtue of a natural impulse toward independence, without other purpose than to reveal the grandeur which hid itself beneath their apparent smallness." Maurice Legendre says: "Spain, by its Conquistadors, was going to seek outside, by sheer energy, the strength which at home she had only potentially and which it was essential for her to realize in order to maintain her independence." Salvador de Madariaga finds in them "the typically Spanish trait: the coexistence of contrary tendencies."

Each of these opinions, even that of Heine, who detested Spain and understood her little, has its share of the truth. Bandits at certain times — crises of panic and greed — the Conquistadors never lost their sense of grandeur. This was one of their contradictions. But the most striking was to have so closely associated the religion of self and the love of country.

The people of Spain, whatever may be her political regime, are the least possible "community-minded." They do not believe in the "collective soul," that invention of sociologists, useful sometimes as a propaganda theme but as sterile as it is theoretical. How could a collection of individuals form a single individual, at least without denying the personal soul? Deny the soul! An old proverb says that every Spaniard *"tiene su alma en su almario"*: a play on words, meaning that he keeps his soul in his closet; it is his own property, a secret thing. Pride and privation: that was the Spaniard of the sixteenth century.

For his soul he was accountable to God alone. Calderon makes the mayor of Zalamea say: "We owe the king our fortune and our life, but honor is the patrimony of our soul. And the soul belongs to God alone." Honor and soul were, for every well-born Spaniard, the supreme freedom. No law, not even the king's will, might prevail against this privilege of making arrangements direct with God and acting accordingly. Hence the individualism of the Conquistadors. Above their local leader, the *visitadores,* and the royal personage there was God, that is to say, the freedom to be themselves. It was Canivet who suggested: "The juridical ideal of Spain would be that every Spaniard should have in his pocket a charter of rights consisting of a single item framed in these brief, clear, and striking terms: 'This Spaniard is authorized to conduct himself as he chooses.' " A joke? Scarcely; for one does not joke about such things beyond the Pyrenees. By this extravagant but unwritten charter every Conquistador shaped his behavior; thus, having concluded an intimate pact with God, he often thought himself exempt from the duty of obedience.

Although fiercely individualistic, the Conquistadors were no less ardently patriotic. Every Spaniard carried in his heart a fragment of Spain and very often bathed it in his solitary tears. Andalusia had provided the first sailors, and Castile the majority of the soldiers. Columbus's sailors were almost all from Palos and Moguer, and the captains of the conquest came from Estremadura. Francisco Pizarro had recruited his companions at Trujillo, his native village; Cortes was from Medellin, Balboa from Jerez de los Caballeros, Valdivia from Villanueva de la Serena. They must have dreamed constantly of their *casa solariega* and the herd at the bottom of the field tilled by the elder brother. Manor houses with nail-studded doors, or huts of slate — the thought evokes them both. That sunburned landscape of Estremadura, with its wide and melancholy horizons, haunted the Conquistadors, and to their conquests they gave the names of home: Medellin, Guadalajara, Trujillo, Caceres, Badajoz, and countless Santiagos. This was the compensation of these voluntary exiles, who were so attached to their homeland that one might have been able, it seems, by scratching the soles of their shoes, to find a scrap of the red clay of the Tierra de Baros.

Under the King's Eye

This Conquistador, brightly daring, taking possession of scraps of empire as he galloped along, and listening to nothing but the promptings of his own heart. . . . His plume could be seen on the narrow roads of the Andes, in the vast grasslands, by the edges of leaden lakes and upon the lava flows, and advancing by night along the rims of craters, white in the moonlight. Could nothing stop him but the fear of God? Yes, the fear of the king, for the Conquistador was not the soldier of God alone. He was the liegeman of the Spanish monarch, and his motto was that of Spain: *un monarca, un imperio, y una espada* (one monarch, one realm, and one sword). There was only one who tried to escape from royal tutelage — *Gonzalo Pizarro,* and he died under the executioner's ax. He who had no fear of cannibals trembled at the thought of incurring the king's wrath. Six thousand miles from Valladolid, his heart froze at the thought of displeasing Charles V. The receipt of a dispatch bearing the royal seal immediately aroused his anxiety. At a single word from the king, he did not hesitate to cross deserts, mountains, and oceans, to take orders, report, or sometimes to give himself up to justice. All, even the greatest, made this humiliating journey. Columbus (three times), Cortès, the Pizarro brothers. . . . The knee had to be bent before the Caesarian monarch if the sheet of parchment legalizing the enterprise was to be secured.

Not a caravel ever left a Spanish port in a westerly direction without a representative of the king aboard. When Columbus left for his first voyage in 1492 — for the unknown, moreover — Rodrigo de Escobedo and Sánchez de Segovia, Royal Notary and Comptroller respectively, had been forced upon him. "Master after God," the Admiral of the Ocean Sea saw the king come between himself and God. Thenceforward, the two faces could make only one. Intoxicated as they were by sudden fortune, the Conquistadors never omitted to put aside a fifth part of their booty for the royal treasury. And if any man swindled the accounts, it was at his own risk and peril: all knew that the garrote awaited the man who took it into his head to defraud the king of his share.

Thus from the beginning of the conquest, even in the opening phase when it was less a matter of conquest than discovery, the Spanish monarchy signified its intention of regarding it as a "royal affair." The first act of the conquest — the *Santa María*'s departure from the port of Palos — was sanctioned by the first administrative act: the charter granted to the Genoese by the Catholic monarchs. The following year, the royal grip on this prey that was scarcely yet imaginable became manifest. A superintendence of Indian affairs was created at Valladolid and immediately established a delegation at Santo Domingo: the first "audience." Then, years later, the *Casa de Contratación* was founded at Seville, with the task of supervising the application of the laws concerning trade with America. It registered the vessels that left or returned to Spain, and legislated at the civil and criminal levels on all disputes concerning traffic with the New World. The Casa de Contratación also decided maritime matters: it maintained the register of crews, fixed the departure dates and destinations of ships, and determined freight and tonnage. Furthermore, the chief pilot performed the duties of controller of navigation, technical adviser, and chief of marine personnel. The Casa was at one and the same time a chamber of commerce, a consular office, a naval school, and a cartographic service.

Eight years after the foundation of the Casa de Contratación, Ferdinand the Catholic created the Royal Council of the Indies — a veritable ministry of the colonies that exercised its jurisdiction over all the affairs of the Indies: civil, military, commercial, and religious. All the officials of the New World, from the highest to the humblest, were subordinate to it. Charles V strengthened the powers of this council and gave it his full confidence, going so far as to delegate to it his signature in all matters of justice, with the exception of nominations to "favors and offices." The seat of the Council of the Indies was at Medina. It was more a directory than an assembly, for there were only seven councilors, including the president and the fiscal attorney. Deliberations and conferences took place behind closed doors, and only the king could be present. Public and secret reports from overseas officials were scrutinized, especially the secret ones; compliments were handed out and penalties fixed. In short, the council administered everything, though from a distance.

One very great long-term concern preoccupied the council: that of giving this still-effervescent America a juridical protection that would insure that one day — God willing — colonization would follow the conquest. The Laws of the Indies answered to this anxiety. In preparing them, the royal advisers created the first colonial law. The majority of these laws were just, though it might be difficult to disentangle the essentials of a legislation whose six thousand articles embraced all the forms of Spanish activity in the New World from the running of schools to bodily hygiene. But respect for the human personality was never lost sight of. Doubtless the men who shaped these laws always kept in mind the spirit of Isabella the Catholic's testament: "That the King, my Lord, the Princess, my daughter, and the Prince, my son, do not permit, or will not be the cause, that the Indians, the inhabitants of the Islands and the mainland, should suffer any injury to their persons or to their property. They will keep watch, on the contrary, that these people shall be treated with justice and kindness."

Humane and just in principle, the Laws of the Indies bore in them the germ of future emancipation. Meanwhile, by extending the system of *fueros* (under the name *cabildos*) to the New World, imperial Spain of the sixteenth century laid the foundations of the South

American democracies. What, in fact, were the cabildos? They were local municipalities whose members could be non-Spanish, but who were obliged to secure office by popular vote. No one, therefore, opposed the fact that there were Indians among the municipal councilors. The members of the cabildos administered the affairs of the commune, looking after public hygiene, the maintenance of roads, and general welfare. The institution of these local assemblies, born of the people, underlines the extent to which the intentions of the Council of the Indies were genuine. Similarly, by creating a third body known as the Consulate of the Indies, the central power manifested its will to regulate the profession of privateering and to prevent its abuse. This multiplicity of agencies and the abundance of legal texts bear witness to the seriousness with which the Spanish sovereigns took their role as protectors and civilizers of the Indies. In this respect they never ceased to nourish high hopes and noble illusions.

The administration in Spain — the Casa de Contratación, the Council of the Indies, and the Consulate of the Indies — was duplicated by a local administration. First the viceroy, appointed directly by the king; this all-powerful person enjoyed royal prerogatives in his territories. Captain general on sea and on land, chief of the departments of justice and finance — in effect, he held absolute power. At the same time, he was obliged, on the expiration of his mandate, to give an exact and faithful account of it. This sincere, quasi-confessional report was in accord with the intentions of the legislators, for it was necessary that officials in the Indies — and especially the high officials — should feel the constant presence of the royal rod.

At the time of Charles V, Spanish America was divided into two viceroyalties, those of Mexico and Peru. New Granada and Río de la Plata, long subordinated to Peru, were not raised to viceroyalty status until much later. Guatemala, Venezuela, Chile, and Cuba were under the leadership of captains general. Provinces of lesser importance were called *gobernaciones* and were administered by governors. Finally, each province comprised districts placed under the command of a *corregidor*. At the head of each commune was an *alcalde*.

In addition to viceroys and captains general, the sovereign also appointed governors and corregidors. These had to pay a deposit before taking up their duties, and firm moral guarantees were required of them. Their powers were rather those of a colonial administrator or an officer for native affairs than of a prefect, since they were skilled in judging the civil and military differences that occurred in the *encomiendas*. In the event of an appeal, the matter was taken before the Royal Audiences, which sat in the capitals. The "auditors," also designated by the king, were subject to very strict rules: they were forbidden to contract marriage in their place of residence, to take part in public ceremonies, to make friends with the Indians, to go into business, or to lend or accept money. Answerable directly to the Council of the Indies, they were not subject to the authority of the viceroy and sometimes even held it in check. In short, the audiences constituted an intermediate echelon between the administration at home and the local governments. Moreover, the king sent "visitors" to the spot for inquiries and to seek information. It may be deduced that he made every effort to keep himself informed of affairs overseas.

The meticulous precautions taken by the Spanish monarchy in choosing colonial personnel, its mistrust of its most experienced servants, the hierarchical chain linking the royal cabinet to the alcalde of the smallest Mexican hamlet, were evidences of its understanding of men. One could not be sure of anybody. By seeking to insure the total independence of the officers entrusted with judging Indians, by demanding their perfect integrity, the monarchy showed its solicitude for the conquered people. "No Indian can be reduced to slavery . . . since all are vassals of the Royal Crown of Castile. . . ." Isabella, Ferdinand, Charles, and, later, Philip II spoke in the same terms, which expressed good faith and a conviction natural to Christian princes brought up on the Gospel, for whom the "racial question" did not exist. It must not be forgotten that the first colonial charter of the Spanish kings proclaimed the equality of Indians and Spaniards before the law. Doubtless it was a symbolic proclamation, yet it revealed a humane preoccupation on the part of its authors to an extent that no other European sovereign had dreamed of. The distinction between natives and subjects was not a Spanish invention.

Although the system was well conceived, it failed in operation. The monarchy, in its naive pride, looked upon the territories of the New World in the same way as upon Milan or Flanders, where it was simply a matter of adapting the administrative scheme of Spain. One reproduced the framework of the royal organization on the map of America, and that was the end of it. That was the first error: dogmatism. The countries were different; the natives spoke unknown languages, and for a long time Spaniards and Indians could converse only by signs. It was only after the second half of the sixteenth century that the conquerors made a sincere effort to understand the mores and mentality of the local people. The monarchy committed a second error — psychological this time — in giving too much credit to the reports of its servants or its favorites — an inevitable weakness if one considers the immense ocean barrier between the colonies and the Ministry of Colonies. Is it surprising, therefore, that certain officials, whose principal function was to aid and protect the Indians, amassed enormous fortunes during their regulation five-year stay, simply by buying back from the natives, at low prices, objects that had been sold to them at high prices and for which they had no use, such as razors, silk stockings, and inkstands? This did not prevent these same officials from ascertaining carefully that mixed marriages were celebrated according to the Roman rites.

One Conquistador sighed maliciously: "*Lo que el Rey manda se obedece, no se cumple*": "What the king orders is obeyed but not executed." This was Belalcazar, the master of Quito. However, Belalcazar's attitude, and that of a few petty tyrants, toward the authority at home was the exception. The Conquistadors' freedom of action was only apparent, and their omnipotence was ephemeral. Attempts at rebellion, even if they succeeded for a while, always ended by being suppressed. A Spanish captain never persisted for long in illegality. The hand of the king, slow to strike, fell sooner or later on the head of the culprit; and the king's eye, though it was such a long way off, never lost sight of the Conquistadors as they marched on.

The Romantics

"Weary of carrying their lofty miseries," "intoxicated by a heroic and brutal dream," "hoping for epic tomorrows": such was the way in which Jose María de Heredia, a Cuban descendant of the Conquistadors (Alonso de Heredia had founded the town of Tolu on the Cauca river), pictured his ancestors steering for Cipango in search of the "fabulous metal." This is the Conquistador adorned with all the romantic accessories; nothing is missing, neither violence nor insupportable pride nor the mirage of gold nor the confusion of instinct and imagination. Another feature common to the romantics was stoicism, sometimes theatrical but most often silent. Arrogant and dignified while they paced up and down the *plazuela* of their native towns, draped in their ragged capes, waiting for adventure, the Conquistadors were even more so when in the very midst of the adventure.

Romantics, indeed, with all the credulity and artless wonder that is associated with the word. Into the extravagant pact they had made with fortune the Conquistadors had brought the passionate quest for risk and the intense curiosity that always made of them something more than old campaigners. In this respect, however, they differ from the romantics, the eternally unsatisfied. The Conquistadors were overwhelmed. For once, the imagination had to admit itself surpassed by reality. No adventurer had ever known such adventure as this, and no actor had ever performed on such a stage. This splendid prize, outstretched beneath their gaze and within their reach, seemed the more beautiful to the conquerors even as the tropical sun burned into their brains. What matter? Atahualpa's treasure and the magnificence of Mexican possessions were not mirages. The enchanted forest emerged from legend to become the tangible virgin forest of America, bathed in twilight shadows. Amadis of Gaul had turned into Pedro de Alvarado; Bernal Díaz del Castillo was about to rewrite a chivalrous novel. With eyes wide open, the Conquistadors lived in a lucid and endless delirium.

The exploits of the Conquistadors have not lacked chroniclers. But what bard will sing of their amours? It was not always the olive-skinned Indian women, their long hair decked out with exotic flowers, stammering childish words, who took the initiative in dalliance. But they did not reject the Spaniards' advances either. Who can say what it was that stirred in the hearts and flesh of these girls or in the wives of the caciques? Submission to the strongest? Curiosity? Sensual comparisons? In any case, no Conquistador was ever repulsed. In order to break their strict moral rules so joyfully on behalf of the Spaniards, to serve these men with such devotion that they sometimes went so far as to betray their brothers, the Indian women must have been great lovers or profligates. We recall that on the very evening of the fall of Cajamarca, the Peruvian women came in a crowd to offer themselves to the victors. Neither Princesses of the Sun nor vestals seemed to harbor the least resentment against those who had scarcely completed "cleaning up" the city. Were they, then, without rancor, these heavy-breasted women with copper-colored skins who did not seem to have the least hatred for the conqueror? Were they yielding to an unfamiliar pleasure, to the prestige of the invader? Or were they simply seeking to put themselves under the protection of a Spanish shield, on the advice of their fathers and husbands?

There was not one Conquistador, even among the greatest, who did not succumb to the Indian women. Hernán Cortés might not have conquered Mexico if he had not begun by subjugating Doña Marina. But it did not rest at that. His residence at Coyoacán was as full of favorites as the Grand Turk's seraglio. Indian women with Spanish names — Doña Inés, Doña Elvira, and many others — shared Malinche's favors. Francisco Pizarro, that graybeard, lived in concubinage with the sister of Atahualpa, his victim. Only Columbus appears to have remained chaste, tortured as he was until the day of his death by his double attachment to his wife and his mistress, Felipa Perestrello y Moniz and Beatriz Enríquez de Harana. All these romantics had their romances, and the history of the conquest is full of picturesque love stories, such as the one that follows.

When Pizzaro landed at Tumbes, Atahualpa and Huáscar were at daggers drawn, but they had not yet taken off their masks. They were watching each other; it was a period of "diplomatic tension." The arrival of the foreign chief in Peru was going to decide the question of war or peace between the two sons of Huayna Capac, but before that, could some solution not be arrived at? The two Inca princes were fully aware that by prolonging their quarrel they were playing into the invader's hands. Atahualpa took the first step. He sent an ambassador to Huáscar with the task of finding some basis for compromise. This man, Quilacou, was one of Atahualpa's most brilliant captains. He reached Cuzco, entered the royal palace, and stood before the legitimate son of the dead emperor. By Huáscar's side stood a young girl who was his mistress: Golden Star. One look between Quilacou and Golden Star was sufficient: they fell hopelessly in love. Quilacou forgot himself, forgot his embassy, and was so daring as to address himself directly to Golden Star. Did he already dream of running off with her? For the moment he was content to smile at her, a rare impropriety that was punished at once. He was driven from the palace, but not before giving the princess the glance of an accomplice: they would meet again!

Meanwhile, negotiations were broken off. Atahualpa's army moved forward, and war began. During the first engagement, Quilacou was gravely wounded and lost consciousness. Rousing from his faint, whom should he see leaning over him but Golden Star. She had abandoned her lover, renounced her position as the favorite of the Inca, and followed the army. In order not to be recognized, she had cut her long hair. Disguised as an adolescent, she mingled with the slaves that carried the baggage and, like them, carried her load. The idyll that had scarcely started at Cuzco unfolded in the midst of the fighting, but it was brief. Both were taken prisoner by the Spaniards and led before Hernando de Soto. Pizarro's captain could recognize true nobility, and he saw at once that the captives were not like the rest of the Indians. He questioned them. Quilacou told their story; De Soto was moved by it and wiped away a tear. The tale was a pretty one, but the woman was prettier still. He took them under his protection. Quilacou died of his wounds, but De Soto married Golden Star, and it proved a marriage of love as well as of profit. Golden Star was in fact the only daughter of a rich Peruvian lord, and she brought her husband a dowry that the most fortunate heiresses of Castile would have envied: gold and silver mines and a multitude of laborers.

On the day Cuzco was taken, Pedro de Barco, a cavalier, entered the gate of the House of the Virgins, who were consecrated to the Sun. There were ten thousand women there! Pedro de Barco set his heart on the one who seemed to him the most beautiful. Passive and smiling, she followed the *caballero*. Was he not the victor? She surrendered. One evening in the main square of Cuzco she observed a number of Spanish soldiers about to cast dice for a golden disk representing the Sun — the effigy of Inti! The vestal could not be witness to such profanation without trembling with horror. The Sun must be saved. This girl, so fragile and so gentle, who had asked nothing of Pedro de Barco until then, was seen to throw herself into his arms, carried away by religious rage. Was he going to allow this sacrilegious game to continue? Had he forgotten that she was still the wife of the Sun? Pedro de Barco shrugged his shoulders. A feminine whim — but he was in love, and what will a man not do for the woman he loves? The Spaniard approached the players, took part in the game, made his throw and won. Pedro de Barco took the shining image back to his wife, but the next day Francisco Pizarro demanded that Pedro de Barco hand over the golden disk, for it had been decided that this symbol of Inca fetichism should be smashed to pieces with hammer blows in the public square before the eyes of the assembled populace. Pedro did not keep them waiting long for his reaction, which was a surprising one for a Spanish cavalier of the sixteenth century. In defiance of discipline and the Faith, he fled with the Indian woman and the disk of the Sun. Love had been stronger than honor.

Pizarro's men rushed in pursuit of the fugitives. The two young people, escorted by a few old priests, took turns carrying the image of the god, but the galloping troop drew nearer. Pedro and his companions reached the shores of Lake Titicaca, but the horsemen were at their heels. Time was short and they had to move fast. They found two pirogues, tied them together with lianas, and laid the golden disk inside. Then they leaped into the boats and drew away from the shore, straining on their oars. Twilight enveloped the raft of the lovers, which went slowly among the rushes. Then torches lit the bank and a boat moved out from it — then two boats, then three. Their wakes traced long luminous tracks on the sacred lake. The two lovers were surrounded, but just as the Spanish boats were about to overtake them, Pedro and his companion lifted the disk and hurled it into the water. Before being captured and without doubt put to death, they had at least saved the god. But instead of sinking to the bottom, the golden disk toppled, rose up, and for an instant stood upright on the waves, no longer yellow, but purple with all the flame of the setting sun. The Spanish cavaliers set up a loud cry of amazement, then the disk tottered, overturned, and sank into the depths. Inti was dead.

While this great drama was taking place, Pedro and the Indian woman had been able to escape from their pursuers and were now beyond reach. It was dark. The hours passed and dawn drew near. Pedro murmured to his love: "The image of your god has sunk. Will it ever cease to haunt the minds of men?" In response the vestal pointed to the horizon and smiled; the first rays of day were beginning to gild the surface of the lake. Having died the day before in crimson glory, the god was reborn in all the youthful beauty of morning.

Under the Pretense of Religion

"So color de religion — van a buscar plata y oro — del encubierto tesoro . . . .": "Under the pretense of religion, they went in search of silver and gold and of hidden treasure." These harsh words of Lope de Vega in his play *El Nuevo Mundo* calls for comment, if not for correction. Certainly the injustices and the crimes committed in the name of religion revolt the heart as well as the conscience. Certainly the Conquistadors used the instruments of the Faith to further their ventures. Thus Ovando, when fighting in Cuba, had given the signal to an ambush by placing his hand on his cross of the Knights of Alcantara, while Valverde warned Pizarro's soldiers that the moment of attack had come by waving the Bible at Atahualpa. The system of *requerimiento* inflicted on the primitive people, the mass baptisms, the conversions *in extremis* that preceded strangulation, the expiatory stake, and the massacres that

ended in the *Te Deum* seem to justify the words of one Indian, exhorted by a monk to die in the Christian faith: "Are there Spaniards in your Paradise? Then I prefer to die a heathen!" Who would dream of denying that the ceremonial of the liturgy often took on the appearance of a funeral procession? But Lope de Vega was wrong on one point: the violent acts of the Conquistadors — abduction, robberies, assassinations — though sometimes performed "in the name of" religion, were never "under the pretense of" religion.

The Conquistadors were sincere. The legality of the enterprise was guaranteed them by pontifical bulls. They had been given to understand that they were leaving for a crusade — the one against Islam having ended but recently — and that after the Jew and the Mohammedan, it was now a question of converting the Heathen. They had been born into a hatred and terror of heresy. They had wept with delight at the capture of Granada, trembled before the Inquisition, and shuddered at the very name of Luther. While still children, they had often spat at the passing of a Moor or set fire to the booth of a Jew. Spain in the sixteenth century was nothing but a vast monastery, noisy with orisons and bells. They had grown up in the shadow of cathedrals and breathed the odor of incense from their earliest years, while the first words they had uttered had been the names of the saints.

The Conquistadors, although for the most part illiterate, had had no need of letters to feel the same fanatical spirit as did the horsemen of the Prophet when they invaded the old Greco-Latin world, or the Crusaders when they spread over the Syrian plains, or their own fathers at the reconquest of Granada. They had been told — they had been convinced — that millions of Indians would burn forever in Hell if they, the Conquistadors, did not bring them the Faith. They believed this quite simply. Religion was for them not a pretext but a banner. The existence of God in three persons, the immortality of the soul, sin, the Last Judgment — it never occurred to any one of them to dispute these facts or even to discuss them. These men of war and passion had retained the faith of little children. Their confessions were sincere, they participated in the Mass not only in the flesh but also in the spirit. The worst of them died in penitence. Pierced by arrows, or with a sword blade in the throat, or tied to the stake under torture, they called loudly for the last rites. *So color de religión*. . . . What an error! No ulterior motive colored the faith of the Conquistadors. They remained men of the Middle Ages. Religious hypocrisy had not yet been invented; it was to turn up later, covering iniquity with its black cloak. The hypocrite is a creature of the seventeenth century.

The Conquistadors believed in God fiercely and unreservedly. But they believed also — above all else! — in the Devil. Now, the New World was the empire of the Devil, a Devil with multiform face, always hideous. The somber Mexican divinities, Huitzilopochtli (the Sorcerer-Hummingbird) and Tezcatlipoca (the Smoking Mirror), the horrible Kinich Kakmo of the Mayas, the Peruvian Viracocha who symbolized boiling lava, the sinister totems of the Araucanians and Diaguites. . . . Why, the medieval demon with short horns, lustful eye, and a tail that was curled like a vine shoot seemed a "good devil" besides such as these! Spaniards who in Estremaduran twilights had taken the flight of a bat for the passing of the Evil One were naturally terrified before these monsters of stone, with bared fangs and gleaming eyes, that seemed to come to fantastic life as night fell. How could they have watched an Aztec ceremony without nausea? The black-robed priests with matted hair, burrowing with their knives in the breasts of their victims, the human skulls piled up at the feet of the teocallis, the cannibal feasts around statues spattered with putrid blood, and the charnel-house stench which all the perfumes of Mexico were never able to hide. . . .

Such things froze the spirits of the Conquistadors, surpassing the nightmares of their childhoods. Satan himself was there, and his worship was celebrated among the dismembered corpses. His maleficent power was honored. He was no longer, as in Spain, the familiar accomplice that could be driven off by a flick of the finger, or the shameful specter slipping furtively through one's conscience but put to flight by a sprinkling of holy water. He was enthroned. Carved in granite, incrusted with precious stones and encircled with golden serpents, he was the superb incarnation of Evil. He glorified sin. Nothing was lacking in their perfect representation of Hell, not even the pots in which certain tribes of the Colombian jungle cooked their enemies alive. This indeed was Satan himself, adorned with all his lugubrious attractions.

Why, therefore, should we be astonished at the reactions of the Spaniards? In the depths of the Indian sanctuaries they could see the Prince of Darkness standing in all his macabre splendor. Looking heavenward, they could distinguish the silvery figure of Saint James galloping across the clouds. The conflict between the true and the false, between good and evil, was manifest in this double apparition. The problem was simple and their duty was clear. The Indians were possessed of the Devil, who had to be exorcised, first by destroying the material evidence of Devil worship. This is why the conquerors, activated by the same blind zeal as early Christians when they shattered the Roman statues, overturned the pre-Columbian idols and burned the ritual articles and the manuscripts that transmitted the sacred tradition — in short, showed a holy ardor to abolish the very memory of the heathen liturgy. This they counted as pious work and a salutary need.

Iconoclasts? Vandals? These epithets would have scandalized the Conquistadors. Who would have applied such words except the agents of Satan who served a vile master? But the Conquistadors did not limit themselves to casting down idols. In order that the exorcism be fully effective, it was not enough to drive away the demons; it was proper also to set up in their places the symbols of the True Faith. Just as holy medals were laid upon flesh that was eaten away with ulcers, the soldiers of Charles V planted crosses on the tops of the teocallis or at crossroads. On the stones that were still spattered with blood from the sacrificial tables, they raised altars to Our Lady of Guadalupe. Tolerance was not for them. Others would follow who would use gentler methods. No one doubts that these booted and armored Christians often lacked the Christian spirit and that charity was almost always missing from their pitiless fervor; but their Faith and their good faith were whole. More even than the love of God and of one's neighbor, the horror of Beelzebub explains certain of the Conquistadors' attitudes, though of course it is understood that to explain is not to absolve.

Gold and Blood

The Conquistadors never ceased to oscillate between the opposing poles of idealism and realism. Were they dreamers or men of action? Does a passion for dreaming master the taste for action? Where does dreaming end and action begin? There is no end to argument on these themes, but the fact remains that from the day the Conquistadors set foot on American soil, they made clear their intention not to be simple voyagers, but to establish themselves there and to remain there. They did not wait until they had finished the war before beginning the peace — by building. During the period between the conquest and colonization, in the middle of the sixteenth century, the conquerors laid the foundations of the colonial edifice which the colonists, later, had the task of completing. To be builders and architects beyond compare, these pursuers of mirages had to be practical men as well.

The first Spanish constructions in the New World were, of course, churches and palaces for the king's representatives, but houses, hospitals, and barracks very quickly arose from the earth as if by magic. Manpower was plentiful and skilled, for masonry and stonework were the arts in which the natives excelled. However, on the instructions of the king himself, the Spaniards at once imposed a special style upon town planning, one that differed completely from the local type of dwelling. This was the famous "checkerboard" plan, inspired by Greco-Latin traditions. The style was simple: a central quadrangular main plaza with a church, municipal buildings, and school. Parallel roads intersected at right angles and formed a regular pattern of squares. Thus the Spaniards transplanted into America an architectural style bequeathed them by their Roman occupiers, who in turn had reproduced Greek models — a curious survival of a scheme some thousands of years old which, revived by Vitruvius and adapted by Hernán Cortés, turned Mexico into a reproduction of the Piraeus.

Had they done nothing but discover the New World, conquer territories, found cities, and teach millions of natives to revere the name of

Christ and that of Charles V, the Conquistadors would have done well by their country. These exploits justified such royal favors as commanderies, the Cross of Santiago, spurs of honor, and marquisates. But the ruler would not have looked on his overseas captains in such a friendly fashion if he had not gained the most precious substance of all: gold. The conquerors were the seekers and purveyors of gold for the kings of Spain.

The Spaniards had always been seekers of gold. Far back into antiquity, in fact, gold mines had been exploited in the Iberian peninsula. Strabo spoke of this in his *Geography*. Pliny was more precise. He explained the technique for the treatment of gold at that time: "It is crushed, washed, burned, ground, and finally treated in a mortar," and that was the method still in use in the sixteenth century. The Spaniards therefore knew that gold could be found either in the form of grains or nuggets, mixed with sand or included in sulphites such as quartz. Grains of gold were extracted from rivers or alluvial deposits. Gold incorporated in sulphites was mined. When the Conquistadors arrived in America, the Indians were also familiar with gold, but they preferred to seek it in the rivers. The process which they commonly used was that of "washing." They ran water over the inclined floor of a sort of trough and into it threw the powdered matter containing the gold. The gold fell to the bottom and was held by a screen. When it was washed clear of particles of soil, the gold was smelted with four times its weight of silver. The resulting alloy was then treated with boiling concentrated sulphuric acid — they used sulphur from volcanoes — which dissolved all metals other than gold. This was the refining process. Both operations were known to the Spaniards, although for refining they also used an older process cited by Pliny, which substituted for sulphuric acid a mixture of copper sulphate, schist, and saltpeter.

Thus the Spaniards knew no more than the Indians about the extraction of gold, but they perfected the system and made it more efficient. To begin with, they discovered a new principle of purification: the "patio amalgamation." The auriferous material was pounded by teams of women and old men. It was then placed on a paved surface called an *arrastra,* surrounded by a rim. Beasts trampled the now muddy mineral. It was sprinkled with water, mercury was added, then a final bath separated the gold from its impurities. The Spaniards were not content merely to improve the technique; they created a gold industry. Under their stimulus, the American earth brought forth its hidden treasure. As the technique of seeking gold in the rivers seemed to them archaic and its results inadequate, the conquerors increased the exploitation of mines. Thousands of natives were allocated to this terrible labor of digging into the mountains, extracting the sulphites with picks, crushing them by hand, and pulverizing them in mills. Then came the washing and the refining: a gentle task compared with that of the slaves of gold beneath the earth.

When the Conquistadors arrived in Mexico, they were surprised to note that the Aztecs extracted only silver. Gold did not seem to be of much interest to them. Doubtless the reserves accumulated by the Aztlan dynasties were sufficient for them, or they thought they had exhausted the resources of the Mexican subsoil. In any case, this did not suit the Spaniards. Would they let the Aztecs rest on the heap of gold piled up by their ancestors? The first concern of the conquerors was to set the Indians to working the gold — without, however, abandoning silver, which was also worth acquiring.

It was Carvajal, an officer under Francisco Pizarro, who discovered the famous Potosi mines in Bolivia, south of La Paz, at nearly 14,000 feet elevation. At the summit of this mountain of silver, the Spaniards built the highest town in the world. Under a colorless sky, houses in the Andalusian style raised their arabesques around the yawning pits. Prison and fortress at the same time, the *Casa de la Moneda* (mint) symbolized — by its heavy door and oppressive silence — the power of the Lion of Castile. Here a whole miserable people, secluded forever, made the king of Spain's silver money. It was better, however — a hundred times better — to live and die between the cyclopean walls of the Casa de la Moneda than to go down into the mines. There men labored as once the slaves of Solomon labored in the Manica mines that were dug for the Queen of Sheba. Some of the Peruvian mines, with their dark figures ceaselessly toiling up and down, recall Michelangelo's "Last Judgment," in which terrorized groups of human beings seem to form a sinister chain.

To smell out gold required enthusiasm and patience. What an event it was when the searcher for gold or silver — the *cateador* — thought he had discovered a mine! All activity in the surrounding country was suspended, shops were shut, the schoolmaster dismissed his pupils, the padre ordered the bells rung, and Indians and Spaniards raced toward the site of the miracle. If the find was confirmed, a feast was held at the very place where the vein had appeared, and if there had been a mistake, everyone returned home, only a little disappointed, so strong had been the emotion. It was a curious fact that Spaniards and natives showed the same joyful excitement, although for the latter gold had no more value — even less, being of secondary utility — than copper or lead. Moreover, for them the discovery of a nugget foretold the martyrdom of the mine. It is probable that the Spaniards communicated to the Indians their fever for gold and that they thought it a good thing to spread the mirage of Eldorado.

The gold thus discovered, extracted, washed, refined, molded into ingots, and placed in chests or barrels, had now to be transported to Spain, and the caravels, which once had been the messengers of hope and the vehicles of the discovery, now played a new role as carriers of gold. The fifteenth century was not ended before a double movement of caravels became organized between Spain and the New World. There were those that set out and those that returned, and those that started were more numerous than those that came back.

In August 1492 three caravels — the *Santa María,* the *Pinta,* and the *Niña* — left the port of Palos. The moment was a solemn one. Repulsed successively by the Portuguese, French, and English, to whom he had offered the keys to the New World, a Genoese adventurer started off on the golden road on behalf of the King of Castile. These three caravels were the first. In 1506 there were twenty-two, in 1507 thirty-two, and in 1508 there were forty-five. There were only seventeen in 1510, but then there arrived at Seville the astonishing news that Grijalva, having landed in Yucatán, had encountered natives who, in exchange for shoddy goods, had given gold — mere crumbs. Some months later, Cortes, who had made contact with Montezuma's emissaries, confirmed the rumor. The consequences of this information were soon manifest: in 1520 seventy-one caravels crossed the Atlantic; and Charles V, for his twentieth birthday, received the respectable amount of about 13 hundredweights of gold from the future victor of Mexico. Eighteen years earlier his grandmother, Isabella the Catholic, had failed to receive a half ton of gold from Bobadilla, governor of Haiti, a large part of the load having been lost en route. In short, the number of ships that were fitted out for the West Indies and the frequency of their crossings varied in proportion to the traffic in American gold.

A departure from Seville about the year 1540: what a bustle upon the quay! The families of the sailors rub shoulders with hidalgos who have financed the expedition, merchants who have provided the merchandise, and Jewish moneylenders seeking last-moment business. Embraces, final injunctions, tears, and the rocking of the caravels in the violet waters of the port.

The time is past when such ships sailed alone, for the experience was a cruel one. In the space of twelve years, only 270 vessels had come back to Spain of the 490 that had left. Nearly half had been lost! Storms, contrary currents, and reefs had taken their toll, but men had been the cause quite as much as nature. First, the fleets of rival nations or those at war — hot or cold — with Spain. French ships, for instance, lay in wait for the caravels near the Canaries. Returning from his third voyage, Columbus just missed being stopped off Cape St. Vincent. Yet more formidable than the regular squadrons of Francis I and Henry VIII were the corsairs, who operated either on their own behalf or on that of the nations who were enemies of Spain and Portugal. In the latter event, they held a commission in good and proper form, and of course levied an honest share of the prize. The danger of piracy was nothing new. Even at the beginning of the century, Ferdinand the Catholic had defended himself by having strong carracks built after the fashion of the Portuguese and by posting armed vessels at the Canaries. But the most serious incident had been that in which Verrazzano the Florentine, sailing in a French ship, had captured three caravels containing Montezuma's treasure, sent to the emperor by Cortés. To provide against such disasters, costly to the treasury and detrimental to Spanish prestige, Charles V had ordered that merchant ships should be convoyed by men-of-war. The sovereign's decision concealed a malicious ulterior motive. While protecting the merchant ships against corsairs, the escorting ships at the same time kept watch over them and brought them safely to the port to which they were consigned. They also brought them back quite faithfully to the port of departure, so there was no longer the opportunity for certain dealers to sell their cargoes in foreign ports. The ships had to unload at Sanlúcar, Seville, or Cádiz under the eyes of the clerks of the Casa de Contratación, and it was not easy to swindle His Majesty's bookkeepers.

The armada of the Indies draws away. It is a proud sight with its graceful caravels and heavy carracks. A captain of highest rank commands the fleet: Blasco Núñez Vela, the future viceroy. The ships are so heavily laden — stuffs of many colors, glass trinkets, gaudy laces — that they sink low into the water. How much will they weigh when all this rubbish has been exchanged for bars of gold! The fleet passes south of the Canaries, meets the trade winds, and steers straight for Cuba. Until now there has been nothing to fear, for the corsairs no longer risk attacking Spanish ships in the middle of the Atlantic. It is not that they have given up the pursuit, but simply that they have moved their hiding place: they now await the ships at the very gates of the New World. For these are indeed gateways which, across the Antillean archipelago, open wide their doors upon America. Two doors: one, the Florida channel between Havana and the Bahamas, gives access to the Gulf of Mexico; and the other, the Windward channel between Cuba and Haiti, commands the entry to the Caribbean Sea. It is by this second route that the galleons reach Nombre de Dios, the point of departure for Peru.

Thus, having reached the islands, the fleet divides into two: one part goes to seek gold in Mexico, while the other steers for the Isthmus of Panama to take delivery of gold from Peru and silver from the Potosí mines. As soon as the news of the arrival of Spanish ships in the port of Nombre de Dios reaches Lima, the viceroy of Peru gives orders for the fleet anchored at Callao to sail up the Pacific coast to Panama. The cargoes of gold and silver are unloaded and transported on muleback across the isthmus to Nombre de Dios, and then there is nothing more to do but fill the caravels.

It was therefore in the region of the Caribbean Sea that the corsairs prowled. They were numerous and of all nationalities. There were Frenchmen, the legendary Brethren of the Coast, established on the small island of Rortuga off the coast of Haiti. They harassed the Spaniards and maintained the French in the West Indies. They were the ancestors of the celebrated *seigneurs* of Haiti, the gentlemen of Guadaloupe, and the fine people of Martinique of the eighteenth century. There were Englishmen, above all: Hawkins of Plymouth, Reneger of Southampton, and Francis Drake, that king of pirates, whom Elizabeth made a knight as a reward for his services. At San Juan de Ulúa and Nombre de Dios, and on the Colombian and Venezuelan coasts at Santa Marta and Cartagena, the raids multiplied. It was not until the reign of Philip II that a Spaniard, Pedro de Menéndez, organized a system of coast guards and protection for the convoys which proved effective for a while. Piracy did not end then, but lasted as long as the Spanish Empire itself. The pirates transmitted the tradition of adventure from one century to another. However much they changed their name, they were always the same: buccaneers in the seventeenth century or filibusters in the eighteenth, they ceased scouring the Caribbean Sea only when the Spaniards no longer passed that way. They always had mysterious and elusive accomplices: the sea, the night, and sometimes runaway slaves — like the *cimarrones* of Panama who, one evening in 1570, carried off one of the last treasures from Peru under the very noses of the Spanish sentries of Nombre de Dios.

The return to Seville: emptied of their trinkets, but heavily laden with Mexican gold and with silver from Potosí, the caravels have set course for Spain. They have passed through the narrow Antillean channels without falling into any corsair ambush, and are now steering in a northerly direction, carried along by the warm waters of the Gulf Stream, discovered by the pilot Alaminos. A flotilla coming straight from Colombia has joined them in the Sargasso Sea and they run alongside the Bermudas. When they reach the Azores, Europe is near. The escorting gunboat fires a shot from time to time to put to flight the pirates who, setting out from Dieppe, La Rochelle, or Saint-Malo, circle the galleons like cormorants. The Spanish coast comes into view, and already assembled on the quay are the officials of the Casa de Contratación to weigh and stamp the king's fifth, the merchants who supplied the cargo, the lords and the prelates, concessionaires of the New World, and the good people of Seville. It is such an exciting moment that social barriers are relaxed. The beggars of Triana and Andalusian dukes are elbow to elbow, and all have their eyes turned westward, awaiting the fleet. And here it is, the torrent of gold and silver which from Vera Cruz, Nombre de Dios, and Cartagena has cut its shining track across the sapphire-blue sea to mingle with the muddy waters of the Guadalquivir. The fleet has arrived.

A torrent of gold and silver it certainly was! Two figures will show its extent. From 1503 (the year in which Columbus completed his fourth voyage) until 1560 (that in which Francisco Fajardo laid the first stones of Caracas), the New World sent Spain 101 metric tons of gold, or nearly 225,000 pounds. Subsequently the exploitation of the Potosí mines must have multiplied the production of silver tenfold. In fact, from 1560 to 1600, 6872 metric tons — well over 15,000,000 pounds — of silver crossed the Atlantic. In forty years Spain received double the stock of silver existing in Europe before Columbus. If to the precious metals are added the Aztec jewels, the emeralds of Bogotá, the pearls of Venezuela, the beaver skins of New Mexico, the precious woods of Guiana, the indigo, vanilla, and cacao of the islands, one might think that Midas and Croesus are small figures besides Charles V. In contrast with such a torrent, the Pactolus was merely a trickle.

But the wealth of Spain was only temporary, and she was not long in feeling the drawbacks of such prodigious wealth. The abundance of gold caused a rise in prices, without an equivalent stimulus to production. A large part of the monetary wealth remained sterile. The great landed proprietors, enriched by speculation, preferred to live on their capital rather than invest it in agricultural works. The nobility, resting on its laurels, disdained labor and allowed its domains to lie fallow. Certain hidalgos of high rank were even to become money-lenders at high rates of interest, instead of increasing the revenues of their estates. Furthermore, a numerous clergy had to be maintained, as well as increasingly heavier administration and the crowd of parasites who encumbered the antechambers of the Escorial in search of pensions or benefices.

Nothing is more costly than a *politique* of grandeur. This does not mean that Spain died of hunger on its heap of gold, but in order to live on the level of a Great Power — that is, to keep her rank in Europe, and especially to provide for the needs of her American empire — she had to buy abroad what she could not make at home: flax and hemp from Normandy, canvas from Brittany, sailcloth from Saint-Brieuc, cloth from England, and hardwood for ship-building from the Baltic. Thus the gold and silver imported from America were exported, in the form of coins, to France, England, and Holland to pay for the merchandise necessary to the homeland and the empire. The consequences of this state of affairs were paradoxical. While the Spain of Philip II and Philip III was at war with the rebellious Low Countries, Anglican England, and Huguenot France, the merchants of those same countries were actively trading with Seville. But that is nothing new! The Spanish imports of goods were so considerable that they had the effect of stimulating the industry of the three enemy nations and contributing to their prosperity. Simultaneously the foe and the client of France, England, and the Low Countries, Spain was to end by being nothing but a dumping-ground for gold between the Atlantic and the Pyrenees until such time as the power founded on the metal yielded irremediably to the power founded on industry.

But before it experienced these vicissitudes, Spain had half a century in which to extract the best part of America's gold. Charles V's plan in 1540 was not only to enrich his inheritance.

He had even more wonderful ambitions. The three crowns he had assumed — those of Charlemagne, of Lombardy, and of the Romans — were not enough. He wanted to dominate the world. While the crowns of the Capetians and the Tudors still shone in the European sky, Charles had not accomplished the task for which he believed he was destined. He needed gold not for investment or to transform into manufactured products, but to pay as ready money for military supplies, soldiers, and arms. In short, he needed gold to make war. Thanks to the immediately available metal, Charles V kept France in check, though she was twice as populous as Spain, much richer in natural resources, and had a regular army of 2500 men-at-arms concentrated on national territory, in contrast to 1900 Spaniards dispersed throughout the Iberian peninsula, the Kingdom of Naples, and Holland. But France was short of specie, while Charles was glutted with it, and thus it was possible for him, by mobilizing the forces of his empire, to bring a permanent threat to bear upon the French and English monarchies. To the 1900 infantry and 3000 light cavalry of his army in time of peace, Charles added several thousands of mercenaries, whom he had the means to buy. One galleon from America paid for a regiment. Charles had won the battle for gold.

A century later, Colbert, that dark, seedy, genial little man, who had been exasperated by Spanish manners, made the following bitter remark: "We see the reigns of Charles V, Philip II, Philip III, and even Philip IV in such abundance of money through the discovery of the West Indies that all Europe has seen the House of a simple Austrian archduke achieve, in the space of sixty or eighty years, sovereignty over all the States of Burgundy, Aragon, Castile, Portugal, Naples, and Milan; has seen her add to all these States the crown of England and Ireland by the marriage of Philip to Mary Tudor; make the Empire almost hereditary; challenge the pre-eminence of our kings to the crown; by secret practices and by arms, place our kingdom in imminent peril of passing into the hands of foreigners; and finally, aspire to the Empire of all Europe — that is, of the whole world." That Spain was rich irritated this French patriot, but that she should spend without thinking provoked him even more. To this devotee of economy, it was something rather immoral and upsetting, for Colbert had no liking for people who lived beyond their means.

One last look at the Conquistadors. We know now how and why they lived. But how did they die? In opulence and glory? One imagines sumptuous places of retirement, or at least comfortable ones, for the captains of the conquest who had returned home with their fortunes made. They would restore the family *solar,* and those who were literate would write their memoirs. Those who were nostalgic for power would hold some honorary position at court; and as for the soldiers — those without rank — they would return to their villages in La Mancha and Estremadura. They would be rich and would buy land, and in the course of endless social gatherings they would relate their campaigns, telling the stories of the Caribbean, of treasure and princesses. They would willingly show their enormous scars, for such wounds were not to be seen every day. Think of it! Scimitars of sharpened obsidian, and darts poisoned with the juice of the manchineel tree! And they would blow out great clouds of smoke from their pipes of Mexican tobacco. . . .

But the reality was quite different. The majority of the Conquistadors died while still in action, by accident, sickness, or violence. Those who survived ended their days in oblivion and, some of them, in poverty. That so melancholy and wretched a fate should have distinguished these enterprises, which at the beginning had been so full of promise, seems scarcely credible. Yet examples abound, and here are some of them, chosen from the most illustrious.

First the Discoverer himself, Christopher Columbus: he died at Valladolid, cast out by the king whose glory he had made. Juan de la Cosa, the father of Atlantic pilots, died riddled with arrows. Núñez de Balboa was beheaded, on his father-in-law's orders. Díaz de Solis was stoned to death. Nicuesa was lost at sea. Ponce de León died of an arrow in the heart. Hernandez de Córdoba was mortally wounded by Indians. Hernando de Soto was carried off by fever. Pedro de Alvarado was crushed by a horse. Juan de Escalante was killed by the natives of Vera Cruz. Hernán Cortés died poor and alone in an Andalusian village. Pánfilo de Narváez was drowned. Pedro de Valdivia was devoured by cannibals. Bastidas was stabbed by one of his own lieutenants. Diego de Ordaz died of sunstroke. Pedro de Mendoza died at sea.

And what happened to the Conquistadors of Peru? Hernando Pizarro ordered Almagro garroted; the latter's son assassinated Francisco Pizarro; Vaca de Castro had the young Almagro beheaded; and Gonzalo Pizarro, before being condemned to death by Gasca, killed Núñez de Vela. Fifty captains were hanged. Not one of those who governed Peru during a quarter of a century, except Gasca, died other than by violence.

We know now that the alliance of Spain and the New World was sealed with blood. We know, too, that those who profited greatly by the venture were not legion. Is it true, then, that wealth acquired by violence never brings happiness and that there is a curse on gold acquired unjustly? A shadow passes over the flamboyant façade of the temple of Mammon: is it the disheveled figure of the goddess Nemesis?

The drama is ended. The curtain falls slowly on a pyramid of corpses, as in the last act of Shakespearean tragedy. It is finished, but another play is about to begin. What is its prologue?

The difficult day of the conquest has just ended in a blaze of gold and blood. *Oro y sangre* — a funeral apotheosis! Night descends upon the battlefield of the Conquistadors, and silence follows. But at dawn, into the shadows that slowly pale, phantoms slip one by one. Then day is here, and the morning light falls gradually upon these new beings, lighting their resolute features with its silver gleam. They wear neither helmet nor breastplate, but robes of monkish homespun or the sober doublets of men of law. They carry no swords, but in their hands is the mason's trowel or the ivory staff of the alcalde or the cavalier's lance. At first there are only a few, but soon a numberless crowd emerges from the shadows. They gather up the dead and bury them. The battlefield has become a cemetery. Then, in serried ranks, elbow to elbow, like the Spartan phalanxes, they move off westward. These are the colonists.

4

A Measure of Decision: The Armada

Epilogue

As Louis B. Wright indicates, Elizabeth I did not chart a direct collision course with Philip II's Spain — she had too great a respect for Spanish power and for the cost war would entail. Instead, Elizabeth tacked back and forth across a hazardous course of occasional covert hostility. English piracy and assistance to the Dutch rebels, rather than any formal, open acts of war — along with the impatience of Philip himself — were responsible for the decisive encounter.

Whether the Armada was in fact a decisive event in European (and thus American) history is the question posed by the late Garrett Mattingly *in his brilliant study,* The Armada. *Professor Mattingly, a distinguished member of the history faculty at Columbia University, and well known for his earlier biography of* Catherine of Aragon, *contends that the Armada enjoys a certain negative importance. It was less a victory for England than a failure for Spain: it denied Philip his dream of restoring Roman Catholicism to England; it withheld from Spain the opportunity of suppressing the Dutch revolt. The Armada, Professor Mattingly suggests, was responsible more for accelerating the decline of Spain than for hastening the colonizing endeavors of England. Despite their victory, the*

Reprinted from Garrett Mattingly, *The Armada* (Boston: Houghton Mifflin Company, 1959), pp. 397–402.

English did not venture abroad until well after they had come to peace terms with Spain in 1604.

Historians agree that the defeat of the Spanish Armada was a decisive battle, in fact one of the Decisive Battles of the World, but there is much less agreement as to what it decided. It certainly did not decide the issue of the war between England and Spain. Though no fleet opposed Drake, and only local defense forces opposed Norris, the English enterprise off Portugal in 1589 ended in disastrous failure, and thereafter the war dragged itself out for nearly fourteen years more, as long, in fact, as Queen Elizabeth lived, and ended in no better than a draw. Some historians say that the defeat of the Armada "marked the decline of the Spanish colonial empire and the rise of the British." It is hard to see why they think so. By 1603, Spain had not lost to the English a single overseas outpost, while the English colonization of Virginia had been postponed for the duration. Nor did the Armada campaign "transfer the command of the sea from Spain to England." English sea power in the Atlantic had usually been superior to the combined strength of Castile and Portugal, and so it continued to be, but after 1588 the margin of superiority diminished. The defeat of the Armada was not so much the end as the beginning of the Spanish navy. The English could raid the Spanish coast, but they were not able to blockade it. Drake and Hawkins had dreamed of bringing Philip to his knees by cutting off his revenues from the New World, but, in fact, more American treasure reached Spain in the years between 1588 and 1603 than in any other fifteen years in Spanish history. In the War of Elizabeth, nobody commanded the seas.

It is sometimes said that the defeat of the Armada produced the mood of buoyant optimism which characterized the Elizabethan temper, and led to the great explosion of literary genius which marked the last fifteen years of Elizabeth's reign.

Come the three quarters of the world in arms
And we shall shock them

from *King John* is usually quoted by way of illustration. Some doubt is cast on the validity of the first part of this assertion, even for those who have no doubts about characterizing with a phrase the whole mood and temper of a people, by the difficulty of demonstrating that "buoyant optimism" was any more prevalent in England in the decade and a half after 1588 than in the decade and a half before. The second part, the assertion of a causal connection between the defeat of the Armada and the flowering of Elizabethan drama, is hard to refute; even harder, except by the method of *post hoc, propter hoc*, to prove. There is no link in England between the Armada campaign and any literary work as clear as one we can find in Spain. According to the accepted story, a maimed veteran of Lepanto, a minor poet, in the confusing weeks before the Armada sailed from Lisbon, got his accounts of collections he was making for the fleet so embroiled that nobody could tell whether he was trying to cheat the crown or not, and in due time he was sent to prison until somebody could straighten out his books. In his enforced leisure, he found time to begin to write *Don Quixote*. Perhaps this proves that defeat may be just as stimulating to genius as victory, a proposition for which history can furnish considerable support. Or perhaps Cervantes and Shakespeare would have written much as they did whether the Armada had sailed or not.

The older historians, Froude and Motley, Ranke and Michelet, who said that the defeat of the Armada decided that the Counter Reformation was not to triumph throughout Europe have a much better case. Perhaps there was nothing that Medina Sidonia could have done to win the naval battle, but Howard could certainly have lost it. Had he done so, perhaps some way could have been found to get Parma's army across to England. Had Parma landed and taken Rochester, as he meant to do, and then marched to London, supported by a victorious Spanish fleet in the Thames, the course of history in England, and on the Continent, might have been altered in any one of a number of ways. Even had Parma failed to conquer England, or to dethrone the queen, just a limited Spanish success might have dealt the cause of Protestantism a serious, possibly even a fatal blow.

It seems more likely, however, that even had the Spaniards snatched a victory at sea, the final picture of Europe, when peace came, would not have been much different. Philip and his militant advisers dreamed of a great crusade which should wipe out heresy and impose on Christendom the king of Spain's Catholic peace. Drake and his fellow Puritans dreamed of spreading the religious revolution throughout Europe until Anti-Christ was hurled from his throne. Both dreams were wide of reality. Neither the Catholic nor the Protestant coalition had the necessary unity, or could dispose of the necessary force. Systems of ideas, though usually self-limiting in their spread, are harder to kill than men, or even than nations. Of all the kinds of war, a crusade, a total war against a system of ideas, is the hardest to win. By its very nature, the war between Spain and England was likely to be indecisive, and, men being what they are, even its object lesson proved to be in vain. Most of Europe had to fight another war, thirty years long, before deciding that crusades were a poor way of settling differences of opinion, and that two or more systems of ideas could live side by side without mortal danger to either.

Nevertheless, the defeat of the Spanish Armada was, in one sense, a decisive event. Less for the combatants than for the onlookers. For the experts on both sides, the outcome at Gravelines was surprising chiefly because the Armada had done as well as it had. But the landsmen, English and Spanish, were less certain which way the scales of victory would incline, and other people were less certain still. France and Germany and Italy had seen the Spanish colossus advance from victory to victory. Providence, God's increasingly obvious design, the wave of the future, seemed to be on the side of Spain, and, as Catholics, French and German and Italian Catholics rejoiced that Spain was clearly the elected champion of God's Church, little as they relished the prospect of Spanish dominance, while Protestants everywhere were correspondingly alarmed and dismayed. When the Spanish Armada challenged the ancient lords of the English Channel on their own grounds, the impending conflict took on the aspect of a judicial duel in which, as was expected in such duels, God would defend the right. The solemnity of the occasion was heightened by the portentous prophecies about the year of the conflict, prophecies so ancient and respectable that even the most enlightened and skeptical could not quite ignore them. So, when the two fleets approached their appointed battleground, all Europe watched.

For the spectators of both parties, the outcome, reinforced, as everyone believed, by an extraordinary tempest, was indeed decisive. The Protestants of France and the Netherlands, Germany and Scandinavia saw with relief that God was, in truth, as they had always supposed, on their side. The Catholics of France and Italy and Germany saw with almost equal relief that Spain was not, after all, God's chosen champion. From that time forward, though Spain's preponderance was to last for more than another generation, the peak of her prestige had passed. France, in particular, after Henry III's coup d'etat at Blois, began to come back to her role of balance against the house of Austria, and so to being the chief guarantor of the liberties of Europe as long as those liberties were threatened by the Habsburgs. Without the English victory at Gravelines and its ratification by the news from Ireland, Henry III might never have summoned the courage to throw off the Leaguer yoke, and the subsequent history of Europe might have been incalculably different.

So, in spite of the long, indecisive war which followed, the defeat of the Spanish Armada really was decisive. It decided that religious unity was not to be reimposed by force on the heirs of medieval Christendom, and if, in doing so, it only validated what was already by far the most probable outcome, why, perhaps that is all that any of the battles we call decisive have ever done. Whether or not Parma could have reconquered Holland and Zeeland for Spain as he had reconquered the southern provinces, we shall never know. After 1588 he never had a chance; too much of his slender force had to go to sustaining the League against Henry of Navarre. The pattern of territorial, ultimately "national" states which was to characterize modern Europe was beginning to emerge, and after 1588 each major state was not only to be free, but increasingly to feel free, to develop its own individual potentialities without conforming to any externally imposed system of beliefs. Since the powers of Europe were not strong enough, and would not be strong enough for centuries, to inflict irreparable harm on one another, the problem of how to combine freedom to differ with safety from utter destruction could be left to the century in which it would arise.

Meanwhile, as the episode of the Armada receded into the past, it influenced history in another way. Its story, magnified and distorted by a golden mist, became a heroic apologue of the defense of freedom against tyranny, an eternal myth of the victory of the weak over the strong, of the triumph of David over Goliath. It raised men's hearts in dark hours, and led them to say to one another, "What we have done once, we can do again." In so far as it did this, the legend of the defeat of the Spanish Armada became as important as the actual event — perhaps even more important.

5

An Experiment in Feudalism

French Canada in the Seventeenth Century

The Anglo-Spanish clash in Europe, and its far-reaching consequences for the North American continent, have tended to overshadow the colonizing ventures of France in America. Exploring the St. Lawrence in the sixteenth century, Jacques Cartier laid the foundation for a flourishing French colony. This success, however, was not soon to be repeated; later efforts by the Huguenots to settle in South Carolina (Port Royal Sound, in 1562) and northern Florida (Fort Caroline, in 1564) met with failure. French settlement was never to approach the English in size; New France represented ambition but little else.

The key to the failure of France in North America lies in the internal structure of French Canada. Dr. Sigmund Diamond, *a historian who teaches in the Department of Sociology at Columbia University, contends that the fatal flaw in New France was feudalism. Re-examining the French efforts to transplant this institution in the New World, Dr. Diamond cites significant differences between the peasant in old and New France which doomed the experiment from its inception. Scarcity of land in Europe had long kept the peasant in his feudal role. In New France, however, land was abundant, while labor was in short supply. As a result, Dr. Diamond maintains, "in North America, the need to recruit a voluntary labor force was the mother of liberty."*

Sigmund Diamond, "An Experiment in 'Feudalism': French Canada in the Seventeenth Century," from *The William and Mary Quarterly*, 3rd Ser., XVIII (1961), 3–34.

The history of sixteenth- and seventeenth-century colonization provides an almost unique opportunity for the study of certain problems in social organization. The very requirement, as in the case of the British and French in North America, to establish settlements "where none before hath stood," or, as in the case of the Spanish in Central and South America, to devise a mode of accommodation with pre-existing societies, imposed the necessity of considering problems of social organization with a clarity and directness rarely before achieved. Nor was this entirely a matter of necessity. The creation of new societies raised thought about appropriate forms of organization to a new level of consciousness, not only because the situation created the need, but also because it created the opportunity. Man had now the possibility, so at least it seemed, of making a fresh beginning. Was it really necessary that he be forever burdened with the residue of the iniquity and folly of past history? Was it not possible to devise a new form of social organization in which at least some of the less desirable characteristics of the old would be eliminated? From consciousness of both necessity and opportunity came the impetus to create forms of social organization appropriate to achieve the ends held by the leaders of colonization ventures — whether corporations, private individuals invested with almost regal authority, or the crown.

How were the members of the new societies to be recruited? How were they to be motivated to accept the obligations attached to their positions in these new societies? How was order to be maintained between persons of different statuses? What should be the proper balance among ethic, reward, and sanction in getting persons to behave in the proper fashion? Would the family detach persons from their loyalty to the colonizing organization, or would it increase their satisfaction with their lot in the New World? What special features of social organization would have to be created to accommodate the new societies to sponsorship by joint-stock companies, and how might these be different in colonies undertaken by individuals or by government?

Simply to state these questions is to suggest that implicit in the history of early modern colonization is the problem of planned social action, and that this history may be re-examined with the view in mind of analyzing the discrepancy between the plan for the new society and the actual outcome of the effort to apply the plan. If, as appears to be the case, the effort to plan certain aspects of a social system may have unanticipated effects elsewhere in the system — effects that may negate the very purposes of the planners — an examination of the sources of these unanticipated effects may reveal to us more than we now know of the ways in which the different parts of a society are related, and how that society worked.

II

In New France, as in Virginia,[1] the first persistent instrument used to achieve the purposes of colonization was the chartered commercial company. Society was brought to both Jamestown and Quebec in the ships of a commercial company, in both cases for the same reasons and with much the same consequences. The form of organization devised by the company proved incapable not only of balancing the somewhat contradictory objectives of the merchants — and others — who invested and the government which patronized, but even of solving the strictly business problem of recruiting the supplies of capital and labor necessary for the survival of the company. To take but one example, the great Company of the One Hundred Associates, the most prominent of several that failed in New France before 1663, undertook by the terms of its charter to transport four thousand settlers between 1627 and 1642. It was, however, unable to devise a form of social organization that could reconcile its own interests in deploying its labor force into the most profitable economic pursuits with the interests of the government in fixing immigrants to the land and in establishing a polity, and with the interests of the population in receiving as many as possible of the rewards for undertaking the hazardous task of bringing society to a wilderness. Colonization under commercial auspices was considered a failure, and with the demise of the company in 1663, it devolved upon the government in France, as it had upon the government in England in the case of the Virginia Company in 1624, to create a more adequate form of social organization. The cost of recruiting a population, of supplying it, of motivating it to work, of defending it against its enemies became a charge upon government and not upon private business.

What followed was a remarkable experiment

[1] Sigmund Diamond, "From Organization to Society: Virginia in the Seventeenth Century," *American Journal of Sociology*, LXIII (1957–58), 457–475. The Virginia Company attempted to establish a form of social organization in which the behavior of the members would be determined entirely by their positions within the organization. It was necessary, however, to offer concessions to recruit a voluntary labor force and once these concessions — land, marriage, political rights — were offered, social relations could no longer be determined exclusively by the positions persons held within a single system, the organization of the company. Each concession created a new status, each new status involved the person in a new relationship imposing its own necessities, and behavior was determined not by a single position within a single relationship, but by all the positions each person held in a network of sometimes complementary, sometimes contradictory relationships.

in creating a society according to plan, an attempt to utilize existing institutions — religion, family, land tenure, law — and to adapt them, under government auspices, to the objectives of the planners and the needs of an immigrant population under frontier conditions. The administrative demands entailed in such an effort were staggering. Hundreds of manuscript volumes of home and colonial decrees and an even larger mass of correspondence, court decisions, and other official documents stand today as mute testimony to the scope of the attempt. What, above all, characterizes the plan is that it bore so clearly the stamp of that passion for rationality — the desire to achieve order, symmetry, and harmony — which is the hallmark of bureaucratic endeavor. It would be anachronistic and yet truthful to describe the objective of the French authorities in Canada after 1663, not as the creation of a society to be governed by political means, but as the creation of an administrative system in which persons would have fixed positions in a table of organization, would behave in the way deemed appropriate for those positions, and would be manipulated, deployed, and disciplined by measures more compatible with the requirements of a formal organization than of a society.

To a degree, of course, this desire to rationalize the operations of the system of governance was already highly developed in France. The attempt of the seigniors of the *ancien régime* to bring order into their own economic activities and into their relations with tenants is by now well known; even better known is the celebrated effort of the monarchy under Louis XIV and his successors to reform the system of administration. What permitted the same effort to be carried even further in Canada was the possibility of beginning at the beginning. Where a society did not already exist, there was no necessity to make the best of a bad situation, to compromise the goal of rationality by having to reckon with the need to adjust to established institutions and traditions.

Instructing the Dauphin in the desirability of recruiting only persons of moderate social position into the civil service, Louis XIV wrote: "It was not to my interest to select subjects of higher degree. It was important that they should not conceive hopes any higher than it pleased me to grant them, something which is difficult among persons of high birth." The tendency betrayed by the King's instructions to regard his civil servants as instruments to aid him in achieving his own purposes had an even wider extension in Canada, for there everyone was looked upon as the King viewed his civil servant, as an agent of the state. The letter of Jean Baptiste Colbert to Marquis Prouville de Tracy upon the latter's assumption of the governorship is exceptional only because Tracy's position in the administration imposed the necessity of greater explicitness. "The first thing that I must insist upon," wrote Colbert, "is that, since the king takes note of all of his affairs, you must address yourself directly to him in making reports and receiving his orders. It would be well for you to observe this in the future, for although I inform him of everything written to me, those, like you, who hold positions of trust ought to have it as a maxim to have their main relationship with His Majesty."

Relying upon the loyalty of their direct subordinates and the self-discipline of the population, the metropolitan authorities aimed at the creation of a society in Canada in which the vast majority of persons would be firmly fixed to the land, would live peaceably in their villages, and would respond obediently to the commands of their superiors. The reins of legitimate power were held firmly in the hands of the administrative authorities and their designated surrogates, and any tendency toward the development of competing authority, even when it conformed to practices already established in France, was rigorously suppressed.[2]

[2] Renaud, *Origines économiques,* 93; Blet, *Colonisation,* 126–127; Mason Wade, *The French Canadians, 1760–1945* (New York, 1955), 18–19; Gérard Filteau, *La Naissance d'une nation* (Montreal, n.d.), I, 79–81. ". . . it is to be feared that as a result of engaging in trade the inhabitants will live a good part of the year in idleness, whereas if they had no such freedom to engage in trade it would be necessary for them to apply themselves in cultivating their lands." Colbert to Talon, Apr. 1, 1666, FOM, Ser. C[11]A, II, fol. 200. As late as the eve of the final struggle with the British for the mastery of Canada, the King of France was still exhorting his officials to make the progress of agriculture their first concern; see, for example, the extracts from the royal correspondence in *Report Concerning Canadian Archives for the Year 1905* (Ottawa, 1906), I, 73, 165, 202.

Every aspect of life in Canada was subject to rational calculation and was alterable by purposeful action. Political institutions, the family, Indian affairs, the range of permissible trades and occupations, the amount of prestige and honor to be associated with each status in the society were all carefully regulated. The behavior of each major segment of the population was prescribed in the minutest detail, even to the point of regulating the order of precedence in religious and secular ceremonies, the appropriate forms of address, and the types of weapons that each might bear. The total corpus of these regulations betrays the assumption, central to the conception of the administrator, that each person is essentially the occupant of a position in an organization and that his behavior can be made to conform to the needs of the system for order and stability.

Precautions were taken that nothing should interfere with the flow of authority in the established chain of command. Though occasional meetings of the population were held to discuss problems and to hear proposed programs, never did these assume the character of representative assemblies; they were *ad hoc* bodies, summoned to listen and not to argue. When, elated by his own cleverness, Governor Louis de Buade, Comte de Frontenac, informed Colbert in 1672 that he had administered an oath of loyalty to the seigniors and, for convenience, to a group of habitants acting on behalf of all, he received a blistering reply. "Since our Kings have long regarded it as good for their service not to convoke the Estates-General of the Kingdom in order perhaps to abolish insensibly this ancient usage, you, on your part, should very rarely, or, to speak correctly, never, give a corporate form to the inhabitants of Canada. You should even, as the colony strengthens, suppress gradually the office of Syndic, who presents petitions in the name of inhabitants, for it is well that each should speak for himself and no one for all."

Nothing was permitted to escape the hawk-like eyes of those responsible for seeing that the colonists behaved according to plan, and no problem was too small to be taken to the highest official. Jérôme de Pontchartrain himself, the minister of colonies in Paris, was called upon to decide disputes involving a cow strayed into someone's garden, a brawl at a church door, the virtue of a certain lady. Colbert had to be informed, as evidence of the degree to which prescriptions for proper behavior were observed, that two captains had been married, one lieutenant engaged, and "four ensigns are in treaty with their mistresses, and are already half engaged." Jean Talon, struck with the thought that population increase might be achieved by the intermarriage of Indians and French, studied the reproductive capacity of Indian women and reported that it was impaired by their nursing children longer than necessary; but, he added, "this obstacle to the speedy building up of the colony can be overcome by a police regulation."

In short, what was planned was a society in which all persons would be under a jurisdiction and patronage that were at once French, royal, and orthodox. Stability would be guaranteed by each person's having a precise place and acting in accordance with the behavior defined as appropriate to that place. The elements of this society were, of course, diverse — government regulation of economic activity, a special system of land tenure, an elaborate code of law, an established church, royal patronage of the institution of the family — and every effort was made to weld them together into an organization in which discipline would be achieved because each man would remain loyal to the institutions to which he was attached.

The fur trade, which had been at once a blessing and a curse to the colony, was the subject of endless consideration by government officials. Although the form of regulation varied, the trade was controlled at virtually all times so as to restrict the number and influence of persons engaged in it. The privileged few were thus to be attached to the government with the ties of gratitude that flow from profit, while the mass of the population would not be diverted from the performance of necessary agricultural tasks. The *coureurs de bois* were to be quarantined so that their lawlessness could not contaminate what was hoped would be an obedient agricultural society. Men who desert the land to enter the forests, said Talon, are men, "without Christianity, without sacraments, without religion, without priests, without laws, without magistrates, sole masters of their own actions and of the application of their own wills. . . ."

Population growth, recognized by government officials as indispensable to increasing agricultural production and, at least indirectly, to reducing the overhead costs of administering the colony, was promoted through immigration, encouragement of marriage, family subsidies, and attempts to mobilize the Indians into the labor force. The policy of "Francisation," which included conversion, domiciliation, intermarriage, and education of the Indians in the ways of the white man, was undertaken in the hope that, made tractable by their re-education, they would swell the labor force. It quickly became evident that the policy had failed, and that population growth would have to come about through immigration and natural increase.

In 1668 Colbert suggested to Talon that those "who may seem to have absolutely renounced marriage should be made to have additional burdens, and be excluded from all honors; it would be well even to add some marks of infamy." The Intendant was quick to take the hint; bachelors were barred from the right to hunt, fish, trade with the Indians, and even to enter the woods. By act of the Sovereign Council of Canada, "any inhabitant having in legitimate marriage ten living children, not priests, *religieux* or *religieuses* shall be paid three hundred livres a year, and those who have twelve shall be paid four hundred livres a year." Young men who married before the age of twenty were given a bonus. Fathers whose sons were not married by the age of twenty or whose daughters were still vestals at the age of sixteen were to be fined and summoned to the court every six months.

But to encourage marriage the government would have to take the initiative in providing women, unless it were willing — which it was not — to tolerate "a thousand disorders in the settlements . . . where the women are very glad to have several husbands and where the men cannot get even one wife." Marriage, it was anticipated, would not only increase the birth rate but would lead to a more settled and orderly life. As in Virginia, therefore, the government assumed the responsibility of shipping from France "demoiselles" for the military officers and what pious Mother Marie de l'Incarnation called "une marchandise mêlée" — mixed goods — for the ordinary settlers, something more than a thousand altogether.

Still, French Canada's population growth, dependent overwhelmingly upon natural increase and very little upon immigration, lagged far behind that of the British North American colonies and even behind Canadian requirements. As late as 1710 Governor Philippe de Rigaud, Marquis de Vaudreuil, complained that there was not enough labor for the seigniors to cultivate even half their estates; six years later he was recommending that condemned salt-smugglers in France be shipped as indentured servants at the expense of the farmers-general. In 1733 Governor Charles de la Boische, Marquis de Beauharnois, and Intendant Gilles Hocquart echoed the complaint: "The scarcity of men, and the high wages of both agricultural and urban labor, considerably diminishes the revenues of landlords and merchants." Despite every effort of a government that exhorted and a people that produced, the population of French Canada amounted to only about 5 per cent of the population south of the St. Lawrence River by the middle of the eighteenth century.

But neither government regulation nor family attachments were, in the view of the French authorities, sufficient to maintain social discipline; religion, too, was counted on to disseminate an ethic calculated to remind each man to keep to his allotted place. From the beginning of New France, the Roman Catholic Church was given major responsibility for enforcing the ban on Protestants in Canada, and the zealousness with which it responded to the task of rooting out unorthodoxy in both its Jansenist and Protestant forms revealed that secular as well as religious discipline was its proper concern. The importance of orthodoxy from the religious viewpoint was self-evident. "On the side of the state," wrote Bishop François Xavier de Laval, "it appears to be no less important. Everyone knows that Protestants in general are not so attached to His Majesty as Catholics. . . . To multiply the number of Protestants in Canada would be to give occasion for the outbreak of revolutions."

Doctrinal conflict was minimized, therefore, by screening prospective immigrants, but the church played a no less significant role in disciplining colonists once they had arrived. The keynote was sounded in a letter from Louis XIV to Bishop Laval: "As I have been informed of your continued care to hold the people in their duty towards God and towards me by the good education you give or cause to be given to the young, I write this letter to express my satisfaction with conduct so salutary, and to exhort you to persevere in it." The nature of this education may be inferred from the list of virtues commended to boys, drawn from the rulebook of the Petit Séminaire in Quebec: "humility, obedience, purity, meekness, modesty, simplicity, chastity, charity, and an ardent love of Jesus and his Holy Mother." All schools but one were under control of the church, and that single exception — the School of Mathematics and Hydrography — passed under its influence early in the eighteenth century.

In its role as custodian of morals and, though its pretensions in this area were disputed, of law, the church went even further. It regulated the style of clothing; it censored books; it established with meticulous accuracy the order of priority of both religious and secular officials on ceremonial occasions; it attacked usury and supported its attack by refusing confession to usurers; it shipped back to France immoral men, including those who were so unmindful of their situation in life as to fall in love with more highly placed girls; and it attempted to cultivate an ethic of obligation and obedience, of simplicity and austerity.

Most important of all, however, it threw the weight of ecclesiastical discipline behind the effort to fix the population into assigned positions; the sanction of excommunication itself was invoked against those who left the land without permission and traded illegally for furs with the Indians. Although there were disputes between secular and religious officials when either tried to exercise authority that pinched the other, they were as one in recognizing the importance of the church in disciplining the inferiors of both, in urging upon them acceptance of a code of belief that would confine their behavior within the limits desired by higher authority. We must "multiply the number of parishes and . . . render them fixed . . . ," wrote Governor Jacques-René de Brissay, Marquis de Denonville, to Colbert in 1685. "This undertaking . . . would be a sure means of establishing schools, with which the *curés* would occupy themselves and thus accustom the children at an early hour to control themselves and become useful." Finally, in its capacity as landowner, the church assumed the rule of model seignior, and attempted by the force of its own example to influence the behavior of other landlords. By 1750 the church held over two million arpents of land, more than one-third of all the grants that had been made.

But the most characteristic institution of the old regime in Canada — the one that gave tone to the entire society — was the seigniorial system. There was much in it that was reminiscent of medieval feudalism, but only reminiscent. Feudalism in France was an organic growth; in Canada it was a transplanted institution, and the French administration saw to it that in the transplanting it was pruned of less desirable characteristics. The French monarchy had established itself in the teeth of feudal opposition and was in no mood now to offer the seigniors sufficient independence and power so as to require repetition of the experience. When Governor Tracy and Intendant Talon drew up their "Project de Règlement" in 1667, they warned that since "obedience and fidelity [two words obscured] are more likely to suffer attenuation in distant provinces of the state than in the neighbors of the Sovereign Authority, which resides mainly in the person of the prince and has more force and virtue there than in any other person, it is the part of prudence to prevent in the establishment of the growing state of Canada all those vexatious revolutions which might render it monarchical, aristocratic, or democratic, or even — by a balanced power and authority between subjects — divide it into parts and give rise to such a dismemberment as France suffered by the creation of such sovereignties within the kingdom as Soissons, Orleans, Champagne, and others." In their concern lies the clue to the essential difference between French and Canadian feudalism. The landed seignior in Canada was entitled to many of the rights possessed by his counterpart in France — potential membership in the nobility; ceremonial rights like fealty and homage; judicial rights like holding private courts; and more lucrative rights such as the collection of rents and mutation fines, the imposition of labor services, and the monopoly of all milling — and the enforcement of these rights was presumably guaranteed by the extension to Canada of the law code known as the Custom of Paris and the beneficent protection of the royal authority. Nevertheless, the position of the Canadian seignior was far different from that of the French.

The right to have a private court was his, but the use of the term *haute, moyenne, et basse justice* in Canada must not delude us into thinking that it held the same meaning as in France. The existence of the competing royal court eventually limited private jurisdiction to relatively simple cases about seigniorial dues and obligations, and even in these the habitant had free right of appeal to the royal court. Nor were the profits of justice as lucrative in Canada as in France; where population was sparse, the opportunity to squeeze income from it in the courts was limited by the small number of cases and by the fear that too much repression would cause the seignior's labor force to move to the lands of a less exacting landlord. "I will not say that the Goddess of Justice is more chaste and impartial here than in France," wrote Baron Louis Armand de la Hontan, "but at any rate, if she is sold, she is sold more cheaply." In Canada the problem was not so much to check the encroachments of the seigniorial courts as to force the reluctant seigniors to accept the profitless and limited jurisdiction the Crown imposed on them.

So, too, the seigniors of Canada had the rights of *banalité* and *corvée*. Under conditions of severely limited population, however, these were drained of most of their significance. The intendants of Canada, conscious of the fact that onerous obligations on the peasantry would hamper immigration, restricted the size of the payments to the seigniors and forced them to improve their mills. So profitless were these rights that, as with private courts, the problem was not so much to control their abuse as to get the seigniors to build mills on their land grants on penalty of losing their monopoly, but for twenty years the seigniors sabotaged enforcement of the decree by not promulgating it. What under other circumstances would have been a profitable privilege was for the Canadian seignior a burdensome cost.

Even the conditions under which he held land and could legitimately demand payments from his sub-infeudees were different from those in France. Squirm though he might, never could the seignior wholly evade the scrutiny of the intendants, who were determined to prevent the payments owed by the *censitaires,* the peasants, from becoming too burdensome. Even more, his power to dispose of his own domain was limited in such a way as to reduce his maneuverability and to make him essentially an agent of the Crown in the achievement of its purposes. After several preliminary gestures, the King, through the Arrêts of Marly in 1711, decreed that all seigniorial grants not settled and developed through sub-infeudation would revert to the Crown, and that the payments to seigniors from sub-infeudated lands must be uniform and limited. In the minds of the administrators, the seigniors were less proprietors than trustees, entitled to occupy the land only if they performed the essential tasks required of them.

Though the Canadian seignior was sometimes able to evade some of the restrictions imposed upon him, there can be little doubt that his rights were more limited than were those of the French. Still, they were believed sufficient to get him to assume the tasks for which the Crown held him responsible — to clear the land, to settle it with farmers, to support the church and the state, and to keep his subordinates in their places. For those who did their tasks well, there was the added incentive of possible ennoblement: We must grant titles, Talon told Colbert in 1670, to "fill the officers and richer seigniors with a new zeal for the settlement of their lands in hope of being recompensed with titles as well." Having deprived the seignior of many of the attributes that permitted him to be a seignior, the King's administrators yet hoped he would act like one.

As with the seigniors, so with the *censitaires.* They, too, had rights and obligations differing somewhat from their brothers' in France. They had to clear the land lest it revert to the seignior; they owed him rent and mutation fines; they worked for him and gave him part of their catch of fish; they paid him deference; they were not allowed to engage in the fur trade. Yet, their duties were less onerous than in France, and they were protected from excessive exploitation by a solicitous officialdom. Besides, the prospect of improvement was such, so it was anticipated, as to induce them willingly, to accept their position. "There are so many strong and robust peasants in France," wrote Father Paul le Jeune, "who have no bread to put in their mouths; is it possible they are so afraid of losing sight of the village steeple, as they say, that they would rather languish in their misery and poverty, than to place themselves some day at their ease among the inhabitants of New France, where with the blessings of earth they will more easily find those of heaven and of the soul?" In short, the seigniorial system in Canada was transformed by the authorities into an agency of land settlement, an instrument for peopling the country, and a mechanism for insuring social stability.

III

How did the system actually work? If long-term stability and social discipline were the objectives desired by the authorities, they were not the objectives attained.

The *sine qua non* of successful colonization was the mobilization of an adequate labor force. In Canada, as in British North America, experiments in the use of forced labor and of the local Indians failed, and it soon became necessary to recruit labor by voluntary means. To do so, however, such substantial concessions had to be made that the real position occupied by the labor force in the new society was utterly different not only from its position in Old World society but even from what the planners of the system had intended.

The companies before 1663 recognized the necessity of offering incentives, but sought to minimize them in an effort to keep costs low. Louis Hébert, the Paris apothecary who became the first settler at Quebec, had been offered full support for himself and his family for a period of two years plus two hundred crowns per year for three years as inducement to emigrate. After he arrived, however, the company imposed harsher terms: he was given only one hundred crowns per year; his entire family and his servant were required to work for the company for three years, after which time he was required to sell all his produce to the company at prices current in France; he could work clearing his land and building his house only when the chief factor did not need his services; he was not to engage in the fur trade; and he was to offer his professional services free of charge to the company.

Samuel de Champlain had been quick to see that the terms were not sufficiently attractive to encourage immigrants. "The Companies having refused to give them the means of cultivating the land," he wrote, "had thus taken away all reason for them to become settlers. At the same time, these Companies gave out that there were numerous families in the country; the truth is that, being entirely useless, they served only to count, and burdened the settlement more than they helped it. . . . That was not the way to create a great desire on the part of anyone to go and people a country, when a man cannot have any free enjoyment of its returns . . . ."

Men who knew the country best, like Father Le Jeune, could only agree with him. Those who emigrate for regular wages, he argued, do not provide the most efficient labor force; they "try to be like some of our neighbors, who, having scarcely passed the line of the Equator, all begin to call themselves Gentlemen, and no longer care to work; if they felt constrained to do it for themselves, they would not sleep over it." The right of ownership, even if limited, was his solution. He explained that immigrants ought to "engage themselves to some family for five or six years on the following conditions:"

> That they should be boarded during all this time without receiving any wages, but also that they should possess entirely and in their own right one-half of all the land they clear. And, as they will need something for their own support, the contract should provide that all they get every year, from the lands they have already cleared, should be shared by half; this half, with the little profits they can make in the Country, would be enough to keep them, and to pay after the first or second year for half the tools which they will use in clearing and tilling the land. Now if four men could clear eight arpents of land a year, doing nothing else, winter or summer, in six years forty-eight arpents would be cleared, of which twenty-four would belong to them. With these twenty-four arpents they could support thirty-six persons, or even forty-eight.

if the land is good. Is this not a way of becoming rich in a little while?[3]

Throughout the long history of New France, the concessions offered to immigrants assumed many different forms, but in the final analysis they amounted to the same thing — the promise, even the guarantee, of social mobility.

Those who came at their own expense had the promise of land and even, if they performed "notable service" in the interests of the authorities, of titles and patents of nobility. If, as now appears to be the case, most of the *engagés* did not have the promise of land at the time they agreed to their contracts of engagement, many did receive land after completion of their term of service; and, in any case, the wages they could expect in Canada allowed them a substantial increase in living standards.

To induce soldiers to remain in Canada after the period of their enlistment, land and financial subsidies were promised according to rank. Nearly 1500 remained, "finding there land that they would not perhaps have had in their own country." For skilled artisans there was not only the guarantee of high wages but, significantly, the promise that they would not forever be tied to the same position. Throughout the entire French occupation of Canada, ordinary craft restrictions on the achievement of mastership were loosened, and the opportunity to return to France in the higher status was freely granted. To be sure, the lure of the carrot was not the only means used; there was also the stick. Servants were forbidden to leave their masters and others to hide them on pain of severe punishment; marriage without consent of the master was banned; artisans were forced to do whatever their masters required, even when that meant working outside their trades; wages of unskilled workers were regulated.

The net effect of the administration's policy was to introduce slackness rather than rigidity into the society, even to the point of seriously compromising its own ability to obtain revenue. The state *corvée* had to be curtailed, eventually suppressed, for fear that word of its existence would restrict emigration from France and would antagonize the labor force, which, in another capacity, was counted on to provide militia service. The billeting of soldiers, always a source of complaint, was progressively limited until in 1683 it was entirely abolished and became a regular fixed charge upon the state. Direct payments in the form of seigniorial rents and ecclesiastical tithes were reduced considerably below the level prevailing in France. Indeed, *liberté* and *tranquillité* — eventually the major objectives of colonial policy — were seen as attainable only by offering concessions to induce a labor force to migrate and increase its productivity. "Such are the means of attracting colonists and keeping them," wrote M. Petit in his treatise on colonization. "But the most important of all is gentleness and moderation in the government, in extending its hands so that the colonists find, at least in the legitimate use of authority, compensations for the harshness of their labor and the sacrifice of their health in establishments recognized as so useful to the state."

Despite all inducements, the population of Canada never reached the desired quantity and quality. From beginning to end, the reports to the authorities bemoaned the scarcity of labor and its lack of discipline. "Sixty indentured servants have been sent to this country again this year with the notion that they would be immediately useful," Intendant Jacques de Meulles wrote to the Marquis de Seignelay, Colbert's son, in 1684. "The oldest is not seventeen, and . . . I believe that those who sent them are making a mockery of us, there being no one of an age to render service." Send us no more gentlemen, Governor Denonville pleaded in 1686, only "sturdy peasants . . . used to hatchet and pickaxe." "We entreat, you, Monseigneur," wrote Beauharnois and Hocquart to Minister Jean-Frédéric Phélypeaux, Marquis de Maurepas, in 1730, "to stop sending libertines to the colony. There is already a very great number, and it is more difficult to restrain them in this country than anywhere else because of the facility they have for escaping and the difficulty of convicting them." By 1712 the seigniory of Isle Perrot, granted in 1672, had only one inhabitant; those of Chicouanne and Boisseau, granted that same year, had none; Pointe du Lac, granted early in the seventeenth century, had one settler; Lussaudière, granted in 1672,

[3] Reuben Gold Thwaites, ed., *The Jesuit Relations and Allied Documents,* IX (Cleveland, 1897), 184–191.

had none; the seigniory of Jacques Cartier, granted in 1649, had only one inhabitant — he fished for eels — and dozens more were so sparsely inhabited as to be profitless to their owners and to the state. The problem of maintaining an adequate labor force was made even more difficult by the flight into the wilderness of those who were expected to remain fixed to the land. Throughout the eighteenth century, when the population of able-bodied adult males was always pathetically small, an average of three hundred men were absent each year, won over to the freedom of forest life, deserters to the English, or seekers after their fortune in Louisiana. Above all, however, the problem of disciplining labor and raising its productivity was exacerbated by the refusal of the population to behave in the expected manner.

The continued loyalty of the seignior to the system depended on his ability to profit from his privileges, and his privileges were such as to require a large and expanding population. But in Canada, unlike France, land was plentiful and people scarce; and the competition was among seigniors for tenants and not among tenants for land. And even the land system itself conspired against the desire of the authorities to fix people to the land and against the ability of the seigniors to make their living from it. The estates, laid out in parallelograms with the short side fronting on the St. Lawrence River, became split up into ever-narrowing ribbons of farms as, with the passage of time, they were divided among heirs; and agricultural productivity suffered accordingly. Instead of wealth and the grandeur of privileged status, poverty was the lot of most seigniors. "It is necessary to help them," wrote Denonville to Seignelay, "by giving them the means of . . . livelihood for, in truth, without that there is great fear that the children of our nobility . . . will become bandits because of having nothing by which to live."

What was a bad situation to begin with was worsened by the propensity of many seigniors to adopt a style of life better in accord with their expectations than with realities. "The Gentlemen that have a Charge of Children, especially Daughters," wrote Baron La Hontan, "are oblig'd to be good Husbands, in order to bear the Expence of the magnificent Cloaths with which they are set off; for Pride, Vanity, and Luxury, reign as much in *New France* as in *Old France*." "One finds here no rich persons whatever," Father Pierre F. X. de Charlevoix wrote. "In New England and the other British colonies there reigns an opulence by which the people seem not to know how to profit; while in New France poverty is hidden under an air of ease which appears entirely natural. The English colonist keeps as much and spends as little as possible; the French colonist enjoys what he has got, and often makes a display of what he has not got."

To persist in behaving in New France in ways that were appropriate to Old France was to fly in the face of reality. When the Sieur de Frédéric, captain in the Carignan-Salières regiment and nephew of its colonel, punished a habitant for complaining to the intendant about injury done to his crops when Frédéric rode over his land, he doubtless felt that the propriety of his behavior could not be impeached. He was, however, returned to France by Intendant Talon. In France, conscience required that sympathy be extended to peasants whose fields were trampled by seigniors. In Canada, the reverse was true: "divers persons so [abuse] the goodness of the seigneurs of this island [Montreal], who allow them such freedom, that they hunt and fish everywhere on the superior's private domain . . . where they kill the pigeons on pretence of their being other game, and break down all the fences, even threatening the overseer, a most worthy man placed there by the seigneur." So widespread was the abuse that the seigniors had to beg the protection of the authorities.

The protection to the ego offered by keeping up appearances at all costs rather quickly reached its limits. Louis Hamelin, the seignior of Grondines, was himself reduced to working his own mill when his miller was called to military service. Even such notable families as Saint-Ours, Verchères, Repentigny, and Aubert de la Chesnaye were impoverished and forced to besiege the King with petitions for military commands, judicial posts, licenses to trade in furs, pensions — anything that might provide income. Others gave up entirely and returned to France. When the owners of the seigniory of Monts-Pelées donated it to the Dames Religieuses de la Miséricorde de Jesus, they wrote wistfully and pathetically: "the present donation is made because the donors find themselves at a very advanced age which does not permit them to work to gain their livelihood and because the little property they have is not sufficient to produce enough income to support them in sickness or in health for the rest of their days; they are, moreover, abandoned by all their relatives and friends." In the circumstances, the seigniors began to behave not as their role prescribed, but as conditions seemed to require.

They violated their obligations to their tenants, attempting to exact from them rights to which they were not entitled. They "grant to their habitants leave to cut timber on the ungranted lands, on condition that they pay 10 per cent of the value of the boards obtained therefrom," Intendant Michel Bégon wrote Victor Marie d'Estrées, president of the Conseil de Marine, in 1716. "When they concede woodlands they reserve for themselves all the oak and pine timber thereon without compensation to the habitants, and they are able to exact any price they please for this wood. . . ." They attempted to squeeze more labor through the *corvée* than they were entitled to, made attractive verbal promises to the habitants and then stiffened the terms in writing, induced tenants to clear land for pasture which they later sold, and extorted illegal payments.

Instead of using land for agriculture and settlement, they used it for speculation. Without themselves making any improvements or insisting that their tenants do so, the seigniors, so the local authorities reported to Paris, encouraged the habitants to buy and sell land so that they might collect the mutation fine that went with every change in ownership. "There will always be some people," Intendant Jean Bochart de Champigny informed Minister Louis de Phélypeaux, Comte de Pontchartrain, in 1691, "who will seek land concessions in distant places . . . for the sole purpose of going there to trade . . . without thought of settling."

Instead of doing their duty in the preservation of law and order, the seigniors connived with lawbreakers. Fearful in Canada as in the Antilles that the establishment of too many taverns would distract workmen and increase delinquency, the authorities sought to use the seigniors as direct agents of social control. "The trade of tavern-keeper has attracted all the rogues and lazy people who never think of cultivating the land," Denonville wrote Seignelay in 1685: "far from that, they deter and ruin the other inhabitants. I believe, Monseigneur, that in the villages, the Seigneur should hire and dismiss the tavern-keeper according to his good and bad conduct, and the Seigneur would be responsible for him. I know of seigneuries where there are only 20 houses and more than half are taverns. . . ." But instead of upholding the law against tavern-keepers, they helped them to break it; as, indeed, they helped others also to break the law. "I must not conceal from you," Intendant Jacques Duchesneau wrote Colbert, "that the disobedience of the *coureurs de bois* has reached such a point that everybody boldly contravenes the King's interdictions. . . . I have enacted ordinances against the *coureurs de bois;* . . . against the gentlemen . . . who harbor them; and even against those who have any knowledge of them, and will not inform the local judges. All has been in vain; inasmuch as some of the most considerable families are interested with them. . . ."

The seigniors broke the law themselves, especially when the authorities put them in such a position that to act in accordance with their status as loyal servant of the state seemed to conflict with the pressures on behavior that followed from their position as seignior. On October 21, 1686, a royal edict ordered all seigniors to establish mills on their property, but for twenty years the law remained a dead letter because, contrary to orders, it was not promulgated by the Superior Council in Quebec.

Above all, the seigniors failed in their obligation to support the social system that they, more than anyone else, were counted on to uphold. In making use of the major opportunity that existed to escape the discipline of the system — participation in the fur trade — they provided an example that others were quick to follow. "These disorders," wrote Denonville, "are much greater in the families of those who are gentlemen or who want to be so, either because of indolence or vanity. Having no other means of subsistence but the forest, because they are not accustomed to hold the plow, the pick, or the ax, their only resource being the musket, they must spend their lives in the woods, where there are no priests to restrain them, nor fathers, nor governors to control them. . . . I do not know, Monseigneur, how to describe to you the attraction that all the young men feel for the life of the savage, which is to do nothing, to be utterly free of constraint, to follow all the customs of the savages, and to place oneself beyond the possibility of correction."

At times even the authorities recognized that a vast discrepancy had developed between the real position of the Canadian seignior and the one he had been given, and the pressure of new necessities was a more powerful influence on behavior than the designs of the administrators. Contrasting the behavior of the Canadians with that of the young men in the Antilles, Beauharnois and Hocquart reported to the King that most Canadians "prefer voyages and trade, which give them the means of livelihood. It is not surprising that the young men of the Islands seek to fill vacancies for the position of councilor, because not only are their customs different from those of the Canadians, but, having been born with money, they are ambitious only for honors. Poverty reigns in Canada; men seek to escape from it and obtain a little comfort."

Conditions that were poison for the seigniors were meat for the *censitaires,* though they, too, disrupted the social organization by refusing to behave in accordance with expectations or even frequently as custom and law dictated. In the design of the administrators, the *censitaires* were intended as a docile and obedient labor force. The very concessions, however, that were offered to entice them into the labor force — concessions that took the form both of direct incentives and limitations on the authority of their seigniorial masters — made it impossible to keep them in their assigned position or to fix their behavior in the desired mold. Their situation in the New World was a very decided improvement over their situation in the Old World, and they acted less in response to old prescriptions than to new imperatives.

In classic feudalism, institutions and rules existed which empowered the seigniors to compel obedience. Marc Bloch has observed:

> Now, in the hands of the seigniors the almost unrestricted exercise of the rights of justice placed an infinitely powerful weapon of economic exploitation. It reinforced their power of command, which in the language of the time . . . was called their "ban." "You can compel us to observe these rules" (those relating to the oven), the inhabitants of a village in Roussillon tell the Templars, masters of the place, in 1246, "even as a seignior can and ought to compel his subjects." . . . Among the multiple applications of this discipline, one of the most significant and, in practice, the most important, was the formation of seigniorial monopolies. . . . With very sure instinct, the jurists, when they began in the thirteenth century to create a theory of society, found themselves in agreement in linking the *banalités* with the organization of justice. The right to judge had been the strongest prop of the right to command.[4]

These were the rules and institutions that permitted the seigniors to maintain distance between themselves and the *censitaires* and that compelled the latter to accept the discipline imposed on them. In Canada, these institutions did not exist — or, at least, they existed in a most attenuated form — and it proved impossible to subject the *censitaires* to a discipline that implied a far wider distance between themselves and their superiors than in fact was the case. Not only were the seigniors' traditional monopolies emptied of meaning and their authority curbed by the administration, but the *censitaires* now competed directly with them in areas that had once been their private preserve. It was the *censitaires,* not the seigniors, who were appointed to the position of *capitaine des milices,* a post that involved the exercise of civil as well as military authority; and the complaints of the seigniors, faced with declining prestige, were to no avail. "You should," wrote Minister Jerome de Pontchartrain to Governor François de Galiffet of Three Rivers, "make the seigniors of the parishes in your jurisdiction understand that the *capitaines des milices* must not communicate to them the orders that they receive from the governors and intendants before executing them; that is not due to them and they have no right to demand it of the *capitaines,*

[4] Marc Bloch, *Les Caractères originaux de l'histoire rurale française* (Paris, 1955), I, 82–84.

who might do so as a matter of courtesy, however, when it is of no interest to the service."

The *censitaires* hunted and fished almost at will, they were occasionally called in to offer advice on government policy, and they were urged to report all "torts, exces, violances" committed by the seigniors. Small wonder, then, they responded to their new situation by surrounding themselves with some of the trappings of the status that had so long been denied them. Though the government appealed to their own self-interest in urging them to concentrate on the production of cattle, pigs, and sheep, and though it imposed ban after ban on the raising of horses, they continued to breed horses and to ride through the countryside, as if in unconscious remembrance of the age-old connection between *cheval* and *chevallerie*.

Even in the area of landownership, they reduced the distance between themselves and the seigniors. In 1712 Gédéon de Catalogne, a military engineer, made a survey of the more than ninety seigniories that then existed in Canada. Excluding those granted to religious orders, it is possible — by comparing the secular owners in 1712 with the original owners — to arrive at some estimate of the degree to which the barriers of privilege and aristocracy were melting away. Of the seventy-six secular grants for which it is possible to find the names both of the persons to whom they were originally granted and who held them in 1712, only forty-five, or 59 per cent, were in the hands of the same families. Of the seigniories issued from 1670 to 1710, 62 per cent remained in the original families. Clearly, time was on the side of mobility. And equally significant, Catalogne's report shows that of the seventy-six secular seigniories in 1712, at least twenty-two were owned by families of bourgeois or lower origin.

Though the intention of the administration and the wish of the seigniors was that the *censitaire* should behave with the oxlike placidity of the peasant, he refused to do so because he was not, in truth, a peasant. As Baron La Hontan wrote: "The peasants there are at their ease. What, did I say peasant? Honorable apologies to these gentlemen! That term, taken in its usual meaning, would put our Canadians into the fields. A Spaniard, if he should be called a rustic, would not wince, nor twirl his mustache more proudly. These people are not wrong after all; they do not pay the salt tax nor the poll tax; they hunt and fish freely; in a word they are rich. Then how can you compare them with our wretched peasants? How many nobles and gentlemen would throw their old parchments into the fire at that price."

That the Canadian *censitaire* had ceased to be a French peasant received stunning confirmation in the eighteenth century, but by then time had run out on the French government. Taking pity on those displaced Acadians who had managed to return to France, the government devised a variety of plans to attach them "à la glebe de France," all of which involved tenurial terms far superior to those of the generality of peasants and at least one of which was drawn up on the basis of the most advanced physiocratic theory. Each attempt to place the Acadians on the land proved a fiasco, for the way in which they had assimilated their own history made them unfit to assume the status of peasant. "I think, really, that the Acadians are mad," wrote the Commissaire Général in 1772. "Do they imagine that we wish to make seigniors of them? The intention of the government is to put them on the level of the cultivators in the provinces where they might be established, giving them the means to subsist by their labor. They seem offended by the fact that we wish to treat them like our peasants."

Not all *censitaires*, of course, did well in Canada. But, whether the peasant profited under the system or suffered under it, how was it possible to retain him in the same subordinate position he had held in France? Indeed, he rejected the very title of *censitaire* because of its connotation of servility and succeeded in having himself referred to even in official documents simply as "habitant." Corresponding to this change in title was a change in his behavior.

Instead of obedience to the seignior, there were "mutinerie et l'indépendence." The state, too, on occasion felt the wrath of its citizens, and even the church, though protected by the loyalty of the people to Catholicism, became the target of popular hostility. When Bishop Laval introduced the French tithe into Canada in 1663, the resistance was so widespread that he was quickly forced to offer concession after concession — reduction from one-thirteenth to one-twentieth and finally to one-twenty-sixth; exemption of fish, eggs, timber, and livestock; and a five-year exemption on newly cultivated land. For more than fifty years the conflict raged between church and inhabitants, and not even the refusal to grant absolution to those who withheld the tithe or who paid in spoiled wheat could quell the "great murmuring at the door of the church." "Many individuals," wrote Duchesneau in 1677, "through plain disobedience . . . and scorn of the church not only refuse to pay the tithes, but are even carried away to the point of violence." As late as 1727 the inhabitants of the parish of St. Antoine-de-Tilly had to be *ordered* by the intendant to pay their tithes to the curé.

Worst of all, their disobedience took the form of wholesale desertion of agricultural tasks. Despite the severe sanctions imposed by church and state, increasing numbers of people, "excited by the bad example of the *coureurs de bois* and by the profits that they had made," left the field for the forest in search of furs. In the year 1680 approximately one-third of the adult male population had escaped the discipline of society by entering the fur trade. At no time does the proportion of the adult male labor force engaged in trapping and hunting seem to have been less than one-quarter or one-fifth. Not only did they deplete an already inadequate labor force, but they infected those who remained with the example of their rebelliousness. "We weare Cesars, being nobody to contradict us," said Pierre Radisson, greatest of all the *coureurs de bois*. If his was a self-image too elevated for the many to aspire to, they felt themselves at least to be captains of their own fate. "The genius of the people of New England," Minister Maurepas wrote to Beauharnois in 1728, "is to work hard at cultivating the land and to establish new settlements one after the other. . . . The inhabitants of New France think differently. They would like always to move forward without getting tangled up in interior settlements, because they gain more and are more independent when they are more remote." "One part of our youth is continually rambling and roving about," wrote Father Charlevoix, "and . . . it infects them with a habit of libertinism, of which they never entirely get rid; at least, it gives them a distaste for labour, it exhausts their strength, they become incapable of the least constraint, and when they are no longer able to undergo the fatigues of travelling . . . they remain without the least resource, and are no longer good for anything. Hence it comes to pass, that arts have been a long time neglected, and great quantity of good land remains still uncultivated, and the country is but very indifferently peopled."

Litigious, independent, insubordinate, the habitants joined the seigniors in making a mockery of the behavior defined for them. No longer were they willing to act as instruments of those who planned the system; they acted now out of concern for their own survival or improvement. At times, as we have seen, they deliberately violated the norms of their society; at times, they violated them unwittingly because, under conditions of rapid change, it became problematic as to how the norms were to be applied. But the society was turned upside down when its sworn defenders themselves subverted it. "Profit, my dear Vergor, by your place," wrote Intendant François Bigot to Louis Du Pont du Chambon, Sieur de Vergor, commandant of Fort Beauséjour; "trim, lop off; all power is in your hands; do it quickly so that you may be able to come and join me in France and buy an estate near mine." Instead of enforcing the laws against illegal fur traders, the intendants permitted them to carry on and they cut themselves in on the profits. They traded in flat violation of the orders they received from Paris. "Trading is prohibited to persons in office," wrote the President of the Navy Board. "They are placed there only to protect it, not to carry on even the most legitimate, and for the strongest reasons should abstain from dealing on concessions and monopolies that they ought to prevent with all their power. . . . What is certain is, that . . . it can only be regarded as criminal on the part of all those who have taken part in it or those who have favored it or even fostered it, and above all for persons employed in the service. . . ."

The circle was complete when what had once been regarded as deviance came later to be recognized as the norm. "I believe," wrote Denonville to Seignelay, "that Monseigneur should not determine to cease to give letters of nobility but that it would be well to give them only to those who will . . . enter into whatever commerce makes a noble in this country." In

1685 the Canadian noblesse — which had been created as the apex of the seigniorial system — was allowed without derogation of rank "to engage in commerce by land as well as by sea, to buy and sell goods wholesale as well as retail." Never did the French nobility obtain such blanket permission to trade, and such permission as they did obtain came later than in Canada.

The medicine, however, only worsened the disease. Trade "serves but to . . . reduce the number of people in the houses; to deprive wives of their husbands, fathers and mothers of the aid of their children . . .; to Expose those who undertake such journeys to a thousand dangers for both their Bodies and their souls. It also causes them to incur very many expenses, partly necessary, partly Useless, and partly Criminal; it accustoms them not to work. . . . It Takes them away from all the holy places. . . . So long as all the young men devote themselves to no other occupation . . . There can be no hope that the Colony will Ever become flourishing . . . for it will always lose thereby What would most enrich it, — I mean the labor of all the young men." Church might mourn and anathematize and King complain and legislate, but the trend could not be reversed. Instead of docility, disobedience was the rule; instead of agriculture, trade; instead of remaining on the land, the people flocked to the cities; instead of simplicity and austerity, the extremes of grinding poverty and the glitter and tinsel "d'un fort bon ton." Canada had become "a tableau of abuses, and not a body of rules."

So disrupted had the society become, then, and so profitless to its sponsors, that only the merchants of the seaport towns of France objected when Canada was lost to the British. On February 10, 1763, the very day the Treaty of Paris was signed, Voltaire wrote Étienne François, Duc de Choiseul: "Permit me to compliment you. I am like the public; I like peace better than Canada and I think that France can be happy without Quebec."

IV

The French government was faced with the twofold problem of maintaining order and stability in Canada and of motivating its subjects to perform the tasks given them. It sought to assign each man a status, the behavior of which was defined and regulated; when men behave according to prescription, each can act toward the other with the certainty that his own behavior will be understood and with the expectation that the other's responses will be the appropriate ones. At the same time, however, the government was faced with the necessity of recruiting a labor force, and the means it used involved offering such a variety of concessions and incentives that the position of the labor force in the society that was actually created was utterly different from its position in the society that had been contemplated. The government of France, like the General Court of the Virginia Company of London, was fully conscious of its problems, but — again like the Virginia Company — the solution it adopted for the problem of motivation made it impossible to solve the problem of order. Rigor and severe discipline, the distinguishing characteristics of the first social order in Canada as in Virginia, broke down in the face of the need to recruit a *voluntary* labor force. By her own actions, France created in Canada a social basis for disobedience, a society in which deviance became the only means of survival and of taking advantage of such opportunities as existed.

In a sense, a drama was taking place on the North American continent that had been played out before in Europe. At various times in late medieval and early modern Europe, especially in periods of considerable stress, the seigniors had to offer concessions to their tenants, even to the point of enfranchisement, to prevent, by their emigration to "free" lands, the loss of their labor force. In 1439 the Hospitaliers de la Commanderie de Bure enfranchised their serfs of Thoisy: "all the 'houses and barns which are at the said Thoisy have been burned and destroyed . . . and no one wants to live . . . in the town . . . in this way everyone withdraws and goes to live in free places.' " In 1628, when the Sire de Montureux-les-Gray, in Comté, freed his serfs, he did not conceal his hope that the "enfranchised village will be 'better inhabited and populated,' and 'consequently,' that the seigniorial rights 'would produce greater revenue.' "

"Misery was sometimes the creator of liberty," says Marc Bloch. So it undoubtedly was in Europe; in North America, the need to recruit a voluntary labor force was the mother of liberty.

Suggested Further Reading: *

Perhaps the best economic history textbook is Herbert Heaton's *Economic History of Europe* (1936), of which chapters 5 through 11 have immediate relevance to the background of discovery and exploration. Among the best studies of the European context for colonization are: W. K. Ferguson, *Europe in Transition, 1300–1520* (1962), E. P. Cheyney, *The Dawn of a New Era, 1250–1453** (1936), and J. H. Parry, *The Establishment of the European Hegemony: 1415–1715** (1961).

For English history in the sixteenth century, see particularly J. B. Black, *The Reign of Elizabeth* (1936), and Sir John Neale's *Queen Elizabeth** (1934). Those who enjoy A. L. Rowse will appreciate his *Sir Richard Grenville of the 'Revenge'* (1957); his *The Elizabethans and America** (1959) is less satisfactory. James A. Williamson is one of the best-known historians of Elizabethan sea power; both *The Age of Drake** (1938) and *Hawkins of Plymouth* are readable and reliable. Willard M. Wallace has written a short, useful biography of *Sir Walter Raleigh* (1959).

There are numerous studies of the explorations of this era: the best general treatment is J. B. Brebner's *The Explorers of North America: 1492–1806** (1933); but see also such special studies as S. E. Morison, *Admiral of the Ocean Sea,* issued in a 2-vol. and 1 vol. edition, 1942, and shortened further in *Christopher Columbus, Mariner** (1955); James A. Williamson, *The Voyages of John and Sebastian Cabot* (1937); S. E. Morison, *Portuguese Voyages to America in the Fifteenth Century* (1940); H. P. Biggar, *The Voyages of Jacques Cartier* (1924); Ernest S. Dodge has written a very readable account of the search for the Northwest Passage (even into the twentieth century), *North-West By Sea* (1961).

For a general treatment of Spanish colonization, see E. G. Bourne, *Spain in America: 1450–1580** (1905), and R. B. Merriman, *The Rise of the Spanish Empire* (4 vols., 1914–34). Paul Horgan gives a new and readable account of *The Spanish Conquistadores* (1963); the best biographies are Herbert E. Bolton's *Coronado, Knight of Pueblos and Plains* (1949), Theodore Maynard's *De Soto and the Conquistadores* (1930), and Lewis Hanke's sympathetic *Bartolomé de Las Casas* (1952).

The literature on the French in North America is limited and often disappointing. John C. Rule has supplied a fine survey of recent writing on the topic, "The Old Regime in America: A Review of Recent Interpretations of France in America," *The William and Mary Quarterly,* 3rd Ser., XIX (1962), 575–600; and W. J. Eccles has reappraised the contributions of Francis Parkman, "The History of New France According to Francis Parkman," *ibid.,* XVII (1961), 163–175. But the most useful books (as opposed to articles) are far from recent: Francis Parkman remains the outstanding contributor, with his *Pioneers of France in the New World* (rev. ed., 1885), *Old Regime in Canada* (1874), and *The Jesuits in North America** (1867) being among the best of his nine volume treatment of *France and England in North America* (1865–1892); see also S. E. Morison's *Parkman Reader* (1955). R. G. Thwaites' *France in America* (1905) is useful, as is G. M. Wrong's *The Rise and Fall of New France* (1928), and W. B. Munro's *The Seigneurs of Old Canada* (1914). The best of the few recent studies are: D. G. Creighton, *Dominion of the North* (1944); G. L. Nute, *Caesars of the Wilderness* (1943); Howard H. Peckham, *Pontiac and the Indian Uprising** (1947); and W. J. Eccles, *Frontenac, the Courtier Governor* (1959). There is a convenient review of the history and characteristics of New France in the first three chapters of Lawrence H. Gipson's *Zones of International Friction* (vol. 5 of *The British Empire before the American Revolution,* 1942).

* See p. 417 for a review of general and multi-volume studies embracing the colonial period of American history. Throughout the bibliographies in this book, items starred are available in paperback form.

PART TWO

Religion in Colonial America

Religion not only played its part in stimulating national rivalries in the sixteenth and seventeenth centuries, but also was a significant force in shaping colonial society. Each American settlement had a positive religious identity: the Spanish and French colonies were citadels of Roman Catholicism; the English, Dutch, and Swedes were as stoutly Protestant. The impulse towards colonization was due partly at least to the desire to propagate the Christian faith and often to extend the influence of a particular sect or denomination.

Freedom and opportunity beckoned: freedom to practice and make secure one's religious faith; opportunity to improve one's economic condition (the two were rarely viewed apart). The British settlements were founded in what Clarence Ver Steeg and others have rightly termed an Age of Faith,[1] when men were engrossed in their relationship to God and the fulfillment of His purpose. If religious divisions had contributed to the execution of one English monarch and the exile of another, it is hardly surprising that similar divisions and doctrinal differences crossed the Atlantic and resulted in a persistent concern with the relations of church and state.

[1] Clarence L. Ver Steeg, *The Formative Years, 1607–1763* (New York, 1964), pp. 74–103.

1

The Puritans

the titles of the Puritan publications of the 1660's and 1670's, Professor Miller notes the sense of uneasiness they convey. He then proceeds to examine the intellectual concepts which the Puritans brought to New England and the changes wrought by their life in America.

I

The Puritan Mission: Errand into the Wilderness

Few men have written as much or as learnedly on the Puritans as the late Perry Miller. *For him the Puritan contribution to American civilization was far more noteworthy than that of the Calvinists.*[1] *In the following essay Professor Miller seeks to portray the Puritans in their intellectual context, to show the sense of mission with which they first came to New England and the manner in which they undertook to execute their purpose.*

This selection, "Errand into the Wilderness," comes from a collection of essays which properly may be regarded as representative of Professor Miller's approach to the Puritans and their legacy. Also outstanding in the collection is "The Marrow of Puritan Divinity" — an essay of singular depth and originality, but of greater length than can be afforded in this volume. "Errand into the Wilderness" was occasioned by the New England exhibition held at the John Carter Brown Library in 1952. Reflecting upon

It was a happy inspiration that led the staff of the John Carter Brown Library to choose as the title of its New England exhibition of 1952 a phrase from Samuel Danforth's election sermon, delivered on May 11, 1670: *A Brief Recognition of New England's Errand into the Wilderness.* It was of course an inspiration, if not of genius at least of talent, for Danforth to invent his title in the first place. But all the election sermons of this period — that is to say, the major expressions of the second generation, which, delivered on these forensic occasions, were in the fullest sense community expression — have interesting titles; a mere listing tells the story of what was happening to the minds and emotions of the New England people: John Higginson's *The Cause of God and His People In New-England* in 1663, William Stoughton's *New England's True Interest, Not to Lie* in 1668, Thomas Shepard's *Eye-Salve* in 1672, Urian Oakes's *New England Pleaded With* in 1673, and, climactically and most explicitly, Increase Mather's *A Discourse Concerning the Danger of Apostasy* in 1677.

All of these show by their title pages alone — and, as those who have looked into them know, infinitely more by their contents — a deep disquietude. They are troubled utterances, worried, fearful. Something has gone wrong. As in 1662 Wigglesworth already was saying in verse, God has a controversy with New England; He has cause to be angry and to punish it because of its innumerable defections. They say, unanimously, that New England was sent on an errand, and that it has failed.

To our ears these lamentations of the second generation sound strange indeed. We think of the founders as heroic men — of the towering stature of Bradford, Winthrop, and Thomas Hooker — who braved the ocean and the wilderness, who conquered both, and left to their

---

Reprinted by permission of the publishers from *Errand Into the Wilderness* by Perry Miller. Cambridge, Mass.: The Belknap Press of Harvard University Press,

[1] For a different appraisal of the Puritan contribution, see James Truslow Adams, *The Founding of New England* (Boston, 1921); Thomas Jefferson Wertenbaker, *The Puritan Oligarchy* (New York, 1947). See also the suggested reading list following this section.

children a goodly heritage. Why then this whimpering?

Some historians suggest that the second and third generations suffered a failure of nerve; they weren't the men their fathers had been, and they knew it. Where the founders could range over the vast body of theology and ecclesiastical polity and produce profound works like the treatises of John Cotton or the subtle psychological analyses of Hooker, or even such a gusty though wrongheaded book as Nathaniel Ward's *Simple Cobler,* let alone such lofty and right-headed pleas as Roger Williams' *Bloudy Tenent,* all these children could do was tell each other that they were on probation and that their chances of making good did not seem very promising.

Since Puritan intellectuals were thoroughly grounded in grammar and rhetoric, we may be certain that Danforth was fully aware of the ambiguity concealed in his word "errand." It already had taken on the double meaning which it still carries with us. Originally, as the word first took form in English, it meant exclusively a short journey on which an inferior is sent to convey a message or to perform a service for his superior. In that sense we today speak of an "errand boy"; or the husband says that while in town on his lunch hour, he must run an errand for his wife. But by the end of the Middle Ages, errand developed another connotation: it came to mean the actual business on which the actor goes, the purpose itself, the conscious intention in his mind. In this signification, the runner of the errand is working for himself, is his own boss; the wife, while the husband is away at the office, runs her own errands. Now in the 1660's the problem was this: which had New England originally been — an errand boy or a doer of errands? In which sense had it failed? Had it been despatched for a further purpose, or was it an end in itself? Or had it fallen short not only in one or the other, but in both of the meanings? If so, it was indeed a tragedy, in the primitive sense of a fall from a mighty designation.

If the children were in grave doubt about which had been the original errand — if, in fact, those of the founders who lived into the later period and who might have set their progeny to rights found themselves wondering and confused — there is little chance of our answering clearly. Of course, there is no problem about Plymouth Colony. That is the charm about Plymouth: its clarity. The Pilgrims, as we have learned to call them, were reluctant voyagers; they had never wanted to leave England, but had been obliged to depart because the authorities made life impossible for Separatists. They could, naturally, have stayed at home had they given up being Separatists, but that idea simply did not occur to them. Yet they did not go to Holland as though on an errand; neither can we extract the notion of a mission out of the reasons which, as Bradford tells us, persuaded them to leave Leyden for "Virginia." The war with Spain was about to be resumed, and the economic threat was ominous; their migration was not so much an errand as a shrewd forecast, a plan to get out while the getting was good, lest, should they stay, they would be "intrapped or surrrounded by their enemies, so as they should neither be able to fight nor flie." True, once the decision was taken, they congratulated themselves that they might become a means for propagating the gospel in remote parts of the world, and thus of serving as stepping-stones to others in the performance of this great work; nevertheless, the substance of their decision was that they "thought it better to dislodge betimes to some place of better advantage and less danger, if any such could be found." The great hymn that Bradford, looking back in his old age, chanted about the landfall is one of the greatest passages, if not the very greatest, in all New England's literature; yet it does not resound with the sense of a mission accomplished — instead, it vibrates with the sorrow and exultation of suffering, the sheer endurance, the pain and the anguish, with the somberness of death faced unflinchingly:

> May not and ought not the children of these fathers rightly say: Our fathers were Englishmen which came over this great ocean, and were ready to perish in this wilderness; but they cried unto the Lord, and he heard their voyce, and looked on their adversitie. . . .

We are bound, I think, to see in Bradford's account the prototype of the vast majority of subsequent immigrants — of those Oscar Handlin calls "The Uprooted": they came for better advantage and for less danger, and to give their posterity the opportunity of success.

The Great Migration of 1630 is an entirely other story. True, among the reasons John Winthrop drew up in 1629 to persuade himself and his colleagues that they should commit themselves to the enterprise, the economic motive frankly figures. Wise men thought that England was overpopulated and that the poor would have a better chance in the new land. But Massachusetts Bay was not just an organization of immigrants seeking advantage and opportunity. It had a positive sense of mission — either it was sent on an errand or it had its own intention, but in either case the deed was deliberate. It was an act of will, perhaps of willfulness. These Puritans were not driven out of England (thousands of their fellows stayed and fought the Cavaliers) — they went of their own accord.

So, concerning them, we ask the question, why? If we are not altogether clear about precisely how we should phrase the answer, this is not because they themselves were reticent. They spoke as fully as they knew how, and none more magnificently or cogently than John Winthrop in the midst of the passage itself, when he delivered a lay sermon aboard the flagship *Arbella* and called it "A Modell of Christian Charity." It distinguishes the motives of this great enterprise from those of Bradford's forlorn retreat, and especially from those of the masses who later have come in quest of advancement. Hence, for the student of New England and of America, it is a fact demanding incessant brooding that John Winthrop selected as the "doctrine" of his discourse, and so as the basic proposition to which, it then seemed to him, the errand was committed, the thesis that God had disposed mankind in a hierarchy of social classes, so that "in all times some must be rich, some poor, some highe and eminent in power and dignitie; others mean and in subjeccion." It is as though, preternaturally sensing what the promise of America might come to signify for the rank and file, Winthrop took the precaution to drive out of their heads any notion that in the wilderness the poor and the mean were ever so to improve themselves as to mount above the rich or the eminent in dignity. Were there any who had signed up under the mistaken impression that such was the purpose of their errand, Winthrop told them that, although other peoples, lesser breeds, might come for wealth or pelf, this migration was specifically dedicated to an avowed end that had nothing to do with incomes. We have entered into an explicit covenant with God, "we haue professed to enterprise these Accions vpon these and these ends"; we have drawn up indentures with the Almighty, wherefore if we succeed and do not let ourselves get diverted into making money, He will reward us. Whereas if we fail, if we "fall to embrace this present world and prosecute our carnall intencions, seekeing greate things for our selves and our posterity, the Lord will surely breake out in wrathe against us be revenged of such a periured people and make us knowe the price of the breache of such a Covenant."

Well, what terms were agreed upon in this covenant? Winthrop could say precisely — "It is by a mutuall consent through a specially overruleing providence, and a more than ordinary approbation of the Churches of Christ to seeke out a place of Cohabitation and Consorteshipp under a due forme of Government both civill and ecclesiasticall." If it could be said thus concretely, why should there be any ambiguity? There was no doubt whatsoever about what Winthrop meant by a due form of ecclesiastical government: he meant the pure Bible polity set forth in full detail by the New Testament, that method which later generations, in the days of increasing confusion, would settle down to calling Congregational, but which for Winthrop was no denominational peculiarity but the very essence of organized Christianity. What a due form of civil government meant, therefore, became crystal clear: a political regime, possessing power, which would consider its main function to be the erecting, protecting, and preserving of this form of polity. This due form would have, at the very beginning of its list of responsibilities, the duty of suppressing heresy, of subduing or somehow getting rid of dissenters — of being, in short, deliberately, vigorously, and consistently intolerant.

Regarded in this light, the Massachusetts Bay Company came on an errand in the second and later sense of the word: it was, so to speak, on its own business. What it set out to do was the sufficient reason for its setting out. About this

Winthrop seems to be perfectly certain, as he declares specifically what the due forms will be attempting: the end is to improve our lives to do more service to the Lord, to increase the body of Christ, and to preserve our posterity from the corruptions of this evil world, so that they in turn shall work out their salvation under the purity and power of Biblical ordinances. Because the errand was so definable in advance, certain conclusions about the method of conducting it were equally evident: one, obviously, was that those sworn to the covenant should not be allowed to turn aside in a lust for mere physical rewards; but another was, in Winthrop's simple but splendid words, "we must be knit togeher in this worke as one man, wee must entertaine each other in brotherly affection." we must actually delight in each other, "always having before our eyes our Commission and community in the worke, our community as members of the same body." This was to say, were the great purpose kept steadily in mind, if all gazed only at it and strove only for it, then social solidarity (within a scheme of fixed and unalterable class distinctions) would be an automatic consequence. A society despatched upon an errand that is its own reward would want no other rewards: it could go forth to possess a land without ever becoming possessed by it; social gradations would remain eternally what God had originally appointed; there would be no internal contention among groups or interests, and though there would be hard work for everybody, prosperity would be bestowed not as a consequence of labor but as a sign of approval upon the mission itself. For once in the history of humanity (with all its sins), there would be a society so dedicated to a holy cause that success would prove innocent and triumph not raise up sinful pride or arrogant dissension.

Or, at least, this would come about if the people did not deal falsely with God, if they would live up to the articles of their bond. If we do not perform these terms, Winthrop warned, we may expect immediate manifestations of divine wrath; we shall perish out of the land we are crossing the sea to possess. And here in the 1660's and 1670's, all the jeremiads (of which Danforth's is one of the most poignant) are castigations of the people for having defaulted on precisely these articles. They recite the long list of afflictions an angry God had rained upon them, surely enough to prove how abysmally they had deserted the covenant: crop failures, epidemics, grasshoppers, caterpillars, torrid summers, arctic winters, Indian wars, hurricanes, shipwrecks, accidents, and (most grievous of all) unsatisfactory children. The solemn work of the election day, said Stoughton in 1668, is "Foundation-work" — not, that is, to lay a new one, "but to continue, and strengthen, and beautifie, and build upon that which has been laid." It had been laid in the covenant before even a foot was set ashore, and thereon New England should rest. Hence the terms of survival, let alone of prosperity, remained what had first been propounded:

> If we should so frustrate and deceive the Lords Expectations, that his Covenant-interest in us, and the Workings of his Salvation be made to cease, then All were lost indeed; Ruine upon Ruine, Destruction upon Destruction would come, until one stone were not left upon another.

Since so much of the literature after 1660 — in fact, just about all of it — dwells on this theme of declension and apostasy, would not the story of New England seem to be simply that of the failure of a mission? Winthrop's dread was realized: posterity had not found their salvation amid pure ordinances but had, despite the ordinances, yielded to the seductions of the good land. Hence distresses were being piled upon them, the slaughter of King Philip's War and now the attack of a profligate king upon the sacred charter. By about 1680, it did in truth seem that shortly no stone would be left upon another, that history would record of New England that the founders had been great men, but that their children and grandchildren progressively deteriorated.

This would certainly seem to be the impression conveyed by the assembled clergy and lay elders who, in 1679, met at Boston in a formal synod, under the leadership of Increase Mather, and there prepared a report on why the land suffered. The result of their deliberation, published under the title *The Necessity of Reformation,* was the first in what has proved to be a distressingly long succession of investigations into the civic health of Americans, and it is probably the most pessimistic. The land was afflicted, it said, because corruption had proceeded apace; assuredly, if the people did not quickly reform, the last blow would fall and nothing but desolation be left. Into what a moral quagmire this dedicated community had sunk, the synod did not leave to imagination; it published a long and detailed inventory of sins, crimes, misdemeanors, and nasty habits, which makes, to say the least, interesting reading.

We hear much talk nowadays about corruption, most of it couched in generalized terms. If we ask our current Jeremiahs to descend to particulars, they tell us that the republic is going on the rocks, or to the dogs, because the wives of politicians aspire to wear mink coats and their husbands take a moderate five per cent cut on certain deals to pay for the garments. The Puritans were devotees of logic, and the verb "methodize" ruled their thinking. When the synod went to work, it had before it a succession of sermons, such as that of Danforth and the other election-day or fast-day orators, as well as such works as Increase Mather's *A Brief History of the Warr With the Indians,* wherein the decimating conflict with Philip was presented as a revenge upon the people for their transgressions. When the synod felt obliged to enumerate the enormities of the land so that the people could recognize just how far short of their errand they had fallen, it did not, in the modern manner, assume that regeneration would be accomplished at the next election by turning the rascals out, but it digested this body of literature; it reduced the contents to method. The result is a staggering compendium of iniquity, organized into twelve headings.

First, there was a great and visible decay of godliness. Second, there were several manifestations of pride — contention in the churches, insubordination of inferiors toward superiors, particularly of those inferiors who had, unaccountably, acquired more wealth than their betters, and, astonishingly, a shocking extravagance in attire, especially on the part of these of the meaner sort, who persisted in dressing beyond their means. Third, there were heretics, especially Quakers and Anabaptists. Fourth, a notable increase in swearing and a spreading disposition to sleep at sermons (these two phenomena seemed basically connected). Fifth, the Sabbath was wantonly violated. Sixth, family government had decayed, and fathers no longer kept their sons and daughters from prowling at night. Seventh, instead of people being knit together as one man in mutual love, they were full of contention, so that lawsuits were on the increase and lawyers were thriving. Under the eighth head, the synod described the sins of sex and alcohol, thus producing some of the juiciest prose of the period: militia days had become orgies, taverns were crowded; women threw temptation in the way of befuddled men by wearing false locks and displaying naked necks and arms "or, which is more abominable, naked Breasts"; there were "mixed Dancings," along with light behavior and "Company-keeping" with vain persons, wherefore the bastardy rate was rising. In 1672, there was actually an attempt to supply Boston with a brothel (it was suppressed, but the synod was bearish about the future). Ninth, New Englanders were betraying a marked disposition to tell lies, especially when selling anything. In the tenth place, the business morality of even the most righteous left everything to be desired: the wealthy speculated in land and raised prices excessively; "Day-Labourers and Mechanicks are unreasonable in their demands." In the eleventh place, the people showed no disposition to reform, and in the twelfth, they seemed utterly destitute of civic spirit.

"The things here insisted on," said the synod, "have been oftentimes mentioned and inculcated by those whom the Lord hath set as Watchmen to the house of Israel." Indeed they had been, and thereafter they continued to be even more inculcated. At the end of the century, the synod's report was serving as a kind of handbook for preachers: they would take some verse of Isaiah or Jeremiah, set up the doctrine that God avenges the iniquities of a chosen people, and then run down the twelve heads, merely bringing the list up to date by inserting the new and still more depraved practices an ingenious people kept on devising. I suppose that in the whole literature of the world, including the satirists of imperial Rome, there is hardly such another uninhibited and unrelenting documentation of a people's descent into corruption.

I have elsewhere endeavored to argue[1] that, while the social or economic historian may read this literature for its contents — and so construct from the expanding catalogue of denunciations a record of social progress — the cultural anthropologist will look slightly askance at these jeremiads; he will exercise a methodological caution about taking them at face value. If you read them all through, the total effect, curiously enough, is not at all depressing: you come to the paradoxical realization that they do not bespeak a despairing frame of mind. There is something of a ritualistic incantation about them; whatever they may signify in the realm of theology, in that of psychology they are purgations of soul; they do not discourage but actually encourage the community to persist in its heinous conduct. The exhortation to a reformation which never materializes serves as a token payment upon the obligation, and so liberates the debtors. Changes there had to be: adaptations to environment, expansion of the frontier, mansions constructed, commercial adventures undertaken. These activities were not specifically nominated in the bond Winthrop had framed. They were thrust upon the society by American experience; because they were not only works of necessity but of excitement, they proved irresistible — whether making money, haunting taverns, or committing fornication. Land speculation meant not only wealth but dispersion of the people, and what was to stop the march of settlement? The covenant doctrine preached on the *Arbella* had been formulated in England, where land was not to be had for the taking; its adherents had been utterly oblivious of what the fact of a frontier would do for an imported order, let alone for a European mentality. Hence I suggest that under the guise of this mounting wail of sinfulness, this incessant and never successful cry for repentance, the Puritans launched themselves upon the process of Americanization.

However, there are still more pertinent or more analytical things to be said of this body of expression. If you compare it with the great productions of the founders, you will be struck by the fact that the second and third generations had become oriented toward the social, and only the social, problem; herein they were deeply and profoundly different from their fathers. The finest creations of the founders — the disquisitions of Hooker, Shepard, and Cotton — were written in Europe, or else, if actually penned in the colonies, proceeded from a thoroughly European mentality, upon which the American scene made no impression whatsoever. The most striking example of this imperviousness is the poetry of Anne Bradstreet: she came to Massachusetts at the age of eighteen, already two years married to Simon Bradstreet; there, she says, "I found a new world and new manners, at which my heart rose" in rebellion, but soon convincing herself that it was the way of God, she submitted and joined the church. She bore Simon eight children, and loved him sincerely, as her most charming poem, addressed to him, reveals:

> If ever two were one, then surely we;
> If ever man were loved by wife, then thee.

After the house burned, she wrote a lament about how her pleasant things in ashes lay and how no more the merriment of guests would sound in the hall; but there is nothing in the poem to suggest that the house stood in North Andover or that the things so tragically consumed were doubly precious because they had been transported across the ocean and were utterly irreplaceable in the wilderness. In between rearing children and keeping house she wrote her poetry; her brother-in-law carried the manuscript to London, and there published it in 1650 under the ambitious title, *The Tenth Muse Lately Sprung Up in America.* But the title is the only thing about the volume which shows any sense of America, and that little merely in order to prove that the plantations had something in the way of European wit and learning, that they had not receded into barbarism. Anne's flowers are English flowers, the birds, English birds, and the landscape is Lincolnshire. So also with the productions of immigrant scholarship: such a learned and acute work as Hooker's *Survey of the Summe of Church Discipline,* which is specifically about the regime set up in America, is written entirely within the logical patterns, and out of the religious experience, of Europe; it makes no concession to new and peculiar circumstances.

The titles alone of productions in the next

[1] See *The New England Mind: From Colony to Province* (1952), Chapter II.

generation show how concentrated have become emotion and attention upon the interest of New England, and none is more revealing than Samuel Danforth's conception of an errand into the wilderness. Instead of being able to compose abstract treatises like those of Hooker upon the soul's preparation, humiliation, or exultation, or such a collection of wisdom and theology as John Cotton's *The Way of Life* or Shepard's *The Sound Believer,* these later saints must, over and over again, dwell upon the specific sins of New England, and the more they denounce, the more they must narrow their focus to the provincial problem. If they write upon anything else, it must be about the halfway covenant and its manifold consequences — a development enacted wholly in this country — or else upon their wars with the Indians. Their range is sadly constricted, but every effort, no matter how brief, is addressed to the persistent question: what is the meaning of this society in the wilderness? If it does not mean what Winthrop said it must mean, what under Heaven is it? Who, they are forever asking themselves, who are we? — and sometimes they are on the verge of saying, who the Devil are we, anyway?

This brings us back to the fundamental ambiguity concealed in the word "errand," that *double entente* of which I am certain Danforth was aware when he published the words that give point to the exhibition. While it was true that in 1630, the covenant philosophy of a special and peculiar bond lifted the migration out of the ordinary realm of nature, provided it with a definite mission which might in the secondary sense be called its errand, there was always present in Puritan thinking the suspicion that God's saints are at best inferiors, despatched by their Superior upon particular assignments. Anyone who has run errands for other people, particularly for people of great importance with many things on their minds, such as army commanders, knows how real is the peril that, by the time he returns with the report of a message delivered or a bridge blown up, the Superior may be interested in something else; the situation at headquarters may be entirely changed, and the gallant errand boy, or the husband who desperately remembered to buy the ribbon, may be told that he is too late. This tragic pattern appears again and again in modern warfare: an agent is dropped by parachute and, after immense hardships, comes back to find that, in the shifting tactical or strategic situations, his contribution is no longer of value. If he gets home in time and his service proves useful, he receives a medal; otherwise, no matter what prodigies he has performed, he may not even be thanked. He has been sent, as the devastating phrase has it, upon a fool's errand, than which there can be a no more shattering blow to self-esteem.

The Great Migration of 1630 felt insured against such treatment from on high by the covenant; nevertheless, the God of the covenant always remained an unpredictable Jehovah, a *Deus Absconditus.* When God promises to abide by stated terms, His word, of course, is to be trusted; but then, what is man that he dare accuse Omnipotence of tergiversation? But if any such apprehension was in Winthrop's mind as he spoke on the *Arbella,* or in the minds of other apologists for the enterprise, they kept it far back and allowed it no utterance. They could stifle the thought, not only because Winthrop and his colleagues believed fully in the covenant, but because they could see in the pattern of history that their errand was not a mere scouting expedition: it was an essential maneuver in the drama of Christendom. The Bay Company was not a battered remnant of suffering Separatists thrown upon a rocky shore; it was an organized task force of Christians, executing a flank attack on the corruptions of Christendom. These Puritans did not flee to America; they went in order to work out that complete reformation which was not yet accomplished in England and Europe, but which would quickly be accomplished if only the saints back there had a working model to guide them. It is impossible to say that any who sailed from Southampton really expected to lay his bones in the new world; were it to come to about — as all in their heart of hearts anticipated —that the forces of righteousness should prevail against Laud and Wentworth, that England after all should turn toward reformation, where else would the distracted country look for leadership except to those who in New England had perfected the ideal polity and who would know how to administer it? This was the large unspoken assumption in the errand of 1630: if the conscious intention were realized, not only would a federated Jehovah bless the new land, but He would bring back these temporary colonials to govern England.

In this respect, therefore, we may say that the migration was running an errand in the earlier and more primitive sense of the word — performing a job not so much for Jehovah as for history, which was the wisdom of Jehovah expressed through time. Winthrop was aware of this aspect of the mission — fully conscious of it. "For wee must Consider that wee shall be as a Citty upon a Hill, the eies of all people are uppon us." More was at stake than just one little colony. If we deal falsely with God, not only will He descend upon us in wrath, but even more terribly, He will make us "a story and a by-word through the world, wee shall open the mouthes of enemies to speake evill of the wayes of god and all professours for Gods sake." No less than John Milton was New England to justify God's ways to man, though not, like him, in the agony and confusion of defeat but in the confidence of approaching triumph. This errand was being run for the sake of Reformed Christianity; and while the first aim was indeed to realize in America the due form of government, both civil and ecclesiastical, the aim behind that aim was to vindicate the most rigorous ideal of the Reformation, so that ultimately all Europe would imitate New England. If we succeed, Winthrop told his audience, men will say of later plantations, "the lord make it like that of New England." There was an elementary prudence to be observed: Winthrop said that the prayer would arise from subsequent plantations, yet what was England itself but one of God's plantations? In America, he promised, we shall see, or may see, more of God's wisdom, power, and truth "then formerly wee have beene acquainted with." The situation was such that, for the moment, the model had no chance to be exhibited in England; Puritans could talk about it, theorize upon it, but they could not display it, could not prove that it would actually work. But if they had it set up in America — in a bare land, devoid of already established (and corrupt) institutions, empty of bishops and courtiers, where they could start *de novo,* and the eyes of the world were upon it — and if then it performed just as the saints had predicted of it, the Calvinist internationale would know exactly how to go about completing the already begun but temporarily stalled revolution in Europe.

When we look upon the enterprise from this point of view, the psychology of the second and third generations becomes more comprehensible. We realize that the migration was not sent upon its errand in order to found the United States of America, nor even the New England conscience. Actually, it would not perform its errand even when the colonists did erect a due form of government in church and state: what was further required in order for this mission to be a success was that the eyes of the world be kept fixed upon it in rapt attention. If the rest of the world, or at least of Protestantism, looked elsewhere, or turned to another model, or simply got distracted and forgot about New England, if the new land was left with a polity nobody in the great world of Europe wanted — then every success in fulfilling the terms of the covenant would become a diabolical measure of failure. If the due form of government were not everywhere to be saluted, what would New England have upon its hands? How give it a name, this victory nobody could utilize? How provide an identity for something conceived under misapprehensions? How could a universal which turned out to be nothing but a provincial particular be called anything but a blunder or an abortion?

If an actor, playing the leading role in the greatest dramatic spectacle of the century, were to attire himself and put on his make-up, rehearse his lines, take a deep breath, and stride onto the stage, only to find the theater dark and empty, no spotlight working, and himself entirely alone, he would feel as did New England round 1650 or 1660. For in the 1640's, during the Civil Wars, the colonies, so to speak, lost their audience. First of all, there proved to be, deep in the Puritan movement, an irreconcilable split between the Presbyterian and Independent wings, wherefore no one system could be imposed upon England, and so the New England model was unserviceable. Secondly — most horrible to relate — the Independents, who in polity were carrying New England's banner and were supposed, in the schedule of history, to lead England into imitation of the colonial order, betrayed the sacred cause by yielding to the heresy of toleration. They actually welcomed Roger Williams, whom the leaders of the model had kicked out of Massachusetts so that his nonsense about liberty of conscience would not spoil the administrations of charity.

In other words, New England did not lie, did not falter; it made good everything Winthrop demanded — wonderfully good — and then found that its lesson was rejected by those choice spirits for whom the exertion had been made. By casting out Williams, Anne Hutchinson, and the Antinomians, along with an assortment of Gortonists and Anabaptists, into that cesspool then becoming known as Rhode Island, Winthrop, Dudley, and the clerical leaders showed Oliver Cromwell how he should go about governing England. Instead, he developed the utterly absurd theory that so long as a man made a good soldier in the New Model Army, it did not matter whether he was a Calvinist, an Antinomian, an Arminian, an Anabaptist or even — horror of horrors — a Socinian! Year after year, as the circus tours this country, crowds howl with laughter, no matter how many times they have seen the stunt, at the bustle that walks by itself: the clown comes out dressed in a large skirt with a bustle behind; he turns sharply to the left, and the bustle continues blindly and obstinately straight ahead, on the original course. It is funny in a circus, but not in history. There is nothing but tragedy in the realization that one was in the main path of events, and now is sidetracked and disregarded. One is always able, of course, to stand firm on his first resolution, and to condemn the clown of history for taking the wrong turning: yet this is a desolating sort of stoicism, because it always carries with it the recognition that history will never come back to the predicted path, and that with one's own demise, righteousness must die out of the world.

The most humiliating element in the experience was the way the English brethren turned upon the colonials for precisely their greatest achievement. It must have seemed, for those who came with Winthrop in 1630 and who remembered the clarity and brilliance with which he set forth the conditions of their errand, that the world was turned upside down and inside out when, in June 1645, thirteen leading Independent divines — such men as Goodwin, Owen, Nye, Burroughs, formerly friends and allies of Hooker and Davenport, men who might easily have come to New England and helped extirpate heretics — wrote the General Court that the colony's law banishing Anabaptists was an embarrassment to the Independent cause in England. Opponents were declaring, said these worthies, "that persons of our way, principall and spirit cannot beare with Dissentors from them, but Doe correct, fine, imprison and banish them wherever they have power soe to Doe." There were indeed people in England who admired the severities of Massachusetts, but we assure you, said the Independents, these "are utterly your enemyes and Doe seek your extirpation from the face of the earth: those who now in power are your friends are quite otherwise minded, and doe professe they are much offended with your proceedings." Thus early commenced that chronic weakness in the foreign policy of Americans, an inability to recognize who in truth constitute their best friends abroad.

We have lately accustomed ourselves to the fact that there does exist a mentality which will take advantage of the liberties allowed by society in order to conspire for the ultimate suppression of those same privileges. The government of Charles I and Archbishop Laud had not, where that danger was concerned, been liberal, but it had been conspicuously inefficient; hence, it did not liquidate the Puritans (although it made halfhearted efforts), nor did it herd them into prison camps. Instead, it generously, even lavishly, gave a group of them a charter to Massachusetts Bay, and obligingly left out the standard clause requiring that the documents remain in London, that the grantees keep their office within reach of Whitehall. Winthrop's revolutionaries availed themselves of this liberty to get the charter overseas, and thus to set up a regime dedicated to the worship of God in the manner they desired — which meant allowing nobody else to worship any other way, especially adherents of Laud and King Charles. All this was perfectly logical and consistent. But what happened to the thought processes of their fellows in England made no sense whatsoever. Out of the New Model Army came the fantastic notion that a party struggling for power should proclaim that, once it captured the state, it would recognize the right of dissenters to disagree and to have their own worship, to hold their own opinions. Oliver Cromwell was so far gone in this idiocy as to become a dictator, in order to impose toleration by force! Amid this shambles, the errand of New England collapsed. There was nobody left at headquarters to whom reports could be sent.

Many a man has done a brave deed, been hailed as a public hero, had honors and ticker tape heaped upon him — and then had to live, day after day, in the ordinary routine, eating breakfast and brushing his teeth, in what seems protracted anticlimax. A couple may win their way to each other across insuperable obtacles, elope in a blaze of passion and glory — and then have to learn that life is a matter of buying the groceries and getting the laundry done. This sense of the meaning having gone out of life, that all adventures are over, that no great days and no heroism lie ahead, is particularly galling when it falls upon a son whose father once was the public hero or the great lover. He has to put up with the daily routine without ever having known at first hand the thrill of danger or the ecstasy of passion. True, he has his own hardships — clearing rocky pastures, hauling in the cod during a storm, fighting Indians in a swamp — but what are these compared with the magnificence of leading an exodus of saints to found a city on a hill, for the eyes of all the world to behold? He might wage a stout fight against the Indians, and one out of ten of his fellows might perish in the struggle, but the world was no longer interested. He would be reduced to writing accounts of himself and scheming to get a publisher in London, in a desperate effort to tell a heedless world, "Look, I exist!"

His greatest difficulty would be not the stones, storms, and Indians, but the problem of his identity. In something of this sort, I should like to suggest, consists the anxiety and torment that inform productions of the late seventeenth and early eighteenth centuries — and should I say, some thereafter? It appears most clearly in *Magnalia Christi Americana*, the work of that soul most tortured by the problem, Cotton Mather: "I write the Wonders of the Christian Religion, flying from the Depravations of Europe, to the American Strand." Thus he proudly begins, and at once trips over the acknowledgment that the founders had not simply fled from depraved Europe but had intended to redeem it. And so the book is full of lamentations over the declension of the children, who appear, page after page, in contrast to their mighty progenitors, about as profligate a lot as ever squandered a great inheritance.

And yet, the *Magnalia* is not an abject book; neither are the election sermons abject, nor is the inventory of sins offered by the synod of 1679. There is bewilderment, confusion, chagrin, but there is no surrender. A task has been assigned upon which the populace are in fact intensely engaged. But they are not sure any more for just whom they are working; they know they are moving, but they do not know where they are going. They seem still to be on an errand, but if they are no longer inferiors sent by the superior forces of the Reformation, to whom they should report, then their errand must be wholly of the second sort, something with a purpose and an intention sufficient unto itself. If so, what is it? If it be not the due form of government, civil and ecclesiastical, that they brought into being, how otherwise can it be described?

The literature of self-condemnation must be read for meanings far below the surface, for meanings of which, we may be so rash as to surmise, the authors were not fully conscious, but by which they were troubled and goaded. They looked in vain to history for an explanation of themselves; more and more it appeared that the meaning was not to be found in theology, even with the help of the covenantal dialectic. Thereupon, these citizens found that they had no other place to search but within themselves — even though, at first, that repository appeared to be nothing but a sink of iniquity. Their errand having failed in the first sense of the term, they were left with the second, and required to fill it with meaning by themselves and out of themselves. Having failed to rivet the eyes of the world upon their city on the hill, they were left alone with America.

II

A Puritan Missionary: Jonathan Edwards and the Great Awakening

By the 1730's, when New England Puritans experienced their Great Awakening, it was apparent that life in America had altered their religion. Puritanism in the eighteenth century differed greatly from that of the seventeenth-century Bible Commonwealth. Still the dominant religious body in New England, the Congregational Church had seen its early vigor and unity seriously reduced. The Half-Way Covenant of 1662 was representative of the issues which divided honest Puritans. Many felt that partial church membership involved a dilution of the true faith. This was the position of Jonathan Edwards in his famous sermons before his Northampton congregation.

Edwards, a gifted theologian and logician, believed salvation to be the main purpose of life and sought a return to the pristine Puritan philosophy of the first settlers of Massachusetts. Not a revivalist in the usual sense, Edwards was, as Perry Miller *makes clear, a harsh and unrelenting critic of the society in which he lived. For the severity of his judgments — and their effect upon his congregation — Edwards was turned out of his pastorate in 1750.*

Although in the year 1740 some fairly flagrant scenes of emotional religion were being enacted in Boston, it was mainly in the Connecticut Valley that the frenzy raged and whence it spread like a pestilence to the civilized East. The Harvard faculty of that time would indeed have considered the Great Awakening a "crisis," because to them it threatened everything they meant by culture or religion or just common decency. It was a horrible business that should be suppressed and altogether forgotten. Certainly they would not have approved its being dignified as a starting-point in a series of great American crises.

As far as they could see, it was nothing but an orgy of the emotions. They called it — in the lexicon of the Harvard faculty this word conveyed the utmost contempt — "enthusiasm." It was not a religious persuasion: it was an excitement of overstimulated passions that understandably slopped over into activities other than the ecclesiastical and increased the number of bastards in the Valley, where already there were too many. And above all, in the Valley lived their archenemy, the deliberate instigator of this crime, who not only fomented the frenzy but was so lost to shame that he brazenly defended it as a positive advance in American culture. To add insult to injury, he justified the Awakening by employing a science and a psychological conception with which nothing they had learned at Harvard had prepared them to cope.

It was certainly a weird performance. Edwards delivered his revival sermons — for example the goriest, the one at Enfield that goes by the title "Sinners in the Hands of an Angry God" and is all that most people nowadays associate with his name — to small audiences in country churches. In these rude structures (few towns had yet prospered enough to afford the Georgian churches of the later eighteenth century which are now the charm of the landscape) the people yelled and shrieked, they rolled in the aisles, they crowded up to the pulpit and begged him to stop, they cried for mercy. One who heard him described his method of preaching: he looked all the time at the bell rope (hanging down from the roof at the other end of the church) as though he would look it in two; he did not stoop to regard the screaming mass, much less to console them.

Of course, in a short time the opinion of the Harvard faculty appeared to be vindicated. In 1740 Edwards had writhing in the churches not only his own people but every congregation he spoke to, and he dominated the entire region. Ten years later he was exiled, thrown out of his church and town after a vicious squabble (the fight against him being instigated by certain of the first citizens, some of them his cousins, who by adroit propaganda mobilized "the people" against him), and no pulpit in New England would invite this terrifying figure. He had no choice but to escape to the frontier, as did so many misfits in American history. He went to Stockbridge, where he eked out his last years as a missionary to a lot of moth-eaten Indians. Because of the works he produced under these — shall we call them untoward? — circumstances, and because he was still the acknowledged leader of the revival movement, he was invited in 1758 to become president of the College of New Jersey (the present-day Princeton), but he died a few weeks after his inauguration, so that his life really belongs to the Connecticut Valley.

One may well ask what makes such a chronicle of frenzy and defeat a crisis in American history. From the point of view of the social historian and still more from that of the sociologist it was a phenomenon of mass behavior, of which poor Mr. Edwards was the deluded victim. No sociologically trained historian will for a moment accept it on Edwards' terms — which were, simply, that it was an outpouring of the Spirit of God upon the land. And so why should we, today, mark it as a turning-point in our history, especially since thereafter religious revivals became a part of the American social pattern, while our intellectual life developed, on the whole, apart from these vulgar eruptions? The answer is that this first occurrence did actually involve all the interests of the community, and the definitions that arose out of it were profoundly decisive and meaningful. In that perspective Jonathan Edwards, being the most acute definer of the terms on which the revival was conducted and the issues on which it went astray, should be regarded — even by the social historian — as a formulator of the propositions that the American society, having been shaken by this experience, was henceforth consciously to observe.

There is not space enough here to survey the Awakening through the vast reaches of the South and the Middle Colonies, nor even to list the intricate consequences for the social ordering of New England. The splintering of the churches and the increase of sectarianism suggest one way in which Americans "responded" to this crisis, and the impulse it gave to education, most notably in the founding of Princeton, is another. Such discussions, however valuable, are external and statistical. We come to a deeper understanding of what this crisis meant by examining more closely a revelation or two from the most self-conscious — not to say the most literate — theorist of the Awakening.

The theme I would here isolate is one with which Edwards dealt only by indirection. He was skilled in the art of presenting ideas not so much by expounding as by vivifying them, and he achieved his ends not only by explicit statement but more often by a subtle shift in emphasis. In this case, it is entirely a matter of divining nuances. Nevertheless, the issue was present throughout the Awakening and, after the temporary manifestations had abated, on this proposition a revolution was found to have been wrought that is one of the enduring responses of the American mind to crisis.

I mean specifically what it did to the conception of the relation of the ruler — political or ecclesiastical — to the body politic. However, before we can pin down this somewhat illusive development, we are confronted with the problem of whether the Great Awakening is properly to be viewed as a peculiarly American phenomenon at all. It would be possible to write about it — as has been done — as merely one variant of a universal occurrence in Western culture. Between about 1730 and 1760 practically all of Western Europe was swept by some kind of religious emotionalism. It was present in Germany, Holland, Switzerland, and France, and in Catholic circles there was an analogous movement that can be interpreted as an outcropping of the same thing, and that the textbooks call "Quietism." And most dramatically, it was present in England with the Wesleys, Whitefield, and Methodism.

Once this international viewpoint is assumed, the American outburst becomes merely one among many — a colonial one at that — and one hesitates to speak about it as a crisis in a history specifically American. What was at work throughout the Western world is fairly obvious: the upper or the educated classes were tired of the religious squabbling of the seventeenth century, and turned to the more pleasing and not at all contentious generalities of eighteenth-century rationalism; the spiritual hungers of the lower classes or of what, for shorthand purposes, we may call "ordinary" folk were not satisfied by Newtonian demonstrations that design in the universe proved the existence of God. Their aspirations finally found vent in the revivals, and in each country we may date the end of a Calvinist or scholastic or, in short, a theological era by the appearance of these movements, and thereupon mark what is by now called the era of Pietism or Evangelicalism.

In this frame of reference, the Great Awakening was only incidentally American. It is only necessary to translate the European language into the local terminology to have an adequate account. In this phraseology, the Great Awakening in New England was an uprising of the common people who declared that what Harvard and Yale graduates were teaching was too academic. This sort of rebellion has subsequently proved so continuous that one can hardly speak of it as a crisis. It is rather a chronic state of affairs. And in this view of it, the uprising of 1740 belongs to the history of the eighteenth century rather than to any account of forces at work only on this continent.

Told in this way, the story will be perfectly true. Because we talk so much today of the unity of Western European culture, maybe we ought to tell it in these terms, and then stop. But on the other hand there is a curiously double aspect to the business. If we forget about Germany and Holland and even England — if we examine in detail the local history of Virginia, Pennsylvania, and New England — we will find that a coherent narrative can be constructed out of the cultural developments in each particular area. The Awakening can be seen as the culmination of factors long at work in each society, and as constituting, in that sense, a veritable crisis in the indigenous civilization.

II

The church polity established in New England was what today we call Congregational. This meant, to put it crudely, that a church was conceived as being composed of people who could certify before other people that they had a religious experience, that they were qualified to become what the founders called "visible saints." The founders were never so foolish as to suppose that everybody who pretended to be a saint *was* a saint, but they believed that a rough approximation of the membership to the Covenant of Grace could be worked out. A church was composed of the congregation, but these were only the professing Christians. The rest of the community were to be rigorously excluded; the civil magistrate would, of course, compel them to come to the church and listen to the sermon, collect from them a tax to support the preacher, but they could not be actual members. Those who qualified were supposed to have had something happen to them that made them capable — as the reprobate was not — of swearing to the covenant of the church. They were able, as the others were not, *physically* to perform the act.

The basic contention of the founders was that a church is based upon the covenant. Isolated individuals might be Christians in their heart of hearts, but a corporate body could not come into being unless there was this preliminary clasping of hands, this taking of the official oath in the open and before all the community, saying, in effect: "We abide by this faith, by this covenant." In scholastic language, the congregation were the "matter" but the covenant was the "form" of the church. They objected above all things to the practice in England whereby churches were made by geography; that a lot of people, merely because they resided in Little Willingdon, should make the church of Little Willingdon, seemed to them blasphemy. That principle was mechanical and unreal; there was no spiritual participation in it — no covenant.

That was why they (or at any rate the leaders and the theorists) came to New England. On the voyage over, in 1630, John Winthrop said to them: "For wee must Consider that wee shall be as a Citty vppon a Hill, the eies of all people are vppon us." They had been attempting in England to lead a revolution; after the king's dismissal of Parliament in 1629 it looked as though there was no longer any hope of revolution there, and so they migrated to New England, to build the revolutionary city, where they could exhibit to Englishmen an England that would be as all England should be.

The essence of their conception was the covenant. As soon as they were disembarked, as soon as they could collect in one spot enough people to examine each other and acknowledge that each seemed visibly capable of taking the oath, they incorporated churches—in Boston, Charlestown, and Watertown, and, even in the first decade, in the Connecticut Valley. But we must always remember that even in those first days, when conviction was at its height, and among so highly selected and dedicated numbers as made up the Great Migration, only about one fifth of the population were found able, or could find themselves able, to take the covenant. The rest of them — with astonishingly few exceptions — accepted their exclusion from the churches, knowing that they were not "enabled" and praying for the grace that might yet empower them.

From that point on, the story may seem somewhat peculiar, but after a little scrutiny it becomes an old and a familiar one: it is what happens to a successful revolution. The New Englanders did not have to fight on the barricades or at Marston Moor; by the act of migrating, they *had* their revolution. Obeying the Biblical command to increase and multiply, they had children — hordes of them. Despite the high rate of infant mortality, these children grew up in New England knowing nothing, except by hearsay and rumor, of the struggles in Europe, never having lived amid the tensions of England. This second generation were, for the most part, good people; but they simply did not have — they could not have — the kind of emotional experience that made them ready to stand up before the whole community and say: "On Friday the 19th, I fell to the earth, and I knew that the grace of God was upon me." They were honest people, and they found it difficult to romanticize about themselves — even when they desperately wanted to.

In 1662 the churches of New England convoked a synod and announced that the children of the primitive church members were included in the covenant by the promise of God to Abraham. This solution was called at the time the Halfway Covenant, and the very phrase itself is an instructive demonstration of the New Englanders' awareness that their revolution was no longer revolutionary. These children, they decided, must be treated as members of the church, although they had not had the kind of experience that qualified their fathers. They must be subject to discipline and censures, because the body of the saints must be preserved. But just in case the authorities might be mistaken, they compromised by giving to these children only a "half-way" status, which made them members but did not admit them to the Lord's Supper.

This provision can easily be described as a pathetic, where it is not a ridiculous, device. It becomes more comprehensible when we realize that it was an accommodation to the successful revolution. Second and third generations grow up inheritors of a revolution, but are not themselves revolutionaries.

For the moment, in the 1660's and 1670's, the compromise worked, but the situation got worse. For one thing, New England suffered in King Philip's War, when the male population was decimated. Then, in 1684, the charter of Massachusetts was revoked, and after 1691 the colony had to adjust itself to the notion that its governor was imposed by the royal whim, not by the election of the saints. Furthermore, after 1715 all the colonies were prospering economically; inevitably they became more and more concerned with earthly things — rum, land, furs. On the whole they remained a pious people. Could one go back to Boston of 1710 or 1720 — when the ministers were asserting that it was as profligate as Babylon — I am sure that one would find it, compared with modern Hollywood, a strict and moral community. Nevertheless, everybody was convinced that the cause of religion had declined. Something had to be done.

As early as the 1670's the ministers had found something they could do: they could work upon the halfway members. They could say to these hesitants: "You were baptized in this church, and if you will now come before the body and 'own' the covenant, then your children can in turn be baptized." Gradually a whole segment of doctrine was formulated that was not in the original theory — which made it possible to address these citizens who were neither outside the pale nor yet snugly inside, which told them that however dubious they might be as saints, visible or invisible, they yet had sufficient will power to perform the public act of "owning the covenant."

With the increasing pressures of the late seventeenth and early eighteenth centuries, the practice of owning the covenant gradually became a communal rite. It was not enough that the minister labored separately with John or Elizabeth to make an acknowledgment the next Sunday: a day was appointed when all the Johns and Elizabeths would come to church and do it in unison, the whole town looking on. It is not difficult to trace through the increasing re-enactments of this ceremony a mounting crescendo of communal action that was, to say the least, wholly foreign to the original Puritanism. The theology of the founders conceived of man as single and alone, apart in a corner or in an empty field, wrestling with his sins; only after he had survived this experience in solitude could he walk into the church and by telling about it prove his right to the covenant. But this communal confession — with everybody doing it together, under the urgencies of an organized moment — this was something new, emerging so imperceptibly that nobody recognized it as an innovation (or rather I should say that some did, but they were shouted down) that by the turn of the century was rapidly becoming the focus for the ordering of the spiritual life of the town.

The grandfather of Jonathan Edwards, Solomon Stoddard of Northampton, was the first man who openly extended the practice of renewal of covenant to those who had never been in it at all. In short, when these occasions arose, or when he could precipitate them, he simply took into the church and up to the Lord's Supper everyone who would or could come. He called the periods when the community responded *en masse* his "harvests," of which he had five: 1679, 1683, 1696, 1712, 1718. The Mathers attacked him for so completely letting down the bars, but in the Connecticut Valley his success was envied and imitated.

The Great Awakening of 1740, seen in the light of this development, was nothing more than the culmination of the process. It was the point at which the method of owning the covenant became most widely and exultingly extended, in which the momentum of the appeal got out of hand, and the ministers, led by Jonathan Edwards, were forced by the logic of evolution not only to admit all those who would come but to excite and to drive as many as possible, by such rhetorical stimulations as "Sinners in the Hands of an Angry God," into demanding entrance.

All of this, traced historically, seems natural enough. What 1740 did was present a number of leading citizens, like the Harvard faculty, with the results of a process that had been going on for decades but of which they were utterly ignorant until the explosion. Then they found themselves trying to control it or censure it by standards that had in fact been out of date for a century, although they had all that while professed them in filial piety. In this sense — which I regret to state has generally eluded the social historian — the Great Awakening was a crisis in the New England society.

Professional patriots, especially those of New England descent, are fond of celebrating the Puritans as the founders of the American tradition of rugged individualism, freedom of conscience, popular education, and democracy. The Puritans were not rugged individualists; they did indeed believe in education of a sort, but not in the "progressive" sense; they abhorred freedom of conscience; and they did not believe at all in democracy. They advertised again and again that their church polity was not democratic. The fact that a church was founded on a covenant and that the minister happened to be elected by the mass of the church — this emphatically did not constitute a democracy. John Cotton made the position of the founders crystal clear when he told Lord Say and Seal that God never ordained democracy as a fit government for either church or commonwealth; although at first sight one might suppose that a congregational church was one, in that the people chose their governors, the truth was that "the government is not a democracy, if it be administered, not by the people, but by the governors." He meant, in short, that even though the people did select the person, the office was prescribed; they did not define its functions, nor was it responsible to the will or the whim of the electors. "In which respect it is, that church government is justly denyed . . . to be democratical, though the people choose their owne officers and rulers."

The conception ran through every department of the social thinking of New England in the seventeenth century, and persisted in the eighteenth up to the very outbreak of the Awakening.

The essence of it always was that though officers may come into their office by the choice of the people, or a number of people, nevertheless the definition of the function, dignity, and prerogatives of the position does not depend upon the intentions or wishes of the electorate, but upon an abstract, divinely given, absolute prescription, which has nothing — in theory — to do with such practical or utilitarian considerations as may, at the moment of the election, be at work among the people.

The divine and immutable pattern of church government was set, once and for all, in the definitive form. The machinery by which a political justice were given in an eternal and New Testament; likewise, the principles of political justice were given in an eternal and definitive form. The machinery by which a particular man was chosen to fulfill these directives (as the minister was elected by the vote of a congregation, or as John Winthrop was made governor of the Massachusetts Bay Company by a vote of the stockholders) was irrelevant. The existence of such machinery did not mean that the elected officer was in any sense responsible to the electorate. He knew what was expected of him from an entirely other source than their temporary passions; he knew what he, upon becoming such a being, should do — as such!

The classic statement, as is widely known, was the speech that John Winthrop delivered before the General Court on July 3, 1645. He had been accused by the democracy of overstepping the limits of his power as a magistrate, and was actually impeached on the accusation. He was acquitted, and thereupon made this truly great declaration. He informed the people that the liberty of the subject may sometimes include, as happily it did in Massachusetts, the privilege of selecting this or that person for office, but that it did not therefore mean the right to tell the officer what he should do once he was installed. The liberty that men enjoy in civil society, he said, "is the proper end and object of authority, and cannot subsist without it." It is not a liberty to do what you will, or to require the authority to do what you want: "It is a liberty to do that only which is good, just, and honest." Who defines the good, the just, and the honest? Obviously, the authority does.

In other words, the theory of early New England was basically medieval. Behind it lay the conception of an authoritative scheme of things, in which basic principles are set down once and for all, entirely before, and utterly without regard for, political experience. The formulation of social wisdom had nothing to do with the specific problems of any one society. It was not devised by a committee on ways and means. Policy was not to be arrived at by a discussion of strategy — for example (in modern terms), shouldn't we use the atomic bomb now? This sort of argument was unavailing, because the function of government was to maintain by authority that which was inherently — and definably — the true, just, and honest.

In Hartford, Connecticut, a colleague of the great Thomas Hooker, the most comprehensive theorist of the Congregational system, summarized the argument by declaring that Congregationalism meant a silent democracy in the face of a speaking aristocracy. There might be something which we call democracy in the form of the church, but the congregation had to keep silent when the minister spoke. And yet, for a hundred years after the death of Hooker, this strange process went on inside the institution. The official theory remained, down to the time of Edwards, that the spokesman for the society — be he governor or minister — told the society, by right divine, what it should or should not do, without any regard to its immediate interests, whether emotional or economic. He had laid upon him, in fact, the duty of forgetting such wisdom as he might have accumulated by living as a particular person in that very community or having shared the hopes and qualities of precisely these people.

What actually came about, through the device of renewing the covenant, was something that in fact completely contradicted the theory. (We must remember that the church was, during this century, not merely something "spiritual," but the institutional center of the organized life.) Instead of the minister standing in his pulpit, saying: "I speak; you keep quiet," he found himself, bit by bit, assuming the posture of pleading with the people: "Come, and speak up." He did not know what was happening. He began to find out only in the Great Awakening, when the people at last and multitudinously spoke up.

III

The greatness of Jonathan Edwards is that he understood what had happened. But note this carefully. He was not Thomas Jefferson; he did not preach democracy, and he had no interest whatsoever in any social revolution. He was the child of this aristocratic, medieval system; he was born to the purple, to ecclesiastical authority. But he was the man who hammered it home to the people that they *had* to speak up, or else they were lost.

Edwards was a Puritan and a Calvinist. He believed in predestination and original sin and all those dogmas which college students hold to be outworn stuff until they get excited about them as slightly disguised by Franz Kafka. Edwards did not submit these doctrines to majority vote, and he did not put his theology to the test of utility. But none of this was, in his existing situation, an issue. Granting all that, the question he had to decide was: What does a man do who leads the people? Does he, in 1740, say with the Winthrop of 1645 that they submit to what he as an ontologist tells them is good, just, and honest?

What he realized (lesser leaders of the Awakening, like Gilbert Tennent, also grasped the point, but none with the fine precision of Edwards) was that a leader could no longer stand before the people giving them mathematically or logically impregnable postulates of the eternally good, just, and honest. That might work in 1640, or in Europe (where to an astonishing extent it still works), but it would not work in Northampton. By 1740 the leader had to get down amongst them, and bring them by actual participation into an experience that was no longer private and privileged, but social and communal.

In other words, he carried to its ultimate implication — this constitutes his "relation to his times," which no purely social historian can begin to diagnose — that slowly forming tendency which had been steadily pressing through enlargements of the ceremonial owning of the covenant. He carried it so far that at last everybody could see what it really did mean. Then the Harvard faculty lifted its hands in horror — because this ritual, which they had thought was a segment of the cosmology of John Winthrop, was proved by Edwards's use to flow from entirely alien principles. For this reason, his own Yale disowned him.

IV

In the year 1748 Edwards's revolutionary effort — his leadership of the Awakening must be seen as a resumption of the revolutionary thrust that had been allowed to dwindle in the Halfway Covenant — was almost at an end. The opposition was mobilizing, and he knew, even before they did, that they would force him out. When the fight had only begun, his patron and friend, his one bulwark in the civil society, Colonel John Stoddard, chief of the militia and warden of the marches, died. There was now no civil power that could protect him against the hatred of the "river gods." Out of all New England, Stoddard had been really *the* outstanding magistrate in that tradition of aristocratic leadership which had begun with Winthrop and had been sustained through a massive succession. As was the custom in New England, the minister gave a funeral sermon; Edwards preached over the corpse of the town's greatest citizen — who happened, in this case, to be also his uncle and his protector. Those who were now certain, with Colonel Stoddard in the ground, that they could get Edwards's scalp were in the audience.

Edwards delivered a discourse that at first sight seems merely one more Puritan eulogy. He told the people that when great and good men like Stoddard are taken away, this is a frown of God's displeasure, which indicates that they ought to reform their vices. This much was sheer convention. But before he came, at the end, to the traditional berating of the populace, Edwards devoted the major part of his oration to an analysis of the function and meaning of authority.

It should be remembered that Winthrop had commenced the New England tradition by telling the people that they had the liberty to do only that which is in itself good, just, and honest; that their liberty was the proper end and object of authority thus defined; that the approbation of the people is no more than the machinery by which God calls certain people to the exercise of the designated powers. And it should also be borne in mind that these powers are given apart from any consideration of the social welfare, that they derive from ethical, theological — *a priori* — considerations.

Jonathan Edwards says that the supreme qualification of a ruler is that he be a man of "great ability for the management of public affairs." This is his first and basic definition! Let us follow his very words, underlining those which carry revolutionary significance. Rulers are men "of great *natural* abilities" who are versed in discerning "those things wherein the *public welfare or calamity consists,* and the proper *means* to avoid the one and promote the other." They must have lived among men long enough to learn how the mass of them disguise their motives, to "unravel the false, subtle arguments and cunning sophistry that is often made use of to defend *iniquity.*" They must be men who have improved their talents by — here are his great criteria — *study, learning, observation,* and *experience.* By these means they must have acquired "skill" in public affairs, "a great understanding of *men and things,* a great *knowledge of human nature,* and of the way of *accommodating* themselves to it." Men are qualified to be rulers if and when they have this "very extensive knowledge of men with whom they are concerned," and when also they have a full and particular understanding "of the *state and circumstances* of the country or people that they have the care of." These are the things — not scholastical articles — that make those in authority "fit" to be rulers!

Look closely at those words and phrases: skill, observation, men and things, state and circumstances — above all, experience! Is this the great Puritan revivalist? It is. And what is he saying, out of the revival? He is telling what in political terms the revival really meant: that the leader has the job of accommodating himself to the realities of human and, in any particular situation, of social, experience. No matter what he may have as an assured creed, as a dogma — no matter what he may be able to pronounce, in the terms of abstract theology, concerning predestination and original sin — as a public leader he must adapt himself to public welfare and calamity. He cannot trust himself to *a priori* rules of an eternal and uncircumstanced good, just, and honest. There are requirements imposed by the office; authority does indeed consist of propositions that pertain to it, but what are they? They are the need for knowing the people, the knack of properly manipulating and operating them, the wit to estimate their welfare, and the cunning to foresee what may become their calamity.

When we are dealing with so highly conscious an artist as Edwards, we not only are justified in submitting so crucial a paragraph to close analysis, we are criminally obtuse if we do not. Most of my effort in my recent studies of him comes down to persuading people to read him. So it becomes significant to note what Edwards does immediately after his radically new definition of the ruler. Following his own logic, he is prepared at once to attack what, in the state and circumstances of the Connecticut Valley, constituted the primary iniquity, from which the greatest social calamity might be expected.

He does it without, as we might say, pulling punches: a ruler must, on these considerations of welfare, be unalterably opposed to all persons of "a mean spirit," to those "of a narrow, private spirit that may be found in little tricks and intrigues to promote their private interest, [who] will shamefully defile their hands to gain a few pounds, are not ashamed to hip and bite others, grind the faces of the poor, and screw upon their neighbors; and will take advantage of their authority or commission to line their own pockets with what is fraudulently taken or withheld from others." At the time he spoke, there sat before him the merchants, the sharp traders, the land speculators of Northampton; with the prompt publication of the sermon, his words reached similar gentlemen in the neighboring towns. Within two years, they hounded him out of his pulpit.

The more one studies Edwards, the more one finds that much of his preaching is his condemnation, in this language of welfare and calamity rather than of "morality," of the rising and now rampant businessmen of the Valley. It was Edwards's great perception — and possibly his greatest value for us today is precisely here — that the get-rich-quick schemes of his contemporaries were wrong not from the point of view of the eternal values but from that of the public welfare. The ruler, he said, must know the "theory" of government in such a way that it becomes "natural" to him, and he must apply the knowledge he has obtained by study and observation "to that business, so as to perform it most advantageously and effectually." Here he was, at the moment his protector was gone, and he knew that he was lost, telling those about to destroy him that the great man is he who leads the people by skill and experiential wisdom, and not by making money.

It is further revealing that, after Edwards had portrayed the ruler in this frame of utility and calculation, when he came to his fourth point he then for the first time said that the authority ought to be a pious man, and only in his fifth and last did he suggest the desirability of a good family. For Winthrop these qualifications had been essentials of the office; for Edwards they were radically submitted to a criterion of utility. "It also contributes to the strength of a man in authority . . . when he is in such circumstances as give him advantage for the exercise of his strength, for the public good; as his being a person of honorable descent, of a distinguished education, his being a man of estate." But note — these are all "useful" because they "add to his strength, and increase his ability and advantage to serve his generation." They serve "in some respect" to make him more effective. It had never occurred to John Winthrop that the silent democracy should imagine for a moment that the elected ruler, in church or state, should be anyone but a pious, educated, honorably descended person, of adequate economic substance. Edwards (who was pious, educated, and very well descended, but not wealthy) says that in some respect these advantages are helps to efficiency.

From one point of view, then, this was what actually was at work inside the hysterical agonies of the Great Awakening. This is one thing they meant: the end of the reign over the New England and American mind of a European and scholastical conception of an authority put over men for the good of men who were incapable of recognizing their own welfare. This insight may assist us somewhat in comprehending why the pundits of Boston and Cambridge, all of whom were rational and tolerant and decent, shuddered with a horror that was deeper than mere dislike of the antics of the yokels. To some extent, they sensed that the religious screaming had implications in the realm of society, and those implications they — being businessmen and speculators, as were the plutocracy of Northampton — did not like.

Again, I would not claim too much for Edwards, and I have no design of inscribing him among the prophets of democracy or the New Deal. What he marks — and what he alone could make clear — is the crisis from which all the others (or most of them) dealt with in this book depend, that in which the social problem was taken out of the arcana of abstract morality and put into the arena of skill, observation, and accommodation. In this episode, the Americans were indeed participating in an international movement; even so, they came — or Edwards brought them — to sharper formulations of American experience. What the Awakening really meant for Americans was not that they too were behaving like Dutchmen or Germans or Lancashire workmen, but that in the ecstasy of the revival they were discovering, especially on the frontier, where life was the toughest, that they rejected imported European philosophies of society. They were now of themselves prepared to contend that the guiding rule of this society will be its welfare, and the most valuable knowledge will be that which can say what threatens calamity for the state.

2

The Quakers

The Culture of Early Pennsylvania

The Quakers, although comparatively few in number, exerted a disproportionately strong influence in the affairs of the colonies. Their

Frederick B. Tolles, "The Culture of Early Pennsylvania," from *The Pennsylvania Magazine of History and Biography* LXXXI (1957), 119–137.

main strength — in terms of both numbers and influence — lay in New Jersey and Pennsylvania, but their activities extended into most of New England and as far south as North Carolina. In William Penn's province the Quakers forged an alliance with the German sects — themselves mostly pacifists — which made them the dominant political power until 1756.

The Quaker experiment in Pennsylvania did not, according to FREDERICK B. TOLLES, *turn out quite as William Penn had hoped. The Quakers in Pennsylvania prospered, became increasingly worldly, made almost a ritual of avoiding ritual, and finally sought to preserve their religious values by quitting the political world altogether. Professor Tolles, who has long been associated with Swarthmore College, suggests that the Quaker problem was the outcome of the "inevitable tension between Christ and culture, between the demands of the Inward Light and the claims of civilization." He argues persuasively that the Quakers made their most notable contribution to colonial — and modern — American culture by creating a province open to all men; each group that settled in Pennsylvania brought its own culture, enriching colonial civilization in the process.*

The founder of Pennsylvania, we must be clear, was neither a narrow-minded religious zealot on the one hand nor a mean-spirited Philistine on the other. William Penn was a man of broad intellectual culture in Matthew Arnold's sense, educated at Oxford, on the Continent, and at Lincoln's Inn; he was a Fellow of the Royal Society and the associate not only of kings and courtiers, but of the reigning intellectuals of the day — men like Samuel Pepys, the diarist; John Locke, the philosopher; Sir William Petty, the political economist. He was a man of wide reading. The list of books he bought to bring to America on his second visit suggests his range; it included the poems of Milton, a copy of *Don Quixote,* the works of John Locke, the latest travel books by William Dampier and Father Hennepin, the Roman histories of Livy and Suetonius. Penn was a good Quaker and a shrewd real-estate promoter, but he was also — though one would scarcely guess it from Benjamin West's canvas — a Restoration egghead, as much at home with the philosophers of the Royal Society as with the Indians of the Pennsylvania forest. The example of such a man was enough to ensure that Pennsylvania would not be a cultural desert. And Penn's commitment to a sophisticated ideal of religious freedom meant that the intellectual life of his colony would never stagnate for want of controversy and the creative clash of opinions.

It is true that, by and large, the English Quakers who sailed with Penn on the *Welcome* or followed him on other ships did not come, as he did, from the leisure class. Quakerism in the seventeenth century took root in the lower orders of society, among the yeoman farmers, husbandmen, artisans, shopkeepers, hired servants, men and women who worked with their hands. The farmers among them, poverty-stricken dalesmen from the moors of northern England, headed straight for the rich uplands of Bucks and Chester counties. (As late as the middle of the eighteenth century, the people of Chester still spoke in a broad Yorkshire dialect.) Within a few years they were producing flour and meat for export. With the proceeds they built those neat stone farmhouses with their projecting pent roofs and door hoods that are so charming when one comes upon them in the midst of the split-levels and ranch houses of Philadelphia's exurbia.

They had little beyond the rudiments of reading and writing, these rural Friends, and few books beyond the Bible and Barclay's *Apology.* They had little time for reading; besides, their Quakerism enjoined upon them a sober, plain way of life. But if their lives seem drab, remember the clean lines, the satisfying proportions, the functional perfection of the stone meetinghouse where they gathered on First Day to worship God in the living silence. In that simple structure form followed function with a faithfulness that Frank Lloyd Wright might have envied, and every superfluity was stripped away to leave its purpose revealed in utter purity. The Pennsylvania Friends even anticipated a favorite device of the modern architect: they installed sliding panels with which they could break up the "flow of space" and convert their oblong meetinghouses into two rooms for the men's and women's meetings for business.

Howard Brinton calls the period from 1700 to 1740 the Golden Age of Quakerism in America. He is thinking primarily of the rural Quakers of Bucks and Chester counties when he describes, with a touch of nostalgia, the "unique Quaker culture" of the period:

> In the Quaker communities the meeting was the center, spiritually, intellectually and economically. It included a library and a school. Disputes of whatever nature were settled in the business sessions of the meeting. The poor were looked after, moral delinquents dealt with, marriages approved and performed . . . . Each group, centered in the meeting, was a well-ordered, highly integrated community of interdependent members . . . . This flowering of Quakerism was not characterized by any outburst of literary or artistic production. Its whole emphasis was on life itself in home, meeting and community. This life was an artistic creation as beautiful in its simplicity and proportion as was the architecture of its meeting houses. The "Flowering of New England" has been described in terms of its literature, but the flowering of Quakerism in the middle colonies can be described only in terms of life itself.[1]

Quaker life in Philadelphia soon fell into a different pattern. Eventually the cleavage between rural and urban Quaker culture would split the Society of Friends into two factions, Hicksite and Orthodox (and one might even suggest that the recent healing of the schism was made easier by the blurring of that sharp line of cleavage in our twentieth century suburban culture). The material basis for the rise of urban Quaker culture was Philadelphia's amazing growth and prosperity. Last of the major colonial cities to be founded, William Penn's "green country town" quickly outstripped New York, Newport, and Charleston, and by 1740 was pressing the much older town of Boston hard for primacy in wealth and population.

By 1740 the Quakers were already a minority group in the Quaker City, but they had been the prime movers in the town's economic expansion and they still controlled a large share of its trade and its visible assets. Most of the early immigrants had been craftsmen and shopkeepers. They practiced the economic ethic of Poor Richard long before Benjamin Franklin, that Johnny-come-lately, arrived in Philadelphia. Working diligently in their callings, they quickly transformed a primitive frontier village into a complex provincial market town and business center. The tons of wheat and flour, the barrels of beef and pork, the lumber, the bales of furs that poured into Philadelphia from the hinterland provided, of course, the substance of Philadelphia's flourishing export trade. But it was the diligence and business acumen of the Quaker merchants that translated those raw goods into prosperity for the whole region.

But prosperity, it must be admitted, had its effects on Philadelphia Quakerism. As wealth increased, plainness in "dress and address" declined, as we noted earlier. As early as 1695 Philadelphia Yearly Meeting was warning its male members against wearing "long lapp'd Sleeves or Coates gathered at the Sides, or Superfluous Buttons, or Broad Ribbons about their Hatts, or long curled Perriwiggs," and cautioning women Friends against "Dressing their Heads Immodestly, or Wearing their Garments undecently . . . or Wearing . . . Striped or Flower'd Stuffs, or other useless and Superfluous Things." Obviously, the Yearly Meeting wouldn't have bothered to discourage its members from wearing these abominations unless some Friends were actually doing so. But the clever Quaker, as we have seen, could find ways to outwit the meeting, could practice conspicuous consumption without violating the letter of the discipline. In other words, the Philadelphia Friends were becoming worldly, and there were Jeremiahs — especially among the country Friends — who insisted that vital Quakerism varied inversely with the prosperity of its adherents.

I am not concerned at the moment with moral judgments. I am concerned with "culture," loosely defined, and I must therefore point out that the Quaker aristocrats of Philadelphia were receptive not only to the fashions of the "world's people," but to their architecture, their books, their ideas as well, though there was always something sober and substantial about Quaker houses, libraries, and intellectual pursuits, as

[1] *Friends for 300 Years* (New York, 1952), p. 184. Quoted by permission of Harper and Brothers.

there was about Quaker clothes. If rural Pennsylvania Quakerism flowered in ordered and beautiful lives, the Quakerism of Philadelphia flowered in many realms of the mind and spirit, particularly in the fields of organized humanitarianism, science, and medicine. Since they had no use for a learned clergy, the Quakers were slow to establish colleges, but the humane and learned institutions which gave Philadelphia its cultural preeminence in the pre-Revolutionary years — the American Philosophical Society, the Library Company, the Pennsylvania Hospital, even the College of Philadelphia, which became the University of Pennsylvania — all owed more than a little to the solid and generous culture of the Quaker merchants.

If I limit myself to mentioning the cultural interests and achievements of just one Philadelphia Quaker — James Logan — it is because he is the one I know best. I shall not contend that Logan was either a typical Philadelphian or a representative Friend. The breadth and reach of his mind would have made him an exceptional man in any time or place; and as for his Quakerism, he sat so loose to it that Philadelphia Monthly Meeting had to deal with him repeatedly for breaches of the discipline. But a résumé of James Logan's contributions in the realm of "high culture" should lay to rest any lingering suspicions that early Philadelphia was a Sahara of the intellect.

Logan came to Philadelphia in 1699 as William Penn's secretary. At one time or another over the next half-century he occupied nearly every responsible public office in the province, including those of chief justice and acting governor. He was Pennsylvania's leading fur merchant, her ablest and most respected Indian diplomat. He was the builder of Philadelphia's most distinguished early Georgian mansion — the house called Stenton, which still stands in its elegant Quaker simplicity amid the ugliness of industrial North Philadelphia. He assembled a library of three thousand volumes which I do not hesitate to call the best-chosen collection of books in all colonial America. Unlike most other colonial libraries, it is still intact at the Library Company of Philadelphia. And unlike many other colonial libraries, it was a scholar's working library. Logan's marginal annotations make it clear how closely he studied his learned books in many tongues. He carried on a correspondence in Latin — the universal language of scholarship — with Dr. Johann Albertus Fabricius of Hamburg, the most erudite classicist of his age, and his commentaries on Euclid and Ptolemy were published in Hamburg and Amsterdam. He made a translation of Cicero's essay on old age which Benjamin Franklin, its publisher, hailed as "a happy omen that Philadelphia shall become the seat of the American Muses." He designed and carried out some experiments on the generation of Indian corn that botanists all over Europe cited for a century or more as proof that sex reared its head in the plant kingdom. He was certainly one of the first Americans to understand and use Sir Isaac Newton's method of fluxions, or calculus. He made contributions to the science of optics, which were published in Holland, and several of his scientific papers were read before the Royal Society of London and printed in its *Philosophical Transactions.* He crowned his intellectual life by writing a treatise on moral philosophy which, unfortunately, was never finished and never published. That treatise, which exists only in fragments, may have been suggested by an offhand remark of the great John Locke that it should be possible to construct a rational science of morals: Logan called it in typical eighteenth century fashion, "The Duties of Man Deduced from Nature."

James Logan, I repeat, was not a typical Philadelphia Quaker, but the example of such a man — and remember, he was the leading public figure of his day — could not fail to stimulate others to the intellectual life. Indeed, the three men who are usually called Philadelphia's first scientists — Benjamin Franklin, John Bartram, the botanist, and Thomas Godfrey, the inventor of the mariners' quadrant — all owed a great deal to Logan's encouragement and patronage.

Here then, were two conflicting, or at least divergent, Quaker cultures in early Pennsylvania. A third — perhaps we should call it a subculture — flourished transiently in the frontier region, west of the Schuylkill, known as the "Welsh Tract." It is difficult to form an accurate picture of the early Welsh community. There are massive works on the subject, but they are all heavily genealogical in emphasis, and read more like stud books than like works of history: they seem more concerned with providing a suitable ancestry for later generations of Philadelphians than with disclosing the actual outlines of life in the Welsh Tract.

Were the settlers of Merion, Haverford, and Radnor rich or poor? We get no clear answer because the truth is obscured by a conflict of myths. On the one hand, to fit the legend of America as a land of opportunity, a haven for the oppressed, they must be poor men, fleeing from persecution. On the other hand, to satisfy our itch for highborn ancestors, they must be aristocrats, country squires, gentlemen to the manner born. The size of some of the early landholdings and the inventories of some personal estates suggest that a few wealthy Welshmen did take up their residence on the Main Line in the 1680's and 1690's. But alongside the purchasers of two and three thousand acres who signed themselves "gentlemen" were scores of yeomen, grocers, tailors, and the like, who settled on one hundred or one hundred fifty acres. The bulk of the Welsh immigrants were probably of "the middling sort" of people who gave the North American colonies and eventually the United States their overwhelming middle-class character.

Neither poverty nor persecution really explains that emigration from Wales which began as soon as William Penn opened the doors of Pennsylvania and lasted till some Quaker communities in Wales were all but depopulated. Professor A. H. Dodd, a learned student of Welsh history, has pointed out that if poverty had been at the root of this folk movement, it would have stemmed from the economically backward regions of Anglesey and Caernarvon rather than from fertile and prosperous Merionethshire, Radnorshire, and Montgomeryshire. And had persecution been the main impetus, the stream of emigration would have slacked off with the coming of toleration in 1689, instead of continuing, as it did, into the next century.

If we would identify the fundamental "cause" of the Welsh migration, we must recognize that it was not the "pushing" factors of poverty or persecution at home, but the strong "pulling" force of a dream — the powerful but delusive dream of a new Wales in the western wilderness, in which, as the Welsh immigrants put it themselves, "we might live together as a civil society to endeavor to decide all controversies and debates amongst ourselves in a Gospel order, and not to entangle ourselves with laws in an unknown tongue." So the first Welsh settlers extracted from William Penn a verbal promise that they should have a 40,000-acre enclave west of the Schuylkill where they could speak their own language, practice their own customs, and hold their own courts in splendid isolation.

Their attempt to transplant their ancient culture and preserve it intact did not prosper. Within a few decades they had lost their identity and merged with the fast-growing American society around them. They blamed William Penn for the failure of their dream. It was true that his governor, confronted with a solid Welsh voting bloc, followed the time-honored principle of divide and rule: he split the Welsh Tract in two by running a county line through the middle of it, throwing Haverford and Radnor into Chester County, leaving only Merion in Philadelphia County. But the experiment, one suspects, was doomed from the start. The Welsh, after all, were a bilingual people, as fluent in English as in their own tongue, and there is little evidence that distinctive Welsh laws or customs were observed in the Tract. It was not long before David ap Rees became David Price, Ellis ap Hugh became Ellis Pugh, and Edward ap John became plain Edward Jones.

It is not clear how long even such national traits as the love of music persisted. Thomas Allen Glenn found it pleasant "to think that often through the wild woodland of Colonial Merion there has echoed the burthen of some ancient British war song, chanted ages ago in battle against the legions of Imperial Rome." But Charles H. Browning, who compiled the fullest account of Welsh life in Pennsylvania, could not find "even a tradition that the Welsh Friends over the Schuylkill were inclined to music, singing and dancing." There is a revealing story about Edward Foulke, one of the pioneer settlers of Gwynedd. While he was still in Wales and not yet joined with the Quakers, people used to collect on Sundays at his house at Coed-y-foel in Merionethshire to join him in song, for Edward was a fine singer.

But he and his wife presently became uneasy in their minds about this idle way of spending the Lord's Day. Thereafter, when his musical friends gathered and he was tempted to "undue levity," he would get out the Bible and read it aloud. It was surprising, says an old account, how quickly "the light and unprofitable portion of his visitors" melted away. When Edward Foulke came to the Quaker settlement of Gwynedd in 1698, it is safe to assume that he left his harp behind. The war songs of the ancient Britons may have rung out in the Merion woods, but the echo that Thomas Allen Glenn thought he caught over the centuries was more likely the sound of the psalms of David sung in the Baptist chapels of the Welsh Tract. In any case there is little reason to think that the Welsh Friends after a few decades in America differed much from their English co-religionists.

The original settlers of Germantown seem to have suffered a like fate. The late Professor William I. Hull was convinced that they were predominantly Dutch, not German, in culture, and Quaker, not Mennonite, in religion. But whatever their origins, they quickly became Philadelphia Friends, like the Welsh. Their very names they Anglicized from Luykens to Lukens, from Kunders to Conard, from Schumacher to Shoemaker. Those Dutchmen who were not assimilated to Anglo-Saxon Quakerism were presently swallowed up by the great tide of Swiss and Germans who came to Pennsylvania after 1709 — the people who, to add to the general confusion, are known as the "Pennsylvania Dutch."

3

The Anglicans

Practical Godliness: An Episcopal Church Without Bishops

The Anglicans were the first successful English settlers in North America. In numbers, they were second only to the Congregationalists; yet no religious denomination has been so neglected by the colonial scholar.

The Church of England was the first religious establishment in the English colonies. It enjoyed the support of royal governors. It was the Church of England *in every sense. But its positive influence upon colonial affairs appears to have been slight. The conservatism of the Elizabethan Church Settlement made the Anglican theology anathema in New England, and its very identity with old England made it suspect in other colonies as well. Its missionary efforts were frequently misdirected, and its lack of a resident bishop resulted in woefully inefficient church administration. Indeed, agitation over the latter question took on political overtones which further complicated the Anglican situation in America.*

And yet the absence of an episcopate in America was not without its advantages. It gave the colonists the opportunity to mold the Church to their local needs and interests and made possible, as Daniel J. Boorstin *(of the University of Chicago) here contends, a con-*

From *The Americans: The Colonial Experience,* by Daniel J. Boorstin. © Copyright 1958 by Daniel J. Boorstin. Reprinted by permission of Random House, Inc.

gregational organization well-suited to Virginian taste.

Virginia was not founded by religious refugees, and the religion of earliest Virginia was not utopian or "purified." The going religion of England was to become part of the life of English gentlemen in America. No fact was more decisive in the history of Virginia and, through Virginians, in shaping the American character. In 1724, the Rev. Hugh Jones, who personally knew the colony, remarked:

> If New England be called a Receptacle of Dissenters, and an Amsterdam of Religion, Pennsylvania the Nursery of Quakers, Maryland the Retirement of Roman Catholicks, North Carolina the Refuge of Run-aways, and South Carolina the Delight of Buccaneers and Pyrates, Virginia may be justly esteemed the happy Retreat of true Britons and true Churchmen for the most Part; neither soaring too high nor dropping too low, consequently should merit the greater Esteem and Encouragement.

The sectarians of New England, Pennsylvania, and Maryland believed that the "purity" of their religion required them to protest against the institutions of the mother country. But even before the others had set up their protesting communities, the Virginians had begun to transplant English religious life to American shores. Although small secessionist movements had troubled English religious life from the Middle Ages, the Roman Catholics were the only major religious group outside the Established Church in England at the time Virginia was founded in 1607. The Church of England, instead of being only one among numerous religious sects, in Virginia was a catholic church, practically coextensive with the community. Many things changed in Virginia between its founding and the later 18th century, but Virginia's religion somehow retained this catholic quality. Theirs was not a violent passion inspiring men to rebuild Zion or to make a City of Brotherly Love, but a quietly pervasive sentiment which suffused the institutions of the colony with a mild aura of divine sanction. The fabric of Virginia society was held together by ancient and durable threads of religion.

"Let others take what courses they please in the bringing up of their posterity," Robert Carter wrote (July 14, 1720) from Rappahannock to the London agent supervising the education of his sons, "I resolve the principles of our holy religion shall be instilled into mine betimes; as I am of the Church of England way, so I desire they should be. But the high-flown up top notions and the great stress that is laid upon ceremonies, any farther than decency and conformity, are what I cannot come into the reason of. Practical godliness is the substance — these are but the shell." In mid-18th-century Virginia this moderate spirit was expressed as much in warm but quiet devotion to the ways of the Established Church as in immunity to the more dramatic appeal of extremists. There were few dissenters of any denomination.

How had this moderation come into being in Virginia? The first explanation was historical. The English Establishment had arisen from a compromise and, in Lord Macaulay's phrase, continued to hold "a middle position between the Churches of Rome and Geneva." This mediating spirit qualified Anglicanism to be the State religion of a liberal society and helps explain its extraordinary vitality. In those days, even in England the emphasis of Anglicanism was traditionally on institutions rather than on doctrines. The catholic character of the church in Virginia simply increased that emphasis.

In Massachusetts Bay, Puritanism became more practical and less interested in dogma than it had been in England. The Puritans in England had been, doctrinally speaking, in a state of siege, but in New England they were free to practice their way of life. Challenged by few theoretical opponents, they showed less interest in sharpening their theological rapiers. The responsibilities of governing New England also dulled the edge of dogma so that by the late 17th century they had begun those prudent compromises which would produce 18th-century Congregationalism and 19th-century Unitarianism.

Anglicanism in Virginia, for similar reasons, was destined to be even more practical and compromising than it had been in England. Virginia was more barren of theological treatises than

New England had been, and Virginians devoted their energies to the institutions of Anglicanism, to the problems of the parish, the vestry, the church-wardens, the assisting of government, the enforcement of morality, and provision for the poor. The practical character which Puritan New England paradoxically achieved by its doctrinal orthodoxy, Anglican Virginia arrived at by its catholicity and its traditionalism.

This practical religious spirit appears, for example, in the planters' libraries, which contained many books about religion. In the library of Edmund Berkeley, a fairly typical planter-aristocrat who died in 1718, of one hundred and thirteen titles, the largest group (thirty-two) dealt with religion. So too in the libraries of William Fitzhugh, Ralph Wormeley II, Richard Lee II, Robert Carter, and William Byrd II, to mention only a few. In these collections, works of theological controversy were extremely rare; religious books consisted mainly of such Anglican guides as Richard Alestree's *The Whole Duty of Man,* or Clement Ellis' *The Gentile Sinner; or, England's Brave Gentleman.* Even the occasional book of religious controversy was likely not to be theological but institutional, concerned with the organization and government of churches.

Although the Church of England, in becoming the Church of Virginia, had not altered its theology one iota, it had undergone a sea-change in institutions. While the ocean insulated Virginia Anglicans from the controversies of the metropolis, wilderness-spaces made a new thing of the English church. The Anglican has commonly been called the "Episcopal" church because it is a church of bishops; but in colonial Virginia there would be no bishops. Anglicanism, in contrast to the dissenting churches, was proverbially a church of hierarchy; but in Virginia congregations became notoriously independent and self-governing. There is surely no better example of the talent of Virginians for adapting English institutions, for bending the outward form without breaking the inner spirit. This transformation was accomplished in two ways: first, by nullifying the power of English bishops in the colony, and second, by diffusing the episcopal power into the local vestries. The Virginia Church did not in fact become truly "episcopal" — that is, it did not acquire a bishop — until 1783, after the separation from England.

During the colonial period the question of whether Virginia should have a bishop had agitated people on both sides of the water. It was generally assumed, although the legal origins were obscure, that the control of the colonial church lay in the hands of the Bishop of London, but the more prudent Bishops refused to assert a control they felt they could not enforce. "For a Bishop to live at one end of the world, and his Church at the other," Bishop Thomas Sherlock (Bishop of London, 1748–1761) wrote, "must make the office very uncomfortable to the Bishop, and in a great measure useless to the people." As a result of legal ambiguities, political ambitions, and hysterical fears, colonial Virginia never had its own bishop; in 1771, the House of Burgesses of Episcopalian Virginia took the same stand against bishops that had been taken by Puritan Massachusetts. The sole tie between the colony and the Mother Church throughout the colonial period was a vaguely empowered official called a Commissary.

Without a bishop in Virginia, every candidate for the Anglican clergy had to go to England to be ordained. "The people of the Country," Bishop Sherlock complained in 1751, "are discouraged from bringing up their Children for the Ministry, because of the hazard and expence of sending them to England to take orders where, they often get the small pox, a distemper fatal to the Natives of those Countrys." English clergymen, arguing for colonial bishops, painted the unhappy plight of young Virginians aspiring to the ministry. "And if they have the fortune to arrive safe, being here without friends, and without acquaintances, they have the sad business to undergo, of presenting themselves unknown to persons unknown, without any recommendation or introduction, except certain papers in their pocket. Are there not circumstances in this case, sufficient to deter every ordinary courage, and to damp the most adventurous spirit?" In 1767, an American writer noted, the trip could not cost less than £100, and, of the fifty-two candidates who had recently gone to England for ordaining, only forty-two had returned in safety.

These hazards and expenses of travel enabled

Virginia Anglicans to build an American church, very different from the English church which they purported to imitate. Without manifestoes, without treatises to defend their position or new dogmas to buttress it, without sounding theological trumpets — and all under the respectable Anglican cloak — Virginians developed their novel institutions. Long before the Revolution, Virginia possessed a congregationalism all its own. It differed from the congregationalism of New England partly because it lacked any explicit theological defense. The ancient hierarchical pile of the Church of England was a defensive facade behind which Virginians built their own modest, self-governing structure. They were so unobtrusive and so successful that the full significance of what they were doing remained long hidden. If they could maintain an "episcopal" church without bishops, what other improving miracles could they not perform?

Before the middle of the 18th century, the Church of Virginia had acquired a fixed character: it was a group of independent parishes, governed in temporal matters by the House of Burgesses and in doctrinal matters by no central authority at all. So far as we know, there was no regular gathering of clergymen and hence no authentic voice of dogma. Under these circumstances the supervision of the clergy and the definition of religious practices fell into the hands of the leading lay members of the parish, who of course believed it was in the best possible hands.

In England an Anglican minister held his post from the bishop; once "inducted" he had a kind of property in his parish. He held it regardless of, sometimes in spite of, the will of the parishioners, and could be removed only by a trial before his bishop. The result was the notorious twin evils of English parish life in the 18th century: "pluralism" or the holding of numerous parishes by a single clergyman; and "absenteeism" or the holding of a parish where the clergyman did not reside, and in some cases had never visited. The unfortunate English parishioner was powerless.

The Virginia remedy was nothing more complicated than the power of each parish through its vestry to choose its own minister and to retain him only so long as he satisfied them. The Anglican laymen of Virginia had not acquired this power by legislation; they simply took advantage of a legal technicality which they quietly transformed into a major institution. Technically, a minister in Virginia came into full possession of his parish and into legal control of the "glebe" (farmland owned by the parish to help support the minister) only after he had been "presented" by the vestry to the Governor and Council and then "inducted" into the living. After induction he had a kind of property in the position; but until that time he held his post at the will of the parish. Practical Virginians, bent on getting their money's worth from their tithes, developed the simple practice of not "presenting" or "inducting" their ministers. Thus the ministers were kept on year-to-year contracts, "which they call by a Name coarse enough," Hartwell, Blair, and Chilton reported with disgust in their *Present State of Virginia* in 1697, "viz. Hiring of the Ministers; so that they seldom present any Ministers, that they may by that Means keep them in more Subjection and Dependence." Thirty years later, the Rev. Hugh Jones still worried over "such Vestry-Men, who erroneously think themselves the Masters of their Parson, and aver, that since they compacted but from Year to Year with him as some have done, they may turn off this their Servant when they will."

But most fears for the Virginia clergy were ill-founded. In 1724 Virginia clergymen had, on the average, served the same parish for twenty years. Yet, of the twenty-eight replying to the Bishop of London's questionnaire in that year, twenty-three had never been "inducted" into their parishes and so, technically, were still on year-to-year tenure.

In England the pauper curate, filling a pulpit for a wealthy absentee who lived comfortably on a distant estate, received treatment befitting his squalor and servility: he ate with the butler and the lady's maid. But in Virginia even the lower clergy had the status of gentlemen. "Any young ministers that intend to marry," Commissary Blair cheerfully reported, "after some proof that they are sober good men, need not fear but that they may match to very good advantage with the Gentlemens daughters of the Countrey." It would be pleasant to report that the Anglican clergy of Virginia were all men of learning and high morals; the fact is that we know too little about the character of individual ministers. But we have no reason to doubt that the Anglican ministers in Virginia parishes were on the whole a conscientious and hard-working lot. In 1759, the Rev. Andrew Burnaby noted that Virginia's sixty-odd clergymen were "men in general of sober and exemplary lives." They were not much inferior to the ministers of other days and were decidedly superior to their English contemporaries.

But the clergyman's life was suffused with the special aroma of the colony, the aroma of tobacco. If there was some exaggeration in saying that the colony had been "founded in smoke," there was much less exaggeration in the remark that in Virginia "the Establishment is indeed Tobacco." In one sense at least, this was literally true, since almost from the beginning the compensation of clergymen had been defined and paid in tobacco. After 1695, the annual salary of a clergyman was fixed by law at 16,000 pounds of tobacco. Since the tobacco in which a minister was paid was that of his particular parish, the money value of his wage depended very much on the quality of that crop. "Some Parishes," the Rev. Hugh Jones lamented, "are long vacant upon Account of the badness of the Tobacco." The minister who found himself in a parish which raised the cruder "Oronoko" type considered himself unfortunate compared with his colleague who preached to parishioners who grew the milder, broader-leaved (and higher-priced) tobacco called "Sweet Scented." When Commissary Blair wrote back to the Bishop of London in 1724 requesting more clergymen for Virginia, he compared the vacancies in "five sweet scented Parishes" with "about double that number of Oranoco ones vacant." The old Virginia parable is still useful for an ambitious clergyman: "The best way to get sweet-scented Tobacco is to use sweet-scented Words."

Virtually the only occasion when ecclesiastical matters became a pressing political issue in colonial Virginia was the so-called "Parson's Cause" (1763). Then Patrick Henry, at the age of 27, first gained popular notice and began his public career. No question of theology or even of church-government was involved, but simply whether, in a period of high tobacco prices, vestries should be permitted to pay their clergymen in the money-values of an earlier age of cheap two-penny tobacco.

"The public or political character of the Virginians," the Rev. Andrew Burnaby sharply reported in 1759, "corresponds with their private one: they are haughty and jealous of their liberties, impatient of restraint, and can scarcely bear the thought of being controuled by any superior power." By the end of the 17th century the practice had become established for the people of the parish, through their vestrymen, to select their own minister. It was actually supported by an opinion of English Attorney General Sir Edward Northey in 1703, but never reached clear judicial decision. After Commissary Blair's bold defense of the principle against Governor Spotswood in 1719, it was never again seriously challenged in colonial Virginia: the parishes went on selecting their own ministers, and employing them on a yearly basis. Thus the battles of the American Revolution, as Bishop Meade has observed, had already been fought in Virginia vestries for a hundred and fifty years. "*Taxation and representation* were only other words for *support and election of ministers*. The principle was the same."

"Self-government" in 18th-century Virginia — in religious no less than in civil matters — was, of course, self-government by the ruling planters on behalf of their servants and neighbors. The parish was their elementary school in the political arts. By law the members of the vestry, not over twelve in number, were supposed to be elected by the parishioners. Since no regular intervals were legally fixed for these elections, however, the ruling planters developed the convenient custom of allowing vestrymen to continue in office indefinitely, until death or resignation. When vacancies occurred, the vestry itself named new members. This self-perpetuating power was important, and the ruling planters were reluctant to give it up. The "rebellious" session of the Virginia Assembly which met under the domination of Nathaniel Bacon in 1676 enacted numerous "reforms," many of which survived; but later Assemblies refused to reenact the requirement that vestrymen be elected every three years. Throughout the 18th century vestries remained self-perpetuating. It was not until 1784, when

Anglicanism was no longer established in Virginia, that regular elections of the vestry were required. During this long period, the only appeal from the decisions of the vestrymen was to the General Court or the Assembly of the colony.

On the whole, these self-elected representatives of the parish did their job well. They met at least twice a year, normally at the home of one of their members. The power to choose the minister and to continue or terminate his employment rested with them. Qualified by education, morals, and property, they appear to have exercised their powers with wisdom and restraint. If Virginia was remarkably free of the absenteeism, pluralism, docility, and corruption which cursed English parishes, if Virginia parishes refused as ministers those from England "who could roare in a tavern and babble in the pulpit," the credit was the vestry's.

The parish, through the vestrymen or their deputies, the church-wardens, wielded some of the powers of a modern sheriff, of a district attorney, and of a grand jury. Among other things, vestrymen had the duty of presenting to the court persons guilty of such moral offenses as drunkenness, blasphemy, profanity, defamation, sabbath-breaking, staying away from divine services, fornication, and adultery. The vestry levied parish taxes, assessed property for their payment, and defined the boundaries of landed property. Once in every four years, under the supervision of the county court, the vestrymen appointed two persons to "procession" the land, that is, to examine and renew old landmarks and to record the bounds in the parish books.

The parish, acting through its church-wardens, was the main social welfare agency. It was the vestry's general duty to call attention to cases of extreme poverty and in the absence of an almshouse to provide for the "poor and impotent" by boarding them at public expense in the homes of willing citizens. The vestry tried to save the parish the support of bastards by binding out the mother, compelling the father to give bond, and indenturing the children till the age of thirty. In the western counties it was the vestry that looked after children orphaned by marauding Indians. Between 1748 and 1752 Augusta Parish, in the Valley where the Indian menace was greatest, found new homes for forty-seven orphans. The people of Norfolk, who saw their town burned on New Year's Day of 1776, had their vestries to thank for relieving their suffering. In the late 17th century it was not unusual for the parish tax-levy to equal three or four times the amount of all other taxes. Just before the Revolution, Truro and Fairfax, the two parishes into which Fairfax County was divided, each had larger budgets than the county government.

No prominent citizen could decently withdraw from churchly institutions, for church duties and civic duties were one. Justices of the county courts were commonly also vestrymen: George Washington, George Mason, and George William Fairfax, all justices of Fairfax County, were all vestrymen of Truro Parish; four of the nine vestrymen of Wicomico Parish who met on Nov. 10, 1757, were justices — and so it went. The officers of the militia, who had to be recommended to the Governor by the county justices, were apt to be these very same men. In 1785 after the Church had been disestablished in Virginia, many powers of the vestry were transferred to the county court, but the leading planters still did the parish jobs in their capacity as county justices.

It would have been strange had not the political and social leaders of Virginia been leading Anglicans. Of the more than a hundred members of the Virginia constitutional convention of 1776, only three were not vestrymen. Two-thirds of all the signers of the Declaration of Independence were members of the Established Church; six were sons or grandsons of its clergymen. During the Revolution the movement toward resistance and independence flourished in the Virginia vestries. When, after the colonial legislature had been dissolved and the county courts abolished, each county was required to elect a small committee of safety to act as a *de facto* government, an Anglican clergyman was elected a member, in many cases president, of that committee in a third of the counties. It is hard to name a leader of the Revolution, including such men as George Washington, James Madison, Edmund Pendleton, and Patrick Henry, who were not securely within the fold of the Church. The fact that there were also outspoken Loyalists like the Rev. Jonathan Boucher who were loyal

Anglicans does not alter the case. For in Virginia a quiet devotion to the English Church — both as a bulwark of things ancient and English and as a local expression of the passion for independence — nourished that very reverence for the British constitution and for the traditional rights of Englishmen which inspired the Revolution.

There is no paradox then in the facts that the leaders of Virginia were almost to a man good Anglicans and that these same Virginians led the Revolution. It has been all too easy to imagine that the "English" church in Virginia, like the British government over the colonies, was shaken by a rationalist, anti-clerical, and anti-traditionalist earthquake with its epicenter somewhere in Europe. Such a view does not square with the facts.

Suggested Further Reading:

The multitude of monographs and biographical studies relating to colonial religion suggests that modern scholars are almost as absorbed with theological problems as were the colonists they study. There are, however, few books which supply a useful overview of colonial religion; the best is W. W. Sweet, *Religion in Colonial America* (1942).

For students of New England Puritanism there is an embarrassment of riches — and some sharply divergent interpretations. James Truslow Adams, *The Founding of New England** (1921), is best known for refuting nineteenth-century concepts of Puritan virtues; he gives much space to deriding Puritan concern with liberty of conscience. Thomas Jefferson Wertenbaker's *Puritan Oligarchy** (1947) is also unsympathetic. Among the more admiring historians of Puritanism are S. E. Morison, *Builders of the Bay Colony,* and *Puritan Pronaos* (1936, reprinted in paperback as *The Intellectual Life of Colonial New England,* 1960); Perry Miller, *Orthodoxy in Massachusetts, 1630–1650* (1933), *The New England Mind: The Seventeenth Century** (1939), and *Jonathan Edwards** (1949); Edmund S. Morgan, *Visible Saints: The History of a Puritan Idea* (1963). See also O. E. Winslow's *Jonathan Edwards, 1703–1758: A Biography* for a very readable, less theologically oriented study. Among other notable biographies are those by Edmund S. Morgan, *The Puritan Dilemma: The Story of John Winthrop** (1958), Richard S. Dunn, *Puritans and Yankees: The Winthrop Dynasty of New England, 1630–1717* (1962), Emery Battis, *Saints and Sectaries* (1962) which discusses the trials and tribulations of Anne Hutchinson. For an interesting account of the Salem witch trial frenzy of 1692, see Marion L. Starkey, *The Devil in Massachusetts** (1949). Two extremely valuable and succinct statements on Puritanism may be found in Alan Simpson's *Puritanism in Old and New England** (1955), and Herbert W. Schneider's *The Puritan Mind** (1958). Lastly there is Clifford K. Shipton's vigorously partisan "A Plea for Puritanism" in *The American Historical Review,* XL (1935), 460–467.

Writings on the Quakers make up in quality their limitations in quantity. The standard reference work is that by Rufus M. Jones, *The Quakers in the American Colonies* (1911), but the most readable recent studies come from the pen of Frederick B. Tolles — see particularly his *James Logan and the Culture of Provincial America* (1957), and *Meeting House and Counting House; The Quaker Merchants of Colonial Philadelphia** (1948). Also valuable is Maxwell S. Burt, *Philadelphia, Holy Experiment* (1945), and Robert Davidson, *War Comes to Quaker Pennsylvania, 1682–1756* (1957). Frederick B. Tolles and E. Gordon Alderfer have edited a convenient selection of Penn's writings in *The Witness of William Penn* (1957). For a recent and highly critical appraisal of the Quakers see Daniel J. Boorstin, "The Inward Plantation," in *The Americans: The Colonial Experience** (1958).

The Anglicans continue to be poorly served by historians. The best and most recent study is G. M. Brydon, *Virginia's Mother Church and the Political Conditions under Which it Grew* (2 vols., 1947–52); also useful is Elizabeth H. Davidson, *The Establishment of the English Church in Continental American Colonies* (1936). But most serious studies of Anglicanism in the colonial period are turgid and dated in style; significantly, when Carl Bridenbaugh began his study of the Episcopate issue, the only scholarly volume on this subject already in print was Arthur Lyon Cross's *The Anglican Episcopate and the American Colonies,* published in 1902; Bridenbaugh's volume makes broad claims for the religious differences he describes in *Mitre and Sceptre: Transatlantic Faiths, Ideas, Personalities, and Politics, 1689–1775* (1962). Wesley M. Gewehr's *The Great Awakening in Virginia, 1740–1790* (1930) throws much light upon Anglican conditions in the mid-eighteenth century, but the best treatment for the earlier period is in article form — William H. Seiler, "The Church of England as the Established Church in Seventeenth Century Virginia," *The Journal of Southern History,* XV (1949), 478–508.

PART THREE

Education in Colonial America

People struggling to survive usually view education as a luxury. Yet in colonial America education was taken very seriously; it was not regarded as a dispensable commodity. At the earliest opportunity New Englanders made far-reaching plans for the education of their children and thus for the future of their society. The citizens of Virginia were far less ambitious in their planning, but through tutors, apprenticeships, and a variety of private schools an educational pattern emerged.

Why did education enjoy so prominent a role in a society so inadequately equipped for its support? Several answers immediately present themselves: the early settlers were predominantly English, anxious to maintain their traditions and culture, and aware that education was a vehicle for what Edward Eggleston called *The Transit of Civilization.* As Bernard Bailyn has noted, "family, community, and church together accounted for the greater part of the mechanism by which English culture transferred itself across the generations." The English colonists drew upon these communitarian-church traditions in education, aided by the happy circumstance that many graduates of Oxford and Cambridge had joined in the Puritan migration of the 1630's. Puritan scholars, as Robert Middlekauff has noted in his recent *Ancients and Axioms,* early recognized that their children would be beneficiaries of such training. And so the colonial village established its school — not just to educate future generations of ministers — but to meet the cultural needs of the community.

If the point of colonial departure in education was usually English, it was still a departure. Throughout the colonial period Americans borrowed culturally from their mother country, but there was also a continuing process of adaptation to their own local needs. The result was a marked diversity in educational arrangements and a dispersion of educational opportunity beyond anything to be found at that time in England. Education at all levels took on an increasingly non-clerical complexion, and the colonial college pursued objectives that were emphatically professional and cultural. The very number of colonial colleges, scattered to meet the needs of the most populous areas, afforded an accessibility to higher education for Americans. Education was available, not systematically, not on a pattern common to all colonies, but through organizations and arrangements that reflected local needs and circumstances.

1

The Character of the Public Schools

I

Free Education in Virginia: The Eaton Free School

The sparse, relatively scattered population of the southern colonies tended to preclude any systematized educational structure, but did create opportunities for well-to-do, public-spirited citizens to furnish independent facilities for the children of their respective communities. There were many free schools. A few were maintained by public funds, but most were sustained by endowments left by such thoughtful citizens as Thomas Eaton, "of the Back River, in the County of Elizabeth Citty" in Virginia.

Here is an early example of Virginia philanthropy: Eaton's property, to the north of present-day Hampton, was well-located and — for its time — represented a sizable bequest. At least Eaton thought it sufficient to support a schoolmaster to instruct the children born within the county, with, perhaps, funds left over for the assistance of "poor, impotent persons."

To all Christian people, to whom these presents shall come, I Thos. Eaton, of the Back River, in the County of Elizabeth Citty (hereby) send Greeting in our Lord God everlasting. Know ye that I, the said Thomas Eaton, being at present weake in body, but whole & p(erfect) in memory, praised bee God out of my owne free wille (and the love) that I beare towards the Inhabitants of the City of Elizabeth Citty, I have for the maintenance of an able Schoolmaster (to) educate and teach the children borne within the said County of Elizabeth Citty — Given, Granted, assigned, set over and confirm, and doo by these presents give, grant, assign, set over and confirm after the time of my decease for the use aforesaid Five hundred acres of land, whereon the sd. Free School shall be kept, being a part of a dividend of six hundred and acres graunted unto me by pattent bearing date the fifth day of June, Anno 1638, Beginning from the beaver Damm. . . . Westerly towards the Head of the Back River & Southerly. . . . Woods, with all houses, edifices, orchards, and Rights to . . . belonging to it, Two negroes called by the names of . . . Twelve Cows and two bulls, Twenty Hoggs young and old, one bedstead, a table, a cheese press, twelve milk trays, an Iron Kettle contayning about twelve gallons, pot rack and pot hooks, Milk Pailes, water tubs, & powdering tubbs, to have and to hold the said land with all other the premises before mentioned for the use afores'd, with all ye male increase thereof for ye maintenance of the said school master, such one as by the Commissioners, Mynister & Churchwardens, whom I doo nominate & appoint as trustees, in trust for the ordering & settling thereof from time to time shall be thought fit, and I, the said Thomas Eaton do further order & appoint that no free education bee allowed but to such children as shal be born within the said County, And that when there shall be found to bee sufficient maintenance for the sd. school master that ye overplus thereof shal be imployed foı the maintenance of poor, impotent persons, Widdowes and Orphans, inhabitants within the said County as by my said Trustees shal be thought fit. All wch the premisses before mentioned to be enjoyed for the use afores'd, without anie manner of claime or demand, disturbance, incumbrance, or hindrance of anie person or persons clayming by, from or under mee forever by the these presents, and further know ye, that I, ye said Thomas Eaton have delivered at the time of the ensealing and

"The Eaton Free School," Announcement of September 19, 1659, from *The William and Mary College Quarterly,* 1st Ser., XI (1903), 19–20.

delivery hereof part of the sd. land in name of all the rest of the premises before mentioned.

In witness whereof I have hereunto set my hand & seal this nineteenth day of September, Anno Dni, 1659.

THO. EATON. (*Seal.*)

Signed, sealed and delivered in the pr'ce of Leonard Yeo, Wm. Hill, Henry Poole.

II

SECONDARY EDUCATION IN THE PURITAN COLONIES

New England's cultural pre-eminence in colonial times has often been challenged by historians. Such writers as James Truslow Adams, Charles and Mary Beard, and Thomas Jefferson Wertenbaker have questioned the level of the New England educational achievement. They have charged that the Puritan purpose was less education than religious and political indoctrination, with results consonant with such limited objectives. Samuel Eliot Morison, for many years professor of American history at Harvard University, has risen to New England's defense. He insists that the Puritans saw education as a benefit to the total life of the commonwealth, as a preparation for service to church or state, and as training for citizenship and service. He notes that the Massachusetts Act of 1647, providing for compulsory common and grammar schools, stemmed from the failure of private efforts to provide universal education; he notes further that the Massachusetts example was widely copied — so that by 1672, with the exception of Rhode Island, all established New England communities were required *to provide education for their children. No one would deny that flaws existed in this arrangement, but enforcement and compliance were widespread by the 1670's.*

CLIFFORD K. SHIPTON'S *enthusiasm for Puritan virtue is well known. He has argued eloquently for the essential tolerance and enlightenment of the Puritan in matters political and theological; he has argued with equal vigor for the civilized nature of secondary education in Puritan New England. The Grammar Schools, he notes, suffered setbacks but survived; their courses of study were ambitious and taxing; they were in no sense* church *schools, since their funds came from secular sources. They were, Dr. Shipton concludes, viable* public *schools in the best sense. Nonetheless Dr. Shipton would not deny the Puritan character of the New England schools: but how could it be otherwise? The schools were administered by Puritan laymen and taught by Puritans; but the quality of learning was generally high, the curriculum humanistic and scholarly.*

Dr. Shipton is well known in many capacities, among them as Director of the American Antiquarian Society at Worcester, Massachusetts, and as the untiring editor and biographer of Sibley's Harvard Graduates.

The accounts of secondary education in the Puritan colonies to be found in the standard texts are somewhat distorted. They have been based on the theses of students of education who rarely have had any general historical training and who have made use of only the readily accessible printed materials, and they are the work of men who, although brilliant writers or sound scholars in their own fields, have not had sufficient grubbing experience in the source materials of the history of this area. Undoubtedly the prevailing ideas are much nearer the truth than was the old idealistic faith in the fathers' achievements in education, but they are in need of a certain amount of qualification.

In the first place, the popular misconceptions in regard to Puritanism have caused the goal of secondary education in early New England to be misunderstood. It is held that the aim of the fathers was not "to make good citizens but to instruct the Christian youth sufficiently that they might search the Scriptures," and that "the newer ideal of an educated citizenry for the benefit of the state" prevailed only when the

Clifford K. Shipton, "Secondary Education in the Puritan Colonies," from *The New England Quarterly* VII (1934), 646–661.

influence of the clergy declined. Of course it is true that the Puritan frequently enunciated the idea, strange to modern writers, that the glory of God, not worldly success, was "the chief end of man." Consequently statutes in support of education were urged on the grounds that learning was "a necessary subservient Means of Religion," without which the colonies would "soon sink into Atheism, gross Darkness and Ignorance." But it is equally true that New England legislatures and town-meetings frequently described their educational legislation as aimed to forward "good literature" and other secular ends. The strongest advocates of "good literature" and the importance of a liberal education for the leaders of the state as well as of the church were the clergy. To choose among a wealth of examples, there was the sermon which John Norton preached in 1708 on the occasion of the election of councillors by the house of representatives, in which he pointed out that "it would be good to take men that are advantaged by Liberal Education, by Knowledge of Affairs abroad, as well as Customs at home; and of the Transactions, and what hath passed in former Ages: without which Knowledge, men will hardly attain to be great States Men." Indeed there were parsons to whom the religious goal was secondary:

> The Education of Youth is a great Benefit and Service to the Publik. This is that which civilizes them, takes down their Temper, tames the Fierceness of their Natures, forms their minds to vertue learns 'em to carry it with a just Deference to Superiors; makes them tractable or manageable; and by learning and knowing what it is to be under Government, they will know the better how to govern others when it comes to their Turn. . . . Yea good Education tends to promote Religion and Reformation as well as Peace and Order. . . .[1]

The *New-England Weekly Journal* for July 13, 1730, published an essay denouncing the neglect of education as an injury to the public: "It is an Evil that starves Posterity, and defrauds our Country of those Persons who with due Care might make an eminent Figure in their respective Posts of Life." The New Englander has not changed his spots; from the time of founding he has regarded education as of value for its own sake and for material as well as for spiritual ends.

One of the favorite ways of proving that the educational system of Puritan New England did not function is to assert that there was a great amount of illiteracy. It is significant that we do not find many seventeenth and eighteenth-century statements to throw light on this point. For all their belief in the importance of education, the fathers did not complain of illiteracy as they did of immorality and irreligion. One of the few people who worried about it was Cotton Mather:

> I know not whether we do, or can at this Day, labour under an iller Symtom, than the too general Want of Education in the Rising Generation; which, if not prevented, will gradually, but speedily, dispose us, to that sort of Criolian Degeneracy, observed to deprave the Children of the most noble and worthy Europeans, when transplanted into America.[2]

But for this same period, the darkest one for New England culture, we have the opinion of Governor Joseph Dudley that every child of ten could read well and every man of twenty write well, and the observation of the generally reliable Neal that "hardly a Child of nine or ten Years old throughout the whole Country" but could "read and write." During the same dark ages a New Englander said that there was not one in a thousand who had not been taught to read. The writer of a secondary work of broad scope may justly feel that he can not afford the space to explain why he chooses to disregard such contemporary evidence on colonial education, but he becomes annoying when he follows modern works of little authority and disregards sound ones in order to prove his thesis. Thus J. T. Adams proves that illiteracy was common by stating that "almost all women" signed by mark.[3] In this he follows Harlan Updegraff[4]

[1] Jeremiah Wise, *Rulers the Ministers of God* (Massachusetts Election Sermon, 1729), 31.

[2] *The Way to Prosperity* (Massachusetts Election Sermon, 1689), 33–34.

[3] J. T. Adams, *Provincial Society, 1690–1763* (New York, 1927), 133.

[4] *Origin of the Moving School in Massachusetts* (New York, 1907), 115.

(who would not have made such a statement had he ever looked into any large *corpus* of New England colonial manuscripts) and ignores one of the best-known works of Massachusetts education, which reports a count of names in the registry books of Suffolk, Essex, and Middlesex counties indicating that about forty per cent. of the women were literate.[5] Nor should the author of a general work on the colonies have missed one of the best works on education in New York, which reports a count of the signatures in the deeds of Suffolk, Massachusetts, for the periods 1653–1656 and 1681–1697 giving the men of that county a literacy score of eighty-nine per cent. in both periods and the women of forty-two and sixty-two respectively.[6] Mr. Adams illustrates to his hundreds of thousands of readers the failure of the New England school system by the fact that in the town of Natick at the end of the seventeenth century "only one child in seventy could read." As one of "the two most authoritative historians of that period" he may perhaps be excused for not knowing that Natick was a famous Indian town without (apparently) a single white inhabitant, but he should have looked up the reference to the town history which shows clearly that the application of the quotation is to the Indians.

The truth is that the failure of the New England school system can not be proved on grounds of illiteracy, for throughout the entire colonial period the level of literacy in Puritan New England remained amazingly high and seems even to have improved in spite of the death of the first generation, the demands of frontier life and of Indian wars, and the great eighteenth-century influx of indentured servants and other immigrants of lower educational achievements than the founders. Either the public school, or some other medium of elementary education, was working well.

Some historians have, failing of concrete evidence, fallen into skepticism of the standards exacted in the Puritan schools. Thomas Jefferson Wertenbaker casts doubt on the grammar-schools by saying that in them the boys were "supposed to make a beginning of Latin."[7] Supposed? Let us meet our misguided friends on their own ground, the cultural dark ages at the turn of the century. At this time, Parson Benjamin Wadsworth of Boston and Andrew Bordman, Harvard steward, were buying copies of Erasmus and Cicero for the grammar-school boys who lived with them, and Master Cheever in the Boston Latin School was having his classes turn *Æsop's Fables* into Latin verse. Although boys began the grind in the Latin grammar-schools at six or ten, they entered college younger than they do to-day, so that to meet the traditional entrance requirements of writing Latin in a pure style and reading any ordinary Greek author, they must have been subjected to a rigorous training. Mr. Wertenbaker finds this hard to believe, and holds that it is improbable that the high entrance standards set by Dunster were adhered to. But the fact is that the evidence points to a raising of the standard in 1655, and the books bought for grammar-school boys by Wadsworth, Bordman, and others, through the whole colonial period, are just the ones calculated to meet these requirements. Obviously if, as has frequently been said, the colleges of colonial New England were no better than grammar-schools, the standards of the secondary schools must have been very low, but the one document that is always cited to prove the low state of collegiate education (the report of the two Dutchmen that they could not converse in Latin with the Harvard students) means nothing in view of the fact that the visitors probably used the continental system of pronunciation. There is a mass of material with which to counterbalance the evidence of the Dutchmen. A Harvard graduate of 1707 wrote to his brother, who was entering in 1713:

> The Business [*sic*] of the 1st year is to perfect your Knowledge in the Greek and Latin and initiate you in the oriental Languages. You must settle it as maxim [*sic*], that unless you can read and understand both Greek and Latin as well as you can English, you will

[5] George H. Martin, *Evolution of the Massachusetts School System* (New York, 1904), 75.

[6] William H. Kilpatrick, *The Dutch Schools of New Netherland* (Washington, 1912), 229. Called to my attention by Professor Carl Bridenbaugh of the Massachusetts Institute of Technology.

[7] Wertenbaker, *The First Americans, 1670–1690* (New York, 1927), 246.

never make a man of any considerable Learning.[8]

If one would compare a Dutch with a New England education, one might take the case of Rowland Cotton, who, with no more formal education than that afforded by a grammar-school and two years at Harvard, needed only three months to take a degree in medicine at the University of Harderwyck. We have no concrete evidence of relaxed standards in the grammar-schools, but we do find efforts to improve teaching methods and text-books, and we do find that the literary attainments of the small merchants, craftsmen, and other middle-class people steadily improved through the colonial period.

Early in the eighteenth century there were signs of public opposition to the compulsory school legislation, and Massachusetts and Connecticut relaxed their statutes. This has caused considerable speculation. It has been said that the free school system was opposed by the wealthy, a statement that finds no support in the papers of the great families. Updegraff says of the colonists that "as a whole they did not want schools," and Adams asserts that "the people were to a great extent opposed to the expenditure of public money for school purposes." If this be true, how does it happen that the first century of the colonial period saw the privately endowed, tuition-supported, "free" schools on the English model replaced by tax-supported "public" schools of the modern American type? Unquestionably, in the war years between 1675 and 1713, a great part of the people felt that they could not afford to support the school program, and even in the days of prosperity that followed, there was a minority that was opposed to taxation for educational purposes. Arguments against the school program are rare. Joseph Belcher of Dedham says that "too many of our unlearned seem to be possessed with prejudice" against schools, and treat them with "coldness, indisposition, not to say opposition," but suggests no reason other than ignorance for their attitude. In the Connecticut election sermon of 1721 Jonathan Marsh gives a glimpse of the group which objected to the educational legislation:

> The Objection made by some against it, is this, that there is too great a Spirit for Learning in the Land; more are brought up to it than will be needed, or find Improvement; hence a snare will be laid for those devoted to it, and Learning will grow into Contempt.[9]

This, of course, referred primarily to Latin school and college education. Such bits certainly do not prove that there was any widespread opposition to the development of the school system other than evasion for financial reasons.

It is not unlikely that much of the seeming opposition on the part of the towns to the keeping of grammar-schools was due to a real difficulty in obtaining competent men at reasonable salaries. At the period in which evasion was at its height, Harvard was turning out only about a dozen graduates a year, for whom there were plenty of pulpits because the even smaller output of the preceding thirty years had caused a shortage of parsons. We know that a few towns which did not keep grammar-schools had applied in vain for masters at Cambridge. But when the Harvard classes increased and Yale opened her doors, the towns had no difficulty in getting bachelors and masters of arts to wield their birch rods. Hadley, for example, had thirty-one teachers in forty-five years, all but the first and the third (he a son of the minister) being college graduates. Of eleven successive Newbury schoolmasters, only the second was not a bachelor of arts. Dedham had twenty-seven in sixty years, all but the first three being fresh from Harvard. By 1725 teachers were advertising for jobs. But, it is argued, the school system could not be healthy when these teachers were being paid salaries which "expressed in modern terms" hardly exceeded sixty or seventy dollars a year. The fact is that those school-masters who were paid no more than twelve or twenty pounds a year were established farmers who kept writing-schools for only a few months. The professional teachers capable of preparing boys for college were, during the period from King Philip's War to the Revolution, usually paid about forty pounds a year. This sum, inadequate for a family in times of inflation, was not bad for a

[8] Massachusetts Historical Society: Prince Papers, 61: 1: 84, 82: Thomas Prince to Nathan Prince, October 2, 1713.

[9] *An Essay* (New London, 1721), 45.

boy fresh from college, and had a purchasing power above that of the average salary of school-teachers in the United States in the twentieth century.

The writers of theses on education trace their stories to the point where Massachusetts and Connecticut relax their educational legislation and the words "grammar-school" disappear from the pages of town histories and printed town records, and then close their monographs with a sorrowful paragraph on the failure of the system of secondary education in Puritan New England. They miss the point that the legislatures, having aimed too high at first, took a second shot which did much more execution among delinquent towns. Frequently, town historians, smelling the Revolution about the time they reach the year 1700 in their story, there drop commonplace education and gallop to the fray. And in the eighteenth century, towns began to delegate school affairs, as a rule, to selectmen or committees, whose reports do not appear in the town records. Yet we know from scattered bits of evidence which no student would be likely to chance upon while writing his thesis, that these towns had schools. In particular the evidence offered by the employment of school-masters proves that the old towns which had been presented for not obeying the school laws during the war years, kept school year in and year out from the peace of Utrecht to the battle of Lexington and Concord. And even on the New Hampshire frontier — take the town of Kingston, for example — one is constantly being surprised by finding the employment of full-time school-masters instructed to teach Latin to all who asked.

This last point is an important one. Too much stress has been laid on the words "Latin grammar-school." Writers have usually proceeded on the thesis that there were three distinct grades of schools in colonial New England — dame schools; English, or writing-schools; and Latin, or grammar-schools. If the town records provide for a Latin or a grammar-school, the town is listed among the sheep; but if the clerk wrote only "school," the town becomes a goat (for statistical purposes). In a few of the largest towns during the seventeenth century such a distinction is justified; in general, and after the legislation of 1690–1710, it is not. Of course the chief purpose of the grammar-school was to prepare boys for college, and when it is remembered that, before the founding of Yale in 1701, Harvard took only a dozen boys a year, on the average, and some of those from outside New England, it is obvious that very few towns would have sufficient Latin students to justify a separate school. Some of the towns required to keep a grammar-school under the old legislation sometimes went a decade without sending a boy to college. In the eighteenth century the school-master's chief business was to teach reading and writing, but he was expected to teach Latin and Greek if any son of the town decided to acquire more education. Here is the explanation of that "constant decline" of the grammar-school in the eighteenth century which some writers report, undismayed by the fact that there were five times as many boys in college in New England in 1740 as there had been in the heyday of the separate grammar-school sixty years before.

In view of these facts, I believe that the eighteenth century saw, not a decline, but a steady improvement in the public school system, making education as far as the classics open to the great majority of children in the Puritan colonies, and as far as the colleges to most boys.

The factors which caused the great revolution in the public school system which occurred between 1650 and 1750 are, in general, well understood. There is, however, a tendency to lay too much stress on internal social evolution and not enough on external forces. The immediate reason for relinquishing the original school statutes was probably the generation-long war which began in 1675. The fact that the prosecution of towns for failing to comply with the school laws increases steadily through the war period — apparently culminating in the third war of the series, after the requirements had been relaxed — shows the connection. It was financial necessity, not simply disregard of the parsons' warning that they were inviting a return to "the Barbarous Age," that led the towns into "Tricks and Shifts whereby the Laws of the Land obliging to the upholding and maintaining of Schools" might be evaded. But over and above the great financial drain and the death of tax-payers on the field of battle, there must be added the fact that Andros let the school laws lapse and discouraged teachers by a license requirement. When Andros fell, Massachusetts attempted to resume the old laws, only to be checked by the privy council, and when matters were finally settled under the new charter, a new deal was an obvious necessity.

Of less importance in the educational revolution than these external factors, and of less importance than the "tyranny of the theocracy" school of historians is inclined to think, was the matter of religious change. Educational ideas, like everything else, were affected by the tendency, once the first generation was off the field, to turn attention from religious to secular matters. But the notion that the schools were the tools of the clergy, and that some four-fifths of the people welcomed the "fall of the theocracy" as an opportunity to get rid of this burden, is absurd. How could the schools be tools of the church when their affairs were managed in town-meetings in which the hypothetical anti-Puritan four-fifths had the ballot? And how did it happen that in 1702, after the four-fifths had been given the province franchise, the general court of Massachusetts gave the clergy authority to pass upon the teachers before the town could hire them? The point is that there was no general hostility to the ministers and no sudden overthrow of their influence to affect the educational situation.

It should be kept in mind that the New England schools were never sectarian, maintained exclusively for the children of the orthodox, as were the first "public" schools of New Amsterdam. Little Baptists and Anglicans were welcome to enjoy the entire educational system from the dame schools through Harvard, even though it was known that their purpose was to preach those minority gospels. Of course the Quakers favored elementary education that each individual might read the Bible in his search for the inner light. Obviously, then, these religious minorities had no reason to oppose the public school system — nor did that ever-growing group which was more interested in the external world than in any religion, for its sons also needed reading, writing, and arithmetic, and even Latin if they contemplated the professions of law and medicine. If these religious minorities did not oppose the school laws on religious grounds, surely the orthodox majority would not, for the complaint of the popular politicians against Harvard in the first quarter of the eighteenth century was that it was not orthodox enough.

In fact, the increase in secular activities increased the demand for public school education. As trade spurted, merchants advertised for apprentices who could read and write; and as fortunes were made, the idea of the importance of a classical education for gentlemen spread. Of all the line of Hutchinsons and Olivers who emerged from the gates of Harvard in the eighteenth century, only one wore the cloth.

The blows which the Puritan colonies received from Indians and the royal government were the occasion of the revolution in the educational system, but the fundamental cause was the frontier, or, more properly, the terrain. Enormous, thinly settled townships led to the invention of moving, or district, schools. The poverty of new towns, where parents could not pay tuition and where there were no rich men to endow schools, led to increasing aid and regulation from the legislatures. And when Connecticut, in 1737, provided that in every new township a certain area be set aside for school purposes, the system peculiar to America may be said to have emerged.

At this point the orthodox accounts of secondary education end, for here end the statutes, records, and town histories, but when one goes on into the newspapers and the manuscript collections it becomes apparent that there was another factor of tremendous importance — the development of the private schools.

The eighteenth century was a period of very swift economic and social change, change at a pace with which the established educational system could not keep up. Formal education is always conservative, lagging behind the times. We have all heard that "business is a trade and has no place in a university." There was no place for technical education in the Puritan public school system; so a rival private school system sprang up to meet the demand of the times. Not long after the turn of the century there appear in Boston private schools teaching geometry, trigonometry, navigation, book-keeping, geography, foreign exchange, and the tongues of trade. The first advertisement for a school of this sort appears in the *Boston News-*

Letter for March 21, 1708–1709, and it is quickly followed by many competitors. At least some of these schools were good, for Isaac Greenwood went to England and studied under a great mathematician for several years before he opened the school from which he was called to occupy the first chair of mathematics at Harvard. The close observation which the town maintained suggests that the master was compelled to be competent. The news of these schools spread to New Hampshire, Rhode Island, and the West Indies, and boys flocked to Boston to attend them.

Unfortunately, we do not have much material on these technical schools, but we do have the account book which Peter Burr kept while running a private school in Boston between 1695 and 1699, and from it we can determine the sort of competition which the town schools were meeting. He charged six or ten shillings a quarter for tuition, more than the New Hampshire boys paid at Cambridge Latin when they came down to prepare for Harvard, but less than the college itself charged. Board and room in the town cost only ten pounds a year, considerably less than at the college, and much less, proportionately, than they would cost to-day. Perhaps that is why these schools became so popular. Burr's students came from good, middle-class families and (this being before the business revival) studied Latin from Tully, Ovid, and Erasmus as did the boys in the public grammar-schools. The great majority of them did not go on to college.

Among those who "began to learn lattin" at Mr. Burr's school were a number of girls. The fact that there was no place for girls in the public school system above the writing-schools has led to some false ideas about their education in colonial times. In Boston, at least, private schools for them abounded, both for day and boarding students, and night sessions were early advertised. Here were taught the classics, advanced composition, and accounts, as well as the more womanly arts. It was probably to such a school that Cotton Mather sent his daughter Katy when he determined to bring her up in a "Knowledge in Physic, and the Preparation, and the Dispensation of noble Medicines," for which a knowledge of Latin was essential. To these schools gentlemen as far away as John Stoddard at Northampton sent their daughters. Many such girls lived in Benjamin Wadsworth's parsonage. Some light is thrown on the schools in the following account, which John Whipple, of Providence, gave of Mary Brattle, a member of the Old South Church and of one of the best families:

> Being in the shopp of Thomas Clarke peutour in boston where came into sayd shopp one called Mary Brattle, and Demaunded of sayd Clarke the key of a house of office and sayd Clarke Denied to Deliver it . . where upon sayd mary Brattle gave sayd Clarke very Taunting speeches . . . called sayd Clark Beggars Bratt, and Cheate: and sayd shee kept a better man to wipe her shoees . . . she also Called the sayd Clarke Rascal, then the sayd Clark bid her gett out of his shopp for you are a pratteing hossey for you had need to have had a hundred pounds Bestooed upon you at a boardeing Schoole to learne manners and breeding. . . .[10]

Of the competition which the public schools faced from charity schools in Boston and such towns as Salem, we know little. These schools were fairly numerous early in the eighteenth century, but then seem to disappear, probably with the development of the idea that education should be paid for by the towns.

Obviously the existence of these private schools makes invalid the conclusions about education which have been drawn from the public schools alone. Some idea of the competition offered by private schools may be gained by public school enrollment in Boston. In 1727 there were two hundred and ten scholars in the grammar-schools and two hundred and twenty in the writing-schools, and one private establishment with one hundred is mentioned. The next decade was one of rapid development for private technical schools. If we average several years at the end of the 1730's and the beginning of the 1740's, we find from the town records that the enrollment had decreased about twenty per cent. in the grammar-schools while increasing nearly one hundred per cent. in the writing-

[10] *Providence Town Records* (Providence, 1892–1895), XVII, 53. According to this lady's obituary, "Her Conversation was always entertaining grave and profitable." *New-England Weekly Journal,* December 24, 1733.

schools. Obviously this reflects the demand for technical education. It is hopeless to attempt to estimate the number of students in private schools, for although the Boston authorities regularly combed the slums to be sure that every child was getting some sort of education, the public school enrollment was hardly ten per cent. of that of a town of the same size to-day. We have no way of calculating the number of children taught by their parents, or apprentices by their masters.

To conclude, it would seem that there was no permanent collapse of secondary education in Puritan New England such as the earlier studies indicated. The public schools, changed in form to meet the new situation, actually improved in the eighteenth century. And the private technical schools of eighteenth-century Boston certainly cared for more students than all the Latin grammar-schools of the seventeenth century combined.

2

The College Enthusiasm

I

The College of William and Mary

The avidity of the colonials for education was markedly demonstrated in the colleges they founded soon after the colonies themselves became established. The Virginia Company had contemplated a university and free school (for the Indians) but nothing came of it. The first successful college, Harvard, traces its beginnings to 1636; the second, William and Mary, to 1693, when (unlike Harvard) it received a royal charter. For its first twenty-five years William and Mary remained largely a grammar school. Anglican in affiliation, the Virginia college owed much to Commissary James Blair, who became its first President. William and Mary proved to be the only college to be established in the southern colonies, but the high hopes surrounding its inception were never even partially realized until the end of the eighteenth century.

During that gentleman's presidency, which began *Anno* 1689, the project of a college was first agreed upon. The contrivers drew up their scheme and presented it to the president and council. This was by them approved, and referred to the next assembly. But Col. Nathaniel Bacon's administration being very short and no assembly called all the while, this pious design could proceed no further.

Anno 1690. Francis Nicholson, Esq., being appointed lieutenant-governor under the Lord Effingham, arrived there. This gentleman's business was to fix himself in my lord's place, and recommend himself to the supreme government. For that end, he studied popularity, discoursing freely of country improvements. He made his court to the people by instituting Olympic games, and giving prizes to all those that should excel in the exercises of riding, running, shooting, wrestling, and backsword. When the design of a college was communicated to him, he foresaw what interest it might create him with the bishops in England, and therefore promised it all imaginable encouragement. The first thing desired of him in its behalf was the calling of an assembly; but this he would by no means agree to, being under obligations to the Lord Effingham, to stave off assemblies as long as he could, for fear there might be further representations sent over against his lordship, who was conscious to himself how uneasy the country had been under his despotic administration.

When that could not be obtained, then they proposed that a subscription might pass through

---

Robert Beverley, *The History and Present State of Virginia* (London, 1722); reprinted in *ibid.*, ed. Louis B. Wright (Chapel Hill: University of North Carolina Press, 1947), pp. 97–100.

the colony to try the humour of the people in general, and see what voluntary contributions they could get towards it. This he granted, and he himself, together with the Council, set a generous example to the other gentlemen of the country, so that the subscriptions at last amounted to about two thousand five hundred pounds, in which sum is included the generous benevolences of several merchants of London.

Anno 1691, an assembly being called, this design was moved to them, and they espoused it heartily; and soon after made an address to King William and Queen Mary in its behalf, and sent the Reverend Mr. James Blair their agent to England, to solicit their Majesties' charter for it.

It was proposed that three things should be taught in this college, viz., languages, divinity, and natural philosophy.

They appointed a certain number of professors, and their salaries.

And they formed rules for the continuation and good government thereof to perpetuity. But of this I shall speak more particularly in the last part of my book, wherein the present state will be considered.

The Assembly was so fond of Governor Nicholson at that time that they presented him with the sum of three hundred pounds as a testimony of their good disposition towards him. But he having an instruction to receive no present from the country, they drew up an address to their Majesties, praying that he might have leave to accept it.

This he took an effectual way to secure by making a promise that if their Majesties would please to permit him to accept it, he would give one half thereof to the college; and so he secured at once both the money and the character of being a generous person.

Their Majesties were well pleased with that pious design of the plantation, and granted a charter, according to their desire; in obtaining which the address and assiduity of Mr. Blair, their agent, was highly to be admired.

Their Majesties were graciously pleased to give near two thousand pounds sterling, the balance due upon the account of quit-rents, towards the founding the college; and towards the endowing of it, they allowed twenty thousand acres of choice land, together with the revenue arising by the penny per pound, on tobacco exported from Virginia and Maryland to the other plantations.

It was a great satisfaction to the archbishops and bishops to see such a nursery of religion founded in that new world; especially for that it was begun in an Episcopal way, and carried on wholly by zealous conformists to the Church of England . . .

. . . With Sir Edmund Andros in 1692 was sent over the college charter and the subsequent Assembly declared that the subscriptions which had been made to the college were due and immediately demandable. They likewise gave a duty on the exportation of skins and furs, for its more plentiful endowment.

The subscription money did not come in with the same readiness with which it had been underwritten. However, there was enough given by their Majesties and gathered from the people to keep all hands at work and carry on the building, the foundation whereof they then laid.

II

King's College, New York

*King's College (later to become Columbia University) was a product of what Ezra Stiles of Yale termed "the College Enthusiasm" of the mid-eighteenth century. Where there were only three colleges before the establishment of Princeton (The College of New Jersey) in 1746, another six had been founded by 1769.** *This "enthusiasm" stemmed partly from the denominational fervor raised by the Great Awakening, partly from the economic prosperity that marked the years between King George's War and the Great War for the Empire (1748–1754), and,*

* The colonial colleges:
1636: Harvard (Congregational)
1693: William and Mary (Anglican)
1701: Yale (Congregational-Presbyterian)
1746: Princeton (Presbyterian)
1751: Pennsylvania (nonsectarian)
1754: Columbia (Anglican)
1764: Brown (Baptist)
1766: Rutgers (Dutch Reformed)
1769: Dartmouth (Congregational)

perhaps in larger measure, from the intellectual interests and ambitions of an increasingly sophisticated colonial society.

Fund raising for King's began as early as 1746. Although an Anglican institution, its governing board included ministers of no less than five denominations. And its curriculum offered science, mathematics, and modern languages — a significant departure from the usual absorption with the classics, history, logic, ethics, and rhetoric.

To such parents as have now (or expect to have) children prepared to be educated in the College of New York.

I. As the gentlemen who are appointed by the Assembly to be trustees of the intended seminary or college of New York have thought fit to appoint me to take the charge of it, and have concluded to set up a course of tuition in the learned languages and in the liberal arts and sciences, they have judged it advisable that I should publish this advertisement to inform such as have children ready for a college education that it is proposed to begin tuition upon the first day of July next at the vestry room in the new schoolhouse adjoining to Trinity Church in New York, which the gentlemen of the vestry are so good as to favour them with the use of in the interim 'til a convenient place may be built.

II. The lowest qualifications they have judged requisite in order to admission into the said college are as follows, viz.: that they be able to read well and write a good legible hand, and that they be well versed in the five first rules in arithmetic, i.e., as far as division and reduction; and as to Latin and Greek, that they have a good construing and parsing to give a good account of two or three of the first select orations of Tully and of the first books of Virgil's *Aeneid* and some of the first chapters of the Gospel of St. John in Greek. In these books, therefore, they may expect to be examined; but higher qualifications must hereafter be expected. And if there be any of the higher classes in any college or under private instruction that incline to come hither, they may expect admission to proportionably higher classes here.

III. And that people may be the better satisfied in sending their children for education to this college, it is to be understood that as to religion, there is no intention to impose on the scholars the peculiar tenets of any particular sect of Christians, but to inculcate upon their tender minds the great principles of Christianity and morality in which true Christians of each denomination are generally agreed. And as to the daily worship in the college, morning and evening, it is proposed that it should ordinarily consist of such a collection of lessons, prayers, and praises of the liturgy of the Church as are for the most part taken out of the Holy Scriptures, and such as are agreed on by the trustees to be in the best manner expressive of our common Christianity. And as to any peculiar tenets, everyone is left to judge freely for himself and to be required only to attend constantly at such places of worship on the Lord's Day as their parent or guardians shall think fit to order or permit.

IV. The chief thing that is aimed at in this college is to teach and engage the children to know God in Jesus Christ and to love and serve Him in all sobriety, godliness, and righteousness of life, with a perfect heart and a willing mind, and to train them up in all virtuous habits and all such useful knowledge as may render them creditable to their families and friends, ornaments to their country, and useful to the public weal in their generations. To which good purposes it is earnestly desired that their parents, guardians, and masters would train them up from their cradles under strict government and in all seriousness, virtue, and industry, that they may be qualified to make orderly and tractable members of this society. And above all, that in order hereunto they be very careful themselves to set them good examples of true piety and virtue in their own conduct. For as examples have a very powerful influence over young minds, and especially those of their parents, in vain are they solicitous for a good education for their children if they themselves set before them examples of impiety and profaneness or of any sort of vice whatsoever.

V[th] and lastly. A serious, virtuous, and industrious course of life being first provided for,

---

Samuel Johnson, advertisement in *The New York Mercury,* June 3, 1754.

it is further the design of this college to instruct and perfect the youth in the learned languages and in the arts of reasoning exactly, of writing correctly, and speaking eloquently; and in the arts of numbering and measuring, of surveying and navigation, of geography and history, of husbandry, commerce, and government; and in the knowledge of all nature in the heavens above us, and in the air, water, and earth around us, and the various kinds of meteors, stones, mines and minerals, plants and animals, and of every thing useful for the comfort, the convenience, and elegance of life in the chief manufactures relating to any of these things. And finally, to lead them from the study of nature to the knowledge of themselves and of the God of nature and their duty to Him, themselves, and one another, and everything that can contribute to their true happiness both here and hereafter.

Thus much, gentlemen, it was thought proper to advertise you of concerning the nature and design of this college. And I pray God it may be attended with all the success you can wish for the best good of the rising generations to which, while I continue here, I shall willingly contribute my endeavours to the utmost of my power.

Gentlemen,

Your real friend and most humble servant,

SAMUEL JOHNSON

N.B. The charge of the tuition is established by the trustees to be only twenty-five shillings for each quarter.

III

COLLEGE FOUNDING IN THE AMERICAN COLONIES, 1745–1775

BEVERLY MCANEAR'S *study of colonial colleges during the thirty years prior to the Revolution deserves the widest possible audience. Here Dr. McAnear examines the forces leading to "the College Enthusiasm," discusses the problems the colleges encountered, and reviews their accomplishments. The colonial college, he concludes, deserves praise for the educational opportunity it afforded, for the public enterprise its very being represented, and for the improvement of secondary education that rising college standards inevitably demanded.*

Beverly McAnear, "College Founding in the American Colonies, 1745–1775," from *The Mississippi Valley Historical Review*, XLII (1955), 24–44.

In the year 1745 there were but three colleges in all of British North America. Yet by the beginning of the Revolution the virus that Ezra Stiles labeled "College Enthusiasm" had so widely infected the American colonists that seven new colleges had been firmly established; plans had been laid for three more which were to open during the Revolution; and at least six abortive projects had been undertaken by responsible people. Thus by 1776 every province and nearly every popular religious sect was planning and had arranged for financial backing for a school of its own. In addition to the older three — Harvard, Yale, and William and Mary — those actually giving instruction were: Dartmouth College in New Hampshire; the College of Rhode Island, now Brown University; King's College, from which Columbia University has descended; Queen's College, soon to bear the name of Rutgers; the College of New Jersey, destined to become Princeton University; the Academy and College of Philadelphia, still living as the University of Pennsylvania; and Newark Academy, ultimately to reappear as the University of Delaware.

This interest in the founding of colleges coincided with a growth of the spirit of rationalism that sought intellectual stimulation in sources other than theological — a spirit eagerly capitalized on by college promoters who urged the establishment of non-sectarian institutions. Sectarian discussion, such as the Old Light-New Light controversy, further spurred on the founding of colleges consecrated to the religious approach of the partisans. Finally, college founding was helped along by the years of prosperity after 1748, which made fund raising easier, and by the growth of civic and humanitarian spirit, which provided the stimulus. Between 1745 and 1765 most of the campaigns were organized by Yale graduates; after 1765 College of New

Jersey men began to take the lead. Men educated in Great Britain and some who were not college men were also among the founders of the new colleges. Except for the role of Harvard graduates in the founding of Dartmouth and the part played by the College of Philadelphia in the establishment of Newark Academy, the graduates of the other American colleges did not figure prominently in the movement.

Regardless of their educational background, college promoters became interested in advancing higher education through affiliation either with a library company or with a church. Most organizers — and they were the most successful — were ministers interested in the advancement of their own sect. Clerical leaders campaigned for Dartmouth, Queen's, New Jersey, Newark, and, in their final stages of organization, for Rhode Island and King's. The reasons emphasized by clerics for establishing colleges were to educate ministers, to raise the level of general culture and morals through the influence of the clerical alumni, and to convert the Indians. They maintained that a college was a religious society whose basic and chief duty was to train its students to be religious and moral men. The study of nature was to be subservient to the inculcation of religion; the one was only a threshold to the other, and religious instruction therefore was to be emphasized. They freely promised toleration to all Protestant Trinitarian sects, but they demanded clerical administration and the dominance of one sect.

Those promoters identified with one of the library companies were usually laymen, often without much formal education. Colleges and libraries were at that time a natural conjunction of interests, for some of the library companies were originally designed as organizations which would not only circulate books but which would also provide popular lecture courses, particularly on scientific subjects. Men affiliated with libraries were concerned with the foundation of Rhode Island, King's, and Philadelphia, and with abortive proposals for colleges at Newport and Charleston. They argued that a college should properly be considered a civil society committed to the duty of training youths for service to the commonwealth, and the value of any type of training was to be measured according to its ultimate usefulness to the graduates in civil life. The best attribute of an educated man was an independent mind; free inquiry was therefore to be encouraged and religious instruction prohibited. To assure freedom, religious toleration and non-sectarianism were to be maintained, and even direct state control was proposed.

To their basic appeal for support each group of promoters added virtually the same arguments. College alumni would provide superior public servants and the very presence of the college and its faculty would raise the cultural level of the province. The students' love of their native province would be protected against the alienation that might result from new attachments formed during their school years in distant parts, and thus the best minds of the colony would be saved for the service of their birthplace. Money would not flow out of the province to enrich the residents of college towns in other provinces. And, finally, a local school would provide a less expensive education for ambitious sons of residents.

Almost inevitably a movement to launch a college aroused religious and political rivalries. Many of the quarrels concerned the sectarian affiliation of the proposed college; and in these contests the Anglicans and Presbyterians were the most combative. In addition to their involvement in the Old Light-New Light controversy raging in the Calvinistic churches, some of the schools became involved in provincial or imperial political questions which had nothing to do with higher education, and some college promoters were confronted with the monopolistic claims of institutions already established. Once aroused by these contentions, factions which had been aligned in the opening days of a college lived on to blight its growth. These feuds account in great measure for the failure of all the newer colleges to gain annual provincial appropriations, and they caused the failure of many of the proposals for new colleges even though neither money nor public interest was lacking.

Factional division usually began with a dispute over the terms of a charter of incorporation and the nomination of the first trustees. Incorporation was necessary to protect the institution's property and to permit the granting of degrees; and the religious loyalties of the trustees usually determined the ecclesiastical affiliation of the college. The founders of New Jersey and Dartmouth objected so stubbornly to the inclusion of royal officers of Anglican faith among the trustees that they were almost denied their charters. A furious battle over the method of organization of the college cost King's thousands of pounds of endowment and all hope of future provincial support.

In drafting their charters, King's, Dartmouth, and Queen's used the College of New Jersey charter of 1748 as a model; Rhode Island drew upon the Harvard and Yale charters, in addition to New Jersey's; and Newark turned to the charter of Pennsylvania. Ironically, no one seems to have known at the time whether the colonial governors had the power to grant charters of incorporation and therefore whether the college charters were valid.

The building lot for the college was invariably provided by a public or semi-public organization in order to attract the college to its town. The difficulties that New Jersey College experienced in its attempts to secure a sizable sum in four different New Jersey villages indicate that the custom was not well established in the 1740's. But it caught on quickly, and Queen's was embarrassed by bids from New Brunswick, Tappan, and Hackensack, while Rhode Island felt obliged to hold an auction to terminate five months of competitive controversy.

As soon as money was available, a college hall, containing classrooms and a dormitory, was erected. To supervise construction, some colleges relied on artisans or amateur architects, but Rhode Island, New Jersey, and Philadelphia retained the services of the Philadelphia architect and builder, Robert Smith. The plans drawn by Smith and William Shippen, a physician and amateur architect of Philadelphia, were repeated elsewhere and virtually created in America the collegiate Georgian style. Essentially their design was an adaptation of that for King's College, Cambridge University. During the twenty-five years before the Revolution, five of these schools spent approximately £15,000 sterling for the erection or remodeling of buildings. "This they chose to do," President John Witherspoon of the College of New Jersey wrote, "though it wasted their Capital, as their great Intention was to make effectual Provision, not only for the careful Instruction, but for the regular Government of the Youth." A pretentious building was also desirable because it afforded publicity, and its inclusion of dormitory space and commons reduced student expenses.

The cost of the original hall invariably reduced the college to a state of near insolvency. Indeed, Philadelphia and Rhode Island invested in their buildings literally the last penny in the till. As a result, trustees tended to limit the materials for classroom demonstrations in physics, surveying, and astronomy. Thanks to the persistence of their presidents, however, by 1775 the scientific instruments of King's, New Jersey, and Philadelphia were equal to or better than those possessed by Harvard, Yale, and William and Mary. The other new colleges owned little or no scientific apparatus.

A greater handicap was the inadequacy of libraries. By the time of the Revolution, the Harvard library, with more than 4,000 volumes, was probably the largest college library in the colonies. Yale was not far behind, but William and Mary must have had less than 3,000. While Philadelphia, King's, and New Jersey, with perhaps 2,000 books each, made at least a respectable showing, library facilities at the other newly established institutions were either virtually or completely non-existent.

Nearly all the books in the libraries of the newer colleges had been presented: none customarily bought more than occasional titles. The only important purchases were three consignments for New Jersey, one of which was so costly that the trustees deemed it an extravagance and charged the bill to the president. To make matters more difficult, these libraries were largely the gifts of benevolent clergymen, and the weight of theology hung heavy upon them. "But few modern Authors, who have unquestionably some Advantages above the immortal ancient, adorn the Shelves," wrote a college official in 1760. "This Defect is most sensibly felt in the Study of Mathematics, and the Newtonian Philosophy." Philadelphia and New Jersey sought to remedy matters by assessing the students a library fee, but the income must have been small.

By the time the trustees of a college had built the hall and provided furniture, scientific equipment, and a library, they had invested approximately £5,000 — perhaps the equivalent of $350,000 today. By 1776 the physical properties of all the infant colleges probably represented the expenditure of something approaching £25,000 — an investment which produced virtually no income, since students' rents could hardly have paid for maintenance.

In assembling a faculty, the trustees were apt to seek a president who had been trained in a British university, but since the necessary income was often lacking they were forced to be content with the product of an American college. The president bore the heaviest share of the burden of the school. He did a good part of the teaching and conducted the college's religious exercises. He was also the chief and sometimes the only administrative officer, and he was obliged to gather money and recruit students. To supplement his income, he often served as the pastor of a neighboring church. Such arrangements were discouraged by the trustees, however, and as the college grew more prosperous, pressure was placed on the president to confine himself to college affairs.

The other members of the faculty (seldom more than three) were usually younger men destined within a few years to be clergymen. Most were American trained, though Anglican schools secured some British-educated tutors. Lack of money prevented the hiring of a more stable, better trained faculty, since almost any profession promised greater returns and better social status. The hardest position to fill was that of the science instructor. Few men with the necessary training were to be found in the colonies, and hence the post was often vacant. Each instructor normally was assigned a given class of students to whom he imparted knowledge on all subjects except the natural sciences. This arrangement demanded, however, that a faculty member undertake a considerable degree of specialization of subject matter, because the curricula emphasized given branches of learning in different years.

One of the president's most perplexing tasks was the enrollment of students. To an even greater extent than the present-day college, colonial institutions relied upon income from tuition to provide vitally needed revenue. But to recruit students, it was necessary to popularize the value of higher education. Prior to 1745 not many parents in the British North American colonies sent their sons to college. This was especially true for the Middle Colonies. To attract public attention, some use was made of printed publicity. Ministers were pressed to act as recruiting agents for the college identified with their sect. Alumni, especially where they were schoolmasters or pastors, were able to help the recruiting for New Jersey, but most of the other colleges were too young to have many graduates.

The overwhelming majority of entrants were attracted by the college nearest their homes. The difficulty and expense of travel, the emotional complications inherent in distant separation from home, and local pride perhaps influenced students and furnished talking points for recruiting agents. But provincialism could be defeated if a distant college offered a cheaper education. Those colleges which grew most rapidly and attracted most students from other provinces were those which charged least. New Jersey and Rhode Island had the lowest charges, and Eleazer Wheelock permitted some Dartmouth students to work for their expenses. Hence these three colleges showed the most rapid increase in enrollment. Apparently New Jersey was also aided by its custom of admitting applicants as juniors, thus waiving costly residence at college for the first two or three years of a boy's work. Philadelphia and King's were the most expensive and therefore always had small student bodies, largely drawn from their immediate vicinity.

Despite ardent campaigning, the enrollment in all these infant colleges was small. The opening class in any one of them could hardly have been more than five to eight boys. Succeeding classes naturally increased enrollment, and the prosperous years of the early 1770's greatly aided recruitment. Even so, most of the newer schools prior to the Revolution had at best an attendance of only forty or fifty students. By all odds, the most successful was New Jersey, which grew to an enrollment of about one hundred. Yet, despite this rapid growth, New Jersey was still smaller than her older rivals, for after 1755 the student bodies of Harvard and Yale had often exceeded one hundred and fifty. Approximately four sevenths of all college students of 1775 were enrolled in the three oldest institutions.

Upon appearance at college, the prospective student was required to pass an entrance examination, usually administered by the president. The requirements of the new colleges seem to have been copied from those of Yale; for Rhode Island, King's, and New Jersey the requirements were almost identical. Essentially, the test demanded ability to translate elementary Latin and Greek and a knowledge of arithmetic — this last being a contemporary innovation. It is doubtful that an applicant was ever sent home, though sometimes extra work was prescribed.

Many of the students admitted were mere boys. From 1750 to 1775 the median age of the entrants at Yale was only sixteen or seventeen; at Philadelphia it was sixteen; and at King's only fifteen. Eleven- and twelve-year-old freshmen were not unknown, and John Trumbull satisfied the Yale entrance examination at the age of seven years and five months. Because of the competition for students the colleges were in danger of becoming grammar schools. As a step toward remedying this difficulty, the governors of King's in 1774 ruled that after the admission of the class of 1778 entrance would be refused any applicant younger than fourteen "except upon account of extraordinary qualifications."

As a general rule, only freshmen were admitted. Though there were exceptions in every college, only Dartmouth, New Jersey, and possibly Philadelphia made a practice of admitting students to advanced standing. These boys had usually studied with a minister because such a training was less expensive than college residence. For admission to advanced standing, the college required payment of fees for the earlier years and passage of an entrance examination. The examination seems to have been largely a formality. Writing to a friend, one such candidate at New Jersey reported: "After examinations on the usual *authors,* when I and they, who were examined with me, received admission into the junior-class, we were told, that we should have been examined on the *Roman antiquities,* if it had not been forgotten." Witherspoon disliked the system and unsuccesfully sought to abolish it.

Rhode Island, King's, and New Jersey also patterned their curricula after the Yale model, a program that reflected the course of study developed in the English dissenting academies. Actually colleges, these institutions had broken away from complete concentration upon the classics and Aristotelianism and had instituted Newtonianism, social sciences, and modern languages. All four colleges required the same course of studies in the first two years: principally Latin, Greek, and Hebrew. That they assigned much more time to these subjects than did the English academies indicates an effort to repair the deficiencies of their matriculants who, compared to their English counterparts, were retarded about a year and a half. In the final two years, the American colleges emphasized natural sciences, mathematics, and metaphysics. President Samuel Johnson at King's apportioned three fourths of the time of juniors and seniors to mathematics and the natural sciences, while Yale provided but one year, and Rhode Island and New Jersey considerably less than a year. To complete the studies for the senior year, Yale provided metaphysics and divinity, and New Jersey and Rhode Island oratory, composition, and almost certainly divinity. This difference in emphasis is partly explained by the desire of the dissenting colleges to train preachers and in part by the lack of scientific equipment and instructors. All devoted some time to logic, ethics, geography, and public speaking.

At Philadelphia a more independent approach to the curriculum was undertaken by President William Smith, who was influenced by Dr. Samuel Johnson, the great English writer, and by Robert Dodsley's *Preceptor.* Nonetheless, the subjects prescribed by Smith were much the same as those offered elsewhere, except that he placed much greater stress upon oratory and the social sciences and did not regularly offer courses on religion.

Between 1765 and 1775 the American institutions showed great capacity to adapt their curricula to trends appearing in the English academies. Stress was placed on English grammar and composition by requiring polished written translations and original products of the students' pens, and greater weight was placed on oratory. English literature, however, was never taught formally. Some schools began to offer modern foreign language as electives, and with their growing popularity classes in Hebrew were deserted. Greater attention was also paid to history by Witherspoon at New Jersey and by President James Manning at Rhode Island, though, as was the case in England, apparently only ancient history was taught. In brief, during these thirty years the college moved to some degree from ancient to modern languages, from divinity to the social sciences, and from metaphysics to natural sciences. Only Dartmouth and King's seemed to find the older ideas the better.

Most colleges organized their courses into a four-year curriculum. Smith, however, instituted at Philadelphia the then current English innovation of a three-year college. In actual fact, Philadelphia's program of study was abbreviated by pushing back into the academy some of the courses taught elsewhere to college freshmen. Newark also seems to have required only three years' residence, but similar experiments in truncation by Witherspoon at New Jersey and Manning at Rhode Island were soon abandoned.

Classes began early and lasted through the day, punctuated by morning and evening prayers. Instruction was based upon recitations from and elaborations of textbooks, though the lecture method was used by some presidents in teaching the seniors. The college library was rarely used by undergraduates, and New Jersey claimed distinction for its policy of encouraging seniors to browse in the library. To stimulate scholarship, King's, New Jersey, and Philadelphia set up prizes to be awarded for excellence in specified subjects, and Manning wanted to adopt the plan at Rhode Island. But the system proved ineffective, and it was allowed to die.

Regular attendance, payment of fees, and proper deportment — or due regret for improper deportment — seemed almost invariably to yield a diploma on the scheduled day. "To the frequent scandal, as well of religion, as learning," wrote a contemporary critic, "a fellow may pass with credit through life, receive the honors of a liberal education, and be admitted to the right hand of fellowship among the ministers of the gospel. . . . Except in one neighbouring province, ignorance wanders unmolested at our colleges, examinations are dwindled to mere form and ceremony, and after four years dozing there, no one is ever refused the honors of a degree, on account of dulness and insufficiency." In 1756 there were 172 students enrolled at Yale, and all but seven eventually received degrees. Elsewhere, virtually automatic progress by the student likewise seems to have been the rule; only at King's and Philadelphia was the mortality rate high.

All the younger colleges claimed to be nonsectarian and insisted that full religious toleration was granted to all Protestants. Therefore all were advertised as "free and Catholic" or as "Catholic, Comprehensive, and liberal." Nevertheless, all students were required to take courses in divinity or the Bible, and all attended college prayers twice a day. College laws also required attendance at church on Sunday. Tolerance demanded that the student be permitted to attend the church of his own choice, though in some instances there was only one church in town. Thus while sectarians could and did freely accuse each other of proselytizing, none could charge these college administrators of ignoring the injunction laid down by one of their trustees that "*Liberty* be not made a Cloak of *Licentiousness*."

Most students lived in the college hall, two or three to a room or suite of rooms. Meals were served in the college refectory, usually situated in the basement of the college hall. The only important meal came at mid-day; it consisted essentially of meat and potatoes. The evening meal was based upon left-overs from noon, and breakfast brought only bread and butter. While this community life was recommended by the college authorities, many students preferred the more expensive but freer method of boarding out in adjacent homes. Such freedom, however, sometimes created special problems of discipline.

Relations between the faculty and the students seem to have been reasonably good, although there were, of course, exceptions. Provost William Smith, of Philadelphia, gained a reputation for harshness; Eleazer Wheelock, of Dartmouth, ruled with the care but without the indulgence of a father; and Robert Harpur, the science instructor at King's, was hated and tormented on general principles. But the newer colleges were free of the student riots which occurred at Harvard and Yale.

The students found their college days profitable and enjoyable, and letters written after graduation to former schoolmates bore the impress of nostalgia. Extracurricular activities revolved around clubs devoted to literary and bibulous exercises. Oratory was perhaps the most popular interest, and students sharpened their oratorical prowess in nightly practice for the seniors' grand performance on commencement day. Singing and the writing of verse were also fashionable; and the score for the New Jersey commencement of 1762 is one of the earliest examples of college music now extant. In their songs and some of their poetry the students frequently gave expression to sentiments which suggest that college pride had already been born.

However valuable students found college life to be, their fathers regarded the expense of maintenance with no little concern. During the years between 1746 and 1772 the charges of the College of New Jersey for room, board, and tuition — £9 a year — were the lowest of any college. But college fees gradually increased, and after 1772 an economical parent found that the lowest bill, £12, was presented by the College of Rhode Island. The highest annual charges made by any of the newer colleges were those of King's — £18. And room, board, and tuition, of course, represented only a fraction of a student's total expenses. Firewood, candles, and washing cost £3 more; books and stationery, clothing and travel, and pocket money, too, increased the cost. Thus in 1775 the lowest cost of educating a boy ranged from £25 to £35 a year; it might easily amount to £55 or even more for spendthrifts. But the highest expense in America was mild compared to charges in England, where advanced education cost over £100 annually.

For colonial days these were large sums in terms of personal cash income. An able carpenter with good employment earned about £50 a year; a captain in the royal army, £136; a college instructor, £100; and a good lawyer, £500. Some relief was afforded by the extension of credit, and only too often greater relief was gained by parents who defaulted payment of the indebtedness. A little money for needy students was raised through church collections and subscriptions by the Baptists at Rhode Island and the Presbyterians at New Jersey. But none of the infant colleges had annually appointed scholars, and it appears that only at Dartmouth did any number of students work to pay their expenses. Therefore, sooner or later, the father had to pay, and clearly only the well-to-do could easily afford to do so. Indeed, some contemporary commentators believed that only the sons of the wealthy should go to college.

The greatest problem faced by the college administrators was that of getting the money necessary to keep the college open, for students' fees paid only a small part of the cost of a boy's education. In their search for the requisite funds, promoters of the new colleges found that tapping the provincial treasury yielded only a trickle of cash. Harvard, Yale, and William and Mary all had been given both grants and annual subventions by their respective provincial governments or by the King. Among the newer colleges, only Dartmouth, King's, and Philadelphia were voted money from public treasuries, and King's alone was treated generously. None ever received an annual public subsidy, despite repeated applications.

Appeals to the general public by means of subscription lists and lotteries brought some funds, and occasional bequests added more; but the receipts from these sources were usually needed to meet recurring deficits. To gain capital for investment, efforts were made to raise funds in Europe and the West Indies. Between 1745 and 1775 the seven new colleges received well over £72,000 in gifts from thousands of people solicited by hundreds of well-wishers. Over the same period approximately two sevenths of these funds were invested in income-producing endowment; about three sevenths were used in meeting current operating expenses; and the remaining two sevenths were absorbed in the erection of buildings. With the exception of King's, which was able to meet its running expenses with the income from its investments, all were operating on deficit budgets after 1770; and at the same time the raising of funds for colleges became increasingly difficult.

The most obvious effect of the work of the pioneer educators who were responsible for the establishment and operation of these newer colleges was the great increase in the number of college-trained men in the colonies. From 1715 through 1745 the three older colleges graduated about fourteen hundred men, but in the following thirty-one years over thirty-one hundred gained bachelors' degrees in British North America. Almost nine hundred of these degrees (28 per cent of the total number) were granted by the seven new colleges. These schools therefore were responsible for about half the increase of college-trained men during these decades.

Behind the growing interest in college attendance was increasing economic prosperity. Each advance in college enrollment followed by three or four years the initial point on a rise of the index of commodity prices. Mounting colonial wealth aided the establishment of colleges in provinces from which the older colleges had drawn few students. Probably over 90 per cent of the graduates of Harvard, Yale, and William and Mary came from eastern New Hampshire, Massachusetts, Connecticut, and Virginia. Rhode Island and the middle provinces were relatively fallow fields, and to the boys in those areas the younger colleges represented opportunity. Therefore, the advance in enrollment beginning in 1769 redounded to the advantage of the newer rather than the older colleges, and from 1769 through 1776 they graduated approximately 40 per cent of the bachelors of arts.

This sudden popular interest in a college degree brought repeated demands that college bills should not be so high as to exclude the sons of the less well-to-do. This insistence sprang in part from a belief that the duty of the college was to open the gates of opportunity to youths of merit regardless of their fathers' social and economic position. One of the college propagandists argued: "The great Inducement to Study and Application . . . is the Hope of a Reward adequate to the Expence, Labour and Pains, taken. In Countries where Liberty prevails, and where the Road is left open for the Son of the meanest Plebeian, to arrive at the highest Pitch of Honours and Preferments, there never will be wanting such Emulation, and of Course great Men. . . . Such at this Day, is Great Britain." Some extended the argument, maintaining that all classes of society needed some type of education beyond that of the common school.

These democratic concepts of education were being applied at the time to a class society which it was assumed educated men would buttress. Such efforts as were made to reduce the barrier of high cost came from the dissenting colleges. Groups of dissenters in England had long aided poor students financially, and the Baptist and Presbyterians in America followed the custom. Furthermore, ministers were badly needed in the colonies and usually they could be recruited only among the sons of farmers. A costly education, therefore, would handicap the Presbyterian and Baptist churches. Inevitably the administrators of dissenting colleges were forced to yield to pressure to keep their fees down, and hence their graduates included a goodly number of sons of artisans and farmers of modest means. Thus the requirements of religious sects gave effect to the demand for democratization of higher education.

One concern of this increased interest in higher education was the improvement of professional training. New Jersey was the first of the younger colleges to build a curriculum designed to train preachers, and it is not surprising, therefore, that about half of the pre-Revolutionary graduates of New Jersey entered the ministry. Rhode Island and Newark followed New Jersey's precedent, and President Smith at Philadelphia read lectures in divinity as a special course for candidates for the ministry. Through the influence of President Witherspoon, New Jersey was also the first of the new colleges to introduce formal graduate training in divinity, a program already long established at William and Mary.

Philadelphia in 1765 and King's in 1767 undertook to supply professional training in medicine, though on an undergraduate level. But physicians had a poor economic and social status, and so the medical schools were never overflowing with students. By 1776, Philadelphia had graduated but ten students and King's twelve. Perhaps it was as well, for one of the abler graduates of King's recommended in his thesis the prescription of a specific he had not the courage to administer.

This advance in educational standards also influenced the legal profession, and in 1756 the New York bar began to demand college work as a requisite for admission. By 1776 one third of those entitled to plead before the provincial courts held the degree of bachelor of arts. Formal training in civil law, the common law, or municipal law was never undertaken in any colonial college, although King's, Philadelphia, and the advocates of the proposed college at Charleston all dreamed and planned for the establishment of such courses.

The colleges likewise raised the standards of secondary education. Throughout the period, criticism of the preparation of college matriculants was constant, and, in an effort to gain more satisfactory material, all the new colleges maintained their own grammar schools. These secondary schools were also essential to the colleges as "feeders" of matriculants. As the years passed, the number of independent grammar schools in the middle and southern provinces increased sharply, and the graduates of the newer colleges, particularly New Jersey, were in great demand as masters.

These college founders also made significant contributions to colonial interdependence. Hundreds of students crossed provincial boundaries to enroll in their alma maters. Half of Newark's enrollment came from provinces other than Delaware; 40 per cent of Philadelphia's from homes outside of Pennsylvania. New Jersey attracted men from North Carolina and Massachusetts. So heavy a migration was a significant change, for the three older colleges had drawn nearly all their students from relatively restricted areas. In the years immediately preceding the Revolution, students migrating northward were passed by northern-born graduates, particularly of Yale and New Jersey, moving to southern provinces. In Virginia and North Carolina, New Jersey men began a new cycle of college founding. Thus the younger colleges stimulated inter-provincial migration of able men, trained in much the same intellectual pattern.

The history of higher education during these three decades, then, is dominated by the establishment of successful colleges and the development of promotional techniques. Each successive college was founded more easily and with better planning than its predecessors; problems were foreseen and precedents were available and accepted. Once opened, they carried on until subjected to military interference during the Revolution. These colleges significantly increased the cultural level of the population and raised the educational standards of the professions. The founders advanced the practice and idea of democratic higher education. They transplanted the essentials of the educational system of the English dissenting academies and saw the system take root; and virtually the entire task had been the accomplishment of men born and bred in America. They believed that they were strengthening the bonds of an empire in which America should be subsidiary, not subordinate to England. From the beginning many had hoped the colleges would further the creation of cultural autonomy in America. In 1770, for example, Ezra Stiles tabulated the various degrees granted by the several American colleges and concluded: "Thus all the learned degrees are now conferred in the American Colleges as amply as in the European Colleges." As the colonial epoch closed, many Americans proudly felt that they had achieved educational self-reliance.

Suggested Further Reading:

The book with which to begin any study of colonial education is Bernard Bailyn's superb short study, *Education in the Forming of American Society** (1960), comprising as it does a brilliant 49-page interpretative essay, followed by a longer bibliographical essay and list of references. Arthur M. Schlesinger Sr. has written an introduction to a new edition of Edward Eggleston's *The Transit of Civilization** (1959); first issued in 1900, this is, as Professor Bailyn has observed, a study in the history of education which deserved more notice than it received when first published.

Education in New England has received greater attention than that in any other colonial region: there are the excellent volumes by S. E. Morison, *The Founding of Harvard College* (1935), *Harvard College in the Seventeenth Century* (2 vols., 1936), and *Puritan Pronaos* (1936); short but illuminating is Robert Middlecauff's *Ancients and Axioms: Secondary Education in Eighteenth-Century New England* (1963); and Edmund S. Morgan's *The Puritan Family* (1944) offers considerable insight into the Puritan views on the family, children, and their education.

Professor Morgan has supplied a similar study of *Virginians at Home: Family Life in the Eighteenth Century** (1952); there is an abundance of useful material in Wesley Frank Craven's *The Southern Colonies in the Seventeenth Century* (1949), and Louis B. Wright's *The Cultural Life of the American Colonies** (1957). Dr. Wright's *First Gentlemen of Virginia** (1940) is excellent on the cultural propensities of the planter class. For a recent and vigorous discussion of some of the more unique qualities of the colonial college, see Daniel J. Boorstin's "Educating the Community" in *The Americans: The Colonial Experience** (1958). Louis L. Tucker has supplied a fine study of a colonial college president in *Puritan Protagonist: President Thomas Clap of Yale* (1962), as has Edmund S. Morgan, in his *The Gentle Puritan: A Life of Ezra Stiles, 1727–1795* (1962).

PART FOUR

Colonial Society

For those historians who seek comfort in safe and secure generalizations, colonial society poses formidable difficulties. Both the attitudes and the pattern of life of the American colonist varied considerably from region to region and often changed markedly from decade to decade. His character and his society, moreover, often have been distorted by the historian's sometimes too eager search for significance. Was colonial society but a pale reflection of the mother country's? Was colonial society uniquely American? Were its intellectual pretensions justified? Perhaps the safest and most accurate answer would be a qualified — but unilluminating — "yes" to all such questions.

Colonial society was naturally affected by its physical environment; it reflected the predominantly English origins of its members; its intellectual achievements were, as often as not, prompted and conditioned by the special economic and political needs of Americans. While eighteenth-century society was the product of the seventeenth, it differed substantially from its predecessor. Economic growth and political maturity brought a developing self-awareness to the colonists and increased their intellectual and cultural self-confidence. Proud of their origins, the colonists were nevertheless determined to shape a society that would be the recognizable product of their American experience.

There remains, however, the necessity for caution when examining society in the colonial period: the historical returns are far from complete. Social history itself is relatively new, and while there have been vast strides in research, much remains unexplored. The pathfinders — Louis B. Wright, Carl Bridenbaugh, Richard H. Shryock, and Brooke Hindle, to name a few — have done their work superbly; but, as Edmund S. Morgan has noted, "we need to study the social groupings in every colony: towns, plantations, counties, churches, schools, clubs, and other groups which occupied the social horizons of the individual colonist."[1] We need, in short, more local studies, more institutional investigations. And we need with these a keener awareness of the English and European social context in which colonial society developed.

[1] Edmund S. Morgan, "The American Revolution: Revisions in Need of Revising," *The William and Mary Quarterly,* 3rd Ser., XIV (1957), 15.

1

Populating the Colonies

I

Indentured Servants and Redemptioners

From the time of the first settlement at Jamestown, Englishmen were concerned with increasing the population of North America. Settlers meant markets; they represented the power to exploit and secure new sources of raw materials; and they formed a bulwark against the incursions of Spanish, French and Dutch imperialism.

Inducements to migrate were never wanting. Economic and religious opportunities offered by the New World persuaded many Englishmen to leave their homes. The device known as "headrights," which assured 50 acres per head to those who subsidized emigrants, attracted the attention of many investors to the southern colonies. But want of adequate financing always remained a fundamental problem: those laborers most powerfully motivated to emigrate were usually those least able to pay for their Atlantic crossing. And free settlers were unwilling to work for wages when afforded the opportunity of farming their own land.

A shortage of labor was a chronic complaint throughout the colonial period of American history and for many years thereafter. Wages rose higher than in England or Europe, for the law of supply and demand operated to the advantage of the working class. Always the problem remained to find a way to meet colonial labor needs — and thus to facilitate the development of a more complex colonial economy.

As Abbot Emerson Smith *makes clear, colonists found in the indentured servant the immediate solution to their labor shortage. Not until the eighteenth century did negro slavery begin to replace the indentured servant, involuntary or redemptionist, on any substantial scale. What were the consequences of this system of temporary white slavery? Socially, the results were mixed. It did accelerate the population growth of the British colonies. It did alleviate the labor shortage. But it brought to America some people of doubtful morals and known criminal tendencies. And ultimately it brought protest from colonial residents who came to resent their shores being exploited as a convenient dumping ground for England's unwanted.*

More than half of all persons who came to the colonies south of New England were servants. The Puritan communities, scanty in their agriculture, chary of favors, hostile to newcomers as they were, received few. Farther south, on the contrary, they were hailed with delight by planters and farmers who wanted cheap labor, by speculators who needed more settlers to validate their grants of land, by colonial proprietors who wished to build up the population. It was universally agreed, said a committee of the Council of Foreign Plantations about 1664, that people were the foundation for the improvement of all Plantations, "and that people are encreased principally by sending of Servants." In they poured, the good, bad, and indifferent together. They formed the principal labor supply of the earlier settlements. Not until the eighteenth century were they superseded in this respect by Negroes, and not until the nineteenth did an influx of free white workers wholly remove the need for indentured labor. In the West Indies, though their value as workers declined more rapidly

Reprinted from Abbot Emerson Smith, *Colonists in Bondage: White Servitude and Convict Labor in America, 1607–1776* (Chapel Hill: University of North Carolina Press, for the Institute of Early American History and Culture, 1947), pp. 4–25. Footnotes deleted by permission of the publisher.

before the competition of Negroes than it did in the continental colonies, they yet continued in demand simply as white men, to bolster up the inadequate numbers of the militia and give some feeling of security against the blacks. Seldom did the supply of good white servants equal the demand.

From the complex pattern of forces producing emigration to the American colonies one stands out clearly as most powerful in causing the movement of servants. This was the pecuniary profit to be made by shipping them. Labor was one of the few European importations which even the earliest colonists would sacrifice much to procure, and the system of indentured servitude was the most convenient system next to slavery by which labor became a commodity to be bought and sold. It was profitable for English merchants trading to the colonies to load their outgoing ships with a cargo of servants, for the labor of these servants could be transferred to colonial planters at a price well above the cost of transporting them. It was profitable to the colonial planter to buy them, for he could rise from mere subsistence to prosperity only by commanding the labor of others beside himself. Hence there was a constantly active stimulant to the emigration of servants, a powerful and resourceful group of merchants and shippers always ready to accept the services of volunteers for the new world, and, what was more important, to bring pressure to bear on doubtful candidates, to advertise the attractions of life in America, and even as a last resort to collect a shipload of labor by forceful means.

It is, of course, not intended to imply that the profitable nature of the trade in servants was the only cause for their going to the colonies. The peopling of the new settlements was a complex phenomenon and the activating forces behind it must be sought also in the expansive spirit of the age, in the economic and social maladjustments in Europe, and in the various obscure motivations of individual personalities. Everyone knows that America was a haven for the godly, a refuge for the oppressed, a challenge to the adventurous. Nor should the fact be forgotten, particularly when dealing with indentured servants, that it was also the last resort of scoundrels. A great many servants went to the colonies simply because, for one reason or another, they wanted to get out of their own country. Even so, they would not have had the opportunity to leave if the peculiar institution of indentured labor had not made it worth the while of shippers to take them.

The English government was well content that the handling of emigration should be in the hands of private business men. It liked to see the establishment and peopling of colonies go slowly forward without requiring from the state either financial commitments or moral responsibility. The government might indeed have taken charge of the migration of poor persons, and have worked out a system of getting them to the colonies which would have been less painful than that which the merchants contrived. Many schemes were drawn up and submitted with this end in view, but nearly all of them were ignored or turned down, and the state transported very few settlers. Even the convicts were handed over to private individuals. They shipped them to Maryland and Virginia and sold them at an excellent profit to the same planters who denounced the English government for allowing them to come at all. In one case, that of Georgia, the proprietors of the venture were liberally assisted with governmental subsidies; in two other instances, those of the Palatine Germans in 1709 and of Halifax in 1749, the government itself directly carried out both transportation and settlement. All three of these state enterprises were justified on the grounds of military and political strategy.

The fact was that although the best political and economic opinion viewed the expansion of empire in general with satisfaction, it was not so certain that emigration was a good thing for the mother country. Mercantilists after about 1660 came to look upon the swarming masses of the poor as forming an indispensable reservoir of labor at home, which ought to be used at home and not dispersed overseas. Emigration was therefore discouraged, though never within the colonial period was it stopped. If this attitude had obtained during the earliest and most critical years of colonization there might have been great difficulty in starting any colonies at all, but when the Virginia Company was commencing its operations people were chiefly impressed with the magnitude and difficulty of the unemployment problem. Various forces had caused a dislocation of the economic life of England, and everyone was made conscious of this dislocation by the large numbers of wandering, idle, and necessitous people who infested the highways and flocked to the cities. Being unable to offer a better explanation for the situation, contemporary opinion attributed the cause to over-population and held that new colonies would provide an outlet for the surplus inhabitants of the mother country. This belief endured long enough to get the new settlements firmly established, but disappeared almost completely after the Restoration. From our present point of view the chief result of this change in opinion was that the servant trade thenceforth got a bad name for depopulating the mother country, found its operations hindered by official obstacles, and transferred much of its activity to Germany, Scotland, and Ireland. Likewise the malodorous reputation which the servant trade has attained in most historical accounts is in part undeserved, for it springs from the testimony of persons who wished to see the business suppressed, and were not averse to arousing public opinion by accusations of kidnapping and other nefarious practices.

Concerning the servants themselves, as individuals in the new world, we do not read very much. Colonial society was not democratic and certainly not equalitarian; it was dominated by men who had money enough to make others work for them. Few of these men were descended from indentured servants, and practically none had themselves been of that class. In studying the servants we drop below the level of distinguished individuals to the undifferentiated body of the people: obscure shopkeepers, field laborers, mechanics, schoolteachers, pioneer farmers in the western valleys. These were the best, but there were many more: men and women who were dirty and lazy, rough, ignorant, lewd, and often criminal. They thieved and wandered, had bastard children, and corrupted society with loathsome diseases. There were still more whose role was most humble of all; they came to America, remained a few days or weeks, and then died of the familiar colonial fever. It would be presumptuous to say that even these contributed nothing, for the process of selection was capricious, and many had to emigrate in order that a portion might survive. This was the cruel system by which the colonies were peopled.

It was under the auspices of the Virginia Company that the customs and habits of indentured servitude were established essentially in the forms which became so familiar to later colonial history. That a man should become a bondservant by legal contract was not strange, for the ancient institution of apprenticeship was well known to all. Its application to colonial requirements had been suggested at least as early as 1582 by Sir George Peckham, who wrote that many people would be glad to go to the settlements and serve for a year for food and clothing only, in the hope that they might thereby amend their estates." The Virginia Company experimented with various forms of contract embodying different terms of agreement, and found to its discomfiture that none of them worked to the profit of the company in London nor to the satisfaction of those who emigrated under them. It was necessary to set most of the colonists free from their servitude and to try a different scheme. The new plan worked no more to the profit of the company than the old one, but it happened that servants were sent to Virginia and transferred to the use of the planters resident there, who reimbursed the company for the expense of transportation. This innovation, which was not deeply meditated nor seriously considered at the time, nevertheless accustomed people to the later practice of "selling" servants. Such a transaction smacked enough of the eastern slave markets to give occasional scandal to delicate-minded observers, but it was the one characteristic of the servant trade which was both indispensable and novel. Hence its development, as well as the other trials and errors of the Virginia Company with their emigrants under bond, must be traced in some detail.

The earliest information which exists of the terms on which people could go to Virginia is contained in a broadside issued by the company in 1609, which held out many false hopes. It announced that since many noble and generous persons were going to the colony, "Therefore, for the same purpose this paper has been made public, so that it may be generally known to all workmen of whatever craft they may be, blacksmiths, carpenters, coopers, shipwrights, turners, and such as know how to plant vineyards . . . and all others, men as well as women, who have any occupation, who wish to go out in this voyage for colonizing the country with people." All such were invited to come to Sir Thomas Smith's house in Philpot Lane, where they would be enrolled, "and there will be pointed out to such persons what they will receive for this voyage, viz. five hundred 'reales' for each one, and they will be entered as Adventurers in this aforesaid voyage to Virginia, where they will have houses to live in, vegetable-gardens and orchards, and also food and clothing at the expense of the Company of that Island, and besides this, they will have a share of all the products and the profits that may result from their labor, each in proportion, and they will also secure a share in the division of the land for themselves and their heirs forever more." A pamphlet published in the same year makes it plain that the division of lands and profits was to be made after seven years, and that each person going to the colony was to be allowed a share equal to that of the investors at home who had put in £12.10.0 apiece.

This first scheme for the transportation of English workers to America is obviously not one of indentured servitude, yet it contains some of the elements of the later system. No wages are to be paid; all rewards are deferred until the end of the seven-year period of labor, and meanwhile the company engages to supply food, clothing, shelter, and a passage to America. The idea of profit-sharing may have seemed generous to those ignorant of conditions in Virginia, but it is scarcely necessary to say that the scheme did not work and the rosy prospects of the broadside proved wholly illusory. Instead of orchards and vegetable gardens the colonists found wretched hardship and want. They were marched out to labor in the fields in gangs, supervised by overseers, and browbeaten by the governor. As all the products of their work went into the common store there seemed to be no reward for individual diligence, and they complained that their condition was actually one of servitude rather than of partnership, as indeed it was. Great numbers died of fever; a few returned to England despite the prohibition of such return by the company, and the tales of these things told at home made it increasingly difficult to get new recruits. When the time eventually came for a division of profits there was nothing worth dividing, and the investors were required to make a new contribution of capital, while the colonists went unrewarded. The company was forced to modify its system, to relax the strictness of the communal arrangements in the settlement, and to introduce limited rights of private property.

These changes were made between 1613 and 1619, and though the precise nature of the earlier ones is difficult to discover, it is plain that tracts of three acres were allotted to some if not to all of the old settlers, for which they paid a rent to the common store of two and a half barrels of corn. By working these tracts they maintained themselves in food, and the service they owed to the company was restricted to one month in the year, while any tobacco they raised individually was traded nevertheless through the company's "magazine." Meanwhile new colonists were sent over, and the most significant development from our present point of view was that some of the partially free tenants were allowed to rent these laborers from the company and employ them as servants, becoming responsible for their maintenance and paying for them at the rate of two and a half barrels of corn apiece per year. The semi-independent farmers had become as desirous of obtaining labor for their own profit as the company had been, and thus was taken a most important step towards the later customs of white servitude.

In the year 1618 new officers took control of the company, new policies were adopted, and Governor Yeardley was sent out to the colony with elaborate instructions for undertaking many reforms. Old settlers were now given substantial amounts of land for their own use, some of them receiving as much as one hundred acres. Later arrivals got less, and paid an annual rent for it to the company, but the principle of individual ownership was accepted and all traces of "servitude" were abolished. New tracts of "public land" were ordered to be laid out: three thousand acres for the governor, twelve thousand for the company, and other amounts for the maintenance of a college, of ministers, and of a fund for converting the Indians to Christianity.

These public lands were to be worked by tenants, most of them newly sent over, and the company now offered fresh proposals to such prospective tenants in these words:

> Every man transported into Virginia, with intent there to inhabit, as Tenants to the Common land of the Company, or to the publike land, shall be freely landed there at the charge of the Company: And shal be furnished with provisions of victuall for one whole yeare next after his arrivall, as also of Cattle: And with apparell, weapons, tooles and implements, both of house and labour, for his necessary use. He shall enjoy the ratable moytie of all the profits that shall be raised of the land on which he shall be Planted, as well Corne and Cattle, as other commodities whatsoever: the other halfe being due to the Owners of the Land.
>
> He shall be tyed by Covenant, to continue upon that Land for the Terme of seaven yeares: which being expired, it shal be in his choyse, whither to continue there or to remove to any other place, at his own will and pleasure.

Thus the company, though it could not bring itself to abandon completely the idea of public lands and collective farming, nevertheless recognized that the old profit-sharing scheme of 1609 would not work again, and endeavored to tempt new emigrants with the promise that they should enjoy half of whatever they could as individuals make their own labors produce. The terms were really very generous.

Beside these tenants the company sent two other classes of emigrants. First were about two hundred poor children taken off the streets of London, for whose transportation the City raised about £500 in 1618 and 1619. These young people, nearly all boys, were distributed among the free colonists as apprentices. Also, beginning in 1619, groups of young women were dispatched to make wives for the planters. The company instructed its officials in Virginia to guard these women carefully, to see that they were not married against their wishes, and to make sure that every colonist who took one remitted the company 120 pounds of tobacco as the price of her passage. To this end the administrators were asked to prevent the girls from falling in love with servants or apprentices.

A year later, in the summer of 1620, the company announced its intention of sending to Virginia "one hundred servants to be disposed amongst the old *Planters,* which they greatly desire, and have offered to defray their charges with very great thankes." Except for the arrangements concerning the young women, this is the first clear example we have of the characteristic transaction of the servant trade: a colonist paying a lump sum to the importer, and thereby acquiring full right and title to the services of the immigrant. Though this is the first evidence of such transactions, there is no reason to doubt that they had been common for at least a year or two before 1620.

The colonists heartily approved of the company's scheme. "Our principall wealth," wrote John Pory from Virginia in 1619, ". . . consisteth in servants," and he told how one planter with six of them had cleared a thousand pounds by one crop of tobacco. The system of tenancy at halves did not work at all well, if indeed it was ever seriously tried, for when the *Bona Nova* arrived with tenants in 1619, the council in Virginia, instead of assigning them to the company and the college land, rented them out to private planters, with the justification that they would thus become acclimated and their overseers learn to know the country. Perhaps the real truth was that the planters could not bear the sight of so much good labor being spent on public and charitable works, and so contrived to secure it for their own profit. Those who did find their way to the public lands were, according to George Sandys, "neither able to sustain themselves nor to discharge their moiety, and so dejected with their scarce provisions . . . that most give themselves over and die of melancholy." Meanwhile the planters made fair profits while the stockholders in London derived little or nothing from their investments. In 1619 the company sent out 650 emigrants, and in 1620 five hundred, but in the autumn of 1621 the deputy of the company reported that capital was nearly exhausted and but few could be shipped that year. Company-promoted emigration rapidly declined, and the dissensions of the directors of the enterprise hastened a collapse which the failure to make a profit seemed to render inevitable. In 1622 an Indian massacre nearly finished the settlement, and it is plain that if the fortunes of the colony and of the company had been identical, Virginia would have been another Roanoke.

The colony was saved because private individuals took over the activities formerly reserved for the company, and made the profits of the free planters themselves the basis of the settlement's life. We have already noted some aspects of this process as reflected in the system of land distribution, and we have seen how from a kind of collective farming project a society of independent farmers had evolved. It remains to show how private enterprise began to participate in the management of emigration from England.

As early as 1617 the company granted to certain groups of men the privilege of transporting settlers to Virginia and establishing them in semi-independent plantations generally called "hundreds." Little is known exactly about these hundreds before 1620, but the rules and regulations obtaining in them seem to have been different from those outside, and their proprietors had the privilege of trading independently of the company's magazine. Their existence marks the first relaxation by the company of its monopolistic control of emigration. What conditions may generally have been offered to prospective settlers in these hundreds we do not know, but from the papers of one of them comes the first genuine servant's indenture which has survived. Four gentlemen who had been granted the right to establish what became known as Berkeley Hundred made on September 7, 1619, the following agreement with one Robert Coopy, of North Nibley in Gloucestershire:

> That the said Robert doth hereby covenant faythfully to serve the said S[r] Willm, Richard George and John for three years from daye of his landinge in the land of Virginia, there to be imployed in the lawfull and reasonable workes and labors of them . . . and to be obedient to such governors his and their assistants and counsell as they . . . shall from tyme to tyme appoynt and set over him. In consideracon whereof, the said S[r] Willm Richard George and John do covenant with the said Robert to transport him (with gods assistance) with all convenient speed into the said land of Virginia at their costs and charges in all things, and there to maintayne him with convenient diet and apparell meet for such a servant, And in thend of the said terme to make him a free man of the said Cuntry theirby to enjoy all the liberties freedomes and priviledges of a freeman there, And to grant to the said Robert thirty acres of land within their Territory or hundred of Barkley. . . .

It happened that Robert decided not to make the voyage, and perhaps that was the reason that this document of indenture was preserved, for it cannot have been unique. The proprietors of Berkeley Hundred as well as other similar groups probably made many such agreements, and in fact the Virginia Company itself may have commonly used the same form.

Presumably these sub-corporations were the first to transport settlers independently of the company itself, but from about 1618 private individuals were also granted land by the company on condition that they transport persons to the colony. This turned out to be one of the most satisfactory methods of encouraging settlement; it became known as the headright system, and was used in nearly every one of the colonies. There is no certain knowledge of when or how it began; a document of December, 1617, may indicate that it had not been worked out at that time. Soon afterwards, however, it became customary to make a grant of fifty acres for each person transported to the colony, and in April, 1623, it was reported to the company that during the past four years, forty-four patents for land had been issued to persons each of whom had agreed to take at least one hundred men to Virginia. During the spring and summer of 1621, according to the company's deputy, nearly one thousand emigrants had gone out, but of these some nine hundred were upon the charge of private men. Doubtless many of these emigrants were servants who did not pay their own passage, and it may be assumed that some of them were "sold" to planters already resident in the colony, but of this there is no direct evidence.

Thus the handling of emigration passed from the hands of the company into those of private individuals, and the unfortunate organization which alone had made the colony possible saw its honors and profits turned over to others. After the massacre of 1622 the courage of the undertaking was gone; the land for the "colledge," situated up the James River nearly as far as present day Richmond, had to be abandoned, while the pious hope of educating the Indians to true religion and civility seemed ironic indeed. The colony itself barely survived that terrible year, but it recovered quickly after the winter had passed, while the company in London went through painful days to its dissolution in 1624. By that time the customs of indentured servitude had been fixed. In 1619 the first legislative assembly in America provided for the recording and enforcing of contracts made with servants before their departure from England, and they became a distinct class in the community. The census of 1624–1625 showed 487 of them in a population of 1,227; the idea of indenturing them in England, bringing them to America, and transferring their services to resident planters for a sum of money or tobacco had become familiar, and the servant trade was ready to bring them in great numbers.

The usual form of indenture was simple. It was a legal contract, by which the servant bound himself well and faithfully to serve the master in such employments as the master might assign, for a given length of time, and usually in a specified plantation. In return the master undertook to transport the servant to the colony, furnish him with adequate food, drink, clothing, and shelter during his service, and perhaps give him a specified reward when his term was ended. In the majority of cases this was all the agreement that was made, but it could be varied at will according to the bargain struck by the two persons concerned. Skilled workmen sometimes secured a clause entitling them to annual wages or providing that they should do no common labor in the fields. A child's indenture might specify that he be given the rudiments of an education or taught a trade. German servants often entered into indentures providing that they be taught to read the Bible in English. The length of service varied considerably; it might be any number of years, but was generally four, and when longer terms were called for it was usually because the servant was a child. Diversity is also found in the "freedom dues"; some indentures named a sum of money, certain tools, clothes, or food, or a plot of land. In all colonies, however, these matters were regulated from early times by custom, and most servants depended upon this custom to direct their lives, contenting themselves with leaving their indentures in common form.

By the year 1636 one could procure printed indentures, with blank spaces left for the names of the servant and master and for any special provisions desired. These forms were entered in the Stationers' Register by Nicholas Bourne, printer, and must have sold well, for in 1661 Bourne's executors petitioned against persons who "during the late disorders" had been illegally producing them. Similar forms were used throughout the colonial period, and one may be quoted here as representative of all servants' indentures:

> This Indenture made the *21st February 1682/3* Between *Rich. Browne aged 33 years* of the one party, and *Francis Richardson* of the other party, witnesseth, that the said *Rich. Browne* doth thereby covenant, promise, and grant to & with the said *Francis Richardson* his Executors & Assigns, from the day of the date hereof, until h*is* first & next arrival *att New York or New Jersey* and after, for and during the term of *foure* years, to serve in such service & imployment, as he the said *Francis Richardson* or his Assigns shall there imploy *him* according to the custom of the Country in the like kind — In consideration whereof, the said *Francis Richardson* doth hereby covenant and grant to and with the said *Richard Browne* to pay for h*is* passing, and to find and allow *him* meat, drink, apparrel, and lodging, with other necessaries, during the said term, & at the end of the said term to pay unto *him according to the Custom of the Country.*
>
> In Witness thereof the parties above mentioned to these Indentures have interchangeably set their Hands and Seals the day and year above written.

The servant took his indenture with him, and a copy might also be furnished to his master or even to the authorities of the plantation where he took up residence. He could be sold for service only according to the terms of the contract, which thus became his protection against an unjust master. In most cases, and especially if the servant was less than eighteen years old, the indenture was chiefly useful to him as a certificate of the length of service required, but if generous freedom dues or any other particularly liberal provisions were included, it became of more obvious value. Colonial courts were always ready to enforce the terms of any servant's indenture which could be produced, and on occasion they even accepted the testimony of a servant's friends who had seen the document and would swear to its terms though it had since been lost. For one living the life of a laborer in the plantations it was not always an easy matter to keep possession of these small scraps of paper.

The pamphleteer John Hammond strongly advised all servants to make their contracts in this manner before leaving England, and to have them properly signed and sealed, so that questions and disappointments after arrival might be reduced to a minimum. After 1682 the English regulations were so strict that this became almost necessary to protect the ship captain from a charge of kidnapping. Yet a great many servants, especially before the turn of the century, went to the colonies without written indentures. Some made verbal agreements with the merchants who shipped them, not realizing that such agreements were of no legal validity and would not be enforced in the colony. On their arrival they were sold as servants because they had not paid their own passages, and to regulate their treatment each colony evolved a certain standard known as the "custom of the country." Sooner or later this custom was set down in statutory law by nearly all colonies, and the earliest of these statutes were to specify the time which servants arriving without indenture should serve. Thus the new arrival, whether with or without previous indenture, found himself fairly well protected against capricious and excessive exploitation, while his importer knew with some exactness what could be expected in years of labor and expense of upkeep.

Few planters could journey to England and select their own servants. Hence they were practically always indentured to a merchant, an emigrant agent, a ship captain, or even to one of the seamen, and then exported like any other cargo of commodities. Upon arrival in the colonies they were displayed on deck, the planters came on board to inspect them, and they were "set over" to the highest bidder. If the servant had a document of indenture, a note of the sale and of the date of arrival was often made on its back, and the transaction was then complete. The invention and acceptance of this system made it possible to handle emigration as a business proposition, and to treat white labor as a commodity. The trade in servants became quite an important part of colonial trade, and the peopling of English America proceeded according to the crudest manifestations of the law of supply and demand. Throughout the colonial period vast numbers of ordinary indentured servants were thus transported to the colonies, while convicts, rogues and vagabonds, political prisoners, all were sold in the plantations as servants, and taken there by merchants as merchandise.

During all of the seventeenth century indentured servitude was practically the only method by which a poor person could get to the colonies or by which white labor could be supplied to planters. About the beginning of the eighteenth century, however, a new scheme made its appearance, and the "redemptioner" took his place alongside the "servant." At first this class of emigrant came generally from the Continent. The movement of Germans and Swiss to the colonies, which had been occasional and scattering since the 1680's, began to assume large proportions in 1708 and 1709. Large numbers of people descended the Rhine to Rotterdam, seeking a passage to the new world, and many of them found when they arrived at the seaport that their financial resources were insufficient to get them the rest of the way. Accordingly, merchants used to take whatever money the emigrant might have left, put him and his goods and his family aboard ship, and contract to deliver them in America. After arrival a certain period of time, commonly fourteen days, was allowed during which the passenger might try to find the balance which was due the shipper, the hope being that he might locate friends who would advance the money. But if the necessary amount could not be found within the time limit then he was to be sold into indentured servitude by the captain of the ship, for an amount sufficient to satisfy his indebtedness. Thus the length of his servitude would depend roughly upon the size of his debt.

The first contemporary references to this method of migration are of no earlier date than

1728, but they indicate that it had been familiar for some time. Though confined at first to Germans, it soon spread across the Channel and was considerably used, particularly by those who transported Irish to Pennsylvania. Many English traveled under redemptionist agreements to the colonies, but the system never wholly replaced the older scheme of indentured servitude among them. Germans, on the other hand, seem rarely to have adopted the seventeenth-century method, and as far as we know nearly all who did not pay their own passage went out as redemptioners. In consequence the total migrations of the eighteenth century consist much more of this class than of ordinary indentured servants.

Between these two methods of transporting persons to the plantations there were certain significant differences which have commonly been overlooked. It is true that once a redemptioner had been sold for his passage money, he became in every respect an indentured servant, and there was no distinction between the two classes. But to the prospective emigrant in Europe, contemplating the possibilities for getting to America, there were virtues in each scheme, and his choice might depend upon his personal circumstances. In the first place, it was customary to supply an indentured servant with food, clothing, and shelter from the time he signed his contract until the end of his term of servitude; destitute persons in Britain, when all other hopes had faded, therefore, could and did sign up as indentured servants and get free of their worst immediate troubles from that moment. Furthermore, since a servant made his agreement before departure he could perhaps secure for himself particularly favorable terms, while the redemptioner, who executed his indenture of servitude after reaching America, was apt to find it necessary to accept whatever was offered.

The most remarkable difference between the two was, however, that the redemptionist system applied generally to people who emigrated in whole families, bringing their goods and chattels with them and seeking a new home. Indentured servants nearly always came singly, in fact English regulations after 1682 required a declaration from each emigrant servant that he was unmarried and without dependents, as well as under no apprenticeship to a master at home. Redemptioners were apt to be people who had raised some money by the sale of their lands or other non-moveable goods; they came in families, and very often one or two members of a family would take the burden of service for the rest. Sometimes parents would come with the expectations of selling the services of their children in order to pay their own passage, while the children would thus become apprentices and learn a trade. At some expense of overstatement the point may be made this way: indentured servants came essentially as cargoes of merchandize representing a supply of labor; redemptioners came essentially as emigrants hopefully transplanting themselves to a new home in America. This statement does not do justice to the aspirations of many servants, but it helps to indicate why the redemptionist system flourished in the eighteenth century, after the colonies had achieved a stable existence such as would be inviting to newcomers, while indentured servants played a greater proportional part during the years of perilous beginnings.

There were, of course, a few times in colonial history when persons were sent to one plantation or another without being under the obligation of labor or servitude, except in so far as labor was obviously necessary to insure their own existence after the supplies furnished by their transporters had run out. When settlers were urgently desired for some locality previously uninhabited they were sometimes established as free men, and given food, shelter and tools for a year with the promise of subsequent land grants. This was the case at Halifax, Nova Scotia, where a settlement was founded by the British government in 1749 for strategic reasons, and over three thousand persons taken out at public expense in the first year, under the supervision of the Board of Trade. The Georgia Trustees, with the considerable financial help of the government, sent 2,127 persons to their colony "on the Charity," and while the motives of the trustees were charitable, those of the government again were strategic. In this case as in that of Halifax, provisions and tools were supplied the colonists for one year. Charitable contributions sent six hundred French Protestants to America in 1687, and about seven hundred more in 1700. On several occasions entrepreneurs secured large grants of American land from the Crown on condition of settling it with certain numbers of Protestant inhabitants; thus for instance de Graffenried settled New Bern in North Carolina with 650 Palatines in 1710, and Jean Peter Pury established some Swiss in Purysburgh, South Carolina, two decades later. Henry McCulloch, a London merchant, petitioned for no less than 1,200,000 acres in North Carolina, and was actually granted such a tract in 1737 on the understanding that he would take 6,000 foreign Protestants there to live. Apparently he did not fulfill his part of the agreement, though he kept the land until the time of the American Revolution. The enormous schemes of Alexander McNutt for the settlement of Nova Scotia in the 1760's gave promise of depopulating Northern Ireland, and were sharply checked by the Privy Council.

None of the above mentioned plans involved the servitude of settlers, and hence they do not come within the province of this study. A few cases involving modification or adaptation of the usual conditions of servitude require some mention, however, and of these the first group is composed of schemes similar to that of the Virginia Company and its "company servants." Essentially this meant, as we have pointed out, that servants worked for a corporation in England instead of for a planter in the colony, and usually they were rewarded with a share of the proceeds of their labors. Thus the Massachusetts Bay Company in its earliest years, the Bermuda Company, and the Providence Company all tried this plan, and in each case it failed just as it had when attempted in Virginia. The Georgia Trustees, besides supplying servants for some of their planters, also tried to use "trust servants" on the common land with no better success. The most grandiose attempt of this kind was that made by the British government itself, when it sent some 3,200 Germans to New York in 1710 for the purpose of making naval stores on the banks of the Hudson. In this case also the project failed, though political conditions at home were in part responsible.

One curious modification of the redemptionist system, which was tried at Halifax, is worth noting. The Board of Trade engaged John Dick of Rotterdam to procure a number of Germans and Swiss for the colony, promising them food and tools for one year, but requiring them to pay their own passage. Dick was unable to find candidates with enough money for this purpose, and the Board, though anxious to have them emigrate, did not wish to pay it for them. Hence it agreed to advance the price of their transportation and since there was no one in the colony able to "redeem" them, it instructed the governor to set them at labor on the public works for such time as it should take them to earn the amount due, calculating their wages at one shilling a day. This was thought a particularly shrewd move because the prevailing wage rate in Nova Scotia was twice the amount allowed the Germans; it had unfortunate results nevertheless, for the foreigners were disgruntled at the bargain, while the price of labor in the colony was so driven down that free workers nearly starved.

While schemes such as these were carrying their hundreds to the plantations, the regular trade in indentured servants and redemptioners was carrying its tens of thousands. This trade was the backbone of the whole migratory movement. Neither imperialist visions and necessities, nor charitable impulses, nor religious enthusiasms, nor the desire for landed possessions kept it going, but simply the fact that colonists wanted white laborers and were willing to pay merchants and ship owners for bringing them.

II

Observations Concerning the Increase of Mankind, Peopling of Countries, &c.

The population of the English colonies rapidly increased. Where there were twenty-five thousand souls in 1640, over a million could be counted a century later, and by 1760 the number of inhabitants had reached one and a half million — a vivid contrast to New France which had only an estimated sixty thousand inhabitants

---

Benjamin Franklin, *Observations Concerning the Increase of Mankind, Peopling of Countries, &c.*, from Albert Henry Smyth, *The Writings of Benjamin Franklin* (New York: The Macmillan Company, 1905–1907), III, 63–73.

at that time.[1] *It was this increase in population which made possible the rapid development of society in the eighteenth century — and which bolstered colonial confidence in the future.*

The occasion for BENJAMIN FRANKLIN'S *famous essay on colonial growth was the passage of the restrictive Iron Act in 1750. Franklin's main theme was that the inexorable increase in the colonial population assured England of steadily growing markets for British manufactures; there was, he urged, no need to restrain colonial iron-masters, "a wise and good mother will not do it. To distress is to weaken, and weakening the children weakens the whole family." He looked forward to the time when there would be more Englishmen in America than in the mother country: England, he argued, should cultivate, not offend, what would become her greatest source of power and wealth.*

1 TABLES of the Proportion of Marriages to Births, of Deaths to Births, of Marriages to the Numbers of Inhabitants, &c., form'd on Obser-vaions (sic) made upon the Bills of Mortality, Christnings, &c., of populous Cities, will not suit Countries; nor will Tables form'd on Observations made on full-settled old Countries, as *Europe,* suit new Countries, as *America.*

2. For People increase in Proportion to the Number of Marriages, and that is greater in Proportion to the Ease and Convenience of supporting a Family. When families can be easily supported, more Persons marry, and earlier in Life.

3. In Cities, where all Trades, Occupations, and Offices are full, many delay marrying till they can see how to bear the Charges of a Family; which Charges are greater in Cities, as Luxury is more common: many live single during Life, and continue Servants to Families, Journeymen to Trades; &c. hence Cities do not by natural Generation supply themselves with Inhabitants; the Deaths are more than the Births.

[1] For a review of the population increase in the colonies, see F. B. Dexter, "Estimates of Population in the American Colonies," American Antiquarian Society *Proceedings,* V, 22–50.

4. In Countries full settled, the Case must be nearly the same; all Lands being occupied and improved to the Heighth; those who cannot get Land, must Labour for others that have it; when Labourers are plenty, their Wages will be low; by low Wages a family is supported with Difficulty; this Difficulty deters many from Marriage, who therefore long continue Servants and single. Only as the Cities take Supplies of People from the Country, and thereby make a little more Room in the Country; Marriage is a little more encourag'd there, and the Births exceed the Deaths.

5. *Europe* is generally full settled with Husbandmen, Manufacturers, &c., and therefore cannot now much increase in People: *America* is chiefly occupied by Indians, who subsist mostly by Hunting. But as the Hunter, of all Men, requires the greatest Quantity of Land from whence to draw his Subsistence, (the Husbandman subsisting on much less, the Gardner on still less, and the Manufacturer requiring least of all), the *Europeans* found *America* as fully settled as it well could be by Hunters; yet these, having large Tracks, were easily prevail'd on to part with Portions of Territory to the new Comers, who did not much interfere with the Natives in Hunting, and furnish'd them with many Things they wanted.

6. Land being thus plenty in *America,* and so cheap as that a labouring man, that understands Husbandry, can in a short Time save Money enough to purchase a Piece of new Land sufficient for a Plantation, whereon he may subsist a Family, such are not afraid to marry; for, if they even look far enough forward to consider how their children, when grown up, are to be provided for, they see that more Land is to be had at rates equally easy, all Circumstances considered.

7. Hence Marriages in *America* are more general, and more generally early, than in *Europe.* And if it is reckoned there, that there is but one Marriage per Annum among 100 persons, perhaps we may here reckon two; and if in *Europe* they have but 4 Births to a Marriage (many of their Marriages being late), we may here reckon 8, of which if one half grow up, and our Marriages are made, reckoning one with another at 20 Years of Age, our People must at least be doubled every 20 Years.

8. But notwithstanding this Increase, so vast is the Territory of *North America,* that it will require many Ages to settle it fully; and, till it is fully settled, Labour will never be cheap here, where no Man continues long a Labourer for others, but gets a Plantation of his own, no Man continues long a Journeyman to a Trade, but goes among those new Settlers, and sets up for himself, &c. Hence Labour is no cheaper now in *Pennsylvania,* than it was 30 Years ago, tho' so many Thousand labouring People have been imported.

9. The Danger therefore of these Colonies interfering with their Mother Country in Trades that depend on Labour, Manufacturers, &c., is too remote to require the attention of *Great-Britain.*

10. But in Proportion to the Increase of the Colonies, a vast Demand is growing for British Manufacturers, a glorious Market wholly in the Power of *Britain,* in which Foreigners cannot interfere, which will increase in a short Time even beyond her Power of supplying, tho' her whole Trade should be to her Colonies: Therefore *Britain* should not too much restrain Manufacturers in her Colonies. A wise and good Mother will not do it. To distress, is to weaken, and weakening the Children weakens the whole Family.

11. Besides if the Manufacturers of *Britain* (by reason of the *American* Demands) should rise too high in Price, Foreigners who can sell cheaper will drive her Merchants out of Foreign Markets; Foreign Manufactures will thereby be encouraged and increased, and consequently foreign Nations, perhaps her Rivals in Power, grow more populous and more powerful; while her own Colonies, kept too low, are unable to assist her, or add to her Strength.

12. 'Tis an ill-grounded Opinion that by the Labour of slaves, *America* may possibly vie in Cheapness of Manufactures with *Britain.* The Labour of Slaves can never be so cheap here as the Labour of working Men is in *Britain.* Any one may compute it. Interest of Money is in the Colonies from 6 to 10 per Cent. Slaves one with another cost £30 Sterling per Head. Reckon then the Interest of the first Purchase of a Slave, the Insurance or Risque on his Life, his Cloathing and Diet, Expences in his Sickness and Loss of Time, Loss by his Neglect of Business (Neglect is natural to the Man who is not to be benefited by his own Care or Diligence), Expence of a Driver to keep him at Work, and his Pilfering from Time to Time, almost every Slave being *by Nature* a Thief, and compare the whole Amount with the Wages of a Manufacturer of Iron or Wool in *England,* you will see that Labour is much cheaper there than it ever can be by Negroes here. Why then will *Americans* purchase Slaves? Because Slaves may be kept as long as a *Man* pleases, or has Occasion for their Labour; while hired Men are continually leaving their masters (often in the midst of his Business,) and setting up for themselves. — Sec. 8.

13. As the Increase of People depends on the Encouragement of Marriages, the following Things must diminish a Nation, viz. 1. *The being conquered;* for the Conquerors will engross as many Offices, and exact as much Tribute or Profit on the Labour of the conquered, as will maintain them in their new Establishment, and this diminishing the Subsistence of the Natives, discourages their Marriages, and so gradually diminishes them, while the foreigners increase. 2. *Loss of Territory.* Thus, the *Britons* being driven into *Wales,* and crowded together in a barren Country insufficient to support such great Numbers, diminished 'till the People bore a Proportion to the Produce, while the *Saxons* increas'd on their abandoned lands; till the Island became full of *English.* And, were the *English* now driven into *Wales* by some foreign Nation, there would in a few Years, be no more Englishmen in *Britain,* than there are now people in *Wales.* 3. *Loss of Trade.* Manufactures exported, draw Subsistence from Foreign Countries for Numbers; who are thereby enabled to marry and raise Families. If the Nation be deprived of any Branch of Trade, and no new Employment is found for the People occupy'd in that Branch, it will also be soon deprived of so many People. 4. *Loss of Food.* Suppose a Nation has a Fishery, which not only employs great Numbers, but makes the Food and Subsistence of the People cheaper. If another Nation becomes Master of the Seas, and prevents the Fishery, the People will diminish in Proportion as the Loss of Employ and Dearness of Provision, makes it more difficult to subsist a Family. 5. *Bad Government and in-*

secure Property. People not only leave such a Country, and settling Abroad incorporate with other Nations, lose their native Language, and become Foreigners, but, the Industry of those that remain being discourag'd, the Quantity of Subsistence in the Country is lessen'd, and the Support of a Family becomes more difficult. So heavy Taxes tend to diminish a People. 6. *The Introduction of Slaves*. The Negroes brought into the *English* Sugar *Islands* have greatly diminish'd the Whites there; the Poor are by this Means deprived of Employment, while a few Families acquire vast Estates; which they spend on Foreign Luxuries, and educating their Children in the Habit of those Luxuries; the same Income is needed for the Support of one that might have maintain'd 100. The Whites who have Slaves, not labouring, are enfeebled, and therefore not so generally prolific; the Slaves being work'd too hard, and ill fed, their Constitutions are broken, and the Deaths among them are more than the Births; so that a continual Supply is needed from *Africa*. The Northern Colonies, having few Slaves, increase in Whites. Slaves also pejorate the Families that use them; the white Children become proud, disgusted with Labour, and being educated in Idleness, are rendered unfit to get a Living by Industry.

14. Hence the Prince that acquires new Territory, if he finds it vacant, or removes the Natives to give his own People Room; the Legislator that makes effectual Laws for promoting of Trade, increasing Employment, improving Land by more or better Tillage, providing more Food by Fisheries; securing Property, &c. and the Man that invents new Trades, Arts, or Manufactures, or new Improvements in Husbandry, may be properly called *Fathers* of their Nation, as they are the Cause of the Generation of Multitudes, by the Encouragement they afford to Marriage.

15. As to Privileges granted to the married, (such as the *Jus trium Liberorum* among the *Romans,*) they may hasten the filling of a Country that has been thinned by War or Pestilence, or that has otherwise vacant Territory; but cannot increase a People beyond the Means provided for their Subsistence.

16. Foreign Luxuries and needless Manufactures, imported and used in a Nation, do, by the same Reasoning, increase the People of the Nation that furnishes them, and diminish the People of the Nation that uses them. Laws, therefore, that prevent such Importations, and on the contrary promote the Exportation of Manufactures to be consumed in Foreign Countries, may be called (with Respect to the People that make them) *generative Laws*, as, by increasing Subsistence they encourage Marriage. Such Laws likewise strengthen a Country, doubly, by increasing its own People and diminishing its Neighbours.

17. Some *European* Nations prudently refuse to consume the Manufactures of *East-India:* — They should likewise forbid them to their Colonies; for the Gain to the Merchant is not to be compar'd with the Loss, by this Means, of People to the Nation.

18. Home Luxury in the Great increases the Nation's Manufacturers employ'd by it, who are many, and only tends to diminish the Families that indulge in it, who are few. The greater the common fashionable Expence of any Rank of People, the more cautious they are of Marriage. Therefore Luxury should never be suffer'd to become common.

19. The great Increase of Offspring in particular Families is not always owing to greater Fecundity of Nature, but sometimes to Examples of Industry in the Heads, and industrious Education; by which the Children are enabled to provide better for themselves, and their marrying early is encouraged from the Prospect of good Subsistence.

20. If there be a Sect, therefore, in our Nation, that regard Frugality and Industry as religious Duties, and educate their Children therein, more than others commonly do; such Sect must consequently increase more by natural Generation, than any other sect in *Britain*.

21. The Importation of Foreigners into a Country, that has as many Inhabitants as the present Employments and Provisions for Subsistence will bear, will be in the End no Increase of People; unless the New Comers have more Industry and Frugality than the Natives, and then they will provide more Subsistence, and increase in the Country; but they will gradually eat the Natives out. Nor is it necessary to bring in Foreigners to fill up any occasional Vacancy in a Country; for such Vacancy (if the Laws

are good, sec. 14, 16,) will soon be filled by natural Generation. Who can now find the Vacancy made in *Sweden, France,* or other Warlike Nations, by the Plague of Heroism, 40 years ago; in *France,* by the Expulsion of the Protestants; in *England,* by the Settlement of her Colonies; or in *Guinea,* by 100 Years Exportation of Slaves, that has blacken'd half *America?* The thinness of Inhabitants in *Spain* is owing to National Pride and Idleness, and other Causes, rather than to the Expulsion of the Moors, or to the making of new Settlements.

22. There is, in short, no Bound to the prolific Nature of Plants or Animals, but what is made by their crowding and interfering with each other's means of Subsistence. Was the Face of the Earth vacant of other Plants, it might be gradually sowed and overspread with one Kind only; as, for Instance, with Fennel; and were it empty of other Inhabitants, it might in a few Ages be replenish'd from one Nation only; as, for Instance, with *Englishmen.* Thus there are suppos'd to be now upwards of One Million *English* Souls in *North-America,* (tho' 'tis thought scarce 80,000 have been brought over Sea,) and yet perhaps there is not one the fewer in *Britain,* but rather many more, on Account of the Employment the Colonies afford to Manufacturers at Home. This Million doubling, suppose but once in 25 Years, will, in another Century, be more than the People of *England,* and the greatest Number of *Englishmen* will be on this Side the Water. What an Accession of Power to the *British* Empire by Sea as well as Land! What Increase of Trade and Navigation! What Numbers of Ships and Seamen! We have been here but little more than 100 years, and yet the Force of our Privateers in the late War, united, was greater, both in Men and Guns, than that of the whole *British* Navy in Queen *Elizabeth's* Time. How important an Affair then to *Britain* is the present Treaty for settling the Bounds between her Colonies and the *French,* and how careful should she be to secure Room enough, since on the Room depends so much the Increase of her People.

23. In fine, a Nation well regulated is like a Polypus; take away a Limb, its Place is soon supply'd; cut it in two, and each deficient Part shall speedily grow out of the Part remaining. Thus if you have Room and Subsistence enough, as you may by dividing, make ten Polypes out of one, you may of one make ten Nations, equally populous and powerful; or rather increase a Nation ten fold in Numbers and Strength.

And since Detachments of *English* from *Britain,* sent to *America,* will have their Places at Home so soon supply'd and increase so largely here; why should the *Palatine Boors* be suffered to swarm into our Settlements and, by herding together, establish their Language and Manners, to the Exclusion of ours? Why should *Pennsylvania,* founded by the *English,* become a Colony of *Aliens,* who will shortly be so numerous as to Germanize us instead of our Anglifying them, and will never adopt our Language or Customs any more than they can acquire our Complexion?

24. Which leads me to add one Remark, that the Number of purely white People in the World is proportionably very small. All *Africa* is black or tawny; *Asia* chiefly tawny; *America* (exclusive of the new Comers) wholly so. And in *Europe,* the *Spaniards, Italians, French, Russians,* and *Swedes,* are generally of what we call a swarthy Complexion; as are the *Germans* also, the *Saxons* only excepted, who, with the *English,* make the principal Body of White People on the Face of the Earth. I could wish their Numbers were increased. And while we are, as I may call it, *Scouring* our Planet, by *clearing America* of Woods, and so making this Side of our Globe reflect a brighter Light to the Eyes of Inhabitants in *Mars* or *Venus,* why should we, in the Sight of Superior Beings, darken its People? Why increase the Sons of *Africa,* by planting them in *America,* where we have so fair an Opportunity, by excluding all Blacks and Tawneys, of increasing the lovely White and Red? But perhaps I am partial to the Complexion of my Country, for such Kind of Partiality is natural to Mankind.

2

Urbanization

One Hundred Years of Urban Growth

When Professor Carl Bridenbaugh *first published his* Cities in the Wilderness *in 1938 he noted with some satisfaction that "historians are now beginning to realize that much that was characteristic of life in the colonies did not necessarily bear the stamp of frontier democracy and individualism." In the past two decades this realization has become a commonplace of historical thinking, thanks in large measure to Professor Bridenbaugh's studies of colonial cities.*[1] *"Commercial as well as agrarian interests dictated political if not also social revolution," he observes, and "most of the intellectual activity and much of the social and political advance of the eighteenth century depended upon an urban rather than a rural environment." If the city never embraced more than ten per cent of the colonial population, it wielded a totally disproportionate influence upon American life.*

It has been remarked that a distinguishing characteristic of European culture in the seventeenth and eighteenth centuries was its concentration in one large urban center. Professor Bridenbaugh's studies would suggest that while there was no such large single center in colonial America, there were at least five of equivalent and proportionate size and significance, each one an important center for "the transit of civilization from the Old World to the New."

[1] See also his *Cities in Revolt* (1955) and *Rebels and Gentlemen: Philadelphia in the Age of Franklin* (1942).

The first hundred years of town history on the American continent witnessed the foundation and gradual development of a truly urban society. The story of American life is customarily regarded as a compound of sectional histories, and in the early colonial period two sections are commonly considered, — the tidewater and the frontier. Yet the tidewater was itself divided, and if we consider the sections as social and psychological rather than as purely geographical entities, it is possible to distinguish three of them, — the rural, agricultural society of the countryside; the restless, advancing society of the frontier; and the urban, commercial society of the larger seaports. Beginning as small specks in the wilderness, the five communities grew from tiny villages into towns, and finally attained the status of small cities. With other village communities of similar interests and outlook which multiplied and grew in the eighteenth century, they emerged as a social and economic "section" extending the length of the Atlantic seaboard, and exhibiting definite urban characteristics in striking contrast to rural farming districts and wilder regions of the frontier. Life in urban areas produced its own peculiar problems to be faced, and the urban viewpoint, based upon continuous close contacts with Europe, derived less from agriculture than from trade. Commercially minded town society looked to the East rather than the West, and was destined from the first to serve as the connecting link between colonial America and its Old World parents.

The future of the colonial towns became immediately evident from the conditions surrounding their birth. Designed as trading communities, they were established on sites most favorable for the pursuit of commerce. They were the western outposts of European commercial expansion in the seventeenth century. City-dwellers from the Old World formed the larger proportion of early town populations, and from the start commercial relations with England or Holland were maintained. Most significantly, the founding process occurred at a time when western Europe, under Dutch and English leadership, was gradually outgrowing and casting off the limitations of medieval feudal economy. Colonial towns grew to maturity in the era of world expansion attending the emergence of modern capitalism, and being new communities, with few irrevocably established customs or traditions, they frequently adapted themselves to the economic drift with more ease and readiness than did the older cities of England. Moreover, the colonizing movement was itself an expression of early capitalistic activity. It called forth organized rather than individual efforts and resources, created new and wider markets for economic development, and opened up seemingly unlimited territories for imperialistic exploitation. It thus produced a marked effect upon Old World economy, accelerating the breakdown of local units of business, and facilitating the formation of larger and more complex organizations of commerce and finance.

The problems which confronted town-dwellers in America were not only those of urban communities, but of a pioneer society as well. Urban development depends largely upon community wealth, and upon the willingness of the group to devote portions of it to projects for civic betterment, or to consent to taxation for this purpose. To a considerable extent the nature of town governments and the extent of authority vested in them conditioned the expenditure of town wealth for community enterprises. Here the colonists were hampered by the traditional nature of the charters of medieval English municipal corporations, whose limitations ill accorded with circumstances in seventeenth and eighteenth century America, especially with the imperious demands for expansion and immediate activity in the New World. In New England towns a new political organization, the town meeting, developed, which exhibited considerable efficiency in the handling of urban problems. This institution was more immediately susceptible to social wants and requirements than were the aristocratic, self-perpetuating corporations founded in America after the example of English municipal governments. Its greater powers of local taxation, and the fact that it placed the spending of public moneys and the enactment of civic ordinances in the hands of those directly affected by these operations, made it a far more effective form of government for dealing with community problems. These problems were the greater, because in the first century of their history the five colonial seaports enjoyed a much more rapid physical growth than did the cities of contemporary Europe. The individual enterprise of American town-dwellers, and the commercial expansion and prosperity they achieved, aided in the solution of these problems of town living, but much of the efficiency and success which attended their efforts may be attributed to the emergence in the New World of a relatively high sense of civic responsibility in the early eighteenth century, at a time when public consciousness in Europe had receded to an extremely low ebb.

The towns were primarily commercial communities seeking treasure by foreign trade, and their economic vitality and commercial demands led to their early breaking the narrow bonds of medieval economic practice to forge ahead on uncharted but highly profitable commercial adventures. All five, during their first century, developed from simple manorial organizations, completely dependent upon European connections, into full-fledged commercial centers, only partially tied to England, and in many cases competing with British cities for a share of imperial traffic. Boston entered early into the West Indian provision trade, thereby setting an example for other American commercial communities. Soon Massachusetts mariners were seeking to monopolize the colonial carrying traffic in ships of their own building, and the profits of carrier and middleman became the basis of the Bay town's prosperity. Her priority in this field gave her an advantage which other seaports did not begin to overcome until the fourth decade of the eighteenth century. A further foundation for urban economic prosperity lay in the existence of an expanding frontier society with its great need for manufactured products. This made possible an earlier development of the towns as distributing centers for a wide hinterland than was the case with English cities like Bristol, Norwich and Exeter, and became in this first century as important a factor in the economic growth of New York, Philadelphia and Charles Town as in that of the New England metropolis. As a producer of staple goods for exchange in trade, Boston, with its limited back country was at a disadvantage. More fortunate were New York with its flour and furs, Philadelphia, with its great staples of wheat, meat and lumber, and Charles Town, which after 1710 found prosperity in the important South Carolina crops of rice and indigo. Eventually the communities enjoying this sound economic backing rose to threaten the supremacy of Boston in colonial trade, while Newport and Philadelphia cut heavily into the Bay town's West India commerce. In the eighteenth century also Newport attained importance in shipbuilding and the slave trade. By 1742 Boston merchants were facing a period of relative decline, while their competitors in other colonial towns found the volume and profits of their traffic steadily mounting.

Continual increase in the volume of colonial trade and enlargement of the territory served by the towns led to greater complexity in commercial relations. In the early years merchants performed all types of business, but toward 1700 their functions began to be more specialized. Retail merchandising having definitely emerged by 1700, the great merchant now dealt chiefly with larger operations of exporting, importing and wholesaling, leaving much of the small trade to the shopkeeper. Demands of trade had by 1710 necessitated the issuance of paper currency in most of the colonies, and the establishment of the colonial post office to serve intercolonial communication. Growing business further led to the creation of insurance offices and some extension of credit facilities. Profits from trade, originally completely absorbed in shipbuilding ventures and industries subsidiary to shipping, now began to create a surplus which sought investment in land, or, in some communities, in the development of certain forms of manufacturing.

Economic prosperity thus made possible the rise of colonial cities. It led to physical expansion of town boundaries, and facilitated dealing with urban problems by corporate effort. Wealth wrung from trade, more than any other single factor, determined the growth of a town society, in which urban amusements and a colonial culture might thrive. This is not, however, to force the history of urban America within the narrow bounds of an exclusively economic interpretation. Social and intellectual development are dependent upon and conditioned by economic progress, but they are not its necessary and inevitable result. They are altered, encouraged or stifled by the action and influence of material forces, but they are not necessarily caused or even initiated solely by economic factors.

When we consider American urban society, apart from its economic aspects, we find it characterized by certain problems affecting it as a unit, and with which as a unit it had to deal. Such problems in general, or collective attempts for their control and regulation, are either absent from or unimportant in rural or frontier societies, but in the case of our urban section they are present, in rudimentary form at least, from its inception. They persist and grow with the maturing of that section, and the means taken for dealing with them further differentiate the urban from other types of society.

Logically, the first of these problems to appear are the physical, and of these the most immediate was housing. As in rural regions this remained for the most part an individual problem, and there are only a few cases on record where even indirectly, by sale or subdivision of land or by encouragement of artisans, the community stepped in to relieve a housing shortage. On the other hand, the laying out and maintaining of a highway system constituted a problem, perhaps the first, which transcended private initiative. Not that the community at any time scorned the assistance of private enterprise; a favorite device, at Boston and elsewhere, throughout the colonial era, was by remission of taxes or grant of other privileges to encourage individuals to open up streets and undertake paving operations for public use at their own charge. But from the beginning public authorities indicated the location of roads, supervised the opening up of new ones, ordered their clearing or partial paving by abutters, and strove to prevent encroachments upon them. At Philadelphia and Charles Town, where some prior power had surveyed and planned the thoroughfares, the first task of local authorities was light; it was more arduous in other communities, where there was no preliminary plan, and where the design had constantly to be expanded and altered to keep pace with town growth. The problems accompanying the mere existence of a highway system, — paving, cleaning and upkeep, — called for full exercise of municipal authority. Sometimes the community exacted from each inhabitant a yearly amount of labor on the streets; in other cases it hired this labor and paid for it outright. In either case it had to levy special taxes, for materials or labor or both. To insure some cleanliness in the streets, it passed mandatory ordinances restricting the conduct of townsmen, impressed the services of carters, and employed public funds for the hire of scavengers. Further to protect the public ways, it restricted and regulated the traffic upon them, especially the weight of cart loads and the width of their wheels. Less necessary but desirable improvements in the highways, like the construction of drains, first came about through private demand and initiative, but as the civic power matured and public funds became available, these too became public functions and responsibilities. In either the municipal or the individual approach to highway problems the towns had good precedent in the Mother Country. In actual execution, especially with regard to refinements like paving and drainage, they seem in some cases to have gone beyond contemporary English cities. With a few exceptions, this generalization does not apply to the corporation governed towns, or to the unfortunately ungoverned metropolis of South Carolina.

Highways may be said to constitute the most rudimentary of public utilities, but there were others, — bridges, wharves, and engineering projects, — of which colonial townsfolk almost immediately felt the need. In the beginning, while municipal authority was politically and financially feeble, these were almost solely the product of private enterprise, but with the gradual tendency of town development they became increasingly matters of public concern. Following Old World precedent, bridges were conceived as parts of the highway system, and hence undoubtedly under public control, but they were usually constructed and operated by private persons or companies, under grant from local or provincial authorities. As the century progressed, in a few cases, notably at Philadelphia and Boston, town governments directly managed the operation and upkeep of bridges. Land reclamation projects, and harbor facilities like lighthouses, pursued a similar history. In the case of wharves, they were either a municipal or a private concern. Most towns maintained a minimum of public docking facilities, while more ambitious wharf projects, like the Long Wharves of Boston and Newport, were only within the capacity of private capital. At Philadelphia public docking facilities were so excellent as to discourage employment of private capital in their erection; at New York, so poor as to require it. Toward the end of the era, when the demands of trade began to make regular transportation between communities desirable, stage and freight routes, too, were operated by private capital, under license, usually from the provincial government.

Fire constitutes a threat especially dangerous to urban communities, and as buildings in colonial towns were from the beginning placed close together, its imminence was immediately felt. The combatting and prevention of fire called forth more than individual efforts from the start. Municipal ordinances required the keeping of fire fighting equipment by all townsmen, regulated their chimneys, forbade bonfires, fireworks, and the housing of explosives in crowded areas. Public authorities had also to make direct outlays for fire fighting equipment of their own, and hire companies for its care and operation. In Boston, Philadelphia and Newport private societies for the protection of property during fires were organized to supplement public agencies. Similarly, water supply for fire uses was a matter of public concern and regulation. Boston, with its crowded streets and buildings of inflammable construction, and its willingness to spend public money and energy for public welfare, was in general far in the forefront with regard to its fire defenses, but by the end of the first century all towns possessed fire engines of the latest European model, and fire fighting regulations equal or superior to those of the average English town.

A distinctive urban function grew in part out of the fire hazards of crowded sections, — the enactment of building regulations. Only public authority could specify the nature of legal building materials as did Boston after the fire of

1679 and the South Carolina Assembly after the Charles Town fire of 1740. Exercise of municipal powers was also necessary to prevent imperfect construction and dangerous neglect of town chimneys and hearths. In addition, conditions of urban congestion led to party-wall regulations like those of Boston and Philadelphia.

Another, more subtle class of problems, those which involved the personal relationships of inhabitants, affected town society from its inception. Intensified by the peculiar conditions of urban life, they required collective rather than individual efforts and powers for their control. Old World experience had taught town-dwellers the immediate need for means of preserving the public peace in settled communities, and the early appearance of constables in all towns supplied the traditional response to that need. For their security after nightfall the towns appointed bellmen or watchmen of varying degrees of efficiency. New York, after developing a highly effective nocturnal police in the seventeenth century, allowed this institution to languish from unwillingness to devote the necessary public funds thereto; other towns were slower in supplying the need, though somewhat more successful by the end of the first century. Efficiency of the watch was in direct ratio to the availability of public funds for its support, — impressment of a citizen's watch having revealed its inadequacy by the turn of the century, — and here the New England towns, with their powers of local taxation, were at a distinct advantage. There are numerous instances, during periods of unusual danger or disturbance like wars or epidemics, when the towns entirely failed in their efforts to preserve nocturnal peace, and their functions had to be taken over by the military arm of the provincial government.

Existence of crime and disorder early became a community concern in urban settlements. Here invitations to lawbreaking existed in the inequalities of wealth and opportunity, and materials for its perpetration in the diverse and unruly elements of town and seaport society. The concentration of people, many of them hardworked and underprivileged, also made for mob disorders, which increased in violence and frequency with the growth of the towns. Presence of sailors, blacks, foreigners, paupers, unpopular religious sects, interlopers in trade, profiteers, and rival political factions, all provided increasing incentives for disorder and violence as the period progressed. Town society clearly soon passed beyond the stage where individual efforts or the force of public opinion could deal with this problem; rather it required the sanctions of the law. Provincial governments passed legislation, and municipal authorities enacted ordinances outlawing offenses against society. Riot acts were drawn up by colonial assemblies, and the local constabulary did its best to round up and confine the perpetrators of disorder and violence. In general, the towns could do little to remove the causes of criminality, and the solution of this peculiarly vexing problem of city life remained as remote in the seventeenth and eighteenth centuries as today.

For punishments, colonial authorities followed a number of Old World precedents, favoring especially the speediest and least expensive methods, — fines, floggings, public humiliation, restitution of stolen goods, and, occasionally, mutilation. In general, their criminal codes were less brutal than those of contemporary Europe. Efforts to make the whole community a partner in the work of law enforcement appeared in the division with informers of the proceeds from fines. Prisons were still generally places of detention for those awaiting trial, though imprisonment as punishment for crime seems to have become more widespread as the period advanced, and save in the case of debtors was probably somewhat more in use in the colonies than in the Old World. The frequency of jail breaks indicates the inefficiency of all colonial prisons, and their inadequacy suggests the absence of more vicious criminal types that troubled older societies. Yet colonial prisons were probably no more inadequate than those of contemporary England, and certainly far less squalid and brutal. Save in the case of Philadelphia in the eighteenth century, the rudimentary penology of the times made no distinction between various classes of offenders, and absence of prison facilities led to frequent misuse of alms and workhouses, wherein pauper and lawbreaker were housed together.

Offenses against the moral and ethical standards which society imposes appear more flagrant in the comparative populousness and congestion of urban environments, and early forced themselves upon the attention of colonial communities. In addition, the psychology of the times made many aspects of the regulation of conduct, manners and dress a legitimate province for the public authority. Early appearance of prostitution in the towns shocked authorities into decreeing harsh penalties for it and similar offenses. With its increasing prevalence in a society which included growingly diverse and uncontrollable elements, they seem everywhere to have become less concerned with the actual offense than with the fear lest the illegitimate offspring become charges to the community. Drunkenness was a prevailing vice, and in all towns the authorities and the better elements fought to eradicate it. Excellent tavern legislation in several of the towns reduced this offense to a minimum, but illegal sale of liquor, and misuse of the legitimate product, continued to baffle municipal authority throughout the period. Sabbath legislation in every town, — as strict in the Anglican South as in Puritan New England, — attempted to insure the sacred character of the Lord's Day. Gambling, card-playing, loitering, idleness, extravagance in dress and behavior, and evidence of frivolity came under the ban of public regulation, either through colony or municipal authority, or as at Philadelphia through the dominant religious group. Especially at Boston and Philadelphia many seemingly innocent amusements suffered from the disapproval of a stern and narrow religion, which served as a powerful and useful supplement to the civic power.

The existence and effects of crime and immorality are intensified in urban communities; so, too, the problem of pauperism. Reports of travelers as to the absence of poverty from colonial towns can only be regarded as comparatively true, for in each town numbers of those unable to care for themselves soon constituted a problem of which the community had to take cognizance. The generally excellent methods with which the towns met this problem indicate a considerable sense of civic maturity and responsibility. New York and Charles Town favored the out-relief method through most of the period, but Boston and Philadelphia had by the end of the century well-regulated and practically self-supporting workhouses, and Newport maintained an adequate almshouse. Considerable direct relief had to be granted, especially at Boston, and in all towns save New York private or religious organizations supplemented the public work of poor relief. Methods to forestall the growth of poverty were devised, such as compulsory apprenticeship of poor children, exclusion of strangers without obvious means of livelihood, and, especially in the New England towns, restriction of immigration. In times of particular stress special devices had to be resorted to, as the distribution of corn or firewood, or a temporary embargo on export of necessary commodities. At Boston, where the problem of poverty became acute in the 1670's and was never thereafter absent, careful registration of all aliens and dependents prevailed, and a public granary was maintained.

The general health, which in rural regions may be privately cared for, early became in urban communities a matter for public concern, and municipal ordinances soon restricted the conduct of inhabitants in matters which might affect the general well-being. Location of wells and privies, and of slaughterhouses and tan pits which might become public nuisances, removal of dumps and disposal of refuse were all subjects of municipal regulation. Similarly, public authorities directed inhabitants in their behavior during epidemics, and enacted quarantine regulations in an attempt to prevent visitations of infectious disease. Toward the end of the century excellent isolation hospitals appeared in several of the towns, erected and operated by the municipality. Despite failure in this period of all attempts to regulate the practice of medicine by town or colony, the medical profession in the towns attained a relatively high development for the times.

In their approach to the physical and social problems of urban life the towns were imitators, not originators. The townsmen came to America with a fund of European experience from which they seldom deviated, and new methods as they employed them had usually first to cross the Atlantic. Poor relief and tavern legislation were directly imported from Great Britain, and the towns might conceivably have done better with their police problem had not Old World precedent served them so exclusively as a guide. Yet it may be said that in several cases there are distinct improvements in the thoroughness with which old methods were employed, and which may usually be traced to the individual civic pride of townsmen, reflected in their municipal governments. This is especially true of communities which enjoyed the town meeting form of government, where, as we have seen, the direct demands of townspeople could effect greater thoroughness and efficiency in dealing with town business, but even in the corporation governments of America there is less indifference to the public welfare than may be noted in contemporary England or Europe. Visitors were impressed with the excellence of poor relief at Boston and Philadelphia, and with Philadelphia's model prison. Fire defences in the towns were a combination of English and Dutch examples, and, especially at Boston, probably unsurpassed for their time. Solution of urban problems in colonial towns was continually hampered by lack of public funds or of necessary authority for obtaining them, — the sad decline of New York's excellent watch is an illustration, — but it was assisted, where public power failed, either politically or financially, by an encouraging growth of civic consciousness among private individuals and nonpolitical organizations. Establishment of private agencies for charity, education, fire protection, improvement of morals, and the like, and the appearance of individual benefactors to the public welfare of the community, in an age not distinguished for civic virtue or interest, is a remarkable and significant accomplishment of town society in colonial America.

Having as they all did a common model and experience, colonial towns exhibit a remarkable similarity in the solution of their urban problems. There are many instances of the failure of a community to provide the usual and accepted necessary solution, but, with the possible exception of Philadelphia's eighteenth century prison, hardly a single example of the development by one town of a unique institution. By the time that local divergences from the original plan might have been expected to appear, communication had sufficiently improved to permit of one town's borrowing from the successful experience of another. The same holds true for privately initiated supplements of municipal endeavor. The Scot's Charitable Society and the Fire Society appear in Boston, copied from European models, and at a later date are further copied by other American towns. In the eighteenth century, because of its long experience in dealing with urban problems, the greater efficiency of its form of government, and its willingness to spend public money for the public good, Boston became the great example, with respect to municipal institutions, for other towns on the continent, but it enjoyed no monopoly of this function. New Yorkers had the fire defences of Philadelphia held up to them as a model, Bostonians were shamed by the excellence of Philadelphia's market, while Charlestonians tried to fashion their city government after the example of the corporation of New York. By the end of the period under review this inter-city exchange of experience had resulted in a striking similarity in municipal institutions, as well as a fairly uniform level of their development. Boston, for the reasons enumerated above, was probably still somewhat in advance in matters of social and material concern, though with its humanitarian agencies Philadelphia was running a close second. Charles Town, within the limits of its governmental incapacity, dealt in fairly efficient fashion with its problems; at Newport, a lesser development of these problems had not yet necessitated any great display of urban consciousness. Even at New York, where political factionalism, a selfish corporation, and the difficulty of amalgamating two languages and nationalities prevented a consistent and devoted attempt to solve the problems of urban living, a comparison of its municipal life with that of older provincial cities of the British Empire would not have resulted in discredit to the former.

The accumulation of economic resources and their concentration in urban units, their direction in commercial ventures which attracted and supported large populations within these units, and the problems of providing for the physical and social well-being of those who thus became city-dwellers, all these aspects of urban development succeeded in bringing forth in America a distinctive society. In constitution, spiritual life, recreational activities, and intellectual pursuits it differed from types of society to be found in other sections of the continent. In respect neither to national origins nor to economic status of their inhabitants did the towns long remain homogeneous. Settled originally by people of the same nation, usually of the same locality, they soon came to include children of other European countries and of another race. Early in their history there could be found small groups of Scots in Boston, French Huguenots in Boston, New York and Charles Town, Welsh in Philadelphia, and a few Jews in every town. Many Germans settled in the 1680's in the environs of Philadelphia, and New York from the time of the first English occupation presented the problem of two peoples, each with their own language, schools and churches, living side by side under government by the numerically weaker group. This incipient cosmopolitanism flowered with the renewed immigration of the early eighteenth century, when all towns received numbers of Scotch-Irish, and the middle and southern cities, especially Philadelphia, large accessions of German exiles. For the most part these strangers were allowed to settle peaceably in colonial towns, whose economic expansion enabled them easily to absorb the newcomers, and though recent arrivals seldom attained social recognition or overcame the barrier of language where it existed, still there was little nativism and small emphasis on the superior advantages of Anglo-Saxon nativity. Such bountiful immigration did, however, lead to many restrictions, especially in the north, where the labor market was well supplied and the poor rates overburdened, to establishment of special churches and social organizations, and in Philadelphia, at least, to common use of the German language in business transactions. By far the greater problem was created by the presence of African Negroes in all towns. In Boston and Newport, where they were used mainly as house servants, and where many of them were free, the problem was negligible. They were subject to various discriminatory rules, such as those which required them to work out their obligations to the community in menial labor rather than by watch or militia duty. But at New York and Charles Town their greater numbers kept constantly present the fear of servile insurrection. At the former town they were the unfortunate objects of such waves of hysteria as the Negro Conspiracy of 1741, and at Charles Town, where they at times equalled the white population in numbers, a severe slave code kept them in subjection.

Social stratification further differentiated urban society from the easy democracy of the back country, where any man might own land and all must work with their hands. Distinctions between the well-to-do and the not-so-rich were perhaps relatively unimportant in the beginning, when society was still so fluid that luck or diligence might elevate a man above his fellows in a short time, but with the accumulation of wealth and economic power in the hands of a few, and the coming in of numbers of artisans, indentured servants and immigrant laborers, class lines tightened and society crystallized into easily recognizable categories of better, middling, and poorer sorts. In all towns native aristocracies were commercial in origin, even at Charles Town where they later sought land as a basis for social distinction. They consolidated their position by means of wealth from successful trading ventures, collecting thereby social prestige and political influence. They lived grandly, dressed gaily, kept horses and coaches, and employed the labor of the less fortunate. The commercial, political and social leadership of the towns was in their hands. Later, as urban life became more sophisticated, they contributed to the development of secular amusements and to the relaxation of earlier strict moral codes. They gained further brilliance by alliance with representatives of British officialdom in America. Below them the middle class, professional people, tradesmen and artisans, lived comfortably but more plainly, enjoying in prosperous times many of the good things of life, but in hard times feeling the pinch far more than did their wealthy neighbors. Steady laborers might know periods of prosperity, but many of them could be squeezed out by the vicissitudes of the economic cycle. They performed the menial labor of the towns, enlisted as common seamen, and constituted a group from which much urban poverty and disorder were recruited. Negro and Indian slaves, mere unprivileged pieces of property, rounded out the caste system as it developed itself in metropolitan America.

Save Newport, each of the towns had originally been dedicated to a dominant Protestant religious organization, but after a century of growth diversity, indifference and actual unbelief came to characterize the religious scene. The complexities of town society were in large measure responsible for this development, for different national or social groups soon evolved their favored sects and denominations. When the ministry could no longer speak with one voice to all elements of town populations, it lost much of its influence, both social and clerical, and the appearance of agnosticism and irreverence was rapid. In general, at the end of the first century, Anglicanism was in all towns the religion of officials and aristocrats; Quakerism and Congregationalism, which had once in their own localities enjoyed this favored position, had joined the ranks of middle class religions, which further included Baptists and Presbyterians; while for the common man a religious refuge was just appearing in the enthusiastic, emotional revivalism of Whitefield. Absence of devotion penetrated all classes; the poorer sort were largely indifferent to the attractions of religion, freethinking characterized such middle class groups as Franklin's Junto, and aristocrats indulged a fashionable Deism. In contrast, a stern and uniform religious fundamentalism for a much longer time characterized the rural communities of the countryside.

Much of their power the quasi-established churches had attained in an age when religious concerns so dominated men's thoughts as to exclude many other aspects of life. But the commercial success of colonial towns altered this singleness of outlook by acquainting townsmen with the delights of secular grandeurs and providing money for their enjoyment. As the age advanced the church step by step gave way before the institution of more attractive secular recreations. Most successful of these, appearing very early and appealing to all classes, was the tavern. Instituted originally as a necessary convenience for strangers and travelers, it soon showed itself to be the resort of all classes of townsmen, the place where they conducted much of their business and where much of their social life was passed. In the eighteenth century coffee houses became as in England the rendezvous of business men and the scene of many commercial transactions. Taverns served not only as places of casual conviviality, but as headquarters for the multifarious clubs into which town social life gradually organized itself. They also offered opportunities for cards, billiards and games of chance, and housed the many traveling shows and exhibitions which the better transportation of the eighteenth century made possible.

Games, contests, tavern recreations, and public celebration of holidays constituted the entertainment of the common man, but for the aristocrats mounting wealth and sophistication were creating more elaborate forms of amusement. To the hearty private dinners and occasional excursions of early days succeeded great public banquets, dances and balls, musical entertainments, and finally, in two of the towns, dramatic presentations. Gradually the commercial aristocracy of the towns, combining with royal officials, evolved a society whose entertainments were artificial, costly, sophisticated and exclusive. But for aristocrat or common man, the vicarious amusements that money could buy, and their variety and attractiveness, differentiated town society from that of the countryside with its simpler, spontaneous pleasures, and tended to draw town-dwellers away from a strict and narrow conception of life as a duty and a task. Copied as they were from the recreations of English society, they also tended to make social life in the towns more like that of the metropolis.

A final characteristic of town society was that it offered to its members a wider intellectual opportunity and challenge than was possible to the man whose life was bounded by his fields or by the hard necessity of clearing away the forest. From earliest childhood opportunities for education, free or otherwise, were open to the town-dweller. Especially was this true of the poor, whose educational needs were largely cared for by religious societies, charity schools, or compulsory apprenticeship. This last system enabled youth of the poorer classes to equip themselves for a trade. In other strata of society young men might fit themselves for business at private vocational schools, for a place in society with private masters, or for higher education for a learned profession at public or private Latin schools or with a private tutor. Young women, too, in the towns might purchase instruction in various fields of learning or merely in the polite arts of feminine society. Also, in the northern English towns, Boston, Newport and Philadelphia, there was from the start a tradition of scholarliness and of respect for intellectual achievement. It followed that a society so trained, constantly in contact by ship with Europe, was alive and ready to adopt the intellectual fashions of the age. Hence, in this first century of American life, most of the intellectual activity, in science, literature and the arts, and what intellectual progress there was, took place in the towns. Only there were there material and opportunity for such activity. And rather than regard the results of that progress with condescension, we should, with James Franklin's subscriber, wonder at the contrary. In comparison with the Augustan Age of eighteenth century London, intellectual and social life in the colonies may seem bare and sterile, but in comparison with the intellectual barrenness of provincial life in England itself, its cultivation and sophistication appear revealed. Urban culture in the eighteenth century was provincial culture at its best, nourished during this period of faltering imitation, which had to precede that of native accomplishment, by constant contact with the vital intellectual currents of England and Europe.

In these various ways the developments of a hundred years of life under relatively urban conditions created a society at once distinct from that of rural regions, whether tidewater or back country, and even further removed from that of the westward reaching frontier. The communal attitude toward the solution of the physical and social problems of diversified populations dwelling together in close propinquity, and the constantly widening outlook which material progress, commercial expansion, and contact with the larger world of affairs made possible, were its distinguishing characteristics. In general, this society was more cooperative and social, less individualistic in its outlook toward problems of daily life, far more susceptible to outside influences and examples, less aggressively independent than the society of frontier America. At the same time it was more polished, urbane, and sophisticated, more aware of fashion and change, more sure of itself and proud of its achievements, more able to meet representatives from the outside world as equals without bluster or apology than the rural society of the colonial back country. Because its outlook was eastward rather than westward, it was more nearly a European society in an American setting. It had appropriated various points on the American continent and transformed them as nearly as possible into likenesses of what it had known at home. It was itself less transformed in the process than might have been expected, because the contact with the homeland never ceased, but rather increased with the passage of years. Its importance to American life as a whole was therefore great. Here were centers of the transit of civilization from Old World to New, — five points at the least through which currents of world thought and endeavor might enter, to be like other commodities assimilated and redistributed throughout the countryside. It was well for the future of national America that its society should not remain completely rural and agricultural, isolated and self-sufficient, ignorant of outside developments and distrustful of new ideas from abroad, as it might well have done had there been no cities. Instead, the five towns provided the nucleus for a wider and more gracious living in the New World.

3

The Pursuit of Culture

The Colonial Struggle Against Barbarism

"For better or for worse," argues Louis B. Wright, *"we have inherited the fundamental qualities of our culture from the British." In*

Reprinted from Louis B. Wright, *Culture on the Moving Frontier* (Bloomington, Indiana: The Indiana University Press, 1955), pp. 15–45.

urban centers and frontier settlements British cultural influences were in evidence, ultimately to assimilate all others. Dr. Wright makes a persuasive case for what he so happily terms "a picket line of English civilization" along the colonial frontier. His evidence is yet far from complete, but he has opened profitable lines of inquiry.

Dr. Wright does not, of course, contend that all colonists were educated, cultured men. He concedes the existence of slothful, backwoods folk, made complaisant by too easy a life in too comfortable a climate. But he is impressed with "the potent minority of culture bearers who plant and cultivate the elements of traditional civilization on each successive frontier."

Dr. Wright may well place too much weight upon the observations of William Byrd II, but he has performed a major service in drawing attention to specific packages among the colonists' intellectual luggage: Americans were *concerned with self-improvement and their attachment to books is only now being appreciated.*

The long struggle to transplant a civilized way of life to the wilderness began with the arrival of the first Englishmen at Jamestown in 1607, and the nature of that struggle was characteristic of that which went on in many later wilderness communities. The early settlers were an unruly lot, more intent upon finding gold or some other quick source of wealth, than upon establishing a stable society. Yet they were not so far gone in greed and sin that they forgot to bring along a parson, one Robert Hunt; and perhaps the first permanent structure erected at Jamestown was a church.

These men, living in a pestilential marsh within earshot and bowshot of the Indians, were not allowed to lapse into savagery. When Captain John Smith sent a detail of gentlemen to chop wood, they blistered their hands and swore at the pain, an offense against decorum which caused their commander to decree a proper punishment — a can of cold water poured down the offender's sleeve for each oath. The picture of Captain Smith or his deputy counting oaths and meting out punishment has in it the elements of comic opera, but it signifies a determination to whip the lawless pioneers into an ordered and decent community.

The rough settlement at Jamestown was not altogether destitute of the symbols of a cultivated life, for the parson, Master Hunt, brought along a library, which, unhappily, he lost by fire, and the next preacher, the Reverend Richard Buck, also had a "library of books." John Pory, a bibulous secretary who came over with Sir George Yeardley in 1619, wrote back to Sir Dudley Carleton that books would be his solace against loneliness in Jamestown, for he had resolved "to mind my own business here, and next after my pen, to have some good book always in store, being in solitude the best and choicest company." He was more fortunate than another settler, one Jacob Bradshaw, who a little later sought the comfort of literature but "received his death at the hands of God by lightning and thunder of heaven as he was lying on a chest and reading in a book." Even literary composition was not unknown in the early days of Jamestown, for not only did some of the newcomers sit down and write back descriptions of the new country, but George Sandys even took time out in 1622 to work on his translation of Ovid's *Metamorphoses,* the earliest contribution to belles-lettres in the English-speaking colonies.

Amidst bitter quarrels, mismanagement, hunger, and death from disease and Indian attacks, the earliest frontiersmen did not completely lose touch with civilization. The majority of the original colonists, to be sure, had small concern with anything except their immediate physical welfare, but a few kept alive the memory of the essentials of a cultivated life. Within a decade after the first settler stepped ashore at Jamestown, a movement was under way to found schools in the colony. By royal decree the Bishops at home collected money for Virginia schools and on May 26, 1619, Sir Edwin Sandys, the treasurer of the Virginia Company, could boast the sum of £1,500 for "that pious work." The Company set aside ten thousand acres for "the university to be planted at Henrico" and another thousand acres for a "college for the conversion of the infidels." Not only were Englishmen in Virginia to be educated but the Indians as well were to share in the benefits of learning, which the seventeenth century equated with godliness.

These ventures attracted so much attention in the next few years that Virginia's education became a favored charity. The Reverend Patrick Copland, chaplain of the East Indiaman, the "Royal James," took up a collection while that vessel was lying off the Cape of Good Hope in 1621 and was able to transmit to the Virginia Company £70 8*s.* 6*d.* which could be used to build a church or a school. It is worthy of note that the officers of the Company decided that a school would be more beneficial and ordered a "public free school, which, being for the education of children and grounding them in the principles of religion, civility of life, and humane learning, served to carry with it the greatest weight and highest consequence unto the plantations."

Although the chief propaganda for Virginia schools, it is true, came from people in England, a few of the colonists themselves helped to further the cause. One of the most famous free schools in Virginia was founded as early as 1635 by the will of Benjamin Symmes, a planter who had done so well that he left two hundred acres of land and eight cows to support a school for children from Elizabeth City and Kiquotan parishes. The education of the Indians, however, for all of the talk about this enterprise, made no headway. The colonists' hope of solving the Indian problem through the pious instruction of the infidels' children vanished in the massacre of 1622 when the Indians fell on the outlying settlements and nearly wiped out the infant colony. The devastation of the college lands gave the projected university at Henrico such a blow that it never recovered.

The plantation system which developed in Virginia and Maryland was not the sort of society calculated to produce a sophisticated culture, and it is proof of the hardiness of the cultural organism that this region actually did see the transplanting of so much of the learning and literate interests which characterized seventeenth- and eighteenth-century England. Instead of settling in towns, the colonists in the Chesapeake Bay area fanned out along the rivers and creeks and established themselves on tobacco farms, invariably called plantations in this region.

In a country cut by rivers and creeks, the waterways became the principal means of transportation, and ships from London and Bristol tied up at the planter's own dock. He shipped his tobacco direct to England and ordered everything he needed from his agent overseas, even leaving to his factor's discretion the choice of a new dress for his wife or a hair ribbon for his daughter. Such conditions of trade discouraged the growth of towns, and towns are generally considered necessary for the development of learning, literature, music and the arts.

These flowers of civilization do not flourish in the cold isolation of the country but require the hothouse air of cities. Even pastoral poetry, which glorifies country life and romanticizes dairymaids, shepherds, and shepherdesses, is written by city dwellers nostalgic for a rural existence that never was. If a dirt farmer has anything to do with dairymaids, shepherds, or shepherdesses, his interests are not likely to run to sentimental reveries or poetry in any meter.

Frontier farmers — and that is what the Virginia and Maryland planters were — of necessity led a busy life. Even when the tobacco planters had laborers, white or slave, to do the roughest work, they nevertheless had an unending task of supervision. If a planter expected to prosper, he had to give his personal attention to the planting and cultivation of the crops, the erection of houses and barns, the preparation and shipping of the tobacco, keeping accounts and records, even the care of the servants themselves, not to mention the bringing up of his children, and public and civic responsibilities. There was no time on a plantation for conventional pastoralism, and precious little time for the cultivation of the mind.

Faced with the hard life exacted by an agricultural economy, weak or indolent folk might have lapsed into barbarism. But the men and women who established themselves in this country were neither weak nor lazy, and they had an almost grim determination to reproduce modes of life which they had respected and honored in the old country. Civilization did not come to the river lands of Virginia and Maryland as a spontaneous growth. It was cultivated with even greater effort than the planters gave to the growing of tobacco and livestock. Men and women worked hard to retain their own intellectual and spiritual inheritance and to pass on to their children the accomplishments and qualities of character which they most admired.

The development of the Tidewater aristocracy in the Chesapeake Bay area is proof of the vitality of the concepts of the country families in England, the country gentry. Pretentious as are the genealogies of many Virginia families, actually their origins are extremely vague. Though many of them think they are descended from some noble or royal ancestor — King Edward III is frequently claimed — most of them have no clear proof of their ancestry on the other side of the Atlantic. Their first American ancestors were immigrants hoping to improve their economic lot, like immigrants in any age; they would not have left England had they been important or prosperous. Marcus Jernegan, weary with listening to fabulous genealogies, once remarked that if Virginians would quit looking for their ancestors in Burke's peerage and start searching the calendars of Newgate Prison they would come nearer finding them. But who the Virginians were before they came to this country is less important than what they became once they were here. Those with enough capital or influence to acquire substantial holdings of land quickly set about establishing themselves as country gentlemen as nearly like the county families of England as they could make themselves. The son of a London grocer or ship chandler, once he had lands in the New World, translated himself into a gentleman, and soon was trying to acquire the accomplishments befitting his station.

The Byrd family is an excellent illustration of this upward progress. They did not reach their social eminence without exertion but their evolution is characteristic of the growth of the new agrarian aristocracy. The first William Byrd was the son of a London goldsmith who married the daughter of a ship captain in the Virginia trade. Sometime around 1670 young Byrd went to Virginia to live with an uncle who had acquired land which he bequeathed to his nephew. Byrd established a trading post on an inherited plantation in Henrico County, not far from the present site of Richmond, and became a shrewd Indian trader. His agents traversed the back country and exchanged pots, pans, guns, and rum for furs. He ran a store from which he supplied other planters with rum, molasses, sugar, barrel staves, household goods, and other products which he imported from the West Indies or England. He also became a slave trader. His land holdings were extensive, and he lavished especial attention on the estate at Westover on the James. But for all of his acquisitiveness and devotion to trade, he was not merely concerned with material things.

The elder William Byrd laid the foundation of the fine library which his son of the same name augmented until it was one of the best in the American colonies. He interested himself in education and served on the building committee of the College of William and Mary, founded in 1693. Lest his own children should grow up uncouth and untrained, he sent William, Susan, and Ursula, the eldest of whom was only a small child, to school in England. To his father-in-law in England, Byrd wrote in 1685 when Ursula was four years old: "My wife hath all this year urged me to send little Nutty [Ursula] home to you, to which I have at last condescended, and hope you'll please to excuse the trouble. I must confess she could learn nothing good here in a great family of Negroes." The Byrds realized that a plantation on the outskirts of civilization, inhabited chiefly with slaves just imported from Africa, would not provide the best opportunities for their children and they were willing to risk separation and hazards of travel across the Atlantic in order that their sons and daughters might receive a proper education.

The challenge of the wilderness was pressing and the response of planters like William Byrd — to use Mr. Toynbee's formula — demonstrated their zeal to overcome the hazards of their intractable environment. They were not going to allow their children to grow up barbarous in the backwoods of Virginia, not even if they had to jeopardize their lives by sending them overseas.

The second William Byrd of Westover in his devotion to learning showed the nature of his own response to the challenge. Young Byrd learned business practices from his father's agents in London, the firm of Perry & Lane.

He also became a member of the Middle Temple where he made friends with literary figures like Congreve, Wycherley, and Nicholas Rowe. A persistent social climber, Byrd also scraped acquaintance with a long roster of nobles and gentry, some of whose portraits he had painted and brought home to Westover where they long served to impress home-keeping Virginians. Byrd's scientific interests were sufficient to gain admittance to the Royal Society where he read a paper on an albino Negro whom he had closely observed.

During a long career devoted to public service in Virginia, William Byrd never relaxed in his effort to maintain his own scholarship and learning. His splendid library at Westover was useful to his neighbors, though Byrd often grudged the loan of a book to a careless friend who might not return it. Thanks to a diary in which he made daily entries we know something of the pleasure which that library gave him, and we also realize the discipline which Byrd imposed upon himself to retain his skill in languages and his familiarity with classical literature. A typical entry, for June 17, 1710, reads:

> "I rose about 5 o'clock and read two chapters in Hebrew and 200 verses in Homer. I said my prayers and ate milk for breakfast. . . . I wrote a letter about my father Parke's will and desired Mr. Perry to give me [credit] for the £1000 which my father Parke ordered him to pay me. I ate roast mutton for dinner. . . . Then I wrote a letter to Mrs. Custis and another to Captain Posford to desire him to deliver my letters at Williamsburg, and his seaman came for them. I read some French till the evening, and then took a walk about the plantation with my wife. Then we returned and ate some milk. Just as we went to bed it began to rain exceedingly and thundered. I said a short prayer and had good health, good thoughts, and good humor, thank God Almighty."

Almost daily, year in and year out, Byrd forced himself to read a little Greek, Latin, and Hebrew. Occasionally he read French or Italian to keep up with the modern tongues. Although a James River plantation in the early eighteenth century was no longer on the literal frontier, it was still remote from the sophistication of cities. It required an effort, beyond that which most men would exert, for Byrd to remain a student of languages and literature and at the same time carry on the busy life of a planter and man of affairs. Finding himself marooned at "Tuckahoe," the Randolph plantation, then in the back country, where he was visiting certain mines, Byrd entertained himself and his hosts by reading aloud *The Beggar's Opera* and discussing comedy. When he was leader of a commission to survey the dividing line between Virginia and North Carolina in 1728, he kept a journal which he transformed into one of the most urbane pieces of writing in colonial America. Byrd brought to rural Virginia a little of the cultivation and literary taste of Augustan England.

The challenge of the wilderness which the Byrd family met so successfully presented a never-ending problem for planters bent upon establishing their families on fresh land in the Chesapeake Bay country. Unless the planter was willing to sink to a level of sodden materialism, he had to keep up a continual struggle against the deadening influences of isolation, loneliness, and the lack of the kind of stimulation which might have come from intellectual associations. Sometimes the plantation environment was almost overwhelming. For example, William Fitzhugh, son of a woolen draper of Bedford, England, who established himself in the wilds of Stafford County, Virginia, in the 1670's, managed to accumulate a fortune, build himself a comfortable house, and surround himself with the trappings of gentility, but he was continually oppressed by the threat of a barbarizing environment. Perhaps the very consciousness of the hazard made him all the more diligent to guard against it. "Society that is good and ingenious," he wrote to a correspondent in London in 1687, "is very scarce and seldom to be come at except in books. Good education of children is almost impossible, and better be never born than ill-bred. But that which bears the greatest weight with me, for I look upon myself to be in my declining age, is the want of spiritual helps and comforts, of which this fertile country in everything else is barren and unfruitful."

To guard against the ill-breeding of his son and heir, Fitzhugh was preparing to send the child, then just four years old, to England when he found a Huguenot minister who undertook to tutor the little boy in French and Latin. Finally when young William was eleven and a half, his father sent him to London with instructions for him to be given a thorough education in Latin, French, English, and other parts of good learning. The father's care was repaid, for the boy grew up to be one of the foremost gentlemen of Virginia and an ornament to the commonwealth.

The elder Fitzhugh imported good books and kept up a correspondence with his fellow Virginians which helped to alleviate the loneliness of his residence in Stafford County. His knowledge of the law was considerable, and his letters are full of commentary on legal theory. Isolated though he was, he helped to emphasize to his fellow planters the importance and the majesty of the English legal tradition as embodied in the common law. Statute law, he commented once to Richard Lee, cannot be understood properly unless one knows the body of the common law. This legal tradition, he insists, "is only to be learned out of ancient authors (for out of the old fields must come the new corn) contrary to opinion of the generality of our judges and practicers of the law here."

Fitzhugh's friend Richard Lee, second of the name in this country, and the founder of the great Lee dynasty, was another who met the challenge of the wilderness and refused to succumb to a life barren of intellectual and spiritual satisfactions. Though Lee's plantation, "Mt. Pleasant," in Westmoreland County, on the Potomac River was then in a remote region, he brought together an excellent library which enabled him to combine the contemplative with the active life. Busy as he was as colonel of the militia, judge of the county court, collector of customs on the Potomac, and member of the Council of State, Lee nevertheless had time for scholarship. Indeed, the multiplicity of his accomplishments and the many sides of his personality make him an exemplification of the Renaissance type of gentleman. So great was his learning that he kept his ordinary notes in Latin, Greek, or Hebrew. When he died, his epitaph declared that "While he exercised the office of magistrate he was zealous promoter of the public good. He was very skillful in the Greek and Latin languages and other parts of polite learning. He quietly resigned his soul to God, whom he always devoutly worshipped, on the 12th day of March, in the year 1714, in the 68th year of his age."

Lee's epitaph suggests the devotion to public service, learning, and religion which characterized the ideal behavior of the planters who were establishing the tradition of English culture in the Tidewater region. Not every planter, it is true, lived up to this high ideal, but the mere fact that it was an ideal and that many planters succeeded in some degree in putting such theories into practice resulted in the establishment of a remarkable society, a society which produced many notable leaders in the generations to come.

Those who failed to meet the challenge also produced a society of their own to which American folklore is much beholden. William Byrd encountered some of them in the backwoods of North Carolina when he was surveying the dividing line. Fertile soil and a benign climate made life so easy that these North Carolinians succumbed to a slothful existence little better than that of the Indians. The men were accustomed to lie snoring in bed through the early hours of the day, Byrd writes. "Then, after Stretching and Yawning for half an Hour, they light their Pipes, and under the Protection of a cloud of Smoak, venture out into the open Air; tho', if it happens to be never so little cold, they quickly return Shivering into the Chimney corner. When the weather is mild, they stand leaning with both their arms upon the corn-field fence, and gravely consider whether they had best go and take a Small Heat at the Hough: but generally find reasons to put it off till another time. Thus they loiter away their Lives, like Solomon's Sluggard."

And Professor Toynbee, describing some of the descendants of these colonial sluggards, finds that "the Appalachian 'mountain people' today are no better than barbarians. They have relapsed into illiteracy and witchcraft. They suffer from poverty, squalor and ill-health. They are the American counterparts of the latter-day white barbarians of the Old World — Riffs, Albanians, Kurds, Pathans, and Hairy Ainus; but whereas these latter are belated survivals of an ancient barbarism, the Appalachians present the melancholy spectacle of a people who have acquired civilization and then lost it." Describing the barbarizing influence of the American frontier, Toynbee quotes the most famous of the historians of the frontier, Frederick Jackson Turner, in support of his ideas about the "spiritual malady of barbarization" in frontier societies.

But both Turner and Toynbee discount or overlook the potent minority of culture bearers who plant and cultivate the elements of traditional civilization on each successive frontier. That was the significance of the planters of the Chesapeake Bay region. These men exerted such a powerful influence and established such a vital civilization, albeit a rural society, that their ideas and concepts dominated a great region for the generations which followed them. The English tradition was so thoroughly established that the South has remained the section of the United States most sympathetic to Britain and things British.

While the Chesapeake Bay agrarians were establishing a picket line of English civilization along their waterways, New Englanders were organizing towns and reproducing the kind of traditional culture which their religion and their mores dictated. Because geographical conditions favored trade and commerce instead of an exclusively agrarian economy, New England became a region of villages and towns instead of a commonwealth of scattered plantations. The mere physical fact of grouping in close communities made the struggle against barbarism much simpler in New England than in the South. Furthermore, many of the New England settlers came as closely knit groups with definite ideas of the kind of society which they proposed to establish. They were simply transferring to what they hoped would be a more favorable environment a religious and social culture which they were determined to defend with all of the resources at their command.

Puritanism, which in some variety predominated throughout New England, was a militant faith, full of vigor and strength. The force and energy of the Puritans' determination to civilize whatever land they occupied affected the whole later course of American history. Whether the Puritans were operating in Boston in 1635 or in San Francisco in 1849, they made their influence felt. The godless trembled and the ignorant soon found themselves being instructed. No Puritan was ever willing to tolerate either devil or dunce.

Although seventeenth-century Puritans had no monopoly of piety and moral rectitude, they practiced more intensely than others certain austere and prudential virtues which coincided with the ideals of the rising middle class. We do not have to agree entirely with Max Weber's famous thesis on capitalism and the Protestant ethic to concede that the Puritan code of behavior was highly effective in developing the doctrine of success which has become a part of the American social dogma. The Puritans were not the only ones who taught the virtues of diligence, thrift, and sobriety, but they emphasized these qualities to such a degree that extravagance became a cardinal sin and work was regarded as a worthy end in itself. Having forsworn waste of either time or money, and having made a virtue of unceasing diligence in his calling, a Puritan, unless he had phenomenally bad luck, could hardly escape material success. Furthermore, he devised an educational system intended to sharpen his wits and make his mind a more effective instrument for dealing with his fellow men. It is small wonder that the Yankee in the nineteenth century became a byword for resourcefulness and shrewdness. Actually he represented the ultimate flowering of the seventeenth-century middle class who were strongly Puritan in their backgrounds.

The political doctrine of Manifest Destiny which played such an important part in westward expansion was a natural outgrowth of the Puritan belief that they were God's chosen people. New Englanders, whether in the seventeenth century or in later periods, have always had a strong conviction of their divine calling to "improve" the world. From the beginning in this country they have been inspired apostles of their particular civilization, and wherever they have gone, from Massachusetts to Ohio and thence to the Pacific Coast, they have displayed a zeal for religion, learning, and social improvement in accordance with their traditional ideas. If we cannot credit Puritan New Englanders with the entire responsibility for civilizing the West, we can discern evidence of their intense activity in nearly every locality. They were a busy and convinced social group, intent upon reproducing their society wherever they went. In most places they succeeded, sometimes too well.

Nothing so clearly illustrates the Puritan determination to reproduce the best of the civilization they had known as their zeal for education. The founding of Harvard College in 1636, only a few years after the first settlements in Massachusetts Bay, is indicative of a crusading attitude toward learning which would endure from that day to this. An often-quoted passage from *New Englands First Fruits* (1643) is worth repeating because it sums up so much of the Puritan attitude: "After God had carried us safe to New England, and wee had builded our houses, provided necessaries for our livelihood, reared convenient places for Gods worship, and setled the Civill Government: One of the next things we longed for, and looked after was to advance Learning and Perpetuate it to Posterity; dreading to leave an illiterate Ministery to the Churches, when our present Ministers shall lie in the Dust. And as wee were thinking and consulting how to effect this great Work; it pleased God to stir up the heart of one Mr. Harvard (a godly Gentleman and lover of Learning, there living amongst us) to give the one halfe of his Estate (it being in all about £1700) towards the erecting of a Colledge: and all his Library: after him another gave £300 others after them cast in more, and the publique hand of the State added the rest: the Colledge was, by common consent, appointed to be at Cambridge, (a place very pleasing and accommodate) and is called (according to the name of the first founder) Harvard Colledge."

The very essence of Protestantism was the doctrine that every individual had a right and obligation to read the Scriptures, and it followed that if he read the Scriptures he had the privilege of drawing his own conclusions about the meaning. Now the Puritans were not a sentimental and soft-headed folk, and they did not subscribe to the notion that interpretation of the Scriptures by anybody, regardless of education, was equally valid. Consequently they were at pains to provide institutions which could supply them with a learned clergy and also assure a laity sufficiently educated to make the most of their religious opportunities. The founding of schools and colleges therefore took on a high religious motive which transcended mere social service. Wherever the Puritans and their descendants have gone, from 1636 to our own day, they have furnished leaders dedicated to education, and their migrations across the continent can be traced by their schoolhouses and their colleges, monuments to a religious ideal. Perhaps the Puritans' most important and most enduring contribution to American society has been a persistent zeal for learning and their equation of religion with education.

So well did the Puritans transplant their culture to New England that some of their colleagues who had remained at home sent their sons to Harvard to drink from a purer fountain than could be found at Oxford and Cambridge during the troublous years of the mid-seventeenth century. Puritan preachers who went out from Harvard, and later, from Yale and other colleges, became great teachers and civilizers of frontier communities. When Puritan communities migrated and established new towns in the Connecticut Valley, or farther westward, the pastor was usually the leader and he and his elders saw to it that the new town reproduced the characteristics of a civilized society as they knew it.

Occasionally Puritan communities went very far afield indeed, as when in 1695 a congregation from Dorchester, Massachusetts, moved to South Carolina and settled a new southern Dorchester. But they carried their traditional beliefs and qualities and re-established them under the warmer South Carolina sun. To save them from the corruption of semitropical ease and Anglican latitudinarianism, Cotton Mather supplied them copiously with sermons of his own composition. Within a few years, the citizens of Dorchester, S.C., procured the passage of an act in the Assembly establishing an elementary school with a provision, however, for the teaching of Latin and Greek. They did not intend to let their children grow up barbarous in the swamps of South Carolina.

The repetition in new communities of the older civilization was of concern to those who remained in the parent hive as well as to the migrants who left. In a letter of instructions, written in 1697 to a group of settlers who went out from Essex County, Massachusetts, to South Carolina, the writer gives some prudent advice: "We do pray and request," he urges, "that you endeavor (and let God help you) to carry and behave yourselves as good and sober men, which we hope you will, and that you will not err from your former conversation, which we have observed to be adorned with prudence and sobriety. Indeed we do rather propose this caution, in that we have been informed that many of New England going into that country have so demeaned themselves as that they have been a scandal to New England and have been an offence to the sober and well minded in Carolina and an ill example unto others. Therefore we pray you will remember you are in this voyage concerned not only for a worldly interest but (though remotely yet really) for the translating Christ's ordinances and worship into that country. Therefore honor God, your [blank in Ms], and your persons by good behavior."

Wherever they went, the Puritans took with them books, not merely pious books, but the basis of humane letters. Even the Separatists who settled Plymouth, most of whom would not be considered learned men, brought along little libraries of surprising diversity. William Brewster, for example, included among his books Machiavelli's *Prince,* Sir Thomas Smith's *The Commonwealth of England and Manner of Government,* Richard Knolles' translation from Bodin, *The Six Books of a Commonwealth,* the *Civil Conversations,* a sort of Emily Post handbook by Stephano Guazzo, and a copy of *A Help to Memory and Discourse,* a manual designed to prevent one's conversation from becoming rude and provincial.

The influence of some of the small private libraries which the New Englanders brought with them and collected after their arrival was incalculable, for they were in effect circulating libraries. John Winthrop, Jr., who became governor of the Connecticut colony, brought a diversified collection of books, including many scientific works. From the time of his arrival in 1631 until his death in 1676, his library was freely used by neighbors and friends. One of these, Jonathan Brewster, read so many books on alchemy that his mind became muddled. Another friend of Winthrop's, Gershom Bulkeley, better balanced than Brewster, read with such discrimination that his tombstone declared him to have been "exquisite in his skill in divinity, physic, and law, and of a most exemplary Christian life." He collected scientific books himself and stimulated scientific observation. In fact, the Puritan interest in science was keen, and even in what then were remote communities, men were keeping up with the discussions in the Royal Society and sometimes contributing their bits of scientific observation. The fact that they lived in compact villages and towns made communication and the exchange of books easy.

But no outpost was too distant to be altogether lacking in reading matter. Boston early had booksellers who supplied the outlying regions. Hezekiah Usher, a merchant, as early as 1642 opened a bookshop in Boston and by 1700 Boston had at least seven booksellers. Other more distant towns also had merchants who sold books as part of their regular stock in trade. Furthermore, peddlers carried books and pamphlets to the very fringes of the wilderness. Cotton Mather realized the civilizing value of the books distributed by peddlers, as an entry in his diary for June 11, 1683, indicates: "There is an old hawker, who will fill this country with devout and useful books if I will direct him. I therefore will direct him, and assist him, as far as I can in doing this." Apparently the peddlers succeeded too well as distributors of literature not precisely to Mather's liking, for he commented a few years later: "I am informed that the minds and manners of many people about the country are much corrupted by foolish songs and ballads which the hawkers and peddlers carry into all parts of the country. By way of antidote, I would procure poetical composures full of piety and such as may have a tendency to advance truth and goodness to be published and scattered into all corners of the land. There may be an extract of some from the excellent Watt's hymns." Mather was keenly aware of the influence of books and was anxious to persuade the booksellers to bring in the right sort of literature, books, as he said in one place, to "serve the interests of truth and piety."

If a Puritan pioneer could take with him no other book, he wanted at least a Bible, which provided him with a whole literature as well as a guide to life. When John Sandbrooke, servant of John Winthrop, in 1638 found that he was to stay ten months on the Isle of Sables with a sealing party he wrote back earnestly requesting "a Bible, a quire of paper, and some sealing wax." Though he thanked God that his stomach could "digest seals, gulls, foxes, owl, and such meat as the Lord is pleased to provide" his spirit could not endure the desolation of the Isle of Sables without a Bible to guide, instruct, console, and entertain him.

The civilizing influence of this one book was incalculable. The English Bible was something more than a religious talisman, a holy book. It was the basis of religious doctrine, to be sure, but the Puritan believed that it also contained the sum of wisdom on every other subject. He read the Bible diligently, quoted it on all occasions, and unconsciously absorbed the rhythms of its prose, its metaphors, and its style. Frontiersmen from John Sandbrooke to Abraham Lincoln owed a great deal more to the Bible than they perhaps realized.

Other religious sects paralleled the New England Puritans in their zeal to maintain the elements of traditional civilization in the backwoods. Indeed, the most notable contribution in the second half of the colonial period was made by Scotch-Irish Presbyterians, chiefly Scots from Northern Ireland. After the turn of the eighteenth century, they poured into America, principally through the port of Philadelphia, though some entered at Charleston, South Carolina, and at other ports. Pushing past the older settlements, they made their way to the back country and fanned out down the river valleys of Pennsylvania and moved on into adjacent territory. They became the typical frontiersmen of the period, the spearheads of white penetration of Indian territory.

The Scots brought with them a deep-seated hatred for the English who had tried to make them conform to the Established Church and had imposed economic restrictions which had hindered their efforts to make a livelihood in Ulster. Bearing a grudge already against the political order which they had known, they were natural revolutionaries and became notable agitators against the English during the prelude to the American Revolution.

But culturally these Scots were exceedingly conservative. They were convinced that the Presbyterian form of church government was the best and that the religious dogma expounded by John Knox was the surest — if not the only — way to salvation. They also had a profound respect for learning, especially classical learning, and their ministers were carriers of this tradition wherever they went. A tough-minded and serious people, they made the establishment of the traditional kirk a concern second only to the elemental needs of food and shelter. Immediately after the erection of churches came the establishment of schools. Long before the American Revolution, the Scots had established a chain of Presbyterian churches and schools along the frontier from New England to Georgia. These fortresses against ignorance and the devil paralleled a chain of blockhouses and forts against the French and Indian. The Scots were as eager to fight one as the other.

Preachers accompanied the settlers into the wilderness and clergymen who held degrees from the University of Edinburgh, and later from Princeton, lived in the same kind of log cabin as those occupied by their far-flung parishioners. These pioneer parsons rode horseback from clearing to clearing, teaching and preaching as they went. They were a fearless group who exerted an enormous influence over their people. Not only were the preachers spiritual guides but they also frequently served as civil and military leaders as well. One of the most famous of the soldier-preachers was the Reverend John Elder, pastor of the church at Derry, Pennsylvania, from 1738 to 1791. Commissioned a captain by the Pennsylvania government, he led a company of rangers and was accustomed to preach with his loaded musket across the pulpit. A graduate of Edinburgh, Elder was a classical scholar equally at home tracing the wanderings of Ulysses or tracking down the most recent Indian marauder.

These hard-riding, long-winded preachers of the Presbyterian faith were the apostles of both religion and learning. They insisted that every child should know at least enough to read the Bible and the Shorter Catechism. They distributed books and tracts. And they taught the children as well as their parents. They were instrumental in stirring up backward settlements to establish neighborhood schools, and they persuaded itinerant schoolmasters to make their way around the circuits which the preachers rode.

Like the Puritans of New England and the Anglicans of Virginia, the Scotch-Irish Presbyterians were concerned lest the supply of learned preachers and teachers fail, and to that end they established academies and colleges to train ministers and laymen. Their first institution of higher learning was the famous "Log College," founded about 1726 by the Reverend William Tennent, Sr. at Neshaminy, Pennsylvania. Tennent, who received his own education at Edinburgh, was skillful in Latin and the other learned languages and his academy taught Latin, Greek, logic, rhetoric, and theology. When George Whitefield, the evangelist, visited the academy in 1739, he reported that "seven or eight worthy ministers of Jesus have lately been sent forth; more are almost ready to be sent, and a foundation is now laying for the instruction of many others." John Blair and Samuel Finley, early presidents of Princeton, were graduates of this frontier academy. The establishment of Princeton in 1746 was inspired by the need of insuring a learned Presbyterian clergy, but the founders provided a broad base of learning and opened the doors to men of all faiths. From Princeton went scores of preachers and teachers to frontier settlements to keep alive the germ of classical culture.

The Scotch Presbyterians on the frontier showed a continuing zeal for the founding of schools and the perpetuation of traditional learning. The maintenance of churches and schools imposed considerable hardships upon a people who had little ready money. For a major portion of their subsistence preachers and teachers could not expect cash but had to accept payment in the products of the country. As tobacco was a medium of exchange in Virginia in the seventeenth century, so whisky became one of the most convenient of assets on the western frontier in the eighteenth. Preachers and teachers were not averse to accepting jugs of rye and corn whisky as contributions toward their upkeep. The Scots who had introduced the art and mystery of distilling whisky from rye and corn mash saw nothing incongruous in devoting a portion of their honored product to the advancement of spiritual and intellectual salvation.

Struggle as colonial Americans might to retain the cultivation of the mother country, they sometimes found themselves fighting a losing battle. The hardships of the wilderness were too great to leave much time for anything except the bitter struggle for survival. The second generation of Americans, even in such literate spots as Boston, appeared to be less cultivated than their elders, but perhaps, as Professor Samuel Eliot Morison has suggested, they merely reflected a prosaic period. A significant fact is that colonial Americans themselves were so conscious of their loss from the dimming of the cultural lamps that they were eternally trying to improve the sources of illumination.

The desire for self-improvement has been one of the most characteristic qualities in Americans from the earliest times to the present day. One has only to read the advertisements of correspondence courses and manuals for self-help in our periodicals to realize how widespread is that appeal today. Benjamin Franklin's *Autobiography* gives a vivid account of the procedure by which one of the greatest colonials educated himself and made himself proficient in the useful knowledge of the past. Franklin is an excellent example of the transmission of ideas from the Old World to the New, for much of his pragmatic philosophy which has so profoundly influenced American thinking had its origin in the ideas of the English middle class of the late sixteenth and early seventeenth centuries.

One of the works that influenced Franklin was *The Spectator* which he read and deliberately imitated. Franklin was not the only American who found the works of Joseph Addison and Richard Steele both entertaining and improving. Few English authors had greater influence upon eighteenth-century Americans than these two, and the reason is not hard to find. Addison and Steele provided sound and "improving" reading matter designed to teach good manners, decorum, decency, and urbanity with the least possible pain to the reader. Their ideas coincided with the common-sense, middle-class notions which dominated most American thinking, whether of the agrarian aristocracy or the trading classes in such centers as Boston and Philadelphia. Implicit in *The Spectator* was the ideal of self-improvement which appealed especially to colonial Americans and became a part of our social dogma.

The Spectator was, of course, only one of many influences which helped to shape second and third generation Americans into the mold of civilized Englishmen. The conscious effort to reproduce English society succeeded almost too well in certain areas. Charleston, South Carolina, for example, did its best to be a replica of London in little and imitated the good as well as the bad qualities of the British capital. Many Charlestonians went to London for business and professional reasons and brought back manners, habits, and customs of the metropolis. Many others imported the current books and periodicals which gave them an insight into the civilized world across the Atlantic.

In all the urban centers in colonial America the same thing was happening. For all of its polyglot population, Philadelphia, the largest of the American towns at the end of the colonial period — and the second city in the British empire — became a center of British culture. That is not to say that German and French influences were invisible, or that Quaker Philadelphians were like Anglican Charlestonians, but that the most important influences at work in that society were English, and London was the focal point from which Philadelphians imported ideas. From the towns and cities along the seaboard, the elements of civilization percolated to the most distant frontiers. Long before the end of the colonial period, British culture was already penetrating the rudest settlements to the west.

4

The Pursuit of Science

I

Eighteenth Century Medicine in America

The connection between natural history and medicine in colonial America was a close one. Every man aspired to be his own physician, and with the aid of his botanical garden he treated himself more economically (and often more effectively) than by employing an unskilled doctor and costly imported drugs. Medical science — in the modern sense — had far to travel in both England and America in the seventeenth and eighteenth centuries, but in the field of public health the colonies can be credited with notable strides.

If, as Dr. Richard H. Shryock *demonstrates in this essay, colonial medicine made significant advances in the eighteenth century, they were more important in form than in substance. The training offered by the Medical College of Philadelphia (founded in 1765) and the medical department of King's College (founded in 1767) was better than that afforded by the earlier, uneven apprenticeship system.*

But confusion rather than progress more often than not marked colonial medical thought. Colonial physicians were handicapped, as Dr. Shryock observes, by the absence of pathological research, by a lack of specialization, and by the demand "for immediate, practical results." Professor Shryock, the author of several studies in

Richard H. Shryock, "Eighteenth-Century Medicine in America," from The American Antiquarian Society *Proceedings,* LIX (1949), 275–292.

the history of medicine (Medicine and Society in America, 1660–1860, *1960), is now Librarian of the American Philosophical Society and professor of history at the University of Pennsylvania.*

One sometimes wishes that the history of our early medicine had been recorded by the patients, rather than by physicians or other learned gentlemen. Those who were ill in Colonial days underwent stern experiences. They were first exposed to the pharmacopeia — no mean hazard in itself. Dr. Holmes later described this situation by observing that:

> The mines have been emptied of their cankering minerals, the vegetable kingdom robbed of all its noxious growths, the entrails of animals taxed for their impurities . . . and all the inconceivable abominations thus obtained thrust down the throats of human beings.

In combination with such dosings, the Colonial patient was subjected to the age-old depletion procedures — bleeding, sweating, and the like. If all this was of small avail, there was no telling what bizarre expedients might be employed. Cotton Mather, in writing to Dr. John Woodward of the Royal Society in 1724, reported the following case history:

> The wife of Joseph Meader . . . had long been afflicted with that miserable *Distemper* known as the *twisting of the guts.* Her physician advised her to swallow a couple of *Leaden Bullets;* upon which after some time, her Pain was abated and the use of her Limbs returned to her.

But, added Mather, "attempts to *swallow Bullets* have not always terminated so well." He recalled a case in which the bullet entered the lung, and added sagely enough: "From which and from other unhappy Experiments, I think, I should endure abundant, before I tried such a remedy."

Upon first encountering such practice, one wonders how our ancestors of only two centuries ago could have submitted to it. Of course, they wanted to believe that it was "good for what ailed them;" and this faith was often sustained by recovery — by the *post hoc, ergo propter hoc* fallacy. But to the modern reader, there seems at first glance no rhyme or reason in that complex thing which was eighteenth century medicine.

First glances are superficial, however, and it is well to look into the matter with more care. Upon further examination, this medicine will be found worthy of some respect; not only as a part of the culture of the times, but because it was in a real sense the precursor of present science. It was in the eighteenth century that the foundations of modern medicine were established; and if American medicine illustrates only the difficulties experienced in laying these foundations, it is still a part of the larger story.

In discussing early American medicine, one must keep in mind (1) the nature of European medicine during the seventeenth and eighteenth centuries, and the means by which this was transmitted to the Colonies, and (2) the social and intellectual circumstances in America which impinged upon medicine once it was established here. For the sake of clarity, the analysis may be broken down into the conventional categories of the history of the public health, of professional institutions, of science, and — last but not least — of medical practice.

The public health in seventeenth- and eighteenth-century England was nothing to boast of from the modern viewpoint. We all know that the country was ravaged by serious epidemics, notably of smallpox and of the plague. It is a truism that death rates were relatively high and life expectancy at birth correspondingly low. One aspect of the transit of Europeans to America which is not usually emphasized, is the fact that they brought with them all their more or less domesticated diseases. Once on this side, moreover, they engaged in a free exchange of their infections with those of the Indians and Negroes; with the result that America served as a melting pot for afflictions heretofore peculiar to three separate continents. This fact helps to explain the toll taken by epidemic diseases among the Colonial populations of all three races. The Indians suffered most; so much so, indeed, that their resulting mortality probably made easier the European occupation of our North American seaboard.

Since few specific diseases were recognized prior to 1800, it is difficult to identify those which harassed the Colonies before that time. The evidence indicates, however, that malaria and the usual respiratory and intestinal infections were responsible for most of the tragic reports in Colonial sources. The most feared epidemics were those of smallpox and diphtheria (European in origin) and of yellow fever (probably of African origin). Why plague failed to make the Atlantic passage is not clear. There were also serious endemic conditions of a non-infectious character, such as scurvy — a reminder of the dietary deficiencies of our ancestors.

Threatened by ever-present illness, Europeans turned for protection to their folk medicine, to physicians, and to the major institutions of Church and State. Certain of these protective patterns do not concern us here, but it should not be forgotten what a role they played in the actual practice of the masses. In the ordinary vicissitudes of illness, the Colonial as well as the English family looked to its folk lore; which involved a blend of home remedies, astrology and other occult practices, and (in America) of notions taken over from Indian "medicine men." They also turned to prayer; a practice which, in one's more cynical moments, might be termed theological prophylaxis and therapy. Yet, apart from the human sympathy which may be accorded this behavior, who can be sure that their faith — whatever its rewards — did not at least have some of the merits now ascribed to psychosomatic medicine?

Governments, in their effort to protect the public health, were handicapped by the state of contemporary medical science. Since epidemics occasioned the chief fear, it was against them that officials took action. Medicine had inherited two theories as to the transmission of epidemics: (1) that these were carried by airs, waters, and food and therefore called for sanitary controls; and (2) that they were transmitted by contagion and therefore indicated isolation, notification, and the destruction of animals. Orthodox medicine tended to uphold the classical emphasis upon sanitation, which was revived during the Renaissance and led in Elizabethan England to the adoption of a respectable sanitary code. This was reflected in Colonial towns by sporadic efforts at street cleaning, inspection of foods, and the like.

Popular feeling, however, leaned towards the medieval contagion theory and was reinforced between 1650 and 1750 by experience with plague and with smallpox. As a result, governments introduced port quarantines, isolated homes, ordered the destruction of animals during epidemics, established pesthouses, and so on. All of these practices were resorted to in Colonial towns, which sometimes even enforced quarantines against neighboring communities.

Town and county authorities in the Colonies also had to assume, against the background of the Elizabethan poor laws, responsibility for sick paupers. Various devices, such as outdoor financial relief or boarding out with the lowest bidders, were employed. The insane were the most troublesome problem here. Boston provided indoor relief in the form of an almshouse as early as 1665; and in 1732 the Philadelphia Almshouse set up an infirmary which in theory provided "state medicine" to the poor. In practice, however, the care given in this and other early institutions was merely custodial in nature. The same was true of the sick who were isolated in town pesthouses.

Since the main defense against disease was resort to private medical practitioners, governments had long been looked to in Europe for some control over this professional personnel. The authorities, in turn, sought the advice of professional organizations in matters of education and licensure. In the England of 1700, the London College of Physicians was authorized to control licensing. This elite body limited its certification to the graduates of Oxford and Cambridge, and so never approved enough men to meet the needs of a tenth of the population. The consequent vacuum was partly filled by licentiates of the apothecaries guild, and by the 1700's apothecaries made up the ranks of ordinary practitioners. Surgeons, overseen by the Surgeon's Guild, were viewed as an inferior group in comparison with the licensed physicians. Since there was no real interference with all sorts of irregulars and quacks, these various forms of licensing meant little in practice.

Hence it is not strange that, in the distant Colonies, governmental control over medical practice almost disappeared. There were occasional acts which reflected the tradition of licensing; for example, the Massachusetts law of 1649 which limited practice to those approved by "such as are skillful in the same art," or by "at least some of the wisest and gravest then present." In the nature of the case, such regulation was vague and ineffective. Most Colonial legislation or court action concerning physicians related to the size of fees rather than to the quality of service.

Some English physicians, including a few university men, came to the Colonies in the 1600's, and introduced the rudiments of respectable practice. Thereafter, the more ambitious students "read medicine" (which was all that was done in the English universities) and apprenticed themselves to older practitioners. Others, who had a flair for the art or were inspired by selfish motives, simply launched themselves into practice. Not until after 1700, did any number of provincials go abroad for formal training. All degrees of reliability were thereafter represented in the Colonial setting; from that of men holding the M.D. from Leyden or Edinburgh, down to the pretense of the most outrageous quacks.

The concept of licensing was never entirely forgotten, and there is evidence that it eventually attracted some support. During the 1760's, New York became the first province to set up a council to license physicians—a body which, incidentally, contained no member of the profession. There is no evidence, however, that this effort — or that of a number of other states during the ensuing half century — was really effective. The general state of things was outlined in the remarks of a New York critic who declared, just before the Revolution, that:

> Few physicians among us are eminent for their skill. Quacks abound like locusts in Egypt. . . . This is the less to be wondered at, as the profession is under no kind of regulation. . . . Any man at his pleasure sets up for physician, apothecary, and chirurgeon. No candidates are either examined or licensed, or even sworn to fair practice.

Against this background, occasional practice by clergymen was not surprising and probably had its merits. Ministers were frequently the only ones who could "read medicine," since before 1700 the greater part of the literature was in Latin. Clerical practice survived incidentally in rural areas well into the eighteenth century — as it did also in England — and traces can be found as late as 1850. Rural conditions in the Colonies also had the effect of imposing all functions upon the general practitioner, so that English distinctions between physicians, surgeons, and apothecaries disappeared.

The lack of a well-trained and licensed profession in the Colonies is usually ascribed to isolation and primitive surroundings. But it must be recalled that English conditions were little if any better. One may therefore attribute the situation in some degree to a lack of respect for medical learning. It was only in large towns that a European degree became an asset after 1700, and it was in these centers that ambitious doctors founded medical institutions both to aid practice and to improve their own status. Philadelphia affords an excellent illustration of these developments between 1750 and 1800; where in imitation of London precedents, leading physicians established the Pennsylvania Hospital, the first native medical school, and the College of Physicians. Patronized by prosperous families, these men acquired wealth and so commanded respect for their social position as well as for their professional standing.

This was not the equivalent, however, of awe for medical learning. The impulse behind the founding of the first hospitals was not primarily a desire to bring medical science to the masses — this, such as it was, could be secured at home. Men sought rather to provide decent care of the poor in terms of charity and of humanitarianism. The truth is that the medical science of the time was unable to guide practice into any more effective channels than those followed by any clever empiric. Exceptions need to be made only in the cases of surgery and obstetrics. The learned physician was actually more dangerous to his patients in some ways than was the self-trained man. In view of these circumstances, it is not surprising that the masses saw little difference between doctors of one sort or another.

What, then, was the nature of this eighteenth-century medicine which reached Americans through Latin and English texts, through the

Transactions of the Royal Society and the early British medical journals, and through direct training in European schools? There is no more complex period in the history of medicine: it may be interpreted, with equal regard to the sources, as an era of lingering medievalism or as an epoch of progress. Perhaps we may characterize the century, as historians are apt to do with any confusing interval, as an era of transition.

In many respects eighteenth-century medicine was far removed from the medieval. Metaphysical perspectives had been discarded, and occult elements had largely disappeared from practice. Although Hippocrates and Galen were cited by physicians, this was because the classic literature still had something to offer; and there was no longer much veneration for authority as such. The respect for original observations which had been inculcated by Bacon was further encouraged by British philosophic empiricism associated with Locke and later with Hume. Precept was closely associated with achievement; the record of eighteenth-century medical investigations was no trivial one. Without reviewing all the various lines of development, let me call attention to one major trend in research which was to lay the foundation for medical science as we now know it.

It is often said that the revival of the Greek anatomic tradition during the Renaissance was the starting point of modern medicine. Actually, it was the combination of this revival with the introduction of new methods of observation (not, themselves, primarily of classical origin) which made all later progress possible. I refer to experimentation, to the use of instruments for aiding the senses, and to quantitative procedures. It is unnecessary to labor the value of experimentation and of measurements in the physiologic research of the seventeenth and eighteenth centuries. One need only recall Harvey and Haller in this connection.

There was little concern about physiologic experimentation in America until Rush encouraged it for a brief time among his students during the early national period. Sporadic interest in experimenting in other fields had appeared earlier than this, however, as in the chemistry of Winthrop the Younger or the immunology of Boylston and Cotton Mather. The latter, moreover — whom I would seriously suggest was the first significant figure in American medicine — employed quantitative procedures in demonstrating the value of inoculation. His figures became a part of the data on which was based the later development of the calculus of probabilities.

Immunology, however, was largely empirical at this stage and was tangential to the major trend in research. This was the continued study of anatomy, a knowledge of which was essential to physiology. But quite apart from this, anatomic investigations revolutionized the concepts of pathology and with these the whole approach to problems of disease. Here one should recall that, along with a sound tradition in anatomy, the moderns had inherited from Greece a speculative pathology in which illness was ascribed either to impurities in the body fluids (the humoral theory) or to conditions of tension in the vascular and nervous systems.

This type of pathology involved little recognition of distinctions between different forms of illness. Although a number of distinct diseases had long been known because of their obviously peculiar symptoms (skin infections, "consumption," gout, and so on), most forms of illness were not recognized as specific and were treated as involving only a state of the body "system." The chief concern was to find cures for these generalized conditions. The humoral theory indicated the common depletion procedures (bleeding, sweating); while the tension thesis called for the use of stimulants and narcotics. The therapy of both schools was reinforced by the employment of the traditional pharmacology — an accumulation in which a little sense was imbedded in a great mass of nonsense. Although there was much talk of the effect of each drug or concoction upon the humors or upon tension, most of these materials were actually of empirical origin and their employment was simply added to depletion procedures for good measure.

This sort of therapy was followed in the Colonies as in Europe, and it was not only ineffective but involved real danger. The more enthusiastic a practitioner was about his pathologic theory, the more was he apt to carry it to logical extremes in heroic practice. Lacking a concept of specific diseases, practitioners could not even recognize the few specifics which had been stumbled upon. Because cinchona bark clearly aided in some fevers, it was tried in all. Whereupon some physicians decided that, since it was supposed to be good for everything, it was really good for nothing.

The speculative pathology not only confused ordinary therapy, but also blocked any development of major surgery. If illness was located in impure body fluids, there was little that surgery could do in the nature of the case. After all, one cannot operate on the blood. Hence surgery remained until after 1800 a matter of superficial emergency measures, such as amputations and the treatment of fractures. Yet the knowledge of anatomy and the instruments necessary to major surgery were available long before this time.

There was no way out of this maze until pathology could be made a natural science. Instead of inquiring what would cure diseases, men must first learn what the diseases were. For only when distinct forms of illness were identified, could one look for their specific causal factors — which would in turn provide clues for their specific cures. Yet the hope of finding immediate remedies was a natural one: it was shared alike by suffering patients and by busy doctors. At this point one encounters an important social influence. The only men who investigated disease were practitioners: there were no scientists who, as in astronomy, could give themselves primarily to research. And just because they were practitioners, physicians who attempted investigations were pressed for time and asked the wrong questions of Nature.

Fortunately, however, a few medical men of the seventeenth century realized — for reasons not entirely clear — that diseases must be discovered before rational cures could be found. Sydenham, for example, gave an impetus to the study of diseases as such. Unfortunately, these at first could be identified only by symptoms (as we still do with the common cold), and symptoms were endlessly confusing. Here, at last, the anatomic tradition began to bring order out of chaos. For the study of normal anatomy led, by internal logic, to the investigation of pathologic anatomy. And by 1760, Morgagni of Padua made it clear that this structural, localized pathology — correlated with symptoms — would yield an identification of specific conditions. Observations made at autopsies, correlated with the antemortem, bedside data, began to break down such vague, symptomatic notions as "inflammations of the chest" into the specific concepts of bronchitis, pneumonia, pleurisy, and so on. Eventually, these distinctions made possible a search for distinct causal factors: a line of development which was successfully exploited by medical bacteriology during the ensuing century.

The significance of research in pathologic anatomy seems never to have been realized in eighteenth-century America. The ideas behind it were doubtless noted in the Colonies by a few individuals who read European works; indeed, the matter was in part explained by Dr. Thomas Bond in a famous lecture at the Pennsylvania Hospital in 1766. But the occasional autopsies performed in American towns reflected only a fear of foul play or a medieval-like curiosity about things in general. Language barriers may have had something to do with the prevailing indifference to Morgagni's work. Perhaps, also, the pragmatic outlook of Americans played a role: pathologic anatomy offered no immediate aid to practice. The busy American doctor wanted therapeutic short-cuts, and had no time for a meditation on the circumstances of death.

Meantime, even before pathology began to identify diseases, there was some speculation as to the causal factors (etiology) of such conditions as were recognized. Here the Greek tradition ascribed much illness to poisons or miasms circulating in the air — the theory upon which their sanitation was predicated. But a new instrument of observation — the microscope — had introduced observers after 1660 to the world of the animalculae. A few men suspected that these little "insects," gaining access to the body, might be the causes of disease. The theory could not be proved in the 1700's, not only because microscopes were imperfect but also because the diseases which would have been checked in this connection were not yet clearly recognized. But speculation and attempted demonstration had meaning: they kept the idea alive until it could be made workable, and occasionally suggested a rational approach to practice.

Did this promising "germ theory" reach the American Colonies? Until recently, we would have doubted it. As far as I know, no prominent physicians so much as mentioned it in the eighteenth century. It is therefore surprising to find that the whole animalcular theory was calmly accepted by none other than Cotton Mather as early as 1723. I am indebted to my student, Mr. O. T. Beall, for this knowledge of Mather's views; as contained in the latter's unpublished manuscript, *The Angel of Bethesda,* which was kindly made available by the American Antiquarian Society. Mather, to be sure, combined this new concept with much of the old speculative pathology. But he viewed the animalcular hypothesis as a most promising one; and, in addition, had some notion of its implications for medical practice. Incidentally, the *Angel* — rarely noticed heretofore by medical historians — seems to have been the first systematic treatise on medicine ever prepared in this country.

Several questions immediately occur. Why was this pioneer American work never published? Failing publication, did it exert any influence? And why was it a theologian and historian, rather than a physician, who prepared this study and who accepted a new theory of etiology a full century before any medical men seem to have done so?

The failure of Americans to participate in the investigation of either pathologic anatomy or the "germ theory" simply reflected their indifference to medical research in general. There were a few notable exceptions, such as the experiments in immunology at Boston with which Mather was associated. But it is remarkable how seldom original studies were undertaken, even by the faculties of the first medical schools. Benjamin Rush lost his interest in experimental physiology and chemistry, after having picked it up at Edinburgh. Dr. John Morgan, of the College of Philadelphia, visited Morgagni at Padua but was not inspired to attempt pathologic studies. Indeed the only American who made serious contributions in pathology, William Charles Wells of Charleston, did his work after fleeing to London as a loyalist. He shares with Franklin and Benjamin Thompson the top honors in Anglo-American science, and was in my opinion as versatile as either of the other two in scientific matters. Not only did Wells do basic work in physics and in medicine, but in an odd moment he tossed off the first known presentation of the Darwinian theory of biologic evolution.

The very fact that these leaders all worked for years in London, suggests that the European center provided stimuli which were rarely present in the American setting. There is no need to explain this contrast here, so far as science in general is concerned, other than to say that it was not simply the result of pioneer conditions on this side. The explanation is more complex than that. But it is, in any case, a mistake to confuse professional progress in eighteenth-century American medicine — which certainly took place — with scientific advances. Boston, New York, and Philadelphia could boast by 1790 of medical institutions comparable to those of London, but no such research was under way in them as was being cultivated in the metropolis.

Although Americans rarely participated in research, they had no difficulty in becoming involved in the confusions and uncertainties of the medical science of that era. This is the other side of the eighteenth-century story. The traditional controversy in speculative pathology related to the humoral versus the tension theory. The influence of Boerhaave at Leyden at first encouraged the humoral tradition among Americans; but Rush later revived the tension theory with vigor. In therapy, men had long been divided between those who advocated leaving cures to Nature and those who demanded interference with Nature. The Dutch influence early in the century promoted some reliance on Nature and correspondingly mild treatments; while Rush and his followers later came to distrust Nature and to demand heroic treatments. From the present viewpoint, American therapy thus went from bad to worse between 1750 and 1800.

A disconcerting phenomenon of this age was the manner in which objective advances in physical science seemed only to revive and complicate speculation in medicine. Thus Newtonian physics, which had systematized dynamics and astronomy, encouraged physicians to go and do likewise in physics. But the only "systems" they could find were the revived pathologic speculations, which represented so many short-cuts across fields of yet unrecognized complexity. The prestige of Newton's physics also encouraged some to urge that all medical problems could be solved by mathematical or physical approaches. This iatro-mathematics had American advocates in Mather (interesting, in a theologian) and in Cadwallader Colden of New York. Mather, who denounced uncertainties and disagreements in medicine as roundly as would Jefferson nearly a century later, urged that the causes and cures of diseases be sought "mathematically" by a study of the "*Laws of Matter and Motion.*" While there was a sound instinct in this advocacy of quantitative procedure, it was of little help at the time; and meanwhile it involved a debate with those who held that biologic phenomena were too complex for quantification.

Related to this issue was the controversy between the vitalists and the mechanists; for the vitalists were inclined to minimize quantitative methods, and the mechanists to favor them. The most active center of the debate was at the University of Halle (1694), where Stahl was the champion of the vitalistic "sensitive soul," and Hoffmann the advocate of a mechanistic conception of the body. Actual research on nervous mechanisms (promising in themselves) only encouraged Hoffmann to ascribe illness to tensions — in other words, to revive this ancient type of pathologic theory. Hoffmann influenced Cullen at Edinburgh, whence Rush brought the thesis to Philadelphia after 1765. The latter subsequently elaborated it into the most popular and also most dangerous "system" in America. In order to overcome tension, he urged that a patient sometimes should be relieved of three-fourths of all the blood in his body!

Here, again, we have what was in a sense retrogression. It will be noted that German influence on American medicine was largely indirect; although a few German doctors came to the Colonies, and various Americans read German works either in Latin or in the vernacular. Only Pennsylvania was directly influenced by German theory or practice. This is well illustrated in the person of Henry Melchior Muhlenberg. Trained at Halle in the days of Stahl and Hoffmann, Muhlenberg avoided extreme support of either of their theories; though his emphasis upon psycho-somatic relationships suggests the impact of Stahl's vitalism on his thought. Coming to America in order to organize the Lutheran churches, the German leader found time to practice medicine on a considerable scale — employing the remedies of Halle in combination with religious exhortation. His approach was different from that of earlier clerical physicians, however, since his university training had introduced him to the spirit of the *Aufklärung.* He rejected crude empiricism and the occult, and practiced only in the absence of those whom he considered as qualified physicians.

A final illustration of the way in which sound investigations often confused medical thought before 1800, is afforded by Rush's advocacy of a tension pathology. It was actually the early effort to identify specific diseases — so desirable in itself — which led him to revert to this ancient speculation *via* Hoffmann and Cullen. For early identification, as noted, was based upon symptoms alone; and these — with their innumerable combinations — had led by the 1780's to lists of over 1500 so-called diseases. Rush decided that order could be restored here only by reverting to the other extreme, in holding that there really was only one disease; that is, an all-pervading hypertension in the vascular system. He failed, as did his compatriots, to see that there was a middle way out of the maze — the correlation of symptoms with pathologic findings which has been mentioned.

Various other examples of the medical confusion caused by even valid research could be cited; for example, the controversy over the relative values of acids and of alkalies as drugs, which was occasioned by studies in chemistry. The truth is that medicine, as already suggested, was unable to use effectively the scientific developments in physics, biology, and chemistry — or the improved methods which made these possible — until it had first discovered with what it was dealing. Its primary subject was human illness, and this was a far more complex phenomenon than were those handled by the physical disciplines. All biologic sciences must first go through a taxonomic stage, since their data must be put in order before they can be employed in research on an analytic level. In botany, this was a matter of identifying and classifying species; in medicine, it involved discovering the diseases. Prior to this, physicians could only accept unverified theories; yet on these theories they based a practice which affected the very lives of the entire population.

Notice that it was again a social factor — the fact that patients could not wait for a sound science — which made it impossible to pursue the internal logic of medicine in an orderly manner. Botanists could postpone theories about the origin of species until a large number of these had been found; but physicians must have their pathologic theories at once if they were to attain any rational approach to practice. Under these circumstances, objective studies in physical science or even in special branches of medicine only enlivened speculation. This was the general picture of American medicine in the eighteenth century. Fortunately, amidst all this confusion, a few Europeans continued the pathologic studies which eventually provided medicine with a sound taxonomy. Such research was on the right track by the end of the eighteenth century; but few physicians — and practically no Americans — were even aware of this.

We should not be too severe, in retrospect, in judging the Americans on this score. All of them were immersed in practice and were handicapped, in addition, by the demand for immediate, practical results which has been noted. Perhaps we should recall the better practitioners as men who were at least devoted to their patients and to their art, and who — in the larger towns — labored successfully to improve the status of their guild. These achievements would prove of value even to future science; since when European research was later imported to these shores, it was essential to have here a profession capable of making the most of it.

II

American Improvement

Just ten years ago the Institute of Early American History and Culture issued a report deploring the lack of historical attention paid to early American science. As Whitfield J. Bell then noted: "the historian who begins to study the early history of science in America must feel he is a stranger in an unknown land." Looking around he would find "the fields sparsely populated; vast areas stretch before him, many of them unworked, some of them uncharted."

Response to this report by scholars was immediate — and productive of much research and writing on colonial science. A major contributor to the literature of this subject has been Professor Brooke Hindle *of New York University. His first book,* The Pursuit of Science, *focuses upon colonial scientific endeavor in the Revolutionary era, stressing the interdependence of English and American men of science. He contends that it was not until the 1730's and 1740's that Americans could afford (as Franklin phrased it) "to cultivate the finer arts and improve the common stock of knowledge." And, as the following selection demonstrates, the colonial concern was (to quote the American Philosophical Society's charter) "the cultivation of useful knowledge," particularly for the advancement of agriculture and trade.*

It was one of the articles of faith of the Enlightenment that science could be applied to the improvement of the material conditions of life. Sir Isaac Newton was not worshipped because of the simple beauty of his laws alone but because he had provided a key which promised to unlock the wisdom of the ages and to permit man to put that wisdom to work. Men became convinced that they might remake the world according to the image of their dreams. It was no accident that Francis Bacon, Lord Verulam, was held in such high esteem despite the dubiousness of his contributions to logic and despite the limited value of his science. Bacon remained the greatest prophet of the application

Reprinted from Brooke Hindle, *The Pursuit of Science in Revolutionary America, 1735–1789* (Chapel Hill: University of North Carolina Press, for the Institute of Early American History and Culture, 1956), pp. 190–215. Footnotes deleted by permission of the publisher.

of science to life — to useful purposes. "Science," he had written, "must be known by its works. It is by the witness of works rather than by logic or even observation that truth is revealed and established. It follows from this that the improvement of man's lot and the improvement of man's mind are one and the same thing."

Not all thinkers and scientists were ready to accept Bacon's identification of truth and utility, but the utilitarian goal was widely acknowledged. The Americans frequently met Bacon's ideas in their press. The Royal Society, which played such an important part in colonial intellectual development, was in some measure a monument to the Baconian ideals, its *Philosophical Transactions* showing a continuing attention to useful knowledge. The London Society of Arts was interested in nothing except immediately and demonstrably useful knowledge. Even the high priest of the natural history circle, Linnaeus, advised his friends to "study that Botany may always be turned to some Beneficial purposes." The historical record did not give a clear indication that science had produced utilitarian results, but there was ample faith that it would do so.

This utilitarian emphasis was particularly welcome in America where youth and necessity gave added prestige to all that was useful. Praise of useful science echoed and re-echoed through the colonies. One magazine declared, "*Rome* was never wiser or more virtuous, than when moderately learned, and meddled with none but the useful Sciences. *Athens* was never more foolish than when it swarmed with Philosophers. . . . Use is the Soul of Study." The physicians, whose study must inevitably be concerned with useful results, were particularly responsive to this emphasis. Dr. John Kearsley prefaced his influential *Observations on the Angina Maligna* with a declaration that must have appeared a mere truism: "It is the duty of every man to aim at being useful." Thomas Paine was quick to express the aspiration as if it were a description of historical process, remarking, " 'Tis by the researches of the virtuoso that the hidden parts of the earth are brought to light, and from his discoveries of its qualities, the potter, the glassmaker, and numerous other artists, are enabled to furnish us with their productions. Artists considered *merely* as such, would have made but a slender progress, had they not been led on by the enterprising spirit of the curious."

The attitude of the colonies' outstanding creative scientist upon this problem is significant. Benjamin Franklin was a product of his time. He became one of the foremost representatives of the Enlightenment in Europe but he attained this eminence without ever losing his American coloration — without ever wanting to. Useful knowledge was important to Franklin as it was to most of his philosophical friends in Europe and to almost all his fellow Americans. When he wrote, "What signifies Philosophy that does not apply to some Use?" he meant just that. He had the faith of a good Baconian that genuine science would ultimately yield useful results. He felt apologetic about the time he had spent upon the useless construction of magic number squares and he felt chagrined until he was able to find something in his electrical experiments "of use to mankind." Franklin's most important scientific investigations were not begun with any specific utilitarian objective. He sought only the truth but he sought it with the conviction that the truth was useful.

There was a wide gulf between the faith of Franklin and Paine that scientific researches would lead to the betterment of mankind and the demand that philosophers focus their efforts upon material improvement. Charles Thomson had expressed the latter view when in 1768 he sought to define "the one end" of the American Society as "the Advancement of useful Knowledge and improvement of our Country." Thomson, however, was not a scientist; he spoke for the merchant and the average literate man. When the American Philosophical Society came to frame a public petition, it revealed a more hazy view of the relationship between the promotion of science and the general welfare. "The experience of ages shews," their petition announced, "that by such institutions, arts and sciences in general are advanced; useful discoveries made and communicated; many ingenious artists, who might otherwise remain in obscurity, drawn forth, patronized and placed in public usefulness; and (what is of great consequence to these young countries, especially in their present situation) every domestic improvement, that may help either to save or acquire wealth, may by such means be more effectually carried on." Whether material improvement could be planned as Thomson seemed to hope or only spurred by the general promotion of arts and sciences, it was clear that utilitarian results were anticipated from the advance of science.

At the same time, some of the academic men were ready to recognize values in science which did not depend upon its ultimate application to material welfare. William Smith called for the promotion of "all those Branches of *Literature* and *Science,* whereby the Mind may be humanized, the Spirit of Religion and Liberty supported, and the Genius of our Country exalted." At the same time that he placed science with the humanities, Smith recognized another equally important category of activity which included "such Mechanic Arts, Inventions and useful Improvements, as tend to shorten Labor, to multiply the Conveniences of Life, and inrich the Community." David Rittenhouse went even further than Smith in picturing astronomy as a humanity, yet at the same time he could remark that he despised the kind of mathematical "juggle, where no use is proposed." Even these men who could see in science values that did not depend upon material betterment, still held high their utilitarian expectations.

The yield of all these exalted hopes was disappointingly meager. Science had not yet reached a stage at which it could offer much help to the farmer, the merchant, or the artisan in the ordinary pursuit of his business. Advances in technics still came by trial and error methods rather than through the application of externally constructed patterns of theory. Except in a few isolated cases, the best that could be done was to attempt to study the most successful practice found in any part of the world and to experiment with new methods as freely and frequently as possible. Knowledge thus attained might then be placed at the disposal of the trade or business in question — though persuading its practitioners to adopt the better methods was still another problem. It was not yet a question of applying scientific knowledge to economic pursuits as Justus Liebig was able to do so successfully with respect to agriculture in the next century. All that could be done was to study practice with the detachment that had been useful in the study of science and to attempt to disseminate the knowledge thus acquired.

This approach was being made in England, particularly in agriculture and the mechanic arts. The Americans learned of it from acquaintance with individual reformers, from their newspapers and magazines, through the efforts of the London Society of Arts, and through the pages of that society's unofficial journal, *Memoirs of Agriculture.* In America, however, despite widespread approval of this process there were only spotty efforts to support it. The American Philosophical Society, with its heavy merchant and nonscientific membership, did turn some of its energies to "the Several Supports of Mankind at large, Agriculture, Manufactures and Commerce." Three of its six committees, Trade and Commerce, Mechanics and Architecture, and Husbandry and American Improvements, dealt with utilitarian pursuits. Most members clearly felt themselves less equipped to do justice to natural philosophy, natural history, and medicine than to "such subjects as tend to the improving of their country, and advancement of its interest and prosperity." This principle of action combined patriotism with personal gain to produce a feeling of exhilaration.

Agriculture was not only the chief support of the American people but it was in dire need of improvement. As early as 1758, the *American Magazine* had suggested that "township companies or societies" be formed to discuss agricultural improvement and to make new experiments. Little was done to introduce the new English practices: the Norfolk system of crop rotation, the marling and pulverizing of the soil, purposeful breeding, and the use of new and better implements. As late as 1775, the perceptive author of *American Husbandry* still saw wasteful practices on every hand and again urged the need for a society specifically devoted to the encouragement of agriculture. Such a society might "settle a plan of operations, which would, in a few years, by means of an annual subscription, given in bounties and premiums, alter the face of things. They might reduce these doubtful points to certainty; they might introduce a better system of rural oeconomy, and be in a few years of infinite service to their country." No such effort was made. The only experimentation was done by enlightened individuals: by Thomas Jefferson in Virginia, William Allen in Pennsylvania, Benjamin Gale in Connecticut, and a handful of others.

Through their magazines and newspapers, the Americans were given a frequent diet of new techniques and new implements, often copied from English and occasionally from French sources. Sometimes they appear to have been inserted merely as space fillers. The *New American Magazine* published in 1760 an article on planting trees that it extracted from the *Philosophical Transactions* of 1669! Yet evidences of the new agriculture were to be found in newspaper advertisements offering new implements for sale and offering to locate marl and instruct in its use. Americans tried new plows and seed drills. They invented harvesting machines, threshing machines, and seed drills of their own. Benjamin Gale of Killingworth, Connecticut received a gold medal from the Society of Arts for the completion of a superior seed drill which his father-in-law, Jared Eliot, had begun. Even so, the practice of the dirt farmer was not much affected.

One of the most serious difficulties was the fact that English experience was not always applicable to the American environment. The extent of land in the colonies, the climate, and the soil differed markedly from England. Intensive farming would have meant economic suicide in America; even the root crops which had proven so beneficial in England did not fare well in America. The problem was recognized in many quarters but the experiments necessary to test the applicability of the English methods were carried out only in a very small part. To the end of the colonial period, Jared Eliot's *Essays upon Field Husbandry* remained the best treatise based upon a knowledge of English methods but written in terms of American experience and experiment.

In the case of crop pests, experience suggested that the insects which attacked American plants were different from those known in Europe. When Thomas Gilpin wrote his paper on the seventeen-year locust, he called it the American locust. The American Philosophical Society published three articles which offered methods of fighting pests. In one of them, Landon Carter, Virginia planter, dealt with the most serious problem, the wheat fly. Much had already been written in England, on the continent, and in America on the control of this or similar insects attacking wheat. Carter was acquainted with some of these writings but he made his own experiments and came up with a method of control by heat that seemed to work well. He was so pleased with the reception of his article that he went on to make more experiments which he reported in the *Virginia Gazette*.

To most of those concerned, agricultural improvement was not primarily a question either of adapting English techniques to America or of attacking specific problems. The widest support was given to the introduction of new crops that offered economic advantage. The natural history circle had been founded in considerable measure upon the desire to introduce American plants to Europe, but a reversal in emphasis was effected when the American Philosophical Society reprinted John Ellis's pamphlet on foreign plants that might be profitably introduced into the colonies. Three other articles in the *Transactions* dealt with new, American sources of table oil, two of them relating experiments in the extraction of oil from sunflower seeds and the third, by John Morel of Georgia, advocating the use of the bene seed. A contemporary letter by George Brownrigg of North Carolina, urging the use of the ground nut or arachis for the same purpose, was published in London in the *Philosophical Transactions*. The American society also published a recipe for currant wine, along with Isaac Bartram's old paper on the distillation of persimmons. Bartram was aware of the use of persimmon beer in the southern back country but what he sought to develop was a rum-like hard liquor. More widespread efforts were made to encourage viniculture, silk culture, and the raising of hemp and flax. These crops had been encouraged from almost the beginning of settlement in America. They were not distasteful to the English nor did they conflict with imperial policy. At the same time, they promised to increase the riches and potentialities of America. Americans of all shades of political opinion could join in supporting the cultivation of new products, convinced that they were acting in the best interests of patriotism.

The culture of grapes for the purpose of making wine had been advocated from an early time in the hope of decreasing the large importation of foreign wine into Britain and her colonies. Some early local success was attained, particularly by the Huguenots who had been settled for that purpose in South Carolina by the British government. After the French and Indian War, encouragement became more general: a bounty was offered by the British government, a premium was announced by the Society of Arts, and in 1769, a vineyard was established by the Province of Virginia. Individuals began to attempt the raising of grapes and the manufacture of wine on a wider scale. One of the most successful was Edward Antill of New Jersey, who was rewarded for his activity by the Society of Arts. In 1768, Antill proposed a most ambitious project through the columns of the *New-York Gazette* and the *Maryland Gazette*. Antill sought subscriptions toward the establishment of a public vineyard from which each province would be able to draw free cuttings. The project failed as did John Leacock's attempt to establish a similar vineyard in 1773 by means of a public lottery. Antill's most lasting contribution was in the form of an eighty-page treatise on viniculture, the best article on the subject to come out of the colonies.

Viniculture was basically a question of skill rather than learning or study, and the men who came closest to success were foreigners who had acquired the techniques in Europe. The two most successful vineyards were established by Frenchmen, each with the aid of Lord Hillsborough. Lewis St. Pierre made his plantings along the Savannah River with such success that he was awarded a gold medal by the Society of Arts. Pierre LeCaux began with a much smaller vineyard on the outskirts of Philadelphia. His enterprise lasted longer despite the withdrawal of Hillsborough's support and the later opposition of the French government. Another considerable vineyard was begun in Virginia by Philip Mazzei who brought with him seeds, cuttings, and plants as well as laborers from Italy. He was enabled to establish himself principally through the assistance of Thomas Jefferson, who induced him to settle on land bordering his own. Mazzei's project failed when his laborers' terms ran out and he himself became involved in the developing Revolution.

Another crop long advocated for mercantilist reasons was hemp, used for cordage, bags, and sails, and even urged in some quarters for clothing. As early as 1735, an Irish pamphlet on flax and hemp was reprinted in Boston, but it was not until the imperial tensions of the 1760's that general interest rose. Parliament established a bounty on hemp in 1765 and Virginia and North Carolina soon followed suit with bounties of their own. While viniculture had attracted the greatest attention in the southern colonies, the raising of hemp was recommended especially to the attention of the northern colonies. It was by order of the Massachusetts Assembly that Edmund Quincy's *Treatise of Hemp Husbandry* was published in 1765. Admittedly a collection from the best European and American accounts, it also contained a description of the extensive experiment in hemp production then being undertaken at Salem. The following year, Boston saw the reprinting of Marcandier's valued work on hemp in an English translation. Even this contained an American element in its "Plan of the *Pennsylvania* Hemp Brake." Hemp was widely attempted, but although its virtues were generously extolled, it did not supplant flax which the hemp advocates considered much less generally useful. Hemp production continued on a limited basis. Madder and tea which also received encouragement failed altogether.

Of all the attempts to introduce new crops, the struggle to establish silk culture was the most dramatic. Like wine and like hemp, silk was a product that Britain and her colonies had to import from foreign lands. For that reason attempts had been made ever since 1621 to establish its production in the colonies. Initial failures in Virginia did not discourage later enthusiasts in Georgia, South Carolina, New York, Connecticut, and Pennsylvania. The pattern of encouragement was extensive, involving premiums for the growth of mulberry trees, bounties as well as premiums on raw silk, favorable instructions to royal and proprietary governors, financial inducements to stimulate the immigration of skilled workers, the establishment of public filatures where silk could be wound from the cocoons, and the printing of numerous accounts, advertisements, and appeals. First and last, it meant the investment of considerable sums of private as well as public money. The whole effort was accelerated during the Seven Years' War when the Society of Arts began to offer premiums in Georgia, Pennsylvania, and Connecticut. After 1765, imperial tensions influenced encouragement, too.

The greatest measure of success was met in Georgia where the proprietors had early fastened upon silk as the most desirable product for that colony. Joseph Ottolenghe, a native of Piedmont, was appointed to direct the silk culture, a filature was built at Savannah, and Italian workers were brought in to do the winding. Maximum production of 1,084 pounds of silk was attained in 1766. In 1767, after having paid out a total of £1,370 in silk premiums nearly all of which went to Georgia, the Society of Arts became discouraged with the results and abandoned its efforts to stimulate silk production in America. In 1769, the parliamentary bounties on silk were reduced. Production had so declined by 1771 that the filature itself was given up. South Carolina never succeeded as well as Georgia, despite the wholehearted cooperation of the provincial assembly in providing a bounty and appropriations toward the erection of two filatures and two spinning factories. Failure was undeniable in both colonies before the Revolution, but in other quarters hope still persisted.

Production of silk in the Northern colonies never equalled that of South Carolina and Georgia. In most of the North, silk culture was promoted only by private individuals. It was in Pennsylvania that the best organized, most literate effort was made in association with America's one learned society. The very men who were most anxious to use science to advance the material welfare of the colonies were in the forefront of the Pennsylvania movement. Ignoring previous failures, a small group of men led by the Reverend Francis Alison began in April 1769 to offer free silk worm eggs to all who would raise them. In May, the *Pennsylvania Journal* and Lewis Nicola's *American Magazine* began to run extracts from Samuel Pullein's standard *Culture of Silk* in the hope that it would "contribute to the Improvement of a Country in an infant State." During the next month, the *Pennsylvania Chronicle* reprinted selections from a French treatise on silk culture. When Dr. Cadwalader Evans wrote to Benjamin Franklin in London for advice, the enterprise was lifted to a new level.

The attention of the American Philosophical Society was turned to the culture of silk when Franklin's reply to Evans was read before it in January, 1770. Franklin transmitted a recent French pamphlet on the subject, promised to get a copy of the act of Parliament establishing the bounty on silk, and outlined the steps to be taken in establishing silk production. He urged that a public filature be established and that the Pennsylvania Assembly be induced to promote the growth of mulberry trees. The society disagreed with the need for mulberry trees since they were native to the province but it did immediately prepare a petition to the assembly asking for aid in establishing the filature and in providing annual premiums to be offered for the ensuing five years.

When the assembly demonstrated a reluctance to appropriate the required £500, even the first year, another approach was made. Two hundred fifty pounds proved easy to collect by way of private subscription. The subscribers then elected a twelve-man board of managers, which was made up exclusively of members of the American Philosophical Society. It at once set to work, established the filature, hired an experienced silk reeler, set the prices it would pay for cocoons at 25 per cent above the market, and offered various premiums to residents of Pennsylvania, Delaware, New Jersey, and Maryland. A rising enthusiasm led to increasing press attention which occasionally did more harm than good. One account had it that if a calf fed on mulberry leaves were killed and the maggots found on the meat were then set on mulberry leaves, they would turn out to be silkworms! Despite such old wives' tales, the first year's operations were reckoned successful when 150 pounds of silk could be exported. Encouraging reports received from England on the quality of the exported silk led the managers to make bigger plans for the following year. The Pennsylvania Assembly proved willing to make a conditional grant of £1,000 to the silk society to be paid as soon as it could be demonstrated that £1,000 had been raised from other sources. The qualification was soon met and the future appeared bright. It even looked as if the New Jersey Assembly might soon grant some encouragement.

The silk society continued its activities right into the war period, offering premiums and exporting silk each year. Franklin handled the affairs of the organization in London, even presenting a dress of American silk to the Queen. At one point, he urged the Americans to protect themselves against future developments by preparing to manufacture the silk cloth themselves, but without effect. The society was responsible for bringing Joseph Ottolenghe to Philadelphia from Georgia and encouraging him to write a little handbook on raising silkworms. Comprehensive directions for breeding silkworms were put together by four of the managers who offered extracts from the works of Samuel Pullein and Pierre de Boissier. Actually, the most original paper to emerge from this whole period was Moses Bartram's study of the life cycle of "native American Silk worms" which had been written before the establishment of the silk society. When newspaper essays and unpublished manuscripts were included, the total literary output was surprising, but it did not save the enterprise from collapse. Humphrey Marshall expressed the proper degree of skepticism when he reported: "Our people Seem to make a great Noise about raising Silk, how it will turn out I know not." When a silk depression hit England in 1772, it turned out rather badly. It was a lost cause when the last list of premiums was offered in May 1776.

There were probably many people throughout the country who wrote some notes on their experiments in silk culture, but it may be doubted that anyone was more careful in this respect than Ezra Stiles at Newport, Rhode Island. He produced a manuscript entitled "Observations on Silk Worms and the Culture of Silk," a narrative account of his experiments with three thousand worms beginning in the summer of 1763. He carried it through to his participation in unsuccessful efforts after the Revolution to revive the culture of silk in Connecticut. The account was embellished with remarks from various Italian and Chinese authorities. It revealed relationships with Philadelphia silk cultivators and with Franklin in London who sent him Chinese prints of silk culture scenes. On one occasion Franklin agreed to sell him enough Pennsylvania silk to permit a dress to be made for his wife entirely of American silk — the Connecticut and Pennsylvania strains no doubt being "indistinguishable." Stiles recorded that the only thing that led him momentarily to neglect his silk worms was his greater absorption with the transit of Venus of 1769.

The effort to establish various manufactures in the colonies was a counterpart of the attempts to alter patterns of agriculture. Manufactures represented only a small part of the American economy, but in the years of tension after the peace of Paris they loomed very large. The encouragement of manufactures had two distinct phases. In the first, the aim was to produce such goods as pig iron, bar iron, potash, and pearl ash which would supplement the economy of the empire. Just as England was anxious to have the colonies produce the agricultural exotics, wine and silk, so it welcomed partly manufactured raw materials that would otherwise have to be imported from foreign nations. The second phase of the American enthusiasm for manufactures involved finished products which were not encouraged in England because they competed with English goods. The Americans made attempts to rediscover the techniques and processes that would permit them to compete with the mother country especially in the manufacture of textiles.

The encouragement of manufactures in the colonies was closely coordinated with the developing Revolutionary movement. Before the imperial reforms that followed the Seven Years' War, the appeal for manufactures had usually been limited to a desire to benefit the poorer elements of the cities which would provide the needed labor. At least the arguments were couched in those terms. After 1764, a series of non-importation movements cut down the supply of British manufactures. The Sugar Act, Stamp Act, Townshend Acts, and finally the Coercive Acts introduced a succession of efforts to stimulate manufactures and to create a preference for American goods. In several colonies, societies offered premiums to aid specified manufactures, town and provincial governments extended encouragement, and home markets flourished. Harvard students demonstrated their patriotism by appearing at commencement in clothes entirely of American manufacture. The use of "foreign Geegaws" was deprecated as Lynn boasted that it produced forty thousand pairs of shoes in a year and Germantown six thousand dozen pairs of stockings. England had early shown its attitude toward this sort of manufacture in the Woolens Act, the Hat Act, and the Iron Act but it did not at this time reply by similar restrictive legislation. In 1766 and 1768 the Board of Trade required reports on manufactures established since 1734 from all colonial governors and in 1774 Parliament prohibited the export of all tools and machinery used in textile manufactures.

Textile manufacture was the most serious problem. Textiles, the foundation of Britain's trade, were at the same time the product the Americans found most desirable to manufacture. The Americans already provided the bulk of their own clothing although little of that got into "trade." Beginning with the New York Society of Arts of 1764, several organizations were formed to manufacture cloth. The most successful of them was the United Company of Philadelphia for Promoting American Manufactures which, soon after its establishment in 1775, had seven hundred people at work making cloth. There was notably less literary activity in connection with cloth manufacture than there was relating to agricultural improvement. There was less interest on the part of the American Philosophical Society and the Royal Society. Occasionally a new textile machine was pictured in a magazine and one plan for a water-powered spinning mill was presented to the American Society. Assembly grants to encourage inventors or to help men duplicate English inventions had some effect.

Less essential products received attention, too. Paper, for example, had been manufactured in the colonies for a long time but the Townshend duty on the importation of paper led to a new effort to increase its production. In New York, the collection of rags was publicized as a patriotic duty. In Boston, rags were bought to sustain the paper mill at Milton; in Connecticut, an assembly bounty kept at least one paper mill in operation; and in Philadelphia, the American Philosophical Society offered premiums for rags with which the manufacture of paper could be extended. The society also gave to William Henry Stiegel a kind of scientific stamp of approval for the flint glass he manufactured. This certificate he was able to use to advantage in his advertising and in his successful appeal for an assembly grant. Another attempt by the Philosophical Society to encourage American manufactures was its request that clays be submitted from all over the country so that the deposits most suitable for pottery could be located. One such specimen, sent from Charlestown in 1772, was adjudged to be particularly good for making crucibles.

Abel Buell of Killingworth, Connecticut, made at this time the first type fonts ever cast in America. When he worked out his plan for producing them in 1769, all printing type had to be imported from England. He won the support of Benjamin Gale, who sent samples of his type to the American Philosophical Society and wrote to the Reverend Ezra Stiles and the Reverend John Devotion of the achievement. The Philosophical Society was pleased with the specimens but it was the Connecticut Assembly that gave Buell support in the form of a loan of £100 without interest. Even with this aid Buell was not able to place his enterprise on a commercial basis nor was a Scottish immigrant in Boston who attempted type founding just a little later. Although Christopher Sower did establish type foundries in Germantown which produced principally gothic type for his German publications, they were not of general importance. Franklin also planned to establish a foundry in Philadelphia with materials he brought back from Europe in 1775, but that undertaking was prevented by the war. Successful production did not begin until after the Revolution when Philadelphia and Hartford became the centers of the trade.

Unlike many of the manufactures encouraged by the Americans in this period, iron production was welcomed by the British — to a degree. The Iron Act of 1750 encouraged the production of pig and bar iron in the colonies by dropping the duty on these products, but at the same time, it prohibited the erection of plants for the production of finished iron products. Iron as a raw material was very much needed in Britain where pig and bar iron were considered semi-finished basic products because they had to be further processed before reaching the consumer. When Jared Eliot found a means of extracting iron from "Black Sea Sand," his discovery was welcomed by the Society of Arts with a gold medal because it looked toward increased production of the American raw material. When Connecticut granted legislative subsidies to sustain steel production that was another matter. Steel was a finished iron product which the English did not want the Americans to make.

Potash, like pig and bar iron, was welcomed by the British. Potash was one of the very limited number of industrial chemicals then in considerable demand. It was used not only in the manufacture of glass and soap but also in bleaching and dyeing which were becoming increasingly important in England with the unfolding of the industrial revolution. The substance was imported by England from the Baltic and the forested regions of Europe. There seemed no good reason why it could not be produced in quantity in America where an abundant supply of timber existed. With that view in mind, Parliament had removed the duty from American potash in 1751, and very shortly after its foundation the Society of Arts began to encourage production by establishing premiums and publicizing methods of manufacture.

Here, if anywhere, was an opportunity for turning science to useful ends, for potash was the product of a series of chemical processes. Potash was an impure form of potassium carbonate. Relatively pure potash went under the name of pearl ash and commanded a higher market price. The processes of manufacture and refinement had been developed on an empirical rather than a theoretical basis; indeed, chemical knowledge did not even permit a satisfactory description of the processes that were involved. Nevertheless, much knowledge had accumulated which could be organized and used by those conversant with it.

In the encouragement of potash there was an endeavor to be as scientific as — in the nature of things — it was possible to be. As early as 1755, an Englishman, Thomas Stevens, was granted £3,000 for a new method of manufacture. Two years later in the Southern colonies he was selling a pamphlet that described that method. On the same trip he succeeded in inducing the Virginia legislature to build a potash furnace at Williamsburg. The Society of Arts sent James Stewart to New England in 1763 and to Maryland in 1771 with the mission of promoting the production of potash and similar alkalis. For years, by paying generous premiums for American potash the society gave some color to its claim to responsibility for the establishment of potash manufacture in the colonies. The best treatises on potash were two published in London, one by W. M. B. Lewis and the other by Robert Dossie, one of the leaders of the Society of Arts. Both of them gave precise descriptions of the methods of production and suggested chemical tests to determine alkalinity. Both were primarily concerned with the American production of potash. The New York Society of Arts also published directions on production and paid out premiums of its own. In 1766, a pamphlet published in Boston described the process for manufacturing pearl ash. The newspapers were full of efforts to promote this manufacture and full of optimism. The *Virginia Gazette* reported that in 1772 the Northern colonies alone exported potash to the value of £200,000 sterling. There is no evidence that the Americans contributed to the knowledge of the chemistry involved in manufacturing and testing potash but the knowledge available was placed at their disposal and used by them to advantage.

Since the improvement of agriculture and manufactures was promoted primarily by the merchant element in the colonies, it was to be expected that specifically commercial demands would also receive some attention from this quarter. Interest was demonstrated in the building of wharfs, the dredging of channels, and general harbor improvement in all of the port cities. At the same time, improvement in ship design was evolving in the colonial trade. More concerted effort, however, was lavished upon internal improvements than upon the elements of foreign trade. Moreover, it was the merchant class — rather than the West which has been traditionally associated with this demand — that was most active in press agitation, legislative lobbying, and the formation of organizations to complete specific improvements. Roads, bridges, and river improvement were all involved, but the most striking attempt to apply science and to use men of science was the proposed construction of canals.

Although there was no canal in any of the colonies, the Americans were kept well informed of the building of many British and continental canals to answer needs which could not have seemed so imperious as their own. After 1765, projects were set on foot in several of the colonies to provide canals where they seemed urgently needed. In North Carolina, an act of assembly provided for opening subscriptions to build a canal that would connect Beaufort and the Neuse River. In Virginia, both legislative and popular support was given to projects for cutting canals around the falls of the James and the Potomac and for connecting the James and York rivers by means of a canal. New England's terrain was less attractive to such projects although Connecticut did devote much attention to the improvement of the Connecticut River and some thought was given to a canal around the falls of the Merrimack River in New Hampshire. Nowhere was there so much enthusiasm for canal construction or so extensive an effort to apply science to the problem as in Philadelphia.

It was Thomas Gilpin, landed Quaker merchant, who began the campaign for a canal to connect the Delaware with the Chesapeake. Gilpin's broad interest in science resulted in papers on the wheat fly, the seventeen-year locust, a hydraulic wind pump, and the migration of herrings. He had twice visited Europe before he purchased a tract of land at the head of Chester Creek on the Maryland eastern shore. There, the utility of a canal of the sort he had seen in his travels became immediately apparent. A relatively short cut would connect the waters of the Delaware with the Chesapeake. Sometime in 1766 or 1767, he began a survey of a canal route from Head of Chester to Duck Creek on the Delaware and subsequently surveyed other routes with the help of some of his Maryland neighbors. In February 1769, Gilpin presented the canal project to the American Philosophical Society of which he was a member.

The strong merchant membership of the Philosophical Society was particularly noticeable in the two committees to which the canal plan was referred. To these men, the canal was no mere academic question. The threat of Baltimore to Philadelphia's control of the rich trade of the interior of Pennsylvania was becoming increasingly clear. The committee sought an intercolonial approach, arguing that the canal would benefit the Marylanders as much as the Philadelphians by the great increase in trade it would promote, but Baltimore merchants were not convinced, charging that the real aim of the whole project was to bring the trade of the Susquehanna to Philadelphia instead of Baltimore. Philadelphia merchants were so attracted to the proposed canal that they quickly subscribed £140 toward a survey of routes.

The initial survey was begun by a committee, four members of which had been appointed by the Philosophical Society and five by the merchants. The best results were assured by the inclusion of two capable surveyors, John Lukens and John Sellers. John Ewing and Joel Bailey were among those who served later in connection with surveys of other routes. Including Gilpin's Chester-Duck Creek survey, estimates were prepared on the cost of five possible routes by which the Delaware and Chesapeake could be united. In its report, the committee favored the building of a barge canal rather than one which could accommodate seagoing ships because the cost of the former was estimated to be only about one-third as great. It also preferred one of the more northerly routes: either the one from Elk River on the Chesapeake to Christiana Creek on the Delaware or that from Elk River to Red Lion Creek on the Delaware. Barge canals along these routes could be constructed at an estimated £19,396 10s and £14,426 respectively, sums not considered beyond the capabilities of the people of that region. At the same time, the committee recommended that the Susquehanna River be improved and that a road be opened between Peach Bottom on the Susquehanna River and the tide waters of Christiana Creek on the Delaware at an estimated cost of £1,500.

The American Philosophical Society accepted the work of the committee and published in its first volume of *Transactions* a summary of its recommendations illustrated by an excellent map showing the routes surveyed. The society labelled the surveys "public-spirited undertakings," having a "tendency to advance the landed and commercial interest of the British colonies in general, and particularly of those Middle Colonies with which they are more immediately connected." Many letters to the Philadelphia newspapers in 1769 and 1770 indicated that there was much support in Philadelphia and the back country for the fulfillment of the proposals but that the Marylanders were distinctly less enthusiastic. When the Pennsylvania Assembly took hold of the problem in 1771, no real hope prevailed that it would be handled in a way to benefit any province but Pennsylvania. A survey under the direction of David Rittenhouse and Samuel Rhoads was instituted for the purpose of finding practical and reasonable routes for navigation or land carriage between the Susquehanna, the Schuylkill, and the Lehigh rivers. One of the most important recommendations of this rough survey called for "Procuring from *Europe* such Assistance as the Importance of the Work may require." This had been Franklin's advice, too, in a letter to Samuel Rhoads, and after Rhoads and Rittenhouse completed the survey, they fully agreed that "Some Experience in works of this kind" was necessary before it would be possible to "estimate the Expence with any Degree of precision." Rittenhouse had great competence in science, but science and practical engineering were widely separated.

For the time, that was the end of the matter. The Susquehanna-Schuylkill Canal was not built until 1828, the Chesapeake-Delaware Canal was not completed until 1829. Throughout the colonies roads were improved, rivers cleared of obstructions, ferries established, and bridges built, but such things had been done for years. Like canals, great bridges also had to wait for future developments although Thomas Gilpin projected a bridge with a three-hundred-foot arch and John Jones of Indian River actually built a model of a suspension bridge designed to support an arch of four hundred feet.

Perhaps Christopher Colles, an immigrant of 1771, was the man best prepared by his knowledge of mathematics and science to apply learning to practical engineering. He called himself an "Engineer and Architect" in an early newspaper advertisement in which he offered to design mills and hydraulic engines at the same time that he proclaimed himself ready to instruct "young Gentlemen, at their Houses, in the different Branches of Mathematics and Natural Philosophy." In 1772, Colles gave one series of lectures on hydraulics in the Hall of the American Philosophical Society in Philadelphia and another on pneumatics. The following year, he offered a more general course in natural philosophy and mechanics from the second floor of the Pennsylvania State House. Colles also demonstrated before the American Philosophical Society a steam engine he had constructed for raising water at a Philadelphia distillery. Despite the fact that he was well considered by the Philadelphia scientists, he drifted to New York in 1774. There he succeeded in getting his plan adopted for a water system using hollow wooden logs as conduits. Except for the war, this ambitious project might have been completed at a time when piped water in America was limited to unusual local situations. In a part of Providence, for example, water was conveyed from an artesian well to the interior of a group of houses where it was available on tap.

The first medal awarded by an American organization for a practical invention came from the Virginia Society for Promoting Useful Knowledge which was founded in Williamsburg, Virginia, on May 13, 1773. It awarded a gold medal to John Hobday in recognition of his threshing machine, a "cheap and simple" device which was credited with a capacity for beating out 120 bushels of wheat in three days. The inventor claimed that it would cost only £15 to duplicate. The curious thing about this award was that the threshing machine was invented before the society was established; it may even have been instrumental in turning the attention of the founders of the society toward the promotion of such useful knowledge. John Page, the most active founder of the society, was among those who in 1772 had sought to get up a subscription to encourage John Hobday to distribute models of his machine through the country.

Indeed, the decision to establish the Virginian

Society for the Promotion of Usefull Knowledge was taken by a group of eight men, including John Page, on November 20, 1772. This was just one day after the original announcement of Hobday's machine was made in Purdie and Dixon's *Virginia Gazette*. The meeting was held in Williamsburg during the session of the legislature — the only time that it was possible to count on finding a large group of intelligent, informed men in any one place in Virginia. Inevitably, the meetings of the new society were thereafter tied to the sessions of the legislature. The establishment of this society came at a peculiarly frustrating time of the Revolutionary struggle, just after the opposition to the Townshend Acts had collapsed. Many Virginians proved ready to support the promotion of useful knowledge, particularly when it promised to benefit their sagging economy.

For a time, the Virginia Society commanded much attention. John Clayton, the now aged author of *Flora Virginica,* was elected president; John Page, vice-president; and the royal governor assumed the post of patron. Some one hundred Virginians accepted membership in an organization which, in a sense, was conceived "in humble imitation of the Royal Society" although from the beginning utilitarian objectives seemed paramount. One early advocate sought to use the writings of Francis Bacon as a guide, pointing to his opinion that the practical arts were based upon the sciences. He lamented the lack of cities in Virginia but felt that planters could, at least, "make Experiments in Agriculture, without Detriment to the usual Course of their Business."

Some papers, meteorological journals, and observations were collected during the ensuing two years when meetings were held with some regularity. After Clayton's death, John Page became president and most of the other offices were given to people associated with the College of William and Mary. A few corresponding members were elected, most of them from among the leadership of the American Philosophical Society. Thought, too, was given to the publication of a volume of scientific papers, but after the granting of the medal to John Hobday, very little of a positive nature was accomplished. With the approach of war, the society declined, never to be revived effectively again.

5

An American Original: The Irrepressible Franklin

I

Further Experiments and Observations in Electricity made in Philadelphia 1748

When Professor Clinton Rossiter of Cornell University sat down to write an essay on Benjamin Franklin, he asked himself, "Can any new thing be written by Benjamin Franklin?"[1] *His ensuing essay and the numerous studies since published both answer Professor Rossiter's question and attest to the many-sided interests and enormous charm of the Philadelphia seer. Not all of the recent studies of Franklin have been as good as that by Professor Rossiter. But paradoxically even a mediocre Franklin book is interesting, provided, that is, the book contains enough Franklin. He opens so many windows upon the colonial scene, and does so with such verve, clarity and wit, that few editors can resist the temptation to let Franklin do their work for them. Nor should they.*

Franklin's curiosity made him a scientist in

Benjamin Franklin, "Further Experiments and Observations in Electricity made in Philadelphia 1748," to Peter Collinson, April 29, 1749; original in the American Academy of Arts and Sciences. Recently reprinted in *The Papers of Benjamin Franklin,* ed. Leonard W. Labaree and Whitfield J. Bell, Jr. (New Haven: Yale University Press, 1961), III, 352–365.

[1] Clinton Rossiter, *Seedtime of the Republic* (New York, 1953), p. 281.

an age when the amateur could still contribute significantly in the field of physics. His mind uncluttered by formal scientific scholarship, Franklin devised his own experiments, invented his own terminology, and made original contributions to the study of electricity. Always, however, Franklin kept in mind the possible practical applications of his discoveries, and it is amusing to know that he planned a picnic in 1748 at which a turkey was to be killed by electrical shock, and roasted on an electrical jack on a fire started by an electrified bottle.

To Peter Collinson.

Sir

I now send you some Further Experiments and Observations in Electricity made in Philadelphia 1748. viz.

§1. There will be the same Explosion and Shock if the electrified Phial is held in one Hand by the Hook, and the Coating touched by the other; as when held by the Coating and touched at the Hook.

§2. To take the charged Phial safely by the Hook, and not at the same Time diminish it's Force, it must first be set down on an Electric per se.

§3. The Phial will be electrified as strongly, if held by the Hook, and the Coating apply'd to the Globe, or Tube, as when held by the Coating and the Hook apply'd.

§4. But the Direction of the Electrical Fire being different in Charging, will also be different in the Explosion. The Bottle charged thro' the Hook will be discharged thro' the Hook. The Bottle charged thro' the Coating, will be discharged thro' the Coating and not otherwise: For the Fire must come out the same way it went in.

§5. To prove this; Take two Bottles that were equally charg'd thro' the Hooks, one in each Hand; bring their Hooks near each other, and no Spark or Shock will follow; because each Hook is disposed to give Fire, and neither to receive it. Set one of the Bottles down on Glass, take it up by the Hook, and apply it's Coating to the Hook of the other; then there will be an Explosion and Shock, and both Bottles will be discharged.

§6. Vary the Experiment, by Charging two Vials equally, one thro' Hook, the other thro' the Coating: Hold that by the Coating which was charged thro' the Hook; and that by the Hook which was charged thro' the Coating. Apply the Hook of the first to the Coating of the other and there will be no Shock or Spark. Set that down on Glass, which you held by the Hook, take it up by the Coating, and bring the two Hooks together; a Spark and Shock will follow, and both Phials be discharged.

In this Experiment the Bottles are totally discharged, or the Equilibrium within them restored. The *Abounding* of Fire in one of the Hooks (or rather in the internal Surface of one Bottle) being exactly equal to the *Wanting* of the other: and therefore, as each Bottle has in itself the *Abounding* as well as the *Wanting*, the Wanting and Abounding must be equal in each Bottle. See §§8, 9, 10, 11. But if a Man holds in his Hands two Bottles, one fully electrified, the other not at all; and brings their Hooks together; he has but half a Shock, and the Bottles will both remain half electrified; the one being half discharged the other half charged.

7. Farther, Place two Vials equally charged on a Table at 5 or 6 Inches Distance; Let a Cork Ball, suspended by a Silk Thread, hang between them. If Vials were both charg'd thro' their Hooks, the Cork, when it has been attracted and repell'd by the one, will not be attracted but equally repell'd by the other. But if the Vials were charged, the one thro the Hook and the thro' the Coating,[1] the Ball when it is repell'd from one Hook will be as strongly attracted by the other, and play vigorously between them, till both Vials are nearly discharg'd.

8. When we use the Terms of *Charging* and *Discharging* the Phial, 'tis in Compliance with Custom, and for want of others more suitable: since We are of Opinion, that there is really no

[1] To charge a Bottle commodiously thro' the Coating, place it on a Glass Stand; form a Communication from the prime Conductor to the Coating, and another from the Hook to the Wall or Floor. When 'tis charg'd remove the latter Communication before you take hold of the Bottle; otherwise great Part of the Fire will escape by it.

more electrical Fire in the Phial, after what is called it's *Charging* than before; nor less after it's *Discharging;* (excepting only the small Spark that might be given to and taken from the Non-electric Matter, if separated from the Bottle, which Spark may not be equal to a 500th. Part of what is called the Explosion) For, if on the Explosion, the Electrical Fire came out of the Bottle by one Part, and did not enter in again by another; then, if a Man standing on Wax and holding the Bottle in one Hand, takes the Spark by touching the Wire Hook with the other, the Bottle being thereby *discharg'd,* the Man would be *charg'd;* or, whatever Fire was lost by one, would be found in the other; since there is no Way for it's Escape. But the Contrary is true.

9. Besides, the Vial will not suffer what is called a *Charging,* unless as much Fire can go out of it one Way as is thrown in by another. A Phial can not be charged, standing on Wax, or Glass, or hanging on the prime Conductor, unless a Communication be form'd between it's Coating and the Floor.

10. But suspend two or more Phials on the prime Conductor, one hanging to the Tail of the other, and a Wire from the last to the Floor: an equal Number of Turns of the Wheel shall charge them all equally; and every one as much as one alone would have been. What is driven out at the Tail of the first, serving to charge the second; what is driven out of the second charging the third, and so on. By this Means, a great Number of Bottles might be charged with the same Labour, and equally high with one alone, were it not that every Bottle receives new Fire and loses it's old with some Reluctance, or rather gives some small Resistance to the Charging, which in a Number of Bottles becomes more equal to the Charging Power, and so repels the Fire back again on the Globe, sooner than a single Bottle would do.

11. When a Bottle is charg'd in the common Way, it's inside and outside Surfaces stand ready, the one to give Fire by the Hook, the other to receive it by the Coating: The one is full and ready to throw out, the other empty and extreamly hungry: yet as the first will not *give out,* unless the other can at the same Instant *receive in;* so neither will the latter *receive in,* unless the first can at the same Instant *give out.* When both can be done at once, 'tis done with inconceivable Quickness and Violence.

12. So a strait Spring (tho' the Comparison does not agree in every Particular) when forcibly bent, must, to restore itself contract that Side, which in the bending was extended, and extend that which was contracted; if either of these two Operations behindered, the other can not be done. But the Spring is not said to be *charged* with Elasticity when bent, and *discharg'd* when unbent; it's Quantity of Elasticity is always the same.

13. Glass, in like Manner, has, within it's Substance always the same quantity of Electrical Fire; and that, a very great Quantity in Proportion to the Mass of Glass, as shall be shewn hereafter. §26.

14. This Quantity, proportioned to the Glass, it strongly and obstinately retains, and will neither have more nor less; tho it will suffer a Change to be made in it's Parts and Situation; that is, We may take away Part of it from one of the Sides, provided we throw an equal Quantity into the other.

15. Yet when the Situation of the Electrical Fire is thus altered in the Glass, when some has been taken from one Side, and some added to the other; it will not be at Rest or in its natural State, till 'tis restored to it's original Equality. And this Restitution can not be made thro the Substance of the Glass, but must be done by a Non-electric Communication formed without, from Surface to Surface.

16. Thus the whole Force of the Bottle and Power of giving a Shock, is in the Glass itself; the Non-electrics in Contact with the two Surfaces serving only to give and receive to and from the several Parts of the Glass; that is, to give on one Side, and take away from the other.

17. This was discovered here in the following Manner. Purposing to analize the electrified Bottle, in Order to find where it's Strength lay; we placed it on Glass, and drew out the Cork and Wire, which, for that Purpose, had been loosly put in. Then taking the Bottle in one Hand, and bringing a Finger of the other near it Mouth, a strong Spark came from the Water, and the Shock was as violent as if the Wire had remained in it; which shew'd that the Force did not lie in the Wire. Then to find if it resided in the Water, being crowded into and con-

densed in it, as confined by the Glass; which had been our former Opinion; we electrified the Bottle again, and placing it on Glass, drew out the Wire and Cork as before, then taking up the Bottle, we decanted all its Water into an empty Bottle, which likewise stood on Glass; and taking up that other Bottle, we expected, if the Force resided in the Water, to find a Shock from it; but there was none. We judged then, that it must either be lost in Decanting, or remain in the first Bottle. The latter we found to be true: For that Bottle on Trial gave the Shock, tho' filled up as it stood with fresh unelectrify'd Water from a Tea Pot. To find then whether Glass had this Property merely as Glass, or whether the Form contributed any Thing to it; we took a Pane of Sash Glass, and laying it on the Hand, placed a Plate of thin Lead on it's upper Surface; then electrified that Plate, and bringing a Finger to it, there was a Spark and Shock. We then took two Plates of Lead of equal Dimensions, but less than the Glass by two Inches every Way, and electrified the Glass between them, by electrifying the uppermost Lead; then separated the Glass from the Lead; in doing which, what little Fire might be in the Lead was taken out; and the Glass being touched in the electrified Part with a Finger, afforded only very small pricking Sparks, but a great Number of them might be taken from different Places. Then dextrously placing it again between the Plates of Lead, and completing the Circle between the two Surfaces, a violent Shock ensu'd. Which demonstrated the Power to reside in the Glass as *Glass;* and that the Non-electrics in Contact served only like the Armature of the Loadstone, to unite the Forces of the several Parts, and bring them at once to any Point desired. It being a Property of a Nonelectric, that the whole Body instantly receives or gives what Electrical Fire is given to or taken from any one of its Parts.

18. Upon this We made what we call'd an *Electrical Battery,* consisting of eleven Panes of large Sash Glass, arm'd with thin leaden Plates, pasted on each Side, placed vertically, and supported at two Inches Distance on Silk Cords; with Hooks of thick Leaden Wire one from each Side standing upright, distant from each other; and convenient Communications of Wire and Chain from the giving Side of one Pane to the receiving Side of the other; that so the whole might be charg'd together, and with the same Labour as one single Pane; and another Contrivance to bring the giving Sides, after charging in Contact with one long Wire, and the Receivers with another; which two long Wires would give the Force of all the Plates of Glass at once thro' the Body of any Animal forming the Circle with them. The Plates may also be discharg'd separately, or any Number together that is required. But this Machine is not much used, as not perfectly answering our Intention with Regard to the Ease of Charging, for the Reasons given §10. We made also, of large Glass Panes, *Magical Pictures,* and self moving animated Wheels, presently to be described.

19. I perceive by the ingenious Mr. Watson's last Book, lately received, that Dr. Bevis had used Panes of Glass to give a Shock before us; tho' till that Book came to Hand, I thought to have communicated it to you as a Novelty. The Excuse for mentioning it here, is, that we try'd the Experiment differently, drew different Consequences from it (for Mr. Watson still seems to think the Fire accumulated on the Non-electric that is in Contact with the Glass pag. 72) and, as far as we hitherto know, have carry'd it further.

20. The Magical Picture is made thus. Having a large Mezzotinto with a Frame and Glass (Suppose of the King, God preserve him) take out the Print, and cut a Pannel out of it, near two Inches all round distant from the Frame; if the Cut is thro' the Picture, tis not the Worse. With thin Paste or Gum Water, fix the Border, that is cut off, on the inside of the Glass, pressing it smoothe and close; then fill up the Vacancy by Gilding the Glass well with Leaf Gold or Brass; gild likewise the inner Edge of the Back of the Frame all round except the Top Part, and form a Communication between that Gilding and the Gilding behind the Glass: then put in the Board, and that side is finished. Turn up the Glass, and gild the foreside exactly over the Back Gilding; and when this is dry, cover it by pasting on the Pannel of the Picture that had been cut out, observing to bring the corresponding Parts of the Border and Picture together; by which the Picture will appear of a Piece as at first, only Part is behind the Glass

and Part before. Hold the Picture horizontally by the Top, and place a little moveable gilt Crown on the Kings Head. If now the Picture be moderately electrified, and another Person take hold of the Frame with one Hand, so that his Fingers touch it's inside Gilding, and with the other Hand endeavour to take off the Crown, he will receive a terrible Blow and fail in the Attempt. If the Picture were highly charg'd, the Consequence might perhaps be as fatal as that of High Treason: For when the Spark is taken thro' a Quire of Paper laid on the Picture, by Means of a Wire Communication, it makes a fair Hole thro' every Sheet; that is thro' 48 Leaves (tho' a Quire of Paper is thought good Armour against the Push of a Sword, or even against a Pistol Bullet) and the Crack is exceeding loud. The Operator, who, to prevent its falling, holds the Picture by the upper End, where the inside of the Frame is not gilt, feels Nothing of the Shock, and may touch the Crown without Danger, which he pretends is a Test of his Loyalty. If a Ring of Persons take a Shock among them the Experiment is called the *Conspiracy*.

21. On the Principle in §7. That the Hooks of Bottles, differently charged, will attract and repel differently, is made an electrical Wheel, that turns with considerable Strength. A small upright Shaft of Wood passes at right Angles thro' a thin round Board of about a Foot Diameter, and turns on a sharp Point of Iron, fixt in the lower End, while a strong Wire in the upper End, passing thro' a small Hole in a thin Brass Plate, keeps the Shaft truly vertical. About 30 Radii of equal Length made of Sash Glass, cut in narrow Strips, issue Horizontally from the Circumference of the Board; the Ends most distant from the Center being about 4 Inches apart. On the End of every one, a Brass Thimble is fixt. If now the Wire of a Bottle, electrified in the Common Way, be brought near the Circumference of this Wheel, it will attract the nearest Thimble, and so put the Wheel in Motion: That Thimble, in passing by, receives a Spark, and thereby being electrified is repell'd and so driven forwards, while a second, being attracted, approaches the Wire, receives a Spark and is driven after the first; and so on till the Wheel has gone once round, when the Thimbles, before Electrified, approaching the Wire, instead of being attracted, as they were at first, are repell'd; and the Motion presently ceases. But if another Bottle, which had been charg'd thro' the Coating be placed near the same Wheel, it's Wire will attract the Thimbles repell'd by the first, and thereby doubles the Force that carries the Wheel round; and not only, taking out the Fire that had been communicated to the Thimbles by the first Bottle, but even robbing them of their natural Quantity, instead of being repell'd when they come again towards the first Bottle, they are more strongly attracted: so that the Wheel mends its Pace till it goes with great Rapidity, 12 or 15 Rounds in a Minute; and with such Strength, as that the Weight of 100 Spanish Dollars, with which we once loaded it, did not seem in the least to retard it's Motion. This is called an *Electrical Jack;* and if a large Fowl were spitted on the upright Shaft, it would be carried round before a Fire with a Motion fit for Roasting.

22. But this Wheel, like those driven by Wind, Water or Weights, moves by a foreign Force, viz. that of the Bottles. The *Selfmoving Wheel,* tho constructed on the same Principles, appears more surprizing. 'Tis made of a thin round Plate of Window Glass, 17 Inches Diameter, well gilt on both Sides, all but two Inches next the Edge. Two small Hemispheres of Wood are then fixt with Cement to the Middle of the upper and under Sides, centrally opposite, and in each of them a thick strong Wire 8 or 10 Inches long, which together make the Axis of the Wheel. It turns horizontally on a Point at the lower End of it's Axis which rests on a Bit of Brass, cemented within a Glass Salt-Seller. The upper End of it's Axis passes thro' a Hole in a thin Brass Plate, cemented to a long strong Piece of Glass, which keeps it 6 or 8 Inches Distant from any Non-electric, and has a small Ball of Wax or Metal on its Top to keep in the Fire. In a Circle on the Table, which supports the Wheel, are fixt 12 small Pillars of Glass, at about 4 Inches Distance, with a Thimble on the Top of each. On the Edge of the Wheel is a small leaden Bullet, communicating by a Wire with the Gilding of the upper Surface of the Wheel: and about 6 Inches from it, is another Bullet, communicating in like Manner with the under Surface. When the Wheel is to be charg'd by the upper Surface, a Communication

must be made from the under Surface to the Table. When it is well chargd it begins to move; the Bullet nearest to a Pillar, moving towards the Thimble on that Pillar; and passing by, electrifies it, and then pushes itself from it: The succeeding Bullet, which communicates with the other Surface of the Glass, more strongly attracting that Thimble, on Account of it's being before electrified by the other Bullet: and thus the Wheel increases it's Motion, till it comes to such a Height, as that the Resistance of the Air regulates it. It will go half an Hour, and make, one Minute with another, 20 Turns in a Minute; which is 600 Turns in the whole: The Bullet of the upper Surface giving in each Turn 12 Sparks to the Thimbles, which makes 7200 Sparks, and the Bullet of the under Surface receiving as many from the Thimbles: these Bullets moving in the Time, near 2500 Feet. The Thimbles are well fixt, and in so exact a Circle, that the Bullets may pass within a very small Distance of each of them. If instead of 2 Bullets, you put 8, 4 communicating with the upper Surface, and four with the under Surface, placed alternately; which 8, at about 6 Inches Distance completes the Circumference; the Force and Swiftness will be greatly increased; the Wheel making 50 Turns in a Minute; but then it will not go so long. These Wheels may perhaps be apply'd to the Ringing of Chimes and Moving Orreries.

23. A small Wire bent circularly, with a loop at each End; Let one End rest against the under Surface of the Wheel, and bring the other End near the upper Surface, it will give a terrible Crack; The Force will be discharg'd, and the Wheel will stop.

24. Every Spark drawn in that Manner from the Surface of the Wheel, makes a round Hole in the Gilding, tearing off a Part of it in coming out; which shews that the Fire is not accumulated on the Gilding, but is in the Glass itself.

25. The Gilding being varnished over with Turpentine Varnish; the Varnish, tho' dry and hard, is burnt by the Spark drawn thro' it, gives a strong Smell and visible Smoke. And when the Spark is drawn thro' Paper, all round the Hole made by it, the Paper will be blackt by the Smoke, which Sometimes penetrates several of the Leaves. Parts of the Gilding, torn off, are also found forcibly driven into the Hole made in the paper by the Stroke.

26. 'Tis amazing to observe in how small a Portion of Glass a great Electrical Force may lie. A thin Glass Bubble about an Inch Diameter, weighing only six Grains, being half filled with Water, partly gilt on the outside, and furnished with a Wire Hook, gives when electrified, as great a Shock as a Man is willing to bear. As the Glass is thickest near the Orifice, I suppose the lower half, which being gilt, was electrified, and gave the Shock, did not exceed two Grains; for it appeared, when broke, much thinner than the upper half. If one of these thin Bottles be electrified by the Coating, and the Spark taken out thro the Gilding, it will break the Glass inwards, at the same Time that it breaks the Gilding outwards.

27. And allowing, for the Reasons before given §§8, 9, 10, that there is no more Electrical Fire in a Bottle after Charging than before, how great must the Quantity be in this small Portion of Glass! It seems as if it were of its very Substance and Essence. Perhaps if that due Quantity of Electrical Fire, so obstinately retain'd by Glass, could be separated from it, it would no longer be Glass, it might loose it's Transparency, or its Fragility, or Elasticity. Experiments may possibly be invented hereafter to discover this.

28. We are surprized at the Account given in Mr. Watson's Book, of a Shock communicated thro' a great Space of dry Ground, and suspect some metalline Quality in the Gravel of that Ground: having found, that simple dry Earth ramm'd in a Glass Tube open at both Ends, and a Wire Hook inserted in the Earth at each End; the Earth and Wires making a Part of a Circle, would not conduct the least perceptible Shock. And indeed when one Wire was electrified, the other hardly shew'd any Signs of it's being in Connexion with it. Even a thoroughly wet Packthread sometimes fails of conducting a Shock, tho' it otherwise conducts Electricity very well. A dry Cake of Ice, or an Iceicle, held between two Persons in a Circle, likewise prevents the Shock, which one would not expect, as Water conducts it so perfectly well. Gilding on a new Book, tho' at first it conducts the Shock extreamly well; yet fails after 10 or a Dozen Experiments; tho' it appears

otherwise in all Respects the same; which we can not account for.

29. There is one Experiment more, which surprizes us, and is hitherto not satisfactorily accounted for. It is this. Place an Iron Shot on a Glass Stand, and let a damp Cork Ball, suspended by a Silk Thread hang in Contact with the Shot. Take a Bottle in each Hand, one that is electrified thro' the Hook, the other thro' the Coating. Apply the *giving* Wire to the Shot, which will electrify it positively, and the Cork shall be repell'd. Then apply the *requiring* Wire, which will take out the Spark given by the other, when the Cork will return to the Shot. Apply the same again, and take out another Spark, so will the Shot be electrified negatively, and the Cork in that Case shall be repell'd equally as before. Then apply the giving Wire, and give to the Shot the Spark it wanted, so will the Cork return: Give it another, which will be an Addition to it's natural Quantity, so will the Cork be repell'd again; And so may the Experiment be repeated, as long as there is any Charge remaining in the Bottles; Which shews that Bodies, having less than the common Quantity of Electricity, repel each other, as well as those that have more.

Chagrin'd a little that We have hitherto been able to discover Nothing in this Way of Use to Mankind, and the hot Weather coming on, when Electrical Experiments are not so agreable; 'tis proposed to put an End to them for this Season somewhat humorously in a Party of Pleasure on the Banks of SchuylKill, (where Spirits are at the same Time to be fired by a Spark sent from Side to Side thro' the River).[2] A Turky is to be killed for our Dinners by the Electrical Shock; and roasted by the electrical Jack, before a Fire kindled by the Electrified Bottle; when the Healths of all the famous Electricians in England, France and Germany, are to be drank in Electrified Bumpers,[3] under the Discharge of Guns from the Electrical Battery.

To Peter Collinson Esqr. F.R.S. London

[2] This was since done.

[3] An electrified Bumper is a small thin Glass Tumbler, near filled with Wine and electrified. This when brought to the Lips, gives a Shock; if the Party be close shaved, and does not breathe on the Liquor.

II

Old Mistresses Apologue

Among Franklin's many virtues was his ability to laugh and make others share his laughter. He knew how to blend wit and wisdom acceptably as have few other public men in America, before or since. His "Old Mistresses Apologue" has enjoyed a checkered career: it was never printed in the nineteenth century — one highly respectable historian thought it "too indecent" for general consumption. Only in the twentieth century has public taste become sufficiently sophisticated to read Franklin's pithy advice on affaires de coeur *with more amusement than shock.*

My dear Friend, June 25, 1745

I know of no Medicine fit to diminish the violent natural Inclinations you mention; and if I did, I think I should not communicate it to you. Marriage is the proper Remedy. It is the most natural State of Man, and therefore the State in which you are most likely to find solid Happiness. Your Reasons against entring into it at present, appear to me not well-founded. The circumstantial Advantages you have in View by postponing it, are not only uncertain, but they are small in comparison with that of the Thing itself, the being *married and settled.* It is the Man and Woman united that make the compleat human being. Separate, she wants his Force of Body and Strength of Reason; he, her Softness, Sensibility and acute Discernment. Together they are more likely to succeed in the World. A single Man has not nearly the Value he would have in that State of Union. He is an incomplete Animal. He resembles the odd Half of a Pair of Scissars. If you get a prudent healthy Wife, your Industry in your Profession, with her good Oeconomy, will be a Fortune sufficient.

Benjamin Franklin, "Old Mistresses Apologue," June 25, 1745; copy in Library of Congress; recently reprinted in *Franklin Papers,* ed. Labaree and Bell, III, 30–31.

But if you will not take this Counsel, and persist in thinking a Commerce with the Sex inevitable, then I repeat my former Advice, that in all your Amours you should *prefer old Women to young ones.* You call this a Paradox, and demand my Reasons. They are these:

1. Because as they have more Knowledge of the World and their Minds are better stor'd with Observations, their Conversation is more improving and more lastingly agreeable.

2. Because when Women cease to be handsome, they study to be good. To maintain their Influence over Men, they supply the Diminution of Beauty by an Augmentation of Utility. They learn to do a 1000 Services small and great, and are the most tender and useful of all Friends when you are sick. Thus they continue amiable. And hence there is hardly such a thing to be found as an old Woman who is not a good Woman.

3. Because there is no hazard of Children, which irregularly produc'd may be attended with much Inconvenience.

4. Because thro' more Experience, they are more prudent and discreet in conducting an Intrigue to prevent Suspicion. The Commerce with them is therefore safer with regard to your Reputation. And with regard to theirs, if the Affair should happen to be known, considerate People might be rather inclin'd to excuse an old Woman who would kindly take care of a young Man, form his Manners by her good Counsels, and prevent his ruining his Health and Fortune among mercenary Prostitutes.

5. Because in every Animal that walks upright, the Deficiency of the Fluids that fill the Muscles appears first in the highest Part: The Face first grows lank and wrinkled; then the Neck; then the Breast and Arms; the lower Parts continuing to the last as plump as ever: So that covering all above with a Basket, and [1. viewing, 2. regarding] only what is below the Girdle, it is impossible of two Women to know an old from a young one. And as in the dark all Cats are grey, the Pleasure of corporal Enjoyment with an old Woman is at least equal, and frequently superior. every Knack being by Practice capable of Improvement.

6. Because the Sin is less. The debauching a Virgin may be her Ruin, and make her for Life unhappy.

7. Because the Compunction is less. The having made a young Girl *miserable* may give you frequent bitter Reflections; none of which can attend the making of an old Woman *happy*.

8[.thly and Lastly] They are *so grateful!!* Thus much for my Paradox. But still I advise you to marry directly; being sincerely
Your affectionate Friend.

III

On Humbling Our Rebellious Vassals

Franklin's wit could be no less devastating when directed at political affairs than when concerned with personal morality or broad social issues (such as The Speech of Polly Baker*). His letters to the press were frequently exercises in biting satire; his* Edict by the King of Prussia *was a magnificent parody of George III's claim to arbitrary rule over the American colonies. The selection which follows is another example of Franklin's humorous acuity and his readiness to ridicule a strong political adversary with a wonderfully earthy turn of phrase.*

To the Printer of the Public Advertiser.

SIR,

Permit me, thro' the Channel of your paper, to convey to the Premier, by him to be laid before his Mercenaries, our Constituents, my own Opinion, and that of many of my Brethren, Freeholders of this imperial Kingdom of the most feasible Method of humbling our rebellious Vassals of North America. As we have declared by our Representatives that we are the supreme Lords of their Persons and Property, and their occupying our Territory at

---

Benjamin Franklin, "On Humbling Our Rebellious Vassals," from *The Public Advertiser,* May 21, 1774; reprinted in *Franklin's Letters to the Press, 1758–1775,* ed. Verner W. Crane (Chapel Hill: University of North Carolina Press, for the Institute of Early American Culture, 1950), pp. 262–264.

such a remote Distance without a proper Controul from us, except at a very great Expence, encourages a mutinous Disposition, and may, if not timely prevented, dispose them in perhaps less than a Century to deny our Authority, slip their necks out of the Collar, and from being Slaves set up for Masters, more especially when it is considered that they are a robust, hardy people, encourage early Marriages, and their Women being amazingly prolific, they must of consequence in 100 years be very numerous, and of course be able to set us at Defiance. Effectually to prevent which, as we have an undoubted Right to do, it is humbly proposed, and we do hereby give it as Part of our Instructions to our Representatives, that a Bill be brought in and passed, and Orders immediately transmitted to G--l G--e, our Commander in Chief in North America, in consequence of it, that all the Males there be c-st-ed. He may make a Progress thro' the several Towns of North America at the Head of five Battalions, which we hear our experienced Generals, who have been consulted, think sufficient to subdue America if they were in open Rebellion; for who can resist the intrepid Sons of Britain, the Terror of France and Spain, and the Conquerors of America in Germany. Let a Company of Sowgelders, consisting of 100 Men, accompany the Army, On their Arrival at any Town or Village, let Orders be given that on the blowing of the Horn all the Males be assembled in the Market Place. If the Corps are Men of Skill and Ability in their Profession, they will make great Dispatch, and retard but very little the Progress of the Army. There may be a Clause in the Bill to be left at the Discretion of the General, whose Powers ought to be very extensive, that the most notorious Offenders, such as Hancock, Adams, &c. who have been the Ringleaders in the Rebellion of our Servants, should be shaved quite close. But that none of the Offenders may escape in the Town of Boston, let all the Males there suffer the latter Operation, as it will be conformable to the modern Maxim that is now generally adopted by our worthy Constituents, that it is better that ten innocent Persons should suffer than that one guilty should escape. It is true, Blood will be shed, but probably not many Lives lost. Bleeding to a certain Degree is salutary. The English, whose Humanity is celebrated by all the World, but particularly by themselves, do not desire the Death of the Delinquent, but his Reformation. The Advantages arising from this Scheme being carried into Execution are obvious. In the Course of fifty years it is probable we shall not have one rebellious Subject in North America. This will be laying the Axe to the Root of the Tree. In the mean time a considerable Expence may be saved to the Managers of the Opera, and our Nobility and Gentry be entertained at a cheaper Rate by the fine voices of our own C-st-i, and the Specie remain in the Kingdom, which now, to an enormous Amount, is carried every Year to Italy. It might likewise be of Service to our Levant Trade, as we could supply the Grand Signor's Seraglio, and the Harams of the Grandees of the Turkish Dominions with Cargoes of Eunuchs, as also with handsome Women, for which America is as famous as Circassia. I could enumerate many other Advantages. I shall mention but one: It would effectually put a Stop to the Emigrations from this Country now grown so very fashionable.

No Doubt you will esteem it expedient that this useful Project shall have an early Insertion, that no Time may be lost in carrying it into Execution.

I am, Mr. Printer,
(For myself and in Behalf of a Number of independent Freeholders of Great Britain)
Your humble Servant,
A FREEHOLDER OF OLD SARUM.

Suggested Further Reading:

For all the many recent monographs dealing with facets of colonial society there have been surprisingly few efforts at a general social history of early America. Louis B. Wright's *Cultural Life of the American Colonies, 1607–1763** remains the only recent survey, but Max Savelle's *Seeds of Liberty* (1948) and Clinton Rossiter's brilliant *Seedtime of the Republic* (1953) are very helpful on colonial thought. Michael Kraus, *The Atlantic Civilization:*

Eighteenth-Century Origins (1949) is excellent on Anglo-American social and intellectual connections; but see also William L. Sachse, *The Colonial American in Britain* (1956).

The best studies of labor in colonial America are Marcus W. Jernegan, *Laboring and Dependent Classes in Colonial America, 1607–1783* (1931), and Richard B. Morris, *Government and Labor in Early America* (1946); S. H. Sutherland, *Population Distribution in Colonial America* (1936) is highly illuminating.

Carl Bridenbaugh has virtually monopolized colonial urban history: cited previously are *Cities in the Wilderness* (1938, rev. ed., 1955), *Cities in Revolt** (1955), with Jessica Bridenbaugh, *Rebels and Gentlemen** (1942), *Seat of Empire: The Political Role of Eighteenth–Century Williamsburg** (1950); also related are his *Myths and Realities: Societies of the Colonial South** (1952), and *The Colonial Craftsman** (1950).

Many new studies attest the importance of the bookish culture of colonial America, but one early monograph still deserves to be listed: Thomas Goddard Wright's *Literary Culture in Early New England* (1920). There are several useful books dealing with colonial libraries, the best being C. Seymour Thompson, *Evolution of the American Public Library, 1653–1876* (1952), and Louis Shores, *Origins of the American College Library*. Two articles of particular merit indicate the common denominators in colonial reading: Joseph T. Wheeler, "Booksellers and Circulating Libraries in Colonial Maryland," *Maryland Historical Magazine*, XXXIV (1939), 111–137, and Caroline Robbins, "Library of Liberty — Assembled for Harvard College by Thomas Hollis of Lincoln's Inn," *Harvard Library Bulletin*, V (1951), 5–23, 181–196. The quickest way to check colonial publishing tastes is to examine Charles Evans, *American Bibliography. . . .* (1903–34) which lists, chronologically, all books published in the colonial period.

No study of colonial science should begin without Whitfield J. Bell's *Early American Science: Needs and Opportunities for Study* (1955). Recent and outstanding are: I. Bernard Cohen, *Some Early Tools of American Science* (1950), Harry Woolf, *The Transit of Venus: A Study of Eighteenth–Century Science* (1959), I. Bernard Cohen, *Benjamin Franklin's Experiments* (1941), and *Franklin and Newton* (1956), John B. Blake, *Public Health in the Town of Boston, 1630–1822* (1959), Ernest Earnest, *John and William Bartram* (1940), Richard H. Shryock and Otho T. Beall, Jr., *Cotton Mather: First Significant Figure in American Medicine* (1954), and Brooke Hindle, *David Rittenhouse* (1964).

PART FIVE

Insurrection and Division

While the spirit of separatism was a commonplace of early American history, it was not until the 1770's that any strong urge to break away from the mother country manifested itself. One reason was inter-colonial rivalries. The greater part of the colonial period was marked by a fierce sense of local loyalties, by distrust and even enmity between colonial neighbors. Many Marylanders, for instance, not only distrusted Virginians, but entertained dark suspicions of each other as well.

The causes of such internal divisions — and the open insurrections they sometimes produced — varied from colony to colony. Frequently these uprisings stemmed from economic and political frustration: as the early settlers grew more prosperous and powerful, they tended to dominate the political life of their province barring newcomers from an equitable voice in the affairs of government. The fact that colonial history was one of continual change, with constant infusions of immigrants and continuous expansion of the economy, made social, class, and political friction inevitable. The wonder is not that there was a Bacon's Rebellion in Virginia, a Leisler Rebellion in New York, persecution of Roman Catholics in Maryland, and Regulator movements in the Carolinas, but that there were not many more such upheavals.

1

Bacon's Rebellion, 1676

The writings of NATHANIEL BACON *and* GOVERNOR BERKELEY *which follow represent opposing and partisan views of the leading characters in the first popular uprising in the English colonies. Bacon's flair for a well-turned phrase is readily apparent; equally so is his sense of outrage with "the mysterious wiles of a powerful cabal," "juggling parasites" who would sooner protect the "darling Indians" than honest settlers. Bacon's "Declaration" was in fact an indictment of Berkeley's onerous and unjust taxes and maladministration. Berkeley's response is that of a patient but abused man, confident of his authority and the correctness of his actions. "Kings have long arms either to reward or punish," he wrote — a prophetic utterance in this instance.*

I

MANIFESTO CONCERNING THE PRESENT TROUBLES IN VIRGINIA

If virtue be a sin, if piety be guilt, all the principles of morality, goodness and justice be perverted, we must confess that those who are now called rebels may be in danger of those high imputations. Those loud and several bulls would affright innocents and render the defence of our brethren and the inquiry into our sad and heavy oppressions, treason. But if there be, as sure there is, a just God to appeal to; if religion and justice be a sanctuary here; if to plead the cause of the oppressed; if sincerely to aim at his Majesty's honour and the public good without any reservation or by interest; if to stand in the gap after so much blood of our dear brethren bought and sold; if after the loss of a great part of his Majesty's colony deserted and dispeopled, freely with our lives and estates to endeavour to save the remainders be treason; God Almighty judge and let guilty die. But since we cannot in our hearts find one single spot of rebellion or treason, or that we have in any manner aimed at the subverting the settled government or attempting of the person of any either magistrate or private man, notwithstanding the several reproaches and threats of some who for sinister ends were disaffected to us and censured our innocent and honest designs, and since all people in all places where we have yet been can attest our civil, quiet, peaceable behaviour far different from that of rebellion and tumultuous persons, let truth be bold and all the world know the real foundations of pretended guilt. We appeal to the country itself what and of what nature their oppressions have been, or by what cabal and mystery the designs of many of those whom we call great men have been transacted and carried on; but let us trace these men in authority and favour to whose hands the dispensation of the country's wealth has been committed. Let us observe the sudden rise of their estates composed with the quality in which they first entered this country, or the reputation they have held here amongst wise and discerning men. And let us see whether their extractions and education have not been vile, and by what pretence of learning and virtue they could so soon come into employments of so great trust and consequence. Let us consider their sudden advancement and let us also consider whether any public work for our safety and defence or for the advancement and propagation of trade, liberal arts, or sciences is here extant in any way adequate to our vast charge. Now let us compare these things together and see what sponges have sucked up the public treasure, and whether it has not been

Nathaniel Bacon, "Manifesto Concerning the Present Troubles in Virginia," and "Declaration of the People," reprinted in *The Virginia Magazine of History and Biography*, I (1894), 55–61. William Berkeley, "Declaration and Remonstrance," May 29, 1676, reprinted in Edward D. Neill, *Virginia Carolarum: The Colony of Virginia under the Rule of Charles the First and Second,* A.D. *1625–*A.D. *1685* (Albany, 1886), pp. 351–357.

privately contrived away by unworthy favourites and juggling parasites whose tottering fortunes have been repaired and supported at the public charge. Now if it be so, judge what greater guilt can be than to offer to pry into these and to unriddle the mysterious wiles of a powerful cabal; let all people judge what can be of more dangerous import than to suspect the so long safe proceedings of some of our grandees, and whether people may with safety open their eyes in so nice a concern.

Another main article of our guilt is our open and manifest aversion of all, not only the foreign but the protected and darling Indians. This, we are informed, is rebellion of a deep dye for that both the governor and council are by Colonel Cole's assertion bound to defend the queen and the Appamatocks with their blood. Now, whereas we do declare and can prove that they have been for these many years enemies to the king and country, robbers and thieves and invaders of his Majesty's right and our interest and estates, but yet have by persons in authority been defended and protected even against his Majesty's loyal subjects, and that in so high a nature that even the complaints and oaths of his Majesty's most loyal subjects in a lawful manner proffered by them against those barbarous outlaws, have been by the right honourable governor rejected and the delinquents from his presence dismissed, not only with pardon and indemnity, but with all encouragement and favour; their firearms so destructful to us and by our laws prohibited, commanded to be restored them, and open declaration before witness made that they must have ammunition, although directly contrary to our law. Now what greater guilt can be than to oppose and endeavour the destruction of these honest, quiet neighbours of ours?

Another main article of our guilt is our design not only to ruin and extirpate all Indians in general, but all manner of trade and commerce with them. Judge who can be innocent that strike at this tender eye of interest: since the right honourable the governor hath been pleased by his commission to warrant this trade, who dare oppose it, or opposing it can be innocent? Although plantations be deserted, the blood of our dear brethren spilled; on all sides our complaints; continually murder upon murder renewed upon us; who may or dare think of the general subversion of all manner of trade and commerce with our enemies who can or dare impeach any of . . . traders at the heads of the rivers, if contrary to the wholesome provision made by laws for the country's safety; they dare continue their illegal practises and dare asperse the right honourable governor's wisdom and justice so highly to pretend to have his warrant to break that law which himself made; who dare say that these men at the heads of the rivers buy and sell our blood, and do still, notwithstanding the late act made to the contrary, admit Indians painted and continue to commerce; although these things can be proved, yet who dare be so guilty as to do it?

Another article of our guilt is to assert all those neighbour Indians as well as others, to be outlawed, wholly unqualified for the benefit and protection of the law, for that the law does reciprocally protect and punish, and that all people offending must either in person or estate make equivalent satisfaction or restitution, according to the manner and merit of the offences, debts, or trespasses. Now since the Indians cannot, according to the tenure and form of any law to us known, be prosecuted, seized, or complained against, their persons being with difficulty distinguished or known; their many nations' languages, and their subterfuges such as makes them incapable to make us restitution or satisfaction, would it not be very guilty to say they have been unjustly defended and protected these many years?

If it should be said that the very foundation of all these disasters, the grant of the beaver trade to the right honourable governor was illegal, and not grantable by any power here present as being a monopoly, were not this to deserve the name of rebel and traitor?

Judge, therefore, all wise and unprejudiced men who may or can faithfully or truly with an honest heart, attempt the country's good, their vindication, and liberty without the aspersion of traitor and rebel, since as so doing they must of necessity gall such tender and dear concerns. But to manifest sincerity and loyalty to the world, and how much we abhor those bitter names; may all the world know that we do unanimously desire to represent our sad and heavy grievances to his most sacred Majesty as our refuge and sanctuary, where we do well know that all our causes will be impartially heard and equal justice administered to all men.

II

The Declaration of the People

For having upon specious pretences of public works, raised unjust taxes upon the commonalty for the advancement of private favourites and other sinister ends, but no visible effects in any measure adequate.

For not having during the long time of his government in any measure advanced this hopeful colony, either by fortification, towns or trade.

For having abused and rendered contemptible the majesty of justice, of advancing to places of judicature scandalous and ignorant favourites.

For having wronged his Majesty's prerogative and interest by assuming the monopoly of the beaver trade.

By having in that unjust gain bartered and sold his Majesty's country and the lives of his loyal subjects to the barbarous heathen.

For having protected, favoured and emboldened the Indians against his Majesty's most loyal subjects, never contriving, requiring, or appointing any due or proper means of satisfaction for their many invasions, murders, and robberies committed upon us.

For having, when the army of the English was just upon the track of the Indians, which now in all places burn, spoil, and murder, and when we might with ease have destroyed them who then were in open hostility, for having expressly countermanded and sent back our army by passing his word for the peaceable demeanour of the said Indians, who immediately prosecuted their evil intentions, committing horrid murders and robberies in all places, being protected by the said engagement and word passed of him, the said Sir William Berkeley, having ruined and made desolate a great part of his Majesty's country, have now drawn themselves into such obscure and remote places and are by their successes so emboldened and confirmed, and by their confederacy so strengthened that the cries of blood are in all places, and the terror and consternation of the people so great, that they are now become not only a difficult, but a very formidable enemy who might with ease have been destroyed, etc. When upon the loud outcries of blood, the Assembly had with all care raised and framed an army for the prevention of future mischiefs and safeguard of his Majesty's colony.

For having with only the privacy of some few favourites, without acquainting the people, only by the alteration of a figure, forged a commission by we know not what hand, not only without but against the consent of the people, for raising and effecting of civil wars and distractions, which being happily and without bloodshed prevented.

For having the second time attempted the same thereby calling down our forces from the defence of the frontiers, and most weak exposed places, for the prevention of civil mischief and ruin amongst ourselves, whilst the barbarous enemy in all places did invade, murder, and spoil us, his Majesty's most faithful subjects.

Of these, the aforesaid articles, we accuse Sir William Berkeley, as guilty of each and every one of the same, and as one who has traitorously attempted, violated and injured his Majesty's interest here, by the loss of a great part of his colony, and many of his faithful and loyal subjects by him betrayed, and in a barbarous and shameful manner exposed to the incursions and murders of the heathen.

And we further declare these, the ensuing persons in this list, to have been his wicked, and pernicious counsellors, aiders and assisters against the commonalty in these our cruel commotions:

Sir Henry Chicherly, Knt.	Jos. Bridger
Col. Charles Wormley	Wm. Clabourne
Phil. Dalowell	Thos. Hawkins, Jr.
Robert Beverly	William Sherwood
Robert Lee	Jos. Page, Clerk
Thos. Ballard	Jo. Cliffe, Clerk
William Cole	Hubberd Farrell
Richard Whitacre	John West
Nicholas Spencer	Thos. Reade

Mathew Kemp

And we do further demand, that the said Sir William Berkeley, with all the persons in this list, be forthwith delivered up, or surrender themselves, within four days after the notice hereof, or otherwise we declare as followeth: that in whatsoever house, place, or ship any of the said persons shall reside, be hid, or protected, we do declare that the owners, masters, or inhabitants of the said places, to be confederates and traitors to the people, and the estates of them, as also of all the aforesaid persons, to be confiscated. This we, the commons of Virginia, do declare desiring a prime union amongst ourselves, that we may jointly, and with one accord defend ourselves against the common enemy. And let not the faults of the guilty be the reproach of the innocent, or the faults or crimes of the oppressors divide and separate us, who have suffered by their oppressions.

These are therefore in his Majesty's name, to command you forthwith to seize the persons above mentioned as traitors to the king and country, and them to bring to Middle Plantation, and there to secure them, till further order, and in case of opposition, if you want any other assistance, you are forthwith to demand it in the name of the people of all the counties of Virginia.

signed
NATH BACON, Gen'l.
By the Consent of the People.

III

DECLARATION AND REMONSTRANCE

The declaration and remonstrance of Sir William Berkeley, his most sacred Majesty's governor and captain-general of Virginia, shows: That about the year 1660 Colonel Mathews, the then governor died, and then in consideration of the service I had done the country in defending them from and destroying great numbers of the Indians without the loss of three men in all the time that war lasted, and in contemplation of the equal and uncorrupt justice I had distributed to all men, not only the Assembly, but the unanimous votes of all the country concurred to make me governor in a time when, if the rebels in England had prevailed, I had certainly died for accepting it. 'Twas, gentlemen, an unfortunate love showed to me, for to show myself grateful for this I was willing to accept of this government again, when by my gracious king's favour I might have had other places much more profitable and less toilsome than this hath been. Since that time that I returned into the country, I call the great God, judge of all things in heaven and earth, to witness that I do not know of anything relative to this country wherein I have acted unjustly, corruptly, or negligently, in distributing equal justice to all men, and taking all possible care to preserve their proprieties and defend them from their barbarous enemies.

But for all this, perhaps I have erred in things I know not of. If I have, I am so conscious of human frailty and my own defects that I will not only acknowledge them, but repent of and amend them, and not, like the rebel Bacon, persist in an error only because I have committed it; and tells me in divers of his letters that it is not for his honour to confess a fault, but I am of opinion that it is only for devils to be incorrigible, and men of principles like the worst of devils; and these he hath, if truth be reported to me of divers of his expressions of atheism, tending to take away all religion and laws.

And now I will state the question betwixt me as a governor and Mr. Bacon, and say that if any enemies should invade England, any counsellor, justice of peace, or other inferior officer might raise what forces they could to protect his Majesty's subjects. But I say again, if, after the king's knowledge of this invasion, any the greatest peer of England should raise forces against the king's prohibition, this would be now — and ever was in all ages and nations — accounted treason. Nay, I will go further, that though this peer was truly zealous for the preservation of his king and subjects, and had better and greater abilities than all the rest of his fellow-subjects to do his king and country service, yet if the king (though by false information) should suspect the contrary, it were treason in this noble peer to proceed after the king's prohibition: and for the truth of this I appeal to all the laws of England, and the laws and constitutions of all other nations in the world. And yet further, it is declared by this Parliament that the taking up arms for the king and Parliament is treason; for the event showed that whatever the pretence was to seduce ignorant and well-affected people, yet the end was ruinous both to king and people, as this will be if not prevented. I do therefore again declare that Bacon, proceeding against all laws of all nations modern and ancient, is rebel to his sacred Majesty and this country; nor will I insist upon the swearing of men to live and die together, which is treason by the very words of the law.

Now, my friends, I have lived thirty-four years amongst you, as uncorrupt and diligent as ever governor was; Bacon is a man of two years among you; his person and qualities unknown to most of you, and to all men else, by any virtuous action that ever I heard of. And that very action which he boasts of was sickly and foolishly, and, as I am informed, treacherously carried to the dishonour of the English nation. Yet in it he lost more men than I did in three years' war; and by the grace of God will put myself to the same dangers and troubles again when I have brought Bacon to acknowledge the laws are above him, and I doubt not but by God's assistance to have better success than Bacon hath had. The reason of my hopes are, that I will take counsel of wiser men than myself; but Mr. Bacon hath none about him but the lowest of the people.

Yet I must further enlarge, that I cannot without your help do anything in this but die in defence of my king, his laws, and subjects, which I will cheerfully do, though alone I do it; and considering my poor fortunes, I cannot leave my wife and friends a better legacy than by dying for my king and you; for his sacred Majesty will easily distinguish between Mr. Bacon's actions and mine, and kings have long arms either to reward or punish.

Now, after all this, if Mr. Bacon can show one precedent or example where such actings in any nation whatever was approved of, I will mediate with the king and you for a pardon and excuse for him; but I can show him a hundred examples where brave and great men have been put to death for gaining victories against the command of their superiors.

Lastly, my most assured friends, I would have preserved those Indians that I knew were hourly at our mercy, to have been our spies and intelligence, to find out our bloody enemies; but as soon as I had the least intelligence that they also were treacherous enemies, I gave out commissions to destroy them all, as the commissions themselves will speak it.

To conclude, I have done what was possible both to friend and enemy; have granted Mr. Bacon three pardons, which he hath scornfully rejected, supposing himself stronger to subvert than I and you to maintain the laws, by which only, and God's assisting grace and mercy, all men must hope for peace and safety. I will add no more, though much more is still remaining to justify me and condemn Mr. Bacon, but to desire that this declaration may be read in every county court in the country, and that a court be presently called to do it before the Assembly meet, that your approbation or dissatisfaction of this declaration may be known to all the country and the king's Council, to whose most revered judgments it is submitted.

Given the 29th day of May, a happy day in the 28th year of his most sacred Majesty's reign, Charles the second, who God grant long and prosperously to reign, and let all his good subjects say amen.

IV

Causes of the Rebellion

Troubles with the Indians occasioned the beginning of Bacon's Rebellion; but problems of political privilege, the questionable role of government officials in the lucrative Indian trade, and the sense of economic exploitation felt by many of Bacon's supporters also contributed to the instability of Virginia in the 1670's. Of less measurable significance, but also

---

Reprinted from Wilcomb E. Washburn, *The Governor and the Rebel: A History of Bacon's Rebellion* (Chapel Hill: University of North Carolina Press, for the Institute of Early American History and Culture, 1957), pp. 153–166. Some footnotes deleted by permission of the publisher.

of importance, was the personal conflict between Bacon and the royal governor.

Few historians would completely endorse earlier interpretations of the Rebellion which depicted it as either a class struggle or an anti-British democratic crusade. Indeed, WILCOMB E. WASHBURN *argues that earlier historians of the Rebellion have ignored or distorted its realities: Berkeley, he believes, was a just and widely admired Governor, while Bacon was a headstrong spoiled young man, rash, intemperate, given to demagoguery. It may be, however, that in seeking to redress the historical balance Dr. Washburn has overdrawn Berkeley's virtues and Bacon's irresponsibility.*

What was the "cause" of Bacon's Rebellion? What motivated the 400 foot and 120 horse who marched with Bacon into Jamestown on June 23, 1767? Romantic historians like to see the rebellion as "a revolt of the lower classes of whites against the aristocratic families who governed Virginia," as "the cause of the poor against the rich, of the humble folk against the grandees."[1]

Unfortunately such simple solutions of the event are simple only because of the one-sided moral and intellectual assumptions of their proponents. Actually, as Professor Craven has written, "no simple answer can be found for the complex problem of Bacon's Rebellion . . . but on one point agreement can be had: the trouble started in a dispute over Indian policy."[2] Craven's views on the complexity of Bacon's Rebellion mark a return to the views held of the event at the time. In the intervening period historians have tended to interpret the rebellion too readily as a forerunner of 1776.

Robert Beverley, writing when memories of the rebellion were still fresh in the minds of the people, gave much thought to the problem of its cause. He wrote:

> The Occasion of this Rebellion is not easie to be discover'd: But 'tis certain there were many Things that concurr'd towards it. For it cannot be imagined, that upon the Instigation of Two or Three Traders only, who aim'd at a Monopoly of the *Indian* Trade,[3] as some pretend to say, the whole Country would have fallen into so much Distraction; in which People did not only hazard their Necks by Rebellion: But endeavor'd to ruine a Governour, whom they all entirely loved, and had unanimously chosen; a Gentleman who had devoted his whole Life and Estate to the Service of the Country; and against whom in Thirty Five Years Experience, there had never been one single Complaint. Neither can it be supposed, that upon so slight Grounds, they would make Choice of a Leader they hardly knew, to oppose a Gentleman, that had been so long, and so deservedly the Darling of the People. So that in all Probability there was something else in the Wind, without which the Body of the Country had never been engaged in that Insurrection.[4]

What this "something else in the Wind" was, Beverley makes a brilliant attempt to answer. He cites the misfortunes suffered by the colony because of the low price of tobacco, the tyranny of the English merchants, the great taxes necessary to throw off the proprietary grants, the restraints on trade caused by the Navigation Acts, and the Indian disturbances. But more important, he relates Virginia's depressed condi-

[1] John Fiske, *Old Virginia and her Neighbours* (Boston, 1897), II, 104. Bernard Bailyn, in a paper entitled "Politics and Social Structure: Virginia in the Seventeenth Century" prepared for the Symposium on Seventeenth-Century Colonial History, Williamsburg, Virginia, April 8–12, 1957, makes a perceptive analysis of the class antagonisms existing at the time. He sees, on the one hand, the "numerically predominant ordinary planters" protesting against the "recently acquired superiority of the leading county families." On the other hand, Bailyn sees a parallel attack by "the dominant local leaders against the prerogatives recently acquired by the province elite, prerogatives linked to officialdom and centered in the Council." That these oppositions existed I have pointed out. That they express "deeper elements" than the more "immediate causes" of "race relations and settlement policy," as Bailyn believes, I deny.

[2] Wesley Frank Craven, *The Southern Colonies in the Seventeenth Century, 1607–1689* (Baton Rouge, 1949), pp. 360–361.

[3] This comment refers to Bacon and his friends.

[4] Robert Beverley, *The History and Present State of Virginia* [1705], ed. Louis B. Wright (Chapel Hill, 1947), p. 74 (Bk. I, chap. iv, sec. 92).

tion to the psychology of the planters and shows how this condition affected their attitude towards the Indians, Governor Berkeley, and the rebel Bacon. It was the Indian disturbances, he finds, which tipped the balance and caused men whose minds were "already full of Discontent" to imagine there was an easy way out by "venting all their Resentment against the poor *Indians*."

Beverley probably came as close to a successful interpretation of the rebellion as anyone since his time. His analysis is also superior to those made before his time. The men who fought in the rebellion were never able to give a satisfactory explanation of why the troubles arose. Philip Ludwell, for example, wrote Secretary of State Sir Joseph Williamson that the rebellion "has been of that Intricate unreasonable Texture that I think it a Taske to hard for me to State in all its Circumstances." Ludwell did not attempt to minimize the extent of the revolt. Just as Berkeley had astounded the commissioners with his report that of above 15,000 persons there were not 500 untainted in the rebellion, so Ludwell reported that the defection was "almost general." The gallant loyalist leader could explain the rebellion only in terms of

> the Lewd dispositions of some Persons of desperate Fortunes Lately Sprang upp amongst us which meeting with People of like Inclinations Easily seduced their willing mindes From their duty and Allegiance to their King, and Indeed from all feare or Respect of God or man Laying before them the Plunder of the best part of the Countrey and the Vaine hopes of takeing the Countrey wholley out of his Majesty's handes into their owne.[5]

Ludwell probably misjudged the causes of the rebellion because, unlike Beverley, the historian, he assumed that the leaders had thought out their plans and knew what they were after. Thus Ludwell commented on Bacon's pitiful Indian campaigns that "It is most Evident he never Intended anything more in it than a Covert under which to Act all his Villanies." If these rather vaguely defined evil aims had not been the rebels' "Cheife Motives," wrote Ludwell, "they had Certainly Understanding Enough to have ledd them a fairer way to presenting their Greivances than on their Swords points."

Richard Lee, one of the more dignified members of the council, was similarly unable to explain the rebellion. Lee suggested that the reason for the "zealous inclination of the multitude" to Bacon was their "hopes of levelling, otherwise all his specious pretences would not have persuaded them. . . ."[6] Lee thus drew a distinction between the reasons for the "zealous inclination" of the people to Bacon and the causes that led Bacon to start the rebellion in the first place. These are two different things, although historians frequently confuse them.

Others, both at the time and more recently, have concluded that Bacon's purpose was to detach Virginia from the Crown of England. The only evidence to support this view is the comment of the minister who attended Bacon at his death and a dialogue between Bacon and a man named John Goode which took place on September 2, 1676, when the rebel leader questioned the captured Goode about the report that two thousand soldiers were on their way to put down the rebellion. Bacon seems to have been trying to reassure himself that his rebels could defeat them even though outnumbered, but Goode matched every advantage with a disadvantage until Bacon found himself defending the thesis that Virginia could maintain its independence against the Crown itself. The discussion can hardly be taken as proof that Bacon was seriously aiming at the independence of the colony. The most that can be said is that he once speculated on the possibility. To Wesley Frank Craven, also, the dialogue "suggests the desperate graspings of a man who already sensed that his cause was lost, and is of interest primarily for Goode's clear statement of the arguments for Virginia's dependence." Craven also underlines Goode's warning to Bacon that " 'your followers do not think themselves en-

[5] Ludwell to Williamson, April 14, 1677, Colonial Office, Series I, Vol. 40, no. 45, in Public Record Office, London (hereafter cited as C. O. I/40, etc.).

[6] Postscript of Richard Lee to letter of Isaac Allerton to Thomas Ludwell, Aug. 4, 1676, in the Henry Coventry Papers at Longleat, estate of the Marquis of Bath (hereinafter cited as Longleat), LXXVII, fol. 161.

gaged against the King's authority, but merely against the Indians.'"

To Governor Berkeley the cause of the rebellion was to be found in the ungovernable will of Nathaniel Bacon rather than in the grievances of the people. In his letter of February 2, 1677, to Secretary of State Henry Coventry he bitterly remarked that in June 1676

> I was Exalted with pride that I had governed this Country fower and twenty yeares in peace and plenty and was most certaine that no pretence of a fault could be alleaged against me. Then did God to humble me and take away the pride of my hart and thoughts rayse this ungrounded (for any real Grevance) and unexpected rebellion against his most sacred Majesty the Country and me. . . .[7]

Berkeley had long prided himself on his justice. In March 1651 he had breathed defiance to the Parliamentary forces that were soon expected to arrive to take over the colony. In a speech to the assembly he urged the burgesses to support him in maintaining the King's government. He asked them

> what is it can be hoped for in a change, which we have not allready? Is it liberty? The sun looks not on a people more free than we are from all oppression. Is it wealth? Hundreds of examples shew us that Industry and Thrift in a short time may bring us to as high a degree of it, as the Country and our Conditions are yet capable of: Is it securety to enjoy this wealth when gotten? With out blushing I will speake it, I am confident theare lives not that person can accuse me of attempting the least act against any mans property. Is it peace? The Indians, God be blessed round about us are subdued; we can onely feare the *Londoners,* who would faine bring us to the same poverty, wherein the *Dutch* found and relieved us; would take away the liberty of our consciences, and tongues, and our right of giving and selling our goods to whom we please.[8]

[7] *William and Mary Quarterly,* 3d ser., 14 (July, 1957), 406.

[8] H. R. McIlwaine, *Journals of the House of Burgesses of Virginia, 1619–1658/59* (Richmond, 1915), p. 76; also in *Virginia Magazine,* I (1893), 77.

Following Berkeley's impassioned oratory, the assembly unanimously passed a series of resolutions denouncing the attempt of Parliament to coerce the rebellious colony, and reaffirming its loyalty to King Charles.

Berkeley was eventually forced to yield to the Parliamentary forces, but so highly was he thought of that in 1660, before the restoration of Charles II, he was proffered the governorship by the house of burgesses. Berkeley refused the burgesses' first offer explaining that he was willing to hold office from the people of Virginia, but never from any English power except that of the Crown. The burgesses thereupon altered their conditions and once more asked him to accept on his own terms. This he did, and, with the unanimous consent of the council, was chosen governor on March 21, 1660.

Seven years later Thomas Ludwell wrote to Lord Arlington:

> nor doe I think there can be a more convincing evidence of his Prudence, and Justice Then that in six years after hee was forced to resigne this Country to the Gennerall unhappy fate of our Nation (a Time when the Enemies of his Loyalty and Virtue would have loaden him with reproaches especially had they had Justice on their side) there was not one man that either publiquely or privately charged him with injustice, or any other fault committed in eight years Government. . . .[9]

In 1673 the council wrote to the King that had the people not loved and reverenced Governor Berkeley they would not have defended the country against the Dutch attacks in the previous years.

> For in this very Conjecture had the People had A Distastefull Governor they would have hazarded the losse of this Countrey, and the rather because they doe believe their Condition would not be soe bad Under the Dutch in Point of Traffique as it is under the Merchants who now use them hardly (even to extremity). But this Governo'r Oppresseth them not, but on the Contrary spends all his revenue amongst them in

[9] Thomas Ludwell to Henry Bennet, Lord Arlington, Sept. 16, 1666, *Virginia Magazine,* 21 (1913), 37.

> Setting up Manufactures to their advantage. . . .[10]

Even Colonel Moryson, one of the commissioners, wrote in 1676 that fifty years' experience had proved Virginia's government "most easy to the people and advantageous to the Crowne, For in all that time there has not been one lawe complain'd of, burdensome to the one or prejudiciall to the Prerogative of the other. . . ."

Some historians, while admitting Berkeley's justice in his early years, have asserted that after the restoration of Charles II the governor gradually became oppressive, greedy, and corrupt.[11] There is not a shred of responsible evidence to support this supposed change. In his proclamation of May 10, 1676, calling for a new election, Berkeley himself boldly challenged anyone to show a just grievance against him during his years as governor. Wrote Berkeley:

> I doe will and require that att the election of the said Burgesses all and every person and persons there present have liberty to present freely to their said Burgesses all such Just Complaints as they or any of them have against mee as Governor for any Act of Injustice by mee done or any reward bribe or present by mee accepted or taken from any person whatsoever and that the same bee by the said Burgesses presented to the Assembly and there duely examined and redressed. And supposeing I whome am head of the Assembly may bee their greatest grevance I will most gladly Joyne with them in a petition to his most Sacred Majesty to appoint a new Governor of Virginia. . . .[12]

He repeated his challenge in his proclamation of May 29, 1676.

Although the many proclamations issued by Bacon and the grievances collected by the commissioners have saturated the consciousness of students of the subject, not one bit of evidence, it should be remembered, was ever found to show that Governor Berkeley was guilty of any act of injustice or bribery. Indeed, he was rarely accused of any specific *act*. Most of the charges against him are the vague political smears with which we are all so familiar today. Historians have accepted them at face value because their own prejudices and assumptions have inclined them to favor a colonial rebel against a representative of imperial Britain. Yet, as Berkeley noted, when he dared the "Baconian" assembly of June 1676 to declare any fault he had ever committed and showed them his petition to the King to send an abler governor, the assembly not only absolved him of all crimes, but begged the King not to remove him from office.

The more prosaic interests of the rebels have rarely been inquired into. It has been assumed that they were selfless patriots fighting a tyrannical government. We are told that Bacon was "a champion of the weak, a rebel against injustice, the fore-runner of Washington, Jefferson and Samuel Adams." Others have compared Bacon to Patrick Henry, to Tiberius Gracchus, to Callimachus, and even to Leonidas at Thermopylae.

It is generally assumed, on the other hand, that the governor and his council were the "grandees" of the colony and that they possessed vast holdings of land while the rest of the colonists eked out a precarious existence on their small plantations. Like so many other assertions about Bacon's Rebellion, this one is not based on a study of the evidence. An investigation of the land holdings of the partisans on both sides reveals a surprising equality between them. The leaders on both sides had large holdings. The followers on both sides had more modest holdings. What is most significant is that the leaders of the rebellion against Governor Berkeley almost invariably owned great tracts of land on the frontier, frequently had a record of oppression and aggression against the neighboring Indians, and occasionally had been punished by Berkeley for their crimes against the natives.

Governor Berkeley strove throughout his career to restrain the aggressiveness of the frontier landowners. But his power was limited.

[10] Virginia council to the King, received Oct. 11, 1673, *Virginia Magazine,* 20 (1912), 236–237.

[11] Thomas Jefferson Wertenbaker, *Patrician and Plebian in Virginia, or the Origin and Development of Social Classes in the Old Dominion* (Charlottesville, 1910), p. 144, cites the years 1660–1676 as "a period of oppression." Most writers see Berkeley gradually becoming oppressive in this period.

[12] C. O. I/36, no. 64, fol. 137.

For one thing he was not in control of the government from 1652 to 1660 when the most unregulated expansion took place. His ability to control expansion was further restricted when, in 1666, he lost the right to allow or disallow individual grants. The assembly successfully challenged his authority to limit the right to acquire land, and "henceforth it was recognised in practice that the Governor had no more power over land grants than that secured by his individual vote in the Council."

The conventional idea that "Berkeley parceled out some handsome estates in a free and easy manner" is simply untrue. Land, in Berkeley's administration, was granted almost entirely under the headright system which authorized a right to fifty acres for each person brought into the colonies. Headrights could be bought and sold, so that a person of means desiring to acquire large acreage could do so. The governor could not disallow such large grants. But, since land acquisition was tied in a fixed ratio to emigration into the colony, estates were relatively modest by eighteenth-century standards. It was only under later governors, when land came to be saleable without presenting headrights, that enormous tracts were amassed by single owners.

Even when Berkeley did have authority to regulate expansion, he fought a losing battle against frontier disregard of the law. When the Indians were forbidden by English law to sell their lands to the whites, for example, their holdings continued nevertheless to be alienated. "Leases" and extortion were two favorite methods. Thomas Ludwell explained the reason for the law forbidding Indian sale by saying that

> whilest the Indians had liberty to sell theire lands the english would ordinaryly either frighten or delude them into a bargaine and for a trifle get away the grownd they should live on, then he comes and settles himselfe there and with his cattle and hoggs destroyes all the corne of the other Indians of the towne. This fills us with complaints and will if not prevented keep our peace for ever uncertaine . . . *this was a great cause of this last warr, and most of those who had thus intruded and were consequently the principall cause of it were notwithstanding amongst the forwardest in the rebellion and complained most of greivances.*[13]

The commissioners, in their "True and Faithful Account" asserted flatly that the breach of the former peace with the Indians "was the Ground of the Rebellion itselfe." Furthermore, the Indian treaty, which was also written by the Berkeley-hating commissioners, confirms Thomas Ludwell's charge that the cause of the breach was principally on the English side. Article 4 of the treaty states that

> Whereas by the mutuall discontents, Complaints, jealousies, and feares of English and Indians occasioned by the violent intrusions of divers English into their lands, forceing the Indians by way of Revenge, to kill the Cattle and hoggs of the English, whereby offence, and injuries being given, and done on boeth sides, the peace of this his Majesties Colony hath bin much disturbed, and *the late unhappy Rebellion by this means in a great measure begunne and fomented. . . .*[14]

The connection between the colonists' itch for land and the Indian "troubles" is a close one. Since the Indian troubles set off the rebellion, it would seem fair to blame the rebellion in great part on those who caused the Indian troubles. But it seems an inescapable conclusion that the English, and particularly the rebellious frontiersmen themselves, were responsible for the Indian troubles. It was the frontiersmen's continuing violation of Governor Berkeley's efforts to settle the Indian-white relationship with fairness to both sides that precipitated the rebellion.

Colonel Moryson, one of the commissioners, was well aware from his period in the Virginia government of the propensity of the frontiersmen to push the Indians off their land. He wrote in 1676 that there had not been a war with the Indians for the previous twenty-five years that had not been caused by the English coveting their land. When, therefore, Moryson and his fellow commissioners were presented the "grievance" of Henrico County that no satisfaction had been obtained against the Indians, they commented: "These Complainants never

[13] Thomas Ludwell to Secretary Coventry, Jan. 30, 1678, Longleat, LXXVIII, fol. 202. My italics.
[14] *Virginia Magazine,* 14 (1907), 291.

consider that the breach of the Peace and occasion of Bloodshed has still been on the side of the English, which was publickly Justified and affirmed in open Court in the face of a very great Assembly, and denyed by none."

The one cause of Bacon's Rebellion that has been consistently overlooked, then, is the aggressiveness of the frontiersmen. The careful Hildreth nearly stumbled onto this conception when he wrote, with unconscious humor, that "the Indian war, the immediate cause of all the late disturbances, seems to have subsided so soon as expeditions against the Indians were dropped." What has caused English and American historians to overlook the frontiersmen's aggressiveness? The reason lies partly in the white historian's unconscious immersion in his racial bias. According to the mythology of the white view of the world, the Indian is ever "primitive," "warlike," and "aggressive," while the "civilized" white man is constantly on guard against his attacks. But the aggressiveness of the frontiersmen has been overlooked for another reason, one based on our idea of our political beliefs. Most of the writers and historians who have dealt with Bacon's Rebellion have written from what they regarded as a "liberal" point of view, and it is part of the mythology of this view of history that the American frontiersman symbolizes America's freedom, democracy, and hatred of oppression. Actually the American frontiersman of the seventeenth century paid scant heed to such ideals. As Professor Abernethy has pointed out, frontier democracy

> cared little for principles or for the rights of the individual. It wished to carry its point, whatever that point might happen to be at any given moment, by popular action; it cared for numbers more than it did for leadership; it despised the superior man — unless he happened to be useful for the time being — just because he was superior; and it strove to put the bottom rail on top, whereas an enlightened government would attempt, as Jefferson wished, to raise the bottom rail toward the top.[15]

It was the tyranny of the temporarily enraged frontiersmen against which Berkeley was struggling in 1676. He was able to win over the elected representatives of that mob in the assembly of June 1676, a brilliant proof of the force of his superior personality. On the great point at issue — Indian policy — that Baconian assembly was soon giving Berkeleian orders. The record of the June Assembly proves that the real grievance against Governor Berkeley was not that he refused to defend the country from the Indians — a ridiculous charge against the conqueror of Opechancanough — but that he refused to authorize the slaughter and dispossession of the innocent as well as the "guilty."

The assembly of February 1677, like that of June 1676, reflected Berkeley's sentiments on the Indian question when it attempted to explain to the King the causes of the rebellion. The February Assembly noted that "the distempered humor predominant in the Common people (the usuall Causes of mutinyes and Insurrections) grounded uppon false humors, Infused by ill affected persons," had been excited by the first incursion of Indians upon the head of Rappahannock River

> wherein about thirty six persons were killed, which Caused greate murmurrings because so speedy A revenge was not taken for it, as theire precipitate desires would have exacted, Not Considering that warrs, are not to bee begunne without Mature deliberation Especially with our neighbours that had long lived, in Amity and good Correspondence with us, and that suddenly it Could not bee well deserned, whether the mischiefe was by them prepetrated, or by Forreignors. . . .

The "giddy multitude" wanted action, the assembly continued, and was not willing to await the meeting of the assembly. Bacon,

> finding the multitude in such distempers . . . did with many false, though specious pretences, declaring to the people, that if they would follow him, hee would destroy the Indians . . . marched forth and Killed many of our friend Indians. . . .[16]

The assembly went on to discuss *how* Bacon got recruits for his design. His method, they noted, was to promise to make the "meanest"

[15] Thomas Perkins Abernethy, *Three Virginia Frontiers* (University, La., 1940), p. 24.

[16] McIlwaine, *Journals of the House of Burgesses, 1659/60–1693*, pp. 73–74.

people "equall with or in better Condition than those that ruled over them. . . ." He tried to fulfill this promise by confiscating the estates of the loyalists and distributing them to the rebels, by setting prisoners at liberty and declaring freedom of all servants of loyalists, and by forcing others to follow him, threatening their ruin if they refused. Bacon's design, the assembly conceived in a wild and improbable guess, was to alienate Virginia from the King's dominion and "subject it to forreigners (as it since Appeares by his owne Coffession to the minister that Assisted at his death . . .)." What motivated Bacon? The assembly could only suggest that "being himselfe of a ruined fortune, ambitious and desiring Noveltyes" had something to do with it.

The preamble to the York County grievances gave a similar explanation of the cause of the rebellion. It justified Governor Berkeley declaring, in the commissioners' words, that "noe oppression of his, was the Rise and occasion of the late Distraction: but that the same proceeded from some disaffected persons, spurning against authoritie, and that the pretence of the dilatory Proceedings against the Indians was onely taken up for a Cloake. . . ." The commissioners agreed: "For the first part we have charity to beleeve it, for before the Warr with the Indians wee can find noe considerable Grievance arising from the Governor, to give the people any just cause of Complaint of his management. . . ."

However difficult it is to judge motives, it is possible to suggest some of the emotions that entered into the rebellion, especially among those who followed Bacon. The Isle of Wight County "opposing grievances" was one of the few documents to express the cause of the rebellion in psychological terms. "Envy, Emulation, Mallice, and Ignorance were the Cheife causes thereof," it stated.

One looks in vain in history books for any recognition that these motives might have had something to do with Bacon's Rebellion. The Bacon-Berkeley fight is traditionally portrayed as another episode in the glorious struggle between the "people" and their "oppressors." As soon as the author's assumptions that Bacon represents the "people" and Berkeley the "oppressors" are established, the narrative rolls smoothly to its intended goal. Actions on the way are judged good or bad not according to what they are but by whom they are done. Bacon's plan to exterminate the weak neighboring Indians is justified by accepting a "guilt" for which there is no proof. Berkeley's attempt to defend the Indian subjects of the King until proof of their guilt might be established is castigated either as administrative incompetency or traitorous greed. Bacon's confiscation of the estates of the loyalists is passed over as one of the necessary steps in the "democratic" revolution. Berkeley's confiscation of the estates of the rebels to support his troops and make up the loyalist losses is denounced as unconscionable, and his hanging of twenty-three of the leading rebels is termed a "reign of terror."

The causes of Bacon's rebellion are complex and profound. They cannot be explained in terms of Berkeley's "greed" and "oppression," Bacon's love of "liberty," the "savagery" of the Indians, or the "patriotism" of the frontiersmen; such explanatory descriptions are meaningless labels pasted on the actors by those who see all history as a morality play. Nor can the rebellion be explained in terms of the concealed identities and mysterious motives of a Gothic romance. Bacon does not change, with the hemispheres, from the spoiled son of a well-to-do English country squire to a dedicated democratic frontier hero. Nor does Governor Berkeley, after being the "Darling of the People" for thirty-five years, suddenly reveal his true identity as their blackest oppressor. Both men remained true to the faults and virtues of their natures.

Nathaniel Bacon would be vastly amused to find himself the sainted hero of the guardians of the liberal traditions of western democratic government. No doubt he would receive the news with an expression of his profane amusement at the idiocy of men. "God damn my blood," he might exclaim; "how easily people are led!"

2

The Paxton Boys of Pennsylvania

A Narrative of the Late Massacres in Lancaster County

The depredations of hostile Indians on the Virginia frontier created the conditions that led to Bacon's Rebellion in 1676. Almost ninety years later history threatened to repeat itself with the Paxton Rebellion in Pennsylvania, which culminated in the massacre of a tribe of peaceful, Christianized Indians near Philadelphia. In both instances, the Indian problem triggered rather than caused the uprising.

In western Pennsylvania the hysteria was prompted by the savage attacks on frontier settlements that were part of the Pontiac conspiracy of 1763. Westerners were inadequately represented in the Pennsylvania assembly, which was dominated by the Quaker faction and which refused to take adequate measures for frontier defense. This did not, to be sure, justify the slaughter at the Conestoga settlement, although few backwoodsmen, during times of border warfare, bothered to differentiate friendly Indians from hostile ones.

Franklin's role in the Paxton Rebellion was that of pacifier and critic. He assisted in turning back the insurgents outside Philadelphia. And he penned his magnificent review of the white man's exploitation of the Indian: "the only crime of these poor wretches seems to have been that they had a reddish-brown skin and black hair. . . ."

These *Indians* were the Remains of a Tribe of the *Six Nations,* settled at *Conestogoe,* and thence called *Conestogoe Indians.* On the first Arrival of the *English* in *Pennsylvania,* Messengers from this Tribe came to welcome them, with Presents of Venison, Corn, and Skins; and the whole Tribe entered into a Treaty of Friendship with the first Proprietor, William Penn, which was to last "as long as the Sun should shine, or the Waters run in the Rivers."

This Treaty has been since frequently renewed, and the *Chain brightened,* as they express it, from time to time. It has never been violated, on their Part or ours, till now. As their Lands by Degrees were mostly purchased, and the Settlements of the White People began to surround them, the Proprietor assigned them lands on the Manor of *Conestogoe,* which they might not part with; there they have lived many years in Friendship with their White Neighbours, who loved them for their peaceable inoffensive Behaviour.

It has always been observed, that *Indians,* settled in the Neighbourhood of White People, do not increase, but diminish continually. This Tribe accordingly went on diminishing, till there remained in their Town on the Manor, but 20 persons, viz. 7 Men, 5 Women, and 8 Children, Boys and Girls.

Of these, *Shehaes* was a very old Man, having assisted at the second Treaty held with them, by Mr. Penn, in 1701, and ever since continued a faithful and affectionate Friend to the *English;* He is said to have been an exceeding good Man, considering his Education, being naturally of a most kind, benevolent Temper.

Peggy was *Shehaes's* Daughter; she worked for her aged Father, continuing to live with him, though married, and attended him with filial Duty and Tenderness.

John was another good old Man; his Son *Harry* helped to support him.

George and *Will Soc* were two Brothers, both young Men.

John Smith, a valuable young Man of the

Benjamin Franklin, *A Narrative of the Late Massacres in Lancaster County,* 1764; reprinted in *Writings of Franklin,* ed. Smyth, IV, 289–298; 308–314.

Cayuga Nation, who became acquainted with *Peggy, Shehaes's* Daughter, some few Years since, married her, and settled in that Family. They had one Child, about three Years old.

Betty, a harmless old Woman; and her son *Peter,* a likely young Lad.

Sally, whose *Indian* name was *Wyanjoy,* a Woman much esteemed by all that knew her, for her prudent and good Behaviour in some very trying situations of Life. She was a truly good and an amiable Woman, had no Children of her own, but, a distant Relation dying, she had taken a Child of that Relation's, to bring up as her own, and performed towards it all the Duties of an affectionate Parent.

The Reader will observe, that many of their Names are *English.* It is common with the *Indians* that have an affection for the *English,* to give themselves, and their Children, the Names of such *English* Persons as they particularly esteem.

This little Society continued the Custom they had begun, when more numerous, of addressing every new Governor, and every Descendant of the first Proprietor, welcoming him to the Province, assuring him of their Fidelity, and praying a Continuance of that Favour and Protection they had hitherto experienced. They had accordingly sent up an Address of this Kind to our present Governor, on his Arrival; but the same was scarce delivered, when the unfortunate Catastrophe happened, which we are about to relate.

On *Wednesday,* the 14th of *December,* 1763, Fifty-seven Men, from some of our Frontier Townships, who had projected the Destruction of this little Commonwealth, came, all well mounted, and armed with Firelocks, Hangers and Hatchets, having travelled through the Country in the Night, to *Conestogoe* Manor. There they surrounded the small Village of *Indian* Huts, and just at Break of Day broke into them all at once. Only three Men, two Women, and a young Boy, were found at home, the rest being out among the neighbouring White People, some to sell the Baskets, Brooms and Bowls they manufactured, and others on other Occasions. These poor defenceless Creatures were immediately fired upon, stabbed, and hatcheted to Death! The good *Shehaes,* among the rest, cut to Pieces in his Bed. All of them were scalped and otherwise horribly mangled. Then their Huts were set on Fire, and most of them burnt down. Then the Troop, pleased with their own Conduct and Bravery, but enraged that any of the poor *Indians* had escaped the Massacre, rode off, and in small Parties, by different Roads, went home.

The universal Concern of the neighbouring White People on hearing of this Event, and the Lamentations of the younger *Indians,* when they returned and saw the Desolation, and the butchered half-burnt Bodies of their murdered Parents and other Relations, cannot well be expressed.

The Magistrates of *Lancaster* sent out to collect the remaining *Indians,* brought them into the Town for their better Security against any farther Attempt; and it is said condoled with them on the Misfortune that had happened, took them by the Hand, comforted and *promised them Protection.* They were all put into the Workhouse, a strong Building, as the Place of greatest Safety.

When the shocking News arrived in Town, a Proclamation was issued by the Governor, in the following Terms, viz.

"Whereas I have received Information, that on *Wednesday,* the Fourteenth Day of this Month, a Number of People, armed, and mounted on Horseback, unlawfully assembled together, and went to the *Indian* Town in the *Conestogoe* Manor, in *Lancaster County,* and without the least Reason or Provocation, in cool Blood, barbarously killed six of the *Indians* settled there, and burnt and destroyed all their Houses and Effects: And whereas so cruel and inhuman an Act, committed in the Heart of this Province on the said *Indians,* who have lived peaceably and inoffensively among us, during all our late Troubles, and for many Years before, and were justly considered as under the Protection of this Government and its Laws, calls loudly for the vigorous Exertion of the civil Authority, to detect the Offenders, and bring them to condign Punishment; I have therefore, by and with the Advice and Consent of the Council, thought fit to issue this Proclamation, and do hereby strictly charge and enjoin all Judges, Justices, Sheriffs, Constables, Officers Civil and Military, and all other His Majesty's liege Subjects within this Province, to make diligent Search and Enquiry after the Authors and Perpetrators of the said Crime, their Abettors and Accomplices, and to use all possible Means to apprehend and secure them in some of the publick Gaols of this Province, that they may be brought to their Trials, and be proceeded against according to Law.

"And whereas a Number of other *Indians,* who lately lived on or near the Frontiers of this Province, being willing and desirous to preserve and continue the ancient Friendship, which heretofore subsisted between them and the good People of this Province, have, at their own earnest Request, been removed from their Habitations, and brought into the County of *Philadelphia* and seated for the present, for their better Security, on the *Province Island,* and in other places in the Neighbourhood of the City of *Philadelphia,* where Provision is made for them at the public Expence; I do therefore hereby strictly forbid all Persons whatsoever, to molest or injure any of the said *Indians,* as they will answer the contrary at their Peril.

"Given under my Hand, and the Great Seal of the said Province, at Philadelphia, *the Twenty-second Day of* December, *Anno Domini One Thousand Seven Hundred and Sixty-three, and in the Fourth Year of His Majesty's Reign.*

"John Penn.

"By his Honour's Command,

"Joseph Shippen, *Jun., Secretary.*

"God save the King."

Notwithstanding this Proclamation, those cruel Men again assembled themselves, and hearing that the remaining fourteen *Indians* were in the Workhouse at *Lancaster,* they suddenly appeared in that Town, on the 27th of *December.* Fifty of them, armed as before, dismounting, went directly to the Workhouse, and by Violence broke open the Door, and entered with the utmost Fury in their Countenances. When the poor Wretches saw they had *no Protection* nigh, nor could possibly escape, and being without the least Weapon for Defence, they divided into their little Families, the Children clinging to the Parents; they fell on their Knees, protested their Innocence, declared their Love to the *English,* and that, in their whole Lives, they had never done them Injury; and in this Posture they all received the Hatchet! Men, Women and little Children were every one inhumanly murdered! — in cold Blood!

The barbarous Men who committed the atrocious Fact, in defiance of Government, of all Laws human and divine, and to the eternal Disgrace of their Country and Colour, then mounted their Horses, huzza'd in Triumph, as if they had gained a Victory, and rode off — *unmolested!*

The Bodies of the Murdered were then brought out and exposed in the Street, till a Hole could be made in the Earth to receive and cover them.

But the Wickedness cannot be covered, the Guilt will lie on the whole Land, till Justice is done on the Murderers. The blood of the innocent will cry to Heaven for vengeance.

It is said that, *Shehaes* being before told, that it was to be feared some *English* might come from the Frontier into the Country, and murder him and his People; he replied, "It is impossible: there are *Indians,* indeed, in the Woods, who would kill me and mine, if they could get at us, for my Friendship to the *English;* but the *English* will wrap me in their Matchcoat, and secure me from all Danger." How unfortunately was he mistaken!

Another Proclamation has been issued, offering a great Reward for apprehending the Murderers, in the following Terms, *viz.*

"Whereas on the Twenty-second Day of *December* last, I issued a Proclamation for the apprehending and bringing to Justice, a Number of Persons, who, in Violation of the Public Faith, and in Defiance of all Law, had inhumanly killed six of the *Indians,* who had lived in *Conestogoe* Manor, for the Course of many Years, peaceably and inoffensively, under the Protection of this Government, on Lands assigned to them for their Habitation; nothwithstanding which, I have received Information, that on the Twenty-seventh of the same Month, a large Party of armed Men again assembled and met together in a riotous and tumultuous Manner, in the County of *Lancaster,* and proceeded to the Town of *Lancaster,* where they violently broke open the Workhouse, and butchered and put to Death fourteen of the said *Conestogoe Indians,* Men, Women and Children, who had been taken under the immediate Care and Protection of the Magistrates of the said County, and lodged for their better Security in the said Workhouse, till they should be more effectually provided for by Order of the Government; and whereas common Justice loudly demands, and the Laws of the Land (upon the Preservation of which not only the Liberty and Security of every Individual, but the Being of the Government itself depend) require, that the above Offenders should be brought to condign Punishment; I have therefore, by and with the Advice of the Council, published this Proclamation, and do hereby strictly charge and command all Judges, Justices, Sheriffs, Constables, Officers Civil and Military, and all other His Majesty's faithful and liege Subjects within this Province, to make diligent Search and Enquiry after the Authors and Perpetrators of the said last-mentioned Offence, their Abettors and Accomplices, and that they use all possible Means to apprehend and secure them in some of the public Gaols of this province, to be dealt with according to Law.

"And I do hereby further promise and engage, that any Person or Persons, who shall apprehend and secure, or cause to be apprehended and secured, any Three of the Ringleaders of the said Party, and prosecute them to Conviction, shall have and receive for each, the public Reward of *Two Hundred Pounds;* and any Accomplice, not concerned in the immediate shedding the Blood of the said *Indians,* who shall make Discovery of any or either of the said Ringleaders, and apprehend and prosecute them to Conviction, shall, over and above the said Reward, have all the Weight and Influence of the Government, for obtaining His Majesty's Pardon for his Offence.

"*Given under my Hand, and the Great Seal of the said Province, at* Philadelphia, *the Second Day of January, in the Fourth Year of His Majesty's Reign, and in the Year of our Lord One Thousand Seven Hundred and Sixty-four.*

"John Penn.

"By his Honour's command,

"Joseph Shippen, Jun., *Secretary.*

"God save the King."

These Proclamations have as yet produced no Discovery; the Murderers having given out such Threatenings against those that disapprove their Proceedings, that the whole Country seems to be in Terror, and no one durst speak what he knows; even the Letters from thence are unsigned, in which any Dislike is expressed of the Rioters.

There are some, (I am ashamed to hear it,) who would extenuate the enormous Wickedness of these Actions, by saying, "The Inhabitants of the Frontiers are exasperated with the Murder of their Relations, by the Enemy *Indians,* in the present War." It is possible; — but though this might justify their going out into the Woods, to seek for those Enemies, and avenge upon them those Murders, it can never justify their turning into the Heart of the Country, to murder their Friends.

If an *Indian* injures me, does it follow that I may revenge that Injury on all *Indians?* It is well known, that *Indians* are of different Tribes, Nations and Languages, as well as the White People. In *Europe,* if the *French,* who are White People, should injure the *Dutch,* are they to revenge it on the *English,* because they too are White People? The only Crime of these poor Wretches seems to have been, that they had a reddish-brown Skin, and black Hair; and some People of that Sort, it seems, had murdered some of our Relations. If it be right to kill Men for such a Reason, then, should any Man, with a freckled Face and red Hair, kill a Wife or Child of mine, it would be right for me to revenge it, by killing all the freckled red-haired Men, Women and Children, I could afterwards anywhere meet with.

But it seems these People think they have a better Justification; nothing less than the *Word of God.* With the Scriptures in their Hands and Mouths, they can set at nought that express Command, *Thou shalt do no Murder;* and justify their Wickedness by the Command given *Joshua* to destroy the Heathen Horrid Perversion of Scripture and of Religion! To father the worst of Crimes on the God of Peace and Love! Even the *Jews,* to whom that particular Commission was directed, spared the *Gibeonites,* on Account of their Faith once given. The Faith of this Government has been frequently given to those *Indians;* but that did not avail them with People who despise Government.

* * *

I will not dissemble that numberless Stories have been raised and spread abroad, against not only the poor Wretches that are murdered, but also against the Hundred and Forty christianized *Indians,* still threatned to be murdered; all which Stories are well known, by those who know the *Indians* best, to be pure Inventions, contrived by bad People, either to excite each other to join in the Murder, or since it was committed, to justify it; and believed only by the Weak and Credulous. I call thus publickly on the Makers and Venders of these Accusations to produce their Evidence. Let them satisfy the Public that even *Will Soc,* the most obnoxious of all that Tribe, was really guilty of those Offences against us which they lay to his Charge. But if he was, ought he not to have been fairly tried? He lived under our Laws, and was subject to them; he was in our Hands, and might easily have been prosecuted; was it *English Justice* to condemn and execute him unheard? Conscious of his own Innocence, he did not endeavour to hide himself when the Door of the Workhouse, his Sanctuary, was breaking open. "I will meet them," says he, "for they are my Brothers." These Brothers of his shot him down at the Door, while the Word Brothers was between his Teeth.

But if *Will Soc* was a bad Man, what had poor old *Shehaes* done? What could he or the other poor old Men and Women do? What had little Boys and Girls done? What could Children of a Year old, Babes at the Breast, what could they do, that they too must be shot and hatcheted? Horrid to relate! And in their Parents Arms! This is done by no civilized Nation in *Europe.* Do we come to *America* to learn and practise the Manners of *Barbarians?* But this, *Barbarians* as they are, they practise against their Enemies only, not against their Friends.

These poor People have been always our Friends. Their Fathers received ours, when Strangers here, with Kindness and Hospitality. Behold the Return we have made them! When we grew more numerous and powerful, they put themselves under our *Protection.* See, in the mangled Corpses of the last Remains of the Tribe, how effectually we have afforded it to them!

Unhappy People! to have lived in such Times, and by such Neighbours! We have seen, that they would have been safer among the ancient *Heathens,* with whom the Rites of Hospitality were *sacred.* They would have been considered as *Guests* of the Publick, and the Religion of the Country would have opereted in their Favour. But our Frontier People call themselves *Christians!* They would have been safer, if they had submitted to the *Turks;* for ever since *Mahomet's* Reproof to *Khaled,* even the cruel *Turks* never kill Prisoners in cold Blood. These were not even Prisoners. But what is the Example of *Turks* to Scripture *Christians?* They would have been safer, though they had been taken in actual War against the *Saracens,* if they had once drank Water with them. These were not taken in War against us, and have drank with us, and we with them, for Fourscore Years. But shall we compare *Saracens* to *Christians?*

They would have been safer among the *Moors* in *Spain,* though they had been Murderers of Sons; if Faith had once been pledged to them, and a Promise of Protection given. But these have had the Faith of the *English* given to them many Times by the Government, and, in Reliance on that Faith, they lived among us, and gave us the Opportunity of murdering them. However, what was honourable in *Moors,* may not be a Rule to us; for we are *Christians!* They would have been safer it seems among *Popish Spaniards,* even if Enemies, and delivered into their Hands by a Tempest. These were not Enemies; they were born among us, and yet we have killed them all. But shall we imitate *idolatrous Papists,* we that are *enlightened Protestants?* They would have even been safer among the *Negroes* of *Africa,* where at least one manly Soul would have been found, with Sense, Spirit and Humanity enough, to stand in their Defence. But shall *Whitemen* and *Christians* act like a *Pagan Negroe?* In short it appears, that they would have been safe in any Part of the known World, except in the Neighbourhood of the CHRISTIAN WHITE SAVAGES of *Peckstang* and *Donegall!*

O, ye unhappy Perpetrators of this horrid Wickedness! reflect a Moment on the Mischief ye have done, the Disgrace ye have brought on your Country, on your Religion, and your Bible, on your Families and Children! Think on the Destruction of your captivated Countryfolks (now among the wild *Indians*) which probably may follow, in Resentment of your Barbarity! Think on the Wrath of the United *Five Nations,* hitherto our Friends, but now provoked by your murdering one of their Tribes, in Danger of becoming our bitter Enemies. Think of the mild and good Government you have so audaciously insulted; the Laws of your King, your Country, and your God, that you have broken; the infamous Death that hangs over your Heads; for Justice, though slow, will come at last. All good People everywhere detest your Actions. You have imbrued your Hands in innocent Blood; how will you make them clean? The dying Shrieks and Groans of the Murdered, will often sound in your Ears: Their Spectres will sometimes attend you, and affright even your innocent Children! Fly where you will, your Consciences will go with you. Talking in your Sleep shall betray you, in the Delirium of a Fever you yourselves shall make your own Wickedness known.

One Hundred and Forty peaceable *Indians* yet remain in this Government. They have, by *Christian* Missionaries, been brought over to a *Liking,* at least, of our Religion; some of them lately left their Nation which is now at War with us, because they did not chuse to join with them in their Depredations; and to shew their Confidence in us, and to give us an equal Confidence in them, they have brought and put into our Hands their Wives and Children. Others have lived long among us in *Northampton* County, and most of their Children have been born there. These are all now trembling for their Lives. They have been hurried from Place to Place for Safety, now concealed in Corners, then sent out of the Province, refused a Passage through a neighbouring Colony, and returned, not unkindly perhaps, but disgracefully, on our Hands. *O Pennsylvania!* Once renowned for Kindness to Strangers, shall the Clamours of a few mean Niggards about the Expence of this *Publick Hospitality,* an Expence that will not cost the noisy Wretches *Sixpence* a Piece, (and what is the Expence of the poor Maintenance we afford them, compared to the Expence they might occasion if in Arms against us) shall so senseless a Clamour, I say, force you to turn out of your Doors these unhappy Guests, who have offended their own Countryfolks by their Affection for you, who, confiding in your Goodness, have put themselves under your Protection? Those whom you have disarmed to satisfy groundless Suspicions, will you leave them exposed to the armed Madmen of your Country? Unmanly Men! who are not ashamed to come with Weapons against the Unarmed, to use the Sword against Women, and the Bayonet against young Children; and who have already given such bloody Proofs of their Inhumanity and Cruelty.

Let us rouze ourselves, for Shame, and redeem the Honour of our Province from the Contempt of its Neighbours; let all good Men join heartily and unanimously in Support of the Laws, and in strengthening the Hands of Government; that Justice may be done, the Wicked punished, and the Innocent protected; otherwise we can, as a People, expect no Blessing from Heaven; there will be no Security for our Persons or Properties; Anarchy and Confusion will prevail over all; and Violence without Judgment, dispose of every Thing.

When I mention the Baseness of the Murderers, in the Use they made of Arms, I cannot, I ought not to forget, the very different Behaviour of *brave Men* and *true Soldiers,* of which this melancholy Occasion has afforded us fresh Instances. The *Royal Highlanders* have, in the Course of this War, suffered as much as any other Corps, and have frequently had their Ranks thinn'd by an *Indian* Enemy; yet they did not for this retain a brutal undistinguishing Resentment against *all Indians,* Friends as well as Foes. But a Company of them happening to be here, when the 140 poor *Indians* above mentioned were thought in too much Danger to stay longer in the Province, chearfully undertook to protect and escort them to *New York,* which they executed (as far as that Government would permit the *Indians* to come) with Fidelity and Honour; and their captain *Robinson,* is justly applauded and honoured by all sensible and good People, for the Care, Tenderness and Humanity, with which he treated those unhappy Fugitives, during their March in this severe Season.

General *Gage,* too, has approved of his Officer's Conduct, and, as I hear, ordered him to remain with the *Indians* at *Amboy,* and continue his Protection to them, till another Body of the King's Forces could be sent to relieve his Company, and escort their Charge back in Safety to *Philadelphia,* where his Excellency has had the Goodness to direct those Forces to remain for some Time, under the Orders of our Governor, for the Security of the *Indians;* the Troops of this Province being at present necessarily posted on the Frontier. Such just and generous Actions endear the Military to the Civil Power, and impress the Minds of all the Discerning with a still greater Respect for our national Government. I shall conclude with observing, that *Cowards* can handle Arms, can strike where they are sure to meet with no Return, can wound, mangle and murder; but it belongs to *brave* Men to spare and to protect; for, as the Poet says,

"Mercy still sways the Brave."

3

The Regulators of North Carolina

Protest and Rebellion in North Carolina, 1765–1771

The movements of the Regulators — rebellious dissidents of the up-country regions in the Carolinas — have, like other colonial upheavals, stimulated considerable argument among historians. Were these movements democratic? Were they directed primarily against British authority? Were they genuine class struggles? Could their leaders be considered to be among the torchbearers of revolutionary democracy?

Actually the Regulators did not fit into a common mold; the South Carolina Regulators had little in common with their neighbors to the north. In South Carolina, there was little real hostility between the tidewater Low Country and the Back Country where the Regulation sought an end to the lawlessness and social disorganization that had followed the defeat of the Cherokees. In South Carolina violence was seen as a means to an end and that end was more, not less, government. Attempts by the Low Country planters to redress Back Country grievances (such as more equitable political representation of the western settlements in Charleston) were made, but encountered British opposition.[1]

In North Carolina the Regulators were less interested in obtaining more democratic representation than insuring that the governor and legislature at New Bern should administer the affairs of the colony in a more just and less corrupt manner. Professor Elisha P. Douglass, *who teaches at the University of North Carolina, sees the very real grievances of the Regulators as a basis for both the impressive strength of Loyalism in the province during the Revolution — most of the gentry espoused separatism — and the later pressure for democratic government in the state. "The victims of exploitation," he writes, "had fruitlessly urged the aristocrats to purge themselves of corruption; by 1776 the feeling grew that the only way to achieve honesty in politics was to keep gentlemen out of office."*

The democratic movements of the Revolution had their inception in the protest against aristocratic domination of government first heard in scattered instances during the late colonial period. The most articulate, comprehensive, and

Reprinted from Elisha P. Douglass, *Rebels and Democrats: The Struggle for Equal Political Rights and Majority Rule During the American Revolution* (Chapel Hill: University of North Carolina Press, 1955), pp. 71–100. Some footnotes deleted by permission of the publisher.

[1] See Richard Maxwell Brown, *The South Carolina Regulators* (Cambridge, Mass., 1963).

violent of these protests was the Regulator agitation in North Carolina. It is not surprising that social conflict should appear in the Carolinas, for there the inconsistencies between natural conditions and political institutions which marked the colonial period were amplified to an unusual degree. In all of the southern colonies there was some dissatisfaction because of the lack of representative local government, the enrichment of the wealthy and the impoverishment of the poor brought about by slavery, and the increasing sectional conflict between yeoman farmers of the piedmont and gentlemen planters of the tidewater. But in the Carolinas the contrast between rich and poor was greater, the sectional division sharper, and the government less suited to the needs and desires of the people. As a result, the history of the provinces during the colonial period was a record of almost continual unrest and occasional violence.

Until 1745 North Carolina was very sparsely settled, but after that time a steady influx of immigrants — many from Pennsylvania — made it the fourth most populous state by 1776. Nearly the entire increase was in the recently formed central and frontier counties, which by the time of the Revolution contained two-thirds of the population.[1] The tide-water counties either remained static or had a much smaller growth. Of the estimated 100,000 population in 1760, 40 per cent was Scotch or Scotch-Irish. Of the remainder, 45 per cent was English and 15 per cent German. Whites outnumbered Negroes more than five to one in the piedmont, and although the whites were a minority in the tidewater area, the vast majority of the population were not slave-holders.

The Germans tended to form centripetal peasant communities and kept themselves apart from the political life of the province. The same was generally true of the Highlanders, who had arrived direct from Britain under the benevolent patronage of the government. During the Revolution, however, many of these Scots became aggressive and determined Loyalists.

Contemporary observers have left unflattering descriptions of the ignorance, indolence, and filth of the yeoman farmers of the Carolinas but at the same time have testified to their rugged individuality and disdain for the social distinctions held in such high esteem by the upper classes. William Byrd wrote that the common people "are rarely guilty of flattering or making any court to their governors, but treat them with all the excess of freedom and familiarity," and the Scottish "lady of quality," Miss Janet Schaw, sniffed at "the disgusting equality" she found in North Carolina.

A population of this type might be expected in time to demand a share in the government of the colony, but the process was hastened by the unrepresentative character of colonial political institutions and the heartless corruption of many of the officials who controlled them. Royal government, instituted in 1729 after the authority of the proprietors had completely broken down, brought a semblance of order to North Carolina, but it also increased the tensions between rulers and ruled which had marked the proprietary period. During the next forty years, while the yeoman farmers by the thousands settled in the piedmont counties of Orange, Rowan, Guilford, Anson, and Mecklenburg, tidewater aristocrats also carved out plantations in the region and some of them, with the help of an aggressive group of lawyers attracted by high profits, inaugurated a systematic exploitation of their poorer neighbors.

The overrepresentation of the eastern counties in the Assembly helped to fasten tighter the aristocratic control of the colony. By a right originating in the Proprietary period, the five small sparsely-populated counties of the Albemarle region — Chowan, Currituck, Pasquotank, Perquimans, and Tyrrell — sent five representatives apiece to the Assembly while the piedmont counties were allotted only two apiece.[2] In the following years the already glar-

[1] Population figures for this period are unreliable, but from the best estimates the colony grew from 24,000 taxables in 1754 to 51,000 in 1769. In 1776 it had nearly 300,000 inhabitants. Evarts B. Greene and Virginia D. Harrington, *American Population before the Federal Census of 1790* (New York, 1932), 159–169.

[2] In 1754 the Privy Council refused to allow the Assembly to limit the number of representatives from the tidewater counties to two apiece. Lawrence F. London, "The Representation Controversy in Colonial North Carolina," *The North Carolina Historical Review,* XI (1934), 268.

ing discrimination against the West increased because the Assembly erected new counties in the piedmont only reluctantly, and then with such extensive boundaries that their population was much greater than that of the tidewater counties. For the privileged tidewater area in 1766 the ratio of representatives to white taxables ranged between 1:100 and 1:150 in some counties; in Orange County it was about 1:1600.

But the ill effects of an unfair system of representation might have been mitigated if the farmers had utilized their power at the polls. Because of the ease of acquiring land many of them could meet the fifty acre qualification for voting. Throughout the colonial period the royal government, anxious to have the province settled, had granted fifty acres as headright to every head of a family desiring it for only the cost of a survey and attendant legal fees. The widespread distribution of property may explain why no demand was made for the abolition of property qualifications until the very eve of the Revolution. Actually, it was more important for the settlers to use intelligently the voting right they possessed than to have it expanded. The trip to the polls on court day was long and arduous, and once one arrived the problem of staying sober was equally difficult. The sheriffs who conducted the elections were sometimes accused of fraud and intimidation. Voting was *viva voce,* of course.

Unfair representation and occasionally rigged elections might have been borne, however, were it not for the heartless corruption common among many of the officials of local government. In the South there was no equivalent of the New England town meeting through which the people could manage local affairs. All authority lay in the hands of the officials connected with the county courts — magistrates, clerks, registers of deeds, sheriffs, and constables. Most of them were nominated by the governor on the recommendation of the county assemblymen and the incumbent office-holders. Through this colonial equivalent of senatorial courtesy the courthouse group was able to control all nominations and pass lucrative offices about among themselves. Hence the designation "ring."

The cost of public services was inordinately high because officials, regarding their offices as investment and paid by fee, tended to overcharge for their services. In nearly every colony there were complaints against such extortion and assemblies attempted to rectify the situation by establishing legal fees and providing penalties for nonobservance. But in North Carolina, at least, legislation of this type appears to have been disregarded.

Exorbitant fees were by no means the only official malpractices. Sheriffs usually defrauded the government in the collection of taxes. Although royal governors complained loudly of this, legislation to bring offenders to book was ineffective, for the connections between courthouse rings and Assembly prevented enforcement. When Tryon succeeded in 1769 in having a thorough accounting made of the colony's finances, a delinquency on the part of the sheriffs was found which amounted to £64,000, £3,000 more than the total taxes collected in the period 1748–1770. It was estimated that sheriffs embezzled more than one half of the annual revenue. Even more flagrant was their defrauding of the poor taxpayer. Sometimes they prevented publication of the tax rate and collected more than the legal amount. If a taxable could not pay — and this was often the case because of the scarcity of money — it was charged that they made distraints of much greater value than the amount of the tax, and, acting in collusion with other members of the courthouse ring, so rigged the vendue sales that insiders bought land and goods at a fraction of their value. If the taxpayer belatedly raised enough money from neighbors to pay his tax and tried to overtake the sheriff on the road in order to rescue his distrained goods, it was asserted that the officer sometimes took by-ways in order to throw the former owner off the track so that he might then sell the goods at a distant town. Any balance from a vendue sale was naturally supposed to be returned to the taxpayer. Herman Husband, usually considered a Regulator leader, declared he never heard of a refund.

If the sheriff acted as executive officer of the county, justices of the peace sitting as the county court were the local legislature and judiciary.[3] Apparently as a group their professional ethics were no higher than those of the sheriffs. Complaints of overcharging were often lodged against them. One method of exacting more than the law allowed apparently used by several types of officeholders was to divide one service for which a fee could be charged into several distinct operations, each carrying a separate fee. Thus Edmund Fanning, Register of Deeds in Orange County, testified in 1768 that he took four fees for registering a conveyance — a single operation according to the letter of the law. Overcharging by lawyers was part of the network of graft which covered every branch of the court's activities. In many cases they occupied official positions and so were able to fill their pockets with both hands.

Because of the greed of lawyers and officials, those who brought their causes before the bench of justice often came as lambs to be shorn. Herman Husband calculated that a litigant in a case for five pounds, after winning on appeal to the Superior Court, would recover fifteen shillings.[4] A writer in the Virginia *Gazette* declared that the cost of six cases for amounts totalling ten pounds was sixty pounds. There is another instance on record where the cost of a court action was fourteen times the amount involved. George Sims, whose *Address to the People of Granville County* was the tocsin of the Regulation, gives a sad description of the farmer within the grip of the law. He presents as a hypothetical case a man who has had execution levied on him by a merchant for a five pound debt secured by a judgment note.[5] Personal effects to the amount of the judgment are seized, but the poor man's troubles are not over. For entering the judgment on the court docket and issuing the execution — "the work of one long minute" — the justice of the peace demands forty-one shillings and five pence. Unable to pay the fee, the unfortunate debtor is confronted with the alternative of a distraint or twenty-seven days work on the justice's plantation. But even after he has worked out his debt to the justice, the poor man's account is not settled. "Stay, neighbor," says Sims, "you must not go home. You are not half done yet. There is the damned lawyer's mouth to stop. . . . You empowered him to confess that you owed five pounds, and you must pay him thirty shillings for that or else to go work nineteen days for that pickpocket . . .; and when that is done you must work as many days for the sheriff for his trouble in levying execution and selling the debtor's goods, and then you can go home to see your living wrecked and tore to pieces to satisfy your merchant."

The settler's plight was even more hopeless when he became involved in a criminal indictment. Defense lawyers, taking full advantage of the predicament of the accused, raised their fees in accordance with the gravity of the charge. Husband declared that when he was arrested in 1768 for participation in a Regulator riot his lawyers made him sign over to them "all the money I had and bonds and notes for £150 more."

For sheer effrontery the corruption in North Carolina resembles the graft uncovered by the muckrakers of the late nineteenth and early twentieth centuries. It lacks the connection with organized crime which has characterized corrupt government in recent times, but in extensiveness and in its implication of leading political figures, it equals the activities of more modern political machines. The activities of the courthouse rings perhaps deserve more censure than those of ward bosses, however, for most corrupt politicians today at least give some thought to the interests of their constituents. It cannot be argued that the sheriffs, magistrates, clerks, and registers of North Carolina were merely exercising prescriptive privileges and for that reason must not be judged by con-

[3] Guess, *County Government,* James Sprunt Historical *Publications,* XI, 31; Tryon estimated in 1767 that there were 516 justices in the colony. These men, mostly planters and lawyers, constituted the governing class. All important county officeholders and the assemblymen were almost invariably chosen from among their number. *Colonial Records,* VII, 481.

[4] Husband, *Impartial Relation, North Carolina Tracts,* 291.

[5] A judgment note empowers a lawyer to confess judgment for the amount of the debt. Thus the creditor, to recover, need not sue on the debt but merely have a justice of the peace issue execution. Obviously, this puts the debtor at the creditor's mercy. From Sims's discussion it seems that the practice was usual in North Carolina. See Judgment Note, *Bouvier's Law Dictionary.*

temporary standards of honesty. Prescriptive dishonesty is dishonesty notwithstanding. They were breaking the law and they knew it. While most prevalent in the piedmont region, corruption probably extended over the whole of the province to a lesser degree. A friend of Samuel Johnston's, the leading conservative of the Revolutionary period, wrote just after the Regulator war that the desire for militant reform had begun to make its appearance in the tidewater country years before. "I should not have been surprised," he said, "if I had heard that your battle of Alamance (the conclusion of the war) had been fought on the banks of the Pasquotank river instead of the Alamance or Haw river." But the extortion in the piedmont region was harder to bear because it was impossible to avoid. New settlers were compelled to go to law to quiet titles and adjust differences with their neighbors. Litigants who won usually paid dearly and losers might see the result of years of work disappear before their eyes. Because of the scarcity of money great numbers of farmers fell into debt, and petty peculation then became a serious drain on their resources. Anyone who refused to go through the processes of the law regarding land titles risked ejectment with total loss of improvements. Considering the gravity of the grievances in North Carolina it is a wonder that the Regulator war did not break out sooner and become more violent than it did.

The first rumblings of discontent came from the piedmont settlers of the Granville District, who not only had to suffer the depradations of corrupt court officials but were compelled to bear with a corrupt land office as well. In 1759 a band of vigilantes kidnapped one of the agents who had systematically pillaged newcomers to the region by charging outrageous prices for land entries and by occasionally granting pieces of land to more than one person. The agent promised restitution but once freed had his kidnappers thrown in jail. This ill-advised action caused a major riot. A mob released the prisoners and feeling ran so high that the government dropped all prosecutions. Although the Assembly bitterly denounced "the torrent of the rioters' licentious extravagances," the Granville District remained turbulent and restless until the outbreak of the Revolution.[6]

The first articulate protest to the corruption in North Carolina government was apparently the pamphlet by the simple farmer, George Sims, *An Address to the People of Granville County,* written in 1765. The *Address* was no invitation to revolt. Sims only asked that the government force the county officials to obey the law. Expressing great admiration for the British Constitution (possibly in an attempt to avoid charges of political radicalism), he advocated that the farmers draft a petition to the Governor asking that the courts be closed until grievances were redressed. But violence should be avoided at all costs. "First let us be careful to keep sober that we may do nothing rashly. Secondly, let us do nothing against the known and established laws of our land that we may not appear as a faction endeavoring to subvert the laws and overturn our system of government. Let us behave with circumspection to the Worshipful Court inasmuch as they represent his Majesty's person, we ought to reverence their authority both sacred and inviolable, except they interpose, and then, Gentlemen, the toughest will hold out the longest."

The only immediate effect of the *Address* was a suit for libel instituted against Sims by the officials of Granville County. In 1766, however, opposition to the rings broke out simultaneously in such widely separated counties as Brunswick, Cumberland, and Granville when settlers in those localities refused to pay taxes.

[6] The District was a strip of territory south of the Virginia border stretching from the ocean on the east to the "South Sea" on the west. The property of the Earl of Granville — the only heir of the original eight proprietors who did not sell his share of the Carolinas to the crown in 1728 — it included the best of the fertile piedmont region and embraced perhaps two-thirds of the population of North Carolina. Although the royal government exercised civil jurisdiction in the area, land was sold by Granville's agents. Their frauds absorbed so much of the revenue from the tract that the Earl closed the land office from 1763 to 1773. He reopened it in the latter year with Governor Martin as agent. The District contained many squatters who were given title to their farms by the Provincial Congress after the outbreak of the Revolution. E. Merton Coulter, *The Granville District,* James Sprunt Historical *Publications,* XIII (1913), No. 2, pp. 38, 46–47, 52–55.

At Hillsborough during the September session of the Orange County Court some of the settlers asked the officials in a public address to attend a conference devoted to a discussion of grievances. The authors cleverly played on the similarity between their grievances and the Stamp Act and pointed out that the sturdy opposition of the Whig leaders to Parliament did not prove that they were incorruptible or justify the activities of the court house rings. "That great good may come of this great designed evil, the Stamp Law, while the Sons of Liberty withstood the Lords in Parliament in behalf of true liberty, let not officers under them carry on unjust oppression in our own province . . . take this as a maxim, that while men are men, though we should see all those Sons of Liberty who have just redeemed us from tyranny set in offices and vested with power, they would soon corrupt again and oppress if they were not called upon to give an account of their stewardship."

The officials were apparently caught off balance by this modest show of spirit and agreed to meet the people at a gathering to be held in October. But in the intervening period they recovered their aplomb and decided to ignore the whole matter. Husband believed they were dissuaded by Edmund Fanning, a Justice of the Peace and the Register of Deeds of Orange County who came to be a symbol of the settlers' grievances. Fanning's character exhibits such marked contradictions that it is impossible to tell whether he was the cause of the farmers' sufferings or the victim of circumstances. Born in Long Island, he graduated from Yale in 1757, studied law in New York, and came to Orange to practice in 1761. He soon grew wealthy, built a fine house in Hillsborough, and became an intimate friend of Governor Tryon. A ditty composed among the Regulators describes his rise to fame and fortune:

When Fanning first to Orange came,
He looked both pale and wan
An old patched coat upon his back,
An old mare he rode on.

Both man and mare wa'nt worth five pounds
As I've been often told,
But by his civil robberies,
He's laced his coat with gold.

Actually, Fanning was not impoverished when he came to Orange and apparently was never guilty of gross fraud or extortion. Put on trial in 1769 at the insistence of the settlers, he was acquitted after nothing more than misconstruction of the fee law could be proved against him. The settlers were not reconciled to the verdict, however, and severely beat him when they broke up the court in 1770. Nevertheless Fanning seemed to be remarkably free from malice, for even after this painful experience he introduced legislation into the Assembly to rectify the Regulators' grievances. He accompanied Tryon to New York in the next year and during the Revolution became an outstanding Loyalist. Successively Lieutenant Governor of Nova Scotia and Governor of Prince Edward Island after the war, he died in London in 1818 a full general in the British army.

When the Orange Assembly delegates and the court officials failed to appear at the meeting requested by the settlers in 1766, those who had gathered to discuss grievances drew up a paper asking for a regular annual gathering at which the court officials would submit to an examination of their accounts and the Assembly delegates receive instructions. The farmers were trying, in a limited sphere, to inaugurate responsible government. They had little chance of success when it came to calling court officials to account, for these were responsible to the Governor, but in claiming the right to control the county delegates they rested their case on the representative character of colonial assemblies so proudly asserted by the members themselves. The instruction of delegates had been practiced for many years in New England and Pennsylvania, yet it had never been common in the South. Hence the authors presented their request with diffidence, noting that instruction "was a thing somewhat new in this county, though practiced in older governments." Like the Sims' *Address,* this paper is remarkable for its generally humble tone. It reasons with the representatives and couches nothing in the form of a demand.

The officials and the delegates might well have agreed to these reasonable requests, for the settlers were asking for no more than the Whigs were demanding from Britain — responsible government and relief from arbitrary taxation. But, in Fanning's words, the court house group in Orange "refused to be arraigned at the bar of the people's shallow understanding." Apparently no meetings were held and the campaign for responsible government came to an end.

The movement was suddenly revived in 1768, however, when the Sheriff of Orange announced that as a result of a recent act of the Assembly he would not travel the county as usual to collect taxes but would receive them at five specified places. Taxables who would not make the journey to pay would be charged two shillings, eight pence for a personal collection. On top of this came a rumor, subsequently verified, that the Assembly had appropriated £15,000 for a new governors' palace. As a result groups of Orange County settlers, taking the name from the Whig organizations, formed "Associations" "for regulating public grievances and abuses of power." In the heat of resentment some of the "Regulators" sent a paper to the court officials announcing their refusal to pay taxes until an accounting was reached. The paper asserted what the pronouncement of 1766 had hinted, ". . . the nature of an officer is a servant to the public and we are determined to have the officers of this county under better and honester regulation than they have been for some time past." Yet the settlers' interpretation of the rights of citizens regarding taxes was considerably more moderate than that of the Whigs. The farmers did not fulminate against taxation without representation but merely observed that "the King requires no money from his subjects but what they are made sensible what use it's for." They concluded by again requesting the assemblymen for a meeting.

The more conservative Regulators drew up a milder protest. Both groups, however, testified to their peaceful intentions. Indeed, the whole object of the Regulators was to force the court officials to obey the law. Nullification and violence were resorted to only when all other means of redressing grievances failed.

The officers made no attempt at conciliation. Deep in embezzlement, they could not submit to an accounting of their funds. Fanning, after an altercation with some settlers over the distraint of a mare, wrote to the governor a grim and exaggerated description of the strength of the Regulators and asserted that their intentions were seditious. Tryon replied by issuing a proclamation calling on them to disperse.

Now sure of the governor's support, Fanning took the drastic step of seizing Herman Husband and William Butler, reputedly the two outstanding leaders of the Regulator movement. Although Husband's name has always been linked to the War of the Regulation, he was apparently not a member of the Association. The Regulators themselves declared he was not one of their number and on one occasion he was called upon to arbitrate differences between them and the officers of Rowan County. Nevertheless, he became so deeply involved in the agitation that in the end he suffered more than many of the actual leaders. Deeply religious, mystical, and eternally in conflict with his environment, he was an incurable radical. Unfortunately, however, he lacked a strong will and courage and so became indecisive and pusillanimous when faced with the demands of leadership.

Born in 1724 on a small farm in Maryland, Husband experienced a soul-searing conversion under the stimulus of the Great Awakening. Reflecting the compelling imagery of Jonathan Edwards, he wrote that "the Flames of Hell, represented with Flames of Sulphur and Brimstone, seemed nothing in comparison of the Wrath of . . . an Angry God." In order to placate Providence he joined the Presbyterian church, but later, convinced that it did not teach the whole truth, became a Quaker. About 1750 he moved to North Carolina. Whether because of, or in spite of his ascetic habits — which were apparently in marked contrast to those of the inhabitants generally — he developed a flourishing plantation near Hillsborough and eventually possessed about 8000 acres. Although disowned by the Quakers — a no doubt inevitable misfortune — he was universally respected because of his honesty, sobriety, and industry.

Husband and Butler were arrested at their homes, and were brought to Hillsborough and threatened with summary execution unless they promised to sever all connections with the Regulators. Under the pressure Husband broke down and promised to cease criticising the officers. Fanning then released him on bail, and Husband prepared to flee the country, for his defection had placed him in such bad odor with the more radical Regulators that he feared for his life. After a period of agonizing indecision, however, he returned to stand trial in the fall of '68 and was acquitted — probably because the government had meanwhile quelled the disturbances which had led to his arrest and was anxious to allay hostility by leniency with offenders.

While Husband was screwing up his courage for his forthcoming trial, the Regulators in Orange County petitioned the governor and council for redress of their grievances. In reply Tryon condemned their activities and called on them to drop their titles of Regulators and Associators and submit to government. He promised, however, that they might prosecute the officers in the courts after peace had been restored. This was by no means a satisfactory response. Tryon's only inducement for the Regulators' return to obedience was to offer a means of redressing grievances which had already been proved fruitless. Of what use to prosecute corrupt officers in courts which were themselves corrupt? Hence the Regulator agitation kept spreading.

Foreseeing open revolt, Tryon then called up a militia force of over 1,000 men which he stationed at Hillsborough. Mainly a gentlemen's affair, this array was officered by six lieutenant generals, two major generals, three adjutant generals, two major of brigades, seven colonels, five lieutenant colonels, four majors, and thirty-one captains. Most of the Council and about 25 per cent of the House held commissions. When the September term of court opened, during which Husband was to be tried, a large number of settlers marched on Hillsborough apparently to prevent the court from sitting; but after viewing the governor's reception committee they disclaimed all intentions of insurrection, handed over their leaders for trial, promised to pay taxes, and dispersed. The court officials, evidently wishing to return to the *status quo ante* without arousing antagonism, either released the leaders or gave them light sentences. Although the governor held to his word and allowed the farmers to bring suit against the officers, most of the suits ended in failure, or, as in the case of Fanning, in a nominal fine.

For a time it appeared that the governor's prompt action had stifled the protests of the piedmont. The sheriff of Orange assured Tryon that farmers were again paying their taxes or suffering distraints with submission. The governor himself informed the home government of the happy ending to the unpleasantness and declared with evident satisfaction, "It is with pleasure I can assure his Majesty not a person of the character of a gentleman appeared among the insurgents."

The Regulator movement was not a complete failure, however, for attempts were made in the Assembly to rectify some outstanding abuses. Fanning, paradoxically, sponsored a bill to lower court costs and stay executions of judgment in suits for small debts. Measures to inaugurate triennial assemblies, regulate elections, and relieve insolvent debtors were brought in, and Fanning, again in the unexpected role of reformer, presented a plan to reduce the Provincial debt and "relieve the present burden of taxation upon the poor." All of these bills were killed either in the House or Council, however. Only one important reform measure became law — an act regulating the sale of distrained goods designed to prevent the frauds of which Sims had complained in his *Address to the People of Granville County*.

On the whole, the tone of the Assembly was unfriendly to the Regulators. It presented an address of lavish praise to Tryon for his part in suppressing the "insurrection." Earlier it had given him additional powers over the militia, raised the fees of justice, and had compelled plaintiffs at the beginning of a case to put up a bond to cover court costs in case they lost their suit — a provision which made it even harder for the poor to sue the rich. Nothing was done to prevent the taking of exorbitant fees, and attempts to make accession to courts easier by dividing Mecklenburg, Orange, and Rowan counties failed, possibly because this would have increased the representation of the back country.

But the Regulator spirit was far from dead in spite of the fiasco of September, 1768. In 1769, two petitions were presented to the government which showed a considerable advance in political thinking. One from Anson County carrying 261 signatures asked for ballot voting, taxation in proportion to wealth, the collection of taxes in commodities, and the printing of money with land as security. The document further requested that all debt cases involving amounts between forty shillings and ten pounds be tried by one justice and a jury with lawyers barred from the courtroom, and that the governor and Council cease making large land grants to individuals who held them for speculation. "Us inhabitants of Orange and Rowan counties" wanted the governor to propose legislation which would prevent lawyers and clerks from holding seats in the House of Commons, put all officers on salary and do away with fees, and make inspection notes on imperishable commodities in warehouses legal tender. The inhabitants also desired regular publication of the laws, division of the large western counties, and the registering of votes on the Assembly journal "so that we may have an opportunity to distinguish our friends from our foes." The petitioners, like those of Anson County, were particularly insistent that the wealthy planters bear more of the tax burden. "For all to pay equal," they wrote, "is with submission, very grievous and oppressive." Polls were the sole basis of taxation in North Carolina and the fact that slaves were also taxable did not alter to any great extent the regressive characteristics of the tax system. Noting that all attempts to bring the extorting officers to book had failed, "partly from their own superior Cunning and partly from our invincible Ignorance," the petitioners asked Tryon to vacate all commissions of present county clerks and install "Gentlemen of probity and Integrity" in their places.

It is evident that the settlers whose only recourse a year before had been to throw themselves on the governor's mercy had matured considerably in political outlook. The proposals to register divisions in the House of Commons, publish the laws and journals, divide the western counties, and inaugurate secret voting were all much-needed reforms adopted in later years. The petitioners' requests for progressive taxation and legal tender secured by nonperishable commodities became elements in the agrarian programs of the nineteenth century culminating in the Populist movement.

This new grasp of political and economic realities on the part of the piedmont farmers bore fruit in the elections of 1769. The middle and frontier counties returned also an entire new slate of delegates. Husband replaced Fanning as a representative of Orange and others of the old guard of whom the Regulators had complained were either defeated or failed of nomination.[7] Tryon soon dissolved the House because of its resolutions on the Townshend Acts, but most of the new members retained their seats in the elections which followed. James Iredell, a Whig who later became a Federalist and a justice of the Supreme Court, declared in 1770 that a majority of the House were "of regulating principles" and were determined upon "a levelling plan." The legislative record of the House gives some justification for this comment. Attorneys' and clerks' fees were again fixed by law and penalties imposed for non-observance, the chief justice was put on salary, the act regulating executions was renewed, and an act to ease court costs in litigation over small debts was passed. The Assembly failed to take the necessary measures for enforcement, however. All penalties were civil and could only be imposed following a suit brought by an injured party. No effective redress of the Regulators' grievances was possible until the government took the responsibility of prosecuting violations of its legislation as criminal acts. The humble farmers of the piedmont naturally hesitated to bring suits in unfriendly courts against officials much better equipped for legal battles than themselves. Therefore it is not surprising that complaints of extortion continued to mount in spite of the remedial legislation of

[7] List of representatives elected in 1766, *Colonial Records*, VII, 342; those elected in 1769, *ibid.*, VIII, 106–107. Among those dropped were Samuel Benton of Granville, of whom Sims had complained, Samuel Spencer of Anson, and John Frohawk of Rowan, both of whom the Regulators detested. The votes on the Orange election were, according to Husband: Fanning, 314; Prior, 445; Husband, 642. Archibald Henderson (ed.), "Herman Husband's Continuation of the Impartial Relation," *North Carolina Historical Review*, XVIII (1941), 65. Although defeated in Orange, Fanning was returned from Hillsborough. The Regulators charged that the town had been given a representative by the governor solely to provide Fanning with an Assembly seat.

the "Regulator" Assembly. A petition from Orange County declared that clerks were still demanding exorbitant fees and that sheriffs were collecting more in taxes than the legal rate required. Although the writers again testified to their peaceful intentions, nevertheless, "If we cannot obtain . . . some security in our properties more than bare humor of officers, we can see plainly that we shall not be able to live under such oppressions and to what extremities this must drive us you can as well judge of as we can ourselves. . . ."

Extremities were closer than possibly either the officers or many of the Regulators realized. When the Orange County Court met in September, 1770, the Regulators invaded the town, pulled the judges from the bench, tried the cases on the docket themselves, and left a summary and blasphemous account of their administration of justice in the court record. News of the riot reached New Bern about the same time as a report that Regulators of Bute and Johnston counties were marching on the capitol to prevent Fanning from taking his seat in the House. Alarm aroused by the possibility of open rebellion apparently led the majority of the members to abandon their "regulating principles." First the delegates expelled Herman Husband for publishing a letter written by the Regulator James Hunter accusing some of the leading men of the province of corruption.[8] Secondly the members passed the Johnston Act — named for the future leader of the conservative Whigs — which made it a felony punishable by death for persons in a riotous crowd of ten or more to refuse to disperse on the order of a sheriff or justice of the peace. Anyone indicted under the act who failed to surrender himself for trial would be outlawed and could be shot on sight. The act was *ex post facto* in that some of its provisions applied to offenses occurring since March, 1770. The object was to punish the perpetrators of the Hillsborough riots.

The Regulators received the Johnston Act as the crowning example of the perfidy of the officers. "The Assembly have gone and made a riotous act," some of them were quoted as saying, "and the people are more enraged than ever. It was the best thing that could be done for the county for now we shall be forced to kill all the clerks and lawyers. . . . If they had not made the Act we might have suffered some of them to live. A Riotous Act! There never was any such act in the laws of England or any other country but France. They brought it from France and they'll bring the Inquisition next."[9] Even the Privy Council agreed that the law was in part at least, unjustifiable. It informed Josiah Martin, Tryon's successor, that the outlawry clause was "irreconcilable with the principles of the constitution, full of danger in its operation and unfit for any part of the British Empire."

The disturbances provided an opportunity for Governor Tryon to stamp out the Regulation by force of arms. When, at his instigation, hand-picked grand juries brought in sixty-two indictments against Regulator leaders in Orange, he arranged a military expedition with the ostensible purpose of seizing the culprits. Two columns, one from the East and one from the West, were to converge on the rebellious county. Gentlemen flocked to the colors. The roster of officers included representatives of almost every important family in the province — men who became the prominent Whig leaders in the Revolution. "With the exception of the Governor and Fanning," says the biographer of Tryon, "nearly every officer of note in the

[8] Hunter implicated two figures of great importance in the future history of the state, Abner Nash and William Hooper. Nash was to serve a term as governor in 1780–1781, and Hooper represented the state in Congress during part of the Revolutionary period. Like Johnston he was an outstanding opponent of democracy. Hunter also asserted that the Regulators would pay no more taxes "until we have some assurance they will be applied toward the support of government." He stressed the fact that the country needed no new laws but only the enforcement of the old ones. Originally printed in the North Carolina *Gazette,* the letter appeared in the Pennsylvania *Journal,* July 11, 1771. A photostatic copy of this latter printing will be found in Regulator Papers, Southern History Collection, University of North Carolina. After his expulsion, Husband was imprisoned for a short time at the instigation of Governor Tryon. Following his release he returned to his plantation in Orange County and, if present at Alamance, fled the field before the conclusion of the battle.

[9] *Ibid.,* 519–520. The Regulators were supposed to have declared that they paid no regard to the laws of the last session. *Ibid.,* 538.

army . . . went heart and soul into the struggle for freedom during the Revolution; and, were the names of this galaxy of patriots omitted from the annals of the fight for independence, little material would be left for the historian of that epoch in North Carolina."[10] Many of these notables had been detested by the Regulators — particularly Abner Nash and Alexander Martin, both of whom were to become governors of the state; John Walker, a future aide-de-camp to Washington; and Francis Nash, a brigadier general during the Revolution who fell at the battle of Germantown. Other unpopular figures who supported Tryon were William Hooper, a future delegate to the Continental Congress, and Richard Henderson, a judge of the Orange County Court during the riot of 1770 and future promoter of the Transylvania Company.

Although the aristocracy breathed fire, there seems to have been little heart for battle among the rank and file. Rednap Howell, a Regulator leader and the possible author of much of the doggerel verse of the movement, wrote that at New Bern the militia broke ranks and declined to serve, and that only seven recruits could be secured in Dobbs County.[11] Most of the Wake County regiment refused to march against the Regulators. Only by threats and cajolery did Tryon succeed here in getting fifty "volunteers." The most effective spur to recruiting was a bounty of forty shillings and good pay during service. By this means, according to an observer friendly to the Regulators, Tryon enlisted an army "of the meaner sort."

To repel Tryon's expected attack a leaderless mob, many of its members without arms, gathered in Orange County. A newspaper writer declared that most of the men were "without principle because they had nothing to lose." But there were others, he said, "who had both property and principles, but with regard to government, were republicans. Such people ever look with jealous eye on public officers and are enemies from principle to that subordination so essential to the being of a well-regulated state. A man genteelly dressed gave them the greatest offense." The writer probably exaggerated the number of political radicals among the Regulators. Few if any of the piedmont settlers had ever indicated dissatisfaction with royal government. But he was more correct in recognizing the elements of class warfare. The yeoman farmers rose against the aristocracy not only as inhabitants of the piedmont but also as common men against gentlemen. As previously indicated, their grievances, although most evident in the western counties, were present to a lesser degree all over the province, and so also the antagonism aroused by these grievances. In the final alignment of forces, the Regulators who fought were apparently all from the piedmont counties, but Tryon's army contained nearly all the gentlemen of prominence in the province.

Tryon succeeded in raising a little over 1,000 men and a second force of about 300 under General Waddell was gathered in the western counties. Some contemporary newspaper accounts pictured the governor as knight in shining armour. "God be thanked they have found a *Tryon,*" declared a writer in the New York *Gazette*. He saw the Regulation as a curtain raiser for social revolution throughout the colonies. A gentleman who took part in the campaign wrote that morale was high in the government forces, and that everyone was determined to "quell this dangerous insurrection and return to their allegiance a body of men who, under the color of redressing nominal grievances, have nothing more in view than overturning the civil government of this province."

Tryon met the perpetrators of this "dangerous insurrection" on the field of Alamance, twenty miles from Hillsborough. General Waddell was not able to make his appearance as planned because of disaffection among his men and the loss of his baggage train. A description of the battle, possibly unreliable in detail but interesting in view of Tryon's difficulties in recruiting, gives the impression that it was a somewhat ludicrous affair because of a general reluctance of both sides to fight. "The two armies marched toward each other with the most profound silence, and such was the indisposition of

[10] Marshall D. Haywood, *Governor William Tryon, and his Administration in the Province of North Carolina, 1765–1771* (Raleigh, 1903), 166.

[11] South Carolina and American General *Gazette,* April 10, 1771. An observer from Bute wrote that although 800 or 900 men turned out for muster, "there was not any would list, but broke their ranks without leave of their commanders and proclaimed for the Regulators." *Colonial Records,* VIII, 552.

either side . . . that the ranks passed each other and were then compelled by a short retreat to regain their respective positions. At the distance of 25 yards apart the contending parties stood and occupied the solemn hour before battle with a verbal quarrel, each party uttering the most violent imprecations and bandying the most abusive epithets. The Regulators shook their clenched hands at the governor and Mr. Fanning and walked up to the artillery with open bosoms, defying them to fire. They were now face to face, each man engaged in a loud and clamorous quarrel with the nearest enemy on the grievances of the people and the virtues of Fanning. It was in vain that the governor roared out the word of command, directing the men to fire. Each loyal soldier was too busily occupied either in an argument or a fist fight to heed the . . . decree."[12] Tryon, possibly fearing that his men would not fight, supposedly rode up and down the line shouting, in the best tradition of eighteenth-century military etiquette, "Fire on them or on me." This perhaps provided an interesting alternative for some of the men in his own ranks. Whether in obedience to his command or not, somewhere a gun went off, and the battle was joined. The Regulators soon took to their heels. The Regulators lost nine killed and numerous wounded. Tryon suffered nine killed and sixty-one wounded.

After the battle the government adopted a policy of summary punishment for known agitators and forgiveness of their followers. Six leading Regulators were hanged after court martial, and one was executed on the field of battle without trial. The others were eventually released. Husband, who had ridden off the field before or during the battle, fled to Maryland. Little or nothing is known about his activities from this time until 1794 when he characteristically became implicated in the Whisky Rebellion. Condemned to death for his part in it, he was later among those pardoned by Washington. He died soon after, a rebel to the last.

Thus ended the War of the Regulation. On the surface it appeared to be a complete victory for the colonial ruling class. The settlers had failed to gain responsible government and their plans for an agrarian program were stillborn. Yet the war was to have important results in the Revolutionary period. The repressed but profound bitterness for the ruling aristocracy emerged in a strong Loyalist movement on one hand and in a demand for democratic government on the other. There can be little doubt that some of the king's irregulars who followed the notorious partisan leader, David Fanning (no kin to Edmund), were avenging the Battle of Alamance. And from those settlers of the piedmont who supported the patriot cause sprang a demand for democratic government when the time came to write a state constitution in 1776. Against the united opposition of royal governor and provincial aristocracy they had no chance at all of securing a permanent redress of their grievances, but when these two allies came to blows over the enforcement of British imperial legislation, the opportunity suddenly arose of obtaining not only responsible government but political equality as well.[13]

[12] Joseph S. Jones, *A Defense of the Revolutionary History of the State of North Carolina from the Aspersions of Mr. Jefferson* (Boston and Raleigh, 1834), 53.

[13] Carl Bridenbaugh argues that the Regulators' grievances were exaggerated and were to some degree pretexts to avoid payment of taxes and submission to the normal restraints of government. I cannot agree. The sharp note of injury and the uniformity of complaints in the voluminous Regulator documents from all over the piedmont cannot be passed off lightly. No doubt the Regulators shared with the rest of mankind an aversion to taxes, but in this instance it must be remembered that a refusal to pay them was the only way they could hope to force a redress of their grievances. They had no political control over local officials and the courts were in the hands of their enemies. Nor were the Regulators' objectives somewhat obscure, as Bridenbaugh asserts. First they wanted local officials to obey the law, and second they wanted certain political and legal reforms which would give a measure of responsible local government. For Bridenbaugh's views see his *Myths and Realities: Societies of the Colonial South* (Baton Rouge, 1952), 160–162. For an estimate more favorable to the Regulators see Hugh T. Lefler and Albert R. Newsome, *North Carolina: the History of a Southern State* (Chapel Hill, 1954), 24–40.

Suggested Further Reading:

The history of colonial unrest can be usefully approached through the study of provincial politics. The newest and best volume yet to appear on this subject is Jack P. Greene's *The Quest for Power: The Lower Houses of Assembly in the Southern Royal Colonies, 1689–1776* (1963). More controversial is the writing of Robert E. Brown; his *Middle Class Democracy and the Revolution in Massachusetts, 1691–1780* (1955) has now been followed by *Virginia, 1705–1786: Democracy or Aristocracy?* (written with B. Katherine Brown, 1964); both books argue for substantial popular participation in colonial politics. Perhaps the most readable study of Virginia politics is Charles S. Sydnor's *Gentlemen Freeholders: Political Practices in Washington's Virginia** (1952).

The literature on Bacon's Rebellion is voluminous, but Thomas Jefferson Wertenbaker's *Torchbearer of the Revolution* (1940) provides a useful foil to Wilcomb E. Washburn's *Governor and the Rebel* (1957); a succinct and dispassionate account is provided by W. F. Craven in *The Southern Colonies in the Seventeenth Century* (1949), chap. 10. For New York, see Jerome R. Reich, *Leisler's Rebellion: A Study of Democracy in New York, 1664–1720* (1953); for Pennsylvania, see *The Paxton Papers,* ed. John R. Dunbar (1957); for the Carolinas, see Richard J. Hooker's *The South Carolina Back-country on the Eve of the Revolution* (1953), Richard Maxwell Brown, *The South Carolina Regulators* (1963) — whom he depicts as prototypes for the American vigilante movements of the nineteenth century, and Carl Bridenbaugh, *Myths and Realities** (1952), pp. 119–196.

PART SIX

The Road to Union, 1643-1774

American efforts to form an inter-colonial union made uneven and unsteady progress. Historians have not been generous to colonial efforts at unification, possibly because they find exasperating the slowness and seeming indifference of the leading actors in this important drama. But hindsight is sometimes an historical liability: the Continental Congress achieved a degree of union at least adequate to insure American survival in 1783.

It is also easy to lose sight of the colonists' perspective on this issue. A union, either organized from within by the colonies themselves, or, as was occasionally attempted, from without by the mother country, was never regarded as inevitable by many Americans. Franklin might urge "Join or Die," but most colonists were not inclined to heed such an imperative. Not one colonial legislature endorsed his Albany Plan of 1754.

In short, the benefits of inter-colonial union are more evident to twentieth-century Americans than to their seventeenth- and eighteenth-century ancestors. Today Americans know for a fact what to James Madison was merely a hope: that a large republic can function effectively. But in the minds of most colonial Americans there existed no precedent for a political union of such size or complexity, and Madison's predecessors as well as his contemporaries can be pardoned for their doubt and hesitancy.

1

The New England Confederation, 1643

Articles of Confederation

Of all the American attempts to organize an inter-colonial union before 1774, that represented by the Confederation of New England proved the most nearly autonomous. Established when the mother country had ample distractions at home, the Confederation was the product of a limited desire for cooperation on the part of the Puritan colonies of Connecticut, New Haven, Plymouth, and Massachusetts. Joint action was certainly facilitated by their common Puritan identity, by England's inability to supply either protection or direction, and, of course, by threats (real and imaginary) from the Dutch, French, and Indians. The Pequot War of 1637 had made its impression.

The deficiencies of the Articles are obvious enough: they created an extremely loose association wherein the decisions of the governing Commissioners were only advisory. The general courts retained full sovereignty and never formally acknowledged the supremacy of the Confederation. Furthermore, the preponderant power and wealth of Massachusetts made her associates in federation somewhat nervous — and angry when, as in 1653, Massachusetts declined to accept a majority decision to wage war on the Dutch in New Netherland.

"Articles of Confederation," August 29, 1643. Reprinted in *Records of the Colony of New Plymouth in New England,* ed. Nathaniel B. Shurtleff, *et. al.* (Boston, 1855–1861), IX, 3–8.

Betweene the plantations vnder the Gouernment of the Massachusetts, the Plantacons vnder the Gouernment of New Plymouth, the Plantacons vnder the Gouernment of Connectacutt, and the Gouernment of New Haven with the Plantacons in combinacon therewith.

Whereas wee all came into these parts of America with one and the same end and ayme, namely, to advaunce the kingdome of our Lord Jesus Christ, and to enjoy the liberties of the Gospell in puritie with peace. And whereas in our settleinge (by a wise Providence God) we are further dispersed vpon the Sea Coasts and Riuers then was at first intended, so that we cannot according to our desire, with convenience communicate in one Gouernment and Jurisdiccon. And whereas we live encompassed with people of seuerall Nations and strang languages which heareafter may proue injurious to vs or our posteritie. And forasmuch as the Natives have formerly committed sondry insolences and outrages vpon seueral Plantacons of the English and have of late combined themselues against vs. And seing by reason of those sad Distraccons in England, which they have heard of, and by which they know we are hindred from that humble way of seekinge advise or reapeing those comfortable fruits of protection which at other tymes we might well expecte. Wee therefore doe conceiue it our bounden Dutye without delay to enter into a present consotiation amongst our selues for mutual help and strength in all our future concernements: That as in Nation and Religion, so in other Respects we bee and continue one according to the tenor and true meaninge of the ensuing Articles: Wherefore it is fully agreed and concluded by and betweene the parties or Jurisdiccons aboue named, and they joyntly and seuerally doe by these presents agreed and concluded that they all bee, and henceforth bee called by the Name of the United Colonies of New-England.

II. The said United Colonies, for themselues and their posterities, do joyntly and seuerally, hereby enter into a firme and perpetuall league of friendship and amytie, for offence and defence, mutuall advise and succour, vpon all just occations, both for preserueing and propagateing the truth and liberties of the Gospel, and for their owne mutuall safety and wellfare.

III. It is further agreed That the Plantacons which at present are or hereafter shalbe settled within the limmetts of the Massachusetts, shalbe forever vnder the Massachusetts, and shall have peculiar Jurisdiccon among themselues in all cases as an entire Body, and that Plymouth, Conneckracutt, and New Haven shall eich of them haue like peculiar Jurisdiccon and Gouernment within their limmetts and in reference to the Plantacons which already are settled or shall hereafter be erected or shall settle within their limmetts respectiuely; prouided that no other Jurisdiccon shall hereafter be taken in as a distinct head or member of this Confederacon, nor shall any other Plantacon or Jurisdiccon in present being and not already in combynacon or vnder the Jurisdiccon of any of these Confederats be received by any of them, nor shall any two of the Confederats joyne in one Jurisdiccon without consent of the rest, which consent to be interpreted as is expressed in the sixth Article ensuinge.

IV. It is by these Confederats agreed that the charge of all just warrs, whether offensiue or defensiue, upon what part or member of this Confederacon soever they fall, shall both in men and provisions, and all other Disbursements, be borne by all the parts of this Confederacon, in different proporcons according to their different abilitie, in manner following, namely, that the Commissioners for eich Jurisdiccon from tyme to tyme, as there shalbe occation, bring a true account and number of all the males in every Plantacon, or any way belonging to, or under their seuerall Jurisdiccons, of what quality or condicion soeuer they bee, from sixteene yeares old to three-score, being Inhabitants there. And That according to the different numbers which from tyme to tyme shalbe found in each Jurisdiccon, upon a true and just account, the service of men and all charges of the warr be borne by the Poll: Eich Jurisdiccon, or Plantacon, being left to their owne just course and custome of rating themselues and people according to their different estates, with due respects to their qualities and exemptions among themselues, though the Confederacon take no notice of any such priviledg: And that according to their different charge of eich Jurisdiccon and Plantacon, the whole advantage of the war (if it please God to bless their Endeavours) whether it be in lands, goods or persons, shall be proportionably deuided among the said Confederats.

V. It is further agreed That if any one of these Jurisdiccons, or any Plantacons vnder it, or in any combynacon with them be envaded by any enemie whomsoeuer, vpon notice and request of any three majestrats of that Jurisdiccon so invaded, the rest of the Confederates, without any further meeting or expostulacon, shall forthwith send ayde to the Confederate in danger, but in different proporcons; namely, the Massachusets an hundred men sufficiently armed and provided for such a service and jorney, and eich of the rest fourty-fiue so armed and provided, or any lesse number, if lesse be required, according to this proporcon. But if such Confederate in danger may be supplyed by their next Confederate, not exceeding the number hereby agreed, they may craue help there, and seeke no further for the present. The charge to be borne as in this Article is exprest: And, at the returne, to be victualled and supplyed with poder and shott for their journey (if there be neede) by that Jurisdiccon which employed or sent for them: But none of the Jurisdiccons to exceed these numbers till by a meeting of the Commissioners for this Confederacon a greater ayd appeare necessary. And this proporcon to continue, till upon knowledge of greater numbers in eich Jurisdiccon which shall be brought to the next meeting some other proporcon be ordered. But in any such case of sending men for present ayd whether before or after such order or alteracon, it is agreed that at the meeting of the Commissioners for this Confederacon, the cause of such warr or invasion be duly considered: And if it appeare that the fault lay in the parties so invaded, that then that Jurisdiccon or Plantacon make just Satisfaccon, both to the Invaders whom they have injured, and beare all the charges of the warr themselves without requireing any allowance from the rest of the Confederats towards the same. And further, that if any Jurisdiccon see any danger of any Invasion approaching, and there be tyme for a meeting, that in such case three majestrats of that Jurisdiccon may summon a meeting at such convenyent place as themselues shall think meete, to consider and provide against the threatned danger,

Provided when they are met they may remoue to what place they please, Onely whilst any of these foure Confederats have but three majestrats in their Jurisdiccon, their request or summons from any two of them shalbe accounted of equall force with the three mentoned in both the clauses of this Article, till there be an increase of majestrats there.

VI. It is also agreed that for the mannaging and concluding of all affairs proper and concerneing the whole Confederacon, two Commissioners shalbe chosen by and out of eich of these foure Jurisdiccons, namely, two for the Mattachusets, two for Plymouth, two for Connectacutt and two for New Haven; being all in Church fellowship with us, which shall bring full power from their seuerall generall Courts respectively to heare, examine, weigh and determine all affaires of our warr or peace, leagues, ayds, charges and numbers of men for warr, divission and spoyles and whatsoever is gotten by conquest, receiueing of more Confederats for plantacons into combinacon with any of the Confederats, and all things of like nature which are the proper concomitants or consequence of such a confederacon, for amytie, offence and defence, not intermeddling with the gouernment of any of the Jurisdiccons which by the third Article is preserued entirely to themselves. But if these eight Commissioners, when they meete, shall not all agree, yet it is concluded that any six of the eight agreeing shall have power to settle and determine the business in question: But if six do not agree, that then such proposicons with their reasons, so farr as they have beene debated, be sent and referred to the foure generall Courts, vizt. the Mattachusetts, Plymouth, Connectacutt, and New Haven: And if at all the said Generall Courts the businesse so referred be concluded, then to bee prosecuted by the Confederates and all their members. It is further agreed that these eight Commissioners shall meete once every yeare, besides extraordinary meetings (according to the fift Article) to consider, treate and conclude of all affaires belonging to this Confederacon, which meeting shall ever be the first Thursday in September. And that the next meeting after the date of these presents, which shalbe accounted the second meeting, shalbe at Bostone in the Massachusetts, the third at Hartford, the fourth at New Haven, the fift at Plymouth, the sixt and seaventh at Bostone. And then Hartford, New Haven and Plymouth, and so in course successiuely, if in the meane tyme some middle place be not found out and agreed on which may be commodious for all the jurisdiccons.

VII. It is further agreed that at eich meeting of these eight Commissioners, whether ordinary or extraordinary, they, or six of them agreeing, as before, may choose their President out of themselues, whose office and worke shalbe to take care and direct for order and a comely carrying on of all proceedings in the present meeting. But he shalbe invested with no such power or respect as by which he shall hinder the propounding or progresse of any businesse, or any way cast the Scales, otherwise then in the precedent Article is agreed.

VIII. It is also agreed that the Commissioners for this Confederacon hereafter at their meetings, whether ordinary or extraordinary, as they may have commission or opertunitie, do endeavoure to frame and establish agreements and orders in generall cases of a civill nature wherein all the plantacons are interested for preserving peace among themselues, and preventing as much as may bee all occations of warr or difference with others, as about the free and speedy passage of Justice in every Jurisdiccon, to all the Confederats equally as their own, receiving those that remoue from one plantacon to another without due certefycats; how all the Jurisdiccons may carry it towards the Indians, that they neither grow insolent nor be injured without due satisfaccion, lest warr break in vpon the Confederates through such miscarryage. It also agreed that if any servant runn away from his master into any other of these confederated Jurisdiccons, That in such Case, vpon the Certyficate of one Majestrate in the Jurisdiccon out of which the said servant fled, or upon other due proofe, the said servant shalbe deliuered either to his Master or any other that pursues and brings such Certificate or proofe. And that vpon the escape of any prisoner whatsoever or fugitiue for any criminal cause, whether breaking prison or getting from the officer or otherwise escaping, upon the certificate of two Majestrats of the Jurisdiccon out of which the escape is made that he was a prisoner or such an offender at the tyme of the escape. The Majestrates or some of them of that Jurisdiccon where for the present the said prisoner or fugitive abideth shall forthwith graunt such a warrant as the case will beare for the apprehending of any such person, and the delivery of him into the hands of the officer or other person that pursues him. And if there be help required for the safe returneing of such offender, then it shalbe graunted to him that craves the same, he paying the charges thereof.

IX. And for that the justest warrs may be of dangerous consequence, espetially to the smaler plantacons in these vnited Colonies, it is agreed that neither the Massachusetts, Plymouth, Connectacutt nor New-Haven, nor any of the members of any of them shall at any tyme hereafter begin, undertake, or engage themselues or this Confederacon, or any part thereof in any warr whatsoever (sudden exegents with the necessary consequents thereof excepted which are also to be moderated as much as the case will permit) without the consent and agreement of the forenamed eight Commissioners, or at least six of them, as in the sixt Article is provided: And that no charge be required of any of the Confederats in case of a defensiue warr till the said Commissioners haue mett and approued the justice of the warr, and have agreed vpon the sum of money to be levyed, which sum is then to be payd by the severall Confederates in proporcon according to the fourth Article.

X. That in extraordinary occations when meetings are summoned by three Majistrats of any Jurisdiccon, or two as in the fift Article, If any of the Commissioners come not, due warneing being given or sent, It is agreed that foure of the Commissioners shall have power to direct a warr which cannot be delayed and to send for due proporcons of men out of eich Jurisdiccon, as well as six might doe if all mett; but not less than six shall determine the justice of the warr or allow the demanude of bills of charges or cause any levies to be made for the same.

XI. It is further agreed that if any of the Confederates shall hereafter break any of these present Articles, or be any other wayes injurious to any one of thother Jurisdiccons, such breach of Agreement, or injurie, shalbe duly considered and ordered by the Commissioners for thother Jurisdiccons, that both peace and this present Confederacon may be entirely preserued without violation.

XII. Lastly, this perpetuall Confederacon and the several Articles and Agreements thereof being read and seriously considered, both by the Generall Court for the Massachusetts, and by the Commissioners for Plymouth, Connectacutt and New Haven, were fully allowed and confirmed by three of the forenamed Confederates, namely, the Massachusetts, Connectacutt and New-Haven, Onely the Commissioners for Plymouth, having no Commission to conclude, desired respite till they might advise with their Generall Court, wherevpon it was agreed and concluded by the said court of the Massachusetts, and the Commissioners for the other two Confederates, That if Plymouth Consent, then the whole treaty as it stands in these present articles is and shall continue firme and stable without alteracon: But if Plymouth come not in, yet the other three Confederates doe by these presents confirme the whole Confederacon and all the Articles thereof, onely, in September next, when the second meeting of the Commissioners is to be at Bostone, new consideracon may be taken of the sixt Article, which concernes number of Commissioners for meeting and concluding the affaires of this Confederacon to the satisfaccon of the Court of the Massachusetts, and the Commissioners for thother two Confederates, but the rest to stand vnquestioned.

In testymony whereof, the Generall Court of the Massachusetts by their Secretary, and the Commissioners for Connectacutt and New-Haven haue subscribed these presente articles, this xixth of the third month, commonly called May, Anno Domini, 1643.

At a meeting of the Commissioners for the Confederacon, held at Boston, the Seaventh of September. It appeareing that the Generall Court of New Plymouth, and the severall Towneships thereof have read, considered and approoued these articles of Confederacon, as appeareth by Commission from their Generall Court beareing Date the xxixth of August, 1643, to Mr. Edward Winslowe and Mr. Will Collyer, to ratifye and confirme the same on their behalf, wee therefore, the Commissioners for the Mattachusetts, Connecktacutt and New

Haven, doe also for our seuerall Gouernments, subscribe vnto them.

JOHN WINTHROP,
Governor of Massachusetts.
THO. DUDLEY,
GEO. FENWICK,
THOMAS GREGSON,
THEOPH. EATON,
EDWA. HOPKINS.

2

The Dominion of New England, 1686-1689

I

THE PRESENT STATE OF AFFAIRS OF NEW ENGLAND

The colonies created the Confederation of New England to meet their own needs; four decades later England, to achieve ends of her own, created the Dominion of New England. The Dominion was a consequence of the Stuart restoration of 1660: Charles II, having secured his defenses at home, turned his attention towards his truculent, near-rebellious subjects in New England. The Dutch Wars intervened to delay the final reckoning, but in 1674 Charles sent an agent, EDWARD RANDOLPH, *to report on conditions in New England. Randolph duly noted violations of the Navigation Acts [see Part Seven], the persecution of the Quakers and Baptists, and the refusal of some New Englanders to take the oath of allegiance to the Crown. His indictment, substantially accurate, was employed in the* quo warranto *judicial proceedings which led to the revocation of the Massachusetts Bay charter in 1684.*

Edward Randolph, "The present state of affairs of New England," May 6, 1677. Reprinted in Robert N. Toppan, *Edward Randolph, including his Letters and Official Papers* (Boston, 1898–1899), II, 265–268.

The present state of the affairs of New England depending before the lords of the Commitee for Plantations are reduced to two heads, viz., matter of law and fact. Matter of law ariseth from the title of lands and government claimed by Mr. Mason and Mr. Gorges in their several provinces of New Hampshire and Maine, and also what right and title the Massachusetts have to either land or government in any part of New England; these are referred to the Lords Chief Justices of the King's Bench and Common Pleas for their opinion.

Matters of fact concern as well his Majesty as Mr. Mason and Mr. Gorges, and against the government of the Massachusetts these following articles will be proved.

1. That they have no right either to land or government in any part of New England and have always been usurpers.

2. That they have formed themselves into a commonwealth, denying any appeals to England, and contrary to other plantations do not take the oath of allegiance.

3. They have protected the late king's murderers, directly contrary to his Majesty's royal proclamation of the 6th of June 1660 and of his letters of 28th June 1662.

4. They coin money with their own impress.

5. They have put his Majesty's subjects to death for opinion in matters of religion.

6. In the year 1665 they did violently oppose his Majesty's commissioners in the settlement of New Hampshire and in 1668 by armed forces turned out his Majesty's justices of the peace in the province of Maine in contempt of his Majesty's authority and declaration of the 10th of April 1666.

7. They impose an oath of fidelity upon all that inhabit within their territories to be true and faithful to their government.

8. They violate all the Acts of Trade and Navigation by which they have engrossed the greatest part of the West India trade whereby his Majesty is damaged in his customs above 100,000 yearly and this kingdom much more.

Reasons inducing a speedy hearing and determination

1. His Majesty hath an opportunity to settle that country under his royal authority with little charge, Sir John Berry being now at Virginia not far distant from New England, and it lies in his way home where are many good harbours free from the worms, convenient towns for quartering of soldiers, and plentiful accommodation for men and shipping.

2. The earnest desire of most and best of the inhabitants (wearied out with the arbitrary proceedings of those in the present government) to be under his Majesty's government and laws.

3. The Indians upon the settlement of that country, it is presumed, would unanimously submit and become very serviceable and useful for improving that country, there being upward of three hundred thousand English Indians? inhabiting therein.

Proposals for the settling of that country

1. His Majesty's gracious and general pardon upon their conviction of having acted without and in contempt of his Majesty's authority will make the most refractory to comply to save their estates.

2. His Majesty's declaration of confirming unto the inhabitants the lands and houses they now possess upon payment of an easy quit-rent and granting liberty of conscience in matters of religion.

3. His Majesty's commission directed to the most eminent persons for estates and loyalty in every colony to meet, consult and act for the present peace and safety of that country during his Majesty's pleasure, and that such of the present magistrates be of the council as shall readily comply with his Majesty's commands in the settling of the country, and a pension to be allowed them out of the public revenue of the country with some title of honour to be conferred upon the most deserving of them, will cause a general submission.

II

Commission to Sir Edmund Andros as Governor of the Dominion of New England

Charles II did not live to see his vigorous colonial policies implemented, and it was left to his less astute brother, James II, to devise and administer the new Dominion of New England. As the royal commissioner to Sir Edmund Andros made explicit, the new administrative unit was to embrace Massachusetts, New Hampshire, Connecticut, Rhode Island, New York, and New Jersey — and eventually Pennsylvania. The powers granted to the new "governor-in-chief" were far-reaching, and, in the opinion of most colonials, entirely too vast and arbitrary.

James the second, by the Grace of God, king of England, Scotland, France, and Ireland, Defender of the Faith, etc. To our trusty and well-beloved Sir Edmund Andros, knight, Greeting: whereas by our commission under our Great Seal of England, bearing date the third day of June in the second year of our reign, we have constituted and appointed you to be our captain-general and governor-in-chief in and over all that part of our territory and dominion of New England in America known by the names of our colony of the Massachusetts Bay, our colony of New Plymouth, our provinces of New Hampshire and Maine, and the Narragansett country or King's Province; and whereas since that time we have thought it necessary for our service and for the better protection and security of our subjects in those parts to join and annex to our said government the neighbouring colonies of Rhode Island and Connecticut, our province of New York and East and West Jersey, with the territories thereunto belonging,

Commission to Sir Edmund Andros as Governor of the Dominion of New England, April 7, 1688. Reprinted in *Documents Relative to the Colonial History of the State of New York*, ed., E. B. O'Callaghan and Berthold Fernow (Albany, 1856–1887), III, 537–542.

as we do hereby join, annex, and unite the same to our said government and dominion of New England. We therefore reposing especial trust and confidence in the prudence, courage, and loyalty of you, the said Sir Edmund Andros, out of our especial grace, certain knowledge, and mere motion, have thought fit to constitute and appoint, as we do by these presents constitute and appoint you, the said Sir Edmund Andros, to be our captain-general and governor-in-chief in and over our colonies of the Massachusetts Bay and New Plymouth, our provinces of New Hampshire and Maine, the Narragansett country or King's Province, our colonies of Rhode Island and Connecticut, our province of New York and East and West Jersey, and of all that tract of land, curcuit, continent, precincts, and limits in America lying and being in breadth from forty degrees of northern latitude from the equinoctial line to the river of St. Croix eastward, and from thence directly northward to the river of Canada, and in length and longitude by all the breadth aforesaid throughout the mainland from the Atlantic or Western sea or ocean on the east part, to the South Sea on the west part, with all the islands, seas, rivers, waters, rights, members and appurtenances thereunto belonging (our province of Pennsylvania and country of Delaware only excepted), to be called and known as formerly by the name and title of our territory and dominion of New England in America.

And for your better guidance and direction we do hereby require and command you to do and execute all things in due manner, that shall belong unto the said office and the trust we have reposed in you, according to the several powers, instructions and authorities mentioned in these presents, or such further powers, instructions, and authorities as you shall herewith receive or which shall at any time hereafter be granted or appointed you under our signet and sign manual, or by our order in our Privy Council, and according to such reasonable laws and statutes as are now in force or such others as shall hereafter be made and established within our territory and dominion aforesaid.

And our will and pleasure is that you, the said Sir Edmund Andros, having, after publication of these our letters patents, first taken the oath of duly executing the office of our captain-general and governor-in-chief of our said territory and dominion, which our Council there or any three of them are hereby required, authorized, and impowered to give and administer unto you, you shall administer unto each of the members of our Council the oath for the due execution of their places and trusts.

And we do hereby give and grant unto you full power and authority to suspend any member of our Council from sitting, voting and assisting therein, as you shall find just cause for so doing.

And if it shall hereafter at any time happen that by the death, departure out of our said territory, or suspension of any of our councillors, or otherwise, there shall be a vacancy in our said Council (any five whereof we do hereby appoint to be a quorum), our will and pleasure is that you signify the same unto us by the first opportunity, that we may under our signet and sign manual constitute and appoint others in their room.

And we do hereby give and grant unto you full power and authority, by and with the advice and consent of our said Council or the major part of them, to make, constitute and ordain laws, statutes and ordinances for the public peace, welfare, and good government of our said territory and dominion and of the people and inhabitants thereof, and such others as shall resort thereto, and for the benefit of us, our heirs and successors. Which said laws, statutes, and ordinances are to be, as near as conveniently may be, agreeable to the laws and statutes of this our kingdom of England: provided that all such laws, statutes, and ordinances of what nature or duration soever, be within three months, or sooner, after the making of the same, transmitted unto us, under our Seal of New England, for our allowance or disapprobation of them, as also duplicates thereof by the next conveyance.

And we do by these presents give and grant unto you full power and authority by and with the advice and consent of our said Council, or the major part of them, to impose, assess and raise and levy such rates and taxes as you shall find necessary for the support of the government within our territory and dominion of New England, to be collected and levied and to be employed to the uses aforesaid in such manner as to you and our said Council, or the major part of them, shall seem most equal and reasonable.

And for the better supporting the charge of the government of our said territory and dominion, our will and pleasure is, and we do by these presents authorize and impower you, the said Sir Edmund Andros, and our Council, to continue such taxes and impositions as are now laid and imposed upon the inhabitants thereof; and to levy and distribute or cause the same to be levied and distributed to those ends in the best and most equal manner, until you shall by and with the advice and consent of our Council agree on and settle such other taxes as shall be sufficient for the support of our government there, which are to be applied to that use and no other.

And our further will and pleasure is that all public money raised or to be raised or appointed for the support of the government within our said territory and dominion, be issued out by warrant or order from you, by and with the advice and consent of our Council as aforesaid.

And our will and pleasure is that you shall and may keep and use our Seal appointed by us for our said territory and dominion.

And we do by these presents ordain, constitute, and appoint you or the commander-in-chief for the time being, and the Council of our said territory and dominion for the time being, to be a constant and settled court of record for the administration of justice to all our subjects inhabiting within our said territory and dominion, in all causes, as well civil as criminal, with full power and authority to hold pleas in all cases, from time to time, as well in pleas of the Crown and in all matters relating to the conservation of the peace and punishment of offenders, as in civil causes and actions between party and party, or between us and any of our subjects there, whether the same do concern the realty and relate to any right of freehold and inheritance, or whether the same do concern the personalty and relate to matter of debt, contract, damage, or other personal injury; and also in all mixed actions which may concern both realty and personalty; and therein, after due orderly proceeding and deliberate hearing of both sides, to give judgement and to award execution, as well in criminal as in civil cases as aforesaid, so as always that the forms of proceedings in such cases and the judgement thereupon to be given, be as consonant and agreeable to the laws and statutes of this our realm of England as the present state and condition of our subjects inhabiting within our said territory and dominion and the circumstances of the place will admit.

And we do further hereby give and grant unto you full power and authority, with the advice and consent of our said Council, to erect, constitute, and establish such and so many courts of judicature and public justice within our said territory and dominion as you and they shall think fit and necessary for the determining of all causes, as well criminal as civil, according to law and equity, and for awarding of execution thereupon, with all reasonable and necessary powers, authorities, fees, and privileges belonging unto them.

And our further will and pleasure is and we do hereby declare that all actings and proceedings at law or equity heretofore had or done, or now depending within any of the courts of our said territory, and all executions thereupon, be hereby confirmed and continued so far forth as not to be avoided for want of any legal power in the said courts; but that all and every such judicial actings, proceeding, and execution shall be of the same force, effect, and virtue as if such courts had acted by a just and legal authority.

And we do further by these presents will and require you to permit appeals to be made in cases of error from our courts in our said territory and dominion of New England unto you, or the commander-in-chief for the time being and the Council, in civil causes: provided the value appealed for do exceed the sum of one hundred pounds sterling, and that security be first duly given by the appellant to answer such charges as shall be awarded in case the first sentence shall be affirmed.

And whereas we judge it necessary that all our subjects may have liberty to appeal to our royal person in cases that may require the same: our will and pleasure is that if either party shall not rest satisfied with the judgment or sentence of you (or the commander-in-chief for the time being) and the Council, they may appeal unto us in our Privy Council: provided the matter in difference exceed the value and sum of three hundred pounds sterling and that such appeal be made within one fortnight after sentence, and that security be likewise duly given by the appellant to answer such charges as shall be awarded in case the sentence of you (or the commander-in-chief for the time being) and the Council be confirmed; and provided also that execution be not suspended by reason of any such appeal unto us.

And we do hereby give and grant unto you full power where you shall see cause and shall judge any offender or offenders in capital and criminal matters, or for any fines or forfeitures due unto us, fit objects of our mercy, to pardon such offenders and to remit such fines and forfeitures, treason and wilful murder only excepted, in which case you shall likewise have power upon extraordinary occasions to grant reprieves to the offenders therein until and to the intent our pleasure may be further known.

And we do hereby give and grant unto you the said Sir Edmund Andros, by yourself, your captains and commanders, by you to be authorized, full power and authority to levy, arm, muster, command, or employ, all persons whatsoever residing within our said territory and dominion of New England, and as occasion shall serve, them to transfer from one place to another for the resisting and withstanding all enemies, pirates, and rebels, both at land and sea, and to transfer such forces to any of our plantations in America or the territories thereunto belonging, as occasion shall require, for the defence of the same against the invasion or attempt of any of our enemies, and then, if occasion shall require, to pursue and prosecute in or out of the limits of our said territories and plantations or any of them; and if it shall so please God, them to vanquish; and, being taken, according to the law of arms, to put to death or keep and preserve alive, at your discretion. And also to execute martial law in time of invasion, insurrection, or war, and during the continuance of the same, and upon soldiers in pay, and to do and execute all and every other thing which to a captain-general doth or ought of right to belong, as fully and amply as any our captain-general doth or hath usually done.

And we do hereby give and grant unto you full power and authority to erect, raise and build within our territory and dominion aforesaid, such and so many forts, platforms, castles, cities, boroughs, towns, and fortifications as you shall judge necessary; and the same or any of them to fortify and furnish with ordnance, ammunition, and all sorts of arms, fit and necessary for the security and defence of our said territory; and the same again or any of them to demolish or dismantle as may be most convenient.

And we do hereby give and grant unto you, the said Sir Edmund Andros, full power and authority to erect one or more court or courts admiral within our said territory and dominion, for the hearing and determining of all marine and other causes and matters proper therein to be heard and determined, with all reasonable and necessary powers, authorities, fees, and privileges.

And you are to execute all powers belonging to the place and office of Vice-Admiral of and in all the seas and coasts about your government; according to such commission, authority, and instructions as you shall receive from ourself under the seal of our Admiralty or from our High Admiral of our foreign plantations for the time being.

And forasmuch as divers mutinies and disorders do happen by persons shipped and employed at sea, and to the end that such as shall be shipped or employed at sea may be the better governed and ordered: we do hereby give and grant unto you, the said Sir Edmund Andros, our captain-general and governor-in-chief, full power and authority to constitute and appoint captains, masters of ships, and other commanders, and to grant unto such captains, masters of ships, and other commanders commissions to execute the law martial, and to use such proceedings, authorities, punishment, correction, and execution upon any offender or offenders who shall be mutinous, seditious, disorderly, or any way unruly, either at sea or during the time of their abode or residence in any of the ports, harbours, or bays of our said territory and dominion, as the cause shall be found to require, according to martial law. Provided that nothing herein contained shall be construed to the enabling you or any by your authority to hold plea or have jurisdiction of any offence, cause, matter, or thing committed or done upon the sea or within any of the havens, rivers, or creeks of our said territory and dominion under your government, by any captain, commander, lieutenant, master, or other officer, seaman, soldier, or person whatsoever, who shall be in actual service and pay in and on board any of our ships of war or other vessels acting by immediate commission or warrant from ourself under the seal of our Admiralty, or from our High Admiral of England for the time being; but that such captain, commander, lieutenant, master, officer, seaman, soldier and other person so offending shall be left to be proceeded against and tried, as the merit of their offences shall require, either by commission under our Great Seal of England as the statute of 28 Henry VIII directs, or by commission from our said High Admiral, according to the act of Parliament passed in the 13th year of the reign of the late king, our most dear and most entirely beloved brother of ever blessed memory (entitled an act for the establishing articles and orders for the regulating and better government of his Majesty's navies, ships of war, and forces by sea) and not otherwise. Saving only, that it shall and may be lawful for you, upon such captains or commanders refusing or neglecting to execute, or upon his negligent or undue execution of any the written orders he shall receive from you for our service and the service of our said territory and dominion, to suspend him, and the said captain or commander, from the exercise of the said office of commander and commit him into safe custody, either on board his own ship or elsewhere, at the discretion of you, in order to his being brought to answer for the same by commission either under our Great Seal of England or from our said High Admiral, as is before expressed. In which case our will and pleasure is that the captain or commander so by you suspended, shall during such his suspension and commitment be succeeded in his said office, by such commission or warrant officer of our said ship appointed by ourself or our High Admiral for the time being, as by the known practice and discipline of our navy doth and ought next to succeed him, as in case of death, sickness, or other ordinary disability happening to the commander of any of our ships, and not otherwise; you standing also accountable to us for the truth and importance of the crimes and misdemeanours for which you shall so proceed to the suspending of such our said captain or commander. Provided also that all disorders and misdemeanours committed on shore by any captain, commander, lieutenant, master, or other officer, seaman, soldier or person whatsoever belonging to any of our ships of war or other vessel acting by immediate commission or warrant from ourself under the Great Seal of our Admiralty or from our High Admiral of England for the time being, may be tried and punished according to the laws of the place where any such disorders, offences, and misdemeanours shall be so committed on shore, notwithstanding such offender be in our actual service and borne in our pay on board any such our ships of war or other vessels acting by immediate commission or warrant from ourself or our High Admiral as aforesaid; so as he shall not receive any protection (for the avoiding of justice for such offences committed on shore) from any pretence of his being employed in our service at sea.

And we do likewise give and grant unto you full power and authority by and with the advice and consent of our said Council to agree with the planters and inhabitants of our said territory and dominion concerning such lands, tenements, and hereditamets as now are or hereafter shall be in our power to dispose of, and them to grant unto any person or persons for such terms and under such moderate quit-rents, services, and acknowledgments to be thereupon reserved unto us as shall be appointed by us. Which said grants are to pass and be sealed by our Seal of New England and, being entered upon record by such officer or officers as you shall appoint thereunto, shall be good and effectual in law against us, our heirs and successors.

And we do give you full power and authority to appoint so many fairs, marts, and markets as you with the advice of the said Council shall think fit.

As likewise to order and appoint within our said territory such and so many ports, harbours, bays, havens and other places for the convenience and security of shipping, and for the better loading and unloading of goods and merchandise as by you with the advice and consent of our Council shall be thought fit and necessary; and in them or any of them to erect, nominate, and appoint custom houses, warehouses, and officers relating thereto; and them to alter, change, place or displace from time to time, as with the advice aforesaid shall be thought fit.

And forasmuch as pursuant to the laws and customs of our colony of the Massachusetts Bay and of our other colonies and provinces aforementioned, divers marriages have been made and performed by the magistrates of our said territory; our royal will and pleasure is hereby to confirm all the said marriages and to direct that they be held good and valid in the same manner, to all intents and purposes whatsoever, as if they had been made and contracted according to the laws established within our kingdom of England.

And we do hereby require and command all officers and ministers, civil and military, and all other inhabitants of our said territory and dominion to be obedient, aiding, and assisting unto you, the said Sir Edmund Andros, in the execution of this our commission and of the powers and authorities therein contained, and upon your death or absence out of our said territory, unto our lieutenant-governor, to whom we do, therefore, by these presents give and grant all and singular the powers and authorities aforesaid to be exercised and enjoyed by him in case of your death, or absence during our pleasure, or until your arrival within our said territory and dominion; as we do further hereby give and grant full power and authority to our lieutenant-governor to do and execute whatsoever he shall be by you authorized and appointed to do and execute, in pursuance of and according to the powers and authorities granted to you by this commission.

And if in case of your death or absence there be no person upon the place, appointed by us to be commander-in-chief; our will and pleasure is that the then present Council of our territory aforesaid, do take upon them the administration of the government and execute this commission and the several powers and authorities herein contained; and that the first councillor who shall be at the time of your death or absence residing within the same, do preside in our said Council, with such powers and preheminences as any former president hath used and enjoyed within our said territory, or any other our plantations in America, until our pleasure be further known, or your arrival as aforesaid.

And lastly, our will and pleasure is that you, the said Sir Edmund Andros, shall and may hold, exercise, and enjoy the office and place of captain-general and governor-in-chief in and over our territory and dominion aforesaid, with all its rights, members, and appurtenances whatsoever, together with all and singular the powers and authorities hereby granted unto you, for and during our will and pleasure.

III

Dominion Interlude

There are several valid ways to analyze the Dominion of New England: it may be regarded merely as an incidental chapter in the abortive attempts at an inter-colonial union, or viewed as one of the persistent Stuart efforts to gain for the English Crown a tighter administration of colonial America. Finally, it may be considered as an interesting "interlude," a three-year void punctuating the end of King Philip's War and the final phase of the hard-dying Confederation of New England.

This last interpretation belongs to Harry M. Ward, *a student of colonial federalism who now teaches at Morehead State College. Professor Ward notes that the Confederation was still very much alive (if inactive) when Andros arrived in 1686, and he points out that the Confederation enjoyed a brief revival upon the overthrow of the despotic Dominion. To what extent the Dominion "increased the horizons for American union" may well be debated. Certainly, as Viola Barnes has observed, the revolt against Andros produced a reaction sympathetic to the Dominion concept.*[1]

The Stuart policy of centralizing government in the colonies under more direct control of the home government had a very real basis, because

Reprinted from Harry M. Ward, *The United Colonies of New England, 1643–1690* (New York: The Vantage Press, 1961), pp. 329–337.

[1] Viola F. Barnes, *The Dominion of New England: A Study in British Colonial Policy* (New York, 1960), pp. 258–261.

of the danger of aggression from their French neighbor to the north. But other practical reasons existed for wanting to consolidate the governments of the colonies. First of all, there was the very great expense of maintaining separate royal governments in the colonies; the colonies [could] not sustain the expense of the many English officials required to come to the colonies. Furthermore, there would be needed effective enforcement of the trade acts and development of naval stores in the New England colonies. The conciliatory policy of President Dudley, and his rivalry with Randolph, was impeding the work of the new government in the Bay, especially Randolph's collection of custom duties. It was not surprising then that as early as June, 1686, Sir Edmund Andros was commissioned Governor of the Dominion of New England, with powers including those of Captain General of all military forces of the Dominion and Vice Admiral of the English navy. The new governor would preside over a territory embracing all of the confederate colonies, Rhode Island, New Hampshire, Maine, and the disputed Narragansett country. Like the Dudley administration in Massachusetts, the Dominion governor was to preside over a council made up of the leading prerogative men in the colonies. Thus the proposals of Randolph in 1681 were put into effect. This bitter opponent of the Puritan oligarchy had written that the appointment of a Governor General over "all the Colonies being 5 in number united under one generall Government" would be more "serviceable to the Crown, and the better enabled to secure themselves and Neighbouring Plantations against any forreign Invasion or Domestick attempts; all of them at present being independent, not one Government haveing authority, or Influence upon another in Civill or Military Affaires." Though the courts of election had already elected Commissioners of the United Colonies for 1686, the establishment of royal government in Massachusetts and subsequently dominion government for the colonies, served sharply to cut off the Confederation. Naturally, with the colonies brought under imperial control and a consolidated administration replacing the cooperative union of the colonies, the New England Confederation could not exist. To have done so would have been rebellion. Thus no Commissioners were chosen during the period of the dominion government from any of the three colonies.

On a bleak December day in 1686, the head of the Stuart contrivance for the Dominion of New England, the paper union of all His Majesty's colonies in the Canaan of the New World, arrived in Boston with two companies of English troops, the first ever to be stationed in America. The arrival of the "Captain Generall, Governour of New England" was a gala occasion. When the Governor had landed he was met by a great crowd of Boston merchants and many other citizens, and all the militia of "Horse and Foot" were drawn up to honor the new Governor. But Governor Andros was not one to be delayed by pomp and circumstance; he had a serious and difficult task, to transform completely the governments of the New England colonies, which could only be done with speed, before an opposition party could be organized. Thus he proceeded immediately to the Town House, the scene of the former government and of the meetings of the Commissioners of the United Colonies when in Boston, where his commission of June, 1686, and subsequent instructions were read. A Council for the colonies was summoned to meet nine days later, and for those officials already present, the oaths of allegiance and office were administered. But the first meetings of the new Council were thinly attended, and of the twenty-six members of the Council, hardly more than six or seven ever appeared, and these being recipients of the Governor's patronage, such as the former Commissioners of the United Colonies, Dudley and Stoughton, who were both appointed judges of the "Superior Court."

The Dominion of New England afforded a sharp contrast to the previous self-governing colonies. The only constitution was that derived from the commission and various instructions to the new governor, which struck at the very heart of local self-government and confined all powers in an administrative agency, without recognition of the right of people to legislate in their own affairs. In effect, the Andros government was to be absolute, invested with full authority to enact laws, levy taxes, and control the militia of the colonies. Andros was authorized to regulate the value of foreign coinage in the colonies, the right of the Bay to continue minting its own coins being disallowed. All laws were to be sent to England for approval, and those disallowed by the King in Council were to be void in the colonies. An alien feature to the laws of New England was the requiring of a quit rent of two shillings and sixpence per hundred acres on all lands to be disposed in the future. "Liberty of Conscience" was to be permitted to all religions, but with special emphasis upon "the exercise of Religion according to the Church of England." Another point of contrast with the former government was the placing of New England on a permanent military basis, whereas formerly the colonies would invest supreme military authority in the colonial councils or the Confederation for the temporary duration of an emergency. But now, with the government under continual control of the Governor-General, the supreme commander of the military forces of the colonies and his administrative council, all affairs of government could at any time be subject to the military arm. Andros recognized the value of maintaining a strong grasp on the military forces in order to bring about effectively the consolidation of the New England governments — using the pretence of threatened invasion from the French in Canada. A vital part in the consolidation of the military resources of the colonies was the establishment of military depots "for receiving and keeping of arms, ammunition, and other public stores."

But the coming of Governor Andros to organize the governments of Massachusetts, New Plymouth, New Hampshire, Maine, and the Narragansett country under one administration still left the envisioned dominion of the northern colonies incomplete. To round out the Dominion of New England, the submission of Connecticut and Rhode Island had to be obtained. Although neither of the two colonies would surrender their charters to Andros, Rhode Island readily acquiesced in the new government by sending its five members to the Andros Council. The River Colony, however, remained obstinate; and, although the surrendering of its charter was not essential to the dissolution of the colonial government, Governor Andros took the position that such action was necessary as a visible sign of submission. Three writs of *quo warranto* were served on the Connecticut colony to surrender its charter, but they were of no avail. Pressure was brought to bear on Connecticut — even Governor Dongan of New York advised the Colony's submission, and indeed, there was little left to do unless Connecticut should take its chances in court, with very little chance for success, since the Massachusetts and the City of London charters had already been vacated.

Governor Andros, to demonstrate his policy (he still harbored a special grievance against Connecticut for that Colony's refusal to allow his contingent of New York troops to participate in the war of the United Colonies against Philip's Indians) decided in October, 1687, to travel down to Hartford and compel the recalcitrant River officials to submit formally to his dominion government. Little notice was given to the Hartford authorities of the coming of the Andros expedition from Boston, and therefore there was not much that could be done except to welcome the dominion governor and his entourage upon their arrival. Andros soon attended a meeting of the General Court, and while a debate was ensuing, with the Connecticut Charter lying upon the table, the lights of the chamber were suddenly extinguished. When the lights came on again, the Charter had vanished. Many a story has been written about the disappearance of the Connecticut Charter — that it was whisked away to the famous Charter Oak, and there remained until popular government was restored in the colony — and many guesses have been made as to who was responsible for this daring maneuver — Allyn, Talcott, Treat, or Wadsworth. Some have doubted the authenticity of the episode altogether. But such discussion is not within the scope of this work; it suffices to note that in any event Governor Andros did not secure the Charter. Nevertheless, he had accomplished for the time being the main object of his mission, for he successfully secured the submission of the Colony. The General Court immediately ceased its jurisdiction, and ordered that the Colony, "being annexed to the Massachusetts and other colonys," proceed "under his Excellencies Government." Three weeks later the Dominion Council declared that the laws of the Council were now in force in the River Colony. In April, 1688, the jurisdiction of the Dominion was extended to embrace New York and the Jerseys — with this last addition considered as one colony. The Dominion of New England covered in one union eight of His Majesty's colonies, a solid phalanx on the northern seaboard.

The powers of the Dominion Governor were now quite formidable. He was to preside over a Council of forty-two members from the representatives of the colonies forming the consolidation. The governor had authority to suspend a Councillor or any members of the militia simply by showing sufficient cause. With only five members making a quorum in the Council, there was virtually no restraint upon the influence of the Governor, who could always count on a loyal few to carry through his policy. Even that odious practice of giving to provincial governors the "power of the press" was initiated, by which all printing had to be licensed by the government. Such an arbitrary government was obviously an anachronism in New England affairs. If Andros had been as wise a politician as he was an able administrator of Stuart policy, he might have had a fair degree of success in consolidating the New England governments on a permanent basis. Playing for the support of not only the prerogative men but also for the moderate party men such as Bradstreet and Stoughton, Governor Andros could have built up real support for the government. He would also have had to be careful not to interfere too directly with the settled institutions of the New Englanders. But resorting to his training as Governor of the province of New York, Andros made the tragic blunder of trying to institute government alien to the New Englanders — of which there could have been no greater error in judging the temperament of a people who on their own had constructed a confederate government.

The Dominion Governor soon found that exercising his authority was an entirely different matter from what it had appeared on paper. Concentrating his efforts on the Bay Colony, the Andros Council proceeded to levy taxes without the consent of an assembly of the people. Public fees were increased, those of the probate some twenty-fold. Town meetings were allowed to meet but once a year. Writs of intrusion forced the landed proprietors to engage in expensive suits to defend their titles; the claims of the Atherton Company in the Narragansett country were again invalidated, as "having been based upon grants extorted through terror from the Indians by the illegal acts of the United Colonies," and Rhode Island was again for the third time given jurisdiction over the King's Province. Many grievances mounted against the Andros government, some of which were merely distasteful to the Puritan manner of doing things. But the investment in the colonial executive of sole powers of taxation, the infringement upon the land system of the colonies, and the regulation of town government aroused the resentment of all the New England colonists, to whatever faction they belonged.

Governor Andros had little time to expand his experiment in consolidation outside the Bay Colony. The protests there had shown that he would have to proceed more cautiously. But meanwhile his time was consumed inspecting the governments under his rule and in raising forces to put down an Indian uprising, again spreading on the northern frontier. The advantages of consolidation from a military point of view were seen when Andros personally headed an expedition of some seven or eight hundred troops to the Maine settlements — a protection to this frontier which the New England Confederation after King Philip's War was unable to afford, and would be unable to do again when the reins of Dominion government would be severed. But the Andros expedition only added to his unpopularity, and he was even accused of creating a war in order to build up his military control.

The Indian problem thus averted the Dominion government from meeting a real test in domestic policy. As for the land grants requiring the payment of quit rents, not more than twenty were actually passed during the entire Andros administration, to give an indication of how little the process of royalization of the New England colonies had progressed. Andro's attention was further distracted by the pressure put on him from New York for a joint expedition of the Dominion colonies against the French in Canada. Nor was there much time to revive the missionary work among the Indians, which had been the province of the Commissioners of the United Colonies. The Lieutenant-Governor of the Dominion, Francis Nicholson, who resided at New York, took it upon himself to visit several of the plantations of praying Indians, but used the opportunity to draft the Indians into military service. Although Eliot, lingering on to the last days in his worldly home, felt that "the work in general seemeth to my soul to be in and well toward a reviving," he sensed that he was "drawing home," which also might have been said of the "Indian Worke" as a whole.

Hardly had Andros returned to Boston from his unfruitful expedition against the northern Indians, than a wave of popular indignation greeted him. Tidings of the landing of William of Orange had reached the New World. The Governor tried unsuccessfully to keep the news from the populace, but the long-awaited overthrow of the Stuart monarchy, accomplished without the shedding of blood, was too great an occurrence in the Puritan colonies to be for long kept secret. The news of the "Protestant Wind" bringing the Prince of Orange (New Englanders through their Puritan heritage had always entertained a closer tie with the Dutch than did their brethren back home) served as a spark to raise the colonists in the Bay in rebellion against the hated regime. The organization of government during the course of the rebellion was in many ways similar to the course of action followed by the American patriots during the era of the Revolution.

On that fateful day of April 18, the very day that the second rebellion began in 1775 in the British march to Concord, about nine o'clock in the morning, the sound of drums echoed throughout the town of Boston. A crowd of townspeople began to crowd about the Town House, eagerly awaiting word from the leading citizens, who as members of Andros' Council were known to be unsympathetic to the Dominion government. About noon a "Declaration of the Gentlemen, Merchants, and Inhabitants of Boston and the Country adjacent" was read, meeting the approval of the people. Like the Declaration of the following century, it enumerated grievances against the arbitrary rule of Andros and conciliar government as a whole. The peroration of this Declaration of the right of revolution, with its expressions of a latent nationalism, is deserving of quotation:

> We do therefore seize upon the persons of those few ill men which have been (next to our sins) the grant authors of our miseries; resolving to secure them for what justice orders from his Highness, with the English Parliament, shall direct, lest, ere we are aware, to find (what we may fear, being on all sides in danger) ourselves to be by them given away to a foreign power, before such orders can reach unto us; for which orders we now humbly wait. In the mean time, firmly believing that we have endeavoured nothing but what mere duty to God and our country calls for at our hands, we commit our enterprise unto the blessing of Him who hears the cry of the oppressed; and advise all our neghbors, for whom we have thus ventured ourselves, to join with us in prayers, and all just actions, for the defence of the land.

The leading men in the revolution of both the moderate and old guard factions put in an appearance at the Town House during this dramatic episode, among whom were counted the former Commissioners of the United Colonies — William Stoughton, Thomas Danforth, Simon Bradstreet, Wait Winthrop — and a new political figure in the Bay, a Commissioner during the revival of the Confederation, Elisha Cooke.

Andros and his retainers took refuge in the castle fort in Boston harbor, but were soon compelled to surrender, and were held as prisoners. Thus, with one easy stroke, rebellion was smoothly accomplished in New England. It has been pointed out that the New England colonies would have revolted against the Andros government whether or not the Glorious Revolution had taken place in the mother country. Evidence given for this position is the careful framing of the "Declaration," which must have taken more than several days during the fury of revolt to have been drawn up. The reasons given for the justification of the revolution in New England, the attempt of Andros to stifle the news of the landing of William of Orange in England and the popular furor over Andros's Indian expedition, only ignited into flames the rebellion that was smouldering under real economic and political grievances.

The New Englanders sought to cover up all traces of the brief period of the Dominion of New England. It was to be nothing more than an unpleasant memory. The records of the

Andros Council were slashed from the official records of the colonies, and the new records of the established colonial governments read as if nothing had happened during the sixteen months of the Andros regime, the time that Connecticut was included in the Dominion, and twenty-eight months for the Massachusetts Colony. Connecticut immediately re-established its charter government, pointing out that it was never revoked, though there was "an interruption to our government" due to the brief dominion status of the colonies. Since Connecticut had felt the brunt of Andros' policies very little, the freemen of the colony had no difficulty in reconvening a court of elections in May and renewing their former government. Plymouth, likewise, soon had its previous government in operation again. But in the Bay, four years of Council government under President Dudley and then under Andros had effected a real severance of the colonial government. To get back on its feet a gradual policy had to be followed: first, as in a later Revolution period, a Council of Safety of the prominent men of the Colony delegated to themselves interim authority of government. The venerable former Governor and Commissioner, Simon Bradstreet, was chosen president of this body; and Wait Winthrop, now of the Bay Colony, who had served as a Connecticut Commissioner with his father during the latter's last year of life, was placed in command of the militia.

From the Massachusetts Council of Safety would emerge the re-establishment of the Colony government and a brief revival of the New England Confederation, both of which would soon be replaced by a new imperial arrangement whereby the one-time Puritan Commonwealth would become a royal colony and Plymouth would cease to exist as a separate colony. But the road to subsequent union of the American colonies was now to be trodden in an ever widening sphere of intercolonial cooperative action. Though the Andros government and succeeding generations failed to contribute in depth to an emerging consciousness for union, the desire for the enlargement of the sphere of cooperation, now embracing all of the New England colonies and New York, was a very definite contribution. Thus the Dominion of New England was more than an unfortunate interlude or interruption; it increased the horizons for American union.

3

The Albany Plan, 1754

I

The Board of Trade Plan, 1754

Interest in inter-colonial union did not die with the overthrow of the Dominion of New England in April, 1689. Although William and Mary, the new sovereigns of Great Britain, did not care to identify themselves with the autocratic experiments of their unpopular predecessor, suggestions for some form of union continued to be offered in profusion. In 1698, William Penn and Charles Davenant addressed the problem; Robert Livingston of New York gave it his attention in 1701; and in 1722 Daniel Coxe offered a proposal strikingly reminiscent of the ill-fated Dominion.

The motivations for union usually varied according to their source. The English were anxious to increase the efficiency of their administration and to enhance the colonial capacity for imperial defense. The colonists were primarily concerned with the French and Indian menace. It was the latter threat which finally led the Duke of Newcastle to order his Board of Trade to formulate suggestions for a firm plan of union. The resultant recommendations were largely restricted to defense, with arrangements whereby the colonies would contribute more

The Board of Trade Plan, 1754. Reprinted in *Documents Relative to . . . New York*, ed. O'Callaghan, VI, 903–907.

substantially to military expenses than had hitherto been the case. Newcastle was by no means enthusiastic about this arrangement since he foresaw undesirable political complications at home which outweighed the negligible benefits of so limited a union.

The Draught of a plan or project for a General Concert to be entered into by His Majesty's several Colonies upon the Continent of North America, for their mutual and common Defence, and to prevent or remove any encroachments on His Majesty's dominions. 9 Aug. 1754.

It is proposed that a Circular Letter or Instruction be forthwith sent to the Governors of all the Colonies upon the Continent of North America to the following purport and effect, viz.

To set forth the danger to which they are exposed from the encroachments and invasions of a foreign Power.

That the only effectual method of putting a stop to these encroachments, and invasions, and preventing the like for the future will be forthwith to agree upon a Plan for maintaining and supporting a proper number of Forts upon the Frontiers, and in such other places as shall appear to be necessary for the general security of the Colonies; for raising and subsisting regular Independent Companies for garrisoning such Forts; For making provision for defraying the expenses of presents for the Indians, and for the other contingent charges of that service, and for putting Indian Affairs under one general direction; and for raising and maintaining troops for the general security, service, and defence of the whole, upon any attack or invasion.

To state the urgent necessity there is, of an immediate Union of the several Colonies upon the Continent, for this purpose.

To direct the Governors forthwith to recommend these points to the serious consideration of their respective Councils and Assemblies, and to propose to them to appoint proper persons, (one for each Colony) subject to the Governor's approbation, to meet at such time, and place, as His Majesty shall appoint, in order to treat and deliberate upon this matter.

That the persons appointed to be the Commissioners for this purpose, be instructed to consider, in the first place, of the number of Forts necessary to be maintained, and supported, and what number of regular forces will be sufficient for garrisoning such Forts, and to prepare an estimate of the annual expense thereof, and of the expense of Presents to the Indians, and other contingent charges attending this Service.

That provision be likewise made in such estimate for maintaining Commissaries to be established by His Majesty in such Forts as shall be thought proper for the regulation and management of Indian Affairs.

That in order to settle these estimates, with the greater exactness the Commissioners be furnished with authenticated Accounts of the particular expense which each Colony has been at, for twenty years last past, for these services, and in what manner the money has been applied and disposed of.

That when the Estimates shall have been settled, the Commissioners do agree upon the quantum of money to be supplied by each Colony for defraying expence of this service.

That in settling such Quantum, regard be had to the number of inhabitants, trade, wealth, and revenue of each Colony; for which purpose the Commissioners are to be furnished with very full and authenticated accounts of these particulars, and of the state of each Colony respectively.

That the said Commissioners do agree that in case of any emergency by invasion, or otherwise, whereon it may be necessary to raise troops for the general defence of the whole, beyond the number upon the ordinary establishment, the expence thereof shall be defrayed by each Colony, according to the proportion each Colony is to bear of the ordinary established Charge for Forts &c.

That the Governors do signify to their respective Councils and Assemblies, that His Majesty will appoint a proper person to be Commander in Chief of all His Majesty's Forts and Garrisons in the Colonies in North America, and of all Troops already raised there, or which may hereafter be raised or sent thither upon any emergency, and also Commissary General for Indian Affairs; and that provision may be made in the estimate for the ordinary established service, for a proper salary for such Commander in Chief.

That it be settled and agreed by the Commissioners at the general meeting, that the said Commander in Chief, and Commissary for Indian Affairs, be impowered from time to time as occasion may require, to draw upon the Treasurer, Collector, Receiver, or other proper officer appointed to receive the Taxes or Duties levyed and raised in each Colony respectively, for such sums of money as shall be necessary for maintaining and supporting the several Forts and Garrisons, making Presents to the Indians, and all other contingent charges, according to the general estimate agreed upon for the ordinary established service &c in proportion to the Quantum settled for each Colony: taking care to transmit annually to each Colony a particular estimate, expressing the particular service for which such draughts are made.

That in all cases of attack or invasion, whereon it may be necessary to raise troops for repelling such invasion or attack, beyond the number on the ordinary Establishment, the estimate of the charge of such troops, of extraordinary presents to the Indians, and of other Contingent Expences, shall be formed by the Governor, Council, and Assembly of the Colony invaded, or attacked, and immediate notice thereof transmitted by the Governor of such Colony with a Copy of the estimate so prepared as aforesaid to the Governors Councils and Assemblys of the other Colonies upon the Continent; and that it be settled and agreed by the Commissioners at the general meeting, that upon such notice so sent, a Commissioner shall be forthwith nominated and appointed to each Colony respectively and meet at such place as the Commander in Chief shall appoint, in order to take into consideration and deliberate upon the aforementioned estimate so prepared by the Colony invaded, with full power to alter the same in such manner as shall be thought expedient, and that when the same shall have been agreed upon by the majority of the Commissioners who shall be there present, any five of which shall make a Quorum, the Commander in Chief shall be impowered by them to draw upon the Treasurer or other proper officer of each Colony for the respective Quotas each Colony is to bear of such expence, in proportion to the ordinary established estimate for Forts &c.

That the draughts of the Commander in Chief as well for the ordinary as extraordinary service to be paid by the Treasurer &c. of each Colony respectively out of any money lying in his hands, in preference to all other services whatever, and that in case it shall so happen that the Treasurer of any Colony shall not have in his hands a sufficient sum to answer such draughts he be empower'd, by the general agreement, to borrow such a sum as shall be necessary; for repayment of which provision is to be forthwith made by the Assembly.

That it be signified, that the said Commander in Chief will be directed to transmit to each Colony once in every year, an account upon oath of all his disbursements for the publick service, and that he will be obliged to account in His Majesty's Exchequer for all money received and disposed of by him.

That each Colony may appoint a Commissioner to view and inspect from time to time, as they shall think proper the state of the several Forts and Fortifications, and of the repairs made thereon, and to make report thereof to the Governor, Council, and Assembly of such Colony respectively, and that each Colony may likewise make Representations from time to time, to the Commander in Chief, of the state of each Colony, and propose to him such measures as shall occur to be necessary for the general good of the whole.

That when the Commissioners have deliberated upon and settled the foregoing points, they do transmit to His Majesty's Secretary of State and to the Commissioners for Trade and Plantations, to be laid before His Majesty, attested copies of all their Minutes and Proceedings, and that they do prepare a Project or draught of a General Convention upon the foregoing Points and transmit copies thereof to the respective Colonies to be forthwith laid before the Governors, Councils, and Assemblies, who are to take the same into immediate consideration, and having made such alterations therein or additions thereto, as they shall think necessary, shall return them to the Commissioners within two months, and when all the copies shall have been returned the Commissioners shall resume their deliberations; and having finally settled the whole the Convention shall be fairly drawn up and signed by each Commissioner and transmitted hither in order to be laid before His Majesty for his approbation.

And in case it shall so happen that any of the Colonies shall neglect to appoint a Commissioner to be present at the General Meeting, or such Commissioner, when appointed, shall neglect or refuse to attend, such neglect or refusall shall not prevent the Commissioners present, (any seven of which to be a Quorum) from proceeding upon the consideration of the foregoing points; but that the Convention shall be proceeded upon, and finally settled and agreed by a Majority of the Commissioners, and when so settled, and ratified by His Majesty, shall be binding upon the whole.

That the Governors be directed to signify to their respective Councils and Assemblies, that His Majesty does not intend to withdraw that part of the expence which the Crown has been usually at, for the security and protection of the Colonies; but that he will be graciously pleased to continue to maintain and subsist such a number of his troops as shall appear to be necessary to be stationed in America; and does also consent that whatever sums of money have been usually given by His Majesty for Indian Services, shall be deducted from the generall estimate, as the share His Majesty is willing to bear of the ordinary establishment for this service, and that upon any great emergency they shall receive such support from His Majesty as shall be thought reasonable upon a due consideration of the Nature of the case and of what the Circumstances and conditions of the Colonies shall seem to require.

II

Plan of Proposed Union

Much controversy has arisen among historians over Franklin's authorship of the Albany Plan; Lawrence Henry Gipson, for instance, has argued a much larger role for Thomas Hutchinson of Massachusetts.[1] *Still, the evidence generally favors Franklin, although it is clear that other plans similar to Franklin's were presented. Certainly, the colonists, faced with the greatest of all crises in the Anglo-French struggle for North America, showed more interest in union than ever before.*

Since 1750, Franklin had been discussing union seriously, and in June, 1754, he drafted his famous "Short Hints towards a Scheme for a General Union of the British Colonies."[2] *This document is practically identical with the scheme of union which was adopted and which here follows.*

July 10, 1754

Plan of a Proposed Union of the Several Colonies of Masachusets-bay, New Hampshire, Coneticut, Rhode Island, New York, New Jerseys, Pensilvania, Maryland, Virginia, North Carolina, and South Carolina. For their Mutual Defence and Security, and for Extending the British Settlements in North America.

That humble Application be made for an Act of the Parliament of Great Britain, by Virtue of which, one General Government may be formed in America, including all the said Colonies, within and under which Government, each Colony may retain its present Constitution, except in the Particulars wherein a Change may be directed by the said Act, as hereafter follows.

PRESIDENT GENERAL

That the said General Government be administred by a President General, To be appointed and Supported by the Crown, and a

GRAND COUNCIL.

Grand Council to be Chosen by the Representatives of the People of the Several Colonies, met in their respective Assemblies.

ELECTION OF

That within Months

"Plan of Proposed Union," 1754. Copies in the Library of Congress and the New York Historical Society. Reprinted in *Franklin Papers,* ed. Labaree and Bell, V, 387–392.

[1] For a listing of published writings on this controversy, see *Franklin Papers,* ed. Labaree and Bell, V, 378n.

[2] The text is in *ibid.,* V, 361–364.

MEMBERS.

after the passing of such Act, the House of Representatives in the Several Assemblies, that Happen to be Sitting within that time or that shall be Specially for that purpose Convened, may and Shall Choose Members for the Grand Council in the following Proportions, that is to say.

Masachusets-Bay	7.
New Hampshire	2.
Conecticut	5.
Rhode-Island	2.
New-York	4.
New-Jerseys	3.
Pensilvania	6.
Maryland	4.
Virginia	7.
North-Carolina	4.
South-Carolina	4.
	48.

PLACE OF FIRST MEETING.

Who shall meet for the first time at the City of Philadelphia, in Pensilvania, being called by the President General as soon as conveniently may be, after his Appointment.

NEW ELECTION.

That there shall be a New Election of Members for the Grand Council every three years; And on the Death or Resignation of any Member his Place shall be Supplyed by a New Choice at the next Sitting of the Assembly of the Colony he represented.

PROPORTION OF MEMBERS AFTER FIRST 3 YEARS.

That after the first three years, when the Proportion of Money arising out of each Colony to the General Treasury can be known, The Number of Members to be Chosen, for each Colony shall from time to time in all ensuing Elections be regulated by that proportion (yet so as that the Number to be Chosen by any one Province be not more than Seven nor less than Two).

MEETINGS OF GRAND COUNCIL.

That the Grand Council shall meet once in every Year, and oftner if Occasion require, at such Time and place as they shall adjourn to at the last preceeding meeting, or as they

CALL.

shall be called to meet at by the President General, on any Emergency, he having first obtained in Writing the Consent of seven of the Members to such call, and sent due and timely Notice to the whole.

SPEAKER.

That the Grand Council have Power to Chuse their Speaker, and shall neither be Dissolved, prorogued

CONTINUANCE.

nor Continue Sitting longer than Six Weeks at one Time without their own Consent, or the Special Command of the Crown.

MEMBER'S ALLOWANCE

That the Members of the Grand Council shall be Allowed for their Service ten shillings Sterling per Diem, during their Sessions or Journey to and from the Place of Meeting; Twenty miles to be reckoned a days Journey.

ASSENT OF PRESIDENT GENERAL.

That the Assent of the President General be requisite, to all Acts of the Grand Council,

HIS DUTY.

and that it be His Office, and Duty to cause them to be carried into Execution.

POWER OF PRESIDENT AND GRAND COUNCIL.

That the President General with the Advice of the Grand Council, hold or Direct all Indian Treaties in which the General Interest or Welfare of the

Colony's may be Concerned;

PEACE AND WAR. And make Peace or Declare War with the Indian Nations. That they make such Laws as they Judge Necessary for regulating all Indian

INDIAN PURCHASES. Trade. That they make all Purchases from Indians for the Crown, of Lands not within the Bounds of Particular Colonies, or that shall not be within their Bounds when some of them are reduced to more Convenient Dimensions.

NEW SETTLEMENTS. That they make New Settlements on such Purchases, by Granting Lands in the Kings Name, reserving a Quit Rent to the Crown, for the use of the General Treasury.

LAWS TO GOVERN THEM. That they make Laws for regulating and Governing such new Settlements, till the Crown shall think fit to form them into Particular Governments.

RAISE SOLDIERS &C. That they raise and pay Soldiers, and build Forts for the Defence of any of the Colonies, and equip

LAKES. Vessels of Force to Guard the Coasts and Protect the Trade on the Ocean, Lakes, or Great Rivers; But they shall not Impress

NOT TO IMPRESS Men in any Colonies, without the Consent of its Legislature. That for these purposes they

POWER TO MAKE LAWS have Power to make Laws And lay and Levy such General Duties, Imposts, or

DUTIES &C. Taxes, as to them shall appear most equal and Just, Considering the Ability and other Circumstances of the Inhabitants in the Several Colonies, and such as may be Collected with the least Inconvenience to the People, rather discouraging Luxury, than Loading Industry with unnecessary Burthens. That they may Appoint

TREASURER. a General Treasurer and a Particular Treasurer in each Government, when Necessary, And from Time to Time may Order the Sums in the Treasuries of each Government, into the General Treasury, or draw on them for Special payments as they find most Convenient;

MONEY HOW TO ISSUE. Yet no money to Issue, but by joint Orders of the President General and Grand Council Except where Sums have been Appropriated to particular Purposes, And the President General is previously impowered By an Act to draw for such Sums.

ACCOUNTS. That the General Accounts shall be yearly Settled and Reported to the Several Assembly's.

QUORUM. That a Quorum of the Grand Council impower'd to Act with the President General, do consist of Twenty-five Members, among whom there shall be one, or more from a Majority of the Colonies.

LAWS TO BE TRANSMITTED. That the Laws made by them for the Purposes aforesaid, shall not be repugnant but as near as may be agreeable to the Laws of England, and Shall be transmitted to the King in Council for Approbation, as Soon as may be after their Passing and if not disapproved within Three years after Presentation to remain in Force.

DEATH OF PRESIDENT GENERAL.

That in case of the Death of the President General The Speaker of the Grand Council for the Time Being shall Succeed, and be Vested with the Same Powers, and Authority, to Continue until the King's Pleasure be known.

OFFICERS HOW APPOINTED.

That all Military Commission Officers Whether for Land or Sea Service, to Act under this General Act under this General Constitution, shall be Nominated by the President General But the Approbation of the Grand Council, is to be Obtained before they receive their Commissions, And all Civil Officers are to be Nominated, by the Grand Council, and to receive the President General's Approbation, before they Officiate; But in Case

VACANCIES HOW SUPPLIED.

of Vacancy by Death or removal of any Officer Civil or Military under this Constitution, The Governor of the Province, in which such Vacancy happens, may Appoint till the Pleasure of the President General and Grand Council can be known. That the Particular Military as well as Civil Establishments in each Colony remain in their present State, this General Constitution Notwithstanding,

EACH COLONY MAY DEFEND ITSELF ON EMERGENCY.

And that on Sudden Emergencies any Colony may Defend itself and lay the Accounts of Expence thence Arisen, before the President General and Grand Council, who may allow and order payment of the same As far as they Judge such Accounts Just and reasonable.

III

The Albany Plan of Union in the Colonies

The Congress at Albany was held at the request of the British Board of Trade to discuss and act on proposals for improved relations with the tribes of the Six Nations. Inter-colonial union was not on the original agenda; indeed, one colony — Maryland — instructed her delegates not *to take any action beyond the field of Indian relations. Just as in Philadelphia in 1787, so too in Albany in 1754 did the delegates exceed their commission: union was discussed as early as June 24, 1754, and by July 10 the Plan had been drafted, approved, and circulated.*

Despite their mounting fear of the French, not one of the eleven colonies expected to participate in the union ratified the Plan. As Robert C. Newbold *demonstrates, the degree of opposition varied. Some colonies feared the new confederation augured a more stringent British rule; others resented the reduction of their authority in provincial affairs, such as taxation, regulation of Indian affairs, and western lands. But two important points must be remembered: there was wide agreement on the need for union — the only disagreements were over its precise form; and, in any case, formal colonial approval was irrelevant, since the Plan required implementation by act of Parliament — and the Duke of Newcastle had decided*

Reprinted from Robert C. Newbold, *The Albany Congress and Plan of Union in the Colonies* (New York: The Vantage Press, 1955), pp. 136–140; 170–171.

against any such move even before copies of the Albany Plan reached London.

It is now clear that the Plan went further than Newcastle had intended, and that he feared the Grand Council, once formally established, would be only slightly less influential than Parliament itself, and might well become the focus of colonial resistance to British rule.[1]

Pennsylvania acted first but gave the plan no support. On August 7, 1754, scarcely a month after the conference adjourned, Governor James Hamilton addressed both branches of the legislature and recommended approval of the project. The assembly, or lower house, ignored his advice, however, and after extensive debate virtually rejected the plan by refusing to refer it to a subsequent session. Franklin, who was absent when the vote was taken, later charged that a certain assemblyman had seized the occasion of his absence to engineer this repudiation of the work of the congress. Although it is impossible to identify this member with certainty, it is reasonable to assume that he was none other than Isaac Norris, Franklin's fellow commissioner. As Speaker, Norris possessed ample influence to defeat approval of the union, which the dominant Quaker faction very likely disliked because of its emphasis on military affairs. In Pennsylvania as in most of the other colonies, the Albany Plan lacked the active and enthusiastic support of the very men who as commissioners had approved it at the congress. With the exception of Franklin, the Pennsylvania representatives at Albany made no effort to back the project in the colony, and one of them, Isaac Norris, as already stated, probably opposed it in the legislature. Had the members of the Albany Congress been as zealous in attempting to win favorable action on the plan in the various provinces as were the delegates to the subsequent constitutional convention in 1787 in seeking ratification of the Constitution, the results might have been different.

Despite the unfavorable attitude of the Pennsylvania lower house, the Albany Plan did not entirely lack support in the colony. The *Maryland Gazette*, on December 5, 1754, published a letter from a Philadelphia merchant to a friend in Maryland in which the writer stressed that the scheme would make the provinces formidable. He pointed out that no one could offer an objection to it that could not also be advanced against any other form of organized government. The merchant felt that the plan protected both the liberties of the people and the rights of the King. If the Pennsylvania legislature had thought the same way, perhaps it would not have so quickly negated the project.

The second government to act conclusively was the charter colony of Connecticut, whose commissioners had quite probably opposed the scheme at Albany. As soon as the legislature reconvened in October 1754, it appointed a committee to study the plan. Reporting quickly, this group urged its rejection. It attacked the extensive authority of the president general and the council, particularly objecting to the right of the president general to nominate and commission all military officers as harmful to the prerogative of the King. Although the fear of endangering the province's charter liberties was probably their chief reason for opposing the project, the committee members quite incongruously directed most of their attack on the threat the plan presented to the King's rights. In addition, the group thought that the scheme would open the way to the importation of military officers from abroad. That this belief was groundless is attested by the fact that the commissioners specifically required the council's approval of all officers selected. Finally, the committee attacked the indiscriminate taxing power of the union both as a dangerous innovation and a violation of the colony's charter privileges. Although listed last, this objection was no doubt the most powerful factor in inducing the group to advise rejection of the plan.

The upper house debated this adverse report on October 2, 1754, and quickly accepted it, listing five reasons that impelled it to reject the plan. These reasons agreed substantially with those offered by the committee. To accomplish the main purposes of the Albany Plan, the members of the upper house submitted some substitute suggestions. They recommended that

[1] See Alison Gilbert Olson, "The British Government and Colonial Union," *The William and Mary Quarterly*, 3rd Ser., XVII (1960), 22–34.

the King appoint suitable persons to manage Indian affairs and regulate the Indian trade. The profits derived from the trade with the Indians could be used for the construction of frontier defenses. In addition, the members urged that the King encourage provincials to settle on land that the government could easily purchase from the savages. These colonists could help secure the loyalty of the Indians and at the same time aid in resisting French onslaughts. By these means, the upper house contended, the Albany Plan's objectives would be achieved without endangering the rights of the colonies. Apparently the self-interest of many legislators in the land-speculating Susquehannah Company accounted for the recommendation for additional settlements. Moreover, it seems certain that this company's activities contributed to the defeat in Connecticut of the plan, which had dared to imply that the extensive western boundaries of provinces like Connecticut that held sea-to-sea charters should be reduced in size. Yet this influence seems secondary to the fear of many legislators that the scheme presented too great a threat to charter-conceded privileges. The lower house concurred in the upper body's reasons for rejection and resolved

> . . . that no application be made in behalf of this Colony to the Parliament of Great Britain for an act to form any such government on the said proposed plan as therein is expressed; and that reasons be offered against any such motion.

After rejecting the plan, the Connecticut legislature directed Governor Fitch to announce its decision to Richard Partridge, the colony's agent in England, and to order him to improve upon the assembly's reasons in an effort to prevent the project's enactment by Parliament. If any of the other provinces sought such approval, the Connecticut legislature requested its agent to seek a hearing before Parliament and, assisted by counsel hired for the purpose, to make full use of the assembly's objections as well as any other pertinent arguments that might be utilized to defeat it.

The legislators also urged Governor Fitch to check on the reaction to the plan of the other colonies, and as far as possible to discourage favorable action by any of them. If any of the governments showed approval, Fitch was directed to furnish Partridge with acceptable revisions of the plan. These were to include a recommendation that the general confederation be divided into two partial unions. The assembly further requested the chief executive to object to the representation allotted to Connecticut under the scheme and to set forth what the true representation should be.

* * *

When the congress concluded its affairs in early July, the Rhode Island legislature was in recess. When it resumed its sessions in the city of Newport on the third Monday of August, the two Rhode Island commissioners, Stephen Hopkins and Martin Howard, Jr., reported on their activities at the conference. They informed their colleagues that the congress had renewed the traditional alliance with the Six Nations. They included in their report a copy of both the "Representation" and the plan of union. Hopkins and Howard made known to the legislators that the commissioners at Albany had judged the project of confederation absolutely necessary, but the report did not recommend that the colony accept the Albany Plan.

After receiving the commissioners' statement, the lower house, on August 21, 1754, accepted it, "reserving to themselves whether they will accede to the General Plan proposed." The upper branch concurred in this the following day.

In 1755, a political opponent of Hopkins, writing under the pseudonym of Philolethes, charged that Hopkins had cunningly presented to the General Assembly

> . . . a Number of Sheets in Folio, in which were contained a Variety of Matters, and the Plan of Union artfully tack'd to the rest, which being read in the Lower House, the Report was received, and in Consequence all their Doings, &c. No doubt, some Advocates of Mr. Hopkins's discovered, the Absurdity of said Plan, which they conceal'd to prevent any Reflections on his Character; However, the Vote of the Lower House was sent to the Governor and Council, who perceived the Fraud, of the Plan's being included with the other Proceedings, and acquainted the Lower House That they concurr'd with their Vote, reserving a further Consideration upon the

Plan of Union. The Lower House confessed the Reserve just.

A study of the legislative records of Rhode Island neither entirely substantiates nor refutes the assertions of Philolethes. Neither the "Journal House of Deputies 1753–54" nor the "Journal of the Senate 1747–55" furnished any certain indication that the upper house had amended the acceptance resolution and referred it back to the lower branch. If this had occurred, the records would ordinarily have contained the phrase "not concurred with," but the "Journal of the Senate 1747–55" has no such notation. Yet one would hesitate to deny Philolethes' charges, for the "Journal House of Deputies" included the reservation clause as an apparent afterthought, the words being closely written in a very narrow space. The "Journal of the Senate," too, appears to have undergone some alterations; several lines following the entry of the record of acceptance are now illegible, having been crossed out. These changes in both official journals prevent a categorical denial of the contentions of Philolethes. Whatever may have been the circumstances, the Rhode Island legislature neither approved nor rejected the Albany Plan when it was first submitted for study.

Because of many other important matters, the legislature did not consider the plan of union during its October session. In December, Governor William Greene received a letter from Richard Partridge, the colony's agent in England, seeking information about the plan, which the mother country was about to study. He wrote:

> The Parliament is like to meet for Dispatch of Business, in about six Weeks Time, when I am apt to think some Application will be made to them, respecting the Union of the several Governments in North-America, Proposals for that Purpose being lately come to hand, as they were agreed on by the Congress at Albany.

Alarmed, Governor Greene forwarded the communication to the upper house, which in turn quickly referred it to the lower branch in an attempt to induce that body to write to England opposing enactment of the plan. Philolethes subsequently charged that some of Hopkins' friends used artifice to prevent the representatives from acting on the project during February. Philolethes accused an unnamed close associate of the commissioner of beseeching a member of the upper chamber not to reject the plan, as such a vote would bring dishonor on both Hopkins and Howard. Whatever the reason, the legislature did not act on the scheme during February.

Hopkins charged that political considerations alone dictated the attacks on the Albany Plan. He accused his opponents, particularly those in the upper house, of allowing the scheme to lie dormant nearly seven months, until the pressure of the coming campaign forced them to resurrect it in order to damage his reputation. As already stated, Philolethes, who took up his pen to refute Hopkins, denied the commissioner's allegations. As there is no other information available, it seems quite likely that some early attempts were made to induce the legislature to reject the Albany Plan. As it was without doubt unpopular in the province because of the supposed threat it presented to the colony's charter privileges, it is difficult to believe that no one made an early attempt to have the legislature oppose the project. Hopkins himself silently testified to its unpopularity when he failed to advocate its adoption in his *A True Representation of the Plan Formed at Albany in 1754,* which he wrote on March 29, 1755, as a defense against his critics.

The Albany Plan's unpopularity in Rhode Island can be traced to the fact that Rhode Island was one of the two real charter governments remaining in North America. Its charter, granted in 1662, permitted the colony to elect its own officials, including the governor. The province naturally feared any innovations that might destroy its great privileges or at least restrict them. Since 1748, much correspondence, alarming to the people, had passed between Rhode Island and British officials. In 1750, some Rhode Islanders had actually petitioned the King to alter the governmental structure by allowing a veto on the acts of the legislature. When Governor William Greene learned of this request, he directed Partridge to oppose the change as dangerous to the colony's liberties.

The governor also instructed him to protest all parliamentary bills that tended to infringe on the province's charter privileges. Two years later, English officials requested Rhode Island to furnish a copy of all its laws then in force. Once more Governor Greene wrote to Partridge and expressed his concern:

> You will easily imagine how much uneasiness the very thoughts of losing our charter liberties creates in the inhabitants of this colony, and how much dependence they must necessarily have on you.

As late as March 7, 1754, Partridge had forewarned the colony, as he had several times before, that satirical remarks concerning charter provinces were being openly repeated in government circles, which indicated that the British government was about to take these provinces in hand for their alleged malpractices. While still alarmed about these reports, Rhode Island received for consideration the plan of union, which, of course, provided for a president general appointed by the King with veto power over the acts of the Grand Council. Even Franklin confessed that the Albany Plan conferred on its officials less power than was already possessed by Rhode Island and Connecticut authorities. Thus these colonies had more to lose than the other governments by the establishment of a new central administration. Is it any wonder that Rhode Island became disturbed and feared for its charter liberties?

Although opposition to the Albany Plan in the province was probably intense, only Philolethes' pamphlet remains to indicate some of the arguments used by the opponents. This political antagonist of Hopkins charged that the project would revoke all the governors' commissions in North America and destroy every colonial charter by imposing an additional authority over the several legislatures. Philolethes stormed:

> We want no arbitrary supream [sic] sovereign Court of Jurisdiction over a free People, to lay Taxes, Imposts, and Duties upon our Land, Trade, and Merchandize [sic]; but are ready when our most gracious Sovereign commands, to oppose the common Enemy.

In addition, Philolethes attempted to stir up interprovincial jealousy by pointing out that the western landowners would make substantial profits when the union erected the frontier forts. Such arguments as these, spread about in a colony already apprehensive about losing its privileges, could scarcely help having a damaging effect.

Mistrustful of innovation and jealous of its charter, Rhode Island especially feared the powers attached to the office of president general. Whoever filled it would be appointed by the King, and enjoy a veto power that even the governor did not possess. Besides, the colony was probably unwilling to submit its affairs to the royal review and administration that the new confederation called for. It is surprising that the Rhode Island legislature did not undertake to reject the plan sooner than February, 1755. Possibly Hopkins' influence in the lower branch and a reluctance to repudiate publicly a project with which he was so closely associated explain the legislature's long delay. As stated before, legislative action began as soon as Governor Greene received Partridge's letter warning the province of the possibility that Parliament might take up the scheme. The lower house, however, apparently delayed the first attempt to go on record as opposed to the plan. While Philolethes was undoubtedly a vehemently partisan witness, it cannot be denied that his explanation for the delayed legislative action was a reasonable one.

Early in March 1755, Governor Greene urged the upper house to indict the Albany Plan as a scheme that would deprive the province of valuable charter rights and over-turn its constitution. The governor recommended that the legislature instruct Partridge to oppose parliamentary enactment of the entire plan or any part of it. Although Philolethes asserted that Greene addressed his request to the upper chamber, the communication appears in the records of that body as its own resolution directed to the members of the House of Deputies, no indication being given that it originated with the governor. The "Journal House of Deputies" furnishes no evidence that the lower house ever actually received the directive. Instead the "Journal" contains the following entry:

> . . . and that in the Letter to the agent he be directed to be upon his Watch & if any Thing should be moved in parliament respecting the

> Plan for an Union of the Colonies formed at Albany which may have a Tendency to infringe on our Privileges that he use his best Endavours to get the same put off till we are furnished with a Copy thereof & have Time to answer the same.

The House of Deputies adopted this weak version of the governor's communication on March 8, 1755, and the upper chamber gave quick concurrence the same day. Probably by this time the upper house had become convinced that this was the only action the deputies would take. Once more Hopkins' influence apparently prevented open repudiation of the Albany plan. Thus the legislature achieved two ends: it did not openly reject the project, and at the same time it successfully warded off the supposed threat to colonial liberties.

Having warned Governor Greene in October that Parliament was likely to consider the plan of union shortly, Partridge wrote again, on December 9, 1754, to say that Parliament had not yet acted on it. On March 8, 1755, he advised the colony that matters remained much the same as before, "nothing having been on ye Carpet in the House of Commons hitherto respecting the Northern Colonies as was expected, about which I am on the Watch." As late as May, 1756, Partridge was informing the colony that Parliament had still done nothing about the project of union. Indeed, Parliament never adopted or even considered the scheme.

Despite the contrary opinions of Osgood and Gipson, Rhode Island never directly rejected the Albany Plan nor advocated its repudiation in England. The most its legislature did was to postpone its examination and request a similar delay in the mother country. Considering the temper of the people, the postponement must be attributed, at least in part, to the influence of Hopkins, who wrote a weak and cautious apology for his activities at the congress.

Despite the legislature's apparent refusal to oppose the plan openly, it would seem that the project was as unpopular in the Rhode Island assembly as it was in that of Connecticut. Both colonies had charters that gave the citizens the right to elect their own governor. With little fear of French attack and already possessing greater power, Rhode Island and Connecticut had the most to lose if Parliament enacted the proposed union into law. Is it any wonder that the project was so repugnant to these two governments? In Connecticut, the opposition took the form of early and emphatic legislative repudiation; in Rhode Island, the antagonism, while intense, did not result in open rejection. Instead, the General Assembly approved an indefinite postponement with the implicit understanding that, if Parliament seriously considered the scheme, the legislature would resume its deliberations on it. If this had become necessary, there seems little doubt that the colony would also have openly rejected it. Since Parliament never debated the plan, nothing further was heard of it in the Rhode Island legislature.

The last of the provinces whose records contain information on the consideration of the Albany Plan is North Carolina. This colony was neither invited to nor represented at the congress. Governor Arthur Dobbs submitted the project to the lower house on December 21, 1754. With the exception of Governor James Hamilton of Pennsylvania, Governor Dobbs was the only provincial executive who was favorably disposed toward the plan. He told the legislators that he hoped they would support the work of the commissioners. If they desired, they could alter or otherwise amend the project, in order that the King might receive their views. After examining the plan of December twenty-fourth, the lower house deferred further consideration until the next session. In the meantime, it ordered that the scheme be printed and copies distributed to all legislators for mature study. The lower house never took any further action on the Albany Plan, for it was virtually dead when the next session convened, on September 25, 1755. Apparently North Carolina confined its action on the project to the lower house, as the proceedings of its upper chamber contain no references to any deliberation on it.

Seven colonies thus publicly examined the Albany Plan. The remaining six, at least in their legislative records, all but ignored it.

* * *

Of the eleven colonies comprehended in the proposed union, not a single one voted legislative approval of it. Some of them, notably Connecticut, New Jersey, and Maryland, vehemently opposed it. Virtually all of them defeated it because they feared it might endanger their rights and privileges. This fear was based in part on previous British attempts to restrict colonial liberties. Some of these rights had been granted through charters or other official documents; others had been assumed or usurped in the passage of time. Many influential colonists feared that the British government might seize upon the confederation as a weapon to curb political autonomy. Accompanying this apprehension was a reluctance on the part of these jealous and independent provinces to surrender to a central government the authority demanded by the Albany Plan. Especially did the legislatures object to conceding the power of taxation, for in granting this they would be giving up, to a great degree, their most potent weapon to curb and restrict the prerogative. To these general motives for rejecting the plan, some of the colonies added local objections as well. Thus New York's lower legislative house opposed the project partly because it took control of Indian affairs away from the Albany commissioners. In Connecticut and Virginia, the provisions relating to western lands seem to have caused much antagonism. This same motive might well have been at work in some of the other colonies, even if undercover. Although most of the provinces greatly feared the danger of a French attack, their apprehension could not overcome their parallel dread of losing some of their privileges, which was probable if the plan was adopted. As a result, although many colonial leaders in 1754 advocated some type of union to withstand the French, they were unable to reach an agreement on the form that union should take, when the time arrived to organize it. The colonial inaction on the Albany Plan convinced Franklin that the provinces would never unite voluntarily. As a consequence, by late 1754 he was advocating compulsory parliamentary association without prior consultation of the colonies. The assemblies had killed all hope of spontaneous confederation. Only coercion, it seemed, could now join the provinces together; but the British government, undoubtedly impressed by the violent legislative reaction to the Albany Plan, refused to accept the challenge and impose either that scheme or one of its own, and thus the colonies remained disunited.

4

The Galloway Plan, 1774

I

Galloway's Plan of Union

The last significant plan of inter-colonial union before independence superficially shared much with the first: Joseph Galloway's Plan of Union was intended to meet an external threat — now presented by the importunities of the mother country — and it was unsuccessful. The occasion for the presentation of the Galloway Plan was the meeting of the First Continental Congress, convened in Philadelphia on September 5, 1774, to discuss the Coercive Acts. It is fair to state that the temper of the members of the Congress was not as moderate as Galloway's. It is also fair to note that Galloway himself was far from being the extreme conservative whom history has represented. "I am," he insisted, "as much a friend of liberty as exists."

The Galloway Plan confirms this. It proposed a federation of the colonies strikingly similar to Franklin's earlier Albany Plan, providing for a President-General, appointed by the Crown, who would regulate inter-colonial affairs through a Grand Council, elected by the colonial legislatures. The startling feature of Galloway's Plan was the requirement that legislation relating to

Galloway's Plan of Union, September 28, 1774. Reprinted in *Journals of the Continental Congress*, ed., Worthington C. Ford (Washington, D.C., 1904), I, pp. 49–51.

inter-colonial affairs be subject to the approval of both *the British Parliament and the colonial Grand Council. The colonies thus would in effect possess an effective veto over British imperial policy. But the colonies were now no longer prepared to accept a legislature specifically "an inferior and distinct branch of the British legislature." By a margin of one vote the Plan was tabled, later to be expunged from the minutes of the Congress.*

RESOLVED. That the Congress will apply to his Majesty for a redress of grievances under which his faithful subjects in America labour; and assure him that the colonies hold in abhorrence the idea of being considered independent communities on the British government, and most ardently desire the establishment of a political union, not only among themselves, but with the mother state, upon those principles of safety and freedom which are essential in the constitution of all free governments, and particularly that of the British legislature; and as the colonies from their local circumstances cannot be represented in the Parliament of Great Britain, they will humbly propose to his Majesty and his two houses of Parliament, the following plan, under which the strength of the whole empire may be drawn together on any emergency, the interest of both countries advanced, and the rights and liberties of America secured.

A Plan of a proposed Union between
Great Britain and the Colonies

That a British and American legislature, for regulating the administration of the general affairs of America, be proposed and established in America, including all the said colonies; within, and under which government, each colony shall retain its present constitution, and powers of regulating and governing its own internal police, in all cases whatsoever.

That the said government be administered by a president-general, to be appointed by the king, and a grand council, to be chosen by the representatives of the people of the several colonies, in their respective assemblies, once in every three years.

That the several assemblies shall choose members for the grand council in the following proportions, viz.

New Hampshire
Massachusetts Bay
Rhode Island
Connecticut
New York
New Jersey
Pennsylvania
Delaware Counties
Maryland
Virginia
North Carolina
South Carolina
Georgia

Who shall meet at the city of
for the first time, being called by the president-general, as soon as conveniently may be after his appointment.

That there shall be a new election of members for the grand council every three years; and on the death, removal or resignation of any member, his place shall be supplied by a new choice, at the next sitting of assembly of the colony he represented.

That the grand council shall meet once in every year, if they shall think it necessary, and oftener, if occasions shall require, at such time and place as they shall adjourn to, at the last preceding meeting, or as they shall be called to meet at, by the president-general, on any emergency.

That the grand council shall have power to choose their speaker, and shall hold and exercise all the like rights, liberties and privileges as are held and exercised by and in the House of Commons of Great Britain.

That the president-general shall hold his office during the pleasure of the king, and his assent shall be requisite to all acts of the grand council, and it shall be his office and duty to cause them to be carried into execution.

That the president-general, by and with the advice and consent of the grand council, hold and exercise all the legislative rights, powers, and authorities necessary for regulating and administering all the general police and affairs of the colonies in which Great Britain and the colonies, or any of them, the colonies in general, or more than one colony, are in any manner concerned, as well civil and criminal as commercial.

That the said president-general and the grand council be an inferior and distinct branch of the British legislature, united and incorporated with it, for the aforesaid general purposes; and that any of the said general regulations may originate and be formed and digested, either in the Parliament of Great Britain, or in the said grand council, and being prepared, transmitted to the other for their approbation or dissent; and that the assent of both shall be requisite to the validity of all such general acts or statutes.

That in time of war, all bills for granting aid to the Crown, prepared by the grand council, and approved by the president-general, shall be valid and passed into a law, without the assent of the British Parliament.

II

Whig Organization and Loyalist Reaction, May 1774–May 1775

It is impossible to do justice to either Galloway or his Plan of Union without attending to the political circumstances surrounding the Plan's creation. In examining the political rivalry between Galloway and John Dickinson, Professor David L. Jacobson *has thrown fresh light upon Galloway's difficulties. The selection which follows shows Galloway anxiously seeking a secure base for colonial rights; this he found in his interpretation of the English constitution, which he conceived as a protector of landed wealth. Galloway saw Parliament as representative of the property interests of England; and it followed that he should seek to establish a similar form of inter-colonial legislature to maintain similar rights for Englishmen in America.*

Galloway's difficulties were many. His known attachment to the British Crown — which he termed "indispensably necessary to the safety and happiness of both" — made his proposals for an American "branch" of Parliament suspect in patriot eyes. Galloway wanted to engender and maintain respect for the mother country and at the same time to obtain security for property in the colonies. But few Americans by this time held much hope for such a compromise. Even the cautious John Dickinson was contemplating "the last Extremity." Galloway's Plan was in fact a valiant attempt to reconcile the irreconcilable, radical in its insistence that "no law should bind America without her consent," but not by now radical enough for the Congress. Disappointed, Galloway began to move towards Loyalism. He wanted no part of a people who were evidently forsaking the guidance of "men of property and character" and following the leadership of those he termed the "very dregs."

Professor Jacobson is presently at the University of California, Davis; he is author of the recently published John Dickinson and the Revolution in Pennsylvania, 1764–1776 *(Berkeley and Los Angeles, Calif., 1965).*

In the several weeks before the meeting of the congress in Philadelphia on September 5, Galloway busied himself with preparing arguments and plans. He put down some of his thoughts in his "Arguments on Both Sides in the Dispute between Great-Britain and her Colonies." The subtitle described the contents: "In which those in Favor of the Power of Parliament to bind the Colonies are stated and answered, and the Rights of the Colonists explained and asserted on *new* and just Principles." In his own words, Galloway emphasized the importance of his subject: "let Candour and Impartiality prevail in every Sentiment. To act otherwise in a Case of so much Weight would be idle and ridiculous. It would be trifling and sporting with the most sacred Things, the Liberties and Welfare of Millions." And this work was indeed as candid and impartial as anything Galloway ever wrote, close to a middle ground and making many concessions to American sympathies and demands. Yet, for some reason, Galloway decided not to make his words available to the public. He circulated his "Arguments on Both Sides" only to friends.

For Galloway, all previous arguments in defense of American liberties seemed unsatisfactory. He was determined to depart from those

Reprinted from David L. Jacobson, "John Dickinson and Joseph Galloway, 1764–1776: A Study in Contrasts," unpublished doctoral dissertation, Princeton University, 1959, pp. 179–191.

"beaten paths"; he could not rely on "refined Distinctions" between taxation and legislation, or taxation for this and taxation for that. In his "humble" opinion, they were only verbal distinctions not corresponding to actual differences in fact. They were inadequate to justify American rights. They had no foundation in history or in proper political theory. The distinctions were not found in the legal sources, not in the statutes or the journals of Parliament. Nor could American claims be securely based on vague general principles: not in "the Law of God and Nature . . . because we are not in [a] State of Nature but of Society — nor 'on the common Rights of Mankind,' because the Rights of Mankind are as different as the Forms and Policy of the Society they live under are different — nor on American charters, because I can find little or nothing in them in Favor of American claims, nor on Acts of Parliament, because the point in Question is the Authority of Parliament." Thus, in less than four hundred words, Galloway rejected the popular colonial arguments and led up to his own historical argument. He thought there was only one possible defense of American freedom: an argument from "the Constitution of the English Government, and the Principals [sic] and Policy upon which it is founded."

Galloway attempted to define the essentials of the English constitution. Parliament had a proper claim to wide authority "from the Necessity of a supreme Power to order, direct and regulate every Member and Part . . . from original Right and Property in the Territory of the Colonies, from the Allegiance due from the People before their Migration, from the Nature of their Charters, and from the Necessity resulting from their present disunited Situation." But there was one distinctive feature of Parliament that kept its absolute authority from becoming tyrannical. The House of Commons represented the landed interests of the kingdom. It thus achieved the most important goal of any government, protection for property, of which land was "the most permanent, unchangeable, and excellent." While the origins of this element in the English government could not be definitely traced, it was certain that Parliament and government since "time immemorial" had derived its real power from the support of the landed interest. Representation for the propertied was in fact the "essence" of the English constitution.

Since the landed interests of the colonies were not represented in Parliament, how could the British legislature legitimately exercise power over America? How could it claim to legislate for unrepresented and propertied people without violating the "essence" of its nature? Galloway's answer was not quite so forthright as it appeared on the surface: it was that the legislature of Great Britain "ought not, upon the Principles upon which it was originally constituted and has continued to exist ever since, to exercise its Jurisdiction over the Colonies." Galloway did not suggest any actual restriction on the absolute power of Parliament; he was simply preparing the way for the argument that its power should be exercised more in conformity with original principles. That goal, the more equitable use of Parliamentary power, might be secured by a plan to associate Americans in the legislative power of the British Parliament.

As the delegates of other colonies arrived in Philadelphia in the first week of September, Galloway sounded out their views and thought he found them compatible with his own. He wrote to his good friend, Governor William Franklin of New Jersey, of his impressions. Galloway had seen only a few of the newcomers, but he found those few men of "Temper and Moderation." The elder Rutledge of South Carolina was amiable and learned. Rutledge had "looked into the Arguments of both Sides more fully than any I have met with, and seems to be aware of all the Consequences which may attend rash and imprudent Measures." Rutledge was apparently thinking of some method for American participation in Parliament. The delegates from New Hampshire also pleased Galloway by their mild manners. Of course, there were some "warm" men, the Bostonians and the younger Rutledge. But Galloway's overall impression was that the majority of the delegates would receive his ideas with "approbation."

Unfortunately for Galloway and his expectations, the Whig leaders of Philadelphia had also been busily contacting the arriving delegates. They met some of the representatives from New England outside of Philadelphia and warned them against trusting Galloway. The Whigs had others of the delegates to dinner, repeating their cautions against Galloway and his kind. And, throughout the first month and a half of the Congress, Dickinson was in continuing contact with the leaders, meeting with them as the most influential of the Pennsylvania Whigs. The New England delegates were also very much impressed by Charles Thomson, who had already been known to them before their arrival as the "Sam Adams of Philadelphia." Thus, many of the congressmen were prepared to side on any crucial issue with Dickinson, Thomson, "the mechanics and citizens in general," rather than with Pennsylvania's official delegates to the First Continental Congress.

As soon as the Congress actually opened on September 5, 1774, Galloway discovered that his opponents had prepared some surprises for him. He wrote to William Franklin again, this time denouncing the "unrest . . . out of doors" which was spoiling his hopes. As one of its first official actions, the Congress had rejected Galloway's choice of a meeting place, the Assembly House, in favor of Carpenter's Hall. Then the delegates ignored his argument that their clerk should come from the membership of the Congress. They decided to go outside and picked none other than Charles Thomson. In so doing, the delegates were quite aware that they had chosen Galloway's "sworn opposite," a man who had been denied a seat in the Congress by Galloway's exercise of power in the Assembly. And, on the first two days of the Congress, Galloway realized that his first sampling of its membership had not been very accurate. Except for his acquaintance, Rutledge, he regarded all the Carolinians and Virginians as being "warm" men. He could find consolation only among the New York delegates. But those men had "as little Expectations of much Satisfaction from the Event of Things" as Galloway himself.

In spite of personal rebuffs and doubts, Galloway decided to remain in the Congress and to present his arguments and plan. On September 8, he addressed a meeting of the committee for stating "rights, grievances, and means of redress." The preceding debate concerned the basis of American claims. Most delegates supported a dual appeal to the British constitution and the laws of nature. But John Rutledge of South Carolina emphatically rejected the idea of rooting the colonial case in anything so vague as natural law. When Galloway rose, he followed Rutledge in attacking the favorite Whig arguments: he rejected the old Whig distinctions and the law of nature. He thought the proper starting point for American arguments might be found in "the constitution of English government," and, particularly, in the principle that "power results from the real property of the society." The conclusion which he reached by his analysis of these concepts was recorded by one diarist in words that should be interpreted with due regard to a similar statement in "Arguments on Both Sides." Galloway summed up: "I have ever thought we might reduce our rights to one — an exemption from all laws made by British Parliament since the emigration of our ancestors. It follows, therefore, that all acts of Parliament made since, are violations of our rights." Most probably, Galloway did not intend this statement as an unequivocal denial of the authority of Parliament over America. He did mean it as a denial of the "equity," the fairness or rightness of Parliament's actions, as a prelude to his argument that the supremacy of the British legislature might be reconciled with principles of right through his plan for constitutional union.

On September 28, Galloway submitted his plan to the Congress. It provided for the creation of a "British and American Government." Within the government, each colony would retain its "present Constitution and powers of regulating and governing its own internal Police in all Cases whatsoever." The government would consist of a royally appointed "president General" and a Grand Council, representing the various colonial Assemblies. The Grand Council would be "an inferior and distinct Branch of the British legislature." It would exercise legislative power where "Great Britain and the Colonies or any of them, the Colonies in general or more than one Colony are in any Manner concerned as well civil and criminal as commercial." Legislative acts within this definition would require the approval of the Grand Council, the President General, and the British Parliament. Thus, the colonies and home country would share authority, "the Assent of both shall be requisite to the validity of all such general Acts or Statutes." The only exception would be in wartime when the Grand Council might make appropriations without the consent of Parliament. Incidentally, the Grand Council was given the privileges of the House of Commons, was to have full control over its own sessions and to choose its own Speaker.

Galloway introduced his plan with a long speech. John Adams recorded one version of this speech in his notes of the debates; Galloway modified his remarks considerably and published them in England in 1780. According to Adams, Galloway objected to any plan for non-importation or non-exportation. Such programs would be too slow in bringing relief and would damage American prosperity. Galloway argued that a properly drawn plan of union might quickly satisfy American grievances and yet give Britain the economic support and obedience it demanded. He traced the imperial dispute to failings on both sides. Americans had been delinquent in answering Parliamentary requisitions. The royal authorities had tried unfortunate methods for enforcing their demands for money. Still, according to Adams' account, Galloway thought the colonies owed allegiance to Great Britain. They were receiving protection, but, unless they somehow recognized the authority of Parliament, they would not be showing proper respect to the home country. The colonies were dangerously near to being independent governments. To avert this possibility and to reunite all parts of the empire, Galloway proposed his plan for a "British-American Legislature." Under its authority, every action affecting the colonies would require their consent as well as that of Great Britain. In Adams' notes, Galloway concluded with a remark which he later omitted from his printed speech. He exclaimed that no men would go further than he "in point of fortune, or in point of blood" to defend his liberty.

In his plan and his speech, Galloway did his best to be conciliatory to what he assumed to be the views of the Congress. He deliberately avoided certain offensive expressions. He did not support two ideas which he personally and privately preferred, American representation in Parliament and the creation of an upper house on the model of the House of Lords in any American legislature. He used arguments which he recognized as dangerous, even subversive, ideas which tended "to an independency of the Colonies, and militate against the maxims that there must be some absolute power to draw together all the will and strength of the Empire." He applauded past American activity, which, at the time, he had actually opposed. He argued, for example, that resistance to the Stamp Act had been undertaken with the "greatest reason and justice." All this Galloway did in the hope that it would make the Continental Congress willing to give an honest hearing to his grand plan for accommodating Parliamentary supremacy with American rights.

But Galloway failed to convince the assembled delegates. In part, this was owing to objections to the plan, legitimate as well as fanciful. Galloway had described his proposed American legislature as an "inferior" branch of Parliament. He had used the hoary argument that within every government, "there must be a supreme legislature," before an audience where many were convinced that the British Empire was held together only by the person of the King. He had suggested that his plan be "humbly" presented to the two houses of Parliament and the King. Richard Henry Lee and Patrick Henry quickly objected to the Galloway program. Henry argued that no assurance of support for the mother country was necessary, that Great Britain already received sufficient compensation for the protection it gave America through control over colonial trade. Then, carried away by his rhetoric, he argued that any American legislature would be subject to the same kind of corruption that had made the House of Commons the willing instrument of a ministry bent on tyranny.

In part, Galloway's defeat was due to the work done by the Pennsylvania Whigs, by the conviction which they helped establish in the minds of the delegates that Galloway was not to be trusted. John Adams recorded his personal view of the place of Galloway in provincial politics. The Galloway faction was similar to "the tribe, in the Massachusetts, of Hutchinsonian Addressers." In the Bay Colony, such men had practiced "Machivelian dissimulation" for a long time and had only recently revealed themselves as real friends of the British ministry. In Pennsylvania, "Dr. Smith, Mr. Galloway,

Mr. Vaughan, and others . . . are now just where the Hutchinsonian faction were in the year 1764," that is, they were still pretending to be true friends of liberty. Patrick Henry had an equally bad opinion of Galloway. The plan for union "would ruin the cause of America." Henry was "very impatient to see such fellows and not be at liberty to describe them in their true colors."

Galloway's plan was really rejected on the same day on which it was offered, but it suffered for some time before being finally dispatched by the Congress. After warm debate on September 28, consideration of the plan was postponed "by a majority of one colony." And the Congress took another step repulsive to Galloway: it endorsed the idea of a non-importation agreement. On the thirtieth, it approved a non-exportation plan. On October 8, the Congress endorsed armed resistance should force be used by the British in Massachusetts. A week later, the delegates adopted a long series of resolutions over Galloway's protest according to his later statement. The fourth of these resolves proclaimed that Americans had "a free and exclusive power of legislation in their several provincial legislatures, in all cases of taxation and internal polity," allowing Parliament to regulate trade only as a matter of expediency. For Galloway, these various measures, the last in particular, seemed to mean that the colonies were approaching independence in all matters. The final blow for him came on or about October 21, 1774. Probably on that day, the Congress dismissed his plan of union and ordered all mention of it expunged from the record. Step by step, the Continental Congress had thus destroyed Galloway's expectations.

Suggested Further Reading:

No general study of inter-colonial union has yet been published, and a synthesis of the scattered monographs and articles in the field is long overdue. Harry M. Ward's *The United Colonies of New England, 1643–1690* (1961) is a useful if unevenly edited study, best in its treatment of the early years of the Confederation of New England. The outstanding work on the Dominion of New England is that by Viola F. Barnes, *The Dominion of New England: A Study in British Colonial Policy* (1923; reprinted, 1960); Michael G. Hall's excellent *Edward Randolph and the American Colonies, 1676–1703* (1960) supplements Dr. Barnes' work and further illuminates the Massachusetts scene; there is also useful material in Kenneth Murdock, *Increase Mather, Foremost American Puritan* (1925). Jack P. Greene has drawn attention to a little-known English plan of union in "Martin Bladen's Blueprint for a Colonial Union," *The William and Mary Quarterly,* 3rd Ser., XVII (1960), 516–530.

For an excellent summary of the imperial problems that led to the Albany Congress, see Lawrence Henry Gipson, *Zones of International Friction . . . 1748–1754* (1942), which is the fifth volume of his *The British Empire before the American Revolution.* Robert C. Newbold's *Albany Congress* (1955) is the only monograph on the subject; a new study is needed which would examine the Congress from the British side as well as the colonial.

Joseph Galloway has had a particularly poor historical press. The closest approach to a biography came over sixty years ago when Ernest H. Baldwin published his series of articles, "Joseph Galloway, the Loyalist Politician," *The Pennsylvania Magazine of History and Biography,* XXVI (1902), 161–191, 289–321, 417–442. Julian P. Boyd's *Anglo-American Union: Joseph Galloway's Plans to Preserve the British Empire, 1774–1788* (1941) is generally excellent but disappointing on the Plan of Union of 1774.

PART SEVEN

Mercantilism and Colonial America

By the seventeenth century England, like most of the new nation-states of Europe, had come to believe that her power — even her very survival — depended upon her wealth. To accumulate riches meant both prosperity and national security, and English society accordingly organized itself and took firm steps both to promote and to regulate its economic life.

This concept of national economic purpose — "an experiment in social engineering," in the words of Lawrence A. Harper — is usually known as mercantilism. It has an obvious relevance both to England's impulse to colonization and to her later administration of those colonies she had established. English leaders viewed colonies as vital sources of raw materials and potentially important markets for English manufactures. The possession and exploitation of colonies would enhance national self-sufficiency, security, and power. A favorable trade balance and the husbanding of specie — gold and silver — were fundamental objectives of English statesmen (and, indeed, of all who subscribed to mercantilist economic theories) throughout the era of the first British empire.

Few Englishmen doubted the essential rightness of the mercantilist economic doctrine; their problems lay only in its implementation. Such problems grew both in number and in complexity as the economy of the American colonies expanded and inevitably came into conflict with England's own interests.

1

The Navigation System

I

The Mercantile Mind

The complexities of mercantilism are hardly restricted to its impact upon Anglo-American relations. Mercantilism posed problems within England as well. For the greater part of the colonial period of American history England was substantially if not predominantly an agrarian nation; and yet, as Professor Harper *shows, England favored legislation primarily to the advantage of the merchant interest. The English gentleman identified trade with wealth, maritime power with security and international significance.*

The following selection is the introductory chapter of Professor Harper's classic study, The English Navigation Laws. *Here he indicates some of the difficulties the English encountered in seeking suitable means of securing their mercantilist objectives.*

Seventeenth-century England faced many of the problems which confront us today. For better or for worse, it encountered the capitalistic system, the problems of unemployment, poor relief, monopolies, and banking. The national debt increased by leaps and bounds, and the public credit was not merely imperiled but actually gave way when the Exchequer stopped making payments in 1672. Relatively speaking there was the same displacement of labor; coal was rapidly becoming a source of power; enclosures were disturbing the agrarians; and the discovery of the New World shifted many of the older channels of trade. International rivalry manifested itself both in the world of trade and on the battlefield. Nations were not afraid that there might be war; peace was considered merely a rest period between wars. Europe was free from strife only eight years in the seventeenth century. England herself engaged in two revolutions and nine foreign wars and was always in fear of foreign competition, first from Spain, then Holland, and thereafter France.

The danger of war explains much that might otherwise be difficult to understand in English mercantilism. It clears up the apparent paradox of the adoption, by a country in which agricultural interests predominated, of legislative programs which redounded principally to the merchants' advantage. The explanation lies in the correlation supposed to exist between national security, bullion, and foreign trade. War was managed "by the power of money," and it was believed that no nation could be "accounted safe, or mistress of its liberties" without an adequate supply. Since England had no gold or silver of her own, she could acquire the bullion upon which the monetary system rested only by exporting more merchandise than she imported. Hence the landed gentry could be persuaded to pass legislation intended to promote a favorable balance of trade. They continually had before them, in one form or another, the warning voiced by Davenant:

> Whenever we lose our trade, we must bid farewel to that wealth and strength which have hitherto enabled us to preserve our liberties, against the designs of Spain and France, . . . want of due circumspection in a point so essential to the very existence of this kingdom, may, perhaps, in less than an age, reduce us to be the prey of some conquerors, notwithstanding our large estates in land, the fertility of our soil, the richness of our product, and the convenience of our ports.

Because of England's insular position, her naval force was recognized to be "the Main Body and Strength of the Nation." It in turn

Reprinted from Lawrence A. Harper, *The English Navigation Laws* (New York: Columbia University Press, 1939), pp. 9–18.

depended upon commerce and navigation, since ships and seamen "like Food to the Body must be dayly renewed." William Potter succinctly summarized contemporary beliefs when he declared "the more Trading doth Encrease in any place, the more Ships multiply in that place . . . the more ships any Nation hath, the more strong they are at sea."

The general view was that England could protect herself, if she would. Contemporary writers declared that England's geographic situation gave her "the Preferrance of the most Valuable Trade in the World"; they proclaimed that the British Isles had better air and better ports than Holland and that they were superior "in their Native Grewth and Production for Commerce; as Rich Soyl is to that which is Barren." One man expressed the general belief when he wrote, "it was said of Old and grounded upon good Reason, that England was a mighty animal that would never die, unless it destroys itself." Even those who believed that "all was out of joint" and that England was losing in the race for international supremacy thought of the country's supposedly desperate plight as a challenge to further endeavor. They exhorted patriots to repent of the habitual fondness for sloth that was blamed for England's being on the "brink of Ruine," to lay aside their vices, and to acquire the virtues of their arch rivals in trade, the Dutch.

Each economic group, however, had its own scheme for promoting the national welfare, and there was often a clash of interests. The desires of the agriculturalist did not always coincide with those of the trader, the manufacturer, or the consumer. Merchants who banded together in chartered companies had conflicts with those who wished freedom of trade. The interests of London and of the outports were not always the same. Merchants trading with Portugal and the countries within the Straits opposed opening a commerce with France for wines; importers from Italy and Turkey quarreled as to the relative merits of their trades; and the "Japaners and Joyners" raised their voices in protest against cabinetwork brought from the East Indies. Even so simple a matter as the voyage of a ship might give rise to conflicts between many divergent interests. The merchants were not always owners of the vessels in which they traded; in fact, they were said to have perhaps "the least share in the Ships of England." They wanted to lower freight rates, while the shipowners wanted to raise them. The owners desired low wages, and the masters and men hoped for high ones.

All were united as to the need for preserving trade and shipping, but they were divided in their views about the means of effecting their ends. Many approached the problem by advocating efforts "to make trade easy and necessary, and thereby to make it our interest to trade." They sought improved harbors, the development of river navigation and internal waterways, the simplification of legal procedure, better regulated insurance, and convoys in time of war. Others advocated usury laws to reduce the interest rate, or plans for the recoinage of the currency, the establishment of banks, and the improvement of credit.

One school of thought wished England to become a "universal merchant" and to serve as an entrepôt for the world's commerce. With this end in view William Stockton proposed that customs duties be replaced by an excise tax payable only when the goods were sold, and therefore not assessable on goods passing through England. Brewster, Child, and others were willing to retain the customs duties but desired a greater rebate of the duty on imported foreign goods, which were later exported, than the moiety then allowed by law. Others argued for the establishment of free ports similar to those at Venice and Leghorn, and one anonymous seventeenth-century writer seemed ready for free trade when he declared:

> It is the Interest of England to send their Product and Manufactory to the best Market, and from thence to bring such Commodities as they cannot purchase cheaper any where else . . . and by this natural Circulation the Nation will be enrich'd. . . .
>
> A Free Trade makes all manner of Commodities cheap; the cheapness of Commodities impowers our People to work cheaper; the cheapness of Work encourages a Foreign Trade; and a Foreign Trade brings Wealth and People, and that alone raises the Price of Lands and Houses.
>
> On the contrary, Prohibitions make Cloath-

ing and every thing else dear; so that the People cannot live without they have a proportionable price for their Labour. And I conceive Prohibitions to be a principal Reason why we Cannot Trade so cheap as our Neighbours do.

The contrary view was taken by those who desired to rely upon the home trade and that founded upon native staples. Carew Reynel argued:

> That the more home Trade, variety of Manufactures, and Husbandries we have within our selves, the more Foreign trade we shall have also . . . home Trade is the foundation of Foreign, and if we are full of home Commodities, every private man will be of a publick spirit to gain Transportation for them.

It irked the author of *The Naked Truth* that England let traders bring "home superfluous Commodities that are purchased with our Bullion, to the hinderance of our own Native Commodities." Another complained of the decrease of England's "own Growth fit for Exportation," and "the double Increase of forreign costly Goods and Commodities brought over more and more from beyond the Seas." The great favorite of such writers was the wool trade, the "Golden Fleece . . . the spring of our Riches," which in 1699 supplied more than a third of England's "universal exports."

Another local industry holding a peculiar fascination for contemporaries was the "great and desirable Rich Trade of Fishing." English interest in this trade was stimulated by irritation at Holland's success in procuring much of her wealth off England's own coasts. It promised a variety of employment, on land in drying and salting the fish and repairing nets and boats, and on sea both directly in fishing and indirectly in carrying the catch to the Mediterranean and in bringing back salt from France. Repeated failures did not deter Parliament from renewing the efforts to promote the fisheries, always regarded in the rather florid language of Misselden as "A Mine of Gold . . . the Mine is deepe, the veines are great, the Ore is rare, the Gold is pure, the extent unlimited, the wealth unknowne, the worth invaluable."

Those who favored home trades usually rated the merits of the short voyage above those of the long voyage. They countered the argument of Mun and others that longer voyages employed more ships, by discussing the need for seamen. Trades pursued near at hand permitted the King to impress both men and ships "at any time for any occasion." Long voyages might keep sailors away when most needed and did not increase the total supply. According to John Cary, it was the short voyages which trained seamen, "both the Imployers and the Imployed being desirous to make their first Tryals on such Voyages. The voyage to Newcastle for coal was reckoned "if not the only, yet the especial Nursery and School of Seamen." Another writer declared it to be the "chiefest in employment of seamen" and "the gentlest, and most open to the landsmen," whereas ships making voyages "far out of the kingdom" were bound by their charter party to the merchant "not to carry but sufficient men, and such as know their labour, and can take their turn at the helm, top, and yard." He also believed that the short trades were the most healthful, and he denounced the trade to the Indies as having been bought at "the price of blood," since it had, according to his figures, cost the lives of more than two thousand of the three thousand men engaged in it.

Tradition supported the advocates of the home trade and short voyages, but potent forces were opposed to them. The lure of sudden riches fired men's imaginations. The amount of gold obtained by Spain in the New World did not diminish in the telling, and Holland was popularly supposed to have found a source of equally fabulous wealth in the East Indies. In days when tales were told of the Dutch measuring their profits by tons of gold, many more doubtless needed than heeded the contemporary dramatist's advice not to exchange the security of "competent certenties" for the dangers of "excellent uncertenties." English sporting instincts were awakened by the elements of hazard and chance involved in conquering new worlds. Commerce with the Continent had, in the minds of the gentry, been tainted by the bargaining and haggling of the market, but the upper classes thought of the new trades as adventures and declared, "the stranger the country, the greater the adventure."

World trade meant colonies, and colonization appealed to many classes. Patriots believed colonies could serve as a base for war with Spain. The religiously inclined thought of the Indians awaiting conversion. Philanthropists found in expansion a solution for England's surplus population. Merchants foresaw new markets, naval leaders an increase of shipping and mariners, and a new source for naval supplies. The argument was advanced that a world-wide trade, founded in part upon colonies, would be freer from interruptions in time of war than the older routes of commerce.

The task of the seventeenth-century mercantilists lay in selecting the best features of all the proposals and in combining as many as possible into a workable scheme. They had no hesitancy in calling upon the government to act; they definitely believed in the virtues of legislation. In periods of depression many found fault, expressly or impliedly, with the rulers of the kingdom, their "negligent or fearful councils" and "weak laws." They declared that "Trade is like a nice and coy Mistress," which one must court and pursue, that "publick spirits and wise measures" are necessary for its conquest, and that to insure its retention it must be "well fixt by a good law."

But we must not think of mercantilism as a system akin to our modern schemes of social planning. Mercantile measures were primarily practical expedients, however well conceived. The cry for legislative action arose from no doctrinaire commitment to the value of legislation, similar to that held by free traders concerning its undesirability. Child, for example, approved of England's Navigation Acts, although he admitted that the Dutch had none and that he had "yet to be informed where the Dutch have missed their proper interest in trade." He defended his position by a doctrine of economic relativity, that

> That which is fit for one nation to do in relation to their trade, is not fit for all; no more than the same policy is necessary to a prevailing army that are masters of the field, as to an army of less force. . . . The Dutch, by reason of their great stocks, low interest, multitude of merchants and shipping, are masters in the field of trade, and therefore have no need to build castles, fortresses, and places of retreat; such I account laws of limitation, and securing of particular trades to the natives of any kingdom.

When mercantilist pamphleteers stopped to consider the point, they recognized that regulatory jurisprudence involved more problems than the enactment of a "good law." As one writer declared, "it were better to have fewer Lawes, with better Execution, than more Lawes, with more trouble and lesse use." Petty recognized the correlation between the value of legislation and the possibility of making it effective when he advised his countrymen that, "as wiser Physicians tamper not excessively with their Patients," so in politics and economics the same method should be used, "rather observing and complying with the motions of nature, then contradicting it with vehement Administrations . . . for '*Naturam expellas furcâ licet usque recurrit.*' " Henry Robinson complained that the laws were "so numerous and intricate . . . that it is not possible to know them all, much lesse keep them in memory, and avoyd the being entangled by them." He wanted to know "whether the Multiplicity of Courts of Justice do not cause a more mischievous Confusion in the World, than the Babilonian of Languages," and he hoped "That some honest publique spirited Lawyer who thoroughly understands the various Meanders, Quirks and subtilities of this over-powering Faculty would anatomize and lay open unto the Nation, how easily it is for the very best Lawes wee have to be evaded and frustrated, and the whole Formality and proceedings to be avoyded and deluded by legall fallacies and tricks."

Most writers, however, were too busy advocating economic panaceas to worry about how they would be carried out. Some of the literature remained merely *ex parte* pleading, but more often the proponents of a particular idea sought to have their work attain the status of a comprehensive treatise on trade by combining various specific proposals that appealed to their fancy, the less able sometimes failing to note that one scheme would nullify another.

Recognition of possible conflicts existing in social regulation between individual interest and the general welfare was usually confined to observations concerning only one-half of the problem. When considering the need for national power, the writers observed that unregulated activity would be designed to bring the greatest gain to particular persons, even at the risk of loss to the nation, "unless Authority interpose, and afford help, as there may be occasion." As Brewster declared, "not only Merchants, but Seamen will Chuse, as all men naturally do, that Employment which brings Profit with least Toil and Labour." Yet at other times the writers realized that since man's actions depend upon personal motivation, individual interests must be conciliated. Thus Child argued in favor of usury laws, that no merchant would drudge in trade if the interest rate were not low enough to keep him from being tempted to turn gentleman and settle on a landed estate. Another writer, opposing such laws, maintained that they would merely cause less money to be loaned. "J. P., Esquire," claimed that prohibitions against the exportation of coin and bullion had never done any good, that the only remedy was to make exportation unprofitable. Sir Francis Brewster declared that "no human Policy and Law can bring men into Arts with Success, and the increase of them, but by Gain, and security of enjoying it."

In so far as seventeenth-century theorists attempted any reconciliation of individual interest and public welfare, it rested on the assumption that there was an ideal balance which, if attained, would secure national prosperity as well as individual advancement. To quote Brewster again: "there needs no trick to promote the true Interest of a Nation, every man will run into it; and he would be a States-man worthy of Honour that did advance the Interest of his Country above that of their Neighbours." Followers of Adam Smith must not misunderstand the nature of the assumption. It did not rely upon any doctrine that the "invisible hand" of Providence would supply the necessary guidance, if only man would not interpose his puny efforts. Mercantilists probably believed as devoutly in the wisdom and omnipotence of the Deity as did Smith, but they placed less reliance upon the assumption, "the Lord will provide," than upon the proverb, "God helps those who help themselves."

II

The Navigation Acts of 1660 and 1663

Of fundamental importance to the English concept of mercantilism was the development and protection of its merchant navy. In 1651, Oliver Cromwell's Parliament decreed that all goods produced in Asia, Africa, and America and destined for England or her possessions must be carried in English-owned ships, manned by crews mainly English, and commanded by English captains. It further stipulated that products from the continent of Europe were to be shipped directly to England from the country of their origin only in English ships or in those of the country which produced them. Finally, the English coastal trade, hitherto nearly monopolized by the Dutch, was to be denied to all foreign shipping.

Several weaknesses in this initial legislation soon became apparent. For one thing, it did not regulate colonial *trade with Europe. For another, the pretensions of the decree were so broad as to provoke doubts of their legality on both sides of the Atlantic. Accordingly one of the first legislative acts of Charles II, recently restored to the English throne, was his approval in September, 1660, of a new, more effective Navigation Law. The provisions of this new act were specific: all imports and exports to and from British possessions were to be transported only in English or colonial bottoms, and those articles of colonial produce on the enumerated list, i.e., cotton, sugar, indigo, dyewoods, ginger, and tobacco, were to be exported only to England or her possessions.*

The Navigation — or Staple — Act of 1663 tightened English control of imperial commerce still further. This measure, designed to keep the colonies "in a firmer dependence" upon the

The Navigation Acts of 1660 and 1663. Reprinted in *Statutes at Large*, ed. Danby Pickering (Cambridge, Eng., 1762–1869), VII, 452–460; VIII, 161–163.

mother country, required that all foreign exports destined for the colonies be transshipped by way of England. Thus England (in theory at least) became the colonies' sole marketplace and brokerage, while simultaneously the flourishing independent colonial import-export trade was to be brought to an end.

The Navigation Act of 1660

For the increase of shipping and encouragement of the navigation of this nation wherein, under the good providence and protection of God, the wealth, safety, and strength of this kingdom is so much concerned; (2) be it enacted by the king's most excellent Majesty, and by the Lords and Commons in this present Parliament assembled, and by the authority thereof, that from and after the first day of December, one thousand six hundred and sixty, and from thence forward, no goods or commodities whatsoever shall be imported into or exported out of any lands, islands, plantations, or territories to his Majesty belonging or in his possession, or which may hereafter belong unto or be in the possession of his Majesty, his heirs, and successors, in Asia, Africa, or America, in any other ship or ships, vessel or vessels whatsoever, but in such ships or vessels as do truly and without fraud belong only to the people of England or Ireland, dominion of Wales or town of Berwick upon Tweed, or are of the built of and belonging to any the said lands, islands, plantations, or territories, as the proprietors and right owners thereof, and whereof the master and three fourths of the mariners at least are English; (3) under the penalty of the forfeiture and loss of all the goods and commodities which shall be imported into or exported out of any the aforesaid places in any other ship or vessel, as also of the ship or vessel, with all its guns, furniture, tackle, ammunition, and apparel; one third part thereof to his Majesty, his heirs and successors; one third part to the governor of such land, plantation, island, or territory where such default shall be committed, in case the said ship or goods be there seized, or otherwise that third part also to his Majesty, his heirs and successors; and the other third part to him or them who shall seize, inform, or sue for the same in any court of record, by bill, information, plaint, or other action, wherein no essoin, protection, or wager of law shall be allowed; (4) and all admirals and other commanders at sea of any the ships of war or other ship having commission from his Majesty or from his heirs or successors, are hereby authorized and strictly required to seize and bring in as prize all such ships or vessels as shall have offended contrary hereunto, and deliver them to the court of admiralty, there to be proceeded against; and in case of condemnation, one moiety of such forfeitures shall be to the use of such admirals or commanders and their companies, to be divided and proportioned amongst them according to the rules and orders of the sea in case of ships taken prize; and the other moiety to the use of his Majesty, his heirs and successors.

II. And be it enacted, that no alien or person not born within the allegiance of our sovereign lord the king, his heirs and successors, or naturalized, or made a free denizen, shall from and after the first day of February, which will be in the year of our Lord one thousand six hundred sixty-one, exercise the trade or occupation of a merchant or factor in any the said places; (2) upon pain of the forfeiture and loss of all his goods and chattels, or which are in his possession; one third to his Majesty, his heirs and successors; one third to the governor of the plantation where such person shall so offend; and the other third to him or them that shall inform or sue for the same in any of his Majesty's courts in the plantation where such offence shall be committed; (3) and all governors of the said lands, islands, plantations, or territories, and every of them, are hereby strictly required and commanded, and all who hereafter shall be made governors of any such islands, plantations, or territories, by his Majesty, his heirs or successors, shall before their entrance into their government take a solemn oath to do their utmost, that every the afore-mentioned clauses, and all the matters and things therein contained, shall be punctually and *bona fide* observed according to the true intent and meaning thereof; (4) and upon complaint and proof made before his Majesty, his heirs or successors, or such as shall be by him or them thereunto authorized and appointed, that any the said governors have been willingly and wittingly negligent in doing their duty accordingly, that the said governor so offending shall be removed from his government.

III. And it is further enacted by the authority aforesaid, that no goods or commodities whatsoever, of the growth, production or manufacture of Africa, Asia, or America, or of any part thereof, or which are described or laid down in the usual maps or cards of those places, be imported into England, Ireland, or Wales, islands of Guernsey and Jersey, or town of Berwick upon Tweed, in any other ship or ships, vessel or vessels whatsoever, but in such as do truly and without fraud belong only to the people of England or Ireland, dominion of Wales, or town of Berwick upon Tweed, or of the lands, islands, plantations or territories in Asia, Africa, or America, to his Majesty belonging, as the proprietors and right owners thereof, and whereof the master, and three fourths at least of the mariners are English; (2) under the penalty of the forfeiture of all such goods and commodities, and of the ship or vessel in which they were imported, with all her guns, tackle, furniture, ammunition, and apparel; one moiety to his Majesty, his heirs and successors; and the other moiety to him or them who shall seize, inform or sue for the same in any court of record, by bill, information, plaint or other action, wherein no essoin, protection or wager of law shall be allowed.

XVIII. And it is further enacted by the authority aforesaid, that from and after the first day of April, which shall be in the year of our Lord one thousand six hundred sixty-one, no sugars, tobacco, cotton-wool, indigoes, ginger, fustic, or other dyeing wood, of the growth, production, or manufacture of any English plantations in America, Asia, or Africa, shall be shipped, carried, conveyed, or transported from any of the said English plantations to any land, island territory, dominion, port, or place whatsoever, other than to such other English plantations as do belong to his Majesty, his heirs and successors, or to the kingdom of England or Ireland, or principality of Wales, or town of Berwick upon Tweed, there to be laid on shore; (2) under the penalty of the forfeiture of the said goods, or the full value thereof, as also of the ship, with all her guns, tackle, apparel, ammunition, and furniture; the one moiety to the king's Majesty, his heirs and successors, and the other moiety to him or them that shall seize, inform, or sue for the same in any court of record, by bill, plaint, or information, wherein no essoin, protection, or wager of law shall be allowed.

XIX. And be it further enacted by the authority aforesaid, that for every ship or vessel, which from and after the five and twentieth day of December in the year of our Lord one thousand six hundred and sixty shall set sail out of or from England, Ireland, Wales, or town of Berwick upon Tweed, for any English plantation in America, Asia, or Africa, sufficient bond shall be given with one surety to the chief officers of the custom-house of such port or place from whence the said ship shall set sail, to the value of one thousand pounds, if the ship be of less burden than one hundred tons; and of the sum of two thousand pounds, if the ship shall be of greater burden; that in case the said ship or vessel shall load any of the said commodities at any of the said English plantations, that the same commodities shall be by the said ship brought to some port of England, Ireland, Wales, or to the port or town of Berwick upon Tweed, and shall there unload and put on shore the same, the danger of the seas only excepted; (2) and for all ships coming from any other port or place to any of the aforesaid plantations, who by this act are permitted to trade there, that the governor of such English plantations shall before the said ship or vessel be permitted to load on board any of the said commodities, take bond in manner and to the value aforesaid, for each respective ship or vessel, that such ship or vessel shall carry all the aforesaid goods that shall be laden on board in the said ship to some other of his Majesty's English plantations, or to England, Ireland, Wales, or town of Berwick upon Tweed; (3) and that every ship or vessel which shall load or take on board any of the aforesaid goods, until such bond given to the said governor, or certificate produced from the officers of any custom-house of England, Ireland, Wales, or of the town of Berwick, that such bonds have been there duly given, shall be forfeited with all her guns, tackle, apparel, and furniture, to be employed and recovered in manner as aforesaid; and the said governors and every of them shall twice in every year after the first day of

January one thousand six hundred and sixty, return true copies of all such bonds by him so taken, to the chief officers of the custom in London.

The Navigation Act of 1663

V. And in regard his Majesty's plantations beyond the seas are inhabited and peopled by his subjects of this his kingdom of England; for the maintaining a greater correspondence and kindness between them, and keeping them in a firmer dependence upon it, and rendering them yet more beneficial and advantageous unto it in the further employment and increase of English shipping and seamen, vent of English woollen and other manufactures and commodities, rendering the navigation to and from the same more safe and cheap, and making this kingdom a staple, not only of the commodities of those plantations, but also of the commodities of other countries and places, for the supplying of them; and it being the usage of other nations to keep their plantations trade to themselves.

VI. Be it enacted, and it is hereby enacted, that from and after the five and twentieth day of March one thousand six hundred sixty-four, no commodity of the growth, production, or manufacture of Europe shall be imported into any land, island, plantation, colony, territory, or place to his Majesty belonging, or which shall hereafter belong unto or be in the possession of his Majesty, his heirs and successors, in Asia, Africa, or America (Tangier only excepted) but what shall be *bona fide,* and without fraud, laden and shipped in England, Wales, or the town of Berwick upon Tweed, and in English built shipping . . . ; and whereof the master and three fourths of the mariners at least are English, and which shall be carried directly thence to the said lands, islands, plantations, colonies, territories, or places, and from no other place or places whatsoever; any law, statute, or usage to the contrary notwithstanding; (2) under the penalty of the loss of all such commodities of the growth, production, or manufacture of Europe, as shall be imported into any of them from any other place whatsoever, by land or water; and if by water, of the ship or vessel also in which they were imported, with all her guns, tackle, furniture, ammunition, and apparel; one third part to his Majesty, his heirs and successors; one third part to the governor of such land, island, plantation, colony, territory, or place, into which such goods were imported, if the said ship, vessel, or goods be there seized or informed against and sued for; or otherwise that third part also to his Majesty, his heirs and successors; and the other third part to him or them who shall seize, inform, or sue for the same in any of his Majesty's courts in such of the said lands, islands, colonies, plantations, territories, or places where the offence was committed, or in any court of record in England, by bill, information, plaint, or other action, wherein no essoin, protection, or wager of law shall be allowed.

VII. Provided always, and be it hereby enacted by the authority aforesaid, that it shall and may be lawful to ship and lade in such ships, and so navigated, as in the foregoing clause is set down and expressed, in any part of Europe, salt for the fisheries of New England and Newfoundland, and to ship and lade in the Madeira's wines of the growth thereof, and to ship and lade in the Western islands of Azores wines of the growth of the said islands, and to ship and take in servants or horses in Scotland or Ireland, and to ship or lade in Scotland all sorts of victual of the growth or production of Scotland, and to ship or lade in Ireland all sorts of victual of the growth or production of Ireland, and the same to transport into any of the said lands, islands, plantations, colonies, territories, or places; anything in the foregoing clause to the contrary in any wise notwithstanding.

VIII. And for the better prevention of frauds, be it enacted and it is hereby enacted, that from and after the five and twentieth day of March one thousand six hundred sixty and four, every person or persons importing by land any goods or commodities whatsoever into any the said lands, islands, plantations, colonies, territories, or places, shall deliver to the governor of such land, island, plantation, colony, territory, or place, or to such person or officer as shall be by him thereunto authorized and appointed, within four and twenty hours after such importation, his and their names and surnames, and a true inventory and particular of all such goods or commodities; (2) and no ship or vessel coming to any such land, island, plantation, colony, territory, or place, shall lade or unlade any goods or commodities whatsoever, until the master or commander of such ship or vessel shall first have made known to the governor of such land, island, plantation, colony, territory, or place, or such other person or officer as shall be by him thereunto authorized and appointed, the arrival of the said ship or vessel, with her name, and the name and surname of her master or commander, and have shown to him that she is an English built ship, or made good by producing such certificate, as abovesaid, that she is a ship or vessel *bona fide* belonging to England, Wales, or the town of Berwick, and navigated with an English master, and three fourth parts of the mariners at least Englishmen, and have delivered to such governor or other person or officer a true and perfect inventory or invoice of her lading, together with the place or places in which the said goods were laden or taken into the said ship or vessel. . . .

III

The Woollen Act, 1699 *and* The Iron Act, 1750

English enforcement of the Navigation system became more strict in the last quarter of the seventeenth century: the acts of 1673 and 1696 ("for the more effectual preventing of frauds") were important links in the tightening chain of economic regulation. But at the beginning of the eighteenth century English control took a new turn: with a steadily increasing interest in manufacturing, England decided upon legislation to protect her carefully cultivated colonial markets.

The first in this series of measures, the Woollen Act of 1699, reflected the priority of the English textile industry. In order to curtail wool manufacturing in Ireland and America ("which will inevitably . . . tend to the ruin of the trade, and the woollen manufactures of this realm"), this measure prohibited the export of wool or woollen products outside the colony of production. Historians generally agree that the Woollen Act was prompted mainly by competition from Ireland rather than America, but it remains a significant declaration of English policy on intra-imperial competition in manufactures. The Hat Act of 1732 followed the pattern set; the prohibition of hat exports, along with restrictions on hat manufacture seriously depressed colonial hatters.

The Iron Act of 1750, while different in detail, is equally representative of the continued English pursuit of mercantilism. True, there was division within England on appropriate legislation: English producers of finished iron products wanted the cheapest raw iron, while English producers of raw iron opposed colonial competition in this commodity. But all iron interests agreed that the colonists should not compete as producers of finished iron goods. The Act of 1750 therefore encouraged the export of colonial raw iron to the English finishing mills, but forbade the erection of new slitting mills in America.

The Woollen Act, 1699. Reprinted in *Statutes at Large,* ed. Pickering, X, pp. 249–256. The Iron Act, 1750. Reprinted in *ibid.,* XX, 97–100.

The Woollen Act

Forasmuch as wool and the woollen manufactures of cloth, serge, bays, kerseys, and other stuffs made or mixed with wool, are the greatest and most profitable commodities of this kingdom, on which the value of lands, and the trade of the nation do chiefly depend; and whereas great quantities of the like manufactures have of late been made, and are daily increasing in the kingdom of Ireland, and in the English plantations in America, and are exported from thence to foreign markets, heretofore supplied from England, which will inevitably sink the value of lands, and tend to the ruin of the trade, and the woollen manufactures of this realm; for the prevention whereof, and for the encouragement of the woollen manufactures within this kingdom. . . .

XIX. And for the more effectual encouragement of the woollen manufacture of this kingdom; be it further enacted by the authority aforesaid, that from and after the first day of December, in the year of our Lord, one thousand six hundred ninety-nine, no wool, wool-fells, shortlings, mortlings, wool-flocks, worsted, bay, or woollen yarn, cloth, serge, bays, kerseys, says, friezes, druggets, cloth-serges, shalloons, or any other drapery stuffs, or woollen manufactures whatsoever, made or mixed with wool or wool-flocks, being of the product or manufacture of any of the English plantations in America, shall be loaden or laid on board in any ship or vessel, in any place or parts within any of the said English plantations, upon any pretence whatsoever; as likewise that no such wool, wool-fells, shortlings, mortlings, woolflocks, worsted, bay, or woollen yarn, cloth, serge, bays, kerseys, says, friezes, druggets, cloth-serges, shalloons, or any other drapery stuffs, or woollen manufactures whatsoever, made up or mixt with wool or wool-flocks, being of the product or manufacture of any of the English plantations in America as aforesaid, shall be loaden upon any horse, cart, or other carriage, to the intent and purpose to be exported, transported, carried, or conveyed out of the said English plantations to any other of the said plantations, or to any other place whatsoever. . . .

The Iron Act

Whereas the importation of bar iron from his Majesty's colonies in America, into the port of London, and the importation of pig-iron from the said colonies into any port of Great Britain, and the manufacture of such bar and pig-iron in Great Britain, will be a great advantage not only to the said colonies, but also to this kingdom, by furnishing the manufacturers of iron with a supply of that useful and necessary commodity, and by means thereof large sums of money, now annually paid for iron to foreigners, will be saved to this kingdom, and a greater quantity of the woollen, and other manufactures of Great Britain, will be exported to America in exchange for such iron so imported; be it therefore enacted by the king's most excellent Majesty, by and with the advice and consent of the Lords Spiritual and Temporal, and Commons, in this present Parliament assembled, and by the authority of the same, that from and after the twenty-fourth day of June, one thousand seven hundred and fifty, the several and respective subsidies, customs, impositions, rates, and duties, now payable on pig-iron, made in and imported from his Majesty's colonies in America, into any port of Great Britain, shall cease, determine, and be no longer paid; and that from and after the said twenty-fourth day of June, no subsidy, custom, imposition, rate, or duty whatsoever shall be payable upon bar-iron made in and imported from the said colonies into the port of London; any law statute, or usage to the contrary thereof in any wise notwithstanding.

IX. And, that pig and bar-iron made in his Majesty's colonies in America may be further manufactured in this kingdom, be it further enacted by the authority aforesaid, that from and after the twenty-fourth day of June, one thousand seven hundred and fifty, no mill or other engine for slitting or rolling of iron, or any plating-forge to work with a tilt hammer, or any furnace for making steel, shall be erected, or after such erection, continued, in any of his Majesty's colonies in America; and if any person or persons shall erect, or cause to be erected, or after such erection, continue, or cause to be continued, in any of the said colonies, any such mill, engine, forge, or furnace, every person or persons so offending, shall for every such mill, engine, forge, or furnace, forfeit the sum of two hundred pounds of lawful money of Great Britain.

2

The Question of Molasses

I

The Molasses Act, 1733

The Molasses Act is historically inconvenient, for it does not fit the mercantilist mold. Its passage did not promote English self-sufficiency. It promised but did not deliver a measure of relief to depressed English planters in the West Indies, who had been complaining bitterly of French and Dutch competition in the sugar markets. The terms of this legislation imposed prohibitive duties on mainland imports of foreign rum, molasses and sugar.

Whereas the welfare and prosperity of your Majesty's sugar colonies in America are of the greatest consequence and importance to the trade, navigation, and strength of this kingdom; and whereas the planters of the said sugar colonies have of late years fallen under such great discouragements that they are unable to improve or carry on the sugar trade upon an equal footing with the foreign sugar colonies without some advantage and relief be given to them from Great Britain; for remedy whereof, . . . be it enacted, . . . that from and after the twenty-fifth day of December, one thousand seven hundred and thirty-three, there shall be raised, levied, collected and paid, unto and for the use of his Majesty, his heirs and successors, upon all rum or spirits of the produce or manufacture of any of the colonies or plantations in America, not in the possession or under the dominion of his Majesty, his heirs and successors, which at any time or times within or during the continuance of this act, shall be imported or brought into any of the colonies or plantations in America, which now are or hereafter may be in the possession or under the dominion of his Majesty, his heirs or successors, the sum of nine pence, money of Great Britain, to be paid according to the proportion and value of five shillings and six pence the ounce in silver, for every gallon thereof, and after that rate for any greater or lesser quantity; and upon all molasses or syrups of such foreign produce or manufacture as aforesaid, which shall be imported or brought into any of the said colonies or plantations of or belonging to his Majesty, the sum of six pence of like money for every gallon thereof, and after that rate for any greater or lesser quantity; and upon all sugars and paneles of such foreign growth, produce or manufacture as aforesaid, which shall be imported into any of the said colonies or plantations of or belonging to his Majesty, a duty after the rate of five shillings of like money, for every hundredweight avoirdupois, of the said sugar and paneles, and after that rate for a greater or lesser quantity.

II

The Colonial Molasses Trade

Few historians have accurately gauged the character of the Molasses Act. Despite its title, scholars have usually focused their attention upon the sugar market to the near exclusion of the more significant product, molasses. Gilman M. Ostrander, *a Michigan State University historian with wide-ranging interests,*[1] *performed a notable service when he examined the mechanics of sugar refining in the eighteenth century. He discovered the key role played by*

The Molasses Act, 1733. Reprinted in *Statutes at Large,* ed. Pickering, XVI, 374.

Gilman M. Ostrander, "The Colonial Molasses Trade," from *Agricultural History,* XXX, (1956), 177–184.

[1] See for example *The Prohibition Movement in California, 1848–1933* (1957), and *The Rights of Man in America, 1606–1861* (1960).

molasses, the inevitable by-product in the refining process. He has demonstrated the colonial need for foreign molasses, and shown how the duty jeopardized the economic well-being of the mainland. Greater interests were involved than the mainland rum industry: molasses was employed throughout the colonies as an essential kitchen commodity — which included brewing molasses beer. Professor Ostrander concludes with an analysis of the role of rum in the famous triangle trade with Africa and the West Indies: while conceding its importance, he contends that it was not the main outlet for colonial rum; the real market was on the mainland itself. Molasses, in short, mattered to the American colonies; the Molasses Act of necessity made smuggling a colonial way of life.

The protests against the Molasses Act of 1733 and the excitement aroused by the Sugar Act of 1764 demonstrated the immense importance of molasses to the commerce of New England and the middle colonies in the eighteenth century. It was not the African rum trade which gave molasses this importance, for relatively little molasses imported to the mainland ever found its way to Africa. The bulk of the import was consumed within the colonies, and for the most part not in the form of rum.

Molasses was important to colonial commerce because it was the only commodity produced in vast quantity by the non-English Caribbean possessions which their governments permitted them to sell to the English. By the mid-eighteenth century, this Caribbean molasses trade, particularly with the French and Dutch sugar colonies, had opened profitable markets for foodstuffs, livestock, lumber, and fish, and various manufactured articles of New England and the middle colonies. In return, the colonials received specie, bills of exchange, and miscellaneous products; but mainly they received molasses, which they were able to adapt to a variety of uses — the manufacture of rum being, no doubt, the most important single use. The chief purpose of the Molasses and Sugar acts was to aid British West Indian molasses producers and rum distillers by cutting off from their New England competitors the chief source of molasses, but the acts incidentally threatened the entire commerce between the mainland colonies and the foreign Caribbean. The Molasses Act remained generally unenforced and was therefore tolerated; the Sugar Act was to some extent enforced, and it drove the colonial merchants to united defiance of British rule in the first major imperial crisis of the pre-Revolutionary era.

Molasses in the eighteenth century had an economic importance to the sugar industry which has since disappeared in the face of technological improvements in the sugar refining process. Modern refining methods produce eight to eleven parts of sugar to one part of molasses, and the molasses residue is suitable only for such uses as cattle feed and industrial alcohol. The manufacture of molasses for kitchen use or for rum distilleries is now a specialized industry. Under eighteenth-century refining methods, on the other hand, as much as three parts molasses was produced to four parts sugar, and on an average it was estimated that the ratio of molasses to sugar was about one to two. The molasses produced under those conditions was suitable for table use or for the rum distilleries. Thus the profitable disposal of the molasses was a major consideration for the eighteenth century sugar planters. The solicitor for the British sugar colonies testified to the Board of Trade in 1750 that,

> It is well known to every one concerned in the Sugar Trade that the Profits of the Planter depend upon the Vent which he finds for his Rum and Molasses for if Sugar only and no Rum or Molasses could be produced from the Sugar Cane it would hardly pay the expense of Culture and making consequently as the Vent of Rum and Molasses is stopt or increased the Sugar Colonies . . . must thrive or decline. . . .

The problems of finding markets or "vents" for molasses increased during the eighteenth century. From the 1640's, when sugar plantations were in operation on Barbados, down through the eighteenth century, English as well as foreign sugar production continued to increase at prodigious rates, while the European market for sugar increased even more rapidly.

"The most striking feature, perhaps, of the British sugar trade in the eighteenth century," according to Frank Wesley Pitman, "was the inadequacy of the supply to meet the effective demand of the empire." The most striking feature of the molasses trade, at least so far as the foreign West Indies were concerned, was the inadequacy of the demand to meet the enormous and ever-increasing supply.

There was practically no market in Europe for molasses; neither England nor France imported it in appreciable amounts. England did import large quantities of West Indian molasses in the form of rum, but the French sugar islands were prohibited from exporting rum to France out of deference to the French brandy interests. Only the English colonies in the Caribbean developed distilleries on a large scale. The French were said to be throwing away a half million gallons of molasses each year in the 1680's for lack of a market. Nor do they appear to have solved the problem through the development of a rum industry in the following century. As late as the 1760's, almost no French rum was imported to the English colonies, even from French islands captured by the British during the Seven Years' War.

The Dutch also do not appear to have developed an important rum industry, even though at the time of the Molasses Act they were producing sufficient quantities of molasses to supply the entire needs of the mainland colonies. In the late colonial period, the New England merchants stated that the distilleries on the foreign sugar islands were of only minor importance to the trade with New England. The one important market for French and Dutch surplus molasses was the English continental colonies which were importing molasses by the late colonial period at the rate of considerably more than four million gallons annually.

The English islands were from the first in a better position to dispose profitably of the molasses by-product. No special restrictions were placed on their rum trade, and the English planters early solved the problem of their molasses surpluses through the development of local distilleries. Rum was distilled in the English sugar islands by the 1650's, and ten years later it had become an important article of export to the English mainland colonies. In 1702, Barbados exported more than two hundred thousand gallons of rum; and in the years that followed, rum production rose as rapidly as sugar production.

By the eve of the Molasses Act, the English sugar planters had solved the problem of molasses surpluses. Every plantation was said to be equipped with a distillery, and the total annual production was estimated to be considerably more than four million gallons. At that time, molasses production was about five million gallons annually, on the basis of a yearly sugar production of one hundred million pounds. At least a gallon of molasses was required to make a gallon of rum, so it is evident that the English planters had little molasses available for export at the time the Molasses Act was passed. West Indian planters claimed this Act was necessary to protect their mainland molasses market from foreign competition. But since they had little molasses for export, this motive can hardly account for their heated support of the Act.

The chief object of the Act seems to have been to protect the mainland market for West Indian rum by depriving the New England distilleries of their source of cheap foreign molasses. The mainland rum market was considered "indispensable to the West Indian planter under the comparative distaste and discouragement of rum as an article of British Consumption," and the English planters were increasingly concerned over the likelihood that the mainland colonies would threaten this market by producing rum for themselves. As Governor Nicholson of South Carolina wrote in the early 1720's,

> . . . the New Englanders . . . are setting up a trade for making rum which they do out of mollasses etc. from Surinam the French Islands and Cape Francois. . . . I suppose they will endeavour to engross all the trade of mollasses from both the former places and also our Islands if so they will furnish all this Continent with rum and how prejudicial this affair will be. . . .

Thus the destruction of the New England rum industry was the main purpose of the Molasses Act, however much the sugar planters might insist that it was merely an effort to protect British molasses from foreign competition in the contest "between Great Britain and

France, which of the two shall be Mistriss of the foreign Sugar Trade." That the Molasses Act would have destroyed the New England rum industry, had it been enforced, is almost certain. At the close of the colonial period, only about one sixteenth of the molasses imported to the mainland came from the British sugar islands.

Throughout the seventeenth century, so far as can be learned from the incomplete naval office records, the mainland molasses trade was confined to the English sugar islands. In the 1660's, a Newport merchant writing his factor in Barbados directed him to send "good Rume and Mallasces: wch is most vendable heare." In the seventies, a factor in Barbados wrote John Winthrop that the Barbadians are "sensable of the greate prejudis which will accrue to them yf they loose the benifitt of those two commodyties, which are vendable in noe part of ye world but New England & Virginea."

The Dutch were the first to threaten this monopoly. The governor of Barbados had written the Board of Trade in the 1670's that "the Dutch are people the planter is not afraid of," and of the imports to Boston recorded in the naval office records for 1687, there is no listing of molasses from the Dutch possessions. In 1707, however, the governor of Barbados wrote the Board of Trade that, "if I bee rightly informed, great quantys of Rum Sugar, and molasses go in returns for their horses flower and other Provisions" to New England from the Dutch possessions. Three years later, it was complained that the Dutch encouraged the trade as much as they could and that there were seldom fewer than four hundred English seamen at Surinam. "Suranam being a large Collony," an agent for the Board of Trade wrote in 1713, "and the Land New and fertile they can make and Vend Sugers much cheaper then any of her Maj[sts]" sugar plantations in America.

In the second decade of the eighteenth century, similar complaints began to be lodged against French competition. Previously the English traders had considered commerce with the French possessions to be illegal, and an English captain testified before a committee of the House of Commons that he had never heard of any trade for rum or molasses with the French Islands before 1714.

An order-in-council was issued in 1713 directing a bill to be prepared for the relief of the sugar islands. The bill, aimed at the Dutch trade, was presented two years later but failed of passage. By that time, the Dutch were supplying the mainland with molasses in large volume. Boston was importing annually more than one hundred thousand gallons of molasses from the Dutch. New York, in those years, was importing about a third as much Dutch molasses as English, as well as a considerable amount from French possessions. From July 1718 to July 1719, Boston imported more molasses from the foreign than from the British possessions, and almost all of the foreign molasses was Dutch.

Meanwhile, French molasses was becoming important in the trade of the English colonies. Writing in 1720, an English merchant stated that the rum, sugar, and molasses trade with the French had increased threefold each year for the last five years. In the 1720's, the Dutch and French West Indian molasses exports to the mainland continued to grow, and the English planters began the agitation which resulted in the passage of the Molasses Act of 1733.

The Molasses Act imposed a prohibitive duty of 9d per gallon on foreign rum and a heavy duty of five shillings per hundredweight on foreign sugar, but these duties aroused little concern among the colonial merchants. A Boston petition of 1764 declared that foreign rum did not enter the New England trade, and a Rhode Island petition declared that the French and Dutch themselves effectively prohibited export of sugar to the mainland, except for small quantities of inferior grade. New York merchants did issue a mild protest against the sugar duty, but for them as for the New England merchants, it was the duty on molasses which was the alarming feature of the act. The duty of 6d per gallon amounted to a one hundred per cent tax, and had it been enforced it would have thoroughly disrupted the colonial commercial life.

In practice, the Molasses Act was systematically violated. A total of £13,702 was collected in duty on foreign molasses during the thirty-one years the law was in effect. This would account for a little more than half a million gallons, an inconsiderable fraction of the foreign molasses that must actually have been imported during the period. Massachusetts, in the mid seventeen-fifties, imported legally less than half as much molasses and rum as it exported, but this fact gives only a hint of the smuggling that took place. Most of the molasses that entered Massachusetts was consumed there, and much of the molasses listed as legally imported was undoubtedly foreign molasses smuggled in via the English sugar islands.

Merchants connived openly with the customs officers. In Salem, the customs officer announced that he was going to charge ten per cent of the legal duties, but in the face of sharp protests, he backed down. In New Jersey, according to Governor Franklin, the customs officers "entered into a composition with the Merchants and took a Dollar a Hogshead or some such small matter." What the customs officers did with the money afterwards, he could not say. Of the collector of the customs at Newport, one merchant wrote another,

> This day settled your account with S. Moore allowing Mr. Letchmore [*sic*] two hundred dollars for his Clearance which I think anuff as he has not charged anyone here more than 150. I have had six myself.

Governor Bernard reported in 1763 that the merchants of Massachusetts had "acted in such a manner as to intitle themselves to all proper favour," but, "if conniving at foreign sugar & molasses, & Portugal wines & fruit, is to be reckoned Corruption, there was never, I believe, an uncorrupt Custom House Officer in America till within twelve months." In Rhode Island, mobs attacked enforcement officers; and in New York, a man was arrested and detained for two years on a false charge, according to his statement, because he informed on a smuggler.

England and France were at war for almost half of the life of the Act. During wartime, the Molasses Act was most nearly enforced, and the relative success of enforcement during the Seven Years' War encouraged the English Government to revise the act and strengthen the means of its enforcement. The result was the Sugar Act, passed in 1764, reducing the duty on foreign molasses to three-pence and providing enforcement measures.

News of the Sugar Act, according to Governor Bernard of Massachusetts, "caused a greater alarm in this country than the taking of Fort William Henry did in 1757." Brown and Company of Rhode Island feared the worst when, after a bad voyage, a company ship returned from Surinam with a load of molasses and faced the prospect of actually paying the new molasses duty. On that occasion, the company managed to avoid paying the duty, and Nicholas Brown wrote that he hoped another of his vessels would be as fortunate, "but how the severity of the officials may be by the time of your arrival we cannot say." The Sugar Act, widely evaded during its two year history, nevertheless was much more successful than its predecessor. Duty was collected on an equivalent of almost two million gallons of molasses. Even so the full duty was not collected. "When the new act was carried into execution," wrote Thomas Hutchinson, "the duty paid on molasses seldom exceeded three-halfpence per gallon. . . ."

The agent for Massachusetts in England estimated that molasses smuggling had been equally expensive during the period of the Molasses Act. Smuggling involved the use of bribes and go-betweens, as well as the risk of capture, particularly in the area of the British West Indies, and these conditions naturally discouraged the trade. Under these circumstances, it seems likely that the Molasses and Sugar acts served the purpose of hampering the mainland trade in foreign molasses, even though the acts were all but universally violated. There is evidence that such was the case. Under the protection of the Molasses Act, the British West Indies exported about a million gallons of molasses annually, according to the Rhode Island merchants. Following the repeal of the Sugar Act, however, exports of British molasses to the mainland dropped to 326,675 gallons in 1768 and four years later to 125,467 gallons out of a total importation of 4,748,228 gallons, according to the customs records. Moreover, rum production on the mainland rose sharply following the repeal of the Sugar Act, surely as a result of the freedom from the restrictions of the act.

In 1766 the Sugar Act was repealed and a one penny per gallon tax was placed on all molasses, British and foreign, imported into the continental colonies. The new law was cordially welcomed by the colonial merchants; and for the first time since the passage of the Molasses

Act, a sufficient volume of legal trade was recorded to indicate widespread obedience to the law. Nevertheless, large-scale smuggling continued. Massachusetts, from 1768 to 1772, imported legally an annual average of 1,678,513 gallons of molasses and exported 1,264,118 gallons of New England rum and molasses. Several years earlier, Boston merchants had declared that 900,000 gallons of molasses and New England rum were consumed each year in Massachusetts. Thus about half a million gallons of molasses must have been smuggled into the colony annually after 1768. Rhode Island actually exported 170,000 gallons more molasses and New England rum annually that it imported legally during the same period. Thus at least three hundred thousand gallons of molasses a year were being smuggled annually into the colony. Brown and Company had ceased smuggling in 1768, but it returned to the practice in 1772.

The large market for molasses in colonial America generally has been attributed almost entirely to the growth of the New England rum industry. Actually, there was a heavy demand for molasses in the colonies before rum distilleries were built in New England, and there was probably never a time when the greater part of the imported molasses was used in the distilleries. In the 1790's, before domestic whiskey had become an important competitor, the New England rum industry enjoyed its period of greatest productivity, but even in that period the distilleries used slightly less than half of the domestic molasses. The rest was used for kitchen purposes.

Molasses had many uses in colonial cooking — in Boston baked beans, Boston brown bread, and Indian pudding in New England, in shoo-fly pie and apple pan-dowdy in Pennsylvania, and in molasses jack and corn pone and molasses in the southern colonies, to name only well-known colonial dishes. It was used for medicinal purposes and in curing meat and pickling fish. It was also widely used in a soft drink called beverige — water flavored with molasses and ginger. Probably its most important use outside the distillery, however, was in the home brewing of small beer.

Molasses beer was easy to make, less expensive than commercial beer, and, as a substitute for impure drinking water, had the advantage of an extremely low alcoholic content. It early became a standard drink throughout the colonies. In 1685, William Penn wrote that, "Our Drink has been Beer and Punch, made of Rumm and Water: Our Beer was mostly made of Molosses, which well boyld, with Sassafras or Pine infused into it, makes a very tolerable drink." He added that, "now they make Mault, and Mault Drink begins to be common, especially at the Ordinaries and Houses of the more substantial People." A traveler in New Jersey at the same time reported that a drink was brewed there "from water and molasses at two shillings like eight shilling beer in England," and in the eighteenth century another traveler in New Jersey wrote that "Beer . . . brewed in the towns is brown, thick and unpalatable," but that "Small beer from molasses . . . is more wholesome, pleasanter to the taste, and milder to the stomach than any small beer of malt." According to the lieutenant governor of Virginia, the chief use of molasses in the southern colonies was in the brewing of beer, and a visitor to Virginia in the late colonial period mentioned molasses beer as widely used there. Molasses was also used in drinks in other combinations. "Blackstrap" was a mixture of rum and molasses, and "whistlebelly vengeance" was a mixture of home brew, molasses, and brown bread crumbs served hot.

Model food budgets submitted to Boston newspapers in 1728 by townspeople included beer as a necessary item of food. One budget allotted seven gallons of molasses annually for a family of nine for cooking purposes alone. Another, which included molasses for the brewing of beer, allotted nine gallons yearly for each member of the family. In New York, a naval officer estimated that molasses was consumed in beer and as a sweetening at the rate of three gallons per capita annually. The manufacture of rum, by comparison, began relatively late in colonial history and probably never consumed the bulk of the molasses imported into the colonies.

The colonial rum industry was confined to New England and the middle colonies, and of these only Massachusetts and Rhode Island produced rum for export on a large scale. Massachusetts, earliest in the rum industry, does not appear to have distilled appreciable amounts of rum in the seventeenth century. By 1717, however, the colony was distilling two hundred thousand gallons annually, according to the customs officer for the port of Boston. By 1750, it supported sixty-three distilleries which, at the average rate of production per still of the early national period, would have accounted for about seven hundred thousand gallons annually. Production increased in the sixties by perhaps one hundred thousand and appears to have almost doubled in the seventies. It was never remotely near the three million gallon production frequently claimed for it by historians. Maximum capacity of a colonial still was estimated to be forty-five thousand gallons annually. On that basis, Massachusetts, in 1750, would have been able theoretically to have produced 2,835,000 gallons annually, a statistic sometimes given as the actual production. However, the Boston merchants themselves stated in 1764 that only 1,500,000 gallons of molasses were imported annually into Massachusetts, and only a part of that was used in the distilleries.

Rhode Island, at the time of the Sugar Act, possessed about thirty distilleries, of which twenty-two were in Newport. At the average rate of production of the post-colonial rum stills, the annual output of Rhode Island would have been about 350,000 gallons. Following repeal of the Sugar Act, production rose to perhaps 500,000 gallons annually. Together, Massachusetts and Rhode Island accounted for three quarters of the entire mainland export of domestic rum in the final years of the colonial period. Distilleries operated in Connecticut also, but little rum was produced there for export even in the late colonial period.

Rum was distilled in New York for local consumption throughout the period of the Molasses Act. There were two distilleries in New York in 1730 and seventeen in 1767, of which twelve were said to have been in constant operation. In Pennsylvania, there were at least seven distilleries late in the colonial period, producing but a small fraction of the rum consumed locally. Little distilling of rum took place in the colonies south of Pennsylvania. Unlike the small whiskey stills which in later years mushroomed up over the back country of the United States, rum stills were large and expensive to build, and the initial cost of establishing one, combined with the sharp competition, discouraged construction outside the commercial centers of the north.

New England rum sold for a little more than half the price of West Indian rum, and cheapness was its chief advantage. It was distilled as quickly as possible from the cheapest available molasses, generally using less molasses per gallon of rum than was the case in the West Indies, and the final product, at times watered considerably, was, according to a visitor from Scotland, "the most shocking liquor you can imagine."

It was produced primarily for domestic consumption, not as part of a "triangle trade" in exchange for slaves in Africa. Massachusetts exported less than five thousand gallons of rum annually to Africa in the 1750's, according to the naval office records. The trade increased in the sixties, and in the seventies Massachusetts was exporting about eighty thousand gallons to the African market, or roughly a twentieth of its production. The total average yearly export of rum to Africa from all of the mainland colonies from 1768 to 1772 was about three hundred thousand gallons, probably about an eighth of the total production for the period. Half of the entire African export was accounted for by Rhode Island, but even Rhode Island exported more than half again as much rum in the coastwise trade as it did to Africa. The Rhode Island merchants in 1763 reported that their African trade, begun in 1723, consumed annually about eighteen hundred hogsheads of rum, enabling them to make annual remittances to England of 40,000. The trade was therefore important, but it was not the main outlet for Rhode Island rum. Of the molasses trade as a whole, the Rhode Island merchants declared that it was vital to the commerce of three hundred and fifty-two ships from that colony in the coastwise trade and about one hundred and fifty in the West Indian trade, compared with but eighteen in the African trade.

The African trade, compared with the coastwise and West Indian trade, was speculative and dangerous and involved competition with English and French traders much more than did the coasting and West Indian trades. The leading Rhode Island firm of Nicholas Brown and Company sent only three ships in the African trade during the colonial period, one of which was lost, another of which proved a financial failure, and the third of which brought a very modest return. By comparison, the Browns found the Caribbean safer and more profitable. It was the West Indian trade, based largely on molasses, that the Browns pursued primarily during the eighteenth century. Similarly, the Hancock firm in Boston, while dealing heavily in the molasses and rum trade, took no part at all, so far as there is evidence, in the African slave trade, preferring closer, more certain markets. At the close of the colonial period, exports of New England rum to Africa were only about equal to the combined exports of New England rum to Pennsylvania and Maryland. The continental colonies themselves provided New England rum with its main market, and even there New England rum was outsold by West Indian rum throughout the colonial period.

The mainland molasses trade developed, not in response to the needs of the slave trade, but as a necessary condition of large-scale commerce with the West Indies, particularly with those areas not permitted to sell sugar to the English colonial traders. Molasses did much to open new markets for the expanding trade of the northern colonies, and the colonists in their turn showed considerable ingenuity in devising uses for it. The acts passed by Parliament at the behest of the English sugar planters were arbitrary, and partly successful efforts to destroy an established commerce which was essential to the well-being of the northern colonies. The Molasses and Sugar acts were designed to aid one group of British colonies at the expense of another. The righteous evasion of these measures by colonial merchants accustomed that group to violate English economic regulation of the molasses trade even after the repeal of the Sugar Act.

3

Tyranny or Benevolence? An Evaluation

Were the Navigation Acts Oppressive?

Disagreement among historians over the impact of the Navigation Acts has become much less pronounced than was once the case. On the one hand George Bancroft pointed to the Navigation Acts as dreadful weapons of English tyranny — a view still supported by Louis M. Hacker. On the other hand George Louis Beer contended that the old colonial system afforded advantages to both parties. Today there is wide agreement that the Acts worked no great hardship upon the American colonies, that few colonists saw them as a serious grievance.

This historical consensus has been reached largely on the basis of the contributions of Lawrence A. Harper, professor of history at the University of California, Berkeley,[1] *and* Oliver M. Dickerson, *former professor and head of the division of social studies at Colorado State College. Dr. Harper has carefully calculated the cost to the colonies of British trade policies; he estimates an annual bill of over $3,000,000 by 1773. But he suggests that colonial advantages came close to balancing the account. Dr.*

Reprinted from Oliver M. Dickerson, *The Navigation Acts and the American Revolution* (Philadelphia: University of Pennsylvania Press, 1951), pp. 31–57.

[1] Lawrence A. Harper, "The Effect of the Navigation Acts on the Thirteen Colonies," in *The Era of the American Revolution,* ed. Richard B. Morris (New York, 1939), pp. 3–39.

Dickerson would go further: he argues that the Navigation Acts were a positive blessing, "the cement of empire."

Certainly there is abundant evidence that both England and her colonies flourished under the mercantilist system, and that the laws were, with the notable exception of the Molasses Act, enforced fairly well. The Navigation Acts were probably more burdensome than Dr. Dickerson is prepared to concede; but not until they were adapted to revenue-raising purposes after 1763 did they become the object of serious colonial irritation. This final phase of British mercantilist rule coincided with a new proclivity for racketeering by customs officials in America: before 1764 officials often pocketed bribes instead of collecting duties, but with tighter administration both bribes and duties were collected. This aspect of the mercantilist story attracts Dr. Dickerson's attention in the second part of The Navigation Acts and the American Revolution. *It helps to recall that the way in which laws are administered can be as important as the laws themselves.*

Bancroft says "American independence, like the great rivers of the country, had many sources, but the headspring which colored all the stream was the Navigation Act." Other writers join in the general condemnation, but few are specific as to just who was hurt and by what provisions of the acts. Let us examine the operation of the system in detail.

Whatever may have been the opinion of some Americans in 1660 in regard to the basic law limiting the carrying trade of the British Empire to English vessels, by 1760 all opposition had disappeared, and a careful search of contemporary newspapers, pamphlets, and other publications discloses no record of anyone seriously proposing an abrogation of that law. Certainly New England, whose fishing, trading, and shipbuilding industry rested upon this law, would not be expected to ask for changes that would bring in the competition of foreign ships. The only sections of the colonial empire that could theoretically have found such a regulation even an imaginary grievance were those engaged in plantation types of industry, where markets were distant and freights heavy.

There may have been a time when freight rates were influenced by the presence or absence of the foreign-owned ships, but after 1700 the expansion of English shipping, especially from New England sources, had become so great that there was ample competition. American ports swarmed with shipping, some owned in England but much more of it in the colonies. In 1768 more than two thousand vessels cleared from the American continental ports for the West Indies alone. By 1771 it required more than one thousand vessels to serve Virginia and Maryland, and over eleven hundred for the two chief ports in Massachusetts, Boston and Salem. In 1770 a total of 4,171 ships, with a combined tonnage of 488,724, cleared from the various continental ports.

The trade to the West Indies was indeed notable, employing more ships with a greater total tonnage than England was using in her trade with Holland, and far more than she used in her direct trade with Norway, Sweden, and the Eastland countries of the Baltic.

In addition, colonial shipping enabled Britain completely to dominate the Mediterranean trade. In 1768 the clearances from American ports for south Europe totaled 436 ships, with a combined tonnage of 37,093. At that time England was only using 23,113 tons in her trade to the Straits of Gibraltar, which encountered less than one per cent of foreign competition. Clearances from America are not included in this figure, so the American tonnage is in addition to the English figure, but is included in the percentage of English ships passing the Straits.

The expansion of colonial shipping continued to the Revolution. By 1775 nearly one third of all the ships in Britain registered as English were colonial built. Instead of being oppressive the shipping clauses of the Navigation Act had become an important source of colonial prosperity which was shared by every colony. As a device for launching ships these clauses were more efficient than the fabled beauty of Helen of Troy's face.

There was another important compensation in having a shipping industry under the British flag adequate for all commercial purposes. The plantation industries, such as tobacco, rice, sugar, and indigo, had to depend upon an annual market of their staple produce and an assured supply of food, clothing, tools, and other necessities that were not produced locally. This supply was dependent wholly upon the annual fleets that visited their ports. So long as England effectually controlled the seas, English shipping could serve them in time of war about as freely as in time of peace. Had they been dependent upon foreign shipping, the outbreak of a war might have meant complete suspension of their industries.

Business of any kind needs stability of conditions under which large investments of capital are made. The plantation colonies were conducted under conditions of as large individual investments of capital as were the manufacturing industries of the time. It was sounder economic practice to pay somewhat higher freight rates, if necessary, than to face the economic losses incident to a dependence upon foreign shipping; besides, there is no proof that freight rates within the British Empire were not as low after 1700 as those outside. Certainly there is no evidence in contemporary publications of any agitation to repeal this provision of the Navigation Act, nor did prominent Americans express any desire for a general relaxation of its major requirements.

Enumeration of commodities of colonial production has been pictured as an outstanding sin of mercantilism. The English continental colonies had three products of major importance, tobacco, rice, and indigo, included in the enumerated list. All were agricultural and were grown commercially only in the southern colonies.

It should be clear that no one would engage in producing enumerated commodities unless he expected to make a profit. If he found his venture unprofitable he could shift his energies to other crops. No one was under any legal compulsion to grow the enumerated products. In spite of the extravagant language that has been used to condemn the system, the grower of enumerated commodities was not enslaved by the legal provisions of enumeration. Obviously growers continued to produce rice, indigo, and tobacco because they made larger cash profits from their cultivation than they could make by using their land, labor, and capital in any other way.

The most cursory examination of these industries reveals that each had its list of wealthy planters who had accumulated fortunes in a few years by growing the enumerated crops. These men and their families were the aristocrats of the South. No similar conditions existed elsewhere in the vast agricultural regions of the colonies. Let us examine the conditions of each industry.

Tobacco

Tobacco, the most important of all colonial exports, suffered from all the disadvantages of other agricultural crops. Late frosts could destroy the tender plants in the seed beds; and early frosts could damage the mature crop before it was harvested. Favorable seasons could produce unusually heavy yields; and heat and lack of moisture could seriously lighten a crop. There were recurring surpluses and shortages. Also there were worms, plant diseases, and soil depletion. All of these and many more were hazards that the grower had to face in colonial times and still does. All are interesting details of the burdens of the tobacco planter, but they have no possible connection with the Navigation Acts. They existed without benefit of law and always will.

Tobacco growers in many cases were debtors. That condition was not peculiar to the tobacco industry and again has no possible connection with enumeration. Farmers who engage in commercial farming always have been in debt and always will be. Farming is a business. It requires land, buildings, equipment, labor, good clothing, and shelter for those engaged in it. Costs for these have to be met for months before a crop can yield any return. Unless inherited, these things had to be supplied by the farmer himself from savings or from borrowings. Most farmers chose the latter course and hoped to make the business ultimately clear itself. In this respect tobacco raising was not different from other business enterprises.

The great assembling and processing markets were in Great Britain, as were also the bankers who supplied the essential working capital. Growing tobacco was one job, marketing it was another. Both were essential parts of the industry.

Tobacco was not only the most important colonial enumerated product, it was an essential source of revenue to the British government. It was one article that could stand enormous taxation without materially reducing its consumption.

Prior to the union with Scotland tobacco could be shipped only to England or Wales; but after 1707 it could go to Scotland as freely as to England. Soon there developed most active competition between Scotch merchants, mostly in Glasgow, and the English tobacco merchants with headquarters in London or the English "outports." The customs service kept three sets of books: one for London, another for the "outports," and a third for Scotland. All of these have to be consulted to get the entire picture. Ireland remained a foreign country so far as tobacco was concerned.

The decade preceding the Revolution was one of rapid expansion for the tobacco planters. American tobacco was supplying a steadily expanding world market. The most important fact in the complicated expanding tobacco trade was the rise of Scotland as a chief primary market (see Table 1). Scottish imports rose from 12,213,610 pounds in 1746 to 48,269,865 pounds in 1771, a growth of more than four hundred per cent in twenty-five years. Finding, serving, and holding an additional market for 36,000,000 pounds of tobacco was a real feat of merchandising. At the same time the London merchants were increasing their importations, but at a slower rate. The merchants in the English "outports" just about held their own. From 1767 to 1771 Scotland imported nearly as much American tobacco as did London and the "outports" combined and remained the chief market to the Revolution. Table 1 shows the course of the tobacco trade for the nine years preceding independence.

Enumeration clearly did not hamper the expansion of the tobacco raising business in America. Any industry that enjoys an expansion of its total production of more than fifty per cent in five years and holds that growth has at least the appearance of prosperity.

This expansion of tobacco raising in America could not have occurred without the aid of the great tobacco marketing centers. The merchants at these centers found and developed new markets in Europe; graded, processed, and repacked the tobacco to suit the varying tastes of tobacco users; supplied, on their own personal security, the liquid capital to buy, ship, and store the annual crops; and found additional funds for loans to planters in America with which they bought land, slaves, and equipment to start new plantations.

The marketing of the tobacco crops each year employed enormous sums. The mere payment to the planter at the lowest price of two pence a pound would have required $4,000,000. In addition there was freight, insurance, export duties, port charges, duties in England, unloading, cartage, warehousing, that had to be paid for. That was only the beginning. No merchandise sells itself. Purchasers had to be found. The tobacco had to be prepared to meet varying demands. Some could be reexported in the original hogsheads in which it was imported. Some had to be made into snuff or various types of smoking and chewing tobacco. A very important tobacco manufacturing industry was

TABLE 1. *Tobacco Importations into Great Britain (in pounds)*

	London	*Outports*	*Scotland*	*Total*
1767	25,723,434	13,417,175	28,937,891	68,078,500
1768	23,353,891	12,103,603	33,237,236	68,694,730
1769	24,276,259	9,480,127	....	....
1770	26,758,534	12,419,503	38,708,809	77,886,846
1771	42,952,725	15,006,771	48,269,865	106,229,361
1772	36,265,788	15,101,682	45,259,675	96,627,145
1773	37,918,111	18,010,718	44,544,230	100,473,059
1774	36,859,641	19,186,837	41,348,295	97,394,773
1775	45,250,505	10,210,997	45,863,154	101,324,656

developing at the centers. A keen set of merchants sought out the varying demands and supplied the tobacco in the form desired. The results are impressive.

At the beginning of the century Spain was an important supplier of tobacco for the English market. She had under her control the finest tobacco lands in the world. But after 1760 Spain was actually importing more than a million pounds of American tobacco annually from Glasgow and London. In addition, American-grown tobacco was being exported to Great Britain, processed, and shipped back to the American colonies to be sold in the very areas where it was originally grown. In 1772 American customers bought more than 500,000 pounds of American tobacco processed in Great Britain, nearly one-fifth of which was imported at New York.

On the eve of the Revolution America was raising tobacco for a world market, created by the merchandising skill of the English and Scottish merchants. Only a small part of the tobacco annually reaching Britain was ultimately consumed there. Johnson says that four-fifths of the total annual importations were reexported. He does not give the source for his statement nor the time when it was true. His estimates for conditions just before the Revolution are much too low. Total British importations in 1772 were 96,627,145 pounds and total exports that year were 92,845,714 pounds, which is more than ninety-five per cent of the imports. The trade through Scotland that year shows an even higher ratio of reexports to imports. In 1772 Scotland imported 45,259,675 pounds of tobacco and exported 44,450,543, leaving only about a million pounds for home consumption, or a little more than two per cent.

The course followed by American tobacco as it traveled from its three great primary markets to its ultimate consumers is shown in tables two and three, one for England and another for Scotland.

Western Europe was the chief market, with France, Holland, and Germany taking more than 76,000,000 pounds in 1772, which was an average year, or more than seventy-five per cent of the total crop exported from America. Scotland was the chief supplier for France and Ireland and a keen competitor for the German, Dutch, and Scandinavian trade. Flanders was almost entirely supplied by the English merchants.

TABLE 2. *Tobacco Reexports from England, 1772*
(in pounds)

Countries to which Exported	*From London*	*From Outports*	*Total from England*
Flanders	3,788,691	710,937	4,499,628
France	7,019,949	2,880,006	9,899,955
Germany	7,579,297	587,156	8,166,453
Holland	16,462,701	2,093,280	18,555,981
Ireland	29,714	1,655,517	1,685,231
Norway and Denmark	616,048	952,972	1,569,020
Spain	854,275	39,281	893,556
Sweden	456,929	990	457,919
Elsewhere	1,805,526	889,588	2,695,114

TABLE 3. *Tobacco Reexports from Scotland, 1772*
(in pounds)

Countries to which Exported	*Amounts*	*Countries to which Exported*	*Amounts*
Flanders	710,937	Norway and Denmark	789,329
France	22,514,188	Spain	130,081
Germany	3,096,706	Sweden	7,914
Holland	14,075,349	Elsewhere	252,930
Ireland	2,873,109		

If the tobacco planters were oppressed by enumeration they should have prospered when freed. But what happened? There was a temporary rise in exports to the pre-Revolutionary levels, but the growers quickly learned that the markets gained for them by the British, and especially by the Scotch, merchants could not be held. An attempt by Jefferson, while Minister to France, to sell tobacco directly to the French government did not succeed. The French complained that the tobacco was not up to grade and canceled the contract. Under the old plan of buying in the great central market at Glasgow they could select just the kind of tobacco that best fitted their needs. There was no such market in America and the growers had neither the experience nor the capital to set up such an organization of their own. Grading by public inspectors proved to be wholly inadequate as compared with the grading in the great merchandising and processing centers.

Instead of thriving, the decades following the Revolution show that tobacco was a sick industry, gradually losing an important part of its former export trade. The Napoleonic wars and the War of 1812 caused wide fluctuations in exportations from year to year; but when these are averaged by five-year periods the steady decline is obvious. The full story of this decline is easily read in Table 4.

The same countries of Europe that bought 96,727,147 pounds of American tobacco in 1772 bought only 68,327,550 pounds fifty years later. Holland was buying only 23,692,034 pounds as contrasted with 32,631,330 in 1772. France had taken 32,414,143 pounds in 1772 but was buying only 4,665,670 fifty years later. Flanders, that had bought 5,210,565 pounds in 1772 was not even mentioned in our exports for 1822. Exports to Germany remained essentially unchanged from what they had been in 1772.

Partially to compensate for the heavy losses in our export market for tobacco in northern Europe new outlets had been found for a little more than six million pounds in other portions of Europe, and additional exports of ten millions of pounds to other parts of the world. Thus there had been some development of direct new markets, but the total market for American tobacco was millions of pounds short of our exports in 1772.

Most of the loss was in drastic reductions in our exports to Scotland. Direct exports to England had shrunk from 51,367,470 pounds in 1772 to 26,740,000 in 1822, but in the same period exports to Scotland had fallen from 45,259,675 in 1772 to only 1,142,000 fifty years later.

The Revolution not only separated the American colonies from official control by the British government, it separated the tobacco planters from the great banking and marketing organizations that had developed their former world market. A very large proportion of the debts due British merchants and creditors after the Revolution were in the southern states. From what we know of the conditions of agriculture, a large percentage of these must have been advances to the tobacco planters. A total of nearly $35,000,000 in such claims was filed before the claims commission created by the Jay Treaty and ultimately compromised in 1802 for $2,664,000. The Scottish merchants seem to have been the chief losers, since they do not again appear prominently in the world tobacco trade. It was three-quarters of a century before the American tobacco industry could replace the great central marketing machinery that had been built up under enumeration.

Rice

Next to tobacco, rice was the most important commercially grown agricultural crop of the

TABLE 4. *Trend of American Tobacco Exports Before and After the Revolution*

Years	*Average Yearly Exports in Pounds*	*Years*	*Average Yearly Exports in Pounds*
1767–1770	71,223,398	1805–1809	54,525,206
1771–1775	100,249,615	1810–1814	51,544,857
1790–1794	99,665,656	1815–1819	84,533,350
1795–1799	70,625,518	1820–1822	79,369,141
1800–1804	85,935,914		

continental colonies. Like tobacco it was enumerated, but on the eve of the Revolution had a free market in Europe south of Cape Finesterre and in America south of Georgia. It was an important crop in the lowlands of South Carolina and Georgia.

It has been assumed by many writers that enumeration imposed a serious burden upon the rice planters. The ascertainable facts do not support this assumption. In the years preceding the Revolution the rice industry was prosperous and expanding. Rice exports from Charleston, South Carolina increased from an average of 80,631 barrels per year for the five years, 1760 to 1764, to an annual average of 120,483 barrels for the years 1770 to 1773. The exports from Georgia, the other important producer of rice, rose from an annual average of 5,152 barrels for the years 1760 to 1764 to an average of 21,910 barrels during the years 1770 to 1773. Planters made fortunes during these years.

American rice growers, like American tobacco planters, were producing for a world market. Where was that market? In 1772 rice exports from America totaled 155,741 barrels; of which 97,563 went to Great Britain, 10,066 to South Europe, and 48,112 to the West Indies. This shows that more than sixty per cent of all American rice exported was finding its world market by way of Great Britain and only about seven per cent was exported to that part of Europe that was free from enumeration.

Something other than mere enumeration was attracting rice to the British markets. In 1773 total British imports were 468,915 hundredweight, of which only 11,842 hundredweight were landed in Scotland. The latter can therefore be eliminated as of any importance as a market for rice, after 1770, although it had been a market of major importance ten years before. The world market centered in England and continued to do so for many years.

Analysis of reexports of rice from Great Britain in 1773 reveals the ultimate market for American rice. A total of 365,325 hundredweight were exported. Of this amount, 242,693 went to Holland; 81,764 went to other parts of Europe north of Cape Finesterre; and 24,684 hundredweight to southern Europe, of which Spain imported 16,657 and Portugal 5,612. Thus, even southern Europe imported more than half as much American rice by way of England as it did directly from the colonies by way of the open market.

What happened to America's world market for rice when the Revolution freed it from enumeration? In 1822, after the world had adjusted itself to peace, our exports of rice totaled 87,089 tierces. Of this amount 40,735 tierces went to Europe; 24,073 of which were imported by the British Isles; 15,526 went to Europe north of Cape Finesterre; and 1,136 tierces to southern Europe. Translating tierces into hundredweight we have the following results: 216,657 hundredweight exported to the British Isles in 1822, as contrasted with 468,915 in 1773; 139,734 hundredweight to continental northern Europe in 1822, as contrasted with 324,407 in 1773; and 10,224 to southern Europe in 1822, as contrasted with combined total direct exports from America and reexports from Great Britain of 69,981 in 1773. Our total European market for rice was only 366,615 hundredweight in 1822, as contrasted with 484,320 exported to the same area fifty years before.

Like the tobacco planters the rice planters faced changed conditions after the Revolution. While England remained their best market, total exports for the five years beginning in 1782 were less than half what they had been in the five-year period before the war. The war had brought to an end a long period of prosperity for the rice industry. Much of the advantage of the old central market in England was lost. Importations were burdened with new duties, although drawbacks on reexportation were permitted. Shipping regulations of other countries hampered our trade. Even our ally, France, would not admit our rice-laden ships to her ports in 1788, so that cargoes bound for that country had to be unloaded at Cowes on the Isle of Wight for transshipment to French vessels.

There is nothing in the evidence to support the theory that the rice planters were handicapped or oppressed by enumeration or that they benefited from the freedom to find markets where they could. The advantages of the one great central market still operated as the magnet to attract imports and exports. The planters not only lost a large part of their former markets, but what was even more serious, they lost the financial help they had received from the British merchants. Freedom involved the necessity of finding their own financing as well as their own markets.

Indigo

Indigo was the third most important enumerated product of the continental provinces. Unlike rice and tobacco, indigo found its ultimate market in Great Britain. It was not only enumerated but was also encouraged by a direct British bounty.

On the eve of the Revolution the indigo planters were very prosperous and production was increasing rapidly, as shown by the tables of exports reported by Sellers and by Gray. Both reports are based upon fragmentary American sources. These show that exports nearly doubled between 1765 and 1773. These estimates are too low. Actual importation by Great Britain in 1773, all certified as produced in the British plantations, was 1,403,684 pounds, or twice that reported by Gray. This is nearly three times the colonial exports reported by Macpherson for 1770, and his reports seem to be based upon official records. Any industry that was so obviously prosperous cannot be called oppressed.

The Revolutionary War quickly brought to a close this period of prosperity for the indigo planters. They soon discovered that the industry could not exist without the former bounties. British aid and encouragement were transferred to Jamaica, which was still within the Empire. American production declined and just about disappeared. By 1822 the reported exports totaled only 3,283 pounds. In the meantime importations of foreign indigo had risen from zero to 1,126,928 pounds, or nearly as much as our exports were in 1773.

The Balance of Trade

The relative values of imports from Great Britain into the colonies and exports from them to the home country are frequently cited as proof of economic exploitation. In the form they are usually given they are misleading. The American colonial empire was one economic whole. The products of the West Indies were used by all of the other colonies and their products in turn supplied the essential needs of the sugar colonies. A far larger number of ships, with a greater tonnage was used in the trade between the continental colonies and the West Indies, than between the former and the mother country, and nearly as great a tonnage as was used for trade between the various continental colonial ports.

The northern colonies with their rum trade were just as much involved in the sugar industry as were the local West India planters. The colonies that supplied the millions of staves to make the sugar and molasses containers were also as directly interested in the sugar industry as were the farmers who supplied meat, grain, beans, peas, and other essential food items. The New England fishermen who marketed their fish in the West Indies may have considered themselves only seamen and fisherfolk but they were actually producing sugar as much as if they worked on the sugar plantations.

To treat imports and exports from one part of the colonial empire as a trade that should balance is as unreal as to set up a similar bookkeeping record for the external trade from New York and California. No one expects the trade of a single state of the Union with the outside world, or with any one other state of the Union, to balance. It is the total trade of the United States that is important. Applying this principle to the trade between Great Britain and her American colonial Empire we get the results shown in table five.

From the above table it is seen that total imports from the colonies exceeded total exports in two of the three years and show a small excess for the three years. It is obvious that imports from the West Indies were being paid for in part by exports to the continental colonies, who in turn supplied exports to the West Indies.

There are some items in the total trade picture that do not appear in the tables. One was the large exports of food and lumber products to southern Europe and the relatively small imports in return. This balance in 1769 amounted to £476,052. These balances helped cover the cost of British imports each year from that area and should be credited to the total colonial exports. Adding to the value of British exports was the steady migration of capital to the continental colonies. Thousands of immigrants were

TABLE 5. *Trade between Great Britain and the American Colonies, 1769–71*

Imported from	*1769*	*1770*	*1771*
Continental Colonies	£1,170,015	£1,129,662	£1,468,941
West Indies	2,792,178	3,131,879	2,717,194
Totals	3,962,193	4,261,541	4,186,135
Grand Total for three years			12,409,869
Exported to			
Continental Colonies	£1,604,760	£2,343,892	£4,586,882
West Indies	1,274,951	1,269,469	1,151,357
Totals	2,879,711	3,613,361	5,738,239
Grand Total for three years			12,231,311

moving to America with their possessions. British capital was being invested in land and various business enterprises. The vast amount of credit extended to American merchants and especially the credits advanced to the planters engaged in producing the three principal enumerated products, tobacco, rice, and indigo, had to be covered at some time by physical exports of British goods. Finally there were the costs of the British standing army and the operations of the British fleet in American waters. These included costs not covered by ordinary exports and involved the actual shipment of bullion to New York, Canada, and the West Indies in 1769 to a total of £16,651.

Limitations on Manufacturing

There were three acts that have been cited as hostile to colonial manufacturing. These are known as the woolens act, the hat act, and the iron bill. The first two applied wholly to shipments by water and the last forbad the creation of new steel furnaces, or forges equipped with tilt hammers or rolling devices for making that metal. The object of the iron bill was to encourage the colonial exportation of pig and bar iron to Britain so as to reduce the dependence upon foreign imports of these basic materials.

Did these laws materially impede the development of manufacturing in the continental colonies? Fortunately we have two thorough, objective studies on this point: one is by Victor S. Clark covering the whole field of manufactures, the other is by Arthur C. Bining dealing specifically with the iron industry. Both of these independent studies are in substantial agreement as to the basic facts. Both agree that British legislation had very little effect in retarding colonial manufacturing. We will discuss each measure separately.

Wool and Woolen Goods

The prohibitions against exporting wool and American-made woolens has generally been referred to as oppressive. The impression given is that Englishmen in America were being treated less well than those in England.

There is no foundation for this inference. England had developed the wool-growing and wool-manufacturing industry far beyond that of other countries in western Europe. It was an economic advantage of first importance — a sort of atom bomb of the seventeenth century. Under no circumstances was England willing to permit her special advantage to get away. To this end there was enacted a long series of laws regulating wool and possible wool exports, commencing with the Restoration under Charles II and extending through the reign of William III. The American woolens act was a minor item in those regulations.

The restraints imposed upon Englishmen in America who engaged in wool growing or processing were mild in comparison with those faced by Englishmen in England.

There, in addition to provisions against the export or shipment of wool similar to those in the American law, the owners of sheep had to give notice of their plans to shear sheep. They also had to report the exact number of fleeces at shearing time and give official notice of any removal from their farms, as no wool could be moved from one place to another without a permit. Buyers in certain areas had to be licensed under bond, and no raw wool could be loaded on a horse cart to be moved by land except in the daytime and at hours fixed by law. All of the above restrictions remained in force until the Revolution and are listed in the same customs manuals with the American regulations.

As has already been pointed out the prohibitions were not upon production or manufacture but upon water export of such goods. Consequently, household and neighborhood production went on unhampered, as did distribution of such products throughout the colonies and the rapidly expanding back country. Little can be added to the extensive studies of Clark. The back country clothed itself. There was very little cloth made for the market. Colonial newspapers, published in the larger port towns, printed very few advertisements of homespun cloth for sale.

There was no effort to compete commercially with imports from the home country. Textile production was still in the handicrafts stage. Weavers were not well paid and spinners very poorly paid. Working in such industries was associated with extreme poverty. It just did not pay to produce cloth under American conditions when goods of as good or better quality could be had from abroad for less money. Where family labor had no commercial value and money and money-crops were scarce there was extensive production.

American conditions remained largely unchanged long after the Revolution. In 1821 woolen goods of American production is not listed among our exports. On the other hand there appears in the list of goods imported into the United States woolen goods of various kinds to a total value of $11,971,933 out of total imports valued at $41,955,134, or nearly thirty per cent of all our imports.

It is obvious that the failure of colonial America to develop a large export of woolen goods and other textiles rested upon factors entirely separate from a parliamentary act of the seventeenth century.

Hats

The hat act did prevent the shipment of hats by water and may have had a temporary effect upon a developing export trade in New England hats. But the act had no effect upon the steady development of hat manufacturing in America. It was more advantageous for hatmakers to migrate with their skills to new neighborhoods than it was to live in one place and make hats for merchants who, in turn, sold them where they could find a market. Hat manufacture, especially of wool, became widely diffused and was so far advanced that Hamilton in his "Report on Manufactures" in 1791, in discussing the wool industry, stated: "Household manufactures of this material are carried on in different parts of the United States to a very interesting extent; but there is only one branch, which as a regular business can be said to have acquired maturity. This is the making of hats." That statement could hardly have been justified concerning any other manufacturing business. The industry was better developed than any other. In 1810 Tench Coxe reported 842 hatteries operating in the United States, some of which were in the western territories of Indiana, Michigan, and Mississippi. The center of the industry was not in New England, but in Pennsylvania, where 532 operating hatteries were reported.

Iron and Steel

The law prohibiting new rolling and slitting mills, plating forges and steel furnaces, passed in 1750, is mentioned in all accounts. In some cases writers have expanded this into an instance of real oppression. Bining, who has made the most detailed study of the colonial iron industry, agrees with Clark that such legislation did not check the development of the iron industry. He even insists that on the eve of the Revolution there were more iron furnaces in operation in America than there were in England and Wales combined and that the total output was greater than that of the iron furnaces of Great Britain. Most of the pots, pans, and other hollow ware used in the colonies were made at local iron works. The growing farming, milling, and extensive wagon transportation demands for iron were absorbing most of the bar iron that could be produced. As a result the British bounties, which attracted increased colonial exports of bar iron from a bare 39 tons in 1761 to a total of 2,234 tons ten years later, proved ineffective after 1771 and exports rapidly declined. The reason was steadily growing demands for domestic use.

Most of the iron works were relatively small and were designed to supply a neighborhood market. In the main they represented personal investments. All of the large colonial iron works were erected by foreign capital and employed imported labor. All of the larger works proved financially unprofitable, largely because of the gradual exhaustion of the local supply of charcoal. That the law was not interfering with the growth of the iron industry is proved by its rapid expansion westward in Pennsylvania and by the fact that the great American Iron Company was set up in 1764 with London capital by Hasenclever, who quickly expended a total of more than a quarter million dollars on the project. It was the largest capital outlay in any colonial manufacturing venture.

Production of steel on a commercial scale came slowly. In 1810 Tench Coxe could report only four steel furnaces in the entire United States with a combined capacity of nine hundred seventeen tons, presumably per year.

Bining did not find a single case where any iron work was discontinued, a slitting mill or steel furnace destroyed, or even an attempted prosecution of an iron works operator. Clark also failed to find a single case in any of the other colonies. An extensive search of the Treasury papers in the Public Record Office in London by the author also failed to reveal a single such prosecution, although there is much material on other clauses of the trade and navigation laws. There is but one conclusion, and that is that the iron industry was not materially hampered by any British legislation and that its development was rapid and continuous.

Other Manufactures

British legislation did not apply to other forms of colonial manufacture except to promote them. Naval stores were encouraged by direct British bounties. The Navigation Acts directly encouraged shipbuilding and all of the allied services such as rope-making, and manufacture of anchor chains, bolts, etc. American distilling of rum was on a large scale as was also sugar refining. Enormous quantities of forest products were worked up and exported to all parts of the empire and to South Europe. Millions of staves and shingles were exported annually. Much furniture shows in the list of exports coastwise and to the West Indies. Thousands of tons of bread and flour were manufactured and exported each year.

The major amount of manufactures, however, do not show in the list of exports as they were produced for domestic consumption and were sold within the colonies in the immediate vicinity where they were made.

While no case can be made for any charge that limitations on colonial manufacture were real, the measures discussed above were a part of the controversy. The iron bill carried a potential threat that real interference with domestic manufactures might be attempted. Thus it produced uneasiness in certain circles in America. The growth of colonial manufactures created a fear in England among workers, capitalists, and trading and shipping circles that unless this movement were checked in America they would lose their best markets and face a future of poverty and high taxes. This was the fear upon which the Americans played with their nonimportation agreements.

Bounties

The bounty system certainly was not an item of complaint on the part of the American producers. As the bounty policy was one of the most important phases of the general mercantile system, it is of course included in any general denunciation of the industrial and commercial relations of the colonies to the mother country.

The following industries were directly dependent upon such bounties: (1) naval stores, including tar, pitch, resin, turpentine, masts, spars, yards, bowsprits, and hemp; (2) lumber; (3) cooperage materials made of white oak; (4) indigo. The bounties were authorized over such periods that producers could plan production intelligently, and merchants in England could count on a continuous, artificially-attracted supply of such products over a period of years. By 1765 the policy of enacting bounty laws for periods of only a few years was abandoned, and laws were passed fixing bounties for periods as great as twenty years. The total sums expended by the British government for bounties on colonial products were very large and extended over a period of nearly seventy years. They were at their highest point on the eve of the Revolution and were reported by the Comptroller General as amounting to £186,144 during the years 1761 to 1776.

Of the four groups of articles that received bounties, all were produced in colonies that revolted; and the sums expended by the British government in behalf of these industries went wholly to the continental group. It was the southern colonies, rather than the northern, that benefited most from this policy. Naval stores other than masts and spars came largely from North Carolina, South Carolina, and Georgia. Indigo grew chiefly in South Carolina and Georgia, and the most desirable lumber and cooperage materials were the products of the colonies south of Pennsylvania. New England supplied mainly masts and spars, and the bounty on these was relatively insignificant.

It should be noted that the policy of granting bounties continued until the close of the colonial period. Those on lumber and cooperage materials were adopted in the reign of George III; in fact, the first bounty on such products was expected to soften the reception of the Stamp Act in America. The framing of bounty laws in permanent form was also a characteristic feature of the legislation of his reign. No part of the commercial policy was more firmly established than that of bounties, and the sugar interests advocated them as more efficient in promoting their favorite industry than tariffs. Below is a very plausible contemporary argument for such a policy.

"Suppose the bounty (on sugar) should be two shillings six pence per hundredweight, and 12,000 hogsheads, at 12 hundredweight each, should be sent to foreign markets, one year with another the bounty will be no more per annum than £18,000. The value of these 12,000 hogsheads at twenty-five shillings per hundredweight will amount to £180,000 sterling, which will be returned to Great Britain; and according to the common course of the sugar trade may be computed as follows, viz.:

It will pay,

For freight to British seamen and shipping	£ 30,000
To factors, insurers, and customs house officers for charges in marketing it	£ 18,000
Merchandise from Great Britain	£ 36,000
Negroes from Guinea, bought chiefly with British and East India goods	£ 24,000
	£108,000
Remains to the sugar planters and merchants	£ 72,000
	£180,000

"This sum of £180,000 that may be thus saved to this nation by the exportation of 12,000 hogsheads of sugar only, amounts to ten times the proposed bounty." In these days of accumulating farm and other surpluses, this argument has a familiar ring.

The same author, while he favored confining the continental colonies to the supply of sugar and molasses available in the British sugar islands, advocated compensatory bounties on the products of those colonies to make up for the losses incident to their exclusion from the direct trade with the foreign sugar islands.

If the bounty policy was a cause of the Revolution, it operated in a decidedly different way from what has been so confidently asserted by those who condemn the Navigation Acts. The bounty payments were a considerable burden upon the exchequer; and, when the load of taxes after 1763 became a matter of public complaint, the existence of the bounties, their continuance, and the impression made upon public opinion by the figures of total payments during the eighteenth century, became an added reason why the people in America, who apparently benefited from such bounties, should assume their fair share in the costs of Empire.

To the extent that the bounties were a burden upon the British taxpayer and an excuse for taxation of the colonies by the home government, they were a cause of the Revolution. They were certainly not a cause in the sense that such payments produced discontent in America.

Several industries practically disappeared at the end of the Revolution because they could not exist without the bounties. As the beneficiaries of the bounty system were essentially all in the thirteen continental colonies that revolted, it is highly probable that the bounty phases of the navigation system produced a conservative element of loyal supporters of the imperial system — at least so far as men permitted themselves to be influenced by their direct economic interests. There may be a direct relation between the British financial encouragement of colonial industries and the loyalist movement in America. It was definitely strongest in those colonies that benefited most directly from this practice.

Preferential Tariffs

The policy of preferential tariffs and export bounties could not have been a cause of economic complaint on the part of Americans, who thus secured access to the best market in Europe on better conditions than other producers. There was no possible ground for complaint on the part of American consumers when the British government allowed drawbacks of its own import and inland duties upon goods exported from England to the colonies, or when it encouraged both production in England and colonial consumption by export bounties, as it did in many cases. These regulations gave the colonies especially favored treatment, and were causes of prosperity and not of complaint.

Influence on General Prosperity

Were the navigation and trade laws so generally burdensome upon the colonies as to interfere with their development, and thus produce general poverty and distress? Again the answer must be negative; just the opposite condition existed. The colonies were prosperous and wages of labor were admittedly higher in the continental colonies than elsewhere in the world.

Population in continental America was doubling every twenty-five years, while in England it was scarcely doubling in a century. In fact the population of England seems to have doubled only once from 1066 to 1600, and again by about 1760, although a very marked increase in population was to characterize the reign of George III. In no other section of the world was there a white population expanding from natural increase so rapidly as in continental America. Marriages occurred early and families were large. The British colonies on the continent were attractive to emigrants, especially from the British Isles, and there are numerous references in the British periodicals, published in the decade, 1765 to 1775, to artisans of all kinds migrating to the new world.

Another measure of their prosperity was the expansion of trade that had occurred during the eighteenth century. Other evidences of wealth were the multiplying educational institutions, churches, newspapers, magazines, and other publications. Many of the finest specimens of colonial church architecture date from the period just before the Revolution.

The wealth acquired by American merchants and planters was a real cause of jealousy on the part of residents in the mother country. There had grown up in America a new race of untitled nobility with estates and palaces that compared favorably with the possessions of the titled classes in England. Their houses were not only well, but even luxuriously, furnished. Their consumption of British and European goods was not limited to necessities, but included luxuries of all kinds. The best evidence of this is the elaborate offerings of goods, including finery of all kinds for both men and women, found in the extensive advertisements in the newspapers of the time. The population of the seaboard was no longer clothed in homespun. Many men wore silk and velvet regularly. Joseph Warren had on his usual silk waistcoat when he was killed at Bunker Hill.

One of the best tests of real prosperity is the rapidity with which a population can sink its public debts following a war. The French and Indian War had been a real world contest so far as the British Empire was concerned. Colonial exertion on the part of the northern colonists, especially, had been on a scale not unlike that of Canada and Australia in the last world war. Many of the colonies levied heavy taxes during the war, and came out with large debts. The total colonial debt according to Charles Lloyd, who prepared the statistical data for the Stamp Act, was £2,600,000. Yet this was sunk so rapidly that in 1765 it was estimated that only £767,000 remained, and the greater part of that would be sunk by 1767.

The estimate of the time within which the colonies could extinguish their remaining obligations was too optimistic; but past accomplishments made a profound impression upon people in England, who could not hope to reduce their own national debt to the level of 1754 in less than a generation.

The ability of the colonies to sink their heavy war debts at the rate of about twenty per cent a year was a startling performance to thoughtful Englishmen. The economic recovery of the American continental colonies was not unlike that of the United States during the first ten years after World War I. The soreness of many British taxpayers, as they looked forward to long years of heavy taxation of their own people, while their fellow citizens across the Atlantic would soon be free from all but the lightest taxes, especially in view of their belief that the war had been fought and the burdens incurred for the benefit of the Americans, was not unlike the feeling aroused over the war debts in the years immediately following World War I.

A few extracts from the extensive contemporary discussion of this subject may give a better understanding of the way many Englishmen viewed America.

> The taxes paid at present by Americans bear no proportion to the burdens of the English. In less than five years, most of their burdens will cease, as their debts will be discharged; there is no hope of relief here, as the total revenue pays only interest and ordinary expenses of government. A future war would increase the taxes to pay interest; Americans have no future wars to dread, as British fleets and armies are a protection against foreign invaders: They can look forward to plenty and security in a wholesome climate and extremely prolific soil. The people of England have to look forward to increasing debts and taxes, frequent wars waged against them because of their burdens, poverty and insecurity, an exhausted people and a deserted country.
>
> England labours under a great load of debt, and heavy taxes; England has a very expensive government to maintain; the Americans have a government of very little expense; and consequently we must dwindle and decline every day in our trade, whilst they thrive and prosper exceedingly. The consequence of this will certainly be that the inhabitants will run away as fast as they can from this country to that, and Old England will become a poor, deserted, deplorable Kingdom — like a farm that has been over-cropped.
>
> It is something remarkable, that ever since the regulations were made last year, concerning the North-American trade, we hardly read a newspaper that does not mention manufacturers of one kind or another going from England, Scotland, or Ireland to settle in those colonies; which, if true, is certainly a matter that should to the last degree prove alarming to these kingdoms.
>
> Your abilities even to share our burthens are unquestionable, seeing that when eight millions of us pay ten millions of taxes, which amounts to twenty-five shillings on each person, three millions of you pay only seventy-five thousand pounds, or six pence on each person, and this in a country where a labouring man gets three times the wages that he does in England, and yet may live on half the expense.
>
> When you tell us that you are unable to pay taxes, pardon us for once in this Address, if we tell you that we do not believe you. . . . For you we submit to monopolies; for you lay restraints on our trade; for you we are taxed; and for you impose similar hardships upon other parts of our dominions.

British officers who served in America were struck by the vast real wealth here: the number of horses, cattle, hogs, farms, thriving cities, bountiful food supplies, and the lavish scale of living they found everywhere in the older parts of the country. Certainly they saw no evidences that the commercial system was reducing the Americans to poverty. On the contrary, they saw evidences of a people acquiring wealth and property more rapidly than elsewhere, with a vision of becoming the richest and most powerful nation in the world. The wealth and prosperity of the Americans was probably one of the causes of the Revolution. It excited both the envy and the fear of some British citizens, and led them to support the taxation policy. It also fired the imaginations of Americans, and led them to think and talk in terms of the vast empire that they conceived would develop here in the next century.

American and British writers prophesied that within half a century the population of the continental colonies and its resultant military and naval strength would exceed that of England. The realization of this fact was one of the reasons for the attempted imperial reorganization between 1763 and 1770, and was largely responsible for serious thinkers abandoning plans for a consolidated imperial legislature made up of representatives from the dependencies as well as the British Isles. Charles Lloyd, Grenville's chief financial lieutenant, urged in 1767 that force should be used to execute the taxation program because, if the Americans were not forced to submit to the authority of Parliament then, their growing strength would make any successful attempts in the future impossible.

No case can be made out for the Navigation Acts as a cause of the Revolution on the grounds that such laws were economically oppressive and were steadily reducing the Americans to a condition of hopeless poverty. It is true that evidences of hard times in the colonies may be found; but such conditions were periodic and were preceded and followed by other periods of over-trading, extravagance, and luxury. There was unquestionably high taxation in some of the colonies during and after the French and Indian War. In places there were price readjustments due to deflation and the termination of large governmental activities. Such conditions were not evenly distributed. There were times when merchants and newspaper publishers complained of slow collections; but such conditions can be found in any region where credit is easy, and they can also be found at times in even the most prosperous countries. The evidence indicates far less depression in the colonies than in the home country in the same years.

It is true that after 1770 there was a serious depression in the tobacco business in a portion of Virginia, which is reflected in the newspapers. In accounting for their economic distress and suggesting possible remedies, the planters in no case charged their distress to the Navigation Acts. Their ideas of what was wrong and of proper remedies sound strangely modern. They charged their economic condition to the too easy credit supplied by the Scottish merchants, and to the organized monopoly of the buyers. One writer seriously proposed active cooperative organizations to handle their tobacco crops, with paid factors in Britain to care for their sales and arrange for their purchases.

Professor Andrews and Professor Schlesinger have assembled a good many items from the correspondence of merchants indicating some economic distress. Such data, however, are not convincing. The conditions complained of are local and periodic where they are not due to the chronic absence of an adequate medium of exchange. They should not be interpreted as indicating a general lack of prosperity for America as a whole, covering the period between 1763 and 1775. They more probably indicate that a tidal movement of prosperous and dull times was characteristic of American economic life long before the formation of the federal government.

Conditions for the period as a whole must be considered. A country that was a Mecca for immigrants; that was importing slaves in large numbers; that was rapidly expanding its settled area into the back country; that could order from overseas expensive marble statues of its favorite English politicians as did South Carolina and New York; that could squander large sums on the public funeral of a royal governor and bury him in a sepulcher as elaborate as was accorded to royalty in England; that could find the funds for better church buildings than it ever had before in its history; that could sink public debts more rapidly than other countries; and whose population could live on a far better scale than similar classes in any other part of the world; was not suffering from economic ills that lead to permanent poverty.

Suggested Further Reading:

As indicated elsewhere in this section the two clearly outstanding scholarly works on English mercantilism and America are Lawrence A. Harper, *The English Navigation Laws* (1939) and Oliver M. Dickerson, *The Navigation Acts and the American Revolution** (1951). Professor Harper's book discusses the Navigation Acts primarily from the administrative viewpoint; he examines their role in the colonies in his excellent essay, "The Effect of the Navigation Acts on the Thirteen Colonies," in *The Era of the American Revolution,* ed. Richard B. Morris (1939). Charles M. Andrews, *The Colonial Period of American History* (4 vols., 1934–38), discusses the acts of trade in his final volume; he sees mercantilism being replaced after 1763 with a new imperialism. Thomas S. Ashton has supplied a stimulating study of relevant economic developments in England: see his *Economic Fluctuations in England, 1700–1800* (1959).

Among more specialized studies highly recommended are: Richard Pares, *Merchants and Planters* (1960), *Yankees and Creoles: The Trade Between North America and the West Indies Before the American Revolution* (1956); Arthur C. Bining, *British Regulation of the Colonial Iron Industry* (1933); Emory G. Evans, "Planter Indebtedness and the Coming of the Revolution in Virginia," *The William and Mary Quarterly*, 3rd Ser., XIX (1962), 511–533; Mack Thompson, *Moses Brown, Reluctant Reformer* (1962); and Bernard Bailyn, *The New England Merchants in the Seventeenth Century** (1955).

PART EIGHT

Context for Revolution

For students of American colonial history the Revolution is possibly the most important single event in nearly two hundred years of English endeavor in the New World. It offers a singularly satisfying climax to an already exciting chronicle; it ends the first British Empire, it marks the beginning of American empire.

Without suggesting that England's relations with her American colonies were previously unflawed, the rapidity of their deterioration in the 1760's is still remarkable. At the close of the War for the Empire in 1763, England stood in victorious splendor, mistress of the greatest empire the world had known. Americans bathed in the reflected glory, proud of their partnership in victory, vastly relieved that the French had been driven from the North American mainland.

The English colonies were indeed the most free, the most nearly self-governing in the modern world. But it was their very familiarity with liberty, with the rights of Englishmen, that led them so easily down the path to independence. In a sense the American Revolution testified to English success, not failure; it was the successful transmission of English ideas of liberty that made possible the Revolution.

"The real American Revolution," according to John Adams, was the "radical change in the principles, opinions, sentiments, and affections of the people." This, thought Adams, was effected between 1760 and 1775, "before a drop of blood was shed." It is to the context for this "radical change" that this section is addressed.

1

A Political Portrait

George III, 1760–1820

Historians seem for ever congratulating themselves upon their enlightenment when they discuss George III and the American Revolution. It is true that they discount the indictment of George that is handed down in the Declaration of Independence. "No longer," write the editors of the New American Nation Series, *"is George III portrayed as a wicked, designing man." But one runs the risk of going to the opposite extreme and finding George no longer portrayed.*

George III did *ascend the British throne in 1760. He* was *the ruler over the American colonies in 1776. His character — and its limitations — are highly relevant to any consideration of the circumstances in which the Revolution broke out. It is important that the reigning British monarch had the disposition "of a conscientious bull in a china shop," that his idea of firmness was a flat refusal to make any concessions to anybody.*[1] *It is important to recall the political and constitutional power of George III in the age of the Revolution, to remember that he largely determined the membership of the Ministries and influenced their policies. Despite the illumination provided by such contrasting historians as Sir Lewis Namier and Herbert Butterfield, there have been few efforts to explore the inner workings of British politics and their real relation to the colonial crises of the 1760's and 1770's.*

Nor is this the immediate purpose of J. H. Plumb, *the Cambridge University historian, in the following essay. Professor Plumb, best known for his monumental biography of Sir Robert Walpole, is here interested in presenting a political portrait of George III as one of a series of remarkable Hanoverian monarchs. The relation of this study to the American scene is incidental and not a major objective. But despite this limitation, the significance of the English political scene for colonial politics comes through with impressive clarity.*

Reprinted from J. H. Plumb, *The First Four Georges* (London: B. T. Batsford Ltd., 1956), pp. 92–124.

[1] Richard Pares, *King George III and the Politicians* (Oxford, Eng., 1953), p. 67.

George III was twenty-two years of age when he succeeded his grandfather but mentally and emotionally he was little more than a boy. His tutors had found him a difficult pupil, not exactly unwilling, but lethargic and incapable of concentration. He was eleven before he could read and at twenty he wrote like a child. He possessed, however, a strongly emotional nature. He was deeply attached to his younger brother, Edward, and could not be parted from him. At eighteen he became infatuated with his mother's friend and adviser, the Earl of Bute, and insisted on making him Groom of the Stole when he obtained his own establishment in 1756. The relationship between George III, his mother, and Bute has been the subject of a great deal of misinterpretation by historians. The situation, however, has been brilliantly clarified by Mr. Romney Sedgwick in his remarkable edition of George III's letters to Bute. Like all heirs to the throne George detested the King's ministers and quickly grew to regard as traitors those of his mother's advisers who, after winning concessions from George II, had, like Pitt, joined the administration. Bute was a man of no consequence and therefore neglected by the Court, and George was able to resent this neglect more strongly because he charged it vicariously with his own resentful loneliness. Bute was exceedingly handsome, well informed, with a taste for natural history, an adroit, easy man, a glaring paragon of those virtues which the young Prince felt himself to lack. Indeed, the prince was very conscious of his own shortcomings and he feared the great burden which the old king's death would place on his shoulders. He implored Bute to help him, longed to be corrected by him, and thought that life would be intolerable and the nation ruined if ever Bute were to quit his side. Nor was their friendship ever to be endangered by the Prince's marriage. When the Prince's heart was touched by the fifteen-year-old daughter of the Duke of Richmond, he rushed to Bute for advice.

> "I submit my happiness to you," he wrote, "who are the best of friends, whose friendship I value if possible above my love for the most charming of her sex; if you can give me no hopes how to be happy I surrender my fortune into your hands, and will keep my thoughts even from the dear object of my love, grieve in silence, and never trouble you more with this unhappy tale; for if I must either lose my friend or my love, I will give up the latter, for I esteme your friendship above every earthly joy. . . . On the whole let me preserve your friendship, and tho' my heart should break, I shall have the happy reflexion in dying that I have not been altogether unworthy of the best of friends tho' unfortunate in other things."[1]

Bute said "no", George obeyed, and prudence triumphed over the "boiling youth" — prudence and that high sense of duty which was to dominate George's strange, cloudy mind until the dark end of his days. He turned away from his natural inclinations and began to search the Almanach de Gotha for a suitable German Protestant princess.

As in marriage, so in all things, George III wished to be controlled by Bute — the one friend whose advice was always right, who never hesitated to mark his faults or to remind him of the immense responsibility of his calling. George III was greatly drawn to the solemnity of his position and gravely pondered the burdens which the Almighty had seen fit to place on his shoulders, of whose weakness he was all too conscious. Only if his dear friend stood constantly by his side had he any hope of being able to fulfil his duty. The need for Bute was greater because George III had been brought up to believe that his grandfather was almost a helpless prisoner in the hands of a gang of unscrupulous politicians, who were eager only for the spoils of office and quite indifferent to the nation's wants. He thought this of one of the most successful ministries the eighteenth century was to know, the ministry of Pitt and Newcastle, which seized half the world's trade and laid the foundation of that empire which was to be so great a source of wealth for Victorian England. Nevertheless, George III sincerely believed that Pitt and Newcastle were leading their country to ruin. Pitt was a traitor, "the blackest of hearts," because he had left the opposition gangs which clustered about the Princess of Wales at Leicester House and taken office with Newcastle. The fact that George himself had done well out of this deal — obtaining his own establishment and Bute as his Groom of the Stole — was ignored. Pitt had joined the enemy and was therefore a detestable traitor. Newcastle was little better; to George III the Pelhams were the symbols of that system of faction which heirs-apparent were led by nature to hate. And his father, his mother, and Bute had strengthened his natural repugnance to his grandfather's ministers.

This, then, was the situation when this young man of twenty-two succeeded his grandfather in 1760. He was infatuated with Bute and detested the ministers whom he had inherited. There is no need to look further than this, as so many historians have done who have swallowed the subtle propaganda of Burke and Horace Walpole and seen in the changes which took place on George III's accession a deliberate attempt to subvert the constitution and bring about a Stuart despotism.

Everyone knew that there would be ministerial changes the moment the old King died. Indeed Pitt was soon assuring Bute that he asked for nothing but Bute's good offices in the new reign to "put me in some honourable by-standing office where I have no responsibility." As expected, the King did everything by Bute, took his advice on every matter, ignoring other ministers with decades of political experience. It seemed natural enough that Bute should fulfil his long-cherished ambition and rise to be First Lord of the Treasury. Alas, for Bute and George

[1] R. R. Sedgwick, *Letters of George III to Lord Bute, 1756–66,* 38–9.

III, the task proved too great for Bute, even though as a peer Bute could not take on the offices of Chancellor of the Exchequer and Leader of the House of Commons which were usually held by the head of the Treasury. The trouble was manifold. In his own way Bute lacked confidence as his King did. Bute too, like George III, was a lonely man. For years he had lived on the fringe of the political world and entirely in opposition. He lacked powerful friends or strong dependents. His group in the Lords and in the Commons was small and a poor match for those tough factions which had successfully waged political warfare since Walpole's day. With the King's unstinted support he could doubtless have won through and created a ministerial position as strong as Walpole's had been, or North's was to be, but he lacked the stomach. His fears and anxieties and his sense of incompetence frayed his nerves, undermined his health, and at last compelled him to give up. He hoped to retain his private influence with the King without its public responsibilities. And for a time the King wished this, too, and consulted Bute secretly on the problems of personalities and politics which arose. Time, however, was working a change in George; time and marriage.

The first year of George III's reign had been taken up almost entirely by the problem of his marriage. Animal passion and the unique sense of public duty in the need for an heir combined to make the matter one of almost neurotic, compulsive frenzy for George III. In the end he settled rashly and unwisely on Charlotte of Mecklenburg-Strelitz, a dim, formidably ugly girl. George himself regretted her plainness. Like his forbears, a sensual man, he was quickly stirred by feminine beauty but, unlike them, his high sense of morality would not allow him to indulge his fancies. Plain and undesirable as she was George III doggedly fulfilled his marital duties, and they bred child after child. On his part it was more an act of will than desire, and the strain on his already unsteady mind is thought to have been a strong contributory cause of those fits of insanity to which he became a prey. Marriage, however, dutiful as it was, weakened his emotional dependence on Bute who, by 1763, had descended from "dearest" to "dear." Marriage and time; for George III was a slow developer and his infatuation with Bute was part of a delayed adolescence. By 1763, this intensely emotional situation had been in existence for seven years, a long time for such relationships, the intensity of which is partly the result of their known, if unavowed, transience. By 1766 George III was clear of Bute. He had taken Pitt back into favour and in so doing expressed a willingness to exclude Bute from affairs. Pitt's ministry marks the emergence of a King not yet, perhaps, mature — in some ways he was never to reach maturity — but he had ceased to be open to new experience; his pattern of life had hardened, his habits were formed, his responsibilities known. He had married, produced heirs, experienced madness, changed and formed ministries, conducted those day to day affairs, private and ceremonial, which were to be the burden of his days. His world was known to him, its terrors diminished with knowledge, and the need for a Bute had passed.

2

The King's relationship with Bute explains much of the early years of his reign, but not all, for the policy which they inaugurated together had vast repercussions. Also George's youth had other consequences than his love for Bute. There was no heir, no Leicester House for the discontented and the disobliged politicians to flock to for plotting and scheming and waiting for their revenge, nor any prospect at all for many long years. True, the King's fit of madness in 1765 provoked a flutter of hope and increased the political stature of his uncle, the Duke of Cumberland, by a few inches, for Cumberland would be Regent if the King went entirely off his head. His quick recovery, however, soon extinguished the awakened ambition. Groups out of office, like Pulteney and Bolingbroke before them, had to fall back on other devices. In effect, there was only one — for the opposition to make such a confounded nuisance of itself that ministries would feel the need to buy it off. And the easiest way of becoming a nuisance was to rouse the public, to bring discredit on the King and his ministers who, it must be said, provided, as we shall see, ample material. The success, however, of these tactics of embarrassment was far, far greater than it might have been; for various reasons. The principal one was the incapacity of Bute. A stronger minister would have quickly made his position in the Lords and the Commons so impregnable that the public mischiefs of the Grenvilles and Pelhams and their kind would have remained mere irritants. They unnerved Bute. He began to imagine for himself the fate of a Buckingham or a Strafford; and so played straight into the opposition's hands. George III himself was as yet too untutored in the political game to be able to strengthen Bute's resolve, as he afterwards strengthened North's. This weakness of will at Court was a most powerful fault and led to that instability at the centre which gave the opposition gangs their opportunity. Instead of being absolutely determined to do without Newcastle, Hardwicke, Pitt, Grenville and the rest, Bute, if not George III, feared that he would fail or, as he himself admirably phrased it, "tho' in the bosom of victory, constantly tread on the brink of a precipice, and this without even the hope of doing good."

Sensing this weakness at the heart of politics, the opposition were soon in full cry and the independents and the cautious place-holders hesitant and watchful; men who should have been tied to Bute's leadership were allowed to wander into the neutral side-lines to await the outcome of the struggle. The fight was bitter because there was much to fight about. When George III ascended the throne in 1760, England had recently enjoyed a year of victories unparalleled in her history, the year of Quebec, Lagos, Minden, and the rest. The City was jubilant and the almost certain prospect of the total humiliation of France was distasteful to few. The years of war had stimulated England's industrial and agricultural production to new levels. A vision of wealth and glory had been dangled before the nation. True, a few grumbled; squires who paid a heavy land tax; clergymen for whom the Hanoverians were still detestable; convinced Tories who had no relish for Whig victories. Bute and George III were, however, determined on peace, peace if need be at any price short of a total return to France of everything England had won. Although the peace took nearly three years to accomplish, their intentions were quite clear to Pitt, who was soon in opposition, declaiming with all his majestic fervour on the folly of such a course. The City merchants were roused to adulation by the fire, the conviction, the sense of destiny which Pitt's words engendered. They knew, as he knew, that Britain's greatness was at stake. The merchants of the City were no longer a small group of extremely wealthy capitalists. Their numbers had grown; the West Indians, the East Indians, the bankers, the brewers, were rarely now the same men under different names as they had been in George I's day. They now tended to be separate powerful groups of merchants, as rich as their forbears but more numerous. And behind the wealthy City fathers were the thickening strata of the professional classes — attorneys, estate-agents, doctors and apothecaries and, more importantly, the new industrialists, the men who were making their fortunes in steel, cotton, coal-mining, porcelain, and the rest, men who believed by instinct that England was destined to great wealth if only her opportunities were not scotched by the incompetence of her King and his ministers. For decades the opposition had denounced the graft and wire-pulling of politics; bitter and virulent pamphlets had exposed abuses in all the institutions of government, usually, it is true, with no desire to reform them, but out of frustration because the writers were denied their enjoyment. In George I's reign and for most of George II's these denunciations carried little weight, for most of the men who felt that they ought to play a part in political life were involved in it one way or another. By 1760, this was no longer true. Every year saw an increase in those men of substance who felt that they ought to have a voice in their country's government and yet were excluded from it. A vigorous press, both provincial and metropolitan, had grown up to cater for these men and their attitude to government is underlined by the fact that opposition newspapers had a far greater circulation than those which respectfully deferred to the politics of the ministry. Hence the opposition, and particularly Pitt, had in this growing politically-minded public a new weapon with which to belabour the King's ministers. Its strength was to increase steadily with each year of the King's reign but quite early its force was demonstrated.

The very knowledge that the King intended peace was sufficient to make him unpopular and when he rode to the City to celebrate his marriage his coach was hissed, whereas Pitt's was received with wild cheering. When at last the Preliminaries of the Peace of Paris came to be debated in 1762, Pitt was so sick and ill that he had to be carried to the House and allowed the indulgence of sitting from time to time during his speech, which lasted for three and a half hours. In him the voice of the City spoke. His denunciations were based entirely on commercial strategy.

> "The ministers seem to have lost sight of the great fundamental principle that France is chiefly if not solely to be dreaded by us in the light of a maritime and commercial power [he told the House], and therefore by restoring to her all the valuable West India islands, and by our concessions in the New foundland fishing, we have given her the means of recovering her prodigious losses and becoming once more formidable to us at sea."

Such words were nectar to the City merchants and they waited for Pitt outside St Stephen's, and cheered him to the echo as he drove home, weary and defeated. Such an acclamation worried both George and Bute; many politicians such as Hardwicke, Newcastle, and Devonshire regarded these manifestations as vulgar and to be deplored. No one, perhaps not even Pitt himself, realised their profound importance. In the same way the sudden eruption of John Wilkes into the political arena failed, too, to make George III or his political advisers realise that the King's inheritance was strangely different from his grandfather's.

3

John Wilkes was a *protégé* of the Earl Temple, the titular head of the Pitt faction. Ugly, witty, vain, he had lived a rake-hellish life on the edge of politics, hoping, as most young men in his situation hoped, that his talents or his nuisance value, or both, would secure him a place and a settled political career. Wilkes, however, lacked birth. His father had been a successful merchant, a self-made man, without even remote connections with gentility. That would not, of itself, have been a disadvantage in a man whose nature was both humble and discreet. Wilkes was neither. He loved display; possessed a cutting tongue which he could never curb. Cocking a snook was second nature with him. His bumptiousness rarely took a fall. Utterly self-confident, he refused to be impressed; his quick eye for a weakness immediately found its expression in a savage phrase. Such a nature was bound sooner or later to find itself in sharp conflict with authority. The moment came with the Treaty of Paris; a client of the Temple-Pitt group, he was naturally its bitter antagonist and he denounced it with unparalleled ferocity in his newspaper, the *North Briton,* and interlaced his denunciation with a few well-directed jibes at George III; in No. 45 he went so far as to hope that the King would not profane St Paul's by attending a thanksgiving service there but stay in his own chapel. Thinking that he had an excellent case of seditious libel, Halifax, the Secretary of State, issued a general warrant for the arrest of the authors, printers, and publishers of the newspaper.

Wilkes responded to this challenge with all the effrontery and brilliance of his nature. He was bundled off to the Tower and from there proceeded not only to claim that he was wrongfully arrested but also to sue Halifax for damages done to his property during its search. Naturally the imagination of the public was caught, and Wilkes became a popular hero. Eighteenth-century society was strongly individualistic, and the attack by a single man, of no particular influence, on the entrenched authority of a corrupt state went to its head like wine. "Wilkes and Liberty" became synonymous. Furthermore he created a focus for discontent, not solely for those prospering middlemen whose disapproval of English government grew yearly, but also for the *sans-culottes,* the journeymen and proletarians who were suffering from the dislocation of trade caused by demobilisation and disarmament. The adulation in which Wilkes was held passed into idolatry when he was triumphant. Mr Justice Pratt declared general warrants illegal, that reasons of state were not pleadable in English courts, that a Secretary of State was as answerable as any other man for his actions. And in the end Wilkes got his damages and Halifax had to pay. This triumph has been acclaimed as victory for liberty, for English law, for the individual, and

Wilkes has become a part of the mythology of English history. Actually the truth was seedier. The legal arguments against Wilkes were as strong as those for him; his luck was to be tried by Pratt, a man whose career had been forwarded by that very political gang to which Wilkes himself belonged. Pratt was a client of Pitt, and an enemy of George III and his ministers. Had Wilkes faced Mansfield, as he easily might, then English liberty and English justice and the right of the individual might have suffered a singular defeat.

Naturally George III was infuriated. He had been insulted and the criminal had escaped. George, like most of his family, was a good hater and "that devil Wilkes" came high on his list. He egged his ministers on to bring the devil to book, and to book he was brought. When the agents of Halifax had looked through his papers they had come across an obscene parody of Pope's *Essay on Man,* called *Essay on Woman.* Probably it was not written by Wilkes, who may only have been responsible for some of the footnotes, but he was certainly responsible for its printing. For this he was expelled from the House of Commons and undoubtedly he would have been convicted had he stood his trial. Instead he fled to France. An act of cowardice? In some ways; yet it must be remembered that Wilkes was a very sick man. Attempts had been made on his life and he had nearly been killed in a duel with a professional thug, possibly hired to involve Wilkes in a fight. Popularity was little protection in a world which contained so many bitterly hostile to him. Had he stood his trial, he would have faced Mansfield, and the sentence would have been as harsh as the law could make it. As it was, he was declared an outlaw and everyone, particularly George III, believed that John Wilkes's career had ended. The lessons of this incident did not register on George III's dark and cloudy mind. Indeed he learnt little from the first five years of his reign, save that Bute was not the man to help him govern, that terrible task imposed on him by the Almighty, on whose discharge, whether good or bad, depended the prosperity of his people. If only he could find strong, dependable ministers who thought as he did, all would be well — his unpopularity would disappear; peace and plenty, happiness for all, and a triumphant monarchy would ensue. So it still seemed.

The fury and bitterness of the London mob, the constant insults offered to Bute, his mother, and himself, the hysterical adulation with which first Pitt, then Wilkes, was acclaimed taught George III nothing. He could not bring himself to regard these things as expressions of a deep discontent, they were the results of machinations of evil men intent on vexing him. Nevertheless, the strains on George III himself had been very great indeed; the failure of Bute to protect him in the struggle for power which was waged about him was a grievous blow. The loss of a sense of protection, an acute awareness of his own isolation, together with the sexual strain of his marriage to so unattractive a woman as the Queen may have been contributory causes of the first mental breakdown which George III suffered in 1765. His attacks of madness took the form of a total flight from reality. No wonder, when sane, he found the detail of life so hard to bear, so vastly fretting, so impossible to control without the help of a strong, guiding hand.

Unfortunately George turned from Bute to his uncle Cumberland, in whose entourage was perched the hawk-eyed Pitt, and within a trice the "blackest of hearts" was the "dear friend" with whom George III could not bear to part. George III had chosen as a friend this time a man far, far more unstable than himself. No sooner had he formed a ministry than Pitt, elevated to Chatham, went mad more profoundly and totally than he had ever been. In his few moments of lucidity he pleaded for release from office, "under a health so broken as renders present application of mind totally impossible." George III would not hear of it; for two years he waited patiently for Chatham's recovery and then did his best to prevent him from resigning, in spite of the fact that his ministry was at loggerheads and the government of the country drifting into chaos. George III had decided that his position would be hopeless without Chatham's aid. The fact that he obtained none mattered not at all — the emotional state of dependence was the critical factor. And when at last Chatham went, George III was transferred at once to the Duke of Grafton, to whom he was soon writing in those clumsy affectionate terms which he had used to Bute, Cumberland, and Chatham. George III's eagerness to adopt at once any man senior to himself, as a father-image, is a measure of his own lack of confidence in the face of duties for which he had an almost exaggerated respect. The happiness, the destiny of his country rested on the wisdom of his conduct and that of his ministers. So far his reign had witnessed little but trials and disappointments and, George III felt, misunderstandings. Wicked men, like Wilkes, had been responsible for leading the nation astray and undermining its confidence in its King. Had George III known that darker days lay ahead of him it is unlikely that his recovery from his madness would have been so quick or so thorough. Not only did Wilkes return to plague him in a more terrible fashion, but the first outbreaks of violence occurred in America, creating a crisis in government such as England had not witnessed for several generations.

4

The colonists' favourite term of abuse was "tyrannical" rather than "unconstitutional" and owing to an unfortunate concatenation of events for George III this sense of "tyranny" was strengthened by the effective protest of Wilkes against general warrants which occurred at this time, so that the cry of "Wilkes and Liberty" echoed in the backwoods of America. Furthermore the propaganda which Wilkes and his supporters were sedulously cultivating, that George himself was the leader in a dark conspiracy to subvert the constitution and deprive Englishmen of their ancient liberties, was swallowed wholesale by the credulous colonists. Nor was the reaction one-sided. The cries of "tyranny" which went up in America struck their own responsive chord in the circle of Wilkes's supporters, bringing new justification to their attitude towards the monarchy. And, in addition, George III had the mischance to become himself the central target of the attacks of the enemies of his ministers. True, to start with these were shared with Bute and his mother, but by 1763 Bute had ceased to be a really effective power in politics. The rapid change of ministries in the next seven years, and the long period of Chatham's incapacity when the ministry was leaderless, all helped to create the illusion that George III himself was the dominant personality in politics and responsible for the policies of his ministers, who lasted only so long as they did his will — and, of course, the illusion was fostered by opposition propaganda. But its effectiveness can be measured by the way it was readily believed both in London and America. The myth that George III was intent on restoring a Stuart despotism was not the fabrication of later historians but a widespread belief which grew out of the conflict with Wilkes and America.[2]

The effect of this well-judged slander was to bring the personality of the King into the bitter political struggles of his reign in a way that was entirely novel in English life. George I and George II had been lampooned on their choice of mistresses, on their predilections for Germans and for Hanover: at times, principally by Chatham, they had been criticised by implication in the House of Commons, but such attacks were intermittent and fleeting. The bulk of abuse had been borne by their ministers. Wilkes and America, and the ruthless exploitation of these conflicts by an unscrupulous opposition, brought George III himself into the political arena. The opposition was certainly unscrupulous — neither Rockingham nor Chatham nor even Grenville had at any time thought deeply about American affairs and although they stuck to their policies with monumental obstinacy, they had, except perhaps for Grenville, stumbled on them by choice. And when they captured office they were responsible in their turn for making the intolerable American situation worse. Yet the fabrications of their hack writers and the diatribes of Junius had a substratum of truth, and there was a certain justice in George III's being dragged into the centre of the stage.

As the King matured in the 'sixties, and as he learned to rule, his opinions became more rigid. At the same time he came to regard the burdens

[2] Cf. *Diary of Sylas Neville,* ed. B. Cozens-Hardy: Neville, a young middle-class man of the same age as George III, had no term of abuse too strong for his monarch or praise too lavish for the Americans — sentiments which were strongly shared by his large circle of acquaintances. Wilkes had compared George III to the Stuarts when talking to Boswell in Naples, 18 Feb. 1765. F. Brady and F. A. Pottle, *Boswell on the Grand Tour, Italy, Corsica, France, 1765–6,* 53.

of his office as awful obligations imposed on him by a Providence more inclined to justice than to mercy. His was a sacred obligation. The power, the might, the empire of Great Britain, the rights of its Kings, the power of its Parliaments, their joint sovereignty, had to be defended at whatever costs, otherwise he would be unworthy of his ancestors or his children. These principles George III grasped with almost lunatic intensity. Hence any compromise with Wilkes or America seemed to him like a sacrilegious weakness, a betrayal of God's trust. The weaker and more unreliable his ministers appeared to be, the more determined George III became to impose his attitude on them. Time and again he tried to obtain assurances before consenting to the appointment of prospective ministers, that they were sound on American policy. And George III's American policy was simple — that the colonists must be reduced to absolute obedience, if need be, by the ruthless use of force. Because his own views were so simple and to him so obviously right, George III was enraged and embittered by opposition and regarded men like Wilkes as little better than agents of the Devil. When it is remembered that the King, although stupid and a little mad, was still the fountain of honour, that his approbation was almost essential for a successful career in church or state, that his character was powerful and intense, and that he was single-minded and obstinate, his presence on the throne can only be regarded as a national disaster. A strong minister might have counterbalanced the unfortunate effects of the King's personality and beliefs, and no one would have been more grateful — if we may believe his own words — than George III to have found a man strong enough to bear his burdens and relieve him of their intolerable weight. His tragedy was to have discovered Lord North at a time when both the question of Wilkes and America were flaring up to a new intensity.

Lord North in life and in death has enjoyed an extremely bad press. During his premiership he was subject to the scathing criticism of Junius — perhaps the ablest and most devastating political commentator this country has known — and to the more urbane but no less effective attacks of Edmund Burke. After his death generations of historians followed their lead. In very recent years attempts have been made to rehabilitate North and to view his career with a charitable eye. No amount of apology can, however, explain away the most glaring fact of all — that he was an utter failure, that during the time that he was leader of the House of Commons the fortunes of his country reached the lowest point in modern history. And worse; at no other time did the House of Commons itself come so near to losing the respect of men of goodwill. One can understand, one can pity North. He possessed many admirable virtues; few men had a greater fund of generosity and loyalty. He was a virtuous husband and a devoted father. The ease, the affability of his nature, made him a persuasive speaker; his droll, sly sense of humour won him many friends and took the edge off the animosity of his enemies. Few men within the closed circle of Court and politics enjoyed a greater popularity. Neither did he lack a certain skill in administration and dexterity in finance. As Chancellors of the Exchequer went in the eighteenth century he was a good one. Yet his defects were large and glaring. The fat, rounded body and soft pig-like face were indicative of more than ease, gentleness and affability; they bespoke an indolence that bordered on disease, a physical incapacity for hard work which made his duties so onerous to him that he often begged George III to release him from his burdens. His body, lacking that hard muscular fibre without which no statesman can hope to dominate either men or events, betrayed his temperament. The same lethargy invaded his mind. He was content to accept ideas, opinions, decisions from others, and the strength of character and the sheer obstinacy of George III were as necessary to him as his ease and kindness were to his monarch. At no time had he either the strength or inclination to take a firm and personal control of affairs; rather he searched for excuses for his unhappy lot, and as events became more dire, pleaded to be relieved of his intolerable burden of office.

It has been maintained that he stayed in office only because George III had paid his debts and that, in return, he had promised never to desert his King. This may contain a half-truth, may easily have been the reason why North excused to himself his own vacillation, and his own inability to solve by a decisive act the unhappy dilemma in which he found himself. But there were deeper causes, and the relationship with George fulfilled many unconscious needs of North's character. Throughout his life, as a child, as a youth, as a married man, North had been subject to his father and ruled decisively by him. As with his monarch there had been the same half-hearted protests, the same bewailing which merely seemed to be a call for further subjection. The situation in which he found himself as prime minister answered some of the deepest needs of his nature.

And as Lord North found George III so George III found Lord North; they were as complementary as notes in a chord. As we have seen, George III had searched all his life for a dependable friend, transferring his hopes to new men as the old ones failed — Bute — Chatham — Grafton and then, at last, North, the weakest yet the most dependable of all. On all major questions — Wilkes, America, and the Rockingham faction — North thought as George III did. Their attitudes were instinctively the same, although in details they might be, at times, slightly at variance. They both had a reverent respect for the idea of monarchy; indeed in some ways North's was even greater than George III's. He was prepared to see the King most actively engaged in business and it was the King himself who often had to urge North to play a larger role in his ministry. Once the relationship became intimate and close, it developed qualities which had been absent from George III's earlier devotions. George III had matured during the 'sixties; marriage and fatherhood had helped to dispel some of his sense of insecurity, but more important than these things was the fact that in his slow, deliberate, painstaking way he had learned thoroughly the business of monarchy. He had grasped the nature of politics and found his way through the labyrinth of patronage and cousinhood, growing to understand what could and could not be done, and realising as he went the immense power of the throne. With North beside him he enjoyed the twofold role of monarch and politician, and here, if anywhere, lies the truth of those charges of personal government which have been levelled against him. He wielded no powers that his ancestors might not have wielded; his regard for constitutional behaviour was as punctilious as one might expect from a Guelph. These things are true. Yet his curiosity, his avid interest, his daily, almost hourly interest, in political activity made him a King with a difference, made him closer to William III or the Stuarts than to his own immediate ancestors. This appetite for politics was sharpened by North's indolent dependence, and because of North's inability to shield his master, men in opposition could not help but feel that the Crown was growing stronger at the expense of the politicians and that dangerous precedents were being created for the future. The tragedy of George III lay in his temperament. His stupidity and obstinacy might have been forgiven, as these same qualities were in his grandfather, if only they had been exercised on the trivialities of politics — the promotion of ensigns, the appointment of deans, or the ritual of the royal lives. But they were not. They were exercised on fundamental questions of policy and personalities — fields in which George II had frequently permitted his own wishes to be overborne without much difficulty. Not that George III was adamant. His hand could be, and was, forced, but the warmth of his temperament made it also seem a far more arduous task to politicians than it had been in George II's day. Certainly it was a task which North used all his skill to avoid.

Across the centuries it is difficult to define or assess the more ephemeral aspects of character. Charm dies with the possessor, but charm is not the only fleeting characteristic of personality. Some men create controversy as others arouse affection. Acts which others can perform without question, gave rise with these men to violent debate. And so it was with George III. Powers which he had every right to exercise seemed despotic when employed by him. It is not remarkable that the grotesque myth that he was aiming at tyranny should have been so widely believed both so early in his reign and for so long after his death.

It was his misfortune that his nature and his actions could be so misinterpreted as to give substance to the belief; and he was dogged by this further handicap, that North instead of shielding him from the calumnies of his enemies strengthened their case by his supine indolence, by his incapacity to extricate himself from a situation that was as tragic for himself as it was for his country. And finally the policy which North pursued with every encouragement from George III ended in utter disaster. Humiliation after humiliation was inflicted on the nation and its institutions brought into grave disrepute. It is time to turn to the sorry tale of their folly.

5

North inherited his first grave problem — John Wilkes. After his expulsion from the Commons in 1764 and subsequent outlawry, Wilkes had decided to remain in France. He drifted to Italy, found a charming but exacting mistress, and frolicked and fooled away his time with that air of serene cynicism which so amazed and entranced his contemporaries. Wilkes had expected to receive a pardon during his erstwhile champion's — Chatham's — ministry. He was disappointed. Chatham in office developed a reverence for the monarchy, greater even than George III's, and in his lucid moments he had not the slightest intention of irritating his King by suggesting a pardon for Wilkes. Wilkes liked wine, loved women, and was obsessed by talk. He found that both Italy and Paris easily satisfied his needs. True, his tastes were expensive. But it was not the lack of money which brought him back in 1768 although he gave this out as the reason. He needed limelight; he longed for the excitement of controversy; in his nature, as with most extravagantly witty men, there was a crude streak of exhibitionism. He timed his return carefully. The ministry under the Duke of Grafton was extremely reluctant to come to grips with Wilkes. They knew well enough his sting. Wilkes, however, made a conflict unavoidable. He stood at the general election in 1768 as candidate for Middlesex and was overwhelmingly successful. There was no avoiding the struggle. The cumbrous process of the law was set in motion, yet it proceeded with great discretion. The outlawry was quashed on technical grounds, but the old conviction of obscene libel could not be evaded. Wilkes was gaoled for eighteen months, which, for an influential man of wealth, was no great hardship. Indeed Wilkes welcomed his incarceration; it made him a martyr and the ministers tyrants. The electors of Middlesex, fed for years on tales of ministerial corruption and jobbery, and recently inflamed with stories of sinister royal intentions to subvert all liberty, adopted Wilkes as a hero. Time and again they elected him with overwhelming majorities, as time and time again the House of Commons declared his election illegal. George III was driven almost to hysteria by the gross misrepresentations of his enemies and by the scorn and vituperation of Junius, who made Wilkes's cause his own.

Wilkes's problem was simply solved. Amidst howls of execration, his opponent — Colonel Luttrell — was declared elected by the House of Commons, and that stopped the seemingly endless inflammatory appeals to the hustings. The justice of such a decision was, naturally enough, hotly debated. The friends of liberty saw in it the end of representative government and clamoured for a reform of the House of Commons, which they came to regard as a complaisant tool of the royal will. More sober men saw the force of Parliament's decision. Over the centuries members had fought for its right to decide the composition of the Commons and to control its membership. The fact that Middlesex was a large and democratic constituency was quite irrelevant. They, themselves, must remain judge and, legally, they had a strong case in rejecting a convicted felon. The alternative to declaring Luttrell elected was to disfranchise Middlesex. The formal, legal case for the ministry and for the Commons was overwhelmingly strong, but only obstinate, blind partisans of the government could refuse to recognise that this was also a case for equity. All knew that the prosecutions against Wilkes had been rigged, that he had been hounded and persecuted for trivial misdemeanours. Tories like Boswell and Johnson, authoritarian Whigs such as Hardwicke and Newcastle, could maintain that Wilkes had endangered the constitution and by his dangerous sallies threatened the throne. The man in the street saw him as a victim of prejudiced authority. And although the ministry solved the problem, it was at an enormous cost. They helped to harden the belief that the House of Commons had become the property of a self-perpetuating and corrupt oligarchy in league with a tyrannical king. In the midst of such tribulations Grafton resigned and North, instead of going with him, undertook the burden of office.

Nor had poor North done with Wilkes. A

few years later, in the midst of his tribulations with the Americans, Wilkes enticed him into a hornets' nest. It was a question of reporting parliamentary debates. Authority once more was on the side of the ministry. Wilkes was entirely in the wrong. Yet so ineptly did the ministry handle this situation that they deeply affronted the City of London, destroying the records of a court of law; indeed, according to Chatham, no lover of Wilkes himself, Parliament behaved like a mob. Once more Wilkes had brilliantly twisted George III's tail. "That Devil Wilkes" maddened the King. The latter realised how dangerous was this constant humiliation of himself, of North, and of Parliament, yet his anger clouded his judgement and the supine North, through negligence, allowed himself to be outmanœuvred.

Yet the American story is a sorrier tale. As with human beings who have ceased to love and grown to hate, no compromise was possible; every gesture of reconciliation was vitiated by a withholding of complete surrender which only led to further suspicion and deeper rancour. And when at last riot gave way to war, George III and his ministers had alienated many loyalists and created a unity amongst the colonists, that, frail as it was, would have been impossible at the start of his reign. And he himself had, unfortunately, become the symbol of tyranny, so that the myth of George III's personal despotism has become almost ineradicable in American history. It is improbable that the most skilful statesman could have found a *modus vivendi,* short of complete independence for the colonies, but it was unfortunate for George III himself that his intransigence turned him into a convenient scapegoat.

The story of the war need not be told. The British began by completely underestimating the strength and determination of the colonists. Sandwich dismissed them as "raw, undisciplined, cowardly men". General Murray thought them "effeminate". More thoughtful men decided that the Americans lacked the financial and economic resources either to succeed in war or to maintain their independence if they procured it. The ugly prognostications of Wilkes and Charles James Fox that Britain's enemies in Europe would aid America and ruin Britain were dismissed as clamour. George III, North, and the bulk of Parliament, including the country gentlemen, now mostly reconciled to the ministry, were united in their determination to teach the rebels obedience. Disaster followed disaster; France and Spain seized their opportunity to inflict a humiliation on their detested rival. Doubts grew, ministers wondered, then resigned. The opposition, sensing the weakness of North and relishing the prospect of office, exploited the government's difficulties to the utmost. The spectral figure of the sick, half-mad Chatham — 'the scarecrow of violence' as he called himself — harangued the Lords on the follies and mismanagements of the war. North, realising that he was caught in circumstances too great for his comprehension, longed to resign, yet his sense of loyalty prevented him from sending more than ambiguous pleas for release which the King rejected. George III could not bear to part with North because that was to recognise his own failure. America would be lost irretrievably and North would be succeeded by a set of men in whom he could place no trust. The situation was more grave, more fraught with danger than many historians will allow. The King held power in his hands. His obstinacy strengthened North; the Court party could dominate the Commons so long as they retained the support of the country gentlemen, whose attitude to America and to libertarian ideals fell little short of the King's. After the passage of Dunning's motion in 1780 in a Committee of the Commons that "the power of the Crown has increased, is increasing, and ought to be diminished", North's fall could only be a matter of time, for into the opposition lobby the country gentlemen had trooped almost to a man.

The need to grant independence and the fall of North were tragic events for George III, and he sat down to draft a message of abdication, so conscious was he of his sense of failure.

> "His Majesty during the twenty-one years he has sate on the throne of Great Britain, has had no object so much at heart as the maintenance of the British Constitution, of which the difficulties he has at times met with from his scrupulous attachment to the rights of Parliament are sufficient proofs. His Majesty is convinced that the sudden change of sentiments of one branch of the legislature

has totally incapacitated him from either conducting the war with effect, or from obtaining any peace but on conditions which would prove destructive to the commerce as well as essential rights of the British nation."[3]

And this was the truth as he saw it. He had a deep regard for the constitution as it was. He never underestimated his own rights and duties; at the same time he held Parliament's sovereignty in the highest regard. The rebellion of the Americans was not only treason to him but treason to Parliament; treason to the ancient, Providential constitution which both he and his advisers had inherited and which it was their sacred duty to protect. Once America had gone, surely, he argued, the rest of the Empire would follow and even Ireland lag not far behind; and the great kingdom which he ruled would moulder away, a prey for the predatory powers of Europe. As Sir Lewis Namier has so cogently phrased it, "He [George III] is defending there the vital interests and essential rights of the British nation." And because he felt that he alone unswervingly followed the path of duty, hampered though he had been by irresponsible, self-seeking men, his failure and its consequences were doubly bitter.

[3] *Correspondence of George III,* ed. Sir John Fortescue, V, 425, No. 3601.

2

The Significance of the Great War for the Empire

The American Revolution as an Aftermath of the Great War for the Empire, 1754–1763

Historians now agree that the Great War for the Empire created many of the conditions that led to the American Revolution; the prospect of scholars agreeing with each other is to be sure a trifle unusual, and in this instance it is to Lawrence Henry Gipson, *gentleman and scholar, that much of the credit must be given.*

Born in 1880, Professor Gipson studied at Idaho, Oxford (a Rhodes scholar), and Yale (under Charles M. Andrews). At present he is enjoying a vigorous retirement from Lehigh University, working a forty-eight hour week on the concluding volume of The British Empire before the American Revolution *(1936–), the tenth volume of which won the Pulitzer Prize in history for 1962.*

To study the problems of the American colonies, contends Professor Gipson, it is necessary to consider their imperial context. This has been the intent of the twelve volumes thus far published on the first British empire.[1] *It was*

Lawrence Henry Gipson, "The American Revolution as an Aftermath of The Great War for the Empire, 1754–1763," *Political Science Quarterly,* LXV (1950), 86–104.

[1] Volumes XI and XII have been recently published (1965); vol. XIII will examine those parts of the Empire which did not throw off dependence upon Great Britain. See Preface, vol. XII.

also the concern of the famous paper Professor Gipson gave at the American Historical Association convention in 1948: here he describes the imperial character of what was once dismissed as "the French and Indian War" or — in England — "the Seven Years' War." He points to the international complications of the struggle outside the Western Hemisphere; he discusses the controversial decisions into which the War forced the British; and he traces the emergence of the problems created by Britain's new imperial responsibilities. While not denying the many sources of Anglo-American friction that antedate the War of 1754–63, Professor Gipson does argue that the War destroyed "the old equilibrium," presenting a new context for old difficulties, with additional headaches built into that new context.

Few historians have gone to such lengths to present both sides of the disputes that led to Revolution. It may be argued that the essential justness of the English case is not strictly relevant; that the colonists' concept of the correctness of their case matters more; but there were two sides to the Revolution, an awareness of which contributes materially to its understanding. Professor Gipson has recently remarked that this essay is "one of the keys to my whole concept of the whole period before the Revolution and so to the series [The British Empire. . . .]." *Accordingly he has made a few clarifications and certain stylistic changes in it for this reprinting. It is this modified version that follows.*

Great wars in modern times have too frequently been the breeders of revolution. The exhausting armed struggles in which France became engaged in the latter half of the eighteenth century led as directly to the French Revolution as did the First World War to the Russian Revolution; it may be said as truly that the American Revolution was an aftermath of the Anglo-French conflict in the New World carried on between 1754 and 1763. This is by no means to deny that other factors were involved in the launching of these revolutionary movements. Before proceeding with an analysis of the theme of this paper, however, it would be well to consider the wording of the title given to it.[1]

Words may be used to disguise or to distort facts as well as to clarify them, but the chief task of the historian is to illuminate the past. He is faced, therefore, with the responsibility of using only such words as will achieve this broad objective of his calling and to reject those that obscure or defeat it. For this reason "the French and Indian War", as a term descriptive of the conflict to which we have just referred, has been avoided in this essay as well as in the writer's series on the *British Empire before the American Revolution*.[2] This has been done in spite of the fact that the term has been employed by most Americans ever since the early days of our Republic and that it therefore has the sanction of long usage — not to mention the sanction of American national tradition, which assigns to the revolt of the thirteen colonies a position of such commanding importance that all other events in American history, both preceding and following it, have been quite subordinated to the War for Independence. In contrast to this traditional interpretation of our history one may affirm that the Anglo-French conflict settled nothing less than the incomparably vital question as to what civilization — what complex cultural patterns, what political institutions — would arise in the great Mississippi basin and the valleys of the rivers draining it, a civilization, whatever it might be, surely destined to expand to the Pacific seaboard and finally to dominate the North American continent. The determination of this crucial issue is perhaps the most momentous event in the life of the English-speaking people in the New World and quite overshadows in importance both the Revolutionary War and the later Civil War, events which, it is quite clear, were each contingent upon the outcome of the earlier crisis.

A struggle of such proportions, involving tre-

[1] This paper was read before the colonial history section of the American Historical Association in December 1948 at the Annual Meeting held in Washington.

[2] The series is published by Alfred A. Knopf, New York, 12 vols., 1939–1965.

mendous stakes, deserves a name accurately descriptive of its place in the history of the English-speaking people, and the title "the French and Indian War", as suggested, in no way fulfills this need. For the war was not, as the name would seem to imply, a conflict largely between English and French New World colonials and their Indian allies, nor was it localized in North America to the extent that the name would appear to indicate. In contrast, it was waged with all their resources both before and after an open declaration of war, by the British and French nations for nine years on three oceans and much of the land washed by the waters of them, and it ultimately brought in both Spain, allied to France, and Portugal, allied to Great Britain. While it involved, it is true, as the name would connote, wilderness fighting, yet of equal, if not of greater, importance in assessing its final outcome was the pouring forth of Britain's financial resources in a vast program of shipbuilding, in the equipment and support of the British and colonial armies and the royal navy, and in the subsidization of allies on the European continent and of the colonies in America. If it also involved the reduction of the fortress of Louisbourg, Fort Niagara, Fort Duquesne, Quebec and Montreal in North America, each in turn to fall to British regulars aided by American provincial troops, these successes, of great significance, were, in fact, really contingent upon the resounding British naval victories in the Mediterranean, off the Strait of Gibraltar, in the Bay of Biscay, and elsewhere, that brought about the virtual extinction of the French navy and merchant marine and thereby presented to France — seeking to supply her forces in Canada and elsewhere with adequate reinforcements and matériel — a logistical problem so insoluble as to spell the doom of her North American empire and of her possessions in India and elsewhere.

If the term "the French and Indian War" meets none of the requirements of accurate historical nomenclature, neither does the term "the Seven Years' War" — a name appropriately enough employed by historians to designate the mighty conflict that raged for seven years in Germany before its conclusion in the Treaty of Hubertusburg in 1763. The principals in this war were Prussia, allied with Great Britain, Hanover, Brunswick and Hesse, facing Austria, most of the Holy Roman Empire, Russia and Sweden, all allied with France and receiving subsidies from her. Although George II, as King of Great Britain and Elector of Hanover, in the treaty of 1758 with Frederick of Prussia, promised not to conclude peace without mutual agreement with the latter, and although large subsidies were annually paid to Prussia as well as to the other continental allies out of the British treasury, and troops were also sent to Germany, it must be emphasized that these aids were designed primarily for the protection of the King's German Electorate. In other words, the British alliance in no way supported the objectives of the Prussian King, when he suddenly began the German war in 1756 by invading Saxony — two years after the beginning of the Anglo-French war. In this connection it should be borne in mind that throughout the Seven Years' War in Germany Great Britain remained at peace with both Russia and Sweden and refused therefore to send a fleet into the Baltic in spite of the demands of Frederick that this be done; nor were British land troops permitted to assist him against Austria, but only to help form a protective shield for Hanover against the thrusts of the French armies. For the latter were determined not only to overrun the Electorate — something that they succeeded in doing — but to hold it as a bargaining point to be used at the conclusion of hostilities with Great Britain, a feat, however, beyond their power of accomplishment. Closely related and intertwined as were the two wars, they were, nevertheless, distinct in their beginning and distinct in their termination.

Indeed, while British historians at length were led to adopt the nomenclature applied by German and other continental historians to all hostilities that took place between 1754 and 1763 in both the Old and New Worlds, American historians, by and large in the past, have rejected, and rightly so, it seems, the name "the Seven Years' War" to designate specifically the struggle during these years in North America with the fate of that continent at stake; so likewise many of them have rejected, as equally inadmissible, the name "the French and Indian War". Instead, the late Professor Osgood employed the title "the Fourth Intercolonial War", surely not a good one; George Bancroft called the war "the American Revolution: First Phase", still more inaccurate in some respects than the names he sought to avoid; Francis Parkman, with the flare of a romanticist, was at first inclined to call it "the Old French War" but finally, under the influence of the great-man-in-history thesis, gave to his two remarkable volumes concerned with it the totally misleading name, *Montcalm and Wolfe;* finally, John Fiske, the philosopher-historian, as luminous in his views as he was apt to be careless in the details of historical scholarship, happily fastened upon the name "the Great War". In the series on the *British Empire before the American Revolution* the writer has built upon Fiske's title and has called it "the Great War for the Empire" in order to emphasize not only the fact that the war was a very great conflict both in its scope and in its lasting effects, as Fiske saw with clearness, but also that, as a war entered into specifically for the defense of the British Empire, it was by far the most important ever waged by Great Britain to this end.

It may be pointed out that later charges, especially by American writers, that the war was begun by Great Britain with less worthy motives in mind, are not supported by the great mass of state papers and the private correspondence of British statesmen responsible for making the weighty decisions at the time — materials now available to the student and which the writer has attempted to analyze in detail in the two volumes of his series that appeared under the title of *Zones of International Friction, 1748–1754.* In other words, the idea that the war was started as the result of European balance-of-power politics or by British mercantilists for the purpose of destroying a commercial rival and for conquering Canada and the French West Indies, and for expelling the French from India, rather than for the much more limited and legitimate objective of affording the colonies — and particularly the new province of Nova Scotia and the Old Dominion of Virginia — protection against the aggressive aims of France, must be dismissed by students brought face to face with impressive evidence to the contrary.

The development of the war into one for the military mastery of the North American continent came with the growing conviction on the part of the British ministers that nothing short of this drastic step would realize the primary aims of the Government, once it had reached the determination to respond to the appeals from the colonies for assistance and to challenge the right of French troops to be planted well within the borders of the Nova Scotia peninsula and at the forks of the Ohio. One may go as far as to state that the acquisition of Canada — as an objective sought by mercantilists to contribute to the wealth of Great Britain — would have seemed fantastic to any contemporary who had the slightest knowledge of the tremendous financial drain that that great possession had been on the treasury of the French King for over a century before 1754. Moreover, the motives that ultimately led, after much searching of heart, to its retention after its conquest by Great Britain were not commercial but strategic and had primarily in view the general security and welfare of the older American colonies.

In view of these facts, not to be confused with surmises, the name "the Great War for the Empire" seems to the writer not only appropriate but, among all the names heretofore applied to the war in question, by far the most suitable that can be used by one concerned with the history of the old British Empire, who seeks earnestly to maintain that standard of exactness in terminology and scholarship which the public has a right to demand of him.

The description just given of the motives that led to the Great War for the Empire, nevertheless, runs counter, as suggested, to American national tradition and most history that has been written in harmony with it by American historians. This tradition had a curious beginning. It arose partly out of Pitt's zealous efforts to energize the colonies to prosecute the war most actively; but there also was another potent factor involved in its creation. Before the conclusion of hostilities in 1763 certain powerful commercial interests — centered particularly at Newport, Rhode Island, Boston, New York City, and to a less extent in Philadelphia — in a desire to continue an enormously lucrative trade with the French West Indies, and therefore with the enemy, all in the face of Pitt's determination to keep supplies from the French armed forces operating in the New World, began to express themselves in terms that implied that the war was peculiarly Great Britain's war and only incidentally one that concerned her colonies and that the French, really friendly to the aspirations of British colonials, were opposed only to the mercantilistic ambitions of the mother country. By 1766 — just twelve years after the beginning of the war and three years after its termination — this extraordinary tradition had become so well established that Benjamin Franklin, astonishingly enough, actually asserted in his examination before a committee of the House of Commons:

> I know the last war is commonly spoke of here as entered into for the defence, or for the sake of the people of America; I think it is quite misunderstood. It began about the limits between Canada and Nova Scotia, about territories to which the crown indeed laid claim, but were not claimed by any British colony. . . . We had therefore no particular concern or interest in that dispute. As to the Ohio, the contest there began about your right of trading in the Indian country, a right you had by the Treaty of Utrecht, which the French infringed . . . they took a fort which a company of your merchants, and their factors and correspondents, had erected there to secure that trade. Braddock was sent with an army to retake that fort . . . and to protect your trade. It was not until after his defeat that the colonies were attacked. They were before in perfect peace with both French and Indians. . . .

By the beginning of 1768 the tradition had been so extended that John Dickinson — voicing the popular American view in his highly important *Letters from a Farmer in Pennsylvania,* No. VIII — felt that he not only could affirm, as did Franklin, that the war was strictly Britain's war and fought for selfish purposes, but could even insist that the acquisition of territory in North America as the result of it "is greatly injurious to these colonies" and that they therefore were not under the slightest obligation to the mother country.

But to return to the last phases of the Great War for the Empire. The British customs officials — spurred into unusual activity in the face of Pitt's demand for the strict enforcement of the Trade and Navigation Acts in order to break up the pernicious practice of bringing aid and comfort to the enemy — were led to employ writs of assistance for the purpose of laying their hands upon goods landed in American ports and secured in exchange for American provisions sent for the most part either directly or indirectly to the French West Indies. Although the British Empire was in the midst of hostilities, most of the merchants in Boston showed bitter opposition to the writs and gave ardent support to James Otis' declaration, made in open court in 1761, that Parliament, whatever its constitutional authority might be in Great Britain, was powerless to extend the use of these writs to America. The importance of this declaration lies not so much in its immediate effect but rather in the fact that it was indicative of the line of attack that would be followed during the developing crisis not only by Otis but also by the Adamses, Warren, Hawley, Hancock, and other popular leaders in the Bay colony as they laid down constitutional restrictions upon the power of Parliament to legislate for America. Further, it is clear that, even before the Great War for the Empire had been terminated, there were those in the province who had begun to view Great Britain as the real enemy rather than France.

Just as clearly related to the war under consideration as the issue over writs of assistance was that growing out of the twopenny acts of the Virginia Assembly. In search of funds for maintaining the frontier defensive forces under the command of Colonel George Washington, the Assembly was led to pass in 1755 and 1758 those highly questionable laws which were as favorable to the tobacco planters as they were indefensively unjust to the clergy. Even assuming the fact that these laws were war measures, and therefore in a sense emergency measures, it was inconceivable that the Privy Council would permit so palpable a violation of contractual relations as they involved. The royal disallowance of the laws in question opened the way for Patrick Henry, the year that hostilities were terminated by the Peace of Paris, to challenge in the Louisa County courthouse the right of the King in Council to refuse approval to a law passed by a colonial assembly — a good law in the judgment of the colony — and to affirm that such refusal was nothing less than an act of tyranny on the part of the King. It was thus resentment at the overturning of Virginia war legislation that led to this attack upon the judicial authority of review by the Crown — an authority exercised previously without serious protest for over a century. It should also be noted that the Henry thesis helped to lay the foundation for the theory of the equality of colonial laws with those passed by Parliament, a theory of the constitution of the empire that most American leaders in 1774 had come to accept in arguing that if the King could no longer exercise a veto over the acts of the legislature of Great Britain, it was unjust that he should do so over those of the colonial assemblies.

But the most fateful aftermath of the Great War for the Empire, with respect to the maintenance of the historic connection between the mother country and the colonies, grew out of the problem of the control and support of the vast trans-Appalachian interior, the right to which was now confirmed by treaty to Great Britain, as well as of the new acquisitions in North America secured from France and Spain. Under the terms of the royal Proclamation of 1763, French Canada to the east of the Great Lakes was organized as the Province of Quebec; most of old Spanish Florida became the Province of East Florida; and those areas, previously held by Spain as well as by France to the west of the Apalachicola and to the east of New Orleans and its immediate environs, became the Province of West Florida. The Proclamation indicated that proper inducements would be offered British and other Protestants to establish themselves in these new provinces. With respect to the trans-Appalachian region, however, it created there a temporary but vast Indian reserve by laying down as a barrier the crest of the mountains beyond which there should be no white settlement except by specific permission of the Crown.

The Proclamation has been represented not only as a blunder, the result largely of carelessness and ignorance on the part of those responsible for it, but also as a cynical attempt by the British ministry to embody mercantilistic principles in an American land policy that in itself ran counter to the charter limits of many of the colonies and the interests in general of the colonials. Nevertheless, this view of the Proclamation fails to take into account the fact that it was the offspring of the war and that the trans-Appalachian aspects of it were an almost inevitable result of promises made during the progress of hostilities. For both in the Treaty of Easton in 1758 with the Ohio Valley Indians, a treaty ratified by the Crown, and in the asseverations of such military leaders as Colonel Bouquet, these Indians were assured that they would be secure in their trans-Appalachian lands as a reward for deserting their allies, the French. As a sign of good faith, the lands lying within the bounds of Pennsylvania to the west of the mountains, purchased by the Proprietors from the Six Nations in 1754, were solemnly released. Thus committed in honor in the course of the war, at its termination what other step could the Cabinet Council have taken? But the Proclamation of 1763 was in opposition to the interests of such groups of land speculators as, for example, the Patrick Henry group in Virginia and the Richard Henderson group in North Carolina, both of whom boldly ignored the Proclamation in negotiating with the Cherokee Indians for land grants. It also led to open defiance by frontiersmen who, moving beyond the mountains by the thousands, proceeded to settle within the Indian reserve — some on lands previously occupied before the beginning of the late war or before the great Indian revolt in 1763, and others on new lands.

The Proclamation Line of 1763 might have become an issue, indeed a most formidable one, between the government of Great Britain and the colonials, had not the former acquiesced in the inevitable and confirmed certain Indian treaties that provided for the transfer of much of the land which had been the particular object of quest on the part of speculators and of those moving westward from the settled areas to establish new homes. Such were the treaties of Hard Labor, Fort Stanwix, Lochaber, and the modification of the last-named by the Donelson agreement with the Cherokees in 1771. Nor did the regulation of the trans-Appalachian Indian trade create serious colonial irritation, especially in view of the failure of the government to implement the elaborate Board of Trade plan drawn up in 1764. The same, however, cannot be said of the program put forward by the ministry and accepted by Parliament for securing the means to maintain order and provide protection for this vast area and the new acquisitions to the north and south of it.

Theoretically, it would have been possible for the government of Great Britain to have dropped onto the lap of the old continental colonies the entire responsibility for maintaining garrisons at various strategic points in North America — in Canada, about the Great Lakes, in the Ohio and Mississippi valleys, and in East and West Florida. In spite, however, of assertions made in 1765 and 1766 by some prominent colonials, such as Franklin, that the colonies would be able and were willing to take up the burden of providing for the defense of America, this, under the circumstances, was utterly chimerical. For it would have involved not only a vast expenditure of funds but highly complicated inter-colonial arrangements, especially in the face of serious inter-colonial rivalries, such as that between Pennsylvania and Virginia respecting the control of the upper Ohio Valley. The very proportions of the task were an insuperable obstacle to leaving it to the colonies; and the colonies, moreover, would have been faced by another impediment almost as difficult to surmount — the utter aversion of eighteenth-century Americans, by and large, to the dull routine of garrison duty. This was emphasized by the Massachusetts Bay Assembly in 1755 in its appeal to the government of Great Britain, after Braddock's defeat, to send regulars to man the frontier forts of that province; the dispatches of Colonel George Washington in 1756 and in 1757 respecting the shameful desertion of militiamen, ordered to hold the chain of posts on the western frontier of Virginia in order to check the frightful French and Indian raids, support this position, as does the testimony in 1757 of Governor Lyttelton of South Carolina, who made clear that the inhabitants of that colony were not at all adapted to this type of work. The post-war task of garrison duty was clearly one to be assumed by regulars held to their duty under firm discipline and capable of being shifted from one strategic point to another as circumstances might require. Further, to be effective, any plan for the defense of the new possessions and the trans-Appalachian region demanded unity of command, something the colonies could not provide. Manifestly this could be done only through the instrumentalities of the mother country.

Confronted with this problem of guaranteeing the necessary security for the extended empire in North America, which it was estimated would involve an annual expenditure of from three to four hundred thousand pounds for the maintenance of ten thousand troops — according to various estimates made by General Amherst and others in 1764 (to be found among the Shelburne Papers) — the British ministry was impelled to raise the question: Should not the colonials be expected to assume some definite part of the cost? Since the government felt that the colonies were in a position to do so and that the stability of these outlying possessions was a matter of greater concern and importance generally to them, by reason of their proximity, than to the people of the mother country three thousand miles away, the answer was in the affirmative. The reason for this is not hard to fathom. The nine years of war had involved Britons in tremendous expenditures. In spite of very heavy taxation during these years, the people were left saddled at the termination of hostilities with a national debt of unprecedented proportions for that day and age of over one hundred and forty million pounds. It was necessary not only to service and to retire this debt, in so far as was possible, but also to meet the ordinary demands of the civil government and to maintain the navy at a point of strength that would offer some assurance that France and Spain would have no desire in the future to plan a war to recover their territorial losses. In addition to all this, there was now the problem of meeting the charges necessary for keeping the new possessions in North America under firm military control for their internal good order and for protection from outside interference.

It may be noted that before the war the British budget had called for average annual expenditures of six and a half million pounds; between the years 1756 and 1766 these expenditures mounted to fourteen and a half million pounds a year on the average and from the latter date to 1775 ranged close to ten million pounds. As a result, the annual per capita tax in Great Britain from 1763 to 1775, without considering local rates, was many times the average annual per capita tax in even those American colonies that made the greatest contribution to the Great War for the Empire, such as Massachusetts Bay and Connecticut — without reference to those colonies that had done little or nothing in this conflict, and therefore had accumulated little in the way of a war debt, such as Maryland and Georgia. The student of the history of the old British Empire, in fact, should accept with great reserve statements to the contrary — some of them quite irresponsible in nature — made by Americans during the heat of the controversy, with respect to the nature of the public burdens they were obliged to carry in the years preceding the outbreak of the Revolutionary War. In this connection a study of parliamentary reimbursement of colonial war expenses from 1756 to 1763 in its relation to public debts in America between the years 1763 and 1775 is most revealing.[3] As to American public finance, all that space will here permit is to state that there is abundant evidence to indicate that, during the five-year period preceding the outbreak of the Revolutionary War, had the inhabitants of any of the thirteen colonies been taxed in one of these years at the average high per capita rate that the British people were taxed from 1760 to 1775, the proceeds of that one year's tax not only would have taken care of the ordinary expenditures of the colony in question for that year but also would have quite liquidated its war debt, so little of which remained in any of the colonies by 1770.[4] Well may John Adams have admitted in 1789 what was equally true in 1770: "America is not used to great taxes, and the people there are not yet disciplined to such enormous taxation as in England."

Assuming, as did the Grenville ministry in 1764, the justice of expecting the Americans to share in the cost of policing the new possessions in North America, the simplest and most obvious way, it might appear, to secure this contribution to a common end so important to Americans and Britons was to request the colonial governments to make definite grants of funds. This was the requisition or quota system that had been employed in the course of the recent war. But the most obvious objections to it were voiced that same year by Benjamin Franklin, who, incidentally, was to reverse himself the following year in conferring with Grenville as the Pennsylvania London agent. In expressing confidentially his personal, rather than any official, views to his friend Richard Jackson on June 25, 1764 he declared: "Quota's would be difficult to settle at first with Equality, and would, if they could be made equal at first, soon become unequal, and never would be satisfactory." Indeed, experience with this system in practice, as a settled method of guaranteeing even the minimum essential resources for the purpose in view, had shown its weakness and utter unfairness. If it could not work equitably even in war time, could it be expected to work in time of peace? It is, therefore, not surprising that this method of securing even a portion of the funds required for North American security should have been rejected in favor of some plan that presented better prospects of a definite American revenue.

The plan of last resort to the ministry was therefore to ask Parliament to act. That Grenville, however, was aware that serious objections might be raised against any direct taxation of the colonials by the government of Great Britain is indicated by the caution with which he approached the solution of the problem of securing from America about a third of the total cost of its defense. The so-called Sugar Act first of all was passed at his request. This provided for import duties on certain West Indian and other products. Colonial import duties imposed by Parliament, at least since 1733, were no innovation. But the anticipated yield of these new duties would fall far short of the desired one hundred thousand pounds. He therefore, in introducing the bill for the Sugar Act, raised the question of a stamp duty but requested postponement of parliamentary action until the colonial governments had been consulted. The latter were thereupon requested to make any suggestions for ways of raising an American fund that might seem more proper to the people than such a tax. Further, it would appear — at least, according to various London advices published in Franklin and Hall's *Pennsylvania Gazette* — that proposals were seriously con-

[3] See Gipson's *British Empire before the American Revolution,* X, Chap. 2. — ed.

[4] *Ibid.,* X, Chaps. 3 and 4. — ed.

sidered by the Cabinet Council during the fall of 1764 for extending to the colonies representation in Parliament through the election of members to the House of Commons by various colonial assemblies. However, it is quite clear that by the beginning of 1765 any such proposals as may have been under deliberation by the ministry, had been put aside when Grenville at length had become convinced that representation in Parliament was neither actively sought nor even desired by Americans. For the South Carolina Commons House of Assembly went strongly on record against this idea in September 1764 as did the Virginia House of Burgesses in December. In fact, when in the presence of the London colonial agents the minister had outlined the objections raised by Americans to the idea of such representation, not one of them, including Franklin, was prepared to deny the validity of these objections. That he was not mistaken in the opposition of Americans at large to sending members to Parliament, in spite of the advocacy of this by James Otis, is clear in the resolutions passed both by colonial assemblies other than the ones to which reference has been made and by the Stamp Act Congress in 1765. Indeed, in 1768 the House of Representatives of Massachusetts Bay went so far in its famous Circular Letter framed in opposition to the Townshend duties as to make clear that the people of that colony actually preferred taxation by Parliament without representation to such taxation with representation.

When — in view of the failure of the colonial governments to suggest any practicable, alternate plan for making some contribution to the post-war defensive program in North America — Grenville finally urged in Parliament the passage of an American stamp bill, he acted on an unwarranted assumption. This assumption was — to paraphrase the minister's remarks to the colonial agents in 1765 — that opposition to stamp taxes, for the specific purpose in mind, would disappear in America both in light of the benefits such provision would bring to colonials in general and by reason of the plain justice of the measure itself; and that, in place of opposition, an atmosphere of mutual goodwill would be generated by a growing recognition on the part of Americans that they could trust the benevolence of the mother country to act with fairness to all within the empire. Instead, with the news of the passage of the Stamp Act, cries of British tyranny and impending slavery soon resounded throughout the entire eastern Atlantic American seaboard. What would have been the fate of the empire had Grenville remained in office to attempt to enforce the act, no one can say. But as members of the opposition to the Rockingham ministry, he and his brother, Earl Temple, raised their voices — one as a commoner, the other as a peer — in warning that the American colonies would inevitably be lost to the empire should Parliament be led to repeal the act in the face of colonial resistance and the pressure of British merchants. Had Parliament determined, in spite of violence and threats of violence, to enforce the act, it might have meant open rebellion and civil war ten years before it actually occurred. Instead, this body decided to yield and, in spite of the passing of the so-called Declaratory Act setting forth its fundamental powers to legislate on all matters relating to the empire, suffered a loss of prestige in the New World that was never to be regained.

But the Stamp Act was not the sole object of attack by colonials. To many of them not only the Sugar Act of 1764 but the whole English pre-war trade and navigation system was equally, if not actually more, obnoxious. Indeed, the unusual energy displayed by the navy and the customs officials, spurred into action by Pitt during the latter years of the war — bringing with it the condemnation in courts of vice-admiralty of many American vessels whose owners were guilty of serious trade violations or even greater crimes — generated a degree of antagonism against the whole body of late seventeenth- and early eighteenth-century restrictions on commercial intercourse such as never had previously existed. It is not without significance that the greatest acts of terrorism and destruction during the great riot of August 1765 in Boston were directed not against the Massachusetts Bay stamp distributor but against those officials responsible for encouraging and supporting the enforcement, during the late war, of the various trade acts passed long before 1754. The hatred also of the Rhode Island merchants, as a group, against the restrictions of the navigation system as well as against the Sugar Act of 1764, remained constant. Moreover, in December 1766 most of the New York merchants, over two hundred in number, showed their repugnance to the way this system was functioning by a strongly worded petition to the House of Commons in which they enumerated an impressive list of grievances that they asked to be redressed. Even Chatham, the great friend of America, regarded their petition "highly improper: in point of time most absurd, in the extent of their pretensions, most excessive; and in the reasoning, most grossly fallacious and offensive." In fact, all the leading men in Great Britain supported the system of trade restrictions.

Nevertheless, the government was now determined — in view especially of the great financial burdens that the late war had placed upon the mother country — to enforce the trade laws now much more effectively than had been done before 1754. To that end in 1767 it passed appropriate legislation in order to secure funds from the colonies by way of import duties so that public officials in America might be held to greater accountability when paid their salaries by the Crown. This attempt to enforce the trade and navigation acts and the passage of the Townshend Acts could have only one result: the combined resistance of those, on the one hand, opposed to any type of taxation that Parliament might apply to America and of those, on the other, desiring to free the colonies of hampering trade restrictions.

The suggestion on the part of the Continental Congress in 1774 that Americans would uphold the British navigation system, if exempted from parliamentary taxation, while a shrewd gesture to win support in England, had really, it would seem, no other significance. For it is utterly inconceivable that the Congress itself, or the individual colonial governments, could have set up machinery capable of preventing wilful violations of the system by those whose financial interests were adversely affected by its operation. Moreover, it is obvious that, by the time the news had reached America that Lord North's ministry had secured the passage of the coercive acts — for the most part directed against Massachusetts Bay for the defiant destruction of the East India Company's tea — leading colonials, among them Franklin, had arrived at the conclusion that Parliament possessed powers so very limited with respect to the empire that without the consent of the local assemblies it could pass neither constitutional nor fiscal legislation affecting Americans and the framework of their governments. It is equally obvious that this represented a most revolutionary position when contrasted with that held by Franklin and the other delegates to the Albany Congress twenty years earlier. For it was in 1754 that the famous Plan of Union was drawn up and approved by the Congress — a plan based upon the view that Parliament, and not the Crown, had supreme authority within the empire, an authority that alone was adequate in view of framers of the Plan to bring about fundamental changes in the constitutions of the colonies in order legally to clothe the proposed union government with adequate fiscal as well as other powers.

In accounting for the radical change in attitude of many leading colonials between the years 1754 and 1774 respecting the nature of the constitution of the empire, surely among the factors that must be weighed was the truly overwhelming victory achieved in the Great War for the Empire. This victory not only freed colonials for the first time in the history of the English-speaking people in the New World from dread of the French, their Indian allies, and the Spaniards, but, what is of equal significance, opened up to them the prospect, if given freedom of action, of a vast growth of power and wealth with an amazing westward expansion. Indeed, it is abundantly clear that a continued subordination of the colonies to the government of Great Britain was no longer considered the asset in the eyes of many Americans by 1774 it had been judged by them to be in 1754, but was rather held to be an onerous liability. What had the debt-ridden mother country to offer in 1774 to the now geographically secure, politically mature, prosperous, dynamic, and self-reliant offspring along the Atlantic seaboard, except the dubious opportunity of accepting new burdens in addition to retaining the old ones? And these burdens would have to be borne in order to lighten somewhat the great financial load that the taxpayers of Great Britain were forced to carry because of obligations the nation had assumed both in the course of the late war and at its termination. If many Americans thought they had a perfect right to profit personally by trading with the enemy in time of war, how much more deeply must they have resented in time of peace the serious efforts made by the home government to enforce the elaborate restrictions on commercial intercourse? Again, if, even after the defeat of Colonel Washington at Great Meadows in 1754, colonials such as Franklin were opposed to paying any tax levied by Parliament for establishing a fund for the defense of North America, how much more must they have been inclined to oppose such taxation with the passing in 1763 of the great international crisis?

At this point the question must be frankly faced: If France had won the war decisively and thereby consolidated her position and perfected her claims in Nova Scotia, as well as to the southward of the St. Lawrence, in the Great Lakes region, and in the Ohio and Mississippi valleys, is it at all likely that colonials would have made so fundamental a constitutional issue of the extension to them of the principle of the British stamp tax? Would they have resisted such a tax had Parliament imposed it in order to provide on an equitable basis the maximum resources for guaranteeing their safety, at a time when they were faced on their highly restricted borders by a militant, victorious enemy having at its command thousands of ferocious redskins? Again, accepting the fact of Britain's victory, is it not reasonable to believe that, had Great Britain at the close of the triumphant war left Canada to France and carefully limited her territorial demands in North America to those comparatively modest objectives that she had in mind at its beginning, there would have been no very powerful movement within the foreseeable future toward complete colonial autonomy — not to mention American independence? Would not Americans have continued to feel the need as in the past to rely for their safety and welfare upon British sea power and British land power, as well as upon British resources generally? In other words, was Governor Thomas Hutchinson of Massachusetts Bay far mistaken when, in analyzing the American situation late in 1773, he affirmed in writing to the Earl of Dartmouth:

> Before the peace [of 1763] I thought nothing so much to be desired as the cession of Canada. I am now convinced that if it had remained to the French none of the spirit of opposition to the Mother Country would have yet appeared & I think the effects of it [that is, the cession of Canada] worse than all we had to fear from the French or Indians.

In conclusion, it may be said that it would be idle to deny that most colonials in the eighteenth century at one time or another felt strongly the desire for freedom of action in a wider variety of ways than was legally permitted before 1754. Indeed, one can readily uncover these strong impulses even in the early part of the seventeenth century. Yet Americans were, by and large, realists, as were the British, and under the functioning of the imperial system from, let us say, 1650 to 1750 great mutual advantages were enjoyed, with a fair division, taking everything into consideration, of the financial burdens necessary to support the system. However, the mounting Anglo-French rivalry in North America from 1750 onward, the outbreak of hostilities in 1754, and the subsequent nine years of fighting destroyed the old equilibrium, leaving the colonials after 1760 in a highly favored position in comparison with the taxpayers of Great Britain. Attempts on the part of the Crown and Parliament to restore by statute the old balance led directly to the American constitutional crisis, out of which came the Revolutionary War and the establishment of American independence. Such, ironically, was the aftermath of the Great War for the Empire, a war that Britons believed, as the Earl of Shelburne affirmed in 1762 in Parliament, was begun for the "security of the British colonies in N. America. . . ."

3

The Philosophy of Revolution

American Political Thought, 1765–1776: The Rights of Man

"The foundation of our Empire was not laid in the gloomy age of Ignorance and Superstition, but at an Epocha when the rights of mankind were better understood and more clearly defined than at any former period. . . ." This reflection of George Washington sums up the political self-confidence of the Revolutionary generation. The colonial patriot was very much the child of the Enlightenment, convinced of the efficacy of man's reasoning powers and of the divine logic of the natural world. Americans inquired carefully into the nature and extent of their rights, and read widely in their quest for basic principles upon which they could rest their claims. They made no claim to originality, they did not seek "new principles, or new arguments, never before thought of," wrote Jefferson defending his Declaration of Independence; the objective was the clarification and identification of a political theory commonplace in the English world.

The precise role of political theory in making the American Revolution can be debated. Clinton Rossiter, *Professor of Government at Cornell University, concedes that Americans were rarely systematic in their enunciation of their political philosophy. Indeed the debates in the Continental Congress reveal that some shied away from any reliance upon "the Law of Nature — because this will be a feeble support." There were colonists who preferred an appeal to something more tangible than philosophy: they looked to their privileges as Englishmen which were "inherent, their Birthright and Inheritance." For many history was a comforting confirmation of the justness of their claims; for many history was a substantiation of their philosophical assumptions.*

From *Seedtime of the Republic,* copyright, 1953, by Clinton Rossiter, pp. 363–381. Reprinted by permission of Harcourt, Brace & World, Inc. Footnotes deleted by permission of the publisher.

The State of Nature

The state of nature — the state of "men living together according to reason without a common superior on earth, with authority to judge between them" — was the point of reference around which Revolutionary thinkers grouped the principles of their political theory. The state of nature was, of course, an old concept, and men raised in the tradition of natural law could accept and use it without feeling any urge to subject it to critical analysis. Most American thinkers were content to mention the state of nature in a sentence or two, then move on briskly to consider those rights which men could be said to enjoy because they had once lived in it. An author writing under the pseudonym "Spartanus" made one of the few attempts to describe this state:

> In the days of Adam and Noah, every man had an equal right to the unoccupied earth, which God said he had given to the children of men. The whole world was before them, there was much more land than they could occupy or enjoy. — Each man had a right to occupy new land where he pleased, and to take wild beasts by hunting. This was what civilians call a state of nature. In this state every man had a right to enjoy himself, a right to his enclosure, to what he took in hunting, and to feed his flocks where he pleased, so that in any of these, he did not interfere with any pre-occupant. In such a state every man had a right to defend himself and repel injuries, as he thought best. . . . Every man had an equal right to judge be-

tween himself & his neighbour, and to do that which was right in his own eyes.

Samuel Cooke was another who elaborated upon the state of nature. Indeed, it would seem that he had two such states in mind:

> In a pure state of nature, government is in a great measure unnecessary. Private property in that state is inconsiderable. Men need no arbiter to determine their rights; they covet only a bare support; their stock is but the subsistence of a day; the uncultivated deserts are their habitations, and they carry their all with them in their frequent removes. They are each one a law to himself, which, in general, is of force sufficient for their security in that course of life.
>
> It is far otherwise when mankind are formed into collective bodies, or a social state of life. Here, their frequent mutual intercourse, in a degree, necessarily leads them to different apprehensions respecting their several rights, even where their intentions are upright. Temptations to injustice and violence increase, and the occasions of them multiply in proportion to the increase and opulence of the society. The laws of nature, though enforced by divine revelation, which bind the conscience of the upright, prove insufficient to restrain the sons of violence, who have not the fear of God before their eyes.

The true state of nature, that is to say, was simply that condition of no positive law and no formal government that preceded the organization of the political community. A few writers followed Hobbes in describing this state:

> The miseries of the state of nature are so evident, that there is no occasion to display them; every man is sensible that violence, rapine, and slaughter must be continually practised where no restraints are provided to curb the inordinancy of self-affection.

Most, however, agreed with Locke that it was "a state of peace, goodwill, mutual assistance, and preservation." All were willing to go one step further with Locke and assert that, although most men in the state of nature were inclined to respect the persons and properties of other men, the want of a superior power to adjust honest differences of opinion and "restrain the sons of violence" rendered it a very precarious existence. The state of nature, like natural man, had much in it that was good, much that was bad. However pleasing the prospect, few men would refuse to abandon it, even fewer seek to return to it. It was a state perhaps "more excellent than that, in which men are meanly submissive to the haughty will of an imperious tyrant," but men would go back to it only to clear the ground for a new government.

It is impossible to say just how seriously the colonists believed in the state of nature as a fact of history. Certainly Americans had more right than most people to talk of the state of nature as if it had been or could be a real situation. Colonial theorists and debaters used this phrase to describe these situations of historical fact: the condition of no government in pre-historic or Biblical times; the situation facing the Pilgrim fathers in Provincetown harbor in 1620 and other unorganized or unauthorized settlements throughout the colonial period; the state of the colonies in 1775, especially after the King had dissolved the compact by sending troops against them; and, following Locke, the relations to one another of "governments all through the world." This was, after all, long before the days of cultural anthropology and social history, and a belief in the state of nature as a fact in the past was perfectly consistent with learning or intelligence, especially since all but a tiny fraction of colonial thinkers seemed to consider this state a pre-political rather than pre-social phenomenon. For men as different in approach as James Otis and Rev. Samuel Cooke society without government — rather than men without society — was the real state of nature.

Most American theorists were more interested in the state of nature as logical hypothesis than as chronological fact. It was far more convenient for them to assume its existence than describe its outlines, and certainly such an assumption called for no explanation from men raised in the Anglo-Christian tradition. The state of nature served as a logical antecedent to at least five major principles of Revolutionary theory, since it permitted the colonists to:

(1) proclaim the prior existence and therefore prior validity of the law of nature, the sys-

tem of natural justice that commands men to love, assist, and respect one another;

(2) describe man's basic nature, by calling attention to those qualities of character he possesses before and despite government or society;

(3) describe man's basic rights, which are therefore considered the gifts of God or nature and not of the community:

> In a state of nature, no man had any *moral* power to deprive another of his life, limbs, property, or liberty; nor the least authority to command or exact obedience from him.
>
> In a state of nature, every man had the sovereign controul over his own person. He might also have, in that state, a qualified property. . . . Over this qualified property every man in a state of nature had also a sovereign control.
>
> No man in the State of Nature can justly take Anothers Property without his Consent.
>
> Man, in a state of nature, has undoubtedly a right to speak and act without controul.

(4) demonstrate the clear necessity of government based on principles of freedom:

> As in a state of nature much happiness cannot be enjoyed by individuals, so it has been conformable to the inclinations of almost all men, to enter into a political society so constituted, as to remove the inconveniences they were obliged to submit to in their former state, and, at the same time, to retain all those natural rights, the enjoyment of which would be consistent with the nature of a free government, and the necessary subordination to the supreme power of the state.

(5) give a mechanistic explanation of the origin of government, in order to free men from the past and let them build new political institutions to suit themselves. "We often read," declaimed a Boston orator,

> of the original contract, and of mankind, in the early ages, passing from a state of nature to immediate civilization. But *what eye* could penetrate through gothic night and barbarous fable to that remote period. Such an eye, perhaps, was present, when the Deity conceived the universe and fixed his compass upon the great deep.
>
> And yet the people of Massachusetts have reduced to practice the wonderful theory. A numerous people have convened in a state of nature, and, like *our ideas* of the patriarchs, have deputed a few fathers of the land to draw up for them a glorious covenant. It has been drawn. The people have signed it with rapture, and have, thereby, bartered, among themselves, an easy degree of obedience for the highest possible civil happiness.

For men anxious to recur to first principles of natural justice the state of nature was a prime philosophical assumption. The dictates of a political theory concerned with limits on political power in behalf of individual liberty demanded that men and their rights be declared logically and chronologically anterior to the organized community. Whatever else it was, the pre-political state of nature was an extremely handy point of reference.

The Law of Nature

The Declaration of Independence was written, the Constitution adopted, and the Republic launched in an age when most men, whether subtle or simple, believed unequivocally in higher law, generally called "the law of nature." If a few men like Bentham doubted or denied, most political theorists — in America, all political theorists — assumed the existence and applicability of "the Laws of Nature and of Nature's God." Thinking colonists realized that they were the latest heirs of a political tradition unrivaled in age and universality. By the time the law of nature had come into their hands, it had assumed many different shapes in the service of many different peoples and purposes. Greek philosophers, Roman jurists, Church fathers, medieval scholastics, Protestant reformers, Continental and English liberals — all these and many others had made rich contributions to the doctrine of natural law. And all had agreed, no matter what their special interpretation of its contents and dictates, that it placed some sort of moral restriction on political power, indeed on all human activity. To understand the place of natural law in Revolutionary thought we must seek brief answers to these questions: What did the colonists consider to be its source? How did they define it? What did it actually mean in terms of their political theory?

Colonial opinion of the ultimate source of

higher law divided into three fairly distinct categories. One group of men held it be of immediately divine origin. For them the higher law was, as Rev. Eliphalet Williams of Hartford told the Connecticut legislature, "the law of God, eternal and immutable." New England preachers, at least the more conservative of them, were the leading members of this group, but it was by no means confined to clerical thinkers. James Otis, for example, considered the law of nature to be "the *unchangeable will of God,* the author of nature, whose laws never vary." For most of these thinkers, if not necessarily for Otis, the commands of higher law were to be found primarily in Scripture. Since the great men of Israel had commanded a variety of things, Eliphalet Williams's law of God was just about as flexible as Samuel Adams's law of nature.

A second group sought, in the tradition of Cicero and Grotius, to secularize higher law. Although they could not quite eliminate the touch of divinity, they were able to thrust God well into the background. Such rationalists in religion as John Adams and Jefferson were willing to concede that God — not necessarily the Christian God — had set the grand machine of nature in motion, but they added quickly that the laws governing this machine had by now become "natural" in the strictest sense: They were at once cause, effect, and expression of nature, an order of things that functioned without divine intervention. Even if God had decreed this order in his original omnipotence, he could no longer tamper with it. Indeed he, too, was bound to respect and follow its laws. The laws of nature that controlled the actions of men were as certain and imperative as those which controlled the movement of the spheres. They were part of the pattern of nature itself, to be discovered by men, whether Christians or pagans, through the use of right reason. Many thinkers, of course, appealed to both "God and nature," a sort of holy duality, but these must be classed finally as believers in natural as contrasted with purely divine law. Reason rather than revelation was their means of discovering the dictates of higher law.

A recent book has argued with some persuasiveness that a few key political theorists adopted a utilitarian rather than metaphysical approach to higher law. When men like James Wilson spoke of the law of nature, we are told, they "appear . . . to have meant, not a transcendental essence, but a practical plan . . . the plan to make possible individual, free, righteous development within a happy and prosperous commonwealth." History, not God or nature, was the source of higher law; experience, not revelation or reason, taught men its commands and penalties. Whether Wilson or any other like-minded colonist was this much of a utilitarian is debatable, but it can be argued that one strong group of American thinkers looked upon the history of liberty and tyranny as the true source of those rules of natural justice which Parliament seemed bent on violating. The higher law that limited political power was simply an experience-proved boundary "built up in the minds of freedom-loving men — not always the same, perhaps, but always on the alert — beyond which it is not safe for governments to go." *Weltgeschichte ist Weltgericht*: History had a way of punishing those men who disregarded its lessons in political freedom.

The colonists revealed the derivative quality of their political theory by quoting English and Continental definitions of the law of nature rather than seeking to define it for themselves. Locke, Pufendorf, Vattel, and Burlamaqui were all called into service for this purpose, but Sir William Blackstone's definition was probably the best known and most widely cited. No young man after 1771 could become a lawyer without reading these words:

> Man, considered as a creature, must necessarily be subject to the laws of his creator, for he is entirely a dependent being. . . . And consequently, as man depends absolutely upon his maker for every thing, it is necessary that he should in all points conform to his maker's will.
>
> This will of his maker is called the law of nature. For as God, when he created matter, and endued it with a principle of mobility, established certain rules for the perpetual direction of that motion; so, when he created man, and endued him with freewill to conduct himself in all parts of life, he laid down certain immutable laws of human nature, whereby that freewill is in some degree regulated and restrained, and gave him also the

faculty of reason to discover the purport of those laws.

Considering the creator only as a being of infinite *power,* he was able unquestionably to have prescribed whatever laws he pleased to his creature, man, however unjust or severe. But as he is also a being of infinite *wisdom,* he has laid down only such laws as were founded in those relations of justice, that existed in the nature of things antecedent to any positive precept. These are the eternal, immutable laws of good and evil, to which the creator himself in all his dispensations conforms; and which he has enabled human reason to discover, so far as they are necessary for the conduct of human actions. Such among others are these principles: that we should live honestly, should hurt nobody, and should render to every one his due; to which three general precepts Justinian has reduced the whole doctrine of law. . . .

This law of nature, being coeval with mankind and dictated by God himself, is of course superior in obligation to any other. It is binding over all the globe in all countries, and at all times: no human laws are of any validity, if contrary to this; and such of them as are valid derive all their force, and all their authority, mediately or immediately, from this original.

The colonists could not possibly have accepted Blackstone's assertion of parliamentary supremacy, but they found his definition of natural law too satisfying to ignore. Indeed, they were delighted to quote a high Tory for their purposes.

The law of nature, whatever its source and however defined, had at least four basic applications or meanings in colonial political theory. First, it was a set of moral standards governing private conduct. There were, it was generally believed, certain rules of human behavior discoverable through reason, experience, or revelation. Justinian had reduced these "immutable laws of good and evil" to three blunt commands; the colonists reduced them further to one: the Golden Rule.

For the greatest of all laws that respect mankind, is, to love our neighbours as ourselves, and do as we would be done by.

Prosperity and happiness were the lot of men who obeyed this law, adversity and sadness the lot of men who did not. Since the good state, the state shaped to the laws of nature, rested on good men, men who obeyed the laws of nature, one of the duties of the political community was to encourage virtue and discourage vice. The cult of virtue, of which we have learned already and will learn again, was an intimate corollary of natural law. The virtuous life was the natural life, just as good government was natural government.

The laws of nature formed a system of abstract justice to which the laws of men should conform. Positive law that ran counter to a community's inherited sense of right and wrong was not only bad law but no law at all, for had not Blackstone himself asserted that "no human laws are of any validity if contrary to . . . the law of nature"? The chief business of an assembly was therefore to search proposed legislation for clauses or commands that outraged accepted notions of abstract justice. A law was a good law, one that demanded obedience, if it was "founded on the law of nature." The British Constitution was the greatest of all systems of government because it was "grounded on the eternal and immutable laws of nature."

But the law of nature, at least in American opinion, was something more than a model of perfection to which positive law should conform. It was also a line of demarcation around the proper sphere of political authority. Governments that pushed beyond it did so at peril of resistance or even revolution. Since the greatest and freest of constitutions was an earthly replica of natural law, any violation of it was both unconstitutional and unnatural. The Massachusetts House of Representatives told the other assemblies "that in all free States the Constitution is fixed; & as the supreme Legislative derives its Power & Authority from the Constitution, it cannot overleap the Bounds of it without destroying its own Foundation." This, of course, was Locke's great message: that government must respect the commands of natural law or release men from obedience. In time Americans came to regard natural law as the one clear restriction on Parliament's power to tax or govern the colonies. Since it was "repugnant to the Laws of Nature . . . for the Subjects of one

State to exercise Jurisdiction over those of another," the people of the second state, in this instance the immediate guardians of those laws, must apply whatever sanctions they had at their command.

Finally and most important, natural law was the source of natural rights. A truly free people, wrote Jefferson, would claim "their rights as derived from the laws of nature, and not as the gift of their chief magistrate" or of the community. Thus it became necessary to establish the existence of natural law in order to provide an unbreachable defense for the rights of man. In the final reckoning, natural law came to be equated with natural rights. Most colonists were so intent upon proving that this law was the one great source and defense of their rights that they used these expressions interchangeably.

In basing their final campaign of resistance to imperial power on "the supreme and uncontrollable laws of nature," the American colonists stood firm in one of their greatest traditions. The higher law, whether proceeding from God or nature, had been part of men's thinking since the first settlements. By the time of the Revolution it was a universally accepted article of faith. If hundreds of New England preachers could declaim upon the law of God and nature, certainly their leading seminary of learning could make General Washington a "Doctor of Laws, the Law of Nature and Nations, and the Civil Law." If a philosopher could invoke "the Laws of Nature and of Nature's God" in behalf of a whole people, certainly one of the least of this people, a runaway servant, could invoke them for release from his contract. Bentham might blast natural law as "nothing but a phrase . . . the natural tendency of [which] is to compel a man by the force of conscience, to rise up in arms against any law whatever that he happens not to like," but Americans seemed not the least bit bothered by its inherent inconsistencies and dangers. The mind of God as read by revelation, the plan of nature as analyzed by right reason, and the history of mankind as interpreted by the scholars of the nation all proclaimed the reality of moral limits on political power. If the rest of the world could not agree that certain truths were self-evident, then the rest of the world was simply ignoring the plain dictates of universal justice.

The Nature of Man

A political thinker's appraisal of man's basic character generally determines the direction of his entire line of thought. We have already had occasion to note this fact in the chapter on John Wise, calling attention to the contrasting views of man and consequent contrasting philosophies of Hobbes and Locke and of Calhoun and Jefferson. Revolutionary theorists devoted special attention to this question. Their sermons and pamphlets are full of assumptions and comments about the natural virtues and vices of the men about them. They were bothered not at all by a lack of scientific psychological data; the lessons of history, properly selected, gave support to all possible shadings of opinion.

The American consensus dictated no particular estimate of the nature of man. Patriot philosophers with identical opinions about the location of sovereignty could entertain the most divergent views about the reasoning powers of men, and a single thinker might advance two or three different estimates within the pages of one tract. A good deal depended, of course, upon the author's immediate purpose. An argument for home rule would lead him to sweeping generalizations about self-reliance and sociability. A tirade against the British ministry would evoke equally broad comments about man's vicious nature. We must remember that the colonists were heirs of several great and contradictory traditions. A son of the Puritans who was also a child of the Enlightenment could be indulged a little confusion on this crucial point.

We may reduce the wide range of opinion on the nature of man to three general attitudes. One small group of thinkers, of whom Jefferson was perhaps the boldest, took the "enlightened" view, considering man a naturally good, decent, friendly, capable person whose troubles were the bitter fruit of a world he had never made. Another, to which many Calvinist preachers belonged, clung to doctrines of sin and depravity, preferring to lay stress on "the ignorance, prejudice, partiality and injustice of human nature." Most thinkers settled down, or oscillated, between these two extremes, finding much that was good and much that was bad in the character of every single man. Said the author of a piece entitled "Loose thoughts on GOVERNMENT":

> In whatever situation we take a view of man, whether ranging the forests in the rude state of his primeval existence, or in the smooth situation of polished society; wheresoever we place him, on the burning sands of Africa, the freezing coasts of Labrador, or the more congenial climes of the temperate zones, we shall every where find him the same complex being, a slave to his passions, and tossed and agitated by a thousand disagreeing virtues and discordant vices.

What exactly were those fundamental traits that Revolutionary theorists found ingrained in man? Which ones were most significant for political organization?

Four qualities that our culture considers "good" were given special stress in the literature of the Revolution: *sociability,* the impulse to associate and co-operate with other men in pursuit of common ends; *love of liberty,* which makes it unnatural and therefore impossible for a man to submit to slavery; *goodness,* the quality of basic human decency that inspires every man to "a love of truth, and a veneration of virtue"; and *rationality,* or *"reasonableness,"* the ability to read, understand, and apply "the eternal laws of natural justice, humanity and equity." Five qualities that we would consider "bad" were stressed with equal vigor, as often as not by the same authors who extolled man's goodness: *selfishness,* the impulse to seek one's own happiness even in defiance of the common good; *depravity,* the quality of sinfulness — of jealousy, injustice, anger, ignorance, deceit, vanity, and intemperance — that lurks in every human soul; *passion,* the refusal to be rational, "as natural to men as reason" itself; *moral laziness,* "Inattention to the real Importance of things," which brings men to slavery contrary to nature and their wills; and *corruptibility,* the inevitable result of "the passion for acquiring power" which operates so "forcibly on the human mind." All these "disagreeing virtues and discordant vices" were thought to be present to some degree in every man, no matter how lofty his station or low his character.

Perhaps the most politically significant of all these qualities was sociability, the urge man feels to associate with other men, even if this means surrendering a substantial part of his original freedom. So pointed was the emphasis placed upon "the social Principle in man" that many thinkers excluded the pre-social state of nature, and therefore natural man, from serious consideration. Man was clearly a social animal, a being "formed for social life." If he had a natural state, that state was society, for "'tis clear that men cannot live apart or independent of each other." Society itself was therefore natural, and few men if any could be said to be in it by free choice. Colonial thinkers were understandably confused in this matter, but it seems clear that the most thoughtful of them made a distinction between society and government. The former was the "natural" result of the presence of a number of men in a certain area; the latter was the mechanistic if inevitable result of an act of will. In short, the contract in Revolutionary thought was governmental, not social.

The one other quality deserving special mention was the transformation that is more than likely to come over man when he is placed in a situation of power. Revolutionary theorists generally agreed with Hamilton that "a fondness for power is implanted in most men, and it is natural to abuse it when acquired." "The history of mankind," wrote James Iredell, "unhappily justifies the strongest suspicion of men in authority." "Every man by nature," echoed Rev. Thomas Allen of Pittsfield, "has the seeds of tyranny deeply implanted within him." Although this belief in man's love of power was not nearly so strong or widely advertised as it was later to be in Federalistic political theory, few authors failed to mention it as a human characteristic, and none went out of his way to deny it specifically. The universal American belief in constitutionalism and the rule of law — indeed in the necessity of a written, comprehensible constitution — derived from this suspicious appraisal of man in authority. No one ever spoke more succinctly to this point than Samuel Adams:

> All men are fond of Power. It is difficult for us to be prevaild upon to believe that we possess more than belongs to us. Even pub-

lick Bodies of men legally constituted are too prone to covet more Power than the Publick hath judgd it safe to entrust them with. It is happy when their Power is not only subject to Controul while it is exercisd, but frequently reverts into the hands of the People from whom it is derived, and to whom Men in Power ought for ever to be accountable.

If man was a composite of good and evil, of ennobling excellencies and degrading imperfections, then one of the chief ends of the community was "to separate his virtues from his vices," to help him pursue his better nature. The achievement of this called for two types of collective action: establishing or encouraging institutions, especially religious and political institutions, that would give free play to his virtues while controlling or suppressing his vices; educating him to recognize the sweet harvest of the one and bitter fruits of the other. True religion encouraged man to suppress his savage impulses; constitutional government forced him to think before acting; sound education taught him the delights of virtue and liberty.

The American colonists . . . had always placed special faith in the efficacy of education. The Revolutionists once again stood firm in the ancient ways by insisting almost unanimously:

> Let the people by all means encourage *schools* and *colleges,* and all the means of *learning* and *knowledge,* if they would guard against *slavery.* For a *wise,* a *knowing* and a *learned* people, are the least likely of any in the world to be enslaved.

Whatever disagreement might have existed over man's other natural or social characteristics, all American thinkers conceded him a capacity for learning. Different men could acquire knowledge in different amounts, but all men could acquire the minimum necessary for survival and citizenship. Man was something more than a fortuitous complex of virtues and vices. He was *educable* — he could learn and be taught. More to the point, he could learn why to cherish virtue and shun vice, how to serve the community and defend liberty. Free government rested on virtue, virtue on knowledge, knowledge on regular techniques of education. It was therefore the business of government "to make provision for schools and all suitable means of instruction." The exigencies of the economy, the weight of tradition, and the unsettled state of the times conspired against general acceptance of the doctrine of free and universal public education, but no political thinker doubted the imperative necessity of community action in this crucial area. The eloquent words of Rev. Phillips Payson expressed American thinking about education for liberty:

> The slavery of a people is generally founded in ignorance of some kind or another; and there are not wanting such facts as abundantly prove the human mind may be so sunk and debased, through ignorance and its natural effects, as even to adore its enslaver, and kiss its chains. Hence knowledge and learning may well be considered as most essentially requisite to a free, righteous government. . . .
>
> Every kind of useful knowledge will be carefully encouraged and promoted by the rulers of a free state. . . . The education of youth, by instructors properly qualified, the establishment of societies for useful arts and sciences, the encouragement of persons of superior abilities, will always command the attention of wise rulers.

Political thinkers naturally emphasized the acquisition of political knowledge. Said John Jay on the inauguration of the New York Constitution of 1777:

> Let virtue, honor, the love of liberty and of science be, and remain, the soul of this constitution, and it will become the source of great and extensive happiness to this and future generations. Vice, ignorance, and want of vigilance, will be the only enemies able to destroy it. Against these provide, and, of these, be forever jealous. Every member of the state, ought diligently to read and study the constitution of his country, and teach the rising generation to be free. By knowing their rights, they will sooner perceive when they are violated, and be the better prepared to defend and assert them.

Others called attention to the mutual dependence of liberty and learning. Education and knowledge were as much the effect as the cause of free government. The infant republic could look forward confidently to intellectual splendor. Dr. David Ramsay was one of many who prophesied:

> Every circumstance concurs to make it probable, that the arts and sciences will be cultivated, extended, and improved, in independent America. . . . Our free governments are the proper nurseries of rhetoric, criticism, and the arts which are founded on the philosophy of the human mind. In monarchies, an extreme degree of politeness disguises the simplicity of nature, and "sets the looks at variance with the thoughts;" in republics, mankind appear as they really are, without any false coloring: In these governments, therefore, attentive observers have an opportunity of knowing all the avenues to the heart, and of thoroughly understanding human nature. The great inferiority of the moderns to the ancients in fine writing, is to be referred to this veil cast over mankind by the artificial refinements of modern monarchies. From the operation of similar causes, it is hoped, that the free governments of America will produce poets, orators, critics and historians, equal to the most celebrated of the ancient commonwealths of Greece and Italy.

Many Americans may have smiled at the grandeur of this hope, but few doubted the capacity of "this numerous, brave and hardy people" to learn the rights and duties of citizenship in a free republic. No characteristic of man had more political significance than his innate capacity for instruction in virtue and freedom.

The natural character of man was an alloy of virtue and vice; his natural state was pure freedom and equality. "All men are, by nature, equal and free," wrote James Wilson; "no one has a right to any authority over another without his consent." Revolutionary thinkers were in virtually unanimous accord on this point. Men might be grossly unequal in appearance, talents, intelligence, virtue, and fortune, but to this extent at least they were absolutely equal: No man had any natural right of dominion over any other; every man was free in the sight of God and plan of nature. The ranks and privileges of organized society were the result of unnatural usurpation, faulty institutions, the dead hand of an ignorant past, or the inevitable division of men into rulers and ruled.

The principle of natural equality was not incompatible with political, social, or economic stratification, but the burden of proof was squarely on advocates of artificial inequality. It was for them to demonstrate that an unequal arrangement was essential to the stability, prosperity, or independence of the community. Conversely, the goal of political science was to discover a political pattern that would recreate the equality of rights and near-equality of property that had preceded the formation of government. The glory of a free constitution was that it reduced these social inequalities to the barest minimum and preserved as much natural equality "as is compatible with the people's security against foreign invasion and domestic usurpation."

It is important to note these two aspects of the doctrine of natural equality to which most Revolutionists subscribed: that equality among men existed within a limited sphere, but that within this sphere all men were created absolutely equal. Each had an equal claim to be free of any earthly power; each could be governed only with his consent. In this sense equality was both an essential feature of human relations and an essential principle of libertarian political theory. It was an article of faith, a challenge to constitution-makers, and the central arrangement of political organization. James Otis was not really joking when he wrote in support of natural equality:

> No government has a right to make hobby horses, asses and slaves of the subject, nature having made sufficient of the two former, for all the lawful purposes of man, from the harmless peasant in the field, to the most refined politician in the cabinet; but none of the last, which infallibly proves they are unnecessary.

The Natural Rights of Man

No political theory, however detached or speculative, ever ranges in perfect symmetry over all great questions of power, organization, and obedience. The political theorist concentrates inevitably upon the problems of his own civilization. His theoretical structure is proportioned to "the felt necessities" of the age rather than to a standard, timeless pattern in which every possible question receives its just due. The political theorists of the Revolution were no exception to this rule. Heirs of a great tradition of personal liberty, children of an age concerned with the individual rather than the community, targets of a policy that seemed to defy the dictates of abstract justice, they used up most of their energy defining the rights of man and devising methods of protecting them. They were individualists because the individual was under fire, limitationists because a government had overleaped its limits, constitutionalists because the existence of their constitution hung in the balance. Above all, they were exponents of natural rights. A legislature claiming the power to bind them in all cases whatsoever had moved decisively against their liberty and property, and they meant to stand and fight this invasion on the broadest possible ground.

The doctrine of natural rights was therefore the hard core of Revolutionary political theory. Like almost all other exponents of higher law, Americans gave this law a content and meaning that suited their practical purpose. The natural rights of man were so useful, even essential, to this purpose that they were willing to equate them with natural law itself. The rights of man, that is to say, not only depended upon or sprang from natural law; they *were* natural law, at least so far as it could be understood by men. In the political theory of the American Revolution natural law was all but swallowed up in natural rights. The dictates, indeed the content, of "the supreme and uncontrollable laws of nature" became "the *absolute* rights of individuals." If a man wished to follow the path of universal justice, he had only to understand and respect these rights. In our own effort to understand the doctrine of natural rights as expounded in the pre-Revolutionary decade we must seek answers to these questions: What exactly was meant by the phrase "natural rights"? What was the source of these rights? What specific rights of man were covered by this concept?

By natural rights the Revolutionists meant simply those rights which belong to man as man. They used several adjectives in addition to "natural" to express the special quality of these rights. They were *natural,* traceable directly to the great plan of nature if not indeed derived from "the great Legislator of the universe"; *absolute,* belonging to man before, outside of, and quite without regard to organized government or society; *eternal,* never varying in content or identity; *essential,* since necessary to man's existence as man; and *unalienable* (or inalienable), "of that importance, that no equivalent can be received in exchange." Inherent, universal, unalterable, inestimable, sacred, indefeasible, fundamental, imprescriptible, divine, God-given, hereditary, and indelible were other adjectives used to stamp the natural rights of mankind with transcendent significance. In the heat of the struggle over the authority of Parliament, some American authors carelessly or designedly confused natural rights with civil or constitutional rights. But more serious thinkers like Otis, Hamilton, and Parsons expressed the true sense of the patriot school when they distinguished those rights which were natural, absolute, eternal, essential, and unalienable from those which were constitutional, civil, social, or relative. The fact or fiction of the state of nature was especially serviceable in clearing up this confusion. In the last analysis, natural rights were different from civil or constitutional rights because they had belonged to man in the state of nature. He had brought them with him into society. He had brought them with him into government. And he would take them with him should he ever return to the state of nature or of natural society. In any case, a fundamental article of the American faith was the belief that every man — no matter what his station, calling, learning, and fortune — had certain natural, unalienable rights. These were "antecedent to all earthly government," incapable of being surrendered to government, and identified with nature or with God himself. Perhaps most important to patriot purposes, they served as the ultimate standard for human laws and the ultimate check upon arbitrary power.

The sources of natural rights were the sources of natural law: God, nature, or history. For the most part colonial theorists were willing to merge God and nature into one magnificent and consecrated source. An occasional author, especially if he occupied a dissenting pulpit, might speak specifically of "natural liberty" as "a gift of the beneficent Creator to the whole human race," but most would have agreed with John

Dickinson's message to the Committee of Correspondence in Barbados:

> Kings or parliaments could not *give* the *rights essential to happiness,* as you confess those invaded by the Stamp Act to be. We claim them from a higher source — from the King of kings, and Lord of all the earth. They are not annexed to us by parchments and seals. They are created in us by the decrees of Providence, which establish the laws of our nature. They are born with us; exist with us; and cannot be taken from us by any human power, without taking our lives. In short, they are founded on the immutable maxims of reason and justice.

Men like Hamilton and Jefferson might have wished to ignore or at least neutralize the hand of God, but they, like Dickinson, were always careful to mention both God and nature. No passage in Revolutionary literature is more justly famous than Hamilton's flamboyant escape from the trap of the Tory argument that New York had no charter and New Yorkers therefore no charter rights:

> THE SACRED RIGHTS OF MANKIND ARE NOT TO BE RUMMAGED FOR AMONG OLD PARCHMENTS OR MUSTY RECORDS. THEY ARE WRITTEN, AS WITH A SUNBEAM, IN THE WHOLE VOLUME OF HUMAN NATURE, BY THE HAND OF THE DIVINITY ITSELF, AND CAN NEVER BE ERASED OR OBSCURED BY MORTAL POWER.

A few writers described the rights of man as "hard-earned." John Adams in particular went deep into the past to remind his readers that these rights, although traceable to God and nature, had in fact been secured in laws and constitutions only after the most bitter struggles against despotism and indifference. He who wished to identify those rights which no government should touch must look not only to "the nature of man" but to the "history of nations." Throughout the political theory of this history-conscious people runs this implicit assumption: Natural and unalienable rights are those basic liberties which are enjoyed and respected wherever men are free, prosperous, and happy. Washington was thinking of rights as the legacy of history rather than the gift of God when he wrote the state governors:

> The foundation of our empire was not laid in the gloomy age of ignorance and superstition; but at an epocha when the rights of mankind were better understood and more clearly defined, than at any former period. The researches of the human mind after social happiness have been carried to a great extent; the treasures of knowledge, acquired by the labors of philosophers, sages, and legislators, through a long succession of years, are laid open for our use, and their collective wisdom may be happily applied in the establishment of our forms of government.

What were these rights which man possessed as man and could never surrender? In the pamphlets, sermons, and documents of this decade almost every conceivable human right — including the right to brew beer at home — was proclaimed to be natural, unalienable, and essential to the good society. But in works that were more political theory than propaganda we find these rights singled out as the legitimate posession of all men everywhere: life, liberty, property, conscience, and happiness.

The right to life was so far above dispute that authors were content merely to mention it in passing. Blackstone had not been able to say much more than that it was "the immediate gift of God, a right inherent by nature in every individual," and no American was going to improve on that celebrated man of the law. The strategic importance of the right to life lay in its great corollary or defense: the law or right of self-preservation. This secondary right made it possible for a single man or a whole nation to meet force with force, to resist all arbitrary invasions of life, liberty, and property.

The natural right to liberty was central to all other rights, and the literature of the Revolution is full of salutes to its blessings and excellencies. "Liberty!" had been the American watchword for so many generations that no author, Whig or Tory, ever doubted in print that it was "in some degree . . . the right of every human creature." Indeed, man without natural liberty was a contradiction in terms. "The god who gave us life," wrote Jefferson to George III, "gave us liberty at the same time." Liberty was defined simply as the freedom and power of each individual to act as he pleased "without restraint or control." From this natural liberty, the freedom from "obligation to obedience," flowed all other liberties that men enjoyed in society.

The colonists, of course, were concerned about specific liberties in the political community rather than the original liberty of man in the state of nature. Most of their discussions of liberty are therefore somewhat confused. Yet we can discover common ideas about natural liberty in even the most occasional apostrophes. A good example of the way in which the colonial theorist dealt with liberty is this communication to "The Sentinel" in the *New-York Gazette:*

> Liberty, as it is the honour and glory of a nation, so also it is their pleasure and happiness. There is not perhaps one temporal blessing bestowed by the supreme being on mankind that is more agreeable when enjoyed; more difficult to be parted with; or more desirable when absent. A love for Liberty seems interwoven with our very nature; and we are always ready to pronounce a people happy or miserable in proportion as they are possessed or destitute of it. . . . There is perhaps nothing in this life more essential to our happiness. It is the state for which we are naturally calculated. It is what we all desire. The absence of it produces positive pain, as well as the presence of it positive happiness. It is the fountain of wealth, and of all real honours. For I cannot conceive of any true dignity a Slave can enjoy; for although he commands a thousand or ten thousand others, he is yet but a Slave himself.

Colonial theorists, even the holders of slaves, concurred generally with this author's assumption that all men were naturally free. Most arguments for abolition of Negro slavery advanced in this decade were based on the doctrine of natural, unalienable liberty.

Perhaps the most interesting subsidiary right that Revolutionary pamphleteers deduced from natural liberty was

> a right, which nature has given to all men, of departing from the country in which chance, not choice has placed them, of going in quest of new habitations, and of there establishing new societies, under such laws and regulations as to them shall seem most likely to promote public happiness.

The natural right of migration was extremely useful to the cause, since it permitted colonists to argue that their ancestors had left England as free agents and had made a fresh contract with the sovereign left behind. Bland and Jefferson were the two most vocal exponents of this radical doctrine, and each made clear that "the natural right of an individual to remove his person and effects wherever he pleases" was a direct corollary of the essential freedom stamped indelibly on man's nature. The hardy migrants of Vermont placed this statement in their first Declaration of Rights:

> All people have a natural and inherent right to emigrate from one State to another, that will receive them; or to form a new State in vacant countries, or in such countries as they can purchase, whenever they think that thereby they can promote their own happiness.

The right to acquire and enjoy property was universally acclaimed in the literature of the Revolution. "The law of nature," wrote "Sidney" in the Norfolk *Virginia Gazette,* "being founded in reason and justice admits of property." Samuel Adams spoke for all American publicists when he told General Conway, "It is acknowledged to be an unalterable law in nature, that a man should have the free use and sole disposal of the fruit of his honest industry, subject to no controul." And elsewhere:

> It is observable, that though many have disregarded life, and contemned liberty, yet there are few men who do not agree that property is a valuable acquisition, which ought to be held sacred. Many have fought, and bled, and died for this, who have been insensible to all other obligations. Those who ridicule the ideas of right and justice, faith and truth among men, will put a high value upon money. Property is admitted to have an existence, even in the savage state of nature. The bow, the arrow, and the tomahawk; the hunting and the fishing ground, are species of property, as important to an American savage, as pearls, rubies, and diamonds are to the Mogul, or a Nabob in the East, or the lands, tenements, hereditaments, messuages, gold and silver of the Europeans. And if property is necessary for the support

of savage life, it is by no means less so in civil society.

Although Locke had several times used the word "property" in the broad sense of everything a man is or has, colonists limited their definition to ownership of things tangible or at least convertible to money. Property in this sense was so essential to the fulfillment of man's promise and powers that it could almost be equated with liberty itself. If Locke included liberty in his definition of property, colonists included property in their definition of liberty. As one anonymous contributor to "The Weekly Dung-Barge" put it, "*Liberty* and *Property* are not only join'd in common discourse, but are in their own natures so nearly ally'd that we cannot be said to possess the one without the enjoyment of the other." This was not because Americans were more materialistic than other people. Quite the contrary, their primary, long-range concern was with political and spiritual aspects of human freedom. But the crisis of the moment, to which their theorizing was directed, was an unprecedented invasion of the right to dispose of property without compulsion: that is, the right of men to be taxed only by representatives of their own choosing. The colonists were no more obsessed than their ancestors or descendants with the great right of "virtuous enjoyment and free possession of property honestly gained." Few thinkers ever doubted, however, that it was a natural right of man, and not a right granted by society. The town of Newburyport spoke for all America when it lectured its representative to the General Assembly:

> That a People should be taxed at the Will of another, whether of one Man or many, without their own Consent in Person or by Representative, is *rank* Slavery. For if their Superior sees fit, they may be deprived of their whole Property, upon any frivolous Pretext, or without any Pretext at all. And a People, without Property, or in the precarious Possession of it, are in no better State than Slaves; for Liberty, or even Life itself, without the Enjoyment of them flowing from Property, are of no Value.

Only two other rights — the right of conscience and the right to happiness — were ever placed by more than one or two authors at the same level of sanctity and universality with life, liberty, and property. In one sense, of course, each of these rights was simply a derivative of natural liberty. Yet, in another and more important sense, they were considered to have an existence of their own. Each was essential to the full expression of man's inherent nature; each was plainly antecedent to society and government. The right to happiness — or at least to pursue happiness without interference — was a logical assumption in the political theory of men to whom rationalism had made a triumphant appeal. Happiness rather than salvation seemed now to be man's chief obsession. Through all the writings of men like Wilson, R. H. Lee, Jefferson, Iredell, and Mayhew runs a firm belief that "the Creator surely wills the happiness of his Creatures," that "God did not make men to be unhappy,"

> that mankind were intended to be happy, at least that God gave them the power of being so, if they would properly exert the means He has bestowed upon them.

Or as Dickinson put it:

> It would be an insult on the divine Majesty to say, that he has given or allowed any man or body of men *a right to make me miserable*. If no man or body of men has *such a right*, I have a *right to be happy*. If there can be no happiness without freedom, I have a *right to be free*.

Jefferson was more than a felicitous penman when he proclaimed the "pursuit of happiness" to be a natural right of man, for by the time of the Declaration most thinkers agreed with him on this point. He was, however, something of a nonconformist in substituting this right for that of property. He alone flirted seriously with the advanced view that property was a social rather than natural right.

The right of conscience, the right of each individual to reach out for God without interference or even assistance from other men, was naturally of prime interest to a people well on the way to full religious liberty. William Livingston reminded his fellow countrymen in these angry words that political interference with a man's religious opinions was a violation of the commands of natural justice:

> Who, in a state of nature, ever dreamed it an inconvenience that every man should choose his own religion? Did the free denizens of the world . . . ever worry one another for not practising ridiculous rites, or for believing things incredible? Did men in their aboriginal condition ever suffer persecution for conscience sake? The most frantic enthusiast will not pretend it. Why then should the members of society be supposed, on their entering into it, to have had in contemplation the reforming an abuse which never existed?

The men of the Revolution may have been given to fantastic hyperbole and astounding ambiguity in discussing their rights and privileges, but there can be no doubt of their sincerity and conviction in placing special value on these five rights: life, liberty, property, happiness, and conscience.

4

Historians and the Revolution

I

The Origin of the Disputes between Great Britain and her Colonies

David Ramsay's *credentials as a historian of the American Revolution are not, at first glance, very impressive. He was a physician, and few medical men have written history with great success; he was a participant in the Revolution, and few participants write good history of the events which they help to shape. And yet Ramsay was a dispassionate and effective writer. His* History of the Revolution of South-Carolina *(2 vols., 1785) excited the admiration of Thomas Jefferson, who arranged for the work's translation and publication in France.*

Ramsay's History of the American Revolution *(2 vols.) was first published in Philadelphia in 1789 and is notable on several counts, as Page Smith's splendid article will detail. Ramsay was sensitive to the impact of the pamphlet campaign that preceded independence: "the pen and the press had merit equal to that of the sword." He gave proper credit to the British for their facility for alienating colonial friends. He drew attention to the formidable task of the revolutionary leadership in both arousing and sustaining popular feelings against the most powerful of imperial nations. The latter, Ramsay observed, was "effected in a great measure by the tongues and pens of the well informed citizens, and on it depended the success of the military operations."*

It is to Ramsay's credit that he could see both sides of the controversy, that he took no satisfaction in its bloody consequences; he did not know precisely where Parliament's power should leave off and colonial sovereignty begin: "happy would it have been had the question never been agitated, but much more so, had it been compromised by an amicable compact, without the horrors of a civil war."

Reprinted from David Ramsay, *The History of the American Revolution* (London, 1793), I, pp. 50–56.

Immediately after the peace of Paris, 1763, a new scene was opened. The national debt of Great Britain then amounted to 148 millions, for which an interest of nearly five millions was annually paid. While the British Minister was digesting plans for diminishing this amazing load of debt, he conceived the idea of raising a substantial revenue in the British Colonies, from taxes laid by the Parliament of the Parent State. On the one hand it was urged, that the late war originated on account of the Colonies — that it was reasonable, more especially as it had terminated in a manner so favourable to their interest, that they should contribute to the defraying of the expences it had occasioned. Thus far both parties were agreed; but Great Britain contended, that her Parliament, as the supreme power, was constitutionally vested with an authority to lay them on every part of the empire. This doctrine, plausible in itself, and conformable to the letter of the British constitution, when the whole dominions were represented in one assembly, was reprobated in the Colonies, as contrary to the spirit of the same government, when the empire became so far extended, as to have many distinct representative assemblies. The Colonists believed that the chief excellence of the British constitution consisted in the right of the subjects to grant, or withhold taxes, and in their having a share in enacting the laws by which they were to be bound.

They conceived, that the superiority of the British constitution, to other forms of government was, not because their supreme council was called a Parliament, but because the people had a share in it by appointing members, who constituted one of its constituent branches, and without whose concurrence, no law, binding on them, could be enacted. In the Mother Country, it was asserted to be essential to the unity of the empire, that the British Parliament should have a right of taxation over every part of the royal dominions. In the Colonies, it was believed, that taxation and representation were inseparable, and that they could neither be free nor happy if their property could be taken from them without their consent. The common people in America reasoned on this subject in a summary way: "If a British Parliament," said they, "in which we are unrepresented, and over which we have no controul, can take from us any part of our property, by direct taxation, they may take as much as they please, and we have no security for any thing that remains, but a forbearance on their part, less likely to be exercised in our favour, as they lighten themselves of the burthens of government, in the same proportion that they impose them on us." They well knew, that communities of mankind, as well as individuals, have a strong propensity to impose on others, when they can do it with impunity, and, especially, when there is a prospect, that the imposition will be attended with advantage to themselves. The Americans, from that jealousy of their liberties which their local situation nurtured, and which they inherited from their forefathers, viewed the exclusive right of laying taxes on themselves, free from extraneous influence, in the same light as the British Parliament views its peculiar privilege of raising money, independent of the crown. The Parent State appeared to the Colonists to stand in the same relation to their local legislatures, as the monarch of Great Britain to the British Parliament. His prerogative is limited by that palladium of the people's liberty, the exclusive privilege of granting their own money. While this right rests in the hands of the people, their liberties are secured. In the same manner reasoned the Colonists, "in order to be stiled freemen, our local assemblies, elected by ourselves, must enjoy the exclusive privilege of imposing taxes upon us." They contended, that men settled in foreign parts to better their condition, and not to submit their liberties — to continue the equals, not to become the slave of their less adventurous fellow-citizens, and that by the novel doctrine of parliamentary power, they were degraded from being the subjects of a King, to the low condition of being subjects of subjects. They argued, that it was essentially involved in the idea of property, that the possessor had such a right therein, that it was a contradiction to suppose any other man, or body of men, possessed a right to take it from him without his consent. Precedents, in the History of England, justified this mode of reasoning. The love of property strengthened it, and it had a peculiar force on the minds of Colonists, 3000 miles removed from the seat of government, and growing up to maturity, in a new world, where, from the extent of country, and the state of society, even the necessary restraints of civil government were impatiently borne. On the other hand, the people of Great Britain revolted against the claims of the Colonists. Educated in habits of submission to parliamentary taxation, they conceived it to be the height of contumacy for their Colonists to refuse obedience to the power, which they had been taught to revere. Not adverting to the common interest which existed between the people of Great Britain and their representatives, they believed, that the same right existed, although the same community of interests was wanting. The pride of an opulent, conquering nation, aided this mode of reasoning. "What," said they, "shall we, who have so lately humbled France and Spain, be dictated to by our own Colonists? Shall our subjects, educated by our care, and defended by our arms, presume to question the rights of Parliament, to which we are obliged to submit?" Reflections of this kind, congenial to the natural vanity of the human heart, operated so extensively, that the people of Great Britain spoke of their Colonies and of their Colonists, as a kind of possession annexed to their persons. The love of power and of property on the one side of the Atlantic were opposed by the same powerful passions on the other.

The disposition to tax the Colonies was also strengthened by exaggerated accounts of their wealth. It was said, "that the American planters lived in affluence, and with inconsiderable taxes, while the inhabitants of Great Britain were borne down by such oppressive burdens as to make a bare subsistence a matter of extreme difficulty." The officers who have served in America, during the late war, contributed to this delusion. Their observations were founded on what they had seen in cities, and at a time, when large sums were spent by government, in support of fleets and armies, and when American commodities were in great demand. To treat with attention those who came to fight for them, and also to gratify their own pride, the Colonists had made a parade of their riches, by frequently and sumptuously entertaining the gentlemen of the British army. These, judging from what they saw, without considering the general state of the country, concurred in representing the Colonists as very able to contribute largely towards defraying the common expences of the empire.

The charters, which were supposed to contain the principles on which the Colonies were founded, became the subject of serious investigation on both sides. One clause was found to run through the whole of them, except that which had been granted to Mr. Penn; this was a declaration, "that the emigrants to America should enjoy the same privileges, as if they had remained, or had been born within the realm;" but such was the subtilty of disputants, that both parties construed this general principle so as to favour their respective opinions. The American patriots contended, that as English freeholders could not be taxed but by representatives, in chusing whom they had a vote, neither could the Colonists: but it was replied, that if the Colonists had remained in England, they must have been bound to pay the taxes imposed by Parliament. It was therefore inferred, that though taxed by that authority, they lost none of the rights of native Englishmen residing at home. The partisans of the Mother Country could see nothing in charters, but security against taxes by royal authority. The Americans, adhering to the spirit more than to the letter, viewed their charters as a shield against all taxes, not imposed by representatives of their own choice. This construction they contended to be expressly recognized by the charter of Maryland. In that, King Charles bound both himself and his successors, not to assent to any bill, subjecting the inhabitants to internal taxation by external legislation.

The nature and extent of the connection between Great Britain and America was a great constitutional question, involving many interests, and the general principles of civil liberty. To decide this, recourse was in vain had to parchment authorities, made at a distant time, when neither the grantors nor grantees of American territory had in contemplation any thing like the present state of the two countries.

Great and flourishing Colonies, daily increasing in numbers, and already grown to the magnitude of a nation, planted at an immense distance, and governed by constitutions resembling that of the country from which they sprung, were novelties in the history of the world. To combine Colonies, so circumstanced, in one uniform system of government with the Parent State, required a great knowledge of mankind, and an extensive comprehension of things. It was an arduous business, far beyond the grasp of ordinary statement, whose minds were narrowed by the formalities of laws, or the trammels of office. An original genius, unfettered with precedents, and exalted with just ideas of the rights of human nature, and the obligations of universal benevolence, might have struck out a middle line, which would have secured as much liberty to the Colonies, and as great a degree of supremacy to the Parent State, as their common good required: But the helm of Great Britain was not in such hands. The spirit of the British constitution on the one hand revolted at the idea, that the British Parliament should exercise the same unlimited authority over the unrepresented Colonies, which it exercised over the inhabitants of Great Britain. The Colonists on the other hand did not claim a total exemption from its authority. They in general allowed the Mother Country a certain undefined prerogative over them, and acquiesced in the right of Parliament to make many acts, binding them in many subjects of internal policy, and regulating their trade. Where parliamentary supremacy ended, and at what point colonial independency began, was not ascertained. Happy would it have been had the question never been agitated, but much more so, had it been compromised by an amicable compact, without the horrors of a civil war.

The English Colonies were originally established, not for the sake of revenue, but on the principles of a commercial monopoly. While England pursued trade and forgot revenue, her commerce increased at least fourfold. The Colonies took off the manufactures of Great Britain, and paid for them with provisions or raw materials. They united their arms in war, their commerce and their councils in peace, without nicely investigating the terms on which the connection of the two countries depended.

A perfect calm in the political world is not long to be expected. The reciprocal happiness, both of Great Britain and of the Colonies, was too great to be of long duration. The calamities of the war of 1755 had scarcely ended, when the germ of another war was planted, which soon grew up and produced deadly fruit.

At that time sundry resolutions passed the British Parliament relative to the imposition of a stamp duty in America, which gave a general alarm. By them the right, the equity, the policy, and even the necessity of taxing the Colonies was formally avowed. These resolutions being considered as the preface of a system of American revenue, were deemed an introduction to evils of much greater magnitude. They opened a prospect of oppression, boundless in extent, and endless in duration. They were nevertheless not immediately followed by any legislative act. Time and an invitation were given to the Americans to suggest any other mode of taxation that might be equivalent in its produce to the stamp act: but they objected, not only to the mode, but the principle, and several of their assemblies, though in vain, petitioned against it. An American revenue was in England a very popular measure. The cry in favour of it was so strong, as to confound and silence the voice of petitions to the contrary. The equity of compelling the Americans to contribute to the common expences of the empire satisfied many, who, without inquiring into the policy or justice of taxing their unrepresented fellow-subjects, readily assented to the measures adopted by the Parliament for this purpose. The prospect of easing their own burdens, at the expence of the Colonists, dazzled the eyes of gentlemen of landed interest so as to keep out of their view the probable consequences of the innovation.

The omnipotence of Parliament was so familiar a phrase on both sides of the Atlantic, that few in America, and still fewer in Great Britain, were impressed in the first instance, with any idea of the illegality of taxing the Colonists.

II

David Ramsay and the Causes of the American Revolution

Apart from the Civil War of 1861–1865, probably no event has attracted the attention of more American historians than the Revolution. It is a familiar adage that each generation writes its own history and that the historical product reflects the intellectual temper of the times. Page Smith, *formerly professor of history at the University of California, Los Angeles, and now Provost of the University of California, Santa Cruz, has himself contributed to the steadily increasing number of Revolution-related histories.*[1] *But in examining David Ramsay's* History of the American Revolution, *Dr. Smith is somewhat less concerned with this early appraisal of the Revolution than with reviewing the strange*

Page Smith, "David Ramsay and the Causes of the American Revolution," from *The William and Mary Quarterly*, 3d Ser., XVII (1960), 51–77.

[1] See Page Smith, *James Wilson; Founding Father, 1742–1798* (1956), and *John Adams* (2 vols., 1962).

course of historical interpretations since Ramsay's work appeared.

For modern-day students, it is useful to make Ramsay's acquaintance, but it is particularly enlightening to have so succinct a review of the historiography of the American Revolution and to encounter anew the shifting interpretations and emphases historians of the Revolution have supplied. Whether Dr. Smith's account proves the need for a healthier respect for contemporary history can be questioned. It does *demonstrate the quality of David Ramsay as a historian. But will the next generation recognize Ramsay's as "the best contemporary history"?*

Much attention has been given recently to the changes that have taken place since the late eighteenth century in historians' interpretations of the causes of the American Revolution.[1] In the same spirit, the causes of the Civil War, the character of Jacksonianism, Woodrow Wilson's New Freedom, and the origins of World War I have all been re-examined. If "revisionism" may be taken as reinterpretation of the generally accepted causes, or significance, or both, of a historical event, the new preoccupation of the historical profession seems to be with the history of successive revisions and is characterized by an effort to relate changing interpretations to the changing times.

Re-examination of the attitudes of successive generations of historians toward the causes of the American Revolution poses most explicitly the problem of historical method. For the thesis of this essay is that the best interpretation of the causes of the Revolution was made in the decade following the treaty of peace in 1783 and that thereafter, as we moved further in time from the dramatic events of the Revolution and brought to bear on the problem all the vast resources of modern scholarship, we moved further and further from the truth about our Revolutionary beginnings.

Among the generation of historians who themselves lived through the era of the American Revolution, David Ramsay is pre-eminent, though by no means atypical. Ramsay (1749–1815) was born in Pennsylvania of Scottish Presbyterian parents and attended the College of New Jersey where his friend Benjamin Rush said of him that he was "far superior to any person we ever graduated at our college . . . I can promise more for him, in every thing, than I could for myself."[2] After graduating from Princeton, Ramsay moved to Charleston, South Carolina, where he began the practice of medicine. He was a prominent patriot, serving in the Continental Congress and taking an active part in the political life of his state.

By all reasonable standards Ramsay, as an actor in those violent times, should have written in an extreme and partisan spirit: caught up in the excitement and emotionalism of the Revolutionary crisis in which England appeared as tyrant and oppressor, he had none of that perspective in time supposedly requisite for an objective and impartial treatment; he had no training as a historian and made no boast of impartiality; the passions which the war aroused had had little time to cool when he began his work; his *History of the American Revolution,* moreover, had a frankly didactic purpose — completed just as the delegates to the Federal Convention finished their work on the Federal Constitution, it was designed to awaken Americans to their responsibilities as citizens under the new government. Finally, he, like many of his fellow eighteenth-century historians, drew heavily and without specific citation from the *Annual Register*. Yet, with all these handicaps (from the viewpoint of orthodox historiography), Ramsay's history is a remarkable achievement. In his analysis and interpretation of the events culminating in the Revolution he showed unusual insight and a keen sense of proportion.

In considering the causes of the conflict between Great Britain and the colonists, Ramsay went back to examine the Puritan attitudes toward church and state, finding in Puritan theology a tradition of opposition to tyranny, which was considered to be contrary "to nature,

[1] Edmund S. Morgan, "The American Revolution: Revisions in Need of Revising," *William and Mary Quarterly,* 3d Ser., XIV (1957), 3–15.

[2] *Letters of Benjamin Rush,* ed. Lyman Butterfield (Princeton, 1951), I, 220.

reason, and revelation."[3] More important in nourishing a spirit of independence in the American colonies, however, was the fact that "the prerogatives of royalty and dependence on the Mother Country, were but feebly impressed on the colonial forms of government." In charter and proprietary colonies the Crown delegated broad powers, and even in the royal provinces the King exercised no more control over the colonists "than over their fellow subjects in England." Thus, "from the acquiescence of the parent state [in the growth of self-government], the spirit of her constitution, and daily experience, the Colonists grew up in a belief, that their local assemblies stood in the same relation to them, as the Parliament of Great Britain to the inhabitants of that island. The benefits of legislation were conferred on both, only through these constitutional channels." In this situation, the colonists claimed as part of their birthright all the benefits of the British constitution, chief among which was that "the people could not be compelled to pay any taxes, nor be bound by any laws, but such as had been granted or enacted by the consent of themselves, or of their representatives."[4]

England had not markedly interfered with the colonists' economic welfare either. Indeed, "the wise and liberal policy of England towards her Colonies, during the first century and a half after their settlement" had exalted them to the pre-eminence they enjoyed at the beginning of the crisis with the Mother Country. England had given the Americans "full liberty to govern themselves by such laws as the local legislatures thought necessary, and left their trade open to every individual in her dominions. She also gave them the amplest permission to pursue their respective interests in such manner as they thought proper, and reserved little for herself, but the benefit of their trade, and that of political union under the same head."[5] Great Britain, Ramsay added, "without charging herself with the care of their internal police, or seeking a revenue from [the colonies], . . . contented herself with a monopoly of their trade. She treated them as a judicious mother does her dutiful children. They shared in every privilege belonging to her native sons, and but slightly felt the inconveniences of subordination. Small was the catalogue of grievances, with which even democratical jealousy charged the Parent State" prior to the Revolutionary crisis. It was Ramsay's conviction that "The good resulting to the Colonies, from their connection with Great Britain, infinitely outweighed the evil."[6]

Among the causes contributing to the breach with Great Britain were such subtle factors as "the distance of America from Great-Britain which generated ideas in the minds of the Colonists favourable to liberty." Moreover, the religion of the great majority of the colonists "nurtured a love for liberty. They were chiefly Protestants, and all Protestantism is founded on a strong claim to natural liberty, and the right of private judgement." There were, in addition, intellectual currents in the age which encouraged libertarian ideals. "The reading of those Colonists who were inclined to books, generally favoured the cause of liberty. . . . Their books were generally small in size, and few in number: a great part of them consisted of those fashionable authors, who have defended the cause of liberty. Cato's letters, the Independent Whig, and such productions, were common in one extreme of the Colonies, while in the other, histories of the Puritans kept alive the remembrance of the sufferings of their forefathers, and inspired a warm attachment, both to the civil and the religious rights of human nature."[7]

The social development of the colonies was likewise, in Ramsay's view, congenial to "a spirit of liberty and independence. Their inhabitants were all of one rank . . . from their first settlements, the English Provinces received impressions favourable to democratic forms of government. . . . A sameness of circumstances and occupations created a great sense of equality, and disposed them to union in any common cause from the success of which, they might expect to partake of equal advantages."[8] The

[3] David Ramsay, *History of the American Revolution,* 1st ed. (Philadelphia, 1789), (London, 1793), I, 8–9. The latter edition is cited throughout this essay.

[4] *Ibid.,* I, 20.

[5] *Ibid.,* I, 17–18.

[6] *Ibid.,* I, 42, 43.

[7] *Ibid.,* I, 29, 30.

[8] *Ibid.,* I, 31, 32–33.

vast majority of the colonists were farmers. "The merchants, mechanics, and manufacturers, taken collectively, did not amount to one fifteenth of the whole number of inhabitants," Ramsay pointed out, adding in characteristically Jeffersonian terms that while "the cultivators of the soil depend on nothing but Heaven and their own industry, other classes of men contract more or less of servility, from depending on the caprice of their customers."[9]

Against this background of maturing colonies, constitutional usage, libertarian ideas, and social equality, the British ministers undertook to tighten the lead strings by which the colonists had heretofore been so loosely guided. The decision of Parliament and the ministers of the Crown to attempt to raise a revenue in the American colonies destroyed at one blow "the guards which the constitution had placed round property, and the fences, which the ancestors of both countries had erected against arbitrary power."[10]

The reaction of the colonists to the Stamp Act was prompt, if unexpected. While the tax worked no considerable hardship on the colonists, public resistance was widespread and apparently spontaneous. The issue was not primarily an economic one, but one of principle — the principle of no taxation without representation for which the Revolution would eventually be fought. The Stamp Act aroused the sentiment for liberty among the Americans as no other pre-Revolutionary issue, and, in Ramsay's words, it became "evident, from the determined opposition of the Colonies, that it could not be enforced without a civil war. . . ."[11]

With the repeal of the Stamp Act, the colonies, "instead of feeling themselves dependent on Great Britain, . . . conceived that, in respect to commerce, she was dependent on them." They were thus "inspired with such high ideas of the importance of their trade, that they considered the Mother Country to be brought under greater obligations to them, for purchasing her manufactures, than they were to her for protection and the administration of civil government." The upshot of repeal was that "the freemen of British America, . . . conceived it to be within their power, by future combinations, at any time to convulse, if not to bankrupt, the nation from which they sprung."[12]

In America, the Revolutionary stage was set. What of England after the Stamp Act? In Ramsay we do not find what we have every reason to expect — a devil theory of the Revolution in which George III and his ministers appear as the malevolent instruments of tyranny and oppression. Pride and inflexibility were the principal shortcomings of the British. " 'What,' said they, 'shall we, who have so lately humbled France and Spain, be dictated to by our own Colonists? Shall our subjects, educated by our care, and defended by our arms, presume to question the rights of Parliament, to which we are obliged to submit?' . . . The love of power and of property on the one side of the Atlantic were opposed to the same powerful passions on the other."[13]

The British task was, at best, not an easy one. "Great and flourishing Colonies . . . already grown to the magnitude of a nation, planted at an immense distance, and governed by constitutions resembling that of the country from which they sprung, were novelties in the history of the world," Ramsay pointed out. "To combine Colonies, so circumstanced, in one uniform system of government with the Parent State, required a great knowledge of mankind, and an extensive comprehension of things. It was an arduous business, far beyond the grasp of ordinary state[smen], whose minds were narrowed by the formalities of laws, or the trammels of office. An original genius, unfettered with precedents, and exalted with just ideas of the rights of human nature, and the obligations of universal benevolence, might have struck out a middle line, which would have secured as much liberty to the Colonies, and as great a degree of supremacy to the Parent State, as their common good required: But the helm of Great Britain was not in such hands."[14]

Ramsay here offers us no evil George III, no tyrannical ministers, no demons and oppressors, but simply well-meaning men caught in a situa-

[9] *Ibid.*, I, 33.
[10] *Ibid.*, I, 47.
[11] *Ibid.*, I, 71.
[12] *Ibid.*, I, 74–75.
[13] *Ibid.*, I, 52–53.
[14] *Ibid.*, I, 54–55.

tion too complex and demanding for their very average talents. His wise and temperate assessment of the British failure has not been improved on. Ramsay here demonstrated not vast research labors but an unusual sense of proportion and capacity for analysis.

Remarkably sensitive to all currents in the tide of Revolutionary agitation, Ramsay paid due attention to the economic motif. Many Americans, he pointed out, especially among the merchant class, found it profitable to oppose British measures. The reaction of the merchants to the threatened importation of East India tea was, in his view, motivated by their fear of losing a profitable trade in smuggled tea. "They doubtless conceived themselves to be supporting the rights of their country, by refusing to purchase tea from Britain," Ramsay wrote, "but they also reflected that if they could bring the same commodity to market, free from duty, their profits would be proportionately greater." Hence the merchants took the lead in denouncing the dutied tea. But "though the opposition originated in the selfishness of the merchants, it did not end there." When the Tea Act of 1773 was passed, the majority of colonists opposed Great Britain on the ground of "principle." They saw it as a scheme "calculated to seduce them into an acquiescence with the views of Parliament for raising an American revenue."[15] In accepting the cheaper tea, they would be accepting the tea tax.

The South Carolina doctor knew likewise that the motives of the patriots, like the motives of all men, were mixed. He offered no picture of a united country rushing to arms in defense of its liberties. "The inhabitants of the Colonies . . . with regard to political opinions," he wrote, "might be divided into three classes; of these, one was for rushing precipitately into extremities. They were for immediately stopping all trade, and could not even brook the delay of waiting till the proposed Continental Congress should meet. Another party, equally respectable, both as to character, property, and patriotism, was more moderate, but not less firm. These were adverse to the adoption of any violent resolutions till all others were ineffectually tried. They wished that a clear statement of their rights, claims, and grievances, should precede every other measure. A third class disapproved of what was generally going on. A few from principle, and a persuasion that they ought to submit to the Mother Country; some from the love of ease, others from self-interest, but the bulk from fear of the mischievous consequences likely to follow. All these latter classes, for the most part, lay still, while the friends of liberty acted with spirit. If they, or any of them, ventured to oppose popular measures, they were not supported, and therefore declined farther efforts. The resentment of the people was so strong against them, that they sought for peace by remaining quiet. . . . The spirited part of the community being on the side of liberty, the patriots had the appearance of unanimity. . . ."[16]

To his summary analysis of the temper of these three classes, Ramsay added a detailed accounting on the basis of section and interest. That three million loyal subjects "should break through all former attachments, and unanimously adopt new ones, could not reasonably be expected. The revolution had its enemies, as well as its friends, in every period of the war. Country, religion, local policy, as well as private views, operated in disposing the inhabitants to take different sides. The New-England provinces being mostly settled by one sort of people, were nearly of one sentiment. The influence of placemen in Boston, together with the connections which they had formed by marriages, had attached sundry influential characters in that capital to the British interest, but these were but as the dust in the balance, when compared with the numerous independent Whig yeomanry of the country."[17] The Quakers of Pennsylvania and the Tory farmers of the Carolina frontier were treated by Ramsay with as much sympathy and understanding as the independent yeomen of New England or the gentlemen planters of the Southern colonies.[18]

"The age and temperament of individuals [Ramsay continued] had often an influence in fixing their political character. Old men were seldom warm Whigs; they could not relish the

[15] *Ibid.*, I, 95, 97.

[16] *Ibid.*, I, 125–126.

[17] *Ibid.*, II, 310.

[18] *Ibid.*, II, 312–313.

changes which were daily taking place; attached to ancient forms and habits, they could not readily accommodate themselves to new systems. Few of the very rich were active in forwarding the revolution. This was remarkably the case in the eastern and middle States; but the reverse took place in the southern extreme of the confederacy. There were in no part of America more determined Whigs than the opulent slaveholders in Virginia, the Carolinas, and Georgia. The active and spirited part of the community, who felt themselves possessed of talents that would raise them to eminence in a free government, longed for the establishment of independent constitutions: but those who were in possession or expectation of royal favour, or of promotion from Great Britain, wished that the connection between the Parent State and the Colonies might be preserved. The young, the ardent, the ambitious, and the enterprising, were mostly Whigs; but the phlegmatic, the timid, the interested, and those who wanted decision were, in general, favourers of Great Britain, or at least only the lukewarm, inactive friends of independence."[19]

Again economic factors exerted a strong influence: "The Whigs received a great reinforcement from the operation of continental money. In the years 1775, 1776, and in the first months of 1777, while the bills of Congress were in good credit, the effects of them were the same as if a foreign power had made the United States a present of twenty million of silver dollars. The circulation of so large a sum of money, and the employment given to great numbers in providing for the American army, increased the numbers and invigorated the zeal of the friends to the revolution."[20]

Even after Lexington, Ramsay pointed out, the colonial leaders, like the great mass of people everywhere, showed the greatest reluctance to take the decisive step toward independence. It was Thomas Paine's *Common Sense* which, more than anything else, nerved the colonies to declare themselves independent of the Mother Country. In an excellent analysis of Paine's pamphlet as propaganda, Ramsay concluded that "in union with the feelings and sentiments of the people, it produced surprising effects. Many thousands were convinced, and were led to approve and long for a separation from the Mother Country. Though that measure, a few months before, was not only foreign from their wishes, but the object of their abhorrence, a current suddenly became so strong in its favour, that it bore down all opposition."[21]

Despite his sensitivity to the more subtle problems of colonial psychology, to self-interest, chance, and the inflexibility of the British government as elements in the Revolutionary crisis, Ramsay grasped firmly, as lying at the heart of the conflict, the constitutional principle. "This was the very hinge of the controversy. The absolute unlimited supremacy of the British Parliament, both in legislation and taxation, was contended for on one side; while on the other, no farther authority was conceded than such a limited legislation, with regard to external commerce, as would combine the interests of the whole empire." "In government," Ramsay added, "as well as in religion, there are mysteries from the close investigation of which little advantage can be expected. From the unity of empire it was necessary, that some acts should extend over the whole. From the local situation of the Colonies it was equally reasonable that their legislatures should at least in some matters be independent. Where the supremacy of the first ended and the independency of the last began, was to the best informed a puzzling question."[22]

David Ramsay's *History of the American Revolution* has been treated at some length in order to provide a base point of interpretation against which the views of later historians may be measured. In addition, Ramsay can be considered an excellent representative of the first generation of Revolutionary War historians. If he outstrips his contemporaries in the depth and perception of his analyses, he stands with them in the main outlines of his interpretation.

The absence of rancor against Great Britain that characterized the histories of Ramsay and William Gordon was apparent in most first

[19] *Ibid.*, II, 314.
[20] *Ibid.*

[21] *Ibid.*, I, 336–337.
[22] *Ibid.*, I, 136; see also I, 48: "As the claim of taxation on one side, and the refusal of it on the other, was the very hinge on which the revolution turned, it merits a particular discussion."

generation histories of the Revolution. Many were journeymen jobs, but the authors, almost without exception, presented fair and balanced narratives of the events leading to the Revolution. One looks in vain for mention of the "long train of abuses and usurpations," or the dark designs "to reduce [the colonies] under absolute despotism" referred to in the Declaration of Independence.[23]

The ablest representative of the second generation of American historians who dealt with the Revolution was George Bancroft. Bancroft allowed his Jacksonian principles to color his interpretation. In him, we find an openly polemical tone. To Bancroft the era of the Revolution was the golden age, the time of giants, the opening act of the extraordinary drama of American democracy. There is thus in his mammoth history much of what appears to modern eyes as rhetorical embellishment. Where his predecessors had been content to describe the events they had observed, Bancroft was an unconscious myth-maker. At the same time he was the first American historian to bring to a study of the Revolution the research techniques of modern scholarship. He was an insatiable collector of source materials, combing European as well as American archives, and, although he wove such materials into a narrative tapestry of vivid colors, he subscribed wholeheartedly to the ideal of scholarly objectivity. "The chronicler of manners and events," he wrote, "can alone measure his own fairness, for no one else knows so well what he throws aside. Indiscriminate praise neither paints to the life, nor teaches by example, nor advances social science. . . . The historian, even more than philosophers and naturalists, must bring to his pursuit the freedom of an unbiased mind."[24]

Yet Bancroft's characters emerge somewhat larger than life and often, one feels, without those human flaws that would make them readily identifiable as real people. The compulsion to create myths was stronger than the good resolutions of the scholar. By the time that Bancroft wrote, the War of 1812 and England's growing power, coupled with her air of arrogant superiority, had exacerbated American feelings. Bancroft spoke of the "haughty feeling" of the Englishman for his American cousin which had outlasted the "period of revolutionary strife," and which, to Bancroft's own day, hung "as a heavy bias on the judgment . . . of Englishmen."[25] In addition, the United States had grown further from Great Britain, and the sense of Englishness that had softened the animosities generated by the Revolution had been largely dissipated by the 1830's.

History, for Bancroft, was the working of Divine Wisdom, and God's eternal principles were discoverable through its study. History traced "the vestiges of moral law through the practice of the nations in every age . . . and confirms by induction the intuitions of reason."[26] Seen in this light, the Revolution appeared as part of God's plan: it was intended for the edification of man and the improvement of society; it ushered in a new and brighter age of human progress.

What in earlier histories had been presented as essentially a misunderstanding between two power systems became, by Bancroft's interpretation, a conscious plan to subvert liberty. George III, in the perspective of a triumphant Whig tradition, was a relentless authoritarian with a "hatred of reform, and an antipathy to philosophical freedom and to popular power."[27]

[23] Some of Ramsay's contemporaries who, like the Carolinian, wrote Revolutionary history of unusual breadth and balance are William Gordon, *History of the Rise, Progress and Establishment of the Independence of the United States of America* . . . (London, 1788); Charles Stedman, *History of the American War* (London, 1794); John Marshall, *Life of George Washington,* 5 vols. (Philadelphia, 1804–07). At the end of the nineteenth century, Orin Grant Libby attacked Gordon and Ramsay as plagiarists, discrediting them as reliable sources on the Revolution: "A Critical Examination of William Gordon's History of the American Revolution," American Historical Association, *Annual Report, 1899* (Washington, 1900), I, 367–388; and "Ramsay as a Plagiarist," *American Historical Review,* VII (1901–02), 697–703. See also William A. Foran, "John Marshall as a Historian," *ibid.,* XLIII (1937–38), 51–64; R. Kent Newmyer, "Charles Stedman's *History of the American War,*" *ibid.,* LXIII (1957–58), 924–934.

[24] George Bancroft, *History of the United States* (Boston, 1876), V, 69–70.

[25] *Ibid.,* V, 73.

[26] *Ibid.,* V, 70.

[27] *Ibid.,* IV, 197–198.

Under his leadership, "Great Britain, allured by a phantom of absolute authority over the colonies, made war on human freedom." If the British Parliament had succeeded "in establishing by force of arms its 'boundless' authority over America," where would "humanity find an asylum?"[28] The struggle was thus a contest between progress and reaction for the soul of man. The Revolution sounded the death knell of "the ages of servitude and inequality," and rang in "those of equality and brotherhood." America's feet were, thereby, set on a "never-ending career of reform and progress."[29]

If Bancroft fixed the image of a wicked King that was to have a long life in American historiography, his political ideals led him into what became in time another classic error. His own free-trade sentiments induced him to count the Acts of Trade and Navigation, some of which dated from the middle of the seventeenth century, as one of the principal causes of the Revolutionary crisis. As a good Democrat and a low-tariff man, he concluded that mercantilism, as expressed in Parliamentary statutes, must have been a bitter grievance to the American colonists. This interpretation became, in the years that followed, one of the most persistently stated "causes" of the Revolution.

We see in Bancroft's history the optimism and self-confidence of Jacksonian democracy allied with the eighteenth-century conception of an orderly universe governed by natural law. His history was drawn from wide sources, scrupulously researched, written with passion and insight; yet it was transformed by a mythos too strong for Bancroft to resist and already moving away from the realistic appraisal of the first generation of historians, already serving the social needs and aspirations of an explosively expanding nation. The image of America's past fixed by Bancroft was a polestar during the tumultuous middle decades of the nineteenth century.

If Bancroft had vices, they were the counterpart of those virtues which won him thousands of readers. His love of the colorful and dramatic, his devotion to democracy and progress, his fine, if to modern tastes over-elaborate, prose style entitle him to a continued hearing by students of American history.

By the turn of the century the ideals of "scientific" history had penetrated the historical profession. Nurtured in the German seminars of Leopold von Ranke and Barthold Niebuhr, the champions of the new history cast a cold eye on the patriotic effusions of a Bancroft. The task of the historian was to recount with dispassionate objectivity "what had happened," ruthlessly suppressing personal prejudices and loyalties wherever possible, leaving the facts to speak for themselves.

Sydney George Fisher's *The Struggle for American Independence* (1908) was the first detailed treatment of the Revolution since Bancroft's history and the first, as Fisher was at some pains to make clear, written under the new scholarly dispensation. Previous historians, he wrote, had never made "any attempt to describe, from the original records, England's exact position with regard to ourselves at the outbreak of the Revolution, except the usual assumption that the Tory statesmen who were in power were either ignorantly stupid, and blind to their own interests, or desperately corrupt and wicked, and that the Whig minority were angels of light who would have saved the colonies for the British empire."[30] Fisher directed his fire primarily at Bancroft and John Fiske, but such a Rhadamanthine judgment was certainly not fair to Bancroft and missed the mark entirely with the first generation of Revolutionary historians.

In attempting to correct what he considered the anti-British prejudices of his predecessors, Fisher stressed the "mildness" of Great Britain and her "spirit of conciliation." "Modern readers of history," he wrote, knew nothing of "the conciliatory measures Great Britain adopted" or "her gentle and mild efforts to persuade us to remain in the empire."[31] The Revolution was "not a contest between a dragon and a fairy," not "a mere accidental mistake on the part of England" resulting in a war brought on "by the king alone against the wishes of the English people." It was, on the contrary, a path "entered upon by the English nation as deliberately and

[28] *Ibid.*, IV, 308.
[29] *Ibid.*, IV, 311, 308.

[30] Sydney George Fisher, *The Struggle for American Independence* (Philadelphia, 1908), I, vii.
[31] *Ibid.*

intelligently as any other imperial expansion they have undertaken and upon principles which for them are still unchangeable."[32]

In explaining the Revolution, Fisher's emphasis was primarily on the character of colonial life which had shaped the New World settlers and in so doing had made independence inevitable. He thus shifted his focus from the immediate causes, such as the Stamp Act, to underlying changes in outlook and ideology. If England was to be exonerated, it was necessary to neutralize the moral and political conflict and to stress, in place of the traditionally offered explanations of the Revolutionary crisis, the "*characterological* divergence" that had developed between England and her colonies. Forces thus take the place of issues. The action of individuals is of little significance, except as a response to these forces, and it is obviously pointless to try to apportion praise or blame for events which move onward, ineluctable and impersonal as the slow passage of a glacier.[33]

While the story of the Revolution lost, by such treatment, much of the drama with which Bancroft had invested it, and perhaps more important, lost its didactic quality — its ability to teach patriotism to the young by inspiring examples — it gained a greater breadth, a wider tolerance, and an insight into the fact that "forces" did indeed exert great influence upon the behavior of individuals and the course of history. If the individual thereby lost in dignity and significance, the recapturing of a deeper awareness of the complexity of historical events was partial compensation.

That Fisher took such a position was, at least in part, a result of the increasing complexity of American society. The sense of exercising control over the course of history, which had been a by-product of the Enlightenment and which during the years of America's buoyant expansion had seemed to find confirmation in our experience as a nation, had declined sharply as the cruel inconsistencies of American capitalism became more apparent. As the American dream at times appeared more of a nightmare than an idyl, historians like Fisher began to see the individual in a diminished role because the individual himself began to feel his role diminished, began to be aware of the harsh shadow of reality that fell across the classic dream.

[32] *Ibid.*, I, xiii.
[33] *Ibid.*, I, 104.

The strongly pro-British inclinations of Fisher, which wore the mask of dispassionate objectivity, appeared even more strongly in the work of many of his contemporaries. There is no question that these Anglophile sentiments were stimulated by the growing world crisis. In the rivalry between Germany and Great Britain for power and empire, the sympathies of many Americans and virtually all historians were with the British. The enthusiasm of Americans of German ancestry for the cause of a nation to which they still looked with pride and affection only served to increase the ardor of the Anglophiles.

Of course, it could be wrong to label all American historians who wrote on the American Revolution in the early decades of the twentieth century as pro-British. Yet it is unquestionably true that such sympathies crept into the "scientific" investigations of the Revolution that were made in these years. We have already seen that Fisher explicitly rejected any devil theory, being determined to exculpate George III as well as his ministers and the English people themselves.

What had been implicit in Fisher — that the underlying causes of the Revolution were primarily economic — was boldly stated by a young historian who had been a student of Frederick Jackson Turner. Arthur M. Schlesinger, in *The Colonial Merchants and the American Revolution, 1763–1776,* spelled out in impressive detail his thesis that the colonial merchants brought on the Revolutionary crisis, albeit unwittingly. Two rival systems of capitalist enterprise, England's and America's, developed inevitable conflicts of interest which precipitated the war for independence. Schlesinger stated this thesis boldly in 1919 in an article summarizing his views on the causes of the Revolution. "In the first years of the republic," he noted, "the tendency of the popular histories and textbooks was to dwell almost exclusively upon the spectacular developments of the struggle and to dramatize the heroism of the patriots."[34] The real explanation for independence, however, was to be found in "the clashing of economic interests and the interplay of mutual prejudices, opposing ideals and personal antagonisms — whether in England or America." These "made inevitable in 1776 what was unthinkable in 1760."[35]

Schlesinger lost no time in presenting his credentials as an historian of the new school. "The shock of American entrance into the Great War," he wrote, brought the American people "to seek a new orientation for the revolutionary struggle," to view "the conflict from the standpoint of scientific detachment."[36] (It apparently did not occur to the writer that this formula might contain a paradox. He offered no explanation of how, in logic, the intense emotions aroused by our participation in World War I could be expected to result in "scientific detachment.") He showed even more of his own particular orientation when he wrote: "At the same time that publicists were questioning the foundations and practices of our modern economic system, a band of devoted research students . . . were employing the ruthless methods of modern scholarship in an effort to make possible a reappraisement" of the Revolution.[37]

If, in the view of American liberal reformers, industrial capitalism had gone sour, all the presuppositions upon which it claimed to be based must be re-examined. The ideals parroted by exploiting entrepreneurs and vulpine politicians must be subjected to the disinterested scrutiny of modern scholarship. That this reappraisal might itself be influenced by the reformist zeal of the reappraisers seems not to have occurred to them. They were secure in the methods and techniques of scientific research which, they seemed to feel, must carry them inevitably to conclusions untainted by personal prejudice or by the liberal temper of their own times.

Against this background, Schlesinger advanced his own highly influential analysis of the Revolutionary crisis. His conclusions were that the merchants, hit in the pocketbook by the tightening of England's imperial policy, promoted the early agitation against Great Britain. It was they who encouraged the radicals' leaders to whip up mobs of angry patriots. Their purpose was to exert, thereby, countervailing pressure against their English rivals and thus win relief from measures which placed their trade under crippling inhibitions. "As a class they [the merchants] entertained neither earlier nor later the idea of independence, for withdrawal from the British empire meant for them the loss of vital business advantages. . . ."[38]

At each stage of the colonial resistance, the merchants stood in the background manipulating the Sons of Liberty. The rhetoric of the radical leaders meant nothing to them; their concern was with profits not principles. But they had calculated without the ambitions of patriot champions and the ardor of the people. The agitation against Great Britain gathered a momentum that swept it onward with a force of its own. Too late the merchants realized that they had summoned up a whirlwind they could not ride. They found it impossible "to reassert their earlier control and to stop a movement that had lost all significance for hard-headed men of business."[39]

The talk of "no taxation without representation," the appeals to Magna Charta, the heated debate over the authority of Parliament — all this was simply flotsam which showed where deeper currents were flowing. "The popular view of the Revolution as a great forensic controversy over abstract governmental rights," Schlesinger wrote, "will not bear close scrutiny."[40]

In a historiography which disclaimed heroes and villains in the name of scientific objectivity, heroes and villains nonetheless crept in. To Schlesinger, as a liberal idealist, those without

[34] Arthur M. Schlesinger, "The American Revolution Reconsidered," *Political Science Quarterly*, XXXIV (1919), 61. Schlesinger's *The Colonial Merchants and the American Revolution, 1763–1776* (New York, 1917), like Charles A. Beard's *An Economic Interpretation of the Constitution of the United States* (New York, 1913), made historians aware of the importance of economic factors in the Revolutionary era.

[35] Schlesinger, "The Revolution Reconsidered," p. 63.

[36] *Ibid.*, p. 61.

[37] *Ibid.*, p. 62.

[38] *Ibid.*, p. 66.

[39] *Ibid.*, p. 71.

[40] *Ibid.*, pp. 76–77.

ideals, that is, the colonial merchants, were the villains. It was not coincidence that the colonial merchants appeared in Schlesinger's book as narrow, self-seeking men, who, in their blind devotion to pounds and shillings, rent the fabric of the British Empire, at the same time that modern-day American captains of industry were testifying before Congressional committees as to their ruthless repression of labor and their callous exploitation of the public. Even George III appears in his familiar role of wicked tyrant. With all his professions of scientific objectivity, Schlesinger, like Bancroft, charges the King with trying to convert the British government to "a personal autocracy."

Having identified the villains, we do not need to look far for the heroes. They are the "proletarian element," the workers in the colonial towns, who were "for the most part unenfranchised," and the sturdy frontiersmen, who "brought to the controversy a moral conviction and bold philosophy which gave great impetus to the agitation for independence" — presumably more moral conviction than could be found among the self-interested elite of the seacoast towns. In Schlesinger's work, tidewater radicals and back-country farmers march side by side toward independence. Exploited by the cunning merchants, they finally seize control and the revolutionary initiative passes "into the hands of the democratic mechanic class," in other words — the workers.

In this formula of Schlesinger's we have a significant union between Turner's frontier thesis, which credited the frontier with all that was liberal, progressive, and uniquely American, and the twentieth-century liberals' idealization of the industrial worker whose spiritual ancestor they perceived in the mechanic class of colonial towns. Here was a "modern" analysis of the causes of the Revolution which for the first time stated the case explicitly for an "economic interpretation," which swept away the argument from "principle," which freed Great Britain from any taint, and which, above all, carried the imprimatur of "scientific" history, self-stamped to be sure, but hardly the less impressive for that.

Arthur Schlesinger's liberal formulary was carried further by Claude Van Tyne in his book, *The Causes of the War of Independence,* published in 1922. Like Schlesinger, Van Tyne saw himself as one of a company of courageous historians, guided by scientific principles and bent on presenting the facts about the Revolution to a people long misled by the distorted accounts of men who put patriotism ahead of the search for objective truth. "For nearly one hundred years after the awakening of the 'spirit of '76' [Van Tyne wrote], the story of the Revolution was told much as the contemporaries had told it, bitterly, with no effort to be impartial or judicial, and no emphasis upon the fundamentals. Men like Bancroft conducted amazing researches in the archives, but rose out of heaps of musty records only to write again of the cunning malevolent King George and his wicked minister, Lord North, enemies of the human race, oppressors of America."

Finally, "here and there a scholar, an investigator" appeared, and "it was these trained investigators who began to get at the truth as to the Revolution. With no aim but to understand, with no desire but to know the truth they worked for forty years — as long as the Chosen People searched for the Promised Land — rewriting the story of the founding of the American Republic. New records, new points of view, new principles of research made new generations of investigators see the Revolution in a new way."[41]

Van Tyne's history is the fruit of all this enlightened industry. In it we find a strong emphasis on the frontier thesis adapted from Turner. For on the frontier "the English race" experienced "a rebirth, the first of these destined to occur perennially as the race marched westward toward the setting sun."[42] In the raw environment of a new continent, "town-bred men became denizens of the wilds." Van Tyne accepted without question Schlesinger's picture of the merchants guiding the early stages of colonial resistance and then dropping out, as "radicals everywhere, from Samuel Adams at the North to Christopher Gadsden in the South, seized the moment of high feeling to carry Amer-

[41] Claude Van Tyne, *England and America: Rivals in the American Revolution* (New York, 1927), pp. 3–6.

[42] Van Tyne, *The Causes of the War of Independence* (Boston, 1922), p. 15.

ica beyond the point where there could be any going back." The conflict became a class struggle. In Massachusetts as in Pennsylvania "the masses [were] pitted against the great merchants." Thus, in 1776, came the climax in the struggle between rich and poor, East and West, those with a vote and those who were voteless, between privilege and the welfare of the common man."[43]

The terms have shifted but we find, nonetheless, familiar echoes of Bancroft in Van Tyne's insistence that the Revolution was "one of the glories of British history," since the colonists, as heirs of all the political accomplishments of England, were simply carrying forward the fight for democracy and political liberty which "England had fostered beyond any other country of the world."[44] And, as in Bancroft, we find an unscrupulous George III drawing on "an inexhaustible treasure of corruption" to obliterate the liberties of the colonists, despite the warnings of Burke, Pitt, Fox, and Camden. The cast has changed somewhat but the final curtain rings down on the same stirring patriotic note.

Two years after Van Tyne's book appeared, Charles McLean Andrews surveyed *The Colonial Background of the American Revolution* in a notable collection of essays. Andrews accepted what had by now become the general view of the Revolutionary crisis: that the basis of the dispute lay in a conflict of interests. The question of colonial rights was "a subject of more or less legal and metaphysical speculation. . . . There is nothing to show," he wrote, "that the somewhat precise and finely spun reasoning of these intellectual leaders had any marked influence on the popular mind."[45] Andrews, like Van Tyne, emphasized the role of the frontier which encouraged individualism and independence, but the conflict remained in its broader outlines a struggle over trade and commerce. We find in Andrews, it must be said, in addition to the residues of many earlier interpretations, a tentativeness and absence of the doctrinaire.

Under the surface of historical investigation the economic interpretation of history had been moving like a subterranean current, influencing individuals in many areas of American history. It was discernible in Arthur Schlesinger's study of the colonial merchants, and in the works of a number of his contemporaries. As applied to the Revolution, however, it was persistently modified in the works we have been concerned with by the naturalistic and romantic gloss of the frontier thesis, and by the fact that even skeptical historians of the scientific school found it extremely difficult to disengage themselves from the mythic elements of the Revolution. However resolutely they started out demolishing, as they boasted, the biased and partisan accounts of earlier historians, they all ended up sounding remarkably like George Bancroft.

In 1954, Lawrence Henry Gipson's *The Coming of the Revolution, 1763–1775,* was published in the *New American Nation Series.* In their introduction, the editors of this series wrote: "During the past half a century the lapse of time and the uncovering of much new evidence have made it possible for scholars to pursue their investigations into the causes of the American Revolution in an atmosphere far less partisan than had prevailed in earlier generations. As a result of this more objective handling of the period of mounting tension that preceded the War of Independence, the rights on both sides of the controversy are more generally conceded." It is Gipson's argument "that the causes of the Revolution stem first from the effort of the British government, faced with vast territorial acquisitions in North America at the end of the Great War for Empire, along with an unprecedented war debt, to organize a more efficient administration on that continent and to make the colonies contribute directly to the support of the enlarged Empire. . . . Secondly, the causes of the breach can be traced to the radically altered situation of the colonies after 1760, by which date they were at long last relieved of the intense pressure previously exerted along their borders by hostile nations."[46] The heart of the issue was a clash of "interests."

From the time of Sydney George Fisher to that of Lawrence Gipson an interpretation of the causes of the American Revolution had slowly

[43] *Ibid.*, pp. 416, 421, 425.

[44] *Ibid.*, p. 478.

[45] Charles McLean Andrews, *Colonial Background of the American Revolution* (New Haven, 1924), p. 135.

[46] Lawrence Henry Gipson, *The Coming of the Revolution, 1763–1775,* in *The New American Nation Series,* ed. Henry Steele Commager and Richard B. Morris (New York, 1954), pp. ix, xii.

taken form. By the early 1950's its outlines seemed, generally speaking, clear and stable and satisfyingly impersonal. The Revolution was the outcome of forces rather than "the result of the actions of wicked men — neither of the King or Lord North, on the one hand, nor of American radicals on the other." The forces were primarily economic and social — the clash between rival systems of mercantilism and the differentiation of the colonists from citizens of the Mother Country through the influence of an agricultural frontier. The problem of dealing with human motivations, decisions, aspirations, and illusions was thus solved by submerging them in the larger currents of history.[47]

On to this settled and orderly scene burst Edmund and Helen Morgan's *The Stamp Act Crisis: Prologue to Revolution*.[48] Their argument, like that of David Ramsay 165 years earlier, hinged on the decisive character of the Stamp Act and threatened at once to undermine the whole painstaking, if jerry-built, structure of interpretation that had been erected by a dozen twentieth-century historians. The Morgans reminded their readers that the Stamp Act aroused an instant and entirely unexpected wave of protest and of determined resistance in the colonies — resistance which could have led to revolution. Never again were the colonists to be so united in opposition to a British measure. The actual cost of the stamp tax to the colonists would have been relatively light. In most places it was never even put into effect so that the colonists had no opportunity to experience it as a material hardship. The opposition was thus almost entirely on the grounds of abstract principle — the constitutional principle of no taxation without representation.

Moreover, the leaders who came forward at the time of the act to direct colonial resistance were the individuals who in most instances carried through to the Revolution and beyond. Of the twenty-six members of the Stamp Act Congress, "only two . . . are known to have become loyalists in 1776. . . . Others who took no part in the congress but led the resistance to the Stamp Act within their own colonies were likewise conspicuous in the revolutionary movement. It seems particularly significant that the parties which brought on the revolution in the two leading colonies, Massachusetts and Virginia, gained their ascendancy at the time of the Stamp Act."[49]

But even more important than the appearance, at the very outset of the controversy, of able and aggressive leaders who continued to lead was "the emergence . . . of well-defined constitutional principles." The colonial assemblies in 1765 "laid down the line on which Americans stood until they cut their connections with England. Consistently from 1765 to 1776 they denied the authority of Parliament to tax them externally or internally; consistently they affirmed their willingness to submit to whatever legislation Parliament should enact for the supervision of the empire as a whole."[50]

In the Morgans' view far too much had been made of the shifts in the colonial position in regard to the powers of Parliament. Historians of the Schlesinger school had pointed to these shifts — from no power to impose internal taxes, to no external taxes for revenue, to no internal or external taxes of any kind, to no right to legislate for the colonies in any case whatever — as an indication that material self-interest rather than principle motivated the colonial actions. On the contrary, the Morgans argued, the colonists did not advance from one position to another under the pressure of Parliamentary enactments. In actual fact the Stamp Act brought at once a

[47] Nineteenth-century historians who dealt with the Revolution such as George Washington Greene, *Historical View of the American Revolution* (Cambridge, 1876), and John Fiske, *The American Revolution* (Cambridge, 1896), wrote in the tradition of George Bancroft. For the twentieth century, no mention has been made of John C. Miller's excellent narrative history, *The Origins of the American Revolution* (Boston, 1943), because it failed to cast new light on the causes of the Revolution. Max Savelle's *Seeds of Liberty: The Genesis of the American Mind* (New York, 1948), in my view, simply applies a cultural-social veneer to older interpretations. Limitations of space have also compelled me to omit consideration of the influence of Sir Lewis Namier and his revisionist school. The Namierists, by rehabilitating George III, reinforced the view of the Revolution as a clash of "forces" or "interests." See Morgan, "American Revolution" for an excellent discussion of the Namier position and some effective counterarguments.

[48] Edmund S. Morgan and Helen M. Morgan, *The Stamp Act Crisis: Prologue to Revolution* (Chapel Hill, 1953).

[49] *Ibid.*, p. 293.

[50] *Ibid.*, p. 295.

denial of the right of Parliament to tax the colonies "without representation." All official statements such as the resolves of the Stamp Act Congress asserted this principle, conceding nothing but a willingness to acquiesce in the Acts of Trade and Navigation in force in 1763. Moreover, a number of colonial leaders at the time of the Stamp Act crisis or soon afterwards came to the conclusion that Parliament had no constitutional authority to legislate for the colonies. But understanding that to press such a view would rouse the deepest suspicions of Parliament and its supporters and alarm all colonial moderates, they kept their peace.

Like Ramsay, the Morgans express the conviction that the growing conflict "was not irretrievable, but that to retrieve it would have required an understanding on each side of the exact limits of the other's claims." While "the English thought that they saw the Americans inching their way toward independence, the Americans thought that they saw a sinister party in England seeking by gradual degree to enslave them."[51] So the crisis moved to its denouement.

If the Morgans' argument in its main outlines is granted, it of course modifies those interpretations which see the Revolution as the more or less inevitable result of a slow process of economic, social, cultural, and political differentiation between the colonies and the Mother Country. The Schlesinger thesis that the merchants used the radical leaders and the mobs simply to gain redress of specific grievances becomes likewise untenable, and the frontier thesis loses much of its force. The Morgans' position, in addition, diminishes the importance of class conflict as an element in the Revolutionary crisis. While class and sectional frictions undoubtedly existed in some of the colonies, they did not become sharply defined until the later years of the war and the postwar period, and they were, in no sense, determinants in the development of the Revolutionary crisis.

In the Morgans' book we have come, in full circle, back to the position of Ramsay and the historians of the first generation. After a century and a half of progress in historical scholarship, in research techniques, in tools and methods, we have found our way to the interpretation held, substantially, by those historians who themselves participated in, or lived through the era of, the Revolution. If it is undoubtedly true that, as Morgan suggests, "George Bancroft may not have been so far from the mark as we have often assumed," it is equally true that Ramsay was closer still.

Once we have picked our way through the bewildering variety of interpretations that successive generations of historians have offered us, we would do well to go back and reread David Ramsay. We cannot fail, I think, to be both puzzled and impressed. How can we account for the remarkable insight, the proportion, and the "objectivity" of this historian who was himself a Revolutionary politician? The historical profession is so deeply committed to the belief that objectivity or perspective is a product of the viewer's distance in time from the events with which he is dealing, that we find it hard to accept the fact that Ramsay offered us a wiser and better balanced interpretation than the most expert and "scientific" of his successors. Nor can we write off Ramsay as a sport, an exception, or an oddity. If he is the best of his generation, he is by no means exceptional in his general attitude toward the events of the Revolution or in his interpretation of those events. It seems to me that we must accept the proposition that, generally speaking, the first generation of historians gave us a more "objective" view of the Revolution than historians have managed to do since.

In justice to later historians, it should, of course be pointed out that the historian's task in interpreting the American Revolution has been more than ordinarily difficult. The America that emerged from the War of Independence was a nation without prehistory in the traditional sense. Having won their independence, the rather loosely knit United States had to find myths and symbols to reinforce and give substance to that national unity which for the first eighty years was so precariously maintained. Myths had, perforce, to be created around the moment of birth. What Homer and the siege of Troy had been to the Greek states of the Periclean Age, George Washington and the campaigns of the Revolution were to nineteenth-century Americans. What Romulus and Remus

[51] *Ibid.*, pp. 291, 290.

and the Twelve Tables of the Law had been for Imperial Rome, the Founding Fathers and the Federal Constitution were for a United States searching in the midst of extraordinary social and economic transformations for unifying symbols.

The American Revolution has, thus, been encrusted with mythic elements and residues which have vastly complicated the task of the historian who wishes to state the truth of the events that took place in that era. The historian, being human and ineluctably partaking of the ideals and values of his own day, has been under the strongest pressure to make the events of the Revolution conform to the particular time spirit of which he himself has been a self-conscious and articulate representative. He has been, therefore, not simply the enemy of the myths, as he would like to see himself, but quite as often the victim, in the sense that he has seldom escaped the temptation to make the Revolution prove something about his own society or about the society which he wishes to see evolve in the future.

It is only fair to add that the aims and aspirations of the generation of historians of which Ramsay was a member were ideally suited to the writing of balanced and judicious history. Federalists, or at least deeply imbued with Federalist doctrines, they were friends of the new Federal Constitution. As enemies of factionalism and party rancor, they sought to write history that would draw the states together. It was thus Ramsay's wish that each state might have "an ingenious learned and philosophical history" so that knowledge of sister states might be widely diffused and the union correspondingly strengthened. As reconcilers, it was the particular responsibility of first generation historians to write accounts so broad and generous that Patriot and Tory, planter and merchant, Northerner and Southerner, could find therein common ground and, joining forces, move forward to the bright future that awaited the new nation. "We are too widely disseminated over an extensive country and too much diversified by different customs and forms of government to feel as one people which we really are," Ramsay wrote his friend, John Eliot. "Had we Belknaps in every state we might become acquainted with each other in that intimate familiar manner which would wear away prejudices, rub off asperities and mold us into an homogeneous people loving esteeming and rightly appreciating each other."[52] Approaching their task in this missionary spirit, Ramsay and his fellows were under the strongest compulsions to write fair and unbiased history. Disunity was the sharpest danger which faced the country, unitary history its best remedy.

In addition, and perhaps most important of all, the historians of the eighteenth century made no distinction between fact and interpretation. Unaware of, or unconcerned with, such divisions, they had not succumbed to the illusion that facts and interpretation were different orders of reality — that if the facts were diligently searched for and assembled the proper interpretation would somehow follow from them. That Ramsay and a number of his contemporaries drew largely from the *Annual Register* suggests a good deal about their attitude toward facts. These, if generally reliable (and there was no better source in the eighteenth century than the *Annual Register*), were of secondary importance; by far the most significant part of the process of writing history was the application of principles of interpretation, or, perhaps better, moral judgment, to the events with which the historian was dealing. The position that the historian took in regard to the treatment of his material did not rest upon "facts" but rather upon an awareness of his responsibility to do justice to the rival groups and conflicting aspirations involved in his story. Ramsay's generation would have spoken of this as a concern with "first principles." If first principles were wrong all subsequent steps, however rational, systematic, or scientific, would simply compound error. It would not have occurred to an eighteenth-century historian to sanctify the facts under the illusion that they contained some measure of saving grace.

Whatever imperfections there may be in Ramsay's facts (and his detractors have not indeed argued that they were at fault but that, in a number of instances, they were taken from the *Annual Register*), it was a poor bargain to get in the place of his work histories which were

[52] Ramsay to John Eliot, Charleston, Aug. 11, 1792, Massachusetts Historical Society, Boston, Mass.

factually impeccable but which lost their grip on the essential meaning of the Revolutionary experience.

On the basis of this brief survey of interpretations of the Revolution it would be very difficult to demonstrate clear and consistent progress in the interpretation of historical events primarily as the result of the longer time-perspectives of successive historians dealing with them. Nor, again, will we find that the opening up of new archives and the discovery of new documents (beyond a certain point, of course), result in notably improved or more acceptable (in any final sense) interpretations.[53]

Indeed, in regard to the Revolution, the most extreme distortions appeared in the work of those historians who made the loudest claims to be "scientific" in their approach. Perhaps these men, believing implicitly in the authority of the data, the "facts" as disclosed by their researches, have been less sensitive to the nature and extent of their own prejudices. The older "prescientific" historians realized that there was no way of evading judgments and were thus quite conscious of the distortion produced by their own personal loyalties and allegiances. The scientific historian, comforted by the illusion of a vast amount of supporting data, might (and obviously in many instances did) have his own predispositions come upon him disguised as the objective results of research.

Beyond all this it must be said that an intelligent contemporary has one advantage over all later investigators. He was there. He saw it happen, felt it, experienced it on many levels. It was part of the complex fabric of his life. Like a seismograph he recorded through the channels of his nervous system and stored in his brain (rather than in a filing cabinet or archive) the emotions, ideas, the realities of his era. And he recorded these, if he was a person of sensitivity and judgment, in roughly the proportion in which they were present in his environment. He could, in addition, push his environment out as widely as the breadth of his mind and his ability to extrapolate from his own immediate experience would carry it. Furthermore, he did not have to mythologize the events or view them through the lens of a later generation with its very different needs and aspirations.

The story of successive interpretations of the American Revolution seems then to bear this moral: There is, or has been so far, no panacea (like scientific method) which can perform for the historian the functions of judgment and analysis. Whatever the historian gains in time-perspective or new materials or specialized monographs, he may well lose through distortions that are the result of his own *Zeitgeist*. He thus fails to approach in any orderly, systematic way the truth in the form of some final, or often, some better interpretation or understanding of the events he is concerned with. We would do well, therefore, to show more respect for the best contemporary history and abandon some of those professional pieties with which we have solaced ourselves in the past. In the struggle for historical understanding there are no final triumphs. Insights once gained will not automatically sustain themselves but must be rediscovered time and again. We cannot solve problems of historical interpretation and then, having reduced the solutions to formulas, pass on to new problems, for the "solved" problems are remarkably full of life, tenacious and enduring.

This being the case, the responsibility is clearly placed where it belongs — on the individual historian. He cannot take refuge from judgments in techniques. His judgments, on the other hand, will be no better than his own capacity for wise insight and human understanding.

Which brings us, properly enough, once more to David Ramsay. Ramsay had certain advantages through his involvement in the events of which he wrote which were denied later historians. Yet, had he not been an individual of far more than ordinary wisdom, he could not have availed himself so successfully of his opportunity. The generosity of mind and spirit which mark his pages, his critical sense, his balanced judgment and compassion are gifts that were uniquely his own and that clearly entitle him to an honorable position in the front rank of American historians.

[53] Herbert Butterfield in an essay entitled, "The Reconstruction of an Historical Episode; the History of an Inquiry into the Origins of the Seven Years War," *Man on His Past* (Cambridge, Eng., 1955), pp. 143–167, has shown how Leopold von Ranke, writing not many years after that war, gave a better analysis of its causes than those made with a longer perspective in time and far greater access to documentary materials.

Suggested Further Reading:

There are several very readable studies of George III; unhappily readability comes often at the expense of accuracy. Among the generally attractive biographies are: J. C. Long, *George III, The Story of a Complex Man* (1960), and C. E. Vulliamy, *Royal George* (1937). Interesting sidelights are provided in L. B. Namier, *The Structure of Politics at the Accession of George III** (2 vols., 1929), and *England in the Age of the American Revolution** (2nd ed., 1961); Richard Pares, *King George III and the Politicians* (1953); Herbert Butterfield, *George III, Lord North and the People, 1779–80* (1949), and *George III and the Historians* (1957, rev. ed., 1959); Charles R. Ritcheson, *British Politics and the American Revolution* (1954); more recent, and very readable, is Bernard Donoughue, *British Politics and the American Revolution: The Path to War, 1773–75* (1964).

Lawrence Henry Gipson explores the immediate consequences of the Great War for the Empire in *The Coming of the Revolution, 1763–1775** (1954), and Howard H. Peckham gives a fine review of the War and its significance in his *The Colonial Wars, 1689–1762* (1964); his earlier account of *Pontiac and the Indian Uprising** (1947) is also excellent; Jack M. Sosin's *Whitehall and the Wilderness* (1961) takes a very detailed look at the making of British western policy after the War. Francis Parkman provides a unique account of *France and England in North America* (9 vols., 1865–92).

Carl L. Becker is still a name with which to conjure when considering the philosophy of the Revolution; his *Heavenly City of the Eighteenth-Century Philosophers** (1932) is a not-so-minor classic, and his *Declaration of Independence** (1922) has hardly been superseded. Randolph G. Adams, *Political Ideas of the American Revolution* (1922) remains useful; Charles H. McIlwain's *The American Revolution: A Constitutional Interpretation** (1923, reissued 1958) discusses the colonists' sense of constitutional justification. But one of the most important studies of the intellectual origins of the Revolution does not exist in independent book form: see Bernard Bailyn's brilliant two-hundred-page introduction to *Pamphlets of the American Revolution* (4 vols., 1965–), I, which owes much to Caroline Robbins and her pathfinding *The Eighteenth-Century Commonwealthman* (1959). Few of these studies can be categorized as light or particularly easy reading.

PART NINE

The American Revolution

" 'Inevitable' results in history," once remarked the noted scholar, Charles H. McIlwain, "are about the last resort of the despairing historian." Recent developments in that widening association of sovereign nations, the British Commonwealth, might well suggest a certain historical logic to eventual independence for the American colonies, but there was little that was inevitable about the Revolution itself. Few Americans contemplated so drastic an action; most hoped to the last that a final rupture with Great Britain might be avoided. By nature they were peace-loving men. "Revolutions are no trifles," John Adams warned. "They ought never to be undertaken rashly."

Any survey of patriot literature will reflect Adams' viewpoint. The reluctance of the colonists even to contemplate revolt and its consequences is everywhere in evidence. Besides revealing a desire for accommodation, their writings often exhibit a confident expectation of a satisfactory settlement. Nor is this surprising. The British government had retreated from the Stamp Act. The Townshend duties had been substantially withdrawn after three tense years. To many patriots it must have seemed that protest and resistance had brought results, that there need be no "last Extremity." After all, they only asked for their rights as Englishmen; surely England would finally concede the rightness — even the conservatism — of their plea?

The American Revolution readily lends itself to a conservative interpretation. Its leaders were frequently more radical in their methods than in their objectives. And the men who made the Revolution were more often than not the men who guided the new nation after Independence. Without entering the controversy over the essential democracy of pre-Revolutionary America, it would seem that recognition of the continuity of its leadership and the moderation for which that leadership stood can contribute helpfully to an understanding of the political and social changes that ensued.

1

The Colonists Argue Their Case

I

A Discourse Concerning Unlimited Submission

Jonathan Mayhew *(1720–66) was the most influential of New England's politically-minded clerics. John Adams identified him as an early advocate of "the principles and feelings for which the Revolution was undertaken." His* Discourse Concerning Unlimited Submission, *the most famous sermon of its kind preached before the Revolution, was the first important public pronouncement on the sacred right and duty of resistance to tyranny.*

The occasion for this sermon was the centennial of the execution of Charles I. Mayhew took vigorous exception to Anglican efforts to portray Charles as a martyred monarch, and began his refutation with some significant remarks on the antiquity of English liberties and the English constitution. England's monarchs, he claimed, were originally enthroned "solely by grant of parliament," and ruled "by the voluntary consent of the people." History had proved the right of all men "to vindicate their natural and legal rights"; this was why Caesar was "cut off in the senate house," and Charles was "beheaded before his own banqueting house." Charles had levied taxes without the consent of his people, set up arbitrary courts, and openly encouraged Popery. "A lawless tyrant," he had "unkinged himself" long before his trial. Here, Mayhew observed, was "a warning to all corrupt councellors and ministers."

Mayhew's sermon, published in London as well as Boston, reached a wide audience, and its usefulness to the patriot cause was acknowledged by a timely reprint in 1775. Shortly before his death in 1766, Mayhew reminded Americans of their need to be alert: "History," he declared, "affords no example of any nation, country, or people long free, who did not take some care of themselves."

Jonathan Mayhew, *A Discourse Concerning Unlimited Submission and Non-resistance to the Higher Powers* (Boston, 1750), pp. 40–55.

This naturally brings us to make some reflections upon the resistance which was made about a century since, to that unhappy prince, KING CHARLES I; and upon the ANNIVERSARY of his death. This is a point which I should not have concerned myself about, were it not that *some men* continue to speak of it, even to this day, with a great deal of warmth and zeal; and in such a manner as to undermine all the principles of LIBERTY, whether civil or religious, and to introduce the most abject slavery both in church and state: so that it is become a matter of universal concern. — What I have to offer upon this subject, will be comprised in a short answer to the following *queries; viz.*

FOR what reason the resistance to king *Charles* the *First* was made?

BY whom it was made?

WHETHER this resistance was REBELLION,[1] or not?

How the *Anniversary* of king *Charles's* death came *at first* to be solemnized as a day of fasting and humiliation?

And lastly,

WHY those of the episcopal clergy who are very high in the principles of *ecclesiastical authority,* continue to speak of this unhappy man, as a great SAINT and a MARTYR?

For what reason, then, was the resistance to king *Charles,* made? The general answer to this inquiry is, that it was on account of the *tyranny*

[1] N. B. I speak of rebellion, treason, saintship, martyrdom, &c. throughout this discourse, only in the *scriptural* and *theological sense.* I know not how the *law* defines them; the study of *that* not being my employment —

and *oppression* of his reign. Not a great while after his accession to the throne, he married a *french catholic;* and with her seemed to have wedded the politics, if not the religion of France, also. For afterwards, during a reign, or rather a tyranny of many years, he governed in a perfectly wild and arbitrary manner, paying no regard to the constitution and the laws of the kingdom, by which the power of the crown was limited; or to the solemn oath which he had taken at his coronation. It would be endless, as well as needless, to give a particular account of all the illegal and despotic measures which he took in his administration; — partly from his own natural lust of power, and partly from the influence of wicked councellors and ministers. — He committed many illustrious members of both houses of parliament to the *tower,* for opposing his arbitrary schemes. — He levied many taxes upon the people without consent of parliament; — and then imprisoned great numbers of the principal merchants and gentry for not paying them. — He erected, or at least revived, several new and arbitrary courts, in which the most unheard-of barbarities were committed with his knowledge and approbation — He supported that more than fiend, arch-bishop *Laud* and the clergy of his stamp, in all their church-tyranny and hellish cruelties — He authorised a book in favor of *sports* upon the *Lord's day;* and several clergymen were persecuted by him and the mentioned *pious* bishop, for not reading it to the people after *divine service* — When the parliament complained to him of the arbitrary proceedings of his corrupt ministers, he told that *august body,* in a rough, domineering, unprincely manner, that he wondered any one should be so foolish and insolent as to think that he would part with the meanest of his servants *upon their account* — He refused to call any parliament at all for the space of twelve years together, during all which time, he governed in an absolute lawless and despotic manner — He took all opportunities to encourage the *papists,* and to promote them to the highest offices of honor and trust — He (probably) abetted the horrid massacre in *Ireland,* in which two hundred thousand protestants were butchered by the roman catholics — He sent a large sum of money, which he had raised by his arbitrary taxes, into *Germany,* to raise foreign troops, in order to force more arbitrary taxes upon his subjects. — He not only by a long series of *actions,* but also in *plain terms,* asserted an absolute uncontroulable power; saying even in one of his speeches to parliament, that as it was blasphemy to dispute what God might do; so it was sedition in subjects to dispute what the king might do. —Towards the end of his tyranny, he came to the house of commons with an armed force,[2] and demanded five of its principal members to be delivered up to him — And this was a prelude to that unnatural war which he soon after levied against his own dutiful subjects; whom he was bound by all the laws of honor, humanity, piety, and I might add, of *interest* also, to defend and cherish with a paternal affection — I have only time to hint at these facts in a general way, all which, and many more of the same tenor, may be proved by good authorities: So that the *figurative* language which St. *John* uses concerning the just and beneficent deeds of our blessed Saviour, may be applied to the unrighteous and execrable deeds of this prince, *viz. And there are also many other things which king Charles did, the which, if they should be written every one, I suppose that even the world itself, could not contain the books that should be written.*[3] Now it was on account of king *Charles's* thus assuming a power above the laws, in direct contradiction to his coronation oath, and governing the greatest part of his time, in the most arbitrary oppressive manner; it was upon this account, that the resistance was made to him, which, at length, issued in the loss of his crown, and of *that head* which was unworthy to wear it.

But by whom was this resistance made? Not by a private *junto;* — not by a small seditious *party;* — not by a *few desparadoes,* who, to mend their fortunes, would embroil the state; — but by the LORDS and COMMONS of *England.* It was they that almost unanimously opposed the king's measures for overturning the constitution, and changing that free and happy

[2] Historians are not agreed, what number of soldiers attended him in this monstrous invasion of the privileges of parliament — Some say 300, some 400; And the author of *The history of the kings of Scotland,* says 500.

[3] John xxi. 25.

government into a wretched, absolute monarchy. It was they that when the king was about levying forces against his subjects, in order to make himself absolute, commissioned officers, and raised an army to defend themselves and the public: And it was they that maintained the war against him all along, till he was made a prisoner. This is indisputable. Though it was not properly speaking the parliament, but the army, which put him to death afterwards. And it ought to be freely acknowledged, that most of their proceeding, in order to get this matter effected; and particularly the court by which the king was at last tried and condemned, was little better than a mere mockery of justice. —

The next question which naturally arises, is, whether this resistance which was made to the king *by the parliament,* was properly *rebellion,* or not? The answer to which is plain, that it was not; but a most righteous and glorious stand, made in defence of the natural and legal rights of the people, against the unnatural and illegal encroachments of arbitrary power. Nor was this a rash and too sudden opposition. The nation had been patient under the oppressions of the crown, even to *long suffering;* — for a course of many years; and there was no rational hope of redress in any other way — Resistance was absolutely necessary in order to preserve the nation from slavery, misery and ruin. And who so proper to make this resistance as the lords and commons; — the whole representative body of the people; — guardians of the public welfare; and each of which was, in point of legislation, vested with an equal, co-ordinate power, with that of the crown?[4] Here were *two* branches of the legislature against *one;* — two, which had law and equity and the constitution on their side, against one which was impiously attempting to overturn law and equity and the constitution; and to exercise a wanton licentious *sovereignty* over the properties, consciences and lives of all the people: — Such a *sovereignty* as some inconsiderately ascribe to the supreme Governor of the world. — I say, inconsiderately; because God himself does not govern in an absolutely arbitrary and despotic manner. The power of this Almighty King (I speak it not without caution and reverence; the power of this Almighty King) is *limited by law;* not, indeed, by *acts of parliament,* but by the eternal *laws* of truth, wisdom and equity; and the everlasting *tables* of right reason; — tables that cannot be *repealed,* or *thrown down* and *broken* like those of *Moses.* — But king *Charles* sat himself up above all these, as much as he did above the written laws of the realm; and made mere

[4] The *english* constitution is originally and essentially *free.* The character which *J. Caesar* and *Tacitus* both given of the ancient *Britains* so long ago, is, That they were extremely *jealous of their liberties,* as well as a people of a *martial* spirit. Nor have there been wanting frequent instances and proofs of the same glorious spirit (in both respects) remaining in their posterity ever since. — in the struggles they have made for liberty, both against foreign and domestic tyrants. — Their kings hold their title to the throne, solely by grant of parliament; i.e. in other words, by the voluntary consent of the people. And, agreably hereto, the prerogative and rights of the crown are stated, defined and limited by law; and that as truly and strictly as the rights of any inferior officer in the state; or indeed, of any private subject. And it is only in this respect that it can be said, that "the king can do no wrong." Being restrained by the law, he cannot, while he confines himself within those just limits which the law prescribes to him as the measure of his authority, injure and oppress the subject. — The king, in his coronation oath, swears to exercise only such a power as the constitution gives him: And the subject, in the oath of allegiance, swears only to obey him in the exercise of such a power. The king is as much bound by his oath, not to infringe the legal rights of the people, as the people are bound to yield subjection to him. From whence it follows, that as soon as the prince sets himself up above law, he loses the king in the tyrant: he does to all intents and purposes, unking himself, by acting out of, and beyond, that sphere which the constitution allows him to move in. And in such cases, he has no more rights to be obeyed, than any inferior officer who acts beyond his commission. The subjects obligation to allegiance *then* ceases of course: and to resist him, is no more *rebellion,* than to resist any foreign invader. There is an essential difference betwixt *government and tyranny;* at least under such a constitution as the *english.* The former consists in ruling according to law and equity; the latter, in ruling contrary to law and equity. So also, there is an essential difference betwixt resisting a tyrant, and rebellion; The former is a just and reasonable self-defence; the latter consists in resisting a prince whose administration is just and legal; and this is what denominates it a crime. — Now it is evident, that king *Charles's* government was illegal, and very oppressive, through the greatest part of his reign; And, therefore, to resist him, was no more rebellion, than to oppose any foreign invader, or any other domestic oppressor.

humor and caprice, which are no rule at all, the only rule and measure of his administration. And now, is it not perfectly ridiculous to call resistance to such a tyrant, by the name of rebellion? — the grand rebellion? Even that — parliament, which brought king *Charles* II. to the throne, and which run *loyally mad,* severely reproved one of their own members for condemning the proceedings of that parliament which first took up arms against the former king. And upon the same principles that the proceedings of this parliament may be censured as wicked and rebellious, the proceedings of those who, since, opposed king *James* II, and brought the prince of *Orange* to the throne, may be censured as wicked and rebellious also. The cases are parallel. — But whatever *some* men may *think,* it is to be hoped that, for their own sakes, they will not dare to *speak* against the REVOLUTION, upon the justice and legality of which depends (in part) his present MAJESTY's right to the throne.

If it be said, that although the parliament which first opposed king Charles's measures, and at length took up arms against him, were not guilty of rebellion; yet certainly those persons were, who condemned, and put him to death; even this perhaps is not true. For he had, in fact, *unkinged* himself long before, and had forfeited his title to the allegiance of the people. So that those who put him to death, were, at most only guilty of *murder;* which, indeed, is bad enough, if they were really guilty of *that;* (which is at least disputable.) *Cromwell,* and those who were principally concerned in the (*nominal*) king's death, might possibly have been very wicked and designing men. Nor shall I say any thing in vindication of the reigning *hypocrisy* of those times; or of *Cromwell's* maladministration during the *interregnum*: (for it is *truth,* and not a *party,* that I am speaking for.) But still it may be said, that *Cromwell* and his adherents were not, properly speaking, guilty of *rebellion;* because he, whom they beheaded was not, properly speaking, *their king;* but a *lawless tyrant.* — much less, are the whole body of the nation at that time to be charged with rebellion on that account; for it was no *national act;* it was not done by a *free* parliament. And much less still, is the nation at present, to be charged with the great sin of rebellion, for what their *ancestors* did, (or rather did NOT) a century ago.

But how came the *anniversary* of king *Charles's* death, to be solemnized as a day of fasting and humiliation? The true answer in brief, to which inquiry, is, that this fast was instituted by way of *court* and *complement* to king *Charles* II, upon the *restoration.* All were desirous of making their court to him; of ingratiating themselves; and of making him forget what had been done in opposition to his *father,* so as not to revenge it. To effect this, they ran into the most extravagant professions of affection and loyalty to him, insomuch that he himself said, that it was a *mad* and *hair brain'd* loyalty which they professed. And amongst other strange things, which his first parliament did, they ordered the *Thirtieth* of *January* (the day on which his father was beheaded) to be kept as a day of solemn humiliation, to deprecate the judgments of heaven for the rebellion which the nation had been guilty of, in that which was no national thing; and which was not rebellion in them that did it — Thus they soothed and flattered their new king, at the expence of their liberties: — And were ready to yield up *freely* to *Charles* II, all that enormous power, which they had justly resisted *Charles* I, for usurping to himself.

The last query mentioned, was, Why those of the *episcopal clergy* who are very high in the principles of *ecclesiastical authority,* continue to speak of this unhappy prince as a *great Saint* and a *Martyr?* This, we know, is what they constantly do, especially upon the 30th of *January;* — a day sacred to the *extolling* of *him,* and to the *reproaching* of those who are not of the *established church. Out of the same mouth* on this day, *proceedeth blessing and cursing;*[5] *therewith bless they their God, even* Charles, *and therewith curse they* the dissenters: And their *tongue can no man tame; it is an unruly evil, full of deadly poison.* King *Charles* is, upon this solemnity, frequently compared to our Lord Jesus Christ, both in respect of the *holiness* of his life, and the greatness and injustice of his *sufferings;* and it is a wonder they do not add something concerning the *merits* of

[5] Jam. iii. 8, 9, 10.

his death also — But *blessed saint* and *royal martyr,* are as humble titles as any that are thought worthy of him.

Now this may, at first view, well appear to be a very strange *phenomenon.* For king *Charles* was really a man black with guilt and *laden with iniquity,*[6] as appears by his crimes before mentioned. He liv'd a tyrant; and it was the oppression and violence of his reign, that brought him to his untimely and violent end at last. Now what of saintship or martyrdom is there in all this! What of saintship is there in encouraging people to *profane* the *Lord's Day?* What of saintship in falsehood and perjury? What of saintship in repeated robberies and depredations? What of saintship in throwing real saints, and glorious patriots, into gaols? What of saintship in overturning an excellent civil constitution; — and proudly grasping at an illegal and monstrous power? What of saintship in the murder of thousands of innocent people; and involving a nation in all the calamities of a civil war? And what of martyrdom is there, in a man's bringing an immature and violent death upon himself, by *being wicked overmuch?*[7] Is there any such thing as grace, without goodness! As being a follower of Christ, without following him? As being his disciple, without learning of him to be just and beneficent? Or, as saintship without sanctity?[8] If not, I fear it will be hard to prove this man a saint. And verily one would be apt to suspect that *that church* must be but *poorly stocked* with saints and martyrs, which is forced to adopt such enormous sinners into her *kalendar,* in order to swell the number.

But to unravel this *mystery of* (*nonsense* as well as of) *iniquity,* which has *already worked* for a *long time* amongst us;[9] or, at least, to give the most probable solution of it; it is to be remembred, that king *Charles,* this *burlesque* upon saintship and martyrdom, though so great an oppressor, was a true friend to the *Church;* — so true a friend to her, that he was very well affected towards the *roman catholics;* and would, probably, have been very willing to unite *Lambeth* and *Rome.* This appears by his marrying a true *daughter* of that true *mother of harlots;*[10] which he did with a dispensation from the *Pope,* that supreme BISHOP; to whom when he wrote, he gave the title of MOST HOLY FATHER. His queen was extremely bigotted to all the follies and superstitions, and to the *hierarchy,* of *Rome;* and had a prodigious ascendency over him all his life It was, in part, owing to this, that he (probably) abetted the massacre of the protestants in *Ireland;* that he assisted in extirpating the *french* protestants at *Rochelle;* that he all along encouraged *papists,* and popishly effected *clergymen,* in preference to all other persons, and that he upheld that monster of wickedness, ARCH-BISHOP LAUD, and the bishops of his stamp, in all their church-tyranny and diabolical cruelties. In return to his kindness and indulgence in which respects, they caused many of the pulpits throughout the nation, to ring with the divine absolute, indefeasible right of kings; with the praises of *Charles* and his reign; and with the damnable sin of resisting the *Lord's anointed,* let him do what he would. So that not *Christ,* but *Charles,* was commonly preached to the people. — In *plain english,* there seems to have been an impious bargain struck up betwixt the *scepter* and the *surplice,* for enslaving both the *bodies* and *souls* of men. The king appeared to be willing that the clergy should do what they would, — set up a monstrous hierarchy like that of *Rome,* — a monstrous inquisition like that of

[6] Isai. i. 4.

[7] Eccles. vii. 17.

[8] Is it any wonder than even persons who do not *walk after their own lusts,* should *scoff* at *such saints* as this, both in the *first* and in the *last days,* even *from everlasting to everlasting?* 2 Pet. iii. 3, 4. — But perhaps it will be said, that these things are MYSTERIES, which (although very true in themselves) *lay-understandings* cannot comprehend: Or, indeed, any other persons amongst us, besides those who being INWARDLY MOVED BY THE HOLY GHOST, have taken a trip across the *Atlantic* to obtain *episcopal ordination and the indelible character.* — However, if these *consecrated gentlemen* do not quite despair of us, it is hoped that, in the abundance of their charity, they will endeavour to *illucidate* these *dark* points; and, at the same time, explain the creed of *another of their eminent saints,* which we are told, that unless we *believe faithfully,* (i.e. *believingly*) *we cannot be saved:* which creed, (or rather *riddle*) notwithstanding all the labours of the *pious* — and *metaphysical* Dr. *Waterland,* remains somewhat *ænigmatical* still.

[9] 2 Thess. ii. 7.

[10] Rev. xvii. 5.

Spain or *Portugal,* — or any thing else which their own pride, and the devil's malice, could prompt them to: *Provided always,* that the clergy would be *tools* to the crown; that they would make the people believe, that kings had God's authority for breaking God's law; that they had a commission from heaven to seize the estates and lives of their subjects at pleasure; and that it was a damnable sin to resist them, even when they did such things as deserved more than damnation. — This appears to be the true key for explaining the *mysterious* doctrine of king *Charles's* saintship and martyrdom. He was a saint, not because he was in his life, a good *man,* but a good *churchman;* not because he was a friend to *Christ,* but the *Craft.* And he was a martyr in his death, not because he bravely suffered death in that cause of truth and righteousness, but because he died an enemy to liberty and the rights of conscience, i.e. not because he died an enemy to *sin,* but *dissenters.* For these reasons it is that all bigotted clergymen, and friends to church-power, paint this man as a saint in his life, though he was such a mighty, such a *royal sinner;* and as a martyr in his death, though he fell a sacrifice only to his own ambition, avarice, and unbounded lust of power. And from prostituting their praise upon king *Charles,* and offering him that incense which is not his due, it is natural for them to make a transition to the dissenters, (as they commonly do) and to load them with that reproach which they do not deserve; they being generally professed enemies both to civil and ecclesiastical tyranny. WE are commonly charged (upon the *Thirtieth of January*) with the guilt of putting the king to death, under a notion that it was our ancestors that did it; and so we are represented in the blackest colours, not only as scismaticks, but also as traitors and rebels and all that is bad. And these *lofty* gentlemen usually rail upon this head, in such a manner as plainly shows, that they are either grossly ignorant of the history of those times which they speak of; or, which is worse, that they are guilty of the most shameful prevarication, slander and falshood. — But every *petty priest,* with a *roll* and a *gown,* thinks he must do something in imitation of his *betters,* in *lawn,* and show himself a *true son* of the church: And thus, through a foolish ambition to appear *considerable,* they only render themselves *contemptible.*

But suppose *our* fore-fathers did kill their *mock* saint and martyr a century ago, what is that to *us* now? If I mistake not, these gentlemen generally preach down the doctrine of the *imputation of Adam's sin to his posterity,* as absurd and unreasonable, notwithstanding they have solemnly subscribed what is equivalent to it in *their own articles of religion.* And therefore one would hardly expect that they would lay the guilt of the king's death upon *us,* altho' *our fore-fathers* had been the only authors of it. But this conduct is much more surprising, when it does not appear that *our* ancestors had any more hand in it than *their own.* — However, bigotry is sufficient to account for this, and many other *phenomena,* which cannot be accounted for in any other way.

Although the observation of this *anniversary* seems to have been (at least) superstitious in its *original;* and although it is often abused to very bad purposes by the established clergy, as they serve themselves of it, to perpetuate strife, a party spirit, and divisions in the christian church; yet it is to be hoped that one good end will be answered by it, quite contrary to their intention: It is to be hoped, that it will prove a standing *memento,* that *Britons* will not be slaves; and a warning to all corrupt *councellors* and *ministers,* not to go too far in advising to arbitrary, despotic measures —

To conclude: Let us all learn to be *free,* and to be *loyal.* Let us not profess ourselves vassals to the lawless pleasure of any man on earth. But let us remember, at the same time, government is *sacred,* and not to be *trifled* with. It is our happiness to live under the government of a PRINCE who is satisfied with ruling according to law; as every other *good prince* will — We enjoy under his administration all the liberty that is proper and expedient for us. It becomes us, therefore, to be contented, and dutiful subjects. Let us prize our freedom; but not *use our liberty for a cloke of maliciousness.*[11] There are men who strike at *liberty* under the term *licentiousness.* There are others who aim at

[11] I Pet. ii. 16.

popularity under the disguise of *patriotism*. Be aware of both. Extremes are dangerous. There is at present amongst *us*, perhaps, more danger of the *latter*, than of the *former*. For which reason I would exhort you to pay all due Regard to the government over us; to the KING and all in authority; and to *lead a quiet and peaceable life.*[12] — And while I am speaking of loyalty to our *earthly Prince*, suffer me just to put you in mind to be loyal also to the supreme RULER of the universe, *by whom kings reign, and princes decree justice.*[13] To which king eternal immortal, invisible, even to the ONLY WISE GOD,[14] be all honor and praise, DOMINION and thanksgiving, through JESUS CHRIST our LORD. AMEN.

II

The Declarations of the Stamp Act Congress

The Stamp Act Congress, initiated by Massachusetts in June, 1765, met in New York in October (7th to 24th). Unlike the Albany Congress, the meeting in New York was neither called nor endorsed by Britain. While only nine of the thirteen colonies were represented, three of the four not in attendance could blame their absence on the refusal of their royal governors to convene the assemblies to elect delegates. New Hampshire alone chose not to participate, but later endorsed the proceedings.

The "declarations of the rights and grievances" were largely the work of John Dickinson of Pennsylvania. For all its moderate tone, the firmness of the "declarations" is unmistakable: the colonists laid claim to "all the inherent rights and liberties" of natural born Englishmen, including "the undoubted right of Englishmen, that no taxes should be imposed on them, but with their own consent." Edmund S. Morgan has rightly criticized the vagueness of "due subordination" to Parliament, but this was the price of unity in the Congress. The colonial appeal was notable in its emphasis upon legal and constitutional rights; the abstractions of philosophy are conspicuously absent.

The members of this congress, sincerely devoted, with the warmest sentiments of affection and duty to his Majesty's person and government; inviolably attached to the present happy establishment of the Protestant succession, and with minds deeply impressed by a sense of the present and impending misfortunes of the British colonies on this continent; having considered as maturely as time would permit, the circumstances of the said colonies, esteem it our indispensable duty to make the following declarations, of our humble opinion, respecting the most essential rights and liberties of the colonists, and of the grievances under which they labour, by reason of several late acts of Parliament.

I. That his Majesty's subjects in these colonies, owe the same allegiance to the Crown of Great Britain, that is owing from his subjects born within the realm, and all due subordination to that august body, the Parliament of Great Britain.

II. That his Majesty's liege subjects in these colonies are entitled to all the inherent rights and liberties of his natural born subjects within the kingdom of Great Britain.

III. That it is inseparably essential to the freedom of a people, and the undoubted right of Englishmen, that no taxes should be imposed on them, but with their own consent, given personally, or by their representatives.

IV. That the people of these colonies are not, and from their local circumstances, cannot be represented in the House of Commons in Great Britain.

V. That the only representatives of the people of these colonies, are persons chosen therein, by themselves; and that no taxes ever have been, or can be constitutionally imposed on them, but by their respective legislature.

The Declarations of the Stamp Act Congress, October 19, 1765. Printed in *Proceedings of the Congress at New York* (Annapolis, 1766), pp. 15–16.

[12] I Tim. ii. 2.

[13] Prov. viii. 15.

[14] I Tim. i. 17.

VI. That all supplies to the Crown, being free gifts of the people, it is unreasonable and inconsistent with the principles and spirit of the British constitution, for the people of Great Britain to grant to his Majesty the property of the colonists.

VII. That trial by jury is the inherent and invaluable right of every British subject in these colonies.

VIII. That the late Act of Parliament, entitled, An Act for granting and applying certain Stamp Duties, and other Duties in the British Colonies and Plantations in America, etc., by imposing taxes on the inhabitants of these colonies, and the said Act, and several other Acts, by extending the jurisdiction of the courts of admiralty beyond its ancient limits, have a manifest tendency to subvert the rights and liberties of the colonists.

IX. That the duties imposed by several late Acts of Parliament, from the peculiar circumstances of these colonies, will be extremely burdensome and grievous, and from the scarcity of specie, the payment of them absolutely impracticable.

X. That as the profits of the trade of these colonies ultimately centre in Great Britain, to pay for the manufactures which they are obliged to take from thence, they eventually contribute very largely to all supplies granted there to the Crown.

XI. That the restrictions imposed by several late Acts of Parliament, on the trade of these colonies, will render them unable to purchase the manufactures of Great Britain.

XII. That the increase, prosperity and happiness of these colonies, depend on the full and free enjoyment of their rights and liberties, and an intercourse with Great Britain, mutually affectionate and advantageous.

XIII. That it is the right of the British subjects in these colonies, to petition the king or either house of Parliament.

Lastly, that it is the indispensable duty of these colonies to the best of sovereigns, to the mother country, and to themselves, to endeavour by a loyal and dutiful address to his Majesty, and humble applications to both houses of Parliament, to procure the repeal of the Act for granting and applying certain stamp duties, of all clauses of any other Acts of Parliament, whereby the jurisdiction of the admiralty is extended as aforesaid, and of the other late Acts for the restriction of American commerce.

III

Letters from a Farmer in Pennsylvania

George Grenville alienated his royal master and was replaced by Lord Rockingham in 1765. Rockingham repealed the Stamp Act with an almost indecent haste in Grenville's opinion, but in 1766 he too was replaced — by Charles Townshend, the dominant figure in the Pitt-Grafton Ministry. In September, 1767, Americans learned of Townshend's colonial program: import duties on glass, lead, paints, paper and tea and new enforcement measures to accompany these taxes. Bostonians lost little time demonstrating their opposition. The reaction in Pennsylvania was less immediate, and it was left to John Dickinson *to awaken Philadelphians with his famous* Letters from a Farmer. *The first appeared in the December 2 issue of the* Pennsylvania Chronicle; *the twelfth and last appeared on February 15, 1768. The popularity of the* Letters *was immediate and startling. Nearly every colonial newspaper ran them, and seven different editions appeared in book form by 1769.*

The first Letter begins gently, modestly, with Dickinson establishing his credentials as a man with "a greater share of knowledge in history, and the laws and constitution of my country than is generally attained by men of my class. . . ." The principal object of this opening Letter was the New York Restraining Act[1]*: New Yorkers, argued Dickinson, "cannot be legally*

Reprinted from John Dickinson, *Letters from a Farmer in Pennsylvania* (Boston: Mein and Fleeming, 1768), pp. 1–8.

[1] The first of the Townshend Acts, the Restraining Act, provided for the suspension of the New York assembly until it complied with the Quartering Act of May, 1765.

deprived of the privilege of making laws, only for insisting on that exclusive privilege of taxation."

My *Dear Countrymen,* I am a farmer, settled after a variety of fortunes, near the banks, of the river *Delaware,* in the province of *Pennsylvania.* I received a liberal education, and have been engaged in the busy scenes of life: But am now convinced, that a man may be as happy without bustle, as with it. My farm is small, my servants are few, and good; I have a little money at interest; I wish for no more: my employment in my own affairs is easy; and with a contented grateful mind, I am compleating the number of days allotted to me by divine goodness.

Being master of my time, I spend a good deal of it in a library, which I think the most valuable part of my small estate; and being acquainted with two or three gentlemen of abilities and learning, who honour me with their friendship, I believe I have acquired a greater share of knowledge in history, and the laws and constitution of my country, than is generally attained by men of my class, many of them not being so fortunate as I have been in the opportunities of getting information.

From infancy I was taught to love humanity and liberty. Inquiry and experience have since confirmed my reverence for the lessons then given me, by convincing me more fully of their truth and excellence. Benevolence towards mankind excites wishes for their welfare, and such wishes endear the means of fulfilling them. Those can be found in liberty alone, and therefore her sacred cause ought to be espoused by every man, on every occasion, to the utmost of his power: as a charitable but poor person does not withhold his *mite,* because he cannot relieve *all* the distresses of the miserable, so let not any honest man suppress his sentiments concerning freedom, however small their influence is likely to be. Perhaps he may "touch some wheel" that will have an effect greater than he expects.

These being my sentiments, I am encouraged to offer to you, my countrymen, my thoughts on some late transactions, that in my opinion are of the utmost importance to you. Conscious of my defects, I have waited some time, in expectation of seeing the subject treated by persons much better qualified for the task; but being therein disappointed, and apprehensive that longer delays will be injurious, I venture at length to request the attention of the public, praying only for one thing, — that is that these lines may be *read* with the same zeal for the happiness of British America, with which they were *wrote.*

With a good deal of surprise I have observed, that little notice has been taken of an act of parliament, as injurious in its principle to the liberties of these colonies, as the STAMP-ACT was: I mean the act for suspending the legislation of New-York.

The assembly of that government complied with a former act of parliament, requiring certain provisions to be made for the troops in America, in every particular, I think, except the articles of salt, pepper, and vinegar. In my opinion they acted imprudently, considering all circumstances, in not complying so far, as would have given satisfaction, as several colonies did: but my dislike of their conduct in that instance, has not blinded me so much, that I cannot plainly perceive, that they have been punished in a manner pernicious to American freedom, and justly alarming to all the colonies.

If the BRITISH PARLIAMENT has a legal authority to order, that we shall furnish a single article for the troops here, and to compel obedience to that order; they have the same right to order us to supply those troops with arms, cloaths, and every necessary, and to compel obedience to that order also; in short, to lay *any burdens* they please upon us. What is this but *taxing* us at a *certain sum,* and leaving to us only the *manner* of raising it? How is this mode more tolerable than the STAMP ACT? Would that act have appeared more pleasing to AMERICANS, if being ordered thereby to raise the sum total of the taxes, the mighty privilege had been left to them, of saying how much should be paid for an instrument of writing on paper, and how much for another on parchment?

An act of parliament commanding us to do a certain thing, if it has any validity, is a tax upon us for the expence that accrues in complying with it, and for this reason, I believe, every colony on the continent, that chose to give a mark of their respect for GREAT-BRITAIN, in complying with the act relating to the troops, cautiously avoided the mention of that act, lest their conduct should be attributed to its supposed obligation.

The matter being thus stated, the assembly of *New-York* either had, or had not a right to refuse submission to that act. If they had, and I imagine no AMERICAN will say, they had not, then the parliament had no *right* to compel them to execute it. — If they had not *that right,* they had *no right* to punish them for not executing it; and therefore had *no right* to suspend their legislation, which is a punishment. In fact, if the people of *New-York* cannot be legally taxed but by their own representatives, they cannot be legally deprived of the privileges of making laws, only for insisting on that exclusive privilege of taxation. If they may be legally deprived in such a case of the privilege of making laws, why may they not, with equal reason, be deprived of every other privilege? Or why may not every colony be treated in the same manner, when any of them shall dare to deny their assent to any impositions that shall be directed? Or what signifies the repeal of the STAMP-ACT, if these colonies are to lose their *other* privileges, by not tamely surrendering that of *taxation?*

There is one consideration arising from this suspicion, which is not generally attended to, but shews its importance very clearly. It was not *necessary* that this suspension should be caused by an act of parliament. The crown might have restrained the governor of *New-York,* even from calling the assembly together, by its prerogative in the royal governments. This step, I suppose, would have been taken, if the conduct of the assembly of *New-York,* had been regarded as an act of disobedience *to the crown alone:* but it is regarded as an act of "disobedience to the authority of the BRITISH LEGISLATURE." This gives the suspension a consequence vastly more affecting. It is a parliamentary assertion of the *supreme authority* of the *British legislature* over these colonies in *the part of taxation;* and is intended to COMPEL *New-York* unto a submission to that authority. It seems therefore to me as much a violation of the liberty of the people of that province, and consequently of all these colonies, as if the parliament had sent a number of regiments to be quartered upon them till they should comply. For it is evident, that the suspension is meant as a compulsion; and the *method* of compelling is totally indifferent. It is indeed probable, that the sight of red coats, and the beating of drums would have been most alarming, because people are generally more influenced by their eyes and ears than by their reason: But whoever seriously considers the matter, must perceive, that a dreadful stroke is aimed at the liberty of these colonies: For the cause of *one* is the cause of *all.* If the parliament may lawfully deprive *New-York* of any of its rights, it may deprive any, or all the other colonies of their rights; and nothing can possibly so much encourage such attempts, as a mutual inattention to the interest of each other. *To divide, and thus to destroy,* is the first political maxim in attacking those who are powerful by their union. He certainly is not a wise man, who folds his arms and reposeth himself at home, seeing with unconcern the flames that have invaded his neighbour's house, without any endeavours to extinguish them. When Mr. *Hampden's* ship-money cause, for three shillings and four-pence, was tried, all the people of *England,* with anxious expectation, interested themselves in the important decision; and when the slightest point touching the freedom of a single colony is agitated, I earnestly wish, that all the rest may with equal ardour support their sister. Very much may be said on this subject, but I hope, more at present is unnecessary.

With concern I have observed that two assemblies of this province have sat and adjourned, without taking any notice of this act. It may perhaps be asked, what would have been proper for them to do? I am by no means fond of inflammatory measures. I detest them. — I should be sorry that any thing should be done which might justly displease our sovereign or our mother-country. But a firm, modest exertion of a free spirit, should never be wanting on public occasions. It appears to me, that it would have been sufficient for the assembly, to have ordered our agents to represent to the King's ministers, their sense of the suspending act, and to pray for its repeal. Thus we should have borne our testimony against it; and might therefore reasonably expect that on a like occasion, we might receive the same assistance from the other colonies.

"Concordia res parvae crescunt."

Small things grow great by concord. —

A Farmer.

IV

The Boston Massacre *and* Dr. Joseph Warren's Funeral Oration

Agitation in Boston over the Townshend duties reached its peak early in 1770. The presence of General Gage's troops in the city both alarmed and infuriated its residents, who, like many Englishmen, had long associated standing armies with tyranny. Feelings ran high and tempers sharpened as townspeople jeered and taunted the British regulars — or "lobster-backs" as they derisively called them. Several ugly incidents had already occurred when, on March 5th, a company of British soldiers, goaded to desperation by the stones and insults of a threatening crowd, fired a volley into their midst.

The Massacre gave Massachusetts its martyrs and furnished the colonists with an effective propaganda issue for years to come. The Boston Gazette *appeared on March 12 with black borders, mourning the five victims of British brutality.*

Beginning in 1771, the anniversary of the Boston Massacre was made the occasion for a public oration, a speech invariably calculated to revive bitter memories and stir up fresh hostility towards the British. Joseph Warren, *a member of the committee that devised the Massacre orations, spoke on two of these occasions. His second oration, delivered in 1775, has suffered undeserved neglect, possibly because it was overshadowed by the increased revolutionary activity in Massachusetts. Warren's speech dwelt extravagantly on the Massacre; few passages are more grisly than his injunction: "take heed, ye orphan babes, lest, whilst your streaming eyes are fixed upon the ghastly corpse,* your feet slide on the stones bespattered with your father's brains." *But it is also interesting to note that Warren gave much time to reviewing the history of colonial rights and their constitutional origins; this at a time when, according to many historians, the colonists had moved to a reliance upon natural rights arguments to justify their grievances against the British Crown. Less than four months after this oration Warren lay dead on the slope of Breed's Hill.*

The Boston Massacre, an account in the *Boston Gazette,* March 12, 1770.

The Boston Massacre

The town of Boston affords a recent and melancholy demonstration of the destructive consequences of quartering troops among citizens in a time of peace, under a pretence of supporting the laws and aiding civil authority; every considerate and unprejudiced person among us was deeply impressed with the apprehension of these consequences when it was known that a number of regiments were ordered to this town under such a pretext, but in reality to enforce oppressive measures; to awe and control the legislative as well as executive power of the province, and to quell a spirit of liberty, which however it may have been basely opposed and even ridiculed by some, would do honour to any age or country. A few persons amongst us had determined to use all their influence to procure so destructive a measure with a view to their securely enjoying the profits of an American revenue, and unhappily both for Britain and this country they found means to effect it.

It is to Governor Bernard, the commissioners, their confidants and coadjutors, that we are indebted as the procuring cause of a military power in this capital. The Boston Journal of Occurrences, as printed in Mr. Holt's *New York Gazette,* from time to time, afforded many striking instances of the distresses brought upon the inhabitants by this measure; and since those Journals have been discontinued, our troubles from that quarter have been growing upon us. We have known a party of soldiers in the face of day fire off a loaden musket upon the inhabitants, others have been pricked with bayonets, and even our magistrates assaulted and put in danger of their lives, when offenders brought before them have been rescued; and why those and other bold and base criminals have as yet escaped the punishment due to their crimes may be soon matter of enquiry by the representative body of this people. It is natural to suppose that when the inhabitants of this town saw those laws which had been enacted for their security, and which they were ambitious of holding up to the soldiery, eluded, they should more commonly resent for themselves; and accordingly it has so happened. Many have been the squabbles between them and the soldiery; but it seems their being often worsted by our youth in these encounters, has only served to irritate the former. What passed at Mr. Gray's rope-walk has already been given the public and may be said to have led the way to the late catastrophe. That the rope-walk lads, when attacked by superior numbers, should defend themselves with so much spirit and success in the club-way, was too mortifying, and perhaps it may hereafter appear that even some of their officers were unhappily affected with this circumstance. Divers stories were propagated among the soldiery that served to agitate their spirits; particularly on the Sabbath that one Chambers, a sergeant, represented as a sober man, had been missing the preceding day and must therefore have been murdered by the townsmen. An officer of distinction so far credited this report that he entered Mr. Gray's rope-walk that Sabbath; and when required of by that gentleman as soon as he could meet him, the occasion of his so doing, the officer replied that it was to look if the sergeant said to be murdered had not been hid there. This sober sergeant was found on the Monday unhurt in a house of pleasure. The evidences already collected show that many threatenings had been thrown out by the soldiery, but we do not pretend to say that there was any preconcerted plan. When the evidences are published, the world will judge. We may, however, venture to declare that it appears too probable from their conduct that some of the soldiery aimed to draw and provoke the townsmen into squabbles, and that they then intended to make use of other weapons than canes, clubs, or bludgeons.

Our readers will doubtless expect a circumstantial account of the tragical affair on Monday night last; but we hope they will excuse our being so particular as we should have been, had we not seen that the town was intending an enquiry and full representation thereof.

On the evening of Monday, being the fifth current, several soldiers of the 29th Regiment were seen parading the streets with their drawn cutlasses and bayonets, abusing and wounding numbers of the inhabitants.

A few minutes after nine o'clock four youths, named Edward Archbald, William Merchant, Francis Archbald, and John Leech, jun., came down Cornhill together, and separating at Doctor Loring's corner, the two former were passing the narrow alley leading to Murray's barrack in which was a soldier brandishing a broad sword of an uncommon size against the walls, out of which he struck fire plentifully. A person of mean countenance armed with a large cudgel bore him company. Edward Archbald admonished Mr. Merchant to take care of the sword, on which the soldier turned round and struck Archbald on the arm, then pushed at Merchant and pierced through his clothes inside the arm close to the armpit and grazed the skin. Merchant then struck the soldier with a short stick he had; and the other person ran to the barrack and brought with him two soldiers, one armed with a pair of tongs, the other with a shovel. He with the tongs pursued Archbald back through the alley, collared and laid him over the head with the tongs. The noise brought people together; and John Hicks, a young lad, coming up, knocked the soldier down but let him get up again; and more lads gathering, drove them back to the barrack where the boys stood some time as it were to keep them in. In less than a minute ten or twelve of them came out with drawn cutlasses, clubs, and bayonets and set upon the unarmed boys and young folk who stood them a little while but, finding the inequality of their equipment, dispersed. On hearing the noise, one Samuel Atwood came up to see what was the matter; and entering the alley from dock square, heard the latter part of the combat; and when the boys had dispersed he met the ten or twelve soldiers aforesaid rushing down the alley towards the square and asked them if they intended to murder people? They answered Yes, by G-d, root and branch! With that one of them struck Mr Atwood with a club which was repeated by another; and being unarmed, he turned to go off and received a wound on the left shoulder which reached the bone and gave him much pain. Retreating a few steps, Mr. Atwood met two officers and said, gentlemen, what is the matter? They answered, you'll see by and by. Immediately after, those heroes appeared in the square, asking where were the boogers? Where were the cowards? But notwithstanding their fierceness to naked men, one of them advanced towards a youth who had a split of a raw stave in his hand and said, damn them, here is one of them. But the young man seeing a person near him with a drawn sword and good cane ready to support him, held up his stave in defiance; and they quietly passed by him up the little alley by Mr. Silsby's to King Street where they attacked single and unarmed persons till they raised much clamour, and then turned down Cornhill Street, insulting all they met in like manner and pursuing some to their very doors. Thirty or forty persons, mostly lads, being by this means gathered in King Street, Capt. Preston with a party of men with charged bayonets, came from the main guard to the commissioner's house, the soldiers pushing their bayonets, crying, make way! They took place by the custom house and, continuing to push to drive the people off, pricked some in several places, on which they were clamorous and, it is said, threw snow balls. On this, the Captain commanded them to fire; and more snow balls coming, he again said, damn you, fire, be the consequence what it will! One soldier then fired, and a townsman with a cudgel struck him over the hands with such force that he dropped his firelock; and, rushing forward, aimed a blow at the Captain's head which grazed his hat and fell pretty heavy upon his arm. However, the soldiers continued the fire successively till seven or eight or, as some say, eleven guns were discharged.

By this fatal manoeuvre three men were laid dead on the spot and two more struggling for life; but what showed a degree of cruelty unknown to British troops, at least since the House of Hanover has directed their operations, was an attempt to fire upon or push with their bayonets the persons who undertook to remove the slain and wounded!

Mr. Benjamin Leigh, now undertaker in the Delph manufactory, came up; and after some conversation with Capt. Preston relative to his conduct in this affair, advised him to draw off his men, with which he complied.

The dead are Mr. Samuel Gray, killed on the spot, the ball entering his head and beating off a large portion of his skull.

A mulatto man named Crispus Attucks, who was born in Framingham, but lately belonged to New-Providence and was here in order to go for North Carolina, also killed instantly, two balls entering his breast, one of them in special goring the right lobe of the lungs and a great part of the liver most horribly.

Mr. James Caldwell, mate of Capt. Morton's vessel, in like manner killed by two balls entering his back.

Mr. Samuel Maverick, a promising youth of seventeen years of age, son of the widow Maverick, and an apprentice to Mr. Greenwood, ivory-turner, mortally wounded; a ball went through his belly and was cut out at his back. He died the next morning.

A lad named Christopher Monk, about seventeen years of age, an apprentice to Mr. Walker, shipwright, wounded; a ball entered his back about four inches above the left kidney near the spine and was cut out of the breast on the same side. Apprehended he will die.

A lad named John Clark, about seventeen years of age, whose parents live at Medford, and an apprentice to Capt. Samuel Howard of this town, wounded; a ball entered just above his groin and came out at his hip on the opposite side. Apprehended he will die.

Mr. Edward Payne of this town, merchant, standing at his entry door received a ball in his arm which shattered some of the bones.

Mr. John Green, tailor, coming up Leverett's Lane, received a ball just under his hip and lodged in the under part of his thigh, which was extracted.

Mr. Robert Patterson, a seafaring man, who was the person that had his trousers shot through in Richardson's affair, wounded; a ball went through his right arm, and he suffered a great loss of blood.

Mr. Patrick Carr, about thirty years of age, who worked with Mr. Field, leather breeches-maker in Queen Street, wounded; a ball entered near his hip and went out at his side.

A lad named David Parker, an apprentice to Mr. Eddy, the wheelwright, wounded; a ball entered in his thigh.

The people were immediately alarmed with the report of this horrid massacre, the bells were set a-ringing, and great numbers soon assembled at the place where this tragical scene had been acted. Their feelings may be better conceived than expressed; and while some were taking care of the dead and wounded, the rest were in consultation what to do in those dreadful circumstances. But so little intimidated were they, notwithstanding their being within a few yards of the main guard and seeing the 29th Regiment under arms and drawn up in King Street, that they kept their station and appeared, as an officer of rank expressed it, ready to run upon the very muzzles of their muskets. The lieutenant-governor soon came into the town house and there met some of his Majesty's Council and a number of civil magistrates. A considerable body of the people immediately entered the council chamber and expressed themselves to his honour with a freedom and warmth becoming the occasion. He used his utmost endeavours to pacify them, requesting that they would let the matter subside for the night and promising to do all in his power that justice should be done and the law have its course. Men of influence and weight with the people were not wanting on their part to procure their compliance with his Honour's request by representing the horrible consequences of a promiscuous and rash engagement in the night, and assuring them that such measures should be entered upon in the morning as would be agreeable to their dignity and a more likely way of obtaining the best satisfaction for the blood of their fellow townsmen. The inhabitants attended to these suggestions; and the regiment under arms being ordered to their barracks, which was insisted upon by the people, they then separated and returned to their dwellings by one o'clock. At three o'clock Capt. Preston was committed, as were the soldiers who fired, a few hours after him.

Tuesday morning presented a most shocking scene, the blood of our fellow citizens running like water through King Street and the Merchants' Exchange, the principal spot of the military parade for about eighteen months past. Our blood might also be tracked up to the head of Long Lane, and through divers other streets and passages.

At eleven o'clock the inhabitants met at Faneuil Hall; and after some animated speeches becoming the occasion, they chose a committee of fifteen respectable gentlemen to wait upon the lieutenant-governor in Council to request of him to issue his orders for the immediate removal of the troops.

The Funeral

Last Thursday, agreeable to a general request of the inhabitants and by the consent of parents and friends, were carried to their grave in succession the bodies of Samuel Gray, Samuel Maverick, James Caldwell, and Crispus Attucks, the unhappy victims who fell in the bloody massacre of the Monday evening preceding!

On this occasion most of the shops in town were shut, all the bells were ordered to toll a solemn peal, as were also those in the neighbouring towns of Charlestown, Roxbury, etc. The procession began to move between the hours of four and five in the afternoon, two of the unfortunate suffers, viz. Messrs. James Caldwell and Crispus Attucks who were strangers, borne from Faneuil Hall attended by a numerous train of persons of all ranks; and the other two, viz. Mr. Samuel Gray, from the house of Mr. Benjamin Gray (his brother) on the north side the Exchange, and Mr. Maverick, from the house of his distressed mother, Mrs. Mary Maverick, in Union Street, each followed by their respective relations and friends, the several hearses forming a junction in King Street, the theatre of the inhuman tragedy, proceeded from thence through the Main Street, lengthened by an immense concourse of people so numerous as to be obliged to follow in ranks of six, and brought up by a long train of carriages belonging to the principal gentry of the town. The bodies were deposited in one vault in the middle burying ground. The aggravated circumstances of their death, the distress and sorrow visible in every countenance, together with the peculiar solemnity with which the whole funeral was conducted, surpass description.

Dr. Joseph Warren's Funeral Oration

The many injuries offered to the town, I pass over in silence. I cannot now mark out the path which led to that unequalled scene of horror, the sad remembrance of which, takes the full possession of my soul. The sanguinary theatre again opens itself to view. The baleful images of terror crowd around me — and discontented ghosts, with hollow groans, appear to solemnize the anniversary of the fifth of March.

Approach we then the melancholy walk of death. Hither let me call the gay companion; here let him drop a farewell tear upon that body which so late he saw vigorous and warm with social mirth — hither let me lead the tender mother to weep over her beloved son — come widowed mourner, here satiate thy grief; behold thy murdered husband gasping on the ground and to complete the pompous show of wretchedness, bring in each hand thy infant children to bewail their father's fate — take heed, ye orphan babes, lest, whilst your streaming eyes are fixed upon the ghastly corpse, *your feet slide on the stones bespattered with your father's brains.* Enough! this tragedy need not be heightened by an infant weltering in the blood of him that gave it birth. Nature reluctant, shrinks already from the view, and the chilled blood rolls slowly backward to its fountain. We wildly stare about, and with amazement, ask who spread this ruin round us? what wretch has dared deface the image of his God? has haughty France, or cruel Spain, sent forth her myrmidons? has the grim savage rushed again from the far distant wilderness? or does some fiend fierce from the depth of hell, with all the rancorous malice which the apostate damned can feel, twang her destructive bow, and hurl her deadly arrows at our breast? no; none of these — but, how astonishing! it is the hand of Britain that inflicts the wound. The arms of George, our rightful king, have been employed to shed that blood, when justice, or the honor of his crown, had called his subjects to the field.

But pity, grief, astonishment, with all the softer movements of the soul, must now give way to stronger passions. Say, fellow-citizens what dreadful thought now swells your heaving bosoms — you fly to arms — sharp indignation flashes from each eye — revenge gnashes her iron teeth — death grins an hideous smile, secure to drench his greedy jaws in human gore — whilst hovering juries darken all the air.

But stop, my bold adventurous countrymen, stain not your weapons with the blood of Britons. Attend to reason's voice — humanity puts in her claim — and sues to be again admitted to her wonted seat, the bosom of the brave. Revenge is far beneath the noble mind. Many, perhaps, compelled to rank among the vile assassins, do from their inmost souls, detest the barbarous action. The winged death, shot from your arms, may chance to pierce some breast that bleeds already for your injured country.

The storm subsides — a solemn pause ensues — you spare, upon condition they depart. They go — they quit your city — they no more shall give offence. — Thus closes the important drama.

And could it have been conceived that we again should have seen a British army in our land, sent to enforce obedience to acts of parliament destructive of our liberty. But the royal ear, far distant from this western world, has been assaulted by the tongue of slander; and villains, traitorous alike to king and country, have prevailed upon a gracious prince to clothe his countenance with wrath, and to erect the hostile banner against a people ever affectionate and loyal to him and his illustrious predecessors of the house of Hanover. Our streets are again filled with armed men; our harbor is crowded with ships of war; but these cannot intimidate us; our liberty must be preserved; it is far dearer than life, we hold it even dear as our allegiance; we must defend it against the attacks of friends as well as enemies; we cannot suffer even Britons to ravish it from us.

No longer could we reflect with generous

Dr. Joseph Warren, Oration of March 5, 1775; printed in Hezekiah Niles, *Principles and Acts of the Revolution* (Baltimore, 1822), pp. 25–29.

pride on the heroic actions of our American forefathers — no longer boast our origin from that far-famed island whose warlike sons have so often drawn their well tried swords to save her from the ravages of tyranny; could we but for a moment entertain the thought of giving up our liberty. The man who meanly will submit to wear a shackle, contemns the noblest gift of heaven, and impiously affronts the God that made him free.

It was a maxim of the Roman people, which eminently conduced to the greatness of that state, never to despair of the commonwealth. The maxim may prove as salutary to us now, as it did to them. Short-sighted mortals see not the numerous links on which the fate of kings and nations is suspended. Ease and prosperity (though pleasing for a day) have often sunk a people into effeminacy and sloth. Hardships and dangers (tho' we forever strive to shun them) have frequently called forth such virtues, as have commanded the applause and reverence of an admiring world. Our country boldly calls you to be circumspect, vigilant, active and brave. Perhaps, (all gracious heaven avert it) perhaps, the power of Britain, a nation great in war, by some malignant influence, may be employed to enslave you: but let not even this discourage you. Her arms, 'tis true, have filled the world with terror: her troops have reaped the laurels of the field: her fleets have rode triumphant on the sea — and when or where, did you, my countrymen, depart inglorious from the field of fight! you too can shew the trophies of your forefathers' victories and your own; can name the fortresses and battles you have won; and many of you count the honorable scars of wounds received, whilst fighting for your king and country.

Where justice is the standard, heaven is the warrior's shield: but conscious guilt unnerves the arm that lifts the sword against the innocent. Britain, united with these colonies, by commerce and affection by interest and blood, may mock the threats of France and Spain: may be the seat of universal empire. But should America, either by force, or those more dangerous engines, luxury and corruption, ever be brought into a state of vassalage, Britain must lose her freedom also. No longer shall she sit the empress of the sea: her ships no more shall waft her thunders over the wide ocean: the wreath shall wither on her temples: her weakened arm shall be unable to defend her coasts: and she, at last, must bow her venerable head to some proud foreigner's despotic rule.

But if, from past events, we may venture to form a judgment of the future, we justly may expect that the devices of our enemies will but increase the triumphs of our country. I must indulge a hope that Britain's liberty, as well as ours, will eventually be preserved by the virtue of America.

The attempt of the British parliament to raise a revenue from America, and our denial of their right to do it, have excited an almost universal enquiry into the right of mankind in general, and of British subjects in particular; the necessary result of which must be such a liberality of sentiment, and such a jealousy of those in power, as will, better than an adamantine wall, secure us against the future approaches of despotism.

The malice of the Boston port-bill has been defeated in a very considerable degree, by giving you an opportunity of deserving, and our brethren in this and our sister-colonies an opportunity of bestowing, those benefactions which have delighted your friends and astonished your enemies, not only in America, but in Europe also. And what is more valuable still, the sympathetic feelings for a brother in distress, and the grateful emotions excited in the breast of him who finds relief, must forever endear each to the other, and form those indissoluble bonds of friendship and affection, on which the preservation of our rights so evidently depend.

The mutilation of our charter, has made every other colony jealous for its own; for this if once submitted to by us, would set on float the property and government of every British settlement upon the continent. If charters are not deemed sacred, how miserably precarious is every thing founded upon them.

Even the sending troops to put these acts in execution, is not without advantages to us. The exactness and beauty of their discipline inspire our youth with ardor in the pursuit of military knowledge. Charles the invincible, taught Peter the great, the art of war. The battle of Pultowa convinced Charles of the proficiency Peter had made.

Our country is in danger, but not to be despaired of. Our enemies are numerous and powerful — but we have many friends — determining to be free, and Heaven and earth will aid the resolution. On you depend the fortunes of America. You are to decide the important question, on which rest the happiness and liberty of millions yet unborn. Act worthy of yourselves. The faltering tongue of hoary age calls on you to support your country. The lisping infant raises its suppliant hands, imploring defence against the monster slavery. Your fathers look from their celestial seats with smiling approbation on their sons, who boldly stand forth in the cause of virtue; but sternly frown upon the inhuman miscreant, who, to secure the loaves and fishes to himself, would breed a serpent to destroy his children.

V

Independence: Jefferson's Notes of Proceedings in the Continental Congress

The sequence of events leading to the decision for Independence is familiar: the Boston Tea Party was answered by the Coercive Acts in 1774; the First Continental Congress adopted the Declaration and Resolves, denouncing the Coercive Acts and insisting upon colonial legislative rights "in all cases of taxation and internal polity," subject to royal approval; bloodshed at Lexington and Breed's Hill was followed by the Declaration of the Causes and Necessities of Taking Up Arms, announcing colonial readiness to die to avoid slavery; in August, 1775, George III declared the colonies in a state of open rebellion; in December the Second Continental Congress reaffirmed its allegiance to George III but repudiated his Parliament; January, 1776, saw the publication of Thomas Paine's Common Sense, *which presented the choice between independence and slavery and attacked the King as the royal brute who had corrupted Parliament, ministry, and even himself. Not until June 7, 1776, did Richard Henry Lee rise to move formally that the Congress declare that "the united Colonies are, and of right ought to be, free and independent States."*

Jefferson's notes do little more than outline the course of the debate, but they do justice to the sense of the arguments advanced. Despite recent military developments, there was considerable opposition in the Congress to an immediate announcement of independence. Jefferson records the fears expressed by James Wilson, John Dickinson and others that unity was essential and not yet achieved, that an alliance was needed and not yet in prospect, that prudence counseled caution. But, notes Jefferson, even the opponents to independence "saw the impossibility that we should ever again be united with Great Britain."

The debate would appear to confirm the persistent reluctance with which Americans embraced their Revolution. Even a conservative could be a staunch patriot when championing ancient liberties; the acid test came in June and July, 1776, when at last a patriot had also to be a Revolutionary. The Congress knew the road it had to travel, but it had difficulty agreeing upon its time for departure.

Jefferson's Notes of Proceedings in the Continental Congress, June 7 to July 2, 1776. Printed in *Journals of the Continental Congress,* ed. Worthington C. Ford (Washington, D.C., 1906), VI, 1087–1093.

In Congress, Friday, June 7, 1776

The delegates from Virginia moved in obedience to instructions from their constituents that the Congress should declare that these United Colonies are and of right ought to be free and independent states; that they are absolved from all obedience to the British Crown, and that all political connection between them and the state of Great Britain is and ought to be totally dissolved; that measures should be immediately taken for procuring the assistance of foreign powers, and a confederation be formed to bind the colonies more closely together.

The house being obliged to attend at that time to some other business, the proposition was referred to the next day when the members were ordered to attend punctually at ten o'clock.

Saturday June 8th they proceeded to take it into consideration, and referred it to a committee of the whole, into which they immediately resolved themselves, and passed that day and Monday the 10th in debating on the subject.

It was argued by [James] Wilson, Robert R. Livingston, E.[dward] Rutledge, [John] Dickinson, and others:

That though they were friends to the measures themselves and saw the impossibility that we should ever again be united with Great Britain, yet they were against adopting them at this time;

That the conduct we had formerly observed was wise and proper now, of deferring to take any capital step till the voice of the people drove us into it;

That they were our power and without them our declarations could not be carried into effect;

That the people of the middle colonies (Maryland, Delaware, Pennsylvania, the Jersies, and N.[ew] York) were not yet ripe for bidding adieu to British connection; but that they were fast ripening and in a short time would join in the general voice of America;

That the resolution entered into by this house on the 15th of May for suppressing the exercise of all powers derived from the Crown had shown, by the ferment into which it had thrown these middle colonies, that they had not yet accommodated their minds to a separation from the mother country;

That some of them had expressly forbidden their delegates to consent to such a declaration, and others had given no instructions, and consequently no powers to give such consent;

That if the delegates of any particular colony had no power to declare such colony independent, certain they were the others could not declare it for them, the colonies being as yet perfectly independent of each other;

That the Assembly of Pennsylvania was now sitting above stairs, their convention would sit within a few days; the convention of New York was now sitting, and those of the Jersies and Delaware counties would meet on the Monday following, and it was probable these bodies would take up the question of independence, and would declare to their delegates the voice of their state;

That if such a declaration should now be agreed to, these delegates must retire and possibly their colonies might secede from the union;

That such a secession would weaken us more than could be compensated by any foreign alliance;

That in the event of such a division foreign powers would either refuse to join themselves to our fortunes, or having us so much in their power as that desperate declaration would place us, they would insist on terms proportionably more hard and prejudicial;

That we had little reason to expect an alliance with those to whom alone as yet we had cast our eyes;

That France and Spain had reason to be jealous of that rising power which would one day certainly strip them of all their American possessions;

That it was more likely they should form a connection with the British court who, if they should find themselves unable otherwise to extricate themselves from their difficulties, would agree to a partition of our territories, restoring Canada to France and the Floridas to Spain to accomplish for themselves a recovery of these colonies;

That it would not be long before we should receive certain information of the disposition of the French court from the agent whom we had sent to Paris for that purpose;

That if this disposition should be favourable, by waiting the event of the present campaign, which we all hoped would be successful, we should have reason to expect an alliance on better terms;

That this would in fact work no delay of any effectual aid from such ally, as, from the advance of the season and distance of our situation, it was impossible we could receive any assistance during this campaign;

That it was prudent to fix among ourselves the terms on which we would form alliance before we declared we would form one at all events;

And that if these were agreed on and our declaration of independence ready by the time our ambassador should be ready to sail, it would be as well as to go into that declaration at this day.

On the other side it was urged by J.[ohn] Adams, [Richard Henry] Lee, [George] Wythe, and others:

That no gentleman had argued against the policy or the right of separation from Britain, nor had supposed it possible we should ever renew our connection; that they had only opposed its being now declared;

That the question was not whether, by a declaration of independence we should make ourselves what we are not, but whether we should declare a fact which already exists;

That as to the people or Parliament of England, we had always been independent of them, their restraints on our trade deriving efficacy from our acquiescence only and not from any rights they possessed of imposing them, and that so far our connection had been federal only and was now dissolved by the commencement of hostilities;

That as to the king, we had been bound to him by allegiance, but that this bond was now dissolved by his assent to the late Act of Parliament by which he declares us out of his protection and by his levying war on us, a fact which had long ago proved us out of his protection, it being a certain position in law that allegiance and protection are reciprocal, the one ceasing when the other is withdrawn;

That James II never declared the people of England out of his protection; yet his actions proved it, and the Parliament declared it;

No delegates then can be denied, or ever want a power of declaring an existent truth;

That the delegates from the Delaware counties having declared their constituents ready to join, there are only two colonies, Pennsylvania and Maryland, whose delegates are absolutely tied up, and that these had by their instructions only reserved a right of confirming or rejecting the measure;

That the instructions from Pennsylvania might be accounted for from the times in which they were drawn, near a twelvemonth ago, since which the face of affairs has totally changed;

That within that time it had become apparent that Britain was determined to accept nothing less than a carte blanche, and that the king's answer to the lord mayor, aldermen, and common council of London, which had come to hand four days ago, must have satisfied everyone of this point;

That the people wait for us to lead the way;

That *they* are in favour of the measure, though the instructions given by some of their *representatives* are not;

That the voice of the representatives is not always consonant with the voice of the people, and that this is remarkably the case in these middle colonies;

That the effect of the resolution of the 15th of May has proved this, which, raising the murmurs of some in the colonies of Pennsylvania and Maryland, called forth the opposing voice of the freer part of the people and proved them to be the majority, even in these colonies;

That the backwardness of these two colonies might be ascribed partly to the influence of proprietary power and connections, and partly to their having not yet been attacked by the enemy;

That these causes were not likely to be soon removed, as there seemed no probability that the enemy would make either of these the seat of this summer's war;

That it would be vain to wait either weeks or months for perfect unanimity, since it was impossible that all men should ever become of one sentiment on any question;

That the conduct of some colonies from the beginning of this contest had given reason to suspect it was their settled policy to keep in the rear of the confederacy, that their particular prospect might be better, even in the worst event;

That therefore it was necessary for those colonies who had thrown themselves forward and hazarded all from the beginning to come forward now also and put all again to their own hazard;

That the history of the Dutch revolution, of whom three states only confederated at first, proved that a secession of some colonies would not be so dangerous as some apprehended;

That a declaration of independence alone could render it consistent with European delicacy for European powers to treat with us, or even to receive an ambassador from us;

That till this they would not receive our vessels into their ports nor acknowledge the adjudications of our courts of admiralty to be legitimate in cases of capture of British vessels;

That though France and Spain may be jealous of our rising power, they must think it will be much more formidable with the addition of Great Britain and will therefore see it their interest to prevent a coalition; but should they refuse, we shall be but where we are; whereas without trying we shall never know whether they will aid us or not;

That the present campaign may be unsuccessful, and therefore we had better propose an alliance while our affairs wear a hopeful aspect;

That to wait the event of this campaign will certainly work delay because during this summer France may assist us effectually by cutting off those supplies of provisions from England and Ireland on which the enemy's armies here are to depend, or by setting in motion the great power they have collected in the West Indies and calling our enemy to the defence of the possessions they have there;

That it would be idle to lose time in settling the terms of alliance, till we had first determined we would enter into alliance;

That it is necessary to lose no time in opening a trade for our people, who will want clothes and will want money too for the payment of taxes;

And that the only misfortune is that we did not enter into alliance with France six months sooner, as, besides opening their ports for the vent of our last year's produce, they might have marched an army into Germany and prevented the petty princes there from selling their unhappy subjects to subdue us.

It appearing in the course of these debates that the colonies of N.[ew] York, New Jersey, Pennsylvania, Delaware, and Maryland were not yet matured for falling from the parent stem, but that they were fast advancing to that state, it was thought most prudent to wait a while for them, and to postpone the final decision to July 1. But that this might occasion as little delay as possible, a committee was appointed to prepare a declaration of independence. The committee were J.[ohn] Adams, Dr. Franklin, Roger Sherman, Robert R. Livingston, and myself. Committees were also appointed at the same time to prepare a plan of confederation for the colonies, and to state the terms proper to be proposed for foreign alliance. The committee for drawing the declaration of independence desired me to do it. It was accordingly done, and being approved by them, I reported it to the house on Friday the 28th of June, when it was read and ordered to lie on the table. On Monday the 1st of July the house resolved itself into a committee of the whole and resumed the consideration of the original motion made by the delegates of Virginia, which being again debated through the day, was carried in the affirmative by the votes of N.[ew] Hampshire, Connecticut, Massachusetts, Rhode Island, N.[ew] Jersey, Maryland, Virginia, N.[orth] Carolina, and Georgia. S.[outh] Carolina and Pennsylvania voted against it. Delaware having but two members present, they were divided. The delegates for N.[ew] York declared they were for it themselves and were assured their constituents were for it but that their instructions, having been drawn near a twelvemonth before, when reconciliation was still the general object, they were enjoined by them to do nothing which should impede that object. They therefore thought themselves not justifiable in voting on either side and asked leave to withdraw from the question which was given them. The committee rose and reported their resolution to the house. Mr. Rutledge of S.[outh] Carolina then requested the determination might be put off to the next day as he believed his colleagues, though they disapproved of the resolution, would then join in it for the sake of unanimity. The ultimate question whether the house would agree to the resolution of the committee, was accordingly postponed to the next day, when it was again moved and S.[outh] Carolina concurred in voting for it. In the meantime a third member had come post from the Delaware counties and turned the vote of that colony in favour of the resolution. Members of a different sentiment attending that morning from Pennsylvania also, their vote was changed so that the whole twelve colonies who were authorized to vote at all gave their voices for it; and within a few days the convention of N.[ew] York approved of it, and thus supplied the void occasioned by the withdrawing of their delegates from the vote.

2

The First American Civil War

I

The Tory Rank and File

"The Loyalists," notes William H. Nelson, *"suffered a most abject kind of political failure, losing not only their argument, their war, and their place in American society, but even their proper place in history." Professor Nelson's study is at least a belated measure of historical recognition; it throws fresh light upon the complex of reasons that made the War for Independence a civil war as well.*

Who were the Loyalists? How numerous were they? Why were they so dismally unsuccessful? These questions do not admit of easy answers. The Loyalists encompassed the entire political and social spectrum. Rich and poor, easterners and westerners, they embraced Loyalism for a wide variety of reasons. There were patriots who could not bring themselves to make a revolution. There were men who felt that British power was invincible and that any rebellion would only lead to disaster. There were still others who simply could not conceive of living their lives out other than under a British monarch. There were, as Professor Nelson observes, no simple determinants.

If their motivations were complex, their numerical strength is no less difficult to estimate. The symmetrical formula of one third patriot, one third Tory, and one third neutral has long been discredited.[1] *Perhaps thirty thousand or more colonists took up arms on behalf of Britain, although Professor Nelson properly admits that "no reliable estimate is possible until more precise studies of individual colonies have been made."*

Finally, why did the Tories fail? Of fundamental importance was their dependence upon the British, who failed to give them adequate support and protection. But another weakness was the Loyalists' frequent agreement with patriot criticism of Britain's colonial policy in the years up to 1775; when open rebellion finally began, the decision of many colonists to remain loyal to the Crown had come too late for them to take effective countermeasures against well-organized patriot forces.

Professor Nelson, who teaches history at the University of Toronto, has a justifiable sympathy for the Loyalists. After Yorktown, he writes, "the Loyalists found themselves with little save their loyalty," and even this had "woefully depreciated in value." But unlike many of their counterparts in other revolutions, they were allowed their lives.

In the folk tales of nineteenth-century America, two kinds of Loyalists were remembered, presumably because a certain romantic interest clung to them. There were the Tory gentlefolk, Royalists who lived in great houses and drove about in fine carriages; and there were fearful outlaws who, in these remembrances, generally travelled with Indians — 'Tories and Indians'. With the disappearance of the frontier and the Indians, the outlaw Tories were forgotten, and historians, in attempting to rationalize the legends of a Tory gentry, slipped into an easy explanation of the Revolution in class terms. By this account, the Tories were either frightened or selfish obligarchs, who had fought the Revolution in order to protect their special privileges. Although traces of this view still sur-

Reprinted from William H. Nelson, *The American Tory* (Oxford, Eng.: Oxford University Press, 1961), pp. 85–115, by permission of The Clarendon Press, Oxford.

[1] See John Alden, *The American Revolution, 1775–1783* (1954), p. 87n.

vive, more recent students have emphasized the dangers of making class generalizations about the Revolution.

Certainly there are a woeful number of exceptions to any generalizations that may be made about the Loyalists. Besides, at first glance, there seems little useful that might be said in the same breath about Governor Hutchinson, say, and a Carolina backwoodsman; or about William Byrd of Westover, and a Brooklyn shopkeeper. Yet if the Tories are to be really understood, and if their dissent from a major decision of their countrymen is to be at all meaningful, an attempt must be made to see them in social rather than in merely individual terms. And it may be that in the very diversity of the Tory ranks there can be found a clue to the identity of the 'army'.

Of all the approaches that might be used in an attempt to separate intelligibly the Loyalists from their Patriot kinsmen, that of occupation or social class seems the least fruitful. There was indeed a Tory oligarchy, but there was also a Whig oligarchy, and if in New England the Tory proportion of ruling families was greater than the Tory proportion of the total population, in the Southern Colonies the reverse was true. Even in New England the Loyalists were hardly the gentry pictured in legend. When an Act of Banishment was passed against some three hundred Loyalists in Massachusetts in 1778, they were listed by trade or profession. About a third were merchants, professional men, and gentlemen; another third were farmers, and the rest were artisans or labourers with a sprinkling of small shopkeepers.

Most random lists of Loyalists show even less evidence of gentility than this. Always the gentlemen, esquires, merchants, and the like are far outnumbered by the yoemen, cordwainers, tailors, labourers, masons, blacksmiths, and their fellows. The social heterogeneity of the New York Tories is evident in the list of people arrested there in June 1776 on suspicion of plotting to assassinate General Washington. These people included the mayor of New York, some other officials and gentlemen, some farmers, several tavern-keepers, a shoemaker, two doctors, several apprentices and labourers, two tanners, a silversmith, a saddler, two gunsmiths, a tallow chandler, a miller, a schoolmaster, a former schoolmaster, a former constable, a 'pensioner with one arm', and one unfortunate man described only as 'a damned rascal'.

Clearly, none of the simpler economic determinants was at work separating Whigs from Tories. Economic influences, however, may account in part for the pattern of geographical distribution that appears when the Loyalist strongholds are considered. The main centres of Tory strength fall into two distinct regions: The first was along the thinly settled western frontier, from Georgia and District Ninety-Six in South Carolina, through the Regulator country of North Carolina and the mountain settlements of Virginia, Pennsylvania, and New York, to the newly-occupied Vermont lands. The other was the maritime region of the Middle Colonies, including western Long Island and the counties of the lower Hudson Valley, southern New Jersey, the three old counties of Pennsylvania around Philadelphia, and the peninsula between Delaware and Chesapeake Bays. There were also locally important concentrations of Tories elsewhere along the Atlantic seaboard: at Charleston, around Wilmington and Norfolk, and around Newport and Portsmouth in New England.

In the West and in the tidal region of the Middle Colonies Loyalists and neutrals may have formed a majority of the population. In the areas of dense agricultural settlement, however, including the plantation country of the Southern Colonies, the thickly settled parts of the Piedmont, and most of New England, Loyalists were comparatively scarce. All that the Tory regions, the mountain and maritime frontiers, had in common was that both suffered or were threatened with economic and political subjugation by richer adjoining areas. The geographical concentration of the Tories was in peripheral areas, regions already in decline, or not yet risen to importance.

It is not difficult to explain the Loyalism of the West. The Appalachian frontiersmen — hunters, trappers, and fur traders — feared the advance of close settlement which would destroy their economy. Like the Indians of the region, many of the frontiersmen were loyal to Britain because the British government was the only force they could rely on to check the rapid advance of agricultural settlement. The tidal region of the Middle Colonies, on the other hand, still had political power, but was in danger of losing it to the more populous districts inland. Moreover, this region formed part of an Atlantic community. It looked eastward; its ties with Britain were closer than its ties with the New West. Even in New England the truly maritime regions seem to have been less than enthusiastic in their support of the Revolution. Newport lacked zeal; Nantucket and Martha's Vineyard were opportunist or neutral, and the Maine coast grew steadily less faithful to the Revolution, until Nova Scotia's Loyalism of necessity was reached.

Whether the St. Lawrence Valley should be considered a separate province, or whether it merely combined the characteristics of a thinly settled and a maritime region, it too was indifferent or hostile to the Revolution. Undoubtedly some of Vermont's capriciousness during the period may be ascribed to the pull of the St. Lawrence. In any case, wherever regions newly or thinly settled touched the sea, there the Revolution was weakest: in Quebec, in Nova Scotia, in Georgia, and in New York where the Hudson carried the Atlantic world into the mountains. Wherever sailors and fishermen, trappers and traders outnumbered farmers and planters, there Tories outnumbered Whigs.

Of course a major insufficiency of such a geographical analysis is that it takes no account of important cultural influences, differences in nationality and religion mainly, that played a great role in the Revolution. The Canadians of the St. Lawrence Valley were suspicious of the Revolution, not only because they lived far outside its physical homeland, but also because they were French and Catholic, and the Revolution seemed to them English and Protestant. No geographic or economic considerations can explain the Tory villages on Long Island, intermingled with Whig villages. The Tory villages were Dutch, while the others had been settled by New Englanders. Here again, legend has done a disservice to students of the Revolution. The Loyalists were seldom more English than the patriots. There were, of course, many British-born Tories whose allegiance to England was habitual and natural. But, apart from these, the Tories more commonly drew their recruits from the non-English than from the English parts of the community. The two most purely English provinces, Virginia and Massachusetts, were the strongholds of the Revolution. It was in the patchwork societies of Pennsylvania and New York that the Tories were strongest.

Among almost all cultural minorities, the proportion of Tories seems to have been clearly higher than among the population at large. The Dutch and Germans seem to have inclined towards supporting the Revolution where they were already anglicized, but not where they had kept their language and separate outlook. In New York, for example, the English-speaking Dutch Reformed congregation was Whiggish, but the Dutch-speaking congregation was Tory, and on such cordial terms with the Anglicans that they were allowed to use St. George's chapel during the British occupation. The Tories praised the loyalty of the French Calvinists at New Rochelle, the only place in the colonies where they had preserved their language, while elsewhere the descendants of the Huguenots were conspicuously active revolutionists.

There seems to have been reason for John Witherspoon's lament that his fellow Scots made bad revolutionists, whether Highlanders in the back country of New York and North Carolina, or Lowlanders along the Virginia and Carolina coast. Even the Ulstermen were tainted with Toryism in the Regulator districts of North Carolina and in the frontier districts of South Carolina. The Loyalism of the Indians is well known, and contemporary opinion held that the Negroes were dangerously Toryfied. Of course people like the Brooklyn Dutch or the South Carolina Germans and Scots may have remained loyal to Britain partly out of political quietism. It is difficult not to believe, however, that they were Loyalists also because they thought Britain would protect them from the cultural aggression of an Anglo-American majority.

In religion, the lines that divided Tories from Whigs were quite clearly drawn. Adherents of religious groups that were in a local minority were everywhere inclined towards Loyalism, while adherents of the dominant local denomination were most often Patriots. In New England not many Congregationalists, in the Middle Colonies not many Presbyterians, in the South not many Episcopalians, were Tories. Conversely, most of the Anglicans in the North were Tories;

so were many Presbyterians in the Episcopalian South. Of the smaller religious groups, most of the Quakers and German Pietists were passive Loyalists, and in New England even the Baptists were accused of 'not being hearty' in the American cause. The reputation the Methodists had for being poor rebels was perhaps not entirely due to the influence of Wesley and other English ministers.

The Catholics and Jews apparently form an exception to the rule that religious minorities leaned towards Toryism. Both seem generally to have supported the Revolution, although among the Jews there were notable exceptions like the Hart family in Newport and the Franks family in Philadelphia. Jonathan Boucher observed that although the Maryland Catholics supported the Revolution in its later stages, they had taken little part at first. It is possible that the Jews and Catholics were in such suspect and habitual minority, that they felt obliged to follow what seemed majority opinion for their own safety.

Taking all the groups and factions, sects, classes, and inhabitants of regions that seem to have been Tory, they have but one thing in common: they represented conscious minorities, people who felt weak and threatened. The sense of weakness, which is so marked a characteristic of the Tory leaders, is equally evident among the rank and file. Almost all the Loyalists were, in one way or another, more afraid of America than they were of Britain. Almost all of them had interests that they felt needed protection from an American majority. Being fairly certain that they would be in a permanent minority (as Quakers or oligarchs or frontiersmen or Dutchmen) they could not find much comfort in a theory of government that assured them of sovereign equality with other Americans *as individuals*. Not many Loyalists were as explicit in their distrust of individualism as, say, Jonathan Boucher, but most of them shared his suspicion of a political order based on the 'common good' if the common good was to be defined by a numerical majority.

A theory that the Loyalists were compounded of an assortment of minority groups does not, of course, preclude their having in total constituted a majority of Americans. Without the social and religious homogeneity, without the common purpose, and without the organic and efficient leadership of the revolutionists, the Loyalists might still have outnumbered them. In this case the Revolution would have been, as it has sometimes been claimed to have been, the achievement of an organized and wilful minority. The problem of discovering how many Tories there were is complicated, moreover, by there having been, between avowed supporters and avowed opponents of the Revolution, a great middle group of passive citizens who had no clear point of view, who hoped perhaps that one side or the other would win, but who wanted above all not to be disturbed. There must have been many like the New Jersey shopkeeper who stood in his door and prayed that whatever happened, he might have peace in his time. There were probably also a good number of sceptics who thought as John Ross of Philadelphia did: 'Let who would be king, he well knew that he should be subject.'

An old and symmetrical guess that a third of Americans were revolutionists, another third Loyalists, and a third neutral, has long been accepted by historians as reasonable. It goes back, presumably, to John Adams's assignment of these relative proportions. But Adams may have been trying, unconsciously, to gain distinction for the revolutionists by maintaining they were a wise minority. In Connecticut, the only colony for which anything like an exact estimate of Tory strength has been made, the hard core of Tories seems to have numbered only about six per cent. of the population. But then, Connecticut was one of two or three colonies where the Tories were weakest. During the Revolutionary War perhaps half as many Americans were in arms for the King, at one time or another, as fought on the side of the Congress. Only in New York is it reasonably certain that the Loyalists numbered half the population. Throughout the Middle Colonies, including New York, the Loyalists may have been almost as numerous as their opponents. In the South, however, they could hardly have amounted to more than a fourth or a third of the population, and in New England to scarcely a tenth. A more reasonable guess than Adams's would be that the Loyalists were a third, and the revolutionists two-thirds of the politically active population of the colonies. No reliable estimate is possible until more precise studies of individual colonies have been made.

The outbreak of open war between the British and the Massachusetts militia threw the Tories, temporarily at least, entirely on the defensive. The shock of the news of Lexington and Concord was shortly transformed into anger at those who did not immediately drop all argument and join the fight against the British. Except along the western frontier, and in parts of the Middle Colonies, there was no doubt that Britain and America, not merely Britain and Massachusetts, were at war, and the Tories, who were now calling themselves Loyalists, were beginning to be regarded as traitors. When the news of the Battle of Lexington reached New York, the mob, after almost ten years' confinement, slipped its chains, looted the arsenal, and raged through the streets. While a few weeks earlier it had been said of the New York Whigs that 'no one dares among gentlemen, to support them', it was now possible for John Adams to write, 'The tories put to flight here . . . such a spirit was never seen in New York.'

As the Whigs luxuriated in their sudden release from the bonds of sober argument, they began to look on the Tories with real impatience. To people with a new faith, especially one being forged in the heat of war, the adherents of the old beliefs are either wicked and will not see, or are superstitious and cannot see. George Washington thought the Loyalists were wicked, and denounced them as 'parricides'. Other revolutionists were more charitable, like one who wrote, 'We may say of Toryism as of Popery, that it is always the same. There are worthy individuals among the professors of both; and a few rare instances of real converts from each, through an increase of knowledge, but the prevailing spirit of the parties is uniform and abiding.'

Just after the adjournment of the First Continental Congress, the local committees of inspection had begun to enforce compliance with the Association. In some localities the whole adult population signed the oath. Everywhere it was used to force Tories either to acquiesce in the measures of the Congress, or to declare themselves open 'enemies of American liberty' and face ostracism. As a Maryland revolutionist put it, the Association acted 'as a powerful emetick to our Tories'. The efficiency of the committees' work rested on years of experience in informal government, going back in many cases to the committees that had enforced the Non-Importation Agreement in 1768.

The Tories naturally resented what they regarded as the high-handed proceedings of the committees, which they usually compared with the methods of the Inqusition. 'In contending for liberty', one man wrote, 'they seem inclinable to engross it all themselves . . . they are arbitrary and even tyrannical in the whole tenour of their conduct; they allow not to others who differ from them the same liberty of thinking and acting that they claim themselves.' In Massachusetts General Timothy Ruggles and a number of other Loyalists sought to promote a Loyalist Association in opposition to the Congress's oath. The Loyalist oath pledged its signers to defend their 'life, liberty and property', and their 'undoubted right to liberty in eating, drinking, buying, selling, communing, and acting . . . consistent with the laws of God and the King'. Signers promised when one of their number was threatened by 'Committees, mobs, or unlawful assemblies', to arm themselves and go to his aid. Lacking the organization of their opponents, however, the promoters of the Loyalist Association seem not to have had much success.

In New England the social pressure to conform was strong, and opposition to the Revolution was usually individual and verbal. Tories often made abject recantations when they were examined by a committee, like that of William Boltwood:

> It evidently appears I have heretofore been unfriendly to my Country; I do hereby publickly acknowledge the offence aforesaid, and ask the foregiveness of all my friends and fellow-countrymen, and promise for the future to act in conjunction with my countrymen, in all ways and methods which shall be judged proper for the recovery of the just rights and privileges of the injured Americans, hoping thereby to gain the friendship of my fellow-subjects, which I have most justly forfeited.[1]

[1] 4 *Am. Arch.* iii. 145.

Thomas Cowden confessed to 'speaking diminutively of the County Congress at Worcester', and other offences; he was truly sorry and 'ready to convince the world' of the sincerity of his conversion by giving his life, if necessary. William Wheton of Stamford, Connecticut, admitted 'damning the honourable Continental Congress', and 'humbly and heartily' begged the forgiveness of God and of the friends to American liberty.

The Committee of Sheffield, Massachusetts, had John and Job Westover brought before it. John had said the Congress was guilty of rebellion against the King, and Job had said Parliament had a right to tax the colonies. When asked which side they would support in a war between Britain and America, John said it was too difficult a question to answer directly, and Job said he supposed an American victory would be worse for America than a British victory. After a long examination, John 'voluntarily and solemnly' engaged to obey the Continental and Provincial Congresses, and the Committee accepted his declaration as satisfactory. Job, however, was declared an enemy of American liberty and the population was advised to have no dealings with him.

Some recantations were obviously forced, like that of Nahum Willard of Worcester, Massachusetts, who was made to say that he had 'from the perverseness of a wicked heart, maliciously and scandalously abused' the Congress, the Selectmen of the town of Worcester, and committees in general. He admitted to being a wicked liar and an enemy to American liberty.

People with influence could appeal against a local committee's decision. The Selectmen of Waltham, Massachusetts, found Abijah Brown guilty of having belittled the general of the Massachusetts army and the committeemen as 'a set of idiots and lunaticks'. But the Provincial Committee of Safety restored him to favour on the grounds that he had temporarily fallen under the influence of 'disaffected antagonists'. Occasionally the revolutionists would run into unexpected opposition, as when the Committee of New Ipswich, New Hampshire, instructed David Hills, a shopkeeper, to reduce his prices. Hills refused, charged the Committee with being arbitrary, and, worst of all, claimed that two leading members of the Committee itself had privately declared against the present proceedings of the colonies, and had said it would have been better to comply with Parliament's requisitions.

Sometimes the local committees themselves lacked the proper spirit. The Portsmouth, New Hampshire, Committee was severely criticized by warm patriots for having arranged to supply a British sloop lying below the town with fresh beef in return for being allowed to bring fresh fish into Portsmouth.

The tug of economic self-interest could be exquisitely sharp. When Stephen Parker of Machias, on the Maine coast, was accused of trading with Nova Scotia in violation of the Association, he apologized to the Council and House of Representatives of Massachusetts Bay in the following words: 'May it please your Honours: Ignorance, inadvertence, and absolute necessity, were the sole cause of my setting foot in the Government of Nova-Scotia.'

One of the most troublesome cases of disaffection in New England was that of Governor Joseph Wanton of Rhode Island. His Toryism was embarrassing since he was not a 'fawning Courtier' like the royal governors, but the duly elected head of a 'perfect Democracy'. Nevertheless, in May 1775 he raised the ghost of Newport's detestable cosmopolitanism by urging the General Assembly of Rhode Island to avoid the 'horrours and calamities of a civil war'. He expressed an ardent desire to see a union between Great Britain and her colonies upon an 'equitable, permanent basis', and advised the Assembly to negotiate separately with Parliament. He said that Rhode Island's happiness and prosperity were founded on its connexion with Britain; 'if once we are separated,' he asked, 'where shall we find another Britain to supply our loss?' The Assembly promptly forbade the oath of office to be administered to Governor Wanton, and provided for the commissioning of militia officers without his signature.

Little escaped the notice of the committees and congresses: the self-constituted General Court of Massachusetts, in the midst of its efforts to raise an army, found time to recommend to the Corporation and Overseers of Harvard College that they 'inquire into the principles' of members of their faculty and dismiss any instructors who appeared to be unfriendly to American liberty. They were also urged not to appoint any teachers, 'but such whose political principles they can confide in'.

The only opposition to the Revolution in New England which threatened to be dangerous was in western Connecticut.[2] The New Haven Town Meeting passed a resolution opposing the taking up of arms. The Ridgefield and Danbury Meetings passed resolutions condemning the measures of the Congress. In a number of towns, among them Reading and New Milford, Loyalist oaths were sworn to by a majority of the inhabitants. The Connecticut Assembly was informed in May 1775 that the 'major part' of a militia company in Waterbury, 'both Officers and Soldiers', was 'totally disaffected to the general cause of American liberty, and that they altogether refuse to adopt the measures advised by the Continental Congress'. This threat was overcome by a promptly and secretly organized expedition of several hundred Whig militiamen from the eastern part of the province who disarmed all the Loyalists in the area around Fairfield and took a dozen Tory leaders prisoner. One Whig wrote with modest satisfaction, 'Our people made them rise about three o'clock in the morning, when there was the greatest confusion imaginable.' The Connecticut Loyalists were caught unprepared and made no resistance, though some escaped across the Sound to Long Island.

In New York the Assembly had been prorogued after it sent its petition to Britain. Before it could meet again, a 'Provincial Congress' had been elected by mass acclamation from a list of nominees put up by the New York Committee. The Provincial Congress brought New York back into the Revolution by appointing delegates to the Continental Congress and taking over the powers of government in New York. Compared with similar irregular congresses in the other provinces, the New York Congress followed a moderate course. It simply resumed the customary practice of the New York conservatives of trying to control the Revolutionary movement by discreet participation in it.

The day after the news of the Battle of Lexington arrived, Lord North's 'Conciliatory Propositions' in answer to the earlier petition of the Assembly, reached New York. To the disappointment of the conservatives, it rejected the Assembly's Memorial. North's Propositions did suggest, instead of outright parliamentary taxation of the colonies, a return to a modified system of requisition, by which Parliament, rather than the Crown, would lay its demands before the colonial assemblies. Ten years before, this might have been acceptable, but in the circumstances no attention was paid to it, and the conservatives were no longer able to hold out high hopes of British conciliation. It was not the first time that Parliament had helped the revolutionists convince America that nothing could be expected from Britain.

The New York Committee and the Provincial Congress both did their best to keep the Revolution from getting out of hand. After the Battle of Lexington the New York Committee advised the people to keep cool, and not deal so harshly with the Tories as to make outright enemies of them. 'In short, gentlemen,' the Committee's address said, 'consider that our contest is for liberty; and therefore we should be extremely cautious how we permit our struggles to hurry us into acts of violence and extravagance inconsistent with freedom'. The Provincial Congress wrote the New York delegates to the Continental Congress urging them to try for a reconciliation, and observed that 'such controversies as we are now engaged in frequently end in the demolition of those rights and privileges which they were instituted to defend'.

The middle road which the New Yorkers were still trying to follow demanded sometimes the drawing of fine distinctions. When in June 1775 the royal governor of New York and General Washington entered New York on the same day on different errands, both received escorts from the Provincial Congress, which instructed a militia colonel to 'have the residue of his Battalion ready to receive either the

[2] The Tories of Worcester County, Massachusetts, were "having frequent meetings in large bodies" in July 1776, but there was no actual insurrection. Collective opposition to the Congress in Massachusetts usually took the form of passive non-co-operation, as when the Barnstable Town Meeting voted (Jan. 1775) against purchasing arms, encouraging the Minutemen, or sending delegates to the Provincial Congress; it endorsed the Association, however. 4 *Am. Arch.* i. 1093, 1250–1.

General or Governor Tryon, whichever shall first arrive, and to wait on both as well as circumstances will allow'. Both Tryon and Washington were cheered in the streets, perhaps by the same crowds.

New York was regarded with suspicion in the other colonies, particularly in New England. A Connecticut man wrote to a friend in New York that it had been said 'your Province would desert us'. He advised the New Yorkers to take care. 'It is no time now to dally, or be merely neutral; he that is not for us is against us . . . If you desert, our men will as cheerfully attack New-York as Boston, for we can but perish.'

General David Wooster, then commanding a small number of Continental troops around New York, wrote to the governor of his own province of Connecticut recalling the 'suspicious light in which the New-York Congress are viewed by the rest of the Continent', and begging that he would not have to serve under them. Wooster had so little confidence in the New Yorkers that he took to sending the 'most Obnoxious' Tories to Connecticut for safe keeping. More direct Connecticut aggression against New York occurred in November 1775 when Isaac Sears rode in with a troop of Connecticut irregulars and destroyed Rivington's press, thus silencing the last press in the colonies open to the Tories. Sears and his men also took a number of New York Tories back to Connecticut as prisoners, including Samuel Seabury. They deposited Seabury and Rivington's type in New Haven and concluded the day 'in festivity and innocent mirth'. In New York even good Whigs like Philip Schuyler and John Jay were annoyed, and the New York Committee petitioned the Provincial Congress protesting the interference of one colony in another's affairs.

The New Englanders were right, however, in thinking the Revolution in New York needed outside help. Only in a few parts of the province, principally Suffolk County (the eastern half of Long Island, settled mainly by New Englanders), part of Ulster County, and the city of New York, could the committees take the kind of coercive action against individual Tories that was commonplace in New England. Even then there were few recantations, and the committees' action was usually mild. Much of the opposition to the Revolution in New York was collective, sometimes involving whole counties. A number of town meetings passed Loyalist resolutions, and many localities refused to send delegates to the Provincial Congress. When, for example, several hundred Westchester County Whigs met at White Plains to choose delegates to the Congress, a much larger number of Tories appeared, denounced the meeting, and marched off singing 'the grand and animating song of "God save great George our King" '.

Peter De Witt wrote that in Dutchess County, 'all are tories, only a few excepted'. The Loyalists went about armed, interfered with the selection of militia officers, 'damned the Congress', and enlisted young men in the British service. The most energetic Tories were the local rivermen, who once threatened to come with an armed vessel and carry off the leading Whigs to the British, and who, until their boats were burnt, were active in taking men down-river to serve with the British. In October 1775 the New York Congress was informed of a conspiracy 'of a great number of people' in the lower Hudson Valley to join the King's troops, and some Loyalists around Peekskill attempted to arm against the Congress, but were disarmed by the local militia.

The adjoining part of New Jersey suspended dealings with Staten Island because the inhabitants 'have manifested an unfriendly disposition towards the liberties of America'. Staten Island sent no delegates to the Provincial Congress, and its people were accused of continuing to trade with the British in defiance of the Association. The Staten Island Committee of Safety itself was accused of favouring men brought before it as Tories. One Whig complained that the Committee allowed the men he had accused to call him 'an informer, cutthroat, dirty rascal, dirty dog, liar, &c.' in their presence, and then dismissed them.

The most serious opposition to the Revolution in New York was on the Atlantic and Appalachian frontiers, respectively: in Queen's County on Long Island, and in Tryon County.[3] Disaffection in Tryon County was the more menacing. The fur trading empire of Sir Wil-

[3] Tryon County at this time included much of upstate New York, while Queen's County included most of the western half of Long Island.

liam Johnson had passed on to his son, Colonel Guy Johnson, who from his capital at Albany could raise the Indians as far as the Great Lakes for a war on the settlers. In addition to his Indians, Colonel Johnson had staunch allies in Sir John Johnson and the Highland Scots settled in Tryon County. In May 1775 Colonel Johnson warned the New York Congress that if the rumoured plan to imprison him was carried out, the Indians would take it as a hostile act and attack the frontier settlements. He offered to observe neutrality if left alone. Receiving no reply, he denounced the Congress and disappeared into the Indian country.

The Highlanders were well armed, and there were rumours that they planned to join the Indians and march down the Hudson Valley, raising the local Tories as they went. In January 1776, however, General Philip Schuyler took several thousand militiamen into Tryon County in a surprise march and disarmed the 'malignant' Scots, taking everything from their dirks and claymores to several four- and six-pound cannon. Six hostages for the Scots' future good behaviour were sent prisoners to Pennsylvania. The Indians were still hoping to remain neutral and did nothing, so the immediate threat of a Loyalist rising on the frontier was dispelled.

Queen's County was not only maritime, but also it was on the cultural frontier between New England and the Middle Colonies. The anti-New-England feelings of its people were genuine and obdurate. The Queen's County towns had refused to send delegates to the Provincial Congress and had passed Loyalist resolutions instead. The man who had been chosen to represent the county in the Provincial Congress did not attend, and explained that since 'the people seemed to be much inclined to remain peaceable and quiet', he thought it would be presumptuous of him to claim to represent them. In the November 1775 elections for the Provincial Congress, the free-holders of Queen's County voted 788 to 221 not to send any deputies at all. In December a great number of the county's inhabitants signed a declaration of neutrality, in which they said they had 'carefully avoided every ostentatious display' of their sentiments, but had reluctantly been compelled to arm themselves against threats of violence. They said they wanted only to remain in peace.

The Continental Congress could not afford to allow the development of a neutrality movement, and therefore decided to make an example of Queen's County. It issued a declaration virtually outlawing the county and denouncing its people for being 'incapable of resolving to live and die freemen'. The Congress resolved that the Loyalists should be disarmed and the 'dangerous' ones confined, and that the names of all dissidents in the county should be published throughout America. All the inhabitants of Queen's County were instructed not to leave the county without a passport issued by the New York Committee of Safety. At the same time as this declaration was issued, a large force of Continental troops was sent in. Lacking any encouragement from the British, the Tories finally allowed themselves to be disarmed without a fight.

Thus by prompt action New York's revolutionists, aided by New Englanders, had secured the two hostile frontiers, mountain and maritime, which in New York were so dangerously close together. The Tories continued to form 'barbarous and infernal plots' and drink 'Damnation to the Congress', but for the time being they were disorganized and helpless. Disaffection in New York did not disappear, but it took more and more the form of passive non-cooperation. This is evident from the difficulty which the new Provincial Congress found in getting a quorum in November 1775. Although the Congress was to have convened on 14 November, by 22 November only four of the twelve counties in the province had sent delegates. The Congress finally met on 6 December, with delegates present from only five counties. New York was waiting to see how the war went.

New Jersey had not played an active part in the revolutionary movement, and was inclined to take its lead from New York or, preferably, from Pennsylvania. The New Jersey Tories, although they preferred neutrality to insurrection, made up perhaps a greater part of the population than in any of the thirteen colonies except New York and Georgia. There were, however, a number of localities which had been settled by New Englanders and were vigorously Whig. The New Jersey revolutionists made up in energy what they lacked in numbers, and maintained a strict discipline over dissidents in areas they controlled. For example, a Quibbletown cooper who had reviled the local committee and the Continental Congress, was stripped naked, 'well coated with tar and feathers' and taken round the village in a cart. A local patriot wrote that this ceremony was conducted 'with that regularity and decorum that ought to be observed in all public punishments'.

The British government had an unusually tenacious champion in New Jersey in the person of the royal governor, William Franklin. Whether or not he was, as his father, Benjamin, maintained, a 'thorough Courtier', Franklin proved himself an unbending Tory. With little encouragement from England, he had done his best to keep New Jersey out of the Revolution. Although he was unable in May 1775 to persuade the Assembly to negotiate separately with Britain, he continued to nurture Tory sentiment in the province. His was the guiding hand behind the petitions which the New Jersey Assembly received in the autumn of 1775, praying that it 'discourage an Independency on Great Britain'. The Assembly replied that reports of independence were groundless, but it nevertheless instructed the New Jersey delegates to the Continental Congress 'utterly to reject any propositions, if such should be made, that may separate this Colony from the Mother Country'. Prodded by Franklin, the Assembly finally overcame its scruples at acting separately from the other colonies, and drafted a petition to the King, 'humbly beseeching him to . . . prevent the effusion of blood; and to express the great desire this House hath to a restoration of peace and harmony'.

Before this petition could be adopted, however, a committee led by John Jay and John Dickinson 'came in great haste' from the Continental Congress and harangued the Assembly on the danger to the American cause of one colony acting separately from the others. Moved by Dickinson's skilful pleading, the Assembly was finally persuaded to drop its petition. Franklin wrote to Lord Dartmouth in despair that, although he was still convinced the majority of people in New Jersey were 'greatly averse to an Independency', he feared independence would be achieved by degrees, and in such a way that the people would not realize what was happening until it was too late to act. Franklin stubbornly held his ground against rising opposition until June 1776 when the New Jersey Provincial Congress had him arrested. He stiffly reaffirmed his loyalty to the King, which, he said, it 'has been the Pride of my Life to demonstrate upon all Occasions'. He was judged a virulent and dangerous enemy to America and was sent to Connecticut, where he was held in close confinement.

In Pennsylvania Galloway's desertion of the Continental Congress had been generally disapproved, and there was little overt Tory activity in 1775. Although, like so many New Yorkers, some of the men of property in Pennsylvania supported the Congress for fear of mob violence, many still supported resistance to Britain out of a genuine attachment to ideas of liberty. Pennsylvania's characteristic attitude seems to have lain somewhere between the calculating cosmopolitanism of New York and the libertarian pride of Virginia. Only a 'perverse, drivelling knot of Quakers' held out with quiet obstinacy against the Congress. The Quakers had deliberately embarrassed the Massachusetts delegates at the First Continental Congress by asking them pointedly about liberty of conscience in New England. When John Adams had tried to justify Massachusetts's laws against the Quakers, Israel Pemberton had said, 'Oh, sir, don't urge liberty of conscience in favour of such laws!'

In 1775 the Philadelphia Friends Meeting sent letters to Quakers all through the Middle Colonies recommending non-participation in all measures of rebellion, and urging them 'constantly to remember, that to fear God, honour the King, and do good to all men, is our indispensable duty'. The Quakers prayed that nothing should break the 'happy connexion' the colonies had with England, 'or tend to introduce persecution and suffering among us'. 'It is not our business', the Philadelphia Meeting decided, to set up governments, 'much less to plot and contrive the ruin or overturn of any of them.' In these ambitious times, for the Quakers alone, the words of Jesus, 'My kingdom is not of this world', had prescriptive meaning.

John Adams thought Maryland was an 'eccentrick Colony'. The Marylanders at the First Congress had usually voted with the Virginians, but had changed sides to support Galloway's Plan. The internal politics of Maryland seem to have been less turbulent in the years before the Revolution, and relations with the British government less strained, than in perhaps any other colony. In addition, some of Maryland's eccentricity may be explained by the partition of the colony by Chesapeake Bay. The Eastern Shore was maritime, in hostile competition with New England, and Tory. The tobacco-growing regions on the western side of the bay were Whig, although, to be sure, living there was one of the most vexatious Tories in the thirteen colonies, that combative advocate of the Church of England, the Reverend Jonathan Boucher.

Boucher had, by his own account, acted as a political manager for Governor Eden and had attempted to handle the Maryland Assembly for him. He had also, as mentioned above, tried to bring the Maryland and Virginia clergy into a common political programme with the Northern clergy, and had in his sermons and writings generally 'endeavoured . . . to check the immense mischief that was impending'. Though bumptious and self-important, Boucher was a man of energy and ability, and had become as obnoxious to Maryland Whigs as Governor Franklin was to those in New Jersey. Finally, after preaching for six months with two loaded pistols lying ready on his pulpit cushion, Boucher was persuaded to leave the colony in order to avoid mob violence. He wrote sadly that his friends were 'as strongly for my flying as I alone was for my not flying'.

More serious politically, though perhaps less serious philosophically than Boucher's disaffection, was that of the Tories of the Eastern Shore. With the possible exception of western Long Island, the Chesapeake peninsula had the highest proportion of Loyalists in the colonies. They seem to have been fairly evenly distributed through the nine Eastern Shore counties of Maryland, the two southern Delaware counties, and the two Virginia counties at the tip of the peninsula. There were reports of imminent Tory insurrections in each of these counties at one time or another during 1775 and the early part of 1776.

In Worcester County, Maryland, a local committee reported in the autumn of 1775 that the friends of liberty there were in a 'very melancholy situation'. They said they had no ammunition, and 'the Tories exceed our number'. The Loyalists were getting arms from a British ship, which they had heard intended to give direct assistance if a sufficient number of signatures to a Loyalist Association was obtained. A Whig officer who was invited to help drill a newly formed militia company found they had their own articles of association. They asked him how he liked them. He replied cautiously that they were something like the articles of his own company, 'they were for their King and Country'. 'Yes,' said one of the militiamen, 'but we are against Boston.' And they 'all huzzaed for the King, and pulled off their hats'.

One day in September 1775, when a Somerset County, Maryland, militia company met for drill, part of the company drew up as usual, but 'one-half or more' drew apart under a certain Isaac Atkinson, and put on red cockades instead of the usual black. Atkinson had ordered his men to bring sharp flints in their guns, and when asked if he meant to oppose the Congress, said he did, 'and offered to lay Mr. Whitear a doubloon he would by that day week have three hundred men to join him in the opposition'. One of his men said, 'Yes, five hundred; for he is the only man that had opened their eyes, and [he] ought to be upheld'. Atkinson said 'that it was rebellion the way the people of Boston were going on, and that he believed the people of Boston wanted a King of their own in America'. He said the present dispute was about religion, 'and was a Presbyterian scheme', and 'a day must be appointed, and they must fight it out'. No day was appointed, however.

There were reports in the spring of 1776 of a thousand Loyalists under arms in Sussex County, Delaware, and some local Whigs wrote that unless troops were sent in to protect them, 'we must be candid enough to inform you, that self-preservation will oblige us either to leave . . . or fall in and run with the current, either of which will be hateful to us'. In Caroline and Dorchester Counties, Maryland, several companies of militia had laid down their arms. In Newcastle County, Delaware, the people were in contact with British ships in the Delaware and were furnishing them with provisions. Some Maryland Whig militiamen who had been sent 'to the assistance of the people' in Accomack and Northampton Counties, Virginia, at the southern tip of the Chesapeake peninsula, reported that they would have little assistance *from* the people, should they need it.

The situation in the Chesapeake country, as well as across Delaware Bay in southern New Jersey, where the people 'would much rather have the Regulars than the Yankees,'[4] was clearly alarming. Yet, as on Long Island, the Loyalists finally lost heart and allowed themselves to be disarmed. They were not confident of getting assistance from the British and, although they were not afraid of the local Whigs, they were impressed by the reputed strength of the revolutionists inland.

In Virginia, except for the two isolated counties on the Chesapeake peninsula, the Tories were most numerous along the coast near Norfolk, and in the sparsely settled counties beyond the Blue Ridge in the West. Many of the coastal Tories were Scots merchants and small planters. The Scots formed an energetic, if often unpopular, part of the population of Virginia, and though not as numerous as the Chesapeake and New Jersey Loyalists, caused much more trouble. Perhaps because many of them were native Britons, they were willing at an early date to take up arms against the Revolution. They obtained supplies from the British naval forces off the coast and fought several small engagements with the Whigs late in 1775. When finally forced to give up Norfolk, they continued to operate from British ships.

The Loyalists on the western frontier of Virginia were mixed Scots, Indians, and Americans, like those in upper New York. Their leader was Major John Connolly, an American who had served with the British in the West Indies during the Seven Years War, and afterwards settled beyond the mountains in West Augusta County in a region still in dispute between Virginia and Pennsylvania. In August 1775 Connolly had made his way across Virginia to Portsmouth where he acquainted the royal governor, Lord Dunmore, with his plans for a general rising of the Indians, French, and Tories of the Appalachian country. Connolly thought that he could stay the winter at Detroit and come up the Ohio in the spring of 1776 with a few regular troops, gather his Loyalists and take Fort Pitt. General Gage authorized him to offer three hundred acres of land to every man who would join him. Connolly hoped that after taking Fort Pitt he could march across Virginia, perhaps enlisting discontented indentured servants, and meet Dunmore at Alexandria. This ambitious scheme, the first part of which may have been feasible, collapsed when Connolly and two Scots friends were arrested by the militia at Frederick, Maryland, on their way back to the West.

North Carolina was a poor province, thinly populated and less active politically than Virginia or South Carolina. Perhaps the most vigorous elements in the population were the New Englanders in the Piedmont and the Scots and English along the coast. There were a good many Scots Loyalists at Wilmington and around Cape Fear, although they were outnumbered by native planters of South Carolina origin. Janet Schaw, a Scotswoman who was visiting relatives in North Carolina in 1775, wrote a vivid account of the plight of the Scots Tories at Wilmington: 'An officer or committeeman enters a plantation with his posse. The Alternative is proposed, Agree to join us, and your persons and properties are safe; . . . But if you refuse, we are directly to cut up your corn, shoot your pigs, burn your houses, seize your Negroes and perhaps tar and feather yourself.'

White Loyalists were not the only enemies of the Revolution in the South. The Whigs were in constant terror of Negro insurrection. There seems to have been some grounds for what a Whig in one of Crèvecœur's *Sketches* said to a Negro boy: 'They say you are a good fellow, only a little Toryfied like most of your colour.' Wherever British ships appeared off the coast in the South, Negroes would row out with provisions, and often Negro men would stay as volunteers. Many Americans were shocked at the fraternization between the British and the Negroes. An American prisoner aboard a British ship in Delaware Bay observed indignantly that three Negro men who had come aboard 'were shaken hands with, and

[4] Loyalist insurrections were reported imminent in Monmouth, Hunterdon, and Bergen Counties, New Jersey in June 1776, and Whig militiamen could not be persuaded to go near the Deal Shore in southern New Jersey for fear the people would turn them over to the British. *Am. Arch.* 4th series, vi. 1630; 5th series, i. 602–3.

kindly received and entertained' by the English, who promised them their freedom when the rebellion was over. British prisoners in New Jersey were accused of 'continually plotting with the Negroes'.[5]

In the spring of 1776 the North Carolina Congress recommended that all masters and owners of slaves on the south side of the Cape Fear River 'remove such male slaves as are capable of bearing arms, or otherwise assisting the enemy, into the country, remote from the sea'. Janet Schaw wrote that the Negroes were going off to the woods around Wilmington. The Whites, she said, were all in arms, 'the patroles going thro' all the town', and searching the Negroes' houses to see that they were all at home by nine at night. She wrote that one Negro was shot and killed by a nervous Whig, but that there was no insurrection, for one reason because the Negroes had no arms.

In some of the western counties of North Carolina many former Regulators were Loyalists. Being old rebels themselves, the Regulators were sceptical of the sudden zeal for liberty of the lowland planters, whom they distrusted more than the British. In an effort to conciliate the Regulators, the North Carolina Provincial Council appointed a committee to 'explain the proceedings of the Congress' to the back country, 'where the People are not well informed', and had been misled by Tory pamphlets distributed by Governor Martin. The explanations were apparently insufficient, because in February 1776 some 1,600 Regulators and Scots Highlanders gathered in arms under the King's standard at Cross Creek. At Moore's Creek Bridge the Loyalists, under the temporary command of Colonel Alexander McLeod, found a smaller force of Whigs in entrenched positions, and the Scots charged them before the Regulators were ready. The Whigs repelled the charge, and the Loyalists fled the field. Most of them were disarmed, and their leaders taken prisoner, soon after.

The back country of South Carolina was even more disaffected than that of North Carolina. In the summer of 1775 the Charleston oligarchs sent William Drayton and the Reverend William Tennent, Charleston's leading dissenting minister, on a mission to District Ninety-Six 'to explain to the People the causes of the present disputes'. At first they made little headway with the Tory leaders. Tennent wrote, 'We soon found the unchangeable malignity of their minds, and the inexpressible pains they are at to blind the people, and fill them with bitterness against the gentlemen, as they are called.' Tennent had, however, true missionary zeal. He and Drayton talked for hours with the principal Tory leader, Thomas Fletchall: 'We honoured him — we laughed with him; then we recurred to argument, remonstrances, and entreaties, to join his Country, and all America.' At first, all Fletchall would say was that 'he would never take up arms against his King or his countrymen, and that the Proceedings of the Congress at Philadelphia were impolitick, disrespectful, and irritating to the King'.

Finally, however, Fletchall agreed to sign a 'Treaty of Neutrality' with Drayton and Tennent. This included a qualified admission of the authority of the Provincial Congress, which the other Tory leaders refused to make. In November 1775, with Fletchall and his men neutral, fighting broke out between the Whig militia and the Tories led by Robert Cunningham. Cunningham's men, though numerically superior to the Whigs, were defeated and disarmed. Drayton ascribed the Tory defeat to lack of leadership, and wrote that if the royal governor, William Campbell, had gone into the back country in the summer of 1775 and led the Tories himself, the 'whole proceedings' of the Provincial Congress might have been overthrown. Campbell, however, had stayed in Charleston, there 'to experience the daily loss of his executive powers; and the little consideration in which he was holden'. The Whigs sealed their victory over the Tories by a generous amnesty in March 1776, by which time many

[5] 4 *Am. Arch.* vi. 811, 1639. Three hundred Negroes took part, with 250 British and 150 Virginia Scots Loyalists, in a landing on Gwin's Island in the Delaware in June 1776. Georgia Negroes were reported running away to join the British. Negroes in southern New Jersey were reported arming themselves. *Ibid.* 811; 5th series, i. 7, 16.

In March 1776 Lord Dunmore organized an 'Ethiopian Corps,' which saw service later in the war. There were many accounts like that of a Marylander who wrote: 'A valuable Negro made his escape from us [to the British] last night, he not being so well guarded as he ought to have been.' *Ibid.* i. 518; ii. 160.

Tories were fighting alongside the Whigs against the Cherokees.

The Indians had been incited to attack the settlements by John Stuart, a South Carolina Tory who was the royal superintendent of Indian affairs in the South. Stuart had a scheme similar to Connolly's for raising the frontiersmen and Indians, and General Gage had apparently hoped to concert both plans with a rising led in upper New York by Guy Johnson. Stuart did persuade the Cherokees to make a general attack in the Carolinas, but the whole plan miscarried when the Indians massacred Tories as well as Whigs. This changed the 'countenance and tone' of some of the Loyalists, a number of whom offered their services to the Charleston government and fought the Indians. The Cherokees were driven back into the mountains, and the active Loyalists were reduced, for the time being, to a few marauding bands.[6]

Everywhere then, in 1775, the Tories were intimidated, disarmed, and defeated, even in districts where they had overwhelming local superiority. Lack of organization, of course, contributed to their failure. This is clear, for example, in the absence of any co-ordination of the several abortive western risings. Had a concerted attack by Tories and Indians been made all along the frontier from New York to Georgia, it might have proved embarrassing to the Congress. Here, however, not only their lack of organization, but also the inherent disparateness of the Tories handicapped them. The alliance between the Cherokees and the South Carolina frontiersmen was uneasy if not unsound. In North Carolina the Regulators and Scots Highlanders mistrusted each other, and none of the frontier Tories had much in common with the stolid farmers of Long Island, or the Chesapeake fishermen.

The Tories were willing enough to fight for their principles and prejudices, as they showed later in the war. But separate grievances can make common cause only when they have a common standard to rally around. The failure, in years gone by, of Tory leaders to provide such a standard was decisive now. In 1775 only the British could have given leadership to the various Tory groups, supplied and reinforced them, and led them into common purpose; this the British were as yet unwilling to attempt. Thus the Loyalist ranks succumbed to the same lack of confidence and direction that had for twenty years unnerved the Tory leaders.

[6] 5 *Am. Arch.* i. 481, 610; ii. 209; *N.Y. Col. Doc.* viii. 159; Samuel Curwen, *Journal and Letters* (New York, 1845), pp. 659–60.

In Georgia, as in Nova Scotia, the very small population was too dependent on British subsidies and protection to be able to afford revolution. Georgia Whigs reported to the Continental Congress that there was little enthusiasm for non-intercourse with Britain in Savannah. 'There were some . . . virtuously for the measures; others strenuously against them; but more who called themselves neutrals than either.' In March 1776, when Georgia was about to resume trade with Britain, the South Carolina Congress sent troops to occupy Savannah. 4 *Am. Arch.* ii. 280; v. 585.

II

The War: The American Revolutionary Army: A French Estimate in 1777

Most Loyalists undoubtedly expected a quick British victory in the American War for Independence. The preponderance of the British military and naval forces over those of the patriots seemed overwhelming — an estimate shared fully by Lord North's Ministry. Such over-confidence combined with inept British generalship contributed substantially to the American victory, no less than did French aid. Neither factor would have mattered much, however, had not the colonists been able to field an army in 1775 and then maintain it despite disheartening defeats.

By any standards, the American military accomplishment was remarkable. The colonists had long nurtured deep suspicions of any military establishment; indeed, their antipathy to standing armies had itself contributed to the Revolution. Washington's army, handicapped by short-term enlistments and unreliable militia

"The American Revolutionary Army: A French Estimate in 1777," ed. Durand Echeverria and Orville T. Murphy, *Military Affairs,* XXVII (1963), 1–7; 153–162.

drafts was rarely a fighting force in any professional sense. Ill-supplied and ill-disciplined, the American army often seemed to survive on hope and luck. "The native American," commented an English general, "is very unfit for and impatient of war." Why then did Washington win? Partly because he made the most of limited opportunities. Moreover, the American army, for all its deficiencies, was much better than the British anticipated.

How much better is an arguable question. At least one contemporary account of a European professional soldier provides a generally favorable portrait, forecasting as early as 1777 an eventual American victory. The author of this appraisal was a young French army officer who visited America for three months in the summer of 1777.[1] *His present editors observe that his report has singular advantages, being the work of a professionally competent observer whose views were not prejudiced by frictions with Congress or the American army.*

Supply

The soldiers are of two sorts, the militia and the regulars. The militiamen are farmers, rich or poor as the case may be, who have been snatched from their plows to fight the enemy. They are dressed comfortably if not richly, according to their means, and have no special uniform. For the most part they wear a coat with one or two waistcoats or vests, a pair of cloth breeches, another pair of duck breeches worn over the first, and hats, stockings, and shoes of whatever sort they choose. In addition they carry on their backs a knapsack for their change of clothing, a blanket, and on the end of a cord a small flat canteen like a cartridge pouch, in which they keep something to drink. I am not including in their dress their military equipment, such as the gun, cartridge pouch, bayonet, and bayonet belt, for which they are paid at the beginning of each campaign and which they buy back by returning the money they have received. Formerly they had to purchase their own food and take care of their other expenses themselves. Now they receive pay, a paltry sum it is true, but about enough to permit them not to be dependent on their families. The tents, cooking pots, etc., are paid for by the government.

The regular soldier presents a quite different appearance, sometimes handsomer and sometimes less so.

When Congress recruited the militia and regular soldiers for only a very short period of service it could not be accused of penny pinching if it did not provide them with clothing, for often a man was discharged before there was time to issue him his enlistment papers and provide him with equipment. Consequently no arrangements were made with suppliers and no warehouses were established, and in short nothing was done to prevent the disadvantages of the unprepossessing appearance of troops dressed according to the whim of the individual soldier.

As supplies, especially of cloth, began to arrive from Europe, the various provinces provided uniforms for as many soldiers as they could. The wild mixture of colors which resulted made the troops look even worse than they had before, and this would still be the case if the efforts of Congress and continued imports from Europe had not speeded up the change over to a standard uniform for all, which makes a much handsomer show. The course of the war brought to a halt this luxury. All the regiments having been expanded in order to meet the growth of the enemy forces, it is not now possible to provide each recruit with the complete uniform he is supposed to have, because of lack of cloth or seasonal shortages. This is the reason for the miserable, motley appearance of the American troops, especially of those under General Washington's command, which has provoked so many comments from Frenchmen accustomed to seeing soldiers neat and well-uniformed even though they may be sick and underfed.

Let us consider, however, in a sensible and objective way whether there is any basis for their ridicule and their sarcastic comments. We know that it is generally true that those who are the most ill-clad are the most impoverished part of a population, but it does not necessarily follow

[1] Tentatively identified as one Louis de Recourt de Ganot (1752–?), a cadet officer in the royal corps of artillery of the French army from 1765 to 1776.

that they are the unhealthiest. If this were so the inhabitants of Auvergne and Saintonge would be the sickliest people in France, and this is obviously not the case. If their diet is not inferior, men somewhat less well-clothed may be just as healthy as anyone else. This is true in the case of the American army. Those soldiers who are well clothed are the ones who when they enlisted were lucky enough to be issued new or used uniforms. If such men present a good appearance it is merely because they happened to be among the first to enlist in the regiment or because they got, from men being discharged, uniforms which happened to fit them. One cannot argue that the well-equipped soldier is healthier than the one who is poorly outfitted since both were formerly in want and ill clad and yet were in good physical condition.

It would obviously be wrong if those not issued uniforms were without adequate protection against the weather while others were as well equipped as our French soldiers. It would be inexcusably inhuman to expose to the rigors of winter in a country as cold as this, men on whose support and courage the defense of the nation depends. This, however, is far from the case, as two most convincing facts prove: First, the soldiers in general are all in good health. And, second, in spite of the hardships they seem to be suffering and the good treatment they would get if they deserted and went over to the enemy, the rate of desertion is very low, in contrast to the high rate in all European armies. So there is nothing real about their apparent sufferings. The truth of this assertion was demonstrated last winter at the Battle of Trenton, when it was the soldiers who urged and practically forced their general to attack the enemy. Surely so clear a proof of valor as this could not be produced by suffering and discontent.

It is of course true that soldiers can be in ill health and courageous at the same time. But you need only question anybody who saw the army parade in Philadelphia or at the camp. He will tell you that though they did not have that perfect alignment which you see in troops who are so identical in stature, headgear, dress, and footwear that each man is indistinguishable from all the others, nevertheless the soldiers, ill-clad as they were for the most part, gave an appearance of health and vigor that one would scarcely expect to see in sick and exhausted troops.

Each regiment has its own uniform. I shall not attempt to list all the various colors, but in general the men wear a jacket-coat, that is, a garment halfway between a long waistcoat and a frockcoat, a white cloth waistcoat, a belt around the coat, breeches, stockings, and whatever footgear the individual prefers. Otherwise they are equipped just about the same as the militia, and those who have been issued little or even nothing in the way of clothing are dressed in no way differently from the militia, though we must remember that the militiaman is often a well-to-do farmer while it has been usually fate, poverty, loose living, or just plain foolishness which has led the regular to enlist.

From the foregoing it is evident that Congress is in no way at fault for having organized the regular army before it found a way to outfit them in uniforms. It is not merely good luck, but good government, good living, and the love of liberty that have made the regulars so healthy and so loyal in spite of the cold and other hardships — sufferings which because of the lack of proper clothing have been far worse than what soldiers normally endure in wartime.

The same circumstances which provided the ships and supplies to organize a naval force gave the material necessary to establish the artillery. When the Royalists were driven out, the Americans seized the forts, arsenals, and all the military stores which the English had been forced to abandon. Thus they turned against the tyrant those arms which he had intended to use against them. The number of cast-iron pieces which they seized was very small, but the wrought-iron guns were numerous enough to arm the frigates in commission and the most important forts, even without the cannon which have been obtained by purchase or from foreign powers since the outbreak of hostilities and the Declaration of Independence. But the captured English guns could not provide the armament for newly constructed forts and for the corps of artillery attached to the various armies, and the astonishing number of guns on privateers. These have been obtained through successful diplomacy and by purchases from European merchants and others.

But guns alone were not enough, and they have been supplemented with so many other military supplies of all sorts, including gunpowder, muskets, bayonets, mortars, bombs, and cannon balls that if the English had been able to establish a tight blockade such as they are maintaining at present, it is quite certain that the colonies would have been already subdued. Instead, the Americans are now well supplied with everything and are able to offer effective resistance and even to assume the offensive.

The cavalry is a special topic. It was organized in response to patriotic demand in the various provinces, which have furnished the money and equipment. Each province has its own regiment, though it is not absolutely necessary that all the men be natives. Any volunteers are accepted, as is the case with infantry regiments. Completely uniformed, the American cavalry presents a much handsomer appearance than the rest of the army. The men are selected so as to be as nearly as possible of the same stature, the officers come from the wealthy classes, and a special effort has been made to obtain those who have been in the King's service. Their mounts, which are rather tall, would not be the equals of our French cavalry horses, either in endurance or strength to resist the shock of battle. From the small use that is made of the cavalry it appears that it serves only for show.

Operations

American military tactics are the product partly of the people's way of life, partly of their military traditions, and partly of their inexperience in this cruel art.

The present inhabitants are, as we know, the descendants of the first settlers, the founding fathers who cleared the land and passed it on to their posterity. As the coastal regions became well populated the colonists felt an urge to extend their settlements by occupying new territories. To do so they found it necessary, in addition to clearing the land, to overcome two closely related obstacles. The first was the hostile Indian. Even when there were no Indian wars the Americans had to be continually on their guard. They always kept their guns within reach, and at the first suspicious sound they would crouch behind a tree, ready for any danger. The other obstacle was the wild animals which inhabited the lands to be settled. They had to hunt them to vary their diet and to get pelts, out of which they made clothing warmer than what they could buy and which provided an additional medium of exchange. These conditions forced the first settlers to become hunters, like the Indians, relying on their guns for their daily food. The children of these pioneers, brought up in this sort of life and sharing from childhood its hardships as well as its joys, naturally learned both by the force of example and out of sheer necessity the ways, the agility, and the vigilance of their fathers. So it is not surprising that the present generation, either through necessity or for pleasure, are still attached to this sort of life and are still masters of all the skills which their fathers were forced to learn. This is the reason that American soldiers can fire a fusillade a hundred times more deadly than that of any other troops in the world. Even when they are retreating or pretending to retreat in order to be in a better position to turn back the enemy, they always lose less men than the opposing force, because nearly every shot is taken deliberately and all of them, officers and men, fire only when they have picked out their target, and they rarely miss.

The excellence of their marksmanship, however, would be an even greater advantage if they could discard their prejudices against conventional tactics and abandon their traditional way of fighting. When confronted by an enemy force they always fall back through the woods, pausing to fire when they have a good target. Each man takes shelter in a ditch or behind a tree, fires from cover, and then immediately runs for a different protected position to wait for a chance for another shot.

These tactics are the result both of their peacetime experience and of their lack of training in the murderous art of war. There is no justification for accusing them of cowardice. How could one expect from such proud and independent men, no matter how much military training they had had, that coolness, that deliberation, that immobility so characteristic of European soldiers? These are valuable military virtues, but they are bought at a high price; for in order to achieve them the European's will, his personality, in fact his very instinct for self-preservation have been stifled and destroyed. In battle he is a mere machine, motionless, without personal feelings, controlled only by hidden springs. Such complete impassiveness constitutes the merit of our soldiers. But if we can forget for a moment our prejudices born of our pride in our past victories, must we not admit that it is far better to command an army of free men fighting for their independence, whose inborn love of liberty is manifested even in their methods of waging war? Such men may be conquered but they will still preserve their spirit of freedom which they have imbibed with their mothers' milk.

This inflexible and independent character, this refusal, so to speak, to surrender to the will of a superior officer, constitutes what might be termed an inevitable disadvantage of the spirit of liberty reigning in America. But there is no reason to consider it, as some have done, a clear or convincing proof of cowardice. For the Americans are still far from being conquered, and if they have lost some battles they have won some hard-fought skirmishes. It is true that they have given ground when faced with the cold steel of disciplined troops, well-trained, advancing in ranks, and that they have indeed sometimes fled from the enemy. Nevertheless, their conduct under fire gives every reason to expect that once they have become accustomed to these unfamiliar tactics and have been tested against them a few times, even under disadvantageous circumstances, their courage, their pride, and especially their newly acquired experience will soon turn them into good soldiers. They will be just as effective as the British troops, who in defeating them will have taught them how to fight, and in the end they will triumph.

We should remember, moreover, a few basic facts: that men are the same everywhere; that Americans are an alert, skillful, hard-working people; that a number of their own native-born officers have demonstrated the ability to conduct successful campaigns; that their army includes officers of all nationalities; that men can always learn from experience and the force of example whenever their own self-interest forces them to do so; that Americans are just as capable as anyone else of perceiving the inadequacies of their present tactics; and finally that they already combine the most fervent patriotism with an incomparable constancy in enduring ice and snow, the lack of the elementary necessities of life, and all the other hardships of war. We shall soon see that there is no reason to accuse them of cowardice for not being able to stand up to an attack by European troops. We shall find that they have learned how to offer effective resistance by adopting sounder tactics and learning how to counter the maneuvers of the enemy. Thus they will force those who have so harshly criticized them to eat their words.

If we merely consider the victories and defeats of the present campaign we shall see the truth of what I have said. The Americans may or may not be as successful as I have ventured to predict. Nevertheless it is impossible not to agree that it is their way of thinking which is the true explanation of their attachment to their own special way of waging war.

The present military successes of the Americans can be ascribed to certain handicaps the English generals have faced: their unfamiliarity with the area of hostilities; their difficulties in obtaining reinforcements and supplies once the armies have advanced inland; the fact that the enemy forces keep steadily increasing, while their own troops are daily depleted;[1] the inevitable exhaustion suffered by soldiers living continually in the forests and without hospitals or recuperation camps where the men might recover from the ill effects suffered from changes in climate and living conditions; the drawn-out, steady fighting in mountainous and unhealthful terrain, where it is necessary to hack out roads even to get at the enemy. To all these difficulties must be added the discontent of foreign troops who have been promised a sure and easy victory and to whom the Americans offer citizenship and good lands if they will desert. It is not surprising if, in spite of the bravery of the

[1] The notion that American strength was growing while British strength was diminishing was probably true for the summer of 1777 when the author was in America. John Richard Alden, *The American Revolution: 1775–1783* (New York, 1954), 116. Unfortunately the American strength relative to British strength did not for long maintain such a favorable growth. See *Ibid.*, 198 and note; and Rupert Hughes, *George Washington: the Savior of the States,* 1777–1781 (New York, 1930) III, 434–435.

Hessian and Royalist troops and the inexperience of the Americans, fortune has favored the Insurgents, for the latter are the more numerous, they are the more effective riflemen, they are fighting in their own land with ample supplies, and they are in a position to encourage desertion among the enemy by offers of rewards and promises of a friendly welcome.

One thing only could forever and completely destroy the hope of an American victory. That would be the capture and dissolution of Congress. In it alone resides the national power. Formed from representatives of all the provinces, it alone makes the laws, causes the money presses to turn, and gives to the rebels the shadow of legislative authority. Once it were suppressed, before the provinces could be informed, elect new deputies, name a president, agree on a capital, we should soon see. . . . But I prefer to suppress the proofs which I could easily give to convince any doubters. The disaster would be all too real. It would bring about the ruin of so many worthy men that I would rather allow myself to be accused of negligence or presumption in discussing this question than to have to repent having suggested an idea which the English themselves have not thought of, and which it would have been so easy for them to have carried out on the night of September 12 of last year.[2]

The same thing is not true, however, of Philadelphia, the possession of which some have incorrectly believed to be all important on the strategy of the present war. Situated at the confluence of the Delaware and the Schuylkill rivers, this city, which before the war was important because of its foreign trade and was expanding each year in wealth and population, is unprotected on the land-side, and the waterfronts are undefended except by the width and depth of the rivers. There is nothing along either river which could stop a victorious army equipped with pontoons and other suitable equipment. The surface of the Schuylkill (which is perhaps once again as wide as the Seine at the Pont Royal at high water) is almost even with the surrounding land, and in all the short and easily fordable course of the stream there is not a single point reasonably well-suited for defense. The Delaware, which is much broader at Philadelphia than the Garonne at Bordeaux, presents a somewhat greater obstacle because of its width. Nevertheless, although its banks are in many places swampy for a long distance inland, there are some spots which would make such good landings and which are so unprotected by high ground that this side of the city likewise can be considered indefensible.

The ease with which Philadelphia can be taken, however, does not prove that its capture is useful or advantageous, for Congress can flee from the city from one side as the enemy enters from the other. It has no arsenals or supply depots of any consequence, and none could easily be established there. Moreover the surrounding bays and rivers, which freeze over in the winter, might make Philadelphia for the Royalists, if they were foolish enough to establish a base there, what the fields of Saratoga were for General Burgoyne. Confined to a restricted and unfortified position from which they could not get out, they would suffer from lack of supplies in the midst of the surrounding plenty, and would soon lose through starvation and shortages the very advantages they had acquired by their bravery and enterprise. So Philadelphia is in no way adapted to serving as a position of strength. The fame that it has had in the present war has come only from the fact that it had been the leading commercial city of the colonies and was chosen by Congress to be the capital of the republic.

Being the handsomest, largest, and richest city on the continent, it won out for these reasons over Boston, Williamsburg, Annapolis, Charleston, etc., though these cities, from the point of view of suitability, defensibility, and magnificence come very close to being able to claim the title of "Mother of the Country," which Philadelphia has been enthusiastically granted in the present crisis.

Personnel

The thirteen provinces, after they had united in a democratic political body, believed they

[2] A reference to the flight of the Continental Congress from Philadelphia before the advancing British army. The correct date, however, was the 19th of September, 1777. Edmund C. Burnett, *The Continental Congress* (New York, 1941), 246–247.

were strong enough to drive out by a sudden, unexpected attack the troops which the British had been maintaining in America for purposes of defense and in well-justified expectation of the revolt which has in fact occurred. It seemed doubtful, however, whether these citizens who had raised the banner of rebellion would be willing to carry through their first efforts at the sacrifice of their own comfort and whether they would continue a prolonged war ruinous to the colonies' agriculture. One special problem was that the soldiers had to return home each year for a few months to take care of the needs of their families. Such fears were prompted by a good understanding of human nature. Men seize blindly upon a new idea that seems to promise desirable rewards, and they recognize the necessary cost and sacrifices only when they are forced to maintain their initial efforts — or when they find they have to begin the task all over again from the beginning. These fears for long kept the provincial assemblies from acting. Even without regular troops they had a reasonable chance, by means of a sudden attack, of driving out the scattered British forces and preventing them from regrouping. But how could they expect to stand up against the troops that would be sent to avenge the initial defeats? The enemy could land without opposition and ravage the country, for there was scarcely a single fort or defensible position capable of stopping them. Moreover, in a land of liberty and equality it was impossible to use the methods of European despotism and force free men to fight against their will for any cause, even one which they believed in. It would have been unjust to have recourse either to a general military service law or to a selective draft by lot in order to compel citizens to serve more than a short period of time and run more than a temporary risk of being killed. There was no justification for inflicting on the people a long and grievous period of military service like that endured by our soldiers, who, once war is declared, even if they are eligible for discharge, must re-enlist and serve for the whole period of hostilities.

According to this reasoning, based on an uncompromising affirmation of complete equality, it was resolved that every man capable of bearing arms would be required to serve for a certain number of days, during which period his fields would be cultivated by the man who was to replace him in the army, or whom he had replaced. Upon the expiration of his term of enlistment he would be under no legal compulsion to re-enlist and he had the right to return to his home after his discharge.

The enactment of this law made it possible to raise a fair-sized army, but it was a poorly trained one and of an impermanent nature. The general never could know exactly how many enlistments were expiring or were about to expire, so that very often when he had counted on a certain number of troops for a battle he found that when the time came to fight he had no soldiers. Yet he could not accuse his men of cowardice, for they were acting according to their contracts with the government. Since they had served out their required enlistments there was no law of equity, reason, or justice which could force them to undergo additional risks or to sign up for a longer period of duty.

The disadvantages of this system of enlistment of the militia, which resulted in General Washington's lack of troops in the winter of 1776–1777 and in the English victories of that year, forced the Continental Congress and the state assemblies to make two changes. First, they extended the period of enlistment for the militia so that every man would serve until the end of the campaign each year or until he had been replaced. Second, they established a certain number of regiments of regular soldiers enlisted for not less than three years or for the duration of hostilities, rather than merely for the period for which the individual volunteered, as had been formerly the practice.

This was the first law of such an oppressive nature to be proposed in the new democracy, and there was considerable difficulty in getting it passed. The measure, however, was supported by a very cogent argument. Regular soldiers had a bad reputation with the general public. The regular regiments were composed entirely of vagabonds and paupers; no enticement or trick could force solid citizens to enlist as regulars, inasmuch as they had to serve as militia anyway. Consequently, it was argued, there could be no danger in making any regulations whatsoever regarding the enlistment of regulars, since a man accepting such an enlistment did so of his own free will and was presumed to understand the conditions. This reasoning led to the acceptance of the principle that a citizen might obligate himself for a prolonged period of service. In order, however, to alleviate the rigors of the law and to compensate for its unfairness it was stipulated that any soldier who volunteered for service as a regular would receive after his discharge full title to a certain amount of uncleared land from his native state or province, thus becoming the owner of a bit of his own country.[3] This truly Roman reward will serve for a long time to increase in every province the number of volunteers; and these men, once they have served out their enlistments, will at least enjoy a tranquil existence and the assurance of a laborious and modest but secure livelihood.

Thus every province has its militia and also its regular provincial regiments, which are allocated to the forts seized from the English, or to the new ones built to protect the province's approaches and harbors, or to the cities requiring troops as a precaution against a Tory uprising or else to the Continental Armies under Washington, the generalissimo.

Such then is the organization of the militia and the regular army. The make-up of the corps of officers needs to be explained in greater detail, and is as follows:

We have seen that at the outbreak of hostilities King George's forces were in complete control of the forts and military posts on the continent. Although the troops were drafted mercenaries and often foreigners, a number of the officers were American colonists. Since they could serve their king just as well in his colonial regiments as in Europe they were not always required, as in France, to endure foreign duty, the unhappy lot so often of the peacetime soldier. These officers, whether or not they had retired from the service, could not help taking sides in their own minds in the quarrel between the royal government and the Americans, since the cause of the latter was their own. The actions of the royalist party, which were aimed at establishing the worst sort of despotism and threatened to wreck the prosperity of the colonies, could not fail to alienate them completely. They loved their native land and were interested in their own welfare. Moreover, they knew they were in disfavor with the Court, and at the same time they were tempted by the rank, dignities, and honors offered by Congress. All these factors contributed to their decision. From such officers came the [Richard] Montgomerys, the [Israel] Putnams, the [George] Washingtons, the De Kassens [*sic*], the [Horatio] Gates, the [John] Sullivans, the [Benedict] Arnolds,[4] and the others of high rank; and in the lower ranks we find all those formerly in the King's service who found it to their advantage to resign and to join so noble a cause, a cause of which they were to become the heroes and protagonists.

This acceptance by the elite of the nation's officers of the responsibilities and risks of the Revolution influenced the majority of the patriotic American officers on duty in Europe to return to serve and defend their native land. But even with these men there were not enough. Subaltern officers were needed, and they were nominated and elected, regardless of their condition or station, by the people and the assemblies in the same way as the members of Congress. The people also granted, as was just, to anyone who could do so the right to raise, equip, and name a regiment of his own and to select all the necessary officers, with the approval of Congress or of the commander-in-chief. Lastly, a number of men were promoted from the ranks of the lower grades to commissions as superior or general officers, either through the process of regular advancement or as a reward for meritorious actions. From all these various sources have come the officers of the American Army.

The fact that the soldiers do not show a sense of discipline and respect for their officers when they are not on guard duty or in ranks can be explained by the national character and by the spirit of liberty, independence, and equality

[3] The bounties of land were granted only to those who enlisted for the duration of the war and not to those who enlisted only for three years. *Journals of the Continental Congress: 1774–1784*, ed. Worthington Chauncey Ford (Washington, D.C., 1906), VI, 945.

[4] Only Richard Montgomery and Horatio Gates had served in the British regular army. Putnam, Sullivan, and Arnold had previously served as officers over colonial militia or volunteer troops. Washington had served on General Braddock's staff, but this commission, signed by Governor Dinwiddie and not by the king, was not a regular army commission.

which these people possess. Yet whenever insubordination becomes too flagrant it is punished, though never as rigorously as in European armies. The punishments inflicted take into account the fact that except for the difference in military rank the offender is the equal of the man he has offended. Penalties which are light in comparison with those usual in our army are sufficient to keep within strict limits any shirking of duty or insubordination. It is certainly reasonable to obviate the shedding of blood, and to prevent that reciprocal hatred inevitably engendered by a condition of absolute subjection which demands of one man a temporary abnegation often impossible for the best of men or the most tractable spirits — even those most thoroughly disciplined to the caprices, rigidities, and injustices of military law — and which at the same time allows the other man unrestricted, arbitrary, despotic power, often uncontrolled by higher authority.

This same lack of discipline and subordination is to be seen in the officer corps, from the most junior lieutenant right up to the generals, for all are the same sort of men in civilian life. The officers, however, are generally better educated than the enlisted men. Moreover, there does not exist the same sense of inferiority or superiority in the attitude of one officer to another, and their relationships are not so formal and are less governed by regulations. Consequently, it is more rarely necessary to discipline or cashier the officers.

It even happens often that when an officer resigns from a regiment or is discharged because of some minor offense, he may join another regiment, so long as there is no doubt as to his honor, honesty, or loyalty. Or else, if he so requests, he may be reinstated in good standing just as if he had never had any trouble and had never given any cause for dissatisfaction. This leniency, which violates all European military traditions, instead of casting discredit on the Americans in fact does them honor. It is convincing proof of their high moral standards and of their determination to adhere to the laws of reason and humanity. For the officer when reinstated is not ashamed to admit his mistake, and he can accept a generous pardon without thinking his honor or reputation has been besmirched. At the same time the superior who, in accordance with their military regulations, permits such an officer to return to duty does not penalize him for the rest of his life for a single offense or because of some personal disagreement between the two of them in which the junior was quite rightly forced to yield.

Such pardons or reinstatements appear all the more necessary and just, when we imagine what might happen to a zealous Whig who has left his family and the comforts of home to rush to the defense of his country. He might find that because of some mistake, some ridiculous trifle, some slight neglect of his duties, or even merely because of some other officer's prejudice against him, he was forced to return home and live out his days in idleness and disgrace. Certainly, he would not be human if such clear injustice on the part of his compatriots did not destroy his enthusiasm for national independence and turn him into the most ardent of Royalists. These are good laws, then, and good principles which put a man back on his feet and save him from despair and treason. They may be in violent contradiction with the military regulations of all other nations in the world, but they promote the welfare of the country, honor humanity, and are to the eternal glory of the men who have adopted them, and who prefer them to all those rules of honor that others defend, tolerate, authorize, and enforce by a system of punishments and rewards. Such a code creates neither better citizens nor better subjects; it only makes men more unjust and more intolerant to one another.

This, then, is that insubordination which has been so violently condemned by French officers who have gone to serve in America. I am not referring to the officers who possess the strength of character befitting their rank and who are self-disciplined, intelligent, fair to their inferiors, and sympathetic to the principle of equality. I mean those who do not understand how an officer should act, who dress up in elaborate uniforms, who cause a lot of trouble — in a word, officers who are a plague to others and no good to their friends. Men of this latter sort are particularly enraged by the fact that they find themselves completely ignored in a country where no consideration is given to birth, name, rank, wealth, or letters of recommendation. For this is a land where honor is paid only to proven merit, and where such tribute is rendered not in words, nor in mere flattery and exaggerated expressions of esteem, but rather in deference and respect for superior merit. It would be well, perhaps, at this point to discuss at some length the French who have gone to America and the motives which took them there.

The French colonies, because they have been the scene of some advantageous marriages for certain officers who have found there opportunities to console widows and old maids weary of celibacy, have long had the reputation of being a good place to make a fortune fast. It has been believed that a man must be singularly lacking in talents if he cannot make a worthwhile match during his tour of duty. But for some time now this attractive myth has been destroyed, and it has finally been recognized that for every one or two officers who have had the luck to make a good marriage in the colonies, a far larger number have been disillusioned and have come back to France to their great chagrin much more unmarried than they expected to be.

Nevertheless many French have conceived these same false ideas about the English colonies. All those who were troubled by poverty and bachelorhood have dashed across the ocean in hopes of putting an end to their complaints. Not one of them, however, has realized his dream. The impoverished have found that, just as in France, making one's fortune by honest means takes a long time. And those who have expected to marry a widow or a rich heiress have found American girls either already engaged or else reserved, retiring, and unapproachable. And the widows, who have turned out to be more sociable but as a rule no less chaste, have avoided them, made fun of their vainglorious talk, laughed at their pretty speeches, and finally snubbed them to their faces by giving their hand to some ordinary American. For they have preferred a man with a background like their own who, combining a simple and honest face with a modest fortune or the reputation of being industrious, was marrying them for themselves and not their money, and who would not make them regret they had said yes so readily. Such has been the fate of those who went to America to make their fortune and "settle down" (this is the word these gentlemen use, though they are incapable of staying put anywhere). They were just as able as anyone else to make a good marriage in France, but they neither could nor should have expected to do so in America so long as they insisted on behaving as though they were still in France.

Disappointed and with their hopes of wealth shattered, they have had to make up their minds either to go back home or else adopt the profession they had claimed they had come to practice. Bred to be proud of their rank and conscious of social distinctions and having lived all their lives in France, they thought, because they found no knights or barons or marquesses in America, that by boasting of their titles they would be able either to obtain commissions at high ranks or at least win a flattering welcome. Most of them, astonished to be received by the members of Congress courteously but without any sort of subservience or deference, began to form of their hosts an unfavorable opinion. They should have stopped to consider that they were 1,500 leagues from home, unknown, without influence, without friends who could recommend them, and in the position of asking for favors. And they should have realized that by the vicissitudes of human affairs values might be different in different countries, and that people might be cordial to someone simply because they liked him and because his presence was useful to the national welfare, but without any intention of doing anything for him. They were incapable, however, of such reflections, for they were not used to thinking on such a high plane. They could not tell the difference between a cool but favorable reception and one which was warm but unfavorable. If we add to all this the fact that it necessarily took a long time to decide on their requests (for Congress, though overwhelmed by business and difficulties, had to vote on the granting of every commission), you will have a good idea of the opinion the typical French officer had of Congress as he received his commission, bonus, and travel expenses. This was the appreciation he felt toward those who had just granted his requests and had taken the risk of rewarding a traitor, a fool, or, as was usually the case, a ne'er-do-well disowned by his family who had fled to America to escape the arm of the law.

Frenchmen, granted commissions of all sorts, and for the most part unable to speak the language of the country, could not be expected to be any happier in the army than they had been in Philadelphia, for they found themselves in the midst of Anglo-Americans who were their equals, their inferiors, and their superiors. No one truckled to them or paid them deference; no one received them with special favors and consideration. In short, they discovered that they could not expect French manners from people who considered themselves all completely equal except for differences in military rank and who always acted according to this principle.

So they complain loudly and continually that Americans violate all the rules of French etiquette, and they claim that this fact is second only to the quality of American officers and the insubordination of American troops as a cause of this dissatisfaction and the misunderstandings which have arisen.

As we have said, the regular army is composed of volunteers serving for three years and the militia is made up of men drafted for a certain period of time; the junior and senior officers are named by the voters, the provincial assemblies, or the colonels of the various regiments, or else are commissioned because of meritorious actions. So it is not surprising to see officers who come from what appears to French eyes to be the lower social classes — merchants, artisans, and farmers — but who are so well-deserving and worthy that their fellow citizens have thought they were only doing them justice in raising them to a rank above that of the average man. Such citizens who have been distinguished from among their equals by their civic virtues are not likely to bring discredit on the positions to which they have been appointed or to the ranks to which they have been promoted. This fact is obvious to the true philosopher, and it has been recognized by certain French officers of high caliber who have fully understood the circumstances. Indeed, if it were not a valid assumption then the system of popular democratic government, which is regarded both by those enjoying its blessings and by those unable to do so as the only true basis for the happiness of man living in society, would be impossible and self-contradictory.

So the corps of the American officers is composed either of deserving and prosperous artisans or of reputable merchants or of farmers loved and esteemed by their neighbors. These are the equals whom the French officers, friendless drifters who have been commissioned more because of their own high opinion of themselves than because of any real merit, have the audacity to despise, and with whom they say they "have been forced to associate." As if these democratic republicans, kings in their own land, were not, whatever else they might be, better than these immigrants. As if these democrats, recognized by their own fellow citizens and honored by the unanimous consent of the nation, did not have besides this first quality of being republicans the additional advantage of being, whatever their class, the chosen representatives of a free people, who have delegated to them power and authority. This is indeed a noble privilege which does great honor to the recipient both because of what it means and because of the reason for which it was given. The Frenchman may despise a man so honored for his social class and he may regard him as inferior and not fit to associate with, but he can never hope to win such honor in his own country.

This, then, together with the complaints about the lack of discipline, is the source of all the vile satires and contemptible complaints which one hears every day in the mouths of the French. They cannot be sensible enough to put aside their stupid national prejudices; and their unreasonable discontent (which they have no right to feel, since here at least they have a chance to be among equals, which is something they can rarely do at home) is one of the greatest obstacles to their establishing a sane and pleasant relationship with the people among whom they have to live.

This is not to say that there are not a certain number of French officers to whom this mild dose of equalitarianism is a matter of indifference, or even a source of great pleasure. But very seldom does one find a Frenchman sensible enough to conform; and the number of malcontents so great that if the unfavorable reports which they promise to make against the Americans — and which, no doubt, they will make — should be taken as approximate pictures of the truth, then no reasonable man would be willing to support the American cause. For you know well from experience, *Quisque clamat de malo, et susurrat de beneficio.*

Those who happen to hear the complaints and

criticisms of these French officers after their return to Europe should consider well the moral character of these accusers and compare them with those whom they condemn. If those in Europe will put aside their political prejudices they will see which is the more reasonable — the man who lives wisely according to the laws of mercy and humanity, or the man who is so full of his own ridiculous national prejudices that he tries to transplant them wherever he goes, who thinks his fondness for his own ways of thinking is quite natural and yet condemns the predilection others may have for their own ideas, who cannot understand the contempt and the indifference his manners inspire, and who, after having revolted common sense and reason, arrives at the verdict that if Americans thought as he does, he would find far less to criticize. The conclusion must be that these French officers have nothing to offer apart from their foibles and their absurd personal and national prejudices, while the Americans, living according to their own principles just as the French live according to theirs, may at least sometimes have justice and reason on their side.

Arguments, it is true, are not facts; but the facts I might present in evidence would be too personal. In order not to offend anyone directly or indirectly, I shall say only this: If Congress has not granted these French officers all they requested, if it has not lived up to all the agreements it made with them regarding their coming to America and their return to Europe, if it has not compensated them for travel and other expenses, if it has not paid them in full for their services, if it has not appointed them to ranks at least a notch higher than those they held in France, if it has discharged them because of protests by native citizens whom they have offended by coming over here and taking ranks to which the Americans had just claims — if any of these allegations are true, then Congress has treated them incorrectly and deserves censure. But the truth is that they have been welcomed as cordially as any stranger could hope to be and that their cases have been handled as quickly as the press of business permitted. Moreover, they have been paid while awaiting their commissions and have been supported and defended against the protests of native citizens.

If under these conditions they seem unable to accustom themselves to the climate and the ways of the people (excepting only those of the fair sex), and to the rudeness and coolness of Americans in general; if their pay, which has proved sufficient for others, is scarcely half enough for them; if they are offended by the lack of discipline in the army and humble birth of American officers; if the soldiers, not knowing French, cannot execute their orders; and finally, if the fine hopes which brought them here have been dispelled and shown to be physically and morally impossible — if these are their complaints, then Congress is in no way responsible for their discontent. Do they have to cast ridicule on people who are doing all in their power to satisfy them and make them happy, when their unpleasant experiences are entirely their own fault? It is not on the Americans that all the blame should fall. It is up to these French officers to get over their natural instability, pride, and presumption and to be as reasonable as the Dutch, Swiss, Prussian, and German officers serving with the Americans. It is up to them to put aside their pettiness, their vainglory, their absurd prejudices. Then they will see that Americans, just like people everywhere, have agreeable manners and that the men are sociable, their wives virtuous, and their daughters well educated. And they will realize that this country, where at the end of the war they will be given, according to their rank, enough land to support them, this country against whose inhabitants they rail so freely, is, if not what they first desired, at least a place where they can settle down, live, and enjoy the pleasures of life just as peaceably as anywhere else.

After what I have just said of the childish discontent and complaints of these French officers, I should be unjust to my nation and to the truth if I were not happy to mention certain others whose good conduct corresponds to the high character, integrity, and lofty purposes which impelled them to go to America.

I refer to those who were motivated by ambition for promotion in France or who went to escape the boredom of garrison duty or sought an opportunity to practice their profession as soldiers to the benefit of their own country (for this revolt of the English colonies is most advantageous to France). These men are behaving correctly in their relations with Congress, the army, and the people as a whole. They are dependent only on themselves; they draw no pay from Congress other than what is necessary to meet their daily expenses, and they do not think of that country as a place to make their fortunes, for they have not gone there with any such intention. Consequently they have not brought in their hearts the seeds of discontent, as the others have. Before entering the American service they had clear and well-founded reasons for hating the enemy they came to fight. Their only complaints are the faulty organization of the army, the lack of discipline, and often also the fact that as gentlemen they are not the equals of artisans or laborers holding like ranks. Reasons as flimsy as these ought not to influence officers who give evidence of such good sense. But in any situation men will necessarily reveal their true natures and display some weakness; and unfortunately we French have so many weaknesses and we believe ourselves so perfect that it is not surprising if in America, as anywhere else, we display our own peculiar faults, our prejudices which we alone defend, our absurd foibles to which we alone cling, and our vices which we alone refuse to admit or justify. . . .

I should describe here the reception given to the Marquis de Lafayette, to General Du Coudray, the hero of the Schuylkill, to the brave Armand de la Rouerie, to General Conway, to General La Balle [*sic*], and to the famous commandant of engineers of the army. But the day will come when the Americans will render sincere and well-deserved eulogies to those who have given loyal service. What I must say, however, after all I have already written about the French who have gone to America, is that no Anglo-American can accuse these men of cowardice, whatever may be their faults. If all the French followed the example of the good behavior and upright conduct of these men whom I have just mentioned, especially La Rouerie and Lafayette, the Anglo-Americans who now hate us for no reason, but merely out of habit, would change their minds. Then they would judge the French not according to their particular faults but rather in relation to the circumstances of the moment, in which any man, as an individual, is just like anyone else and should be forgiven whatever faults, real or imaginary, he may appear to have. . . .

It is impossible to give the exact figure of the number of men in the American forces. An estimate, however, of the militia, artillerymen, regulars, and cavalrymen in the four armies which have been operating during this campaign and also in the detached bodies of troops stationed at various points would come to the following figures: 21,000 men in the Northern Army on the fourteenth of October; 14,000 in General Putnam's army; 10,000 in the army in Rhode Island; 12,000 under General De Kaissen [*sic*] at Elizabethtown; and 30,000 in General Washington's army.[5] These figures do not include the militia of the states close to the theater of war, who can be called up within twenty-four hours, or the troops which each province needs to guard its ports, roadsteads, passes, and cities. It is clear that the Americans can be conquered only by a major offensive. If they do not win the war the reason will be the superiority of the Hessian troops over undisciplined soldiers who have not had sufficient training in the execution of mass maneuvers; it will not be because of any lack of bravery under fire.

In this connection, I hope that the shortcom-

[5] These figures totaling 87,000 troops operating during the campaign of 1777 represent nearly 50 per cent of the arms-bearing population of all the American colonies. Even if such a number could have been raised it is doubtful that they could have been supplied with arms and provisions. During the summer of 1778, when Washington commanded the "largest body of regular troops ever assembled under the American banner," he had only 16,782 rank and file fit for duty. Douglas Southall Freeman, *George Washington: A Biography* (New York, 1951), III, 442; Rupert Hughes, *George Washington: The Savior of the States, 1777–1781* (New York, 1930), III, 410; Fitzpatrick, *Writings of George Washington,* XII, 230. The aggregate enrollment for the year 1777, counting all of the militia who served as long as two months, may have reached 68,000, but such a total does not represent effective strength, which was considerably weaker. Hughes, *George Washington,* III, 434. For more accurate estimates of the American forces mentioned above consult Fitzpatrick, *Writings of George Washington,* IX, 278; X, 52n., 195; Leonard Lundin, *Cockpit of the Revolution* (Princeton, 1940), 333–335, and *passim;* John Richard Alden, *The American Revolution: 1775–1783* (New York, 1954), 119–120; and Freeman, *George Washington,* IV, 520.

ings of the Americans, for which they have been justly criticized, will no longer be exaggerated by politically-minded censors and by eyewitnesses. Men need only the experience of defeats in order to learn how to defend themselves properly and to acquire the military effectiveness usually necessary in order to inspire respect in the enemy. As soon as the Americans have suffered a few reverses the contempt which certain Frenchmen have had for their bravery will quickly vanish, and we may expect to see no further displays of lack of initiative and inexperience. . . .

3

The Revolution Measured

I

The American Revolution Considered as a Social Movement

Until some forty years ago most historians were satisfied to study the American Revolution within a political or military frame of reference. The battles, the constitutional experiments, the diplomacy of the Revolution were well attended; but the social and economic implications of the struggle were largely neglected. John Franklin Jameson *was among the first historians to write on the social history of the Revolution. While he raised many more questions than he answered, such questions had hitherto been all too rarely asked.*

Jameson's scholarly inquiries were concerned with the broad social changes which took place in America between 1776 and 1783 as a result of the Revolution — in the suffrage, the redistribution of landholdings, anti-slavery sentiments, farming, manufactures, finance, and commerce. While more exhaustive research is still required in many of these fields, Jameson's early work retains its significance.

J. Franklin Jameson, *The American Revolution Considered as a Social Movement* (Princeton: Princeton University Press, 1926), pp. 56–70.

It was natural that in the development of certain classes of manufacture the Revolution should have a peculiar importance. There were arms and munitions of war to be provided, for instance. Great Britain in 1774 forbade the exportation of fire-arms, gun-powder, and other military stores. Some manufacture of them had already begun in the colonies. But now Congress and the state Committees of Safety took hold of the matter as a thing of vital importance in the struggle. For the making of gunpowder, saltpeter was collected from old cellars and stables. As for arms, though the Americans had not made them in great numbers, they had become very skilful in the art, as was natural in a nation so full of hunters. Governor Richard Penn, in his examination before the House of Lords just as the war was beginning, stated, in reply to the inquiries of the Duke of Richmond, that the casting of iron and brass cannon at Philadelphia had been carried to great perfection, and that the workmanship and finish of the small arms was all that could be desired. Rifles were made in the colonies at that time which were thought as good as any that were imported. Gunsmiths were numerous. But in this, as in other trades, there was little organization. Each gunsmith worked for himself, or perhaps had two or three men to help him, so that the committees of Congress had to make their contracts for small quantities, and place them here and there with individuals, and, after all, to get most of their arms from Europe.

In 1778 the government armory at Springfield was established, where the works would be remote from the incursions of the enemy. For a similar reason, much gun-making was carried on in Maryland. To stimulate the manufacture of such things, Congress called upon the states to exempt from taxation all who were engaged in them. That they were sometimes at the greatest straits for material, may well be imagined, when all the ordinary channels of trade were closed or perverted. We hear of one foundry idle for a long time from sheer want of copper. A few days before the battle of Brandywine, messengers were sent to the mills of the Dunkers or German "Brethren" at Ephrata for a supply of paper for cartridges. The mill's products happened to be exhausted, so far as clean paper was concerned. But the fraternity also did a printing business, and had on hand an edition of Fox's *Book of Martyrs,* in sheets, then ready for the bindery. They generously placed this mass of printed paper at the service of their country, and in the ensuing battle the good old martyrologist, in the form of cartridges, went up in smoke and flames for the good cause, like the martyrs of whom he wrote.

Paper-mills increased enormously during the Revolutionary period. One important reason for this was the great increase of newspapers. There were thirty-seven in 1776. In 1789 there were probably over a hundred. The addiction of the American to this sort of reading was already remarkable. "All these people," says the Duke of LaRochefoucauld of the people of the house at which he was stopping in Marlborough, Massachusetts, "busy themselves much with politics, and from the landlord down to the housemaid they all read two newspapers a day."

It will perhaps hardly be imagined that, of the manufactures which the Revolution directly affected, one of those most highly stimulated was that of salt. Before the Revolution, the saline deposits of central New York and of the remoter interior had not yet been reached, and salt was almost altogether procured from abroad. It was an article of prime importance to the Americans, partly because of the great amounts used in the fisheries, partly because it was much given to cattle, and largely also because our fathers made so enormous use of salted provisions and exported so many barrels of them. The chief supply of salt had been obtained by the ships which went out with lumber, fish and other provisions, and tobacco. When they came back, they often brought coarse salt as ballast, from the ports of southern Europe, the Canary or Madeira or West Indian Islands.

The interruption of this trade produced a distressing scarcity of salt. It rose to six dollars a bushel. Many attempts were made, all along the shore of the Atlantic, to procure salt by boiling sea-water in kettles. Finally, an enterprising sailor residing upon Cape Cod conceived the idea of making salt more economically, after the manner followed in the Mediterranean, by evaporation by the sun's heat acting on sea-water in large and shallow vats. Soon many such went into operation, and the wind-mills by which the salt water was pumped up became a noteworthy feature of the not-too-varied scenery of the Cape. This particular manufacture, being of necessity carried on in positions near the sea, was more than ordinarily exposed to the destructive attacks of the British. But it developed in the United States a considerable industry.

On the other hand, the war destroyed for the time that which had been before the war the chief of American manufactures for exportation, namely, shipbuilding. Writers in that time and since have been fond of declaiming against the oppressiveness of the Navigation Acts. Their burden was in many ways difficult to bear — or would have been had they not been so systematically and successfully evaded by the enterprising colonists. But it is certain that they fostered American shipbuilding in the highest degree. In the years 1769, 1770, and 1771, nearly four hundred vessels a year, large and small, were built in the colonies. When the war broke out, 400,000 tons of colonial-built shipping were employed in the general commerce of Great Britain. The severing of the political connection with England deprived American shipwrights of this advantage, and for a time their trade languished, but after the peace it recovered with surprising swiftness.

It is not possible to dwell upon all the varieties of manufacture which the Revolution called into existence or stimulated in America, though it would be pleasant to speak of the development of the piano-forte, whose prodigious frequency in all subsequent times might easily deceive unwary travellers into the belief that we were a musical people. The leading manufactures when the war ended, suffice it to say, were, beside those that have been mentioned, those from iron and leather, and that of glass. Europeans believed that, when the artificial stimulus produced by the war was withdrawn, many of these would not continue to succeed. Dr. Cooper, an intelligent and fair-minded man, thought it would be a long time before manufactures of woollen, linen, and cotton goods, or of pottery, would succeed. Wages were too high. "I have no doubt, however," he says, "of the success of a glass manufacture, a gunpowder manufacture, of a paper maker, a paper stainer, a letter founder, a manufactory of all the heavy kinds of iron-work, such as castings from the ore, pig iron, bar iron, rolling mills, slitting mills, and the making of nails." Of most of these there were already examples in the country by the year 1789. To illustrate the increase of mills of various sorts, the Duke of LaRochefoucauld says that, ten years after the Revolution, Brandywine Creek, in the seven or eight miles of its short course through Delaware, turned about sixty mills.

But it should be understood that but a small part of the manufacturing enterprise which the Revolution evoked expended itself in manufacturing establishments. The bulk of American manufacturing was after all domestic. In most parts of the country by far the greatest part of the clothing was made in the household. When Tench Coxe investigated this subject, a few years later, he said that typical neighborhoods of twenty families rich and poor, in Virginia, showed in one case domestic manufactures of the value of $1670 in one year, in the other of $1791. For another evidence of this extent, we know that there were forty-one fulling-mills in New Jersey at a time when there were in that state no established manufactories of cloth, none, that is, other than the domestic; also, that one shop in Philadelphia, a few years after the Revolution, sold in one year fifteen hundred sets of spinning-wheel irons.

This domestic mode was often employed in trades to which we should hardly think of its being applicable now. Take for instance, the manufacture of nails. It was one of those branches in which the country earliest became independent of British supplies, and one of those in which the effects of the war were first felt among British manufacturers — at least so said Lord Dudley in the House of Peers in 1776. Yet it was in very large part, if not chiefly, a domestic manufacture. In one of the first debates in the House of Representatives, Fisher Ames of Massachusetts said: "This manufacture, with very little encouragement, has grown up very remarkably. It has become common for the country people in Massachusetts to erect small forges in their chimney corners, and in winter, and on evenings when little other work can be done, great quantities of nails are made, even by children. These people take the rod-iron of the merchant and return him the nails, and in consequence of this easy mode of barter, the manufacture is prodigiously great." This bit may serve to show us that, if it seems a long distance from these humble beginnings to the vast industrial development of today, nevertheless the industry and grit were already present which were in time to make this the greatest manufacturing country of the world.

If we turn now to the consideration of internal trade, it is easy to see that here the war could do little but harm to the industrial life of the country. A comparatively poor country, being compelled to manage an expensive war, of necessity had recourse to large issues of paper money. Millions upon millions were sent forth. Each one of the thirteen states issued notes which competed for circulation with those of the Continental Congress. In December 1778, the Continental bills, then considerably exceeding a hundred millions in amount, had depreciated until they were worth only a twentieth part of their face value. Yet Congress maintained the certainty of their redemption, and resolved "that any contrary report was false, and derogatory to its honor." In August 1779, a paper dollar was worth only three or four cents in silver. In December it was worth less than two and a half cents. "A wagon-load of money," it was said, "would scarcely purchase a wagon-load of provisions." In April 1781, Congress proposed an exchange of the old bills for new, at the rate of forty dollars for one, and the measure was received with favor, though it wiped out at one stroke thirty-nine fortieths of such debt as was represented by the paper money. A Philadelphia wag made a blanket for his dog out of the Continental paper, and paraded him upon the street in that array.

Under such circumstances it was hardly to be expected that trade should flourish, even in regions which did not feel heavily the pressure of war and were not in danger from incursions or depredations of the enemy. Prices went up and up. Conventions of counties, and finally conventions at which several states were represented, met, for instance at Providence, at Springfield, at Hartford, and at Yorktown, and attempted to bolster up the failing credit of the paper money by laws declaring that the prices of commodities should not rise above certain figures enumerated upon their lists. Nevertheless prices rose. Economic laws were stronger than those of state legislatures, however resolute and patriotic. In 1781 we find quotations of shoes at twenty pounds a pair, milk at fifteen shillings a quart, potatoes at ninety shillings a bushel, rum at forty-five shillings a quart, corn at forty dollars a bushel, a cow at $1200.

The depreciation, of course, bore hardest upon men who lived upon salaries, or in other ways had fixed incomes. Dr. Ezra Ripley, who was settled over the parish of Concord, Massachusetts, in 1788, gives a vivid account of his trials in his *Half-Century Discourse* preached in 1828. He says: "With all his exertions in various ways, as teaching scholars, manual labor, etc., your pastor could not have waded through, had it not been for a particular event in Providence, and the long credit given him by one benevolent trader (Deacon John White) in town." For those whose deacons were not benevolent, as no doubt sometimes happened, there must have been many privations while the currency was in this disordered condition.

It should be remembered, also, how lacking in the colonies were the most ordinary facilities for the transaction of large business. Transportation was in an almost primitive condition. It casts a flash of light upon the provinciality of American life at the time of the Declaration of Independence, to reflect that at that time there was not a single bank in the whole country. The first organized bank in the United States, the Bank of North America, had its origin in a meeting of citizens of Philadelphia, in June 1780, to devise means of furnishing supplies to the army, then in a state of great destitution. It was then resolved to open a "security subscription to the amount of £300,000, Pennsylvania currency, real money." Robert Morris subscribed ten thousand pounds to this fund, and Tom Paine five hundred dollars. Morris made the plan for the Bank of North America, which was chartered by Congress on the last day of the year 1781. The charter permitted a capital of ten million dollars, but individuals paid in only $85,000, and the government, which subscribed $250,000, paid in only $50,000. The bank began its career with $300,000. Besides this pioneer bank, which is still in existence, only two others had come into operation in 1789, the Massachusetts Bank in Boston, and the Bank of New York.

One branch of American industrial life made great gains because of the war, to which we have not yet alluded, and that is maritime commerce. Under all the restrictions imposed by the Navigation Acts, American commerce had been constantly growing, and there were even merchant princes in some of the greater ports, or traders so esteemed in that day. The war interrupted commerce greatly, of course. It could not fail to do so, in view of the prodigious navy of Great Britain. Nevertheless it furnished the maritime development of the nation, and that in two ways, first by stimulating privateering adventure, and secondly by removing legal restrictions and opening a free course to American shipping into all parts of the world save those under British control. Privateering was of course a mode of warfare, but the impulse that led men into it was largely commercial, or at least that same love of gain which also inspired commerce.

The Americans were old hands at privateering. In the War of the Spanish Succession, in the Spanish war of 1739, the French war of 1744, and especially in the French and Indian War, the business had attained prodigious proportions. In 1745, Captain Simeon Potter, of Bristol, Rhode Island, sailing in the *Prince Charles of Lorraine,* had ravaged fifteen hundred miles of territory on the Spanish Main. In one cruise, in 1759 and 1760, Abraham Whipple of Rhode Island captured twenty-three prizes, valued at a million dollars. Now when the Revolution broke out the memory of these exploits and receipts was still fresh, and New England had many skilful seamen idle because of the serious interruption to the fisheries which had been caused by the presence of the British warships off the coast. Here was all the material for a great development of privateering enterprise.

Sometimes it is difficult to distinguish, in the maritime history of the Revolution, what was naval endeavor, carried on in government vessels, which was war, from that which was carried on in private vessels, which was half war, half business. But it seems clear that the privateering successes of the Revolution quite overshadowed those obtained by the vessels of the federal and state governments, and that they made more impression upon the enemy. Service on a privateer was more attractive to bold sailors, for it offered prospects of greater gains. So great were the profits that New England shipping interests, it is said, were never more prosperous than in the last years of the war. In 1781 Salem alone had fifty-nine vessels, carrying four thousand men. In the year preceding, the Admiralty Court of the Essex district of Massachusetts had condemned 818 prizes. In the single month of May 1779 eighteen prizes were brought into New London. In the course of the whole war more than five hundred privateers were commissioned by the various states, and probably as many as ninety thousand Americans were, first and last, engaged in these voyages, a number of men almost as great as served in the army, and greater than that of the army in any single year save one. Two-thirds of these men were from Massachusetts, the rest from the other New England states and from the Delaware river.

A good notion of the importance of the privateers' exploits may be gained from the fact that in 1776 insurance on cargoes going from the West Indies to England rose to twenty-eight per cent of the value of the ship and goods. Special types of vessels were developed for these purposes, and American designs in shipbuilding permanently benefited. "Thousands of schemes of privateering," wrote John Adams, "are afloat in American imaginations." At the end of that year, 1776, no less than two hundred and fifty West Indiamen had been captured, and the injury already done to the West India trade was estimated in England at £1,800,000. Robert Morris is said to have raised his fortune to between £300,000 and £400,000 by such ventures. Abraham Whipple, in the *Providence,* once fell in with a large convoy of English merchantmen bound from the West Indies to England. He disguised his vessel, or concealed her character, so that he boldly entered the fleet as one of their number. After dark on each of ten successive nights he boarded and captured some vessel from the convoy. Upon each of these he put a small prize crew and sent it away secretly to Boston. Eight of them reached that port, and their cargoes sold for more than a million dollars. Beside exploits in the nearer waters, the privateers sought their gain in remoter seas. Even the waters around Britain were not safe from them, and the privateer *General Mifflin* hovered around the North Cape and took seven or eight English vessels on their way to Archangel.

All this would have various effects upon the development of regular commerce. It would immensely stimulate boldness and enterprise on the part of captains and sailors. If when peace was made they could bring themselves down from these sublime heights of romantic adventure to the sober level of peaceful trade at all, it must be trade with a spice of adventure in it at least.

One of the least happy avenues through which this spirit of venture found expression was the revival of the African slave trade. In years just before the outbreak of hostilities that traffic was flourishing. During the war importations into the Continental colonies ceased almost entirely. The natural effect in the West Indies was a glut of the market. Peace was promptly followed by a great revival of the trade. Not only had the planters been deprived during seven years of the opportunity for their customary buying, but they had also lost many of their negroes by the depredations of the invading army. So rapid was the increase in importations into South Carolina that by 1785 that state was once more debating the wisdom of curtailing the traffic, at least for a time. During the course of the debate it was stated that 7000 negroes had been imported into Charleston since the peace. The assembly passed a law forbidding importations, effective in 1787. In Rhode Island a law was passed forbidding any citizen of the state to take part in the trade. Thereafter any participation in it by Rhode Islanders was illicit and furtive.

In forms more respectable a pronounced taste for longer voyages, for trade with remoter regions, is found among seamen when the war ended. In 1783 men began to talk in Salem of the China trade. The Orient had for them something of the same charm which it had exercised upon the minds of Prince Henry the Navigator and Vasco da Gama. If the traders themselves had no gift of any but prosaic expression, who shall say, nevertheless, that there was not a poetic element in this looking toward a wider horizon for the expansive influence of the young republic?

At all events the new trade went on. In 1784 Captain John Green, in the *Empress,* sailed direct from New York to Canton. The *Grand Turk,* Captain West, made a voyage that year to the Cape of Good Hope, and in 1785 to the Isle of France and Canton. So rapidly was the trade pushed that in 1789, only four years later, a British observer reports that, of eighty-six ships in the harbor of Canton, fifteen were American. Brissot says that in that same year forty-four vessels sailed out of Boston alone for the Northwest Coast, the East Indies, and China. Many of these ships were in the command of boys under twenty-one.

The incentive to the trade was the enormous profits which might be made by these direct voyages to regions with which the colonies had traded only indirectly. The usual profit on muslins and calicoes from Calcutta was a hundred per cent. The ship *Benjamin Silsbee* took less than $1,000 worth of plain glass tumblers to the Isle of France, and sold them for $12,000. Ebenezer Parsons, a younger brother of Chief Justice Parsons, sent vessels from Gloucester to the Indies, which then carried cargoes of coffee around to Smyrna, making large profits, sometimes as much as three hundred or four hundred per cent. Everyone knows the story of Lord Timothy Dexter and his cargo of warming-pans, but that was of a later time.

But beside such effects as arose from heightened boldness and enterprise, the Revolution affected American commerce in another and very substantial way. It is familiar that, among the grievances that gave rise to the Revolution, none was more insisted upon than the Navigation Acts. These purported to confine the commerce of the colonies for the benefit of the mother country. Most colonial products could be sent abroad only to English ports. It is quite true that the laws were extensively evaded; nevertheless they did operate to some extent. Therefore the Declaration of Independence brought to American commerce a release from fetters. The commerce of the world, except with England, was thrown open to the new United States. Even before independence was declared, the Continental Congress had so far relaxed the American Association as to permit the export of produce to all countries not under British rule, and free trade in all goods not of British origin. New channels of trade were thus at once opened. Shipments of tobacco and other staples were made to France, Spain, and Holland, either directly or through the West Indian possessions of those countries, which had a great demand for American lumber, fish, and salted meat. Indirectly, it proved possible to keep up a trade, though at some risk in case of discovery, with the British West Indies also. The intermediary was St. Eustatius, a little Dutch island of the Caribbean group, which had a good roadstead and was a free port. Here the goods of the revolted colonies of the mainland could be exchanged against those of the still loyal colonies of the West Indies, much to the advantage of both, for we are told that the cessation of the ordinary supplies from the mainland colonies had caused in Jamaica alone the starvation of fifteen thousand negroes. When Rodney captured St. Eustatius in 1781, sober authorities estimated the value of the capture at more than three million pounds sterling.

By all such means, American commerce began to recover from the first shocks and losses of war. In April 1777, a Boston merchant writes: "Though our money has depreciated, the internal strength of the Country is greater than when the war began; and there is hardly a town that has not more ratable polls than at that time. And though many individuals suffer, yet the farmer and the bulk of the people gain by the war; and Great Britain therefore ought not to think of ever getting a peace without allowing independence." That the people who surrounded him were not without the comforts and even the luxuries of life is evident from other passages in his letters. French silks, cambrics, etc., are called for. "I would observe," he says, "that people dress as much and as extravagantly as ever. The ladies lay out much on their heads, in flowers and white gauze; and hoop petticoats seem crawling in."

II

The American Revolution Considered as a Social Movement: A Re-Evaluation*

Jameson's study of the social and economic changes brought about by the Revolution has, inevitably, been subject to the challenge of modern scholarship. Frederick B. Tolles *of Swarthmore College has examined the new research and, in its light, has thoughtfully reappraised the Jameson lectures.*

Professor Tolles suggests that Jameson tended at times to overstatement, that his generalizations were frequently in need of qualification, that his research was, in some instances, too confined. It should be noted, however, that Jameson is not without his defenders among contemporary historians;[1] *Professor Tolles has found that in certain areas further investigation has served to bolster Jameson's conclusions, to clarify his statements, or to stimulate further historical inquiries.*

Sometimes a single essay, a monograph, or a series of lectures makes historiographical history. It was so in 1893 when Frederick Jackson Turner read his paper on "The Significance of the Frontier in American History." It was so again in 1913 when Charles A. Beard published his *Economic Interpretation of the Constitution.* And it was so in 1925 when J. Franklin Jameson delivered his four lectures at Princeton on "The American Revolution Considered as a Social Movement."

At first glance the comparison with Turner and Beard may seem strained. We are accustomed to think of Jameson as a scholar's scholar, a kind of indispensable historical midwife — curator and editor of manuscripts, director of other men's research, editor of the *American Historical Review* — not as a pathbreaker, an innovator. But this is to do him less than justice. *The American Revolution Considered as a Social Movement* stands as a landmark in recent American historiography, a slender but unmistakable signpost, pointing a new direction for historical research and interpretation. Before Jameson, the American Revolution had been a chapter in political, diplomatic, and military history, a story of Faneuil Hall and Lexington, Independence Hall and Valley Forge, Versailles and Yorktown. After Jameson, it became something different, something greater — a seismic disturbance in American society, a sudden quickening in the American mind.

The American Revolution, like the French, Jameson believed, was accompanied by social and cultural changes of profound significance.

> The stream of revolution, once started, could not be confined within narrow banks, but spread abroad upon the land. Many economic desires, many social aspirations were set free by the political struggle, many aspects of colonial society profoundly altered by the forces thus let loose. The relations of social classes to each other, the institution of slavery, the system of landholding, the course of business, the forms and spirit of the intellectual and religious life, all felt the transforming hand of revolution, all emerged from under it in shapes advanced many degrees nearer to those we know.[1]

No more than Turner's or Beard's was Jameson's notion wholly new. Just a year earlier, in his massive volume on *The American States during and after the Revolution,* Allan Nevins had devoted fifty pages to the task of demonstrating in impressive detail that "a social and intellectual revolution" occurred between Lexington and Yorktown.[2] Nearly twenty years before, Carl Becker had described the Revolution as a two-

---

Frederick B. Tolles, "The American Revolution Considered as a Social Movement: A Re-evaluation," from *The American Historical Review,* LX (1954), 1–12.

* Read at the meeting of the Pacific Coast Branch of the American Historical Association, held at the University of California at Davis, December 28–30, 1953.

[1] For one of the most recent defenses of the Jameson thesis, the student is referred to R. R. Palmer, *The Age of the Democratic Revolution* (Princeton, N.J., 1959), I, 188–89.

[1] *The American Revolution Considered as a Social Movement* (Princeton, 1926), p. 11.

[2] New York, 1924, chap. x.

fold contest: for home-rule on the one hand, for "the democratization of American politics and society" on the other.[3] As far back as 1787, Benjamin Rush had perceived that the American revolution was bigger than the American war, that the real revolution was in "the principles, morals, and manners of our citizens," and that, far from being over, that revolution had only begun.[4]

Jameson's view of the Revolution was not new, but no one hitherto had marshaled the evidence so compactly, conveyed it so lucidly, or argued from it so persuasively. Perceptive historians immediately greeted his little volume as a gem of historical writing — "a truly notable book," Charles A. Beard called it, ". . . cut with a diamond point to a finish, studded with novel illustrative materials, gleaming with new illumination, serenely engaging in style, and sparingly garnished with genial humor."[5]

The influence of this little book with the long title has grown steadily. A year after its publication, the Beards summarized its thesis in their widely read *Rise of American Civilization*.[6] Jameson's emphasis on social factors harmonized perfectly with the intellectual and political climate of the 1930's. In 1940, after the author's death, a second edition appeared, and in 1950 a third — an unusual tribute to a set of academic lectures. With the passage of a quarter-century, the book has achieved the standing of a minor classic.[7] One will find hardly a textbook that does not paraphrase or quote Jameson's words, borrow his illustrations, cite him in its bibliography. The notion of the Revolution as a social upheaval has achieved the final seal of acceptance: it has been taken over by the historical novelists — by such writers as Kenneth Roberts and Howard Fast, to name two rather unlikely bedfellows.

Jameson, one suspects, had no idea he was writing a classic. His aim was simply to challenge American historians by opening new windows on the Revolutionary era, suggesting new directions for future research, throwing out tentative hypotheses for others to test. Over the past quarter-century historians have risen to his challenge with a flood of articles, monographs, academic dissertations, and full-dress histories bearing on one or another of his propositions. But the average textbook-writer, one is tempted to believe, has not got beyond Jameson. The time has come to go back and ask how Jameson's original thesis stands up in the light of all this detailed research; what modifications, if any, must be made; what further extensions, if any, are possible.

Jameson disposed his arguments under four rubrics — the status of persons, the land, industry and commerce, thought and feeling. If we recognize, as he did, that such divisions are purely arbitrary, we may adopt his procedure.

American society, he suggested, was measurably democratized during the Revolution. The upper stratum, the old colonial aristocracy, was largely liquidated — by banishment, voluntary exile, or impoverishment. New groups rose to the surface to take their places. "In most states the strength of the revolutionary party lay most largely in the plain people," and the social changes which they brought about naturally tended "in the direction of levelling democracy."

[3] *The History of Political Parties in the Province of New York* (Madison, Wis., 1909), p. 5.

[4] *American Museum,* I (1787), 9. Jameson quoted part of this well-known passage but ascribed it, for some reason, to "a writer in South Carolina." *American Revolution,* p. 29.

[5] *New Republic,* XLVII (Aug. 11, 1926), 344. In the *American Historical Review* discussion of the book was relegated to the "Minor Notices," perhaps because of its brevity, more likely because of the modesty of the managing editor — J. Franklin Jameson. The reviewer, Allan Nevins, called its scholarship "impeccable," its style "polished," its outlook "broad and thoughtful." XXXII (1926–27), 167–68.

[6] New York, 1927, I, 291–96.

[7] In a recent poll, in which 103 historians were asked to name the ten best historical works published between 1920 and 1935, Jameson's *American Revolution* got twenty-six votes. The pollster, analyzing the returns, observed that a brief book stood at a disadvantage in the poll but offered the comment, for whatever it might be worth, that Jameson's book showed "the best vote-getting record per word." John Walton Caughey, "Historians' Choice: Results of a Poll on Recently Published American History and Biography," *Mississippi Valley Historical Review,* XXXIX (September, 1952), 293, 299. W. Stull Holt's figures on the number of copies sold — only 1,356 in the quarter-century since first publication — suggest that the book may deserve the name of classic in a Pickwickian sense — a work that everyone knows about but few read. "Who Reads the Best Histories?" *Ibid.,* XL (1954), 617.

Broadening of the suffrage elevated "whole classes of people . . . in their social status," and the revolutionary philosophy of liberty wrought improvements in the condition of the most debased class in America — the Negro slaves.[8]

Recent studies of individual states and regions seem to suggest that Jameson was too sweeping when he equated colonial aristocrats with Loyalists and implied that this group was erased from American society. In eastern Massachusetts it was perhaps true that "a majority of the old aristocracy" emigrated.[9] But in the central and western part of the state the oldest, most respected families chose the Whig side and remained to perpetuate their local rule in the days of the early Republic.[10] In New Hampshire, except around Portsmouth, society had never been highly stratified, and the Tory emigration bore away few outstanding individuals.[11] In Connecticut, where "the native aristocracy of culture, wealth, religion, and politics" tended to be loyal to the crown, at least half of the Tories never left the state. Others were welcomed back even before the war was over. Within six months of the peace treaty, New Haven was openly extending an invitation to former Loyalists to return, and President Ezra Stiles of Yale College was grumbling about efforts "silently to bring the Tories into an Equality and Supremacy among the Whigs."[12] In New York and Philadelphia, many prominent merchants — perhaps the majority — were Loyalists, or at least "neutralists," and they stayed on in such numbers as to give a definite tone to postwar society, politics, and business in these important centers.[13] In Maryland, the "internal" Revolution turns out to have been a struggle between one group of aristocrats — planters, merchants, lawyers — and another; the "plain people" took little part in the conflict and the resultant social shifts were minimal.[14] In Virginia, of course, most of the "F.F.V.'s" were Whigs, and their control of politics was to continue through the days of the "Virginia dynasty."[15] In the North Carolina back country it was the "plain people" — the old Regulators — who were most stubbornly Loyalist.[16] Clearly Jameson's generalizations about the fate of the old aristocracy must be qualified.[17]

What about the new democracy of the Revolutionary period? Unquestionably a sense of dignity and importance came to the common man — the small farmer, the town artisan — as a result of his revolutionary activities and the limited extension of the suffrage. But before we can say with assurance how democratic the new society was, we must answer the prior question: how undemocratic was the old? No one will dispute the fact that provincial society was stratified, that class distinctions existed, that political and social equality were hardly dreamed

[8] Jameson, pp. 25, 26.

[9] *Ibid.*, p. 22.

[10] In the inland counties, finds Lee N. Newcomer, "no internal upheaval" accompanied the Revolution. *The Embattled Farmers: A Massachusetts Countryside in the American Revolution* (New York, 1953), pp. 86–87. Nor do the Tories of this region "fit readily into any definite categories or groups." In Ashfield, for instance, the Baptists, whom historians are accustomed to lump among the Whigs, tended to remain loyal because they had found royal authority friendly in their fight against the "standing order." *Ibid.*, p. 59.

[11] Richard F. Upton, *Revolutionary New Hampshire* (Hanover, N.H., 1936), p. 130.

[12] Oscar Zeichner, "The Rehabilitation of Loyalists in Connecticut," *New England Quarterly,* XI (1938), 308–30. Stiles's comment is found in his *Literary Diary,* ed. F. B. Dexter (New York, 1901), III, 111.

[13] "The return of former Loyalists to participation in the life and politics of [New York City] was comparatively rapid," concludes Sidney I. Pomerantz, *New York: An American City, 1783–1803* (New York, 1938), p. 90. The early relaxation of the Pennsylvania test laws, originally designed to exclude Loyalists from voting and holding office, undoubtedly hastened the conservative triumph in that state. Robert L. Brunhouse, *The Counter-Revolution in Pennsylvania, 1776–1790* (Harrisburg, 1942), pp. 179–80.

[14] Philip A. Crowl, *Maryland during and after the Revolution* (Baltimore, 1943), chap. 1.

[15] See Charles S. Sydnor, *Gentlemen Freeholders: Political Practices in Washington's Virginia* (Chapel Hill, 1952), chap. 1.

[16] Robert O. DeMond, *The Loyalists in North Carolina during the Revolution* (Durham, N.C., 1940), pp. 34–50.

[17] For a recent summary of the postwar status of Loyalists see Merrill Jensen, *The New Nation: A History of the United States during the Confederation, 1781–1789* (New York, 1950), pp. 265–81. For a more subtle social analysis of the Tory group than Jameson was able to give in his limited space see Evarts B. Greene, *The Revolutionary Generation* (New York, 1943), pp. 211–30.

of. A recent brilliant study of electoral practices in colonial Massachusetts raises, however, some questions. By means of ingenious statistical methods and samplings of contemporary opinion, the author of this study has shown rather convincingly that, in the Bay Colony at least, practically all adult males had the vote. Massachusetts society before 1776, he concludes, was "very close to a complete democracy." And he hints of further revisions to come. "As for the 'internal revolution' in other colonies," he says, " — perhaps we should take another look. There is more than a hint in the records that what applies to Massachusetts applies without too much change to other colonies as well."[18]

Though the Negro slave received some indirect benefits from the Revolution, the indentured servant, Jameson found, received none. Nor has subsequent research uncovered any important evidence that he overlooked.[19] While he was dwelling on the negative side, Jameson might have mentioned another large dependent class that gained nothing in status as a result of the Revolution. Even before independence was declared, that doughty feminist Abigail Adams was writing to her husband in Congress: "By the way, in the new code of laws which I suppose it will be necessary for you to make, I desire you would remember the ladies and be more generous and favorable to them than your ancestors." Her husband wrote back, as much in earnest as in jest: "Depend on it, we know better than to repeal our masculine systems."[20] It was to be nearly three quarters of a century before the Declaration of Independence would be revised by a group of determined ladies at Seneca Falls to read: "All men and women are created equal." Both negative and positive evidence, then, suggests that the Revolution made less difference in the status of persons in America than Jameson believed.

The doctrine that underlies Jameson's second lecture is, quite explicitly, economic determinism: "political democracy," he says flatly, "came to the United States as a result of economic democracy." The movement for manhood suffrage which reached its fruition in Jacksonian America, he maintains, was rooted in a peculiarly American type of land tenure — the system of small holdings or what he chooses to call "peasant proprietorship." This system the Revolution fixed upon the nation when it swept away the royal restrictions, the archaic manorial laws and usages which had encumbered the land throughout the colonial period. There was, he makes clear, "no violent outbreak," no bloody massacre of landlords as in France a decade later. Still, "in a quiet, sober, Anglo-Saxon way a great change was effected in the land-system of America between the years 1775 and 1795."[21] Specifically, the changes were of three sorts: the discontinuance of quitrents and of the king's right to mast-trees, the abolition of primogeniture and entail, the confiscation and distribution of the Tory estates.

The importance of the quitrents and the king's "broad arrow" was probably more symbolic than real. Jameson himself admitted this: payment of quitrents, he pointed out, was "largely evaded"; the law giving the king's surveyors the right to reserve the tallest, straightest pine trees for the Royal Navy "was not rigorously enforced."[22] Still, no historian will deny the importance of an emotion-laden symbol, and Jameson insists, quite rightly, that the quitrent and the king's "broad arrow" were symbols of an obsolete and alien feudalism, that until they were done away with, private property was not private property.

There is high authority, of course, for attaching great significance to the abolition of primogeniture and entail in Virginia — the authority

[18] Robert E. Brown, "Democracy in Colonial Massachusetts," *New England Quarterly,* XXV (1952), 291–313.

[19] William Miller, "The Effects of the American Revolution on Indentured Servitude," *Pennsylvania History,* VII (1940), 131–41; Samuel McKee, Jr., *Labor in Colonial New York* (New York, 1935), pp. 175–78.

[20] Charles Francis Adams, ed., *Familiar Letters of John Adams and His Wife Abigail Adams during the Revolution* (New York, 1876), pp. 149, 155. Mary Beard points out that the legal subjection of women to men was actually buttressed after the Revolution by the steadily growing weight of Blackstone's authority in the United States. *Woman as Force in History* (New York, 1946), chaps. v, vi. See also Elizabeth Cometti, "Women in the American Revolution," *New England Quarterly,* XX (1947), 329–46.

[21] Jameson, pp. 41, 42, 48–49.

[22] *Ibid.,* pp. 50, 51.

of Thomas Jefferson. But these gestures too, it now appears, were more important in the realm of symbol than of economic reality. In point of fact, neither primogeniture nor entail operated to any important degree in Virginia. Recent research has shown that most estates in the Old Dominion were not entailed but could be freely alienated. And primogeniture was mandatory only if the property-owner died intestate. Most Virginia planters were careful to make wills. By their wills they often distributed their property among all their sons, and sometimes even their daughters. So Jefferson, in the words of his most authoritative biographer, "did not destroy the country gentry as a group with the blows of his mighty ax, and there is insufficient reason to believe that he wanted to." What he did was merely to "remove legal vestiges of Old World aristocracy." The sweeping conclusion reached by a recent student of this problem in Virginia may well apply to other colonies: "No radical change of custom in devising estates resulted from the abolition of primogeniture and entail."[23]

On the confiscation of Loyalist lands much has been written of late years. The evidence has not been canvassed for all the states, but a definite conclusion seems to be emerging: that considerably less diffusion and democratization of landownership resulted from the breakup of these estates and their disposition in small parcels than Jameson supposed.

The most intensive study has been centered on the southern counties of New York, where the DeLanceys, the Bayards, the Philipses held sway in colonial times over their vast baronies. When the revolutionary New York government seized the estates and sold them off, some of the land, to be sure, went to former tenants and other landless individuals. But the bulk of it was bought up by wealthy patriots and merely augmented the domains of rival families like the Livingstons, Schuylers, and Roosevelts. "While it is true," concludes the author of this study, "that the disposal of the loyalist estates effected a greater diffusion of ownership, it is questionable whether it went far toward a radical redistribution of landed wealth and a new social and economic order."[24]

The same thing seems to have been true in Maryland, where wealthy Whig planters and speculators bought up a large proportion of the desirable Tory lands in Baltimore and Frederick counties. Nor is the story greatly different in western Massachusetts or New Hampshire. The South Carolina confiscation law, in the opinion of a contemporary, was actually "so framed that a man who wants land has no chance to get any," for the state required security which only the wealthy landowner could provide.[25]

The case of North Carolina is instructive. The authority on the Loyalists of that state, noting that the confiscated lands were sold in plots averaging two hundred acres, concludes with Jameson that the confiscations "tended to make the Revolution economic and social as well as political."[26] From his own evidence, however, one could draw the equally justified inference that many a wealthy patriot took advantage of the bargain prices to increase his holdings and consequently his social status. The largest Tory estate was that of the great speculator Henry McCulloh — some 40,000 acres. Of the ninety purchasers of McCulloh's lands thirty-four bought more than one tract. Some acquired as many as ten or fifteen, thereby creating estates as large as 5,000 acres. Robert Raiford purchased parcels from five different Tories and put together an estate of more than a thousand acres. The 3,600-acre estate of Thomas Hooper passed almost intact to John McKinsey. Before a final

[23] Dumas Malone, *Jefferson the Virginian* (Boston, 1948), pp. 252–57; Clarence R. Keim, "Influence of Primogeniture and Entail in the Development of Virginia," University of Chicago, *Abstracts of Theses, Humanistic Series,* V (1928), 289–92.

[24] Harry B. Yoshpe, *The Disposition of Loyalist Estates in the Southern District of the State of New York* (New York, 1939), p. 60. Thomas C. Cochran earlier arrived at a similar conclusion in his *New York in the Confederation* (New York, 1932), p. 64. E. Wilder Spaulding, on the contrary, emphasizes the democratizing effects of the confiscations (*New York in the Critical Period* [New York, 1932], p. 70), and feels that Yoshpe's evidence really supports this thesis (see his review of Yoshpe in the *American Historical Review,* XLV [1939–40], 899–900).

[25] Crowl, chap. 11; Newcomer, p. 151; Upton, p. 172; Aedanus Burke to Arthur Middleton, July 6, 1782, *South Carolina and Genealogical Magazine,* XXVI (1925), 203.

[26] DeMond, p. 180.

generalization can be made about the social effects of the confiscations in North Carolina, we need to know more about the previous economic status of the purchasers.[27]

The largest estate to be confiscated in America, as Jameson pointed out, was that of the Penn family. By the Divesting Act of 1779 the Pennsylvania legislature assumed control of twenty-one and a half million acres — all the ungranted lands which by royal charter had belonged to the proprietors. But this proprietary land, from which the Penns had never received any income, was comparable, surely, to the ungranted crown lands which fell into the hands of the other commonwealths. Much more significant is the fact that the private manors, the "proprietary tenths," of the Penns, amounting to more than 500,000 acres, together with the quitrents on them, were specifically "confirmed, ratified and established for ever" in the hands of the Penn family — and this by the most "radical" of all the revolutionary legislatures![28]

Clearly, there are two ways of reading the evidence concerning the confiscation and sale of Loyalist lands. Jameson, who was arguing a thesis, chose to stress the "democratizing" effects. But there were other social consequences of an opposite tendency — the aggrandizement of certain individuals and families already well entrenched, the opportunities opened for speculation — and we shall not understand all the social results of this great sequestration of lands until we assess these as well.

In particular, until someone has studied the social effects of land speculation in the Revolutionary and post-Revolutionary era as Professor Paul W. Gates has done for a later period, we shall not know whether the operations of the speculators hastened or delayed settlement, encouraged or hindered the system of small holdings. Meanwhile, we may note that Professor Abernethy considers the Virginia land office act of 1779 (drafted, incidentally, by Thomas Jefferson) "a colossal mistake," a blow to economic democracy, and a retarding influence on settlement because it played into the hands of speculators and thus *prevented* the diffusion of land in small holdings. By this act, he says, "democracy was defeated in Virginia at the moment when it might have had its birth."[29]

Land speculation was, of course, a form of business enterprise. And business enterprise, it is now clear, took a sharp spurt as a direct result of Revolutionary conditions. That Jameson should have perceived and stressed this in 1925 is sufficiently remarkable. His chapter on "Industry and Commerce" undoubtedly opened the eyes of many American historians to the economic facts which, as everyone now recognizes, are as crucial in the history of a war as the political, diplomatic, and military facts.

Some of the new economic paths which the Revolution opened, turned out to be blind alleys. Postwar interest in the improvement of agriculture, reflected in the sudden popularity of farmers' societies, proved to be short-lived and relatively ineffectual.[30] In some regions the wartime growth of manufacturing, which Jameson noted, was choked off by the postwar flood of cheap British goods, which he neglected to mention.[31]

But in other ways enterprise burgeoned and flourished under wartime and postwar conditions. Opportunities for quick gains in privateering and profiteering, the opening of new markets, the expansion of the credit system, the injection of new supplies of specie into the economy as a result of foreign borrowing, the rise of new business groups around men like Jeremiah Wadsworth, William Duer, Robert Morris, the very idea (a new one for Americans) of large-scale business association — all these were constructive economic forces generated by

[27] The list of real estate confiscated and sold is printed by DeMond in an appendix (pp. 240–50).

[28] *The Acts of the General Assembly of the Commonwealth of Pennsylvania* (Philadelphia, 1782), p. 260.

[29] Cf. Gates, "The Role of the Land Speculator in Western Development," *Pennsylvania Magazine of History and Biography*, LXVI (1942), 314–33; Thomas P. Abernethy, *Western Lands and the American Revolution* (New York, 1937), p. 228.

[30] Jameson implies (pp. 79–80) that French influence was chiefly responsible for this sudden burst of interest in scientific farming. Actually, the major inspiration came from England. See Frederick B. Tolles, "George Logan and the Agricultural Revolution," *Proceedings of the American Philosophical Society*, XCV (1951), 590.

[31] Jensen holds, however, that there was no real collapse in manufacturing, only a temporary recession. *The New Nation*, pp. 219–27.

the Revolution.[32] Especially important were the rise of banking and the spread of incorporation. In the words of one economic historian, the Bank of North America, which opened in Philadelphia in 1782, "was identified with the American Revolutionary 'settlement,' — as the Bank of England was with that of the 'Glorious Revolution.' "

The same scholar gives us some revealing statistics on the chartering of business corporations: "In contrast with the half-dozen American business charters granted in the entire colonial period, eleven were issued in the United States between 1781 and 1785, twenty-two between 1786 and 1790, and 114 between 1791 and 1795."[33] Economic facts of this order have led one writer to treat the American Revolution as "the triumph of American mercantile capitalism."[34] Whether or not one wishes to adopt this view, it is clear, as Jameson dimly perceived, that the Revolution loosed potent new forces in the American economy. How these forces were related to the social and political democracy which Jameson saw as products of the Revolution remains to be studied.

When he turned from the hard facts of economic history to the impalpable realm of "thought and feeling," Jameson was less at home. Yet even here he opened vistas which a generation of intellectual and cultural historians have explored with profit. The greater part of his final lecture is concerned with the effect of independence on the churches — with disestablishment and the separation of church and state, with the reorganization of the churches on a national basis, with the wartime decline of religious life and the postwar spread of liberal theologies. Subsequent research has added little to Jameson's account of these matters, except to fill in details.[35] What Jameson did — and it was no trifling achievement — was to bring American church history within the purview of American historians — to take, as it were, the first steps toward giving this neglected orphan child a home and a standing within the family of historical disciplines.

Certain of his insights, naturally, have proved more fruitful than others. His *obiter dictum* to the effect that military men can never again play the part in public life that they played after the Revolution falls strangely on our ears, who have known the proconsulate of MacArthur, the foreign ministry of Marshall, the Presidency of Eisenhower. Curiously, Jameson found little evidence of educational advance in the Revolutionary era, except for the founding of new colleges. Had he taken a broader view of education, he might have recognized a number of important developments directly or indirectly related to wartime experience: the improvement of medicine (including dentistry) and of medical education;[36] the emergence of civil engineering from military engineering; the founding of Judge Tapping Reeve's "law school" at Litchfield, Connecticut, in 1784; the diffusion of scientific knowledge through the revived activity of the American Philosophical Society and the founding of the American Academy of Arts and Sciences; the popularity of pamphleteering as a form of mass education; and — not least important — the informal education, the widening of horizons, that resulted from wartime mobility, from the fact that, for the first time, many Americans rubbed elbows — and minds — not only with Europeans but with other Americans.[37] The school of intellectual and cultural

[32] Robert A. East, *Business Enterprise in the American Revolutionary Era* (New York, 1938), chap. II.

[33] *Ibid.*, pp. 285, 288.

[34] Louis Hacker, *The Triumph of American Capitalism* (New York, 1940), chap. XIII.

[35] Here Jameson had the benefit of E. F. Humphrey's solidly documented, probably little-read monograph on *Nationalism and Religion in America* (Boston, 1924). One added comment which he might have made — for it would have fitted his emphasis on French influences — was that the French alliance and the hope of enlisting Canadian support brought some improvement in the legal status of Roman Catholics and a more tolerant attitude toward them. See Evarts B. Greene, *Religion and the State: The Making and Testing of an American Tradition* (New York, 1941), pp. 76–78; Sister M. Augustana Ray, *American Opinion of Roman Catholicism in the Eighteenth Century* (New York, 1936), p. 348.

[36] Fielding H. Garrison says flatly: "The War of Independence was the making of medicine in this country." *An Introduction to the History of Medicine* (4th ed.; Philadelphia, 1929), p. 376.

[37] Dixon Ryan Fox ("Culture in Knapsacks," in *Ideas in Motion* [New York, 1935] pp. 37–76) emphasizes contacts with foreigners and foreign ideas; Evarts B. Greene ("Some Educational Values of the American Revolution," *Proceedings of the*

historians which has sprung up in the last quarter century has made much of the "intellectual democracy" and the "cultural nationalism" which Jameson vaguely perceived as concomitants, in the realm of "thought and feeling," of the American Revolution.[38]

The danger here as elsewhere is that the historian, misled by his enthusiasm for the concept of "revolution," will posit too abrupt a set of changes, will pay too little attention to the evidences of historical continuity. Jameson himself did not altogether avoid this pitfall. For example, he wrote that "Joel Barlow's *Vision of Columbus*, or President Stiles's celebrated election sermon on *The United States Elevated to Glory and Honor*, could not possibly have been written twenty years earlier."[39] If he meant by this that the idea of the United States as an independent nation was not entertained in the 1760's, the statement is obviously correct, though hardly startling. If he meant that before 1775 no American felt or expressed love for the land, pride in its people, confidence in its future, he was just as obviously wrong. For one finds strong feelings of American patriotism in a pre-Revolutionary poem like Freneau and Brackenridge's "The Rising Glory of America," written in 1771, in the sermons of Samuel Davies and Jonathan Mayhew in the 1750's, even in Judge Samuel Sewall's proud paean to his beloved Plum Island, Crane Pond, and Turkey Hill as far back as the last decade of the seventeenth century.[40] Indeed the points at which the supports to Jameson's thesis seem weakest — where for example he argues for sharper changes in the political and social status of individuals than can be justified on the evidence — are precisely those points at which he overlooked or underestimated dynamic forces already present in the society of late colonial America.

Still, a historian who fashions so useful a conceptual tool, who popularizes so fruitful a hypothesis, who enlarges so notably our understanding of a significant era in American history, can be forgiven a few oversights, a few overstatements. Basically, the "Jameson thesis" is still sound, and, what is more important, still vital and suggestive, capable of still further life, still greater usefulness. Jameson, after all, did much more than give us a new approach to the American Revolution. He formulated and cogently applied to a particular period an important general thesis — "the thesis that all the varied activities of men in the same country and period have intimate relations with each other, and that one cannot obtain a satisfactory view of any one of them by considering it apart from the others."[41] For this he deserves homage as one of the founders of American social and cultural history.

Suggested Further Reading:

Any serious investigation of the American Revolution entails study of the documents and pamphlets that chart the progress towards independence. S. E. Morison edited a collection of *Sources and Documents Illustrating the American Revolution, 1764–1788** (1923; 2nd ed., 1929; paperback ed., 1965); and, as noted elsewhere, Bernard Bailyn has edited, with impeccable style and scholarship, *Pamphlets of the American Revolution* (4 vols., 1965–).

The role of the clergy in the Revolution has been effectively presented by Alice M. Baldwin, *The New England Clergy and the American Revolution* (1928, reprinted 1958) and exhaustively examined by Carl Bridenbaugh, *Mitre and Sceptre* (1962). For an outstanding biography of Jonathan Mayhew, see Charles W. Akers, *Called unto Liberty; a Life of Jonathan*

American Philosophical Society, LXVIII [1929], 185–94) stresses the association of Americans with men from other states.

[38] Merle Curti, *The Growth of American Thought* (New York, 1943), chap. VI.

[39] P. 120.

[40] See the excellent chapter "Of Loyalties and of the British American Nation" in Max Savelle, *Seeds of Liberty: The Genesis of the American Mind* (New York, 1948), pp. 553–82; also Merle Curti, *The Roots of American Loyalty* (New York, 1946), chap. I. For the Sewall passage, which appeared in his *Phaenomena quaedam Apocalyptica ad Aspectum Novi Orbis configurata* (1697), see Perry Miller, *The New England Mind: From Colony to Province* (Cambridge, Mass., 1953), pp. 189–90.

[41] Jameson, p. 158.

Mayhew (1964). John Dickinson awaits a modern biographer, but there are two useful essays in *Early Dickinsoniana* (Dickinson College, 1961). John Cary has written a fine biography of *Joseph Warren, Physician, Politician, Patriot* (1961). For a readable account of the causes of the Revolution and the developments that brought about independence, John C. Miller's *Origins of the American Revolution* (1943) remains unchallenged. But the volumes by Lawrence Henry Gipson, *The Coming of the Revolution** (1954), and John Alden, *The American Revolution** (1954), are often more detailed and more accurate. Bernhard Knollenberg's *Origin of the American Revolution: 1759–1766** (1960) is exciting in its attention to English politics in this period. David Hawke has recently supplied a lively account of the genesis, drafting, and ratification of the Declaration of Independence in *A Transaction of Free Men* (1965). Studies of the Loyalists are still confined to the scholarly journals; but Douglass Adair and John A. Schutz have edited *Peter Oliver's Origin & Progress of the American Rebellion* (1961), a work unhappily unconsulted by the best modern study of the Loyalists, William H. Nelson's *The American Tory** (1961).

The military side of the Revolution is apparently irresistible to historians. The best general studies are: Claude H. Van Tyne, *War of Independence* (1929), John C. Miller, *Triumph of Freedom, 1775–1783* (1948), Willard M. Wallace, *Appeal to Arms** (1951), and Christopher Ward, *War of the Revolution* (1952). A random selection of special studies must include John R. Alden, *General Gage in America* (1948), William B. Willcox, *Sir Henry Clinton* (1964), Don Higginbotham, *Daniel Morgan* (1961), and Paul H. Smith, *Loyalists and Redcoats* (1964). The best brief account of the war is Howard H. Peckham's *The War for Independence** (1958). Excellent on the British side are Piers Mackesy, *The War for America, 1775–1783* (1964), and John Shy, *Toward Lexington: The Role of the British Army in the Coming of the American Revolution* (1965).

A few of the important (but not necessarily readable) studies of domestic aspects of the Revolution are listed in the notes to Professor Tolles' essay; among the more notable are: Allan Nevins, *American States during and after the Revolution, 1775–1789* (1924), Philip A. Crowl, *Maryland during and after the Revolution* (1943), Robert E Brown, *Middle-Class Democracy and the Revolution in Massachusetts 1691–1780* (1955), *Virginia 1705–1786: Democracy or Aristocracy* (1964), and Lee N. Newcomer, *The Embattled Farmers: A Massachusetts Countryside in the American Revolution* (1953). But we have an embarrassment of riches in the abundance and the quality of historical writing dealing with the era of the American Revolution; the foregoing is only a sampling.

PART TEN

Confederation and Constitution

It is a historical axiom that wars are won on the battlefield and lost at the conference table. The American Revolution survived both hazards. While the victory at Yorktown did not destroy the British armies in North America, it did dissolve Great Britain's determination to maintain the struggle. At the peace conference, America was the beneficiary of Lord Shelburne's generous terms which were designed to weaken the Franco-American alliance. Despite such successes the War for Independence could well have been lost. Had the Second Continental Congress not devised a form of union adequate to the new nation's immediate needs, its military and diplomatic successes alike would have been futile. American survival ultimately depended upon the character of American union.

Between 1776 and 1787 Americans debated and after much hesitation adopted two vastly different forms of federal union. Both proved to be remarkably effective. Each confronted specific national needs and substantially satisfied them; each reflected the circumstances of its creation and adoption; and each proved adaptable to drastic changes in those circumstances. The first constitution — the Articles of Confederation — supplied sufficient central government direction to win the War. But while adequate to secure victory and to resolve the sectional conflicts over western lands, the Confederation was inadequate as an instrument for directing domestic and foreign policy after the war.

Perhaps the crowning accomplishment of the Articles of Confederation was the Constitution that superseded it: the Articles were a necessary preface to the more distinctly national government that followed, in the sense that they reassured Americans by demonstrating that national government was both desirable and useful. Fearful of tyranny, be it imposed from London or from Philadelphia, Americans needed such reassurance.

1

The First Constitution

An Appraisal

The Articles of Confederation served as the first constitution of the "United States of America" from 1781 to 1789. Debate on the provisions of this document lasted from June, 1776, until March, 1781, an indication that the particularism that had impeded colonial efforts at union did not vanish upon the announcement of independence.

What were the chief characteristics of the Confederation period and in what respects was its constitution found wanting? These questions have been the subject of considerable historical debate. Almost eighty years ago John Fiske termed this The Critical Period of American History (1888), *and argued that the fate of the new nation then hung in the balance. In Fiske's opinion, lack of federal sovereignty seriously jeopardized the unity of the United States. Charles A. Beard disputed Fiske's view, suggesting it was a "phantom of the imagination produced by some undoubted evils which could have been remedied without a political revolution." In this opinion* Merrill Jensen *of the University of Wisconsin concurs. He sees the Articles of Confederation as "a natural outcome of the revolutionary movement within the American colonies"; the nation did indeed face serious problems, but the government structure created by the Articles could not be held responsible for them.* The New Nation — *the volume which followed Professor Jensen's study of* The Articles of Confederation — *was a reality, the achievement of the Confederation; the period 1781–1789 was one of progress and accomplishment. It was, however, marred fatally by the failure of the "true federalists" to realize the need for sustained leadership and union if their association of sovereign states was to survive.*

Professor Jensen's interpretation has not gone unchallenged. Without accepting the Fiske view in toto *many historians now see the Confederation period as one critical for the ultimate resolution of the Revolution. Richard B. Morris, who has written a brilliant essay on Shays' Rebellion, depicts the period 1776–1789 in the context of the divisions among the revolutionaries. So divided were they on all issues except independence from Great Britain that victory could hardly settle anything beyond freedom from British rule; the real radicals, suggests Professor Morris, were not "true federalists" like Richard Henry Lee and Samuel Adams, but nationalists like Alexander Hamilton and James Madison.*

Obviously there remain disagreements on the true role of the Confederation; equally obviously some disagreements stem from problems in semantics. The "Critical Period," as Professor Jensen contends, may have been less than perilous; but it is nothing less than complex.

Reprinted with permission of the copyright owners, the Regents of the University of Wisconsin, from Merrill Jensen, *The Articles of Confederation*, 1940, the University of Wisconsin Press.

The Articles of Confederation were the constitution of the United States from 1781 to 1789, when the Confederation Congress held its last session and turned over the government of the thirteen states to the new national government. The fact that the Articles of Confederation were supplanted by another constitution is no proof either of their success or of their failure. Any valid opinion as to the merits of the Articles must be based on a detailed and unbiased study of the confederation period. Though no such comprehensive study has yet been made, it is possible to draw certain tentative conclusions by approaching the history of the period from the point of view of the American Revolution within the American states rather than from the point of view that the Constitution of 1787 was a necessity, the only alternative to chaos.

An analysis of the disputes over the Articles of Confederation makes it plain that they were not the result of either ignorance or inexperience. On the contrary, they were a natural outcome of the revolutionary movement within the American colonies. The radical leaders of the opposition to Great Britain after 1765 had consistently denied the authority of any government superior to the legislatures of the several colonies. From 1774 on, the radicals continued to deny the authority of a superior legislature whether located across the seas or within the American states. The reiteration of the idea of the supremacy of the local legislatures, coupled with the social and psychological forces which led men to look upon "state sovereignty" as necessary to the attainment of the goals of the internal revolution, militated against the creation of such a centralized government as the conservative elements in American society desired. It can be said that the constitution which the radicals created, the Articles of Confederation, was a constitutional expression of the philosophy of the Declaration of Independence.

Today "states' rights" and "decentralization" are the war cries of the conservative element, which is not wielding the influence in national affairs it once did and still longs to do. But in the eighteenth century decentralization and states' rights meant local self-government, and local self-government meant a form of agrarian democracy. The mass of the population was composed of small farmers, who in the long run could control the politics of their individual states. Since this was the belief of the fathers of the constitution of 1787, who were thus in substantial agreement with the radical leaders of 1776, the testimony might very well be regarded as conclusive.

The writing of the Articles of Confederation brought to the fore political issues that were to be of vast significance in the history of the United States. Many a debate in later years was merely a reiteration or an elaboration of arguments used in 1776 and 1777. Those ideas upon which it is necessary to place the inadequate but necessary label of "conservative" were as well expressed in 1776 as in 1787, and often by the same men: John Dickinson and James Wilson, for instance. The vital change which took place between 1776 and 1787 was not in ideas nor in attitudes but in the balance of political power. The radical organization which had brought about the Revolution disintegrated with success, for the radicals had won their real goal, local self-government. Radical leaders returned to their states to enjoy the results of their efforts unhampered by a central government of extensive power. The conservatives, on the other hand, made only occasional gains in the states, as in Massachusetts, where their rule was met by open rebellion in 1786. In other states the attack upon their position was a slow but sure process, as in Virginia. Some of them had realized in 1776 that centralization was their protection: a central government to suppress internal rebellions, to regulate trade, and to control the actions of the state governments as the British government had controlled the colonial governments.

The fight for centralization did not stop with the completion of the Articles of Confederation. Discontent with the document was expressed in the private correspondence of such conservative leaders as Washington, Dickinson, Charles Carroll, Robert Morris, Gouverneur Morris, James Wilson, and Alexander Hamilton. Even before they were finally ratified Hamilton proposed a revolutionary convention to create the kind of government the conservatives wanted. Once the Articles had been ratified, many serious attempts were made to amend them in such a way as to strengthen the central organization. These attempts at amendment failed, as did efforts to "interpret" into the Articles certain "nationalistic" ideas foreign to both the purpose and character of the document. Even if such amendments had been adopted, the constitution would not have been satisfactory to the conservative element, for it was impossible to change its nature by mere amendment. From the conservative point of view it was the wrong *kind* of government. Even if Congress had been given a limited income, as was proposed in various amendments, the central government would still have been a federal government and therefore inadequate in conservative opinion. The alterations proposed during the Confederation period were not fundamental, for they did not touch the vital question of the distribution of power between the states and the central government. The vast field of undefined and unenumerated powers lay with the states. Congress could function only within an area of precisely delegated and carefully limited authority. It was the creature of the state governments and thus, ultimately, of the electorate of the states.

Centralized government with a legal veto on state laws, the power to enact general and uniform legislation, and the power to use arms to subdue rebellious social groups within the states, had disappeared with the Declaration of Independence. The Articles of Confederation were designed to prevent its reappearance, and for this reason were not, and never could be, adequate from the point of view of the conservatives, who wanted the essence of the British imperial system restored in the American states.

John Dickinson and his conservative committee had sought to lay the legal foundation of such a system in their first draft of articles of confederation. The document was involved and legalistic to the point of obscurity, but it was an obscurity which would lend itself readily to multiple interpretation. Legally, ultimate authority lay with the central government, for only one conditional guarantee was given to the states, and only one specific restraint was placed on Congress. The states were guaranteed the control of their "internal police" in matters where such control did not interfere with the Articles of Confederation. Congress was restrained only from levying taxes other than those for support of the post office. This was a great but not insurmountable obstacle in the way of centralization. The important point is that the vital area of undefined and unenumerated powers fell within the domain of the central government, as Thomas Burke demonstrated to Congress in 1777.

The final draft of the Articles of Confederation was, as James Wilson said in the convention in 1787, "how different." Certain powers and no others were delegated to Congress. No phrase in the document could be construed as making the central government supreme over the states. Nothing remotely resembling such phrases as "obligation of contract," "supremacy of the laws," "necessary and proper," or "general welfare" were to be found in it. The control of war and foreign affairs was expressly granted to Congress, as was the power to regulate the trade with Indians who were not members of any of the states, but Congress might not infringe upon the right of any state to legislate upon matters within its own limits. Congress was given the power to regulate the value of both its coinage and that of the states, but no control over the emission of paper money by the states. Congress was a court of last appeal, or rather a board of arbitration, in disputes between one state and another, and between private individuals claiming lands under different grants. Congress was given charge of the post office and the regulation of weights and measures. These were its "sole and exclusive" powers. In addition, it was given the authority to appoint a committee of the states to sit during the recess of Congress and the power to control its own organization and sessions.

Eighteenth-century radicals looked upon the desire for office as a disease which fed upon office-holding. Hence they were careful to provide that Congress should never become an association of office-holders. No one could be a member of Congress for more than three out of any six years. No one could be president of Congress for more than one year out of any three; thus no individual would be likely to acquire much prestige as head of the central government. The delegates were subject to recall at any time by the state governments which had selected them, and hence were usually responsive to the will of their electorates as expressed in the state legislatures. This serves to explain why so many votes in Congress were often inconsistent with a given delegate's political and economic views.

The Articles of Confederation placed few restraints upon the states, and even these tended to be qualified out of existence. No state could receive or send embassies or enter into alliances or treaties without the consent of Congress. No two or more states could enter into a confederation without the consent of Congress. No state could levy imposts or duties which might interfere with stipulations in treaties made by Congress. No treaty made by Congress, on the other hand, could interfere with the right of a state to subject foreigners to the same imposts and duties as were levied on its own citizens. The states were not to keep vessels of war in peacetime unless Congress deemed it to be necessary for purposes of defense. Neither could a state maintain troops unless Congress considered them necessary to garrison forts. States were forbidden to declare war without the consent of Congress except where sudden invasion would permit of no delay. Letters of marque and reprisal were to be granted only after a declaration of war by Congress and under conditions laid down by it. None of these restraints was a serious check upon the sovereignty of the states.

Between the states there was complete equality. Every state was required to have at least two representatives in Congress, and it might have as many as seven, though each delegation was to have only one vote. When more than two delegates from a state were present, the state's vote was decided by the majority of the delegation. If the vote was a tie, the state had no vote. Citizens of any state were allowed to emigrate freely to another. Extradition of criminals was provided for. The Articles declared that each state should give full faith to the judicial proceedings of every other state. Except in these things the states were not responsible to one another. The union that had been created was a federal union of equal states in which the central organization was carefully subordinated to the members of it.

The Articles of Confederation were designed to prevent the central government from infringing upon the rights of the states, whereas the Constitution of 1787 was designed as a check upon the power of the states and the democracy that found expression within their bounds. The character of the Articles of Confederation was the result of two realities: the reality of the psychological and legal independence of the states, and the reality of the belief that democracy was possible only within fairly small political units whose electorate had a direct check upon the officers of government. Such a check was impossible where the central government was far removed from the control of the people by distance and by law. The independence of the states was a product of colonial history. The distrust of centralization, of government spread over a great area, was the product of both political theory and practical experience. The rise of radicalism had been checked often enough to teach the radicals that central governments, however democratic in form, were fundamentally undemocratic in action.

This government, the product of the forces which brought about the American Revolution, failed not because it was inadequate but because the radicals failed to maintain the organization they had created to bring about the American Revolution. The radical movement was essentially a movement of parties within states, and their political and social aims were to a great extent local. To achieve their purpose, local independence, unity of all the states had been necessary. What the radicals failed to see was that they must continue their union if they were to maintain their local independence under the Articles of Confederation. Thomas Burke of North Carolina expressed the radical view admirably. Congress, he said, was a general council instituted for the purpose of opposing the usurpations of Great Britain and of conducting a war against her, of forming necessary foreign alliances, directing the army and navy, and making binding treaties. Since this was the nature of Congress and its powers, it eliminated "all pretence for continuance of a Congress after the war is concluded, or of assuming a power to any other purposes."

Thus when the radicals had won their war, most of them were well content to go home and continue with the program of action they had started long before the war began. The thwarting of that program by the local conservatives and the British government had been one of the major causes of the Revolution. Needless to say, the motives of the radicals were not always the highest or the most disinterested, but their program was essentially democratic in tendency, for it widened the bases of political power and it declared that men should be bound only by those laws to which they had given their consent. Above all, when that program was idealized, as in the Declaration of Independence, it declared that the purpose of government was the protection of the life, liberty, and happiness of the individual, and when it did not fulfill this ideal it should be overthrown. Such a revolution was a practical possibility in a state unchecked by an outside and superior authority. Such an authority was rendered impossible by the Articles of Confederation.

What the radicals did not see was that the conservative elements in American society had learned a bitter lesson at the hands of the radicals. They too could call conventions. They too could paint dark pictures of the times and blame the supposed woes of the country on the Articles of Confederation, as the radicals had blamed the British government before 1776. They too could, and did, adopt the radical theory of the sovereignty of the people; in the name of the people they engineered a conservative counter-revolution and erected a nationalistic government whose purpose in part was to thwart the will of "the people" in whose name they acted. They too could use one name while pursuing a goal that was the opposite in fact. Thus, although the purpose of the conservatives was "nationalistic," they adopted the name "Federalist," for it served to disguise the extent of the changes they desired. True, the government they created had a good many "federal" features, but this was so because the conservatives were political realists and had to compromise with the political reality of actual state sovereignty.

What the conservatives in their turn failed to see was that the government they created might be captured by the radicals united on a national scale. Madison in *The Federalist* wrote that such a union was impossible, though he shortly helped to bring it about when faced with the workings of the government under the Constitution of 1787.

Wise old John Adams probably had the last word. Writing in 1808, he declared, "I have always called our Constitution a game at leapfrog."

2

The Second Constitution: Economic and Intellectual Origins

I

Charles Beard and the Constitution: A Critical Review of Forrest McDonald's *We the People* with a Rebuttal by Forrest McDonald

Forrest McDonald *begins his book* We the People *with the remark that before the advent of Frederick Jackson Turner and Charles A. Beard the study of history was largely confined "to what Beard called 'barren political history.'" While somewhat of an overstatement, Professor McDonald correctly appraises the impact of Turner and Beard. No study of the second United States constitution can ignore Beard's contribution to its understanding — and few studies agree upon just what Beard's contribution happens to be.*

Beard, as Professor McDonald puts it, "made one great and lasting contribution" — he demonstrated that "American political history has not taken place in a vacuum," least of all an eco-

---

Jackson T. Main, "Charles Beard and the Constitution: A Critical Review of Forrest McDonald's *We the People*," with a Rebuttal by Forrest McDonald, from *The William and Mary Quarterly*, 3rd Ser., XVII (1960), 86–110. Reprinted with permission of the authors and the Institute of Early American History and Culture, Williamsburg, Virginia.

nomic vacuum. Beard did not insist that an economic interpretation was the interpretation. Nor did he pretend to be definitive. Historians, like politicians, are much inclined to criticize each other for sins of omission as well as commission. Beard has been attacked for what he did not say as well as for his undoubted inaccuracies. McDonald, it seems fair to add, is one of Beard's more constructive and fair-minded critics; he is persuaded that an economic study of the origins of the Constitution of 1787 makes intelligible many of the forces that produced it; however, he questions the correlation between economic interests and voting behavior; he regards the Constitution as "the product of a number of conflicting elements" with few substantive changes except the replacement of the Congress of the Confederation.

Professor Jackson T. Main *clearly takes exception to McDonald's general criticism of Beard, to his economic categorization, and to his methodology. Main's own study of* The Antifederalists *(1961) argues against any simplistic account of the Confederation period, but he does find for a fundamental antagonism between the commercial and the non-commercial elements in America, a division McDonald declines to recognize.*

If, after reading Main's review of McDonald and McDonald's retort, the student of the Constitution emerges bewildered and uncertain, that is as it should be. No subject is more confusing, less certain. But at least historians are aware of their problems and are at last addressing them. It seems safe to say that Professor Main's recent study, The Social Structure of Revolutionary America *(1965), along with Professor McDonald's eagerly-anticipated second volume,* E Pluribus Unum *(1965), will not only stoke the fires of controversy, but generate some illumination as well as heat.*

Professor McDonald is presently with Brown University; Professor Main has taught at San José State College and the University of Maryland.

It is a little strange that, when dozens of monographs during two-score years have profitably used Beard's interpretation of the Constitution, an attempt utterly to refute him has aroused scarcely a whimper of protest. Nobody would insist that Beard's thesis be accepted in its entirety, but his fundamental idea — that the Constitution reflected the economic interests of the large property holders who wrote it — has survived much research, and any book which challenges it ought to be examined with a cautious and a skeptical eye. If Forrest McDonald's *We the People: The Economic Origins of the Constitution* (Chicago, 1958), is so scrutinized, it will be found that Beard has survived the attack. Since a complete criticism would require a volume of equal length, this discussion will review only a few of the most important aspects.[1]

Beard's work was an early attempt to test the hypothesis "that economic elements are the chief factors in the development of political institutions."[2] He therefore assembled data concerning the real and personal property owned by those who wrote the Constitution and those who favored its ratification. Since, as he wrote, a complete survey "would entail an enormous labor," Beard relied chiefly on secondary accounts and published documents, except that he did undertake to identify the holders of the Federal debt. In addition, he discussed the political ideas of the members of the Federal Convention insofar as these related to his general purpose. This chapter is not discussed by McDonald. Beard found that most of the members of the Convention were lawyers, that they came from towns or regions near the coast where public securities were concentrated, that they were not farmers, and that they would be economically benefited by ratification because they possessed public securities, land held for speculation, money at interest, slaves, or property in

[1] The essay is based upon material gathered for a study of post-Revolutionary politics. The objective is not to defend Beard *in toto,* for much that he wrote has been proved erroneous, nor is it to present an alternative hypothesis, but to examine critically this particular attack upon Beard's thesis and thereby to clear the way for future interpretations.

[2] *An Economic Interpretation of the Constitution of the United States* (New York, 1913), p. 6.

commerce, manufacturing, and shipping. The same observations applied to the Federal members of the various state ratifying conventions. In general, the division on this issue "was between substantial personality interests on the one hand and the small farming and debtor interests on the other."

McDonald set himself the task of testing Beard's conclusions. In doing so he made far greater use of primary materials and has substantially increased our knowledge, especially concerning the economic interests of the men involved. It is this contribution which immediately impresses the reader and has led to the general praise which the book has hitherto received. Nevertheless the research is far from complete. The facts cited are those which tend to refute Beard, while those which would support his views are often omitted; and the interpretation of the facts is likewise open to dispute.

The first part of the book attempts to prove that the Federal Convention, far from reflecting exclusively the ideas of certain well-to-do economic groups, was a truly representative body. McDonald seeks first to show that the delegates came from most of the major geographical areas; second, that they reflected all "shades of political opinion"; and third, that they themselves were of diverse economic interests, often in debt, less rich than Beard had suggested, and less influenced by ownership of public securities.

The first contention is "proved" by defining geographical areas in a way which achieves the desired result and by counting as present at the Convention anyone who was chosen as a delegate even when he did not attend. This faulty methodology may be illustrated by the case of Massachusetts. On the basis of physical location one might expect that the major areas would be described as (1) the maritime coast and its immediate hinterland, (2) Maine, and (3) the agricultural, upland interior, with perhaps (4) the Connecticut Valley towns distinguished as a fourth section. Such a division would reflect political and economic realities, for the seacoast towns were in fact usually opposed to those of the interior, while the lower Connecticut Valley usually supported the east and Maine went its own way. If this were done, then of the four delegates who attended, three came from the east and one from the Valley, leaving most of the state, including Maine and all of the interior, unrepresented. However, McDonald divides the coastal towns into four separate areas in such a way that all but one of them were represented; counts Rufus King as doubling for Maine as well as Newburyport, although King no longer lived in either place (being in fact a resident of New York) and had left Maine when he was twelve; considers that a group of interior towns connected with Boston were present through Francis Dana, although Dana did not attend the Convention; and concludes that six out of the nine areas into which he divides the state were represented at Philadelphia. In this manner the fundamental fact, which Beard recognized, is concealed, namely, that the commercial east coast was represented and the agrarian west was not. In like fashion he says that three out of four New Hampshire regions were represented, although the only two delegates who attended were from Portsmouth and Exeter, both within ten miles of the coast!

In Virginia as in Massachusetts, McDonald divides the Tidewater eastern part of the state into four separate areas, all represented; in addition the "Upper James" is counted present through Edmund Randolph who lived in Richmond, a fall-line town; and the rest of the interior is also considered to be present through Patrick Henry, who did not attend. McDonald can then cheerfully concede that the three sections west of the Blue Ridge were not represented, for he has discovered a majority of six out of nine. It can be argued with equal if not superior evidence that in truth all of Virginia's delegates to the Convention represented only one section: the Tidewater, or perhaps more accurately the eastern river valley area, leaving four sections to be counted as not present.

McDonald's proof that "all shades of political opinion" were present rests upon his division of the country into "factions," which are supposed to include all political groupings. He then finds that most of the major factions were represented. The argument depends, of course, upon whether the idea of "factions" adequately describes post-Revolutionary politics, and whether his particular identification of factions is valid. His conclusions therefore follow only if his definitions be accepted and if in addition it is granted that all those chosen as delegates should be counted even though they rejected the election. Massachusetts may again serve as an illustration. McDonald finds two major factions, led by John Hancock and James Bowdoin, and several minor ones headed by Samuel Adams, Theodore Sedgwick, Benjamin Lincoln, Benjamin Austin, and the Cushing family. Since both of the major factions were represented, he declares his point proved. But Massachusetts politics cannot be explained in terms of the personal leadership of individuals, of whom all but one lived near the coast, and that one (Sedgwick) a supporter of the conservative, commercial Bowdoin group. What about the vast majority of small interior towns? Surely a delegation which contained not a single man to express the views of small farmers — not a Shaysite or Shaysite sympathizer — did not reflect all of the various political opinions, but fundamentally only one. Similarly in Virginia, McDonald declares that "all four major and three independent factions were represented." But R. H. Lee and Henry did not attend, so that even accepting his definition of factions the true figure is two out of four major groups. Moreover, once again there was not a single delegate who spoke for the small farmers. In state after state the only "factions" represented were those of the mercantile, large landholding, well-to-do easterners, and it certainly is not true that the Convention represented all shades of political opinion. Once again Beard's analysis is the more nearly correct one.

The attempt to refute Beard's views concerning the property interests of the delegates is equally open to question, even though McDonald has gathered much additional data. The refutation is attempted by placing the emphasis upon those facts which depreciate the property held and by continually minimizing the delegates' wealth. Now every historian is required to select such facts as he believes significant and to arrange them in such a way as to convey a meaning: to interpret. Yet it is not always easy for the reader to remember that he is being presented an interpretation rather than an exact re-creation of reality. It will be instructive to compare, in a few cases, the accounts given by Beard and McDonald. The latter emphasizes that Robert Morris was heavily in debt and died bankrupt; Beard barely mentions this and concentrates upon describing his great wealth in 1787. Beard stresses James Wilson's large estate, McDonald his debts and ultimate poverty. To McDonald, Hamilton was "perpetually in debt"; to Beard, he is the principal spokesman for the rich, who "lived well, and had a large income." Madison is depicted by McDonald as the owner of "560 ill-kept acres," by Beard as the son of a wealthy planter, relieved thereby from the necessity of earning a living (actually the Madison estate included 5,748 acres and 99 slaves). Richard Bassett appears in *We the People* as a man of moderate means who lived "in comfort"; in Beard he is one of the wealthy men of the state who "entertained lavishly." In a number of other instances the two accounts differ, sometimes radically.

Throughout *We the People,* men of means are made to appear quite the opposite. Hamilton, Robert Morris and Wilson were not the only ones to die in debt; so also did Nathaniel Gorham, who in 1787 — the date that matters — was one of the country's wealthiest men. We read that Pierce Butler, who owned 143 slaves, was "in rather desperate circumstances." William Houstoun, "the richest member of the Georgia delegation," could scarcely support himself, the implication being that the rest of the delegates from that state must have been truly impoverished; yet in truth Houstoun was one of the wealthy planter aristocracy with extensive lands. Gouverneur Morris's family estate is called "magnificent" when he fails to inherit it, but in the next paragraph, having passed into Morris's hands, it becomes "debt-laden." Jared Ingersoll, we read, had in 1787 "besides a wealthy father-in-law, a moderately successful practice, a fourth interest in a 30-ton sloop in the coasting trade, *and little else*" (italics mine). Edmund Randolph was in "great need," "beset with economic difficulties," impoverished it seems by thousands of acres and over a hundred slaves. Indeed to McDonald the rich man had less wealth than the poor, for we learn that John Rutledge's 243 slaves "were apparently more of a burden than an asset." When a man's basic wealth enabled him to borrow money in a time of great currency shortage, this is interpreted as a sign of poverty. Washington becomes "land- and slave-poor," a debtor, who borrowed $10,000 to cover expenses when he went to

New York as President. McDonald lists thirteen members who were "debtors for significant amounts" and whose condition "ranged from acute embarrassment to desperation and outright bankruptcy," including such impecunious figures as Rutledge, Robert Morris, James Wilson, Washington, Madison, Randolph, Butler, Houstoun, and both Pinckneys.

This is absurd. If the reader will take the trouble to examine the facts which McDonald himself provides, the true situation will become apparent. The fact is that over two dozen of the sixty-five elected delegates, and more than half of those who signed the Constitution, were rich, and others were well-to-do. Not more than nine — less than one-seventh of the elected delegates — were of only modest means. Almost all of the delegates, moreover, were merchants, large landholders, or lawyers representing these groups, comprising precisely what Beard said they were: a "consolidated economic group."

McDonald also attempts to disprove the influence of public securities upon the Founders. The real question, it might be urged, is not whether a member of the Convention held securities, but the distribution of these in the country at large and the extent to which delegates reflected the desires of security holders. However, since Beard did not do this, McDonald is justified in restricting his inquiries to the holdings of the delegates. In doing so he emphasizes that few of them held large amounts, and he tries, by gratuitous remarks, to disparage the importance of the profit received. Nicholas Gilman made $500 which is "roughly $10 per month from 1787 to 1791." Rufus King made "only" about $1,300 in four years. Thomas Fitzsimons retained "only" $2,668.10 worth. Oliver Ellsworth's profit of $3,240 "would hardly seem large enough to write a Constitution to protect," and McDonald's concession that in Ellsworth's case the motive probably did exist merely emphasizes the impression he conveys that in all other cases no such amount would suffice. It was Beard's point, however, that even a small holding might well create sympathy with the needs of public creditors. The question was not, he wrote, "how many hundred thousand dollars accrued to them," but whether they represented "distinct groups whose economic interest they understood and felt in concrete, definite form through their own personal experience with identical property rights." Furthermore the stake of the delegates was by no means as small as McDonald implies. No argument can conceal the fact that nearly half of the delegates made over $500 each from the appreciation of these certificates, and no fewer than thirteen held $5,000 worth apiece (face value) in 1787. It would certainly seem that once again Beard is closer to the mark than McDonald.[3]

In addition to this effort to reinterpret the nature of the Convention, McDonald tries to disprove Beard's contention concerning the alignment for and against ratification — "to test," as he puts it, "the validity of Beard's class struggle interpretation," by demonstrating through a description of the members of the ratifying conventions that men on both sides had the same economic interests and the same amount of property. In his anxiety to prove his point, McDonald sometimes (1) minimizes the property held by Federalists and exaggerates that owned by Antifederalists; (2) defines, in ways open to question, the professions of men on both sides so as to make it appear that they were of similar status; (3) omits, doubtless inadvertently, some relevant biographical data; (4) prints summary tables which appear to support his views, but neglects to publish tables which might have proved the contrary; and lastly (5) includes those facts which support his opinions but overlooks some which do not. The reader is drawn into an uncritical acceptance of all this because McDonald has done some excellent research and goes into great detail upon subjects which uphold his interpretation.

[3] There are other interpretations in these chapters which might be challenged. The author is eager to note whenever a delegate voted for paper money or on behalf of debtors, ignoring any contrary behavior. The reader is usually not informed of the circumstances, which perhaps were not always known to McDonald. Langdon's vote for paper money was actually cast in behalf of a measure which was favored by many creditors as an alternative to something worse: a paper money plan so conservative that it was negatived by all of the soft money towns. Moreover Langdon spoke out strongly against state issues of paper money. See Richard B. Morris, "Insurrection in Massachusetts," in *America in Crisis,* ed. Daniel Aaron (New York, 1952), p. 48. The quote from Beard is from *An Economic Interpretation,* p. 73.

The first chapter of the three (chapters five, six, and seven) devoted to this subject is the least liable to objection. Most of the states discussed did not contain a large Antifederal party, and so, few challenging comparisons are made. There are, however, some doubtful generalizations,[4] and the discussion of the Connecticut ratifying convention introduces the line of argument which McDonald follows throughout. It is emphasized that the wealthy Federalist merchant Jeremiah Wadsworth had to give up some of his tax-delinquent land, and this is evidently supposed to cast doubt upon his financial position. Nearly everyone, rich or poor, was affected by the financial difficulties of the period. The question therefore is not who was in financial straits at the time — everybody was — but whether Federalists or Antifederalists had more property. In this case the fact of greatest significance is that Wadsworth was the richest man in the state. In the ratifying convention, we are told, both sides came from "similar economic backgrounds" in spite of the fact that twenty-nine out of thirty-three lawyers and ten out of twelve merchants were Federalists. The admission that among Antifederalists "less than half as many were public security holders" turns out to be McDonald's way of expressing the fact that forty-five Federalists and only six Antifederalists held part of the national debt.

Chapter six will furnish most of the examples of the way in which the true situation is disguised. The treatment of the alignment in Pennsylvania is typical. Property held by the Federalists is minimized. Robert Coleman is listed merely as the "proprietor of an ironworks"; one would not guess that this was the Elizabeth Furnace, which covered part of a 4,000-acre property, and that Coleman was one of the wealthy men of the state. Less than justice is done to the holdings of such men as Yeates and Rush, while Neville and Scott certainly cannot be characterized merely as frontier farmers, for both were men of means, economic leaders of their community. Colonel Thomas Bull, whom McDonald calls a farmer, managed an iron furnace so successfully that he was able to erect a fine mansion, a gristmill, a sawmill, and a blacksmith shop, and to retire. On the other hand, among the Antifederalists, Nicholas Lotz, who was a weaver, becomes "the proprietor of a clothing business." Adam Orth is called an iron manufacturer although he did not own a forge until 1793. James Martin is stated to have been engaged in "miscellaneous promotional and speculative deals" elevating him above the farmer rank, but these high-sounding phrases mean, upon examination, only that he owned a couple of small farms and some public securities. Federalists such as Barclay, Neville, and Scott, who outdealt Martin by a wide margin, remain merely "farmers." Summarizing his information in a table, McDonald introduces an occupation called "manufacturing capitalist," which turns out to mean someone who had a mill, the idea evidently being that these small property holders should be considered among the economic elite. Six Federalists and seven Antifederalists are placed in this category, which makes it appear that, if anything, the Antifederalists were more likely to be "capitalists." But the fact is that six additional Federalists, identified only as farmers, also had mills (Allison, Bull, Hannum, J. Morris, Wynkoop, and Yardley). In addition, if the Antifederalist Whitehill is elevated out of the farmer ranks because he owned an inn, the same ought to apply to the Federalist Barclay. The total result is that McDonald's summary table is misleading, for whereas it states that 35 per cent of the Federal ratifiers were farmers, the true figure, accepting his definition of what constituted a farmer, is 15 per cent.

McDonald also tries to demonstrate that the Antifederalists held more public securities than their opponents by comparing the certificates held by the delegates. The fact that a few of the important Antifederalists owned certificates really proves little. Popular parties typically derive their leadership from men of large property, and in nearly every state, including Pennsylvania, the Antifederalists were led by men of means. A few of them were indeed large holders, but the evidence is strong that most of the securities were owned by Federalists. Philadelphians owned as much as 90 per cent of the

[4] McDonald theorizes that the states which were weak supported, and those which were strong opposed, the Constitution. There may be some validity to this, although an attempt to prove it universally true forces the author to insist, against much contrary evidence, that Connecticut and Maryland were weak whereas Rhode Island and New Hampshire were strong.

debt, and Philadelphians of all professions and classes were Federal; pro-Constitution candidates to the ratifying convention received an average of 1,200 votes each compared with 160 each for the Antifederalists.[5] Among the largest ($10,000 plus) holders whose political affiliations could be determined, three out of five were Federalists.

Finally (and this is the most important point of all), whereas only two or three Antifederal delegates were men of large property, more than a dozen of their opponents were wealthy. In short the delegates on both sides did not hold "about the same amounts of the same kinds of property." Again Beard is more nearly correct than McDonald.

A similar procedure is followed in the case of Massachusetts. Federalists are downgraded and their property minimized. Elijah Dwight was more than a retail shopkeeper; he was a prominent and wealthy judge. Ebenezer Janes, who is called a maker of gravestones, was also a miller and a deacon who had an imposing house. T. J. Skinner, "carpenter," was a prominent Williamstown merchant. John Ashley, identified by McDonald merely as a farmer, was a merchant, a lawyer, and a large landowner (and Harvard, 1754). Noah Porter, also called a farmer, had the first chair in town, later added a chaise, had £100 loaned at interest, was Harvard 1761, and was sheriff of Hampshire County. Tristam Dalton was not just a lawyer but a wealthy merchant who married the daughter of another wealthy merchant. Morison writes that when Dalton went to New York as one of Massachusetts' first senators, he drove "in Newburyport style, in his own four-horse coach, emblazoned with the Dalton arms, and attended by servants in the Dalton livery." Other examples could be given. Among the Federalists whom McDonald could not identify, George Payson of Walpole and Moses Richardson of Medway were both innkeepers, while John Winthrop and Caleb Davis were both prominent merchants of Boston. On the Antifederal side there are also some errors on the assigning of occupations.

An important question of interpretation concerns the category of "gentleman-capitalists," who were "men of means, large landowners, renters, money-lenders, and investors in various local business ventures." Among the thirteen Federalists identified as such, many undoubtedly belong to this group, among them Francis Dana, Benjamin Greenleaf (who was from Newburyport, incidentally, not Salem), Nathaniel Barrell, Benjamin Lincoln, William Pynchon, William Heath, and Richard Cranch. Whether all or even any of the fifteen Antifederalists are properly assigned to this category is of course a matter of judgment, but it is clear from the records that they did not as a group compare in wealth with their Federal equivalents.

McDonald's summary table and his conclusions, being based in part upon doubtful facts, can be seriously challenged. If the changes in occupation noted above are made, it appears that thirty merchants and tradesmen favored ratification and only eight opposed it. At the other end of the social scale most of the men whose occupations are unknown may safely be presumed to have been farmers, and if they are added to those known to have been such, then 38 per cent of the Federalists and 58 per cent of the Antifederalists were farmers. Therefore, despite McDonald, the Federalists were not more successful in winning the support of these men. McDonald omits any mention of the relative property holdings of the opposing sides, but it is certainly important to observe that almost all of the wealthy men in the convention were Federal. He does concede that the vast majority of public security holders favored ratification. His figures (in assembling which he has done a real service) show, indeed, that only three Antifederalists held $500 worth whereas forty-one Federalists did so. Outside of the convention, virtually all of the securities were concentrated in Boston and a few other seacoast centers; most of the large owners were merchants and, insofar as their politics are known, they were Federalists.

South Carolina is discussed without providing the usual table summarizing the alignment. Had such a table been constructed it might have caused McDonald to modify his conclusions.

[5] McDonald argues that this vote represented the decision of mechanics, artisans, and tradesmen, but clearly the merchants had voted the same way. Contemporary testimony is unanimous on this point. For example, David Redick to William Irvine, Sept. 24, 1787, Irvine Papers, Vol. IX, Historical Society of Pennsylvania, Philadelphia; statement of George Bryan, Bryan Papers, *ibid.*

Two key generalizations are offered. First, "The majorities by which merchants, factors, lawyers, planters, and farmers favored ratification was for each group about the same as the overall majority in the convention — about two to one." Let us accept the data given, but among the Federalists changing John Chesnut and Henry Laurens from planters to merchants and John Kean from unknown to merchant. The proportions are as follows: merchants, 3:1 for ratification; among artisans and mechanics, 7:1, lawyers 5:1, doctors 5:1, and large planters 3:1, but in significant contrast small planters and farmers 2:1 *against* ratification. The truth therefore is diametrically opposed to his statement. Secondly, he continues, "They had, proportionately, about the same amounts of the same kinds of property." Let us construct our own table of slave-ownership, since none is furnished:

	Federalists	*Antifederalists*
unknown	18	8
none	2	2
1–9	16	21
10–19	25	14
20–49	23	13
50–99	30	12
100 plus	35	3

It will be seen that 43.6 per cent of the Federalists and only 20.5 per cent of the Antifederalists owned fifty slaves.[6] So also the very great majority of large landholders and of large public security holders were Federalists. Once again McDonald's conclusions are contrary to the evidence.

Chapter six closes with a discussion of the ratification in New Hampshire. The shortage of biographical information prevents any confident generalizations. McDonald concedes that public securities were held mainly by the Federalists. All of the merchants in the convention were Federalists; 60 per cent of the Antifederalists and 53 per cent of the Federalists were farmers or of unknown occupation. No summation is made of the proportion of large property holders on either side, although such information as is provided makes it obvious that the Federalists had far more wealth, a conclusion which contemporaries shared.

To summarize the critique of this key chapter, the true situation is as follows: in all four of these states, among members of the conventions, (1) merchants and those connected with the commercial interest favored ratification by an overwhelming margin, (2) farmers took the opposite side, (3) public security holders were predominantly Federal, (4) the Federalists had far more property. This is precisely what Beard argued, yet McDonald, through the omission of pertinent data and the distortion, doubtless unconscious, of the facts he does give, arrives at an opposite conclusion.

The analysis which has been presented here could be extended through the third chapter on ratification, but enough has perhaps been said to prove the points at issue. A few additional remarks may be made. In Virginia, the delegates held properties in counties other than those which they represented, and these are not always noted — twenty-five Federalists and seventeen Antifederalists had more property than is shown. Some errors are made in regard to the professions of the delegates: among the Federalists, Simms, Z. Johnston, and Tomlin were merchants; T. Lewis, McClerry, and Bushrod Washington were lawyers; while Antifederalists R. Williams and R. Lawson were also lawyers. Federal delegates did have more slaves than the Antifederalists, and more of them were large public security holders, but it is true that the division of property among the delegates in the Virginia convention was more equal than was ordinarily the case. McDonald's concluding generalizations, as elsewhere, do not always follow from the evidence. The discussion of New York's ratification also contains some errors. His description of the convention delegates omits altogether the wealthy Federalist lawyer Richard Morris, while Philip Livingston was a merchant in addition to his other occupations. The impression is given that Federalist John Hobart was merely a debtor, but in fact he inherited a considerable estate. As usual the conclusion is drawn that the members were about equal in wealth and economic interest. No table is provided, so it is necessary to construct one:

[6] Most of the eighteen Federalists whose property in slaves is unknown lived in the eastern part of the state and probably were slaveowners.

	Federal	elected Anti, voted Fed.	elected Anti, did not vote	Anti-federal
merchants	5	1	0	0
lawyers and large landowners	3	3	0	1
lawyers	5	0	4	7
large landowners	2	1	1	2
millers	0	1	0	1
obscure men	4	3	2	9
farmers	0	3	0	6

Obviously there was no such equality. It should also be noted that on the final alignment eleven Federalists and six Antifederalists held public securities worth over $500.

The last three chapters consider the economic origins of the Constitution from a more general point of view, and some more general criticisms are in order. In the first place, it can be seen from the foregoing that the attack upon Beard has been unsuccessful. The Federal Convention did not represent all or even most of the economic interests and political opinions. Analysis of the delegates to the ratifying conventions shows conclusively that the influence of the merchants, lawyers, and large landowners was pro-Constitution while most farmers were on the other side; that the Federalists held far more wealth than their opponents; and that the influence of public security holders was strongly on the side of ratification. The evidence upon which the final interpretative chapters is based therefore lacks validity and the conclusions themselves are of course invalid.

A second general criticism concerns the introductory paragraphs which precede the descriptions of the delegates in each state. These are designed to analyze some of the local factors which were involved in the ratification process. In some cases McDonald has uncovered new materials, and parts of his introductions are very good, but they usually deal with only a few of the causative factors. Those which do not support his general thesis are omitted, although the reader is sometimes left with a different impression. Particular attention is given to the state paper money controversy, in discussing which McDonald tries to show that the Federalists were more deeply in debt than the Antifederalists and that they supported debtor bills. Several observations must be made here. The first is that by selecting particular votes and ignoring others, the evidence is "stacked." In the case of South Carolina, for example, all of the attention is concentrated on the debates in 1785. Yet it is conceded that two years later the planters had changed their minds (indeed the situation in 1785 was abnormal, not typical). It would seem pertinent therefore to examine a series of votes recorded on economic matters during 1787–88, in which the sectional division, correlating with the vote on the Constitution, is revealed. Secondly, the fact that men borrowed money, as did the South Carolina planters, does not make them debtors in the Beardian sense. The difference between the man of means, who borrows of his free will, or to avoid disposing of some of his less fluid wealth (as Washington borrowed £10,000), and the small property holder, who unwillingly falls into debt, or is forced to borrow from one creditor in order to pay another, is fundamental; and to treat them alike is as absurd as it would be to condemn United States Steel because its indebtedness is greater than that of a corner filling station. Thirdly, McDonald's anxiety to prove that Federalists were debtors leads him into some misstatements. We are informed for example that "virtually all of the fourteen delegates" from the Shenandoah Valley were debtors, but according to his source only five were in debt. Fourthly, in spite of what McDonald says, paper money advocates did tend to oppose the Constitution: (1) most of the Antifederal strength in Connecticut came from paper money districts, (2) the correlation in Massachusetts exceeds 80 per cent, (3) the correlation in New Hampshire is not high, but it exists, (4) the paper money forces in Rhode Island were Antifederal, (5) the alignment in New York is well known, (6) the correlation in North Carolina is very high (the situation there is not described by McDonald), and (7) paper money supporters in both Maryland and Virginia usually opposed ratification. There are certainly many cases in which the generalization does *not* hold, but it cannot be denied altogether. To do so, finally, is also to ignore a great deal of contemporary testimony. If the debtors did not, on the whole, oppose, and the creditors did not, by and large, support the Constitution, it would come as a great surprise to informed observers on both sides.[7]

Another general critical observation stems from what is in many ways an excellent suggestion: namely, that the economic aspects of the Constitution be studied by classifying Americans in terms of their occupations, of which McDonald distinguishes four major categories and over two dozen subgroups. Beyond doubt this kind of an investigation is needed and will be most rewarding. However, American society in 1787–88 can be structured in other ways than by occupation, of which one of the most important is by class, or (if the existence of classes be denied) at least by relative income or property held. It is not sufficient to distinguish, for example, between the occupations of subsistence farmers and merchants unless it is recognized also that the former were poor by comparison with the latter. Despite McDonald, it can be maintained that the Constitution was written by large property owners and that the division over its acceptance followed, to some extent, class lines. There is much evidence that this was the case, and the thesis is stated explicitly in many contemporary letters and newspaper articles. At the very least the subject warrants investigation, and no program for research can be successful which ignores it.

A final point: the procedure adopted by McDonald and others of conducting their research with the intent of disproving someone's thesis is not likely to reveal the truth, because one's conclusions are prejudiced in advance. The facts cf history do not, as a rule, all point inescapably in a single direction; interpretations are made by balancing the evidence. When one sets out deliberately to gather evidence on only one side the desired result can generally be achieved, for along the way first the "facts" and then the judgment are unconsciously distorted. McDonald has done much valuable research, and his errors are doubtless honest errors; yet no better example can be found of the pitfalls inherent in this methodology. (Beard, of course, can be criticized on the same basis, but this does not justify the method.) The full story of the Constitution and its ratification remains to be written. Until this is done, the historian seeking an interim interpretation will be better advised to follow Beard than McDonald.

[7] Incidentally it should be added that if, as McDonald maintains, the Constitution did not prevent the states from issuing paper, makers and opponents alike thought that it did.

Forrest McDonald's Rebuttal

It is with some reluctance that I undertake a reply to Jackson T. Main's critique of *We the People,* for with much of what Mr. Main says I entirely agree. Like him, I have been distressed by the absence of critical reviews of the book (I have seen only two, and he wrote both).[1] Like him, I have been surprised that an attempt to correct some of the errors, misinterpretations, and overemphases in Charles A. Beard's pioneering work (by no means an attempt "utterly to refute" it) has, in Mr. Main's words, "aroused scarcely a whimper of protest." Furthermore, Mr. Main has, in some instances, correctly pointed out some of my factual errors, though he has missed others that I have discovered since publication. The book, it should be said, is based upon several thousand scraps of miscellaneous information, most of it obscure and much of it drawn from sources that were not written with the most scrupulous accuracy, and though I triple-checked each statement of fact some errors were inevitable. Thus where Mr. Main himself has been accurate (which is not always), I gratefully accept the correction.

With other parts of his review, however, I am less happy. Though I feel that chapter two — on factions and areas represented in the Philadelphia Convention to which Mr. Main devotes approximately one-fifth of his paper — is the weakest part of the book, as well as not being entirely germane, Mr. Main's undocumented comments about it seem to me as naive as they

[1] Mr. Main's first review appeared in *The Nation,* June 13, 1959, pp. 538–539.

are inaccurate. Most of his observations here concern Massachusetts. My analysis of that state was based upon the tabulation and mapping of every vote, popular and legislative, cast on state-wide issues from 1781 to 1790, and upon an intensive study of the patterns of internal trade and transportation. And, until he or someone else goes through this material, I shall prefer to believe what I have derived from my research rather than his bare assertion that I am wrong.

Similarly, I am unhappy with Mr. Main's practice of building logical conclusions upon self-contradictory assumptions, and changing his assumptions to suit his convenience. For example, consider the matter of how property holding is supposed to have influenced attitudes toward the Constitution. At the outset he approves Beard's assertion that the line of division for and against the Constitution was between substantial personalty interests on the one hand and real property interests (particularly small farmers) and debtors on the other. However, Mr. Main omits Beard's explicit qualification that what was meant was personality *other than slaves*. Later, he goes on to construct a new definition of division that entirely abandons Beard's fundamental distinction between personalty and realty. To Mr. Main the fight becomes one between rich guys and poor guys. And even as he shifts the main argument, Mr. Main finds it convenient to change assumptions frequently. At one point he is with Beard on the proposition that it is not so much the *amount* of public security or other personalty holdings that counts; rather, what "really" matters is merely having had experience with various kinds of property, as a result of which "even a small holding might well create sympathy" with the needs of suffering public creditors or other personalty groups. Two paragraphs later he changes his mind and decides that what is really important is neither who was suffering nor who had experience with different kinds of property, "but whether Federalists or Antifederalists had more property." As this bewildering display of illogic proceeds, it is difficult for me to understand just what thesis Mr. Main is defending. It is certainly not Charles A. Beard's thesis.

But let us get down to specifics. Mr. Main's first volley, after his critique of my second chapter, is directed against my account of the economic interests of the members of the Philadelphia Convention. He begins with a reluctant admission that my sketches contain "much additional data." But he then forgets this and compares my analysis of the delegates with Beard's, as if we were merely placing different emphasis (mine a distorted emphasis) upon precisely the same data. To substantiate his charge, he mentions by name thirteen of the delegates, and asserts that I attempted to depreciate their property holdings. He made an unfortunate choice. If the reader will compare my statements with Beard's on these thirteen delegates, he will find that I have shown at least eight of them to have had considerably *more* property than Beard had indicated. I found and reported that all four delegates from South Carolina had far more property than Beard had stated: Butler had 112 more slaves than Beard had said (about this, more later); Beard credited Rutledge with only 26 slaves, whereas I show the number to have been 243; Beard records Charles Pinckney as holding 52 slaves, which I corrected to 111, and C. C. Pinckney as holding only 45 slaves, which I revised upward to 70. In addition, I found and reported considerable personal property holdings, overlooked by Beard, in the cases of Houstoun, Wilson, Ingersoll, and Randolph. Yet it is in precisely these cases that Main charges me with twisting Beard's data so as to depreciate the property holdings of the delegates. To quote a phrase used by Mr. Main, "This is absurd." But if he had chosen a different set of delegates, or considered them all, the result would have been the same, since for a vast majority of the delegates I found and reported more property than did Beard.

As to the use of adjectives to disparage property holdings, Mr. Main makes great sport over my characterizing Edmund Randolph as in "great need," "beset with economic difficulties," and, in Mr. Main's words, "impoverished it seems by thousands of acres and over a hundred slaves." Main neglects to tell us that Beard himself described Randolph as a man "burdened with debt," "apparently never very prosperous," and one whose slaves "had long been an incumbrance."

My aim was not to depreciate but to clarify

and fill in the details, details which were, in the main, unavailable when Beard wrote his book. To illustrate, let us consider the case of Pierce Butler, one of Mr. Main's thirteen. Beard described Butler as a plantation aristocrat; so do I (pp. 81–82). But because of the paucity of available manuscripts when he wrote, Beard was able to add only two items of factual information, both of which happened to be wrong. He lists Butler as owning only thirty-one slaves. I corrected this, revising Beard upward, not downward, and showed that Butler owned 143 slaves. But then I went on to add more precise data about Butler's economic affairs during the years 1783–87. Butler was financially embarrassed. Just after the war he had negotiated a large loan in Holland on the security of his very large plantation, but then misfortune overtook him. He suffered a succession of crop failures and it was not until the crop of 1787, harvested and marketed some months after the Convention, that he began to pay off his postponed obligations. From 1785 to 1787 he was rich but a debtor — a debtor, unable to pay his debts — and during 1785 and 1786 his perilous circumstances led him to vote for an issue of paper money, for the Pine Barren Act, and for various other emergency measures for the relief of debtors. Beard's polarization of his data in this instance was, in my opinion, justifiable and probably unavoidable. Mr. Main's effort to re-polarize is neither.

As to the problems that confront a debtor, Mr. Main is extremely confused.[2] The seriousness or safety of a debtor's situation do not depend upon the amount of his debt or of his other property, but upon whether he is in a position to pay when debts fall due.[3] Mr. Main's distinction between "the man of means, who borrows of his own free will, or to avoid disposing of some of his less fluid wealth, and the small property holder, who unwillingly falls into debt, or is forced to borrow from one creditor in order to pay another," is not, as he asserts, "fundamental." It is merely inaccurate. Some of the largest debtors of all are precisely described by his statement about the "small property holder," and many of the small property holders borrowed of their own free will to avoid selling their farms or other holdings. Bray Hammond settled this myth of the poor debtor in his work published two years ago, and if Mr. Main has not read Hammond's work, he should.

Before passing on to the next section of Mr. Main's effort, one might observe that regarding the Philadelphia Convention, Main neglects to mention that in my summary I drew the extremely reserved conclusion that Beard's analysis merely requires "a large number of qualifications." He also neglects to mention that I state (p. 95) that, though the value of the agricultural holdings of the delegates far outweighed their personalty, delegates having personalty interests outnumbered delegates having primarily realty interests thirty-one to twenty-four. He also neglects to consider my fourth chapter, in which it is rather conclusively demonstrated, I believe, that there was virtually no correlation between economic interests and voting behavior in the Convention. One would suspect that Mr. Main is attacking one book and defending another without having read either.

The rest of Mr. Main's efforts are devoted to my chapters on ratification. He begins with another demonstration that he has apparently not read my book. My description of Jeremiah Wadsworth's condition, Main speculates, "is evidently supposed to cast doubt upon his financial position." To anyone who can comprehend the English language, the passage in question, if read in context (pp. 138–140), is a description of Connecticut's economic problems during the Confederation period, pointing out

[2] In his review in *The Nation,* Mr. Main said, in effect, that what counts is not debts but assets. Apparently he thought the matter over between the two pieces and realized what his corner grocer could have told him: that it is neither of these, but the net difference between assets and liabilities, that is the criterion of the economic worth of a man or a company. But apparently he did not give the matter much further thought.

[3] The classic example is seen in the collapse of the so-called Insull Empire in 1932. Middle West Utilities, the Insulls' major holding company, controlled well over a billion dollars of property, and its debts were nowhere near that figure, but it went into bankruptcy because it was unable, at the critical moment in the summer of 1932, to meet a ten million dollar note maturity. Mr. Main might gain some understanding of the economics of the subject on which he writes if he were to study the problems that American business has faced during various periods of financial stringency.

why Connecticut had abundant economic reasons for supporting the Constitution. It forms the primary basis for my conclusion that, with only minor modifications (particularly that the majority of Connecticut's farmers apparently favored ratification), Beard's thesis is applicable in the case of Connecticut.[4]

Otherwise Mr. Main focuses upon my chapter six, concerning ratification in Pennsylvania, Massachusetts, South Carolina, and New Hampshire. As to Massachusetts, I see no point in quibbling, for Mr. Main's efforts are again beside the point. If he will read the "Significance of the Data" chapters which he dismisses without a hearing, he will learn that in chapters eight and ten I conclude that for Massachusetts, as for Connecticut — but only for these two states — Beard's thesis is fundamentally sound, though it can be clarified in numerous details.

As to Pennsylvania, rather than argue with Mr. Main's corrections, and point out where he is often, though sometimes subtly, mistaken, let us suppose that he is correct in every detail. If one applies Mr. Main's suggested corrections to my summary table regarding the Pennsylvania delegates (p. 181), one learns that the Federalists and anti-Federalists were economically even more nearly equal than I had indicated! That is, in every respect except public security holdings, which Beard regarded as the superdynamic element in the ratification. Nothing Main has said is designed to, or could, alter the facts (a) that 73.9 per cent of the anti-Federalists in the Pennsylvania ratifying convention held securities, as against 50 per cent of the Federalists; (b) that the average and mean holdings of the anti-Federalists were far greater than those of the Federalists; and (c) that the twenty-three anti-Federalists in the convention held, between them, securities of a face value greater than those of the forty-six Federalists combined.

In his comments regarding South Carolina, Mr. Main demonstrates that he is no better at arithmetic than he is at reading. First he corrects my lists of merchants, adding Chesnut, Laurens, and Kean as Federalist merchants. Since I do not have available the source he cites for Chesnut, I accept that correction for present purposes. Regarding Laurens, however, Mr. Main is some years out of date, for Laurens had definitely retired from mercantile activity before 1788. As to Kean (whom Main mistakenly says he is transferring from the "unknown" classification, whereas actually I have classified him as a planter), it depends upon the Kean we are talking about. John Kean, merchant (obviously the one to whom Main refers, since he cites the *Biographical Directory of the American Congress* as his source), was born and lived in Charleston; he died in 1795. The other John Kean, a planter (and obviously a different person, since the tax records for St. Helena's Parish indicate that he was alive in 1798), was the one to whom I referred, and he lived in St. Helena's Parish. I assumed that the latter was the delegate to the ratifying convention, since the delegate represented St. Helena's, not Charleston. I may be wrong, but I have seen no evidence demonstrating it. This means that we add 1 merchant, not 3, to the Federalist ranks, and that at best Mr. Main may be 33⅓ per cent accurate, roughly the extent to which he is accurate throughout. But even if he were right in asserting that 3 should be added, that would bring the total number of Federalist merchants to 9, as opposed to 4 anti-Federalist merchants. Nine to four, according to Mr. Main's system of reckoning, is equivalent to 3 to 1.[5] Similarly, from his own table, constructed from my data, he concludes that small planters and farmers in South Carolina opposed the Con-

[4] At the close of this paragraph Mr. Main justifiably takes me to task for saying that among anti-Federalists in Connecticut "less than half as many were public security holders." I should have said that the percentage of anti-Federalists who held securities was less than half that among the Federalists (the percentages were 15 and 35.1 respectively). Upon checking I find that this is what I did say in my first draft, but the important distinction was edited out somewhere along the way, probably because the phraseology in the original was so awkward. The phrasing as it appears in the book distorts the meaning. In another part of the book I did a similar thing, with the result that I said "direct" instead of "inverse" in describing the ratio of one thing to another.

[5] If he will refigure, he will find that his corrections, had they been valid, would have given the Federalists 69 per cent of the merchants. Since they had 67 per cent of the total vote, Main's revisions would actually make my statement more accurate than it is.

stitution, 2 to 1. He does not define small planters and farmers. If this mean those owning less than 10 slaves, the number (according to Mr. Main's table) is 23 anti-Federalists to 18 Federalists. Twenty-three to eighteen is, according to Mr. Main's system of reckoning, equivalent to 2 to 1. If he means those owning 19 slaves or less, the number (according to Mr. Main's table) is 37 anti-Federalists to 43 Federalists. Thirty-seven, according to Mr. Main's system of reckoning, is twice as many as 43. Similarly, regarding the artisans and mechanics in the convention, all 7 of whom were Federalists, 7 to 0 is, according to Mr. Main's system of reckoning, equivalent to 7 to 1. Finally, having arrived at these various ratios by a method unknown to ordinary mortals, Mr. Main is ready for comparisons. To disprove my statement regarding (1) merchants, (2) factors, (3) lawyers, (4) planters, and (5) farmers, Main compares his own ratios for (1) merchants, (2) artisans and mechanics, (3) lawyers, (4) doctors, (5) large planters, and (6) small planters. He thus places his logic on a footing with his arithmetic.

In summarizing South Carolina Mr. Main overlooks two small details: that 68.5 per cent of the anti-Federalists held securities, as against 41.6 per cent of the Federalists; and that 26.8 per cent of the Federalists had borrowed state paper money, whereas only 10.9 per cent of the anti-Federalists had borrowed paper money. Please let us remember that Beard maintained that it was personalty other than slaves, and particularly public securities, that was the dynamic element in the ratification, and that it was friends of paper money who furnished the principal leadership against ratification.

Next Mr. Main takes up New Hampshire. Except for the snide aside that I "concede that public securities were held mainly by Federalists (as a matter of fact I "conceded" nothing throughout; I merely reported the facts as I found them), Main has nothing to argue about here. He does neglect to mention, however, that only 7 of the 104 voting delegates in the convention, 6 of them Federalists, held any securities at all. The interesting thing about Main's paragraph on New Hampshire is that he states that more than half (53 per cent) of the Federalists were farmers, then tells us in the very next paragraph that he has just demonstrated that an overwhelming majority of the farmers in this and three other states opposed the Constitution. (This after having previously suggested changes in the Pennsylvania sketches that would still leave a majority of the farmers in that convention opposed to ratification, and after suggesting no changes whatever as to the numbers of farmers in the South Carolina convention.)

It is by similar reasoning Mr. Main draws the other three conclusions in this last paragraph about the chapter in question. For example, regarding securities: I reported that in Massachusetts, which had a large number of security holders, and in New Hampshire, which had a small number, security holders favored ratification. I also reported that in Pennsylvania and South Carolina, where there were large numbers of security holders, a far greater percentage of anti-Federalists than of Federalists held securities. Mr. Main says nothing even aimed at contradicting this information. But he summarizes what he has said by telling us that he has just shown that "public security holders were predominantly Federal." This paragraph is too ludicrous for description.

After this bit of nonsense, Mr. Main has little in the way of substantive comment, and certainly not enough to warrant further discussion here. Instead, let us consider the paper as a whole. Suppose we assume that even his most fanciful and maladroit claims were well founded; what would be the result? Main concedes that I was right, or close to it, in four of the five states considered in chapter five; he admits that in Virginia (per his own researches), despite my being guilty of making some miscellaneous factual errors, property was pretty evenly distributed between the contending sides; and finally, he allows North Carolina and Rhode Island to go entirely unchallenged. Even if we give Mr. Main New Hampshire, which he does not really claim, this means that Main concedes that Beard was wrong in at least seven of the thirteen states. It seems to me that even if I were as bad as Mr. Main makes out, it remains a certainty that Beard's thesis cannot hold up. After all, a general interpretation that is at best, and by admission of its staunchest defender, more than 50 per cent invalid is not the most universal truth imaginable. The essential point of my book was just that: Beard's fundamental error (not an uncommon one in our profession) lay in attempting to postulate a single, uniform system of interpretation for an event that was just too complex to admit of such.

Charles A. Beard made one great and lasting contribution to American historiography: he pointed out something that should have been obvious, that American political history has not taken place in a vacuum. To convey this simple truth to the diehards in his profession, Beard found it expedient to employ radical means. He polarized his data, almost to the point of suggesting that politics unfold according to mechanistic economic laws, calculable with a slide rule. The great irony is that many of his fellows and followers, lacking his imagination, failed to profit from his contribution because they took for Gospel the means by which he made it. My humble effort was directed at getting us back on the path. Apparently Mr. Main prefers the wilderness.

II

"THAT POLITICS MAY BE REDUCED TO A SCIENCE": DAVID HUME, JAMES MADISON, AND THE TENTH FEDERALIST

The Constitution had intellectual as well as economic origins. The men who led and sustained the American Revolution did so with an appeal to reason and the justification of history; the Founding Fathers drew upon these same sources in their investigation of the constitutional needs of the United States in the 1780's.

Professor DOUGLASS ADAIR, *of the Claremont Graduate School, has contributed greatly to our present understanding of the intellectual bases of the Constitution of 1787. Taking James Madison's famous tenth* Federalist Paper *as his point of departure, Professor Adair has examined both the intellectual problems that faced the makers of the Constitution and the character of their response. He notes the irony of Charles A. Beard's esteem for the tenth* Federalist *in particular. Beard declared that its philosophy of government was the basis for his famous* An Economic Interpretation, *and ever since Beard scholars have turned to the tenth* Federalist *for an explanation of the "ultimate meaning" of the Constitution itself.*

What does the tenth Federalist *say? In it Madison argued that there were two methods for resolving the problem of factionalism — which he, and others, regarded as a principal threat to stable government: remove the causes or control the effects. Any effort to remove the causes, he feared, would entail the destruction of liberty since men would always entertain different opinions and interests; indeed, Madison saw positive virtue in this natural diversity of interest. The proper solution, concluded Madison, was to control faction, rather than to attempt its destruction.*

Madison did not, as Beard suggested, reject theories as unimportant in politics; on the contrary, his tenth Federalist, *arguing as it does that the very size of the United States and the variety of its conflicting interests could guarantee stability and justice in the new Constitution of 1787, represents theorizing of a very high order.*

To Professor Adair the germ of Madison's famous theory of the extended republic may be found in David Hume's Essays. *To both Hume and Madison the study of man — which meant the study of history — illuminated the problems of the present and made possible their resolution for the future. This is not to suggest in turn a slavish attachment to the past on the part of the Founding Fathers; they were in fact criticized for their willingness to experiment — "We know of no instance in History," wrote Richard Henry Lee and William Grayson in 1789, "that shew a people ruled in Freedom when subject to an individual Government, and inhabiting a Territory so extensive as that of the United States."*

Douglass G. Adair, " 'That Politics May Be Reduced To A Science': David Hume, James Madison, and the Tenth *Federalist*," from *The Huntington Library Quarterly*, XX (1957), 343–360.

In June 1783, the war for American independence being ended, General Washington addressed his once-famous circular letter to the state governors with the hopeful prophecy that if the Union of the States could be preserved, the future of the Republic would be both glorious and happy. "The foundation of our Empire was not laid in the gloomy age of Ignorance and Superstition," Washington pointed out, "but at an Epocha when the rights of mankind were better understood and more clearly defined, than at any former period; the researches of the human mind after social happiness, have been carried to a great extent, the treasures of knowledge, acquired by the labours of Philosophers, Sages, and Legislators, though a long succession of years, are laid open for our use, and their collected wisdom may be happily applied in the Establishment of our forms of Government . . . At this auspicious period, the United States came into existence as a Nation, and if their Citizens should not be completely free and happy, the fault will be intirely their own."

The optimism of General Washington's statement is manifest; the reasons he advances for this optimism, however, seem to modern Americans a century and a half later both odd and naive, if not slightly un-American. For Washington here argues in favor of "the Progress of the Human Mind." Knowledge gradually acquired through "researches of the human mind" about the nature of man and government — knowledge which "the gloomy age of Ignorance and Superstition" did not have — gives Americans in 1783 the power to new-model their forms of government according to the precepts of wisdom and reason. The "Philosopher" as Sage and Legislator, General Washington hopes, will preside over the creation and reform of American political institutions.

"Philosopher" as written here by Washington was a word with hopeful and good connotations. But this was 1783. In 1789 the French Revolution began; by 1792 "philosophy" was being equated with the guillotine, atheism, the reign of terror. Thereafter "philosopher" would be a smear-word, connoting a fuzzy-minded and dangerous social theorist — one of those impractical Utopians whose foolish attempts to reform society according to a rational plan created the anarchy and social disaster of the Terror. Before his death in 1799 Washington himself came to distrust and fear the political activities of philosophers. And in time it would become fashionable among both French conservatives and among all patriotic Americans to stress the sinister new implications of the word "philosophy" added after 1789 and to credit the French philosophers with transforming the French Revolution into a "bad" revolution in contrast to the "good" non-philosophical American Revolution. But this ethical transformation of the word still lay in the future in 1783. Then "philosophy" and "philosopher" were still terms evoking optimism and hopes of the high tide of Enlightenment on both sides of the Atlantic.

Dr. Johnson in his *Dictionary* helps us understand why Washington had such high regard for philosophy as our war for independence ended. "Philosophy," according to the lexicographer, was "knowledge natural or moral"; it was "hypothesis or system upon which natural effects are explained." "To philosophize," or "play the philosopher," was "to search into nature; to enquire into the causes of effects." The synonym of "Philosophy" in 1783 then was "Science"; the synonym of "Philosopher" would be our modern word (not coined until 1840) "Scientist," "a man deep in knowledge, either moral or natural."

Bacon, Newton, and Locke were the famed trinity of representative great philosophers for Americans and all educated inhabitants of Western Europe in 1783. Francis Bacon, the earliest prophet of philosophy as a program for the advancement of learning, had preached that "Knowledge is Power" and that Truth discovered by Reason through observation and free inquiry is as certain and as readily adapted to promote the happiness of human life, as Truth communicated to mankind through God's direct revelation. Isaac Newton, "the first luminary in this bright constellation," had demonstrated that Reason indeed could discover the laws of physical Nature and of Nature's God, while John Locke's researches into psychology and human understanding had definitely channeled inquiry toward the discovery of the immutable and universal laws of Human Nature. By the middle of the eighteenth century a multitude of researchers in all the countries of Europe were seeking, in Newtonian style, to advance the bounds of knowledge in politics, economics, law, and sociology. By the middle of the century the French judge and *philosophe* Montesquieu had produced a compendium of the behavioral sciences, cutting across all these fields in his famous study of *The Spirit of the Laws*.

However, Washington's assurance that already scientific knowledge about government had accumulated to such an extent that it could be immediately applied to the uses of "Legislators," pointed less toward France than toward Scotland. There, especially in the Scottish universities, had been developed the chief centers of eighteenth-century social science research and publication in all the world. The names of Francis Hutcheson, David Hume, Adam Smith, Thomas Reid, Lord Kames, Adam Ferguson, the most prominent of the Scottish philosophers, were internationally famous. In America the treatises of these Scots, dealing with history, ethics, politics, economics, psychology, and jurisprudence in terms of "system upon which natural effects are explained," had become the standard textbooks of the colleges of the late colonial period. At Princeton, at William and Mary, at Pennsylvania, at Yale, at King's, and at Harvard, the young men who rode off to war in 1776 had been trained in the texts of Scottish social science.

The Scottish system, as it had been gradually elaborated in the works of a whole generation of researchers, rested on one basic assumption, had developed its own special method, and kept to a consistent aim. The assumption was "that there is a great uniformity among the actions of men, in all nations and ages, and that human nature remains still the same, in its principles and operations. The same motives always produce the same actions; the same events follow from the same causes. . . . Would you know the sentiments, inclinations, and course of life of the Greeks and Romans? Study well the temper and actions of the French and English . . ." — thus David Hume, presenting the basis of a science of human behavior. The method of eighteenth-century social science followed from this primary assumption — it was historical-comparative synthesis. Again Hume: "Mankind are so much the same, in all times and places, that history informs us of nothing new or strange in this particular. Its chief use is only to discover the constant and universal principles of human nature, by showing men in all varieties and situations, and furnishing us with materials from which we may form our observations and become acquainted with the regular springs of human action and behavior."[1] Finally, the aim of studying man's behavior in its comparative-historical manifestations was for the purpose of prediction — philosophy would aid the legislator in making correct policy decisions. Comparative-historical studies of man in society would allow the discovery of the constant and universal principle of human nature, which, in turn, would allow at least some safe predictions about the effects of legislation "almost as general and certain . . . as any which the mathematical sciences will afford us." "Politics" (and again the words are Hume's) to some degree "may be reduced to a science."

By thus translating the abstract generalizations about "philosophy" in Washington's letter of 1783 into the concrete and particular type of philosophy to which he referred, the issue is brought into new focus more congenial to our modern understanding. On reviewing the specific body of philosophical theory and writing with which Washington and his American contemporaries were familiar, we immediately remember that "the collected wisdom" of at least some of the Scottish academic philosophers was applied to American legislation during the nineteenth century. It is obvious, for example, that the "scientific predictions," based on historical analysis, contained in Professor Adam Smith's *An Inquiry into the Nature and Causes of the Wealth of Nations* (London, 1776), concerning the role of free enterprise and economic productivity, was of prime significance in shaping the relations of the state with the American business community, especially after 1828. Washington's expectations of 1783 were thus accurate in the long-run view.[1a]

[1] David Hume, "Of Liberty and Necessity," in *An Enquiry Concerning Human Understanding* (London, 1748).

[1a] The theoretical and prophetic nature of Adam Smith's classic when it was published in 1776 is today largely ignored by both scholars and spokesmen for the modern American business community. In 1776, however, Smith could only theorize from

It is the purpose of this paper, however, to show that Washington's immediate expectations of the creative role of "philosophy" in American politics were also accurate in the period in which he wrote. It is thus the larger inference of the following essay that "philosophy," or "the science of politics" (as defined above), was integral to the whole discussion of the necessity for a *more* perfect Union that resulted in the creation of the American Constitution of 1787.

It can be shown, though not in this short paper, that the use of history in the debates both in the Philadelphia Convention and in the state ratifying conventions is not mere rhetorical-historical window-dressing, concealing substantially greedy motives of class and property. The speakers were making a genuinely "scientific" attempt to discover the "constant and universal principles" of any republican government in regard to liberty, justice, and stability.

In this perspective the three hundred pages of comparative-historical research in John Adams's *Defence of the Constitutions of the United States* (1787), and the five-hour closely argued historical analysis in Alexander Hamilton's Convention Speech of June 18, 1787, were both "scientific" efforts to relate the current difficulties of the thirteen American republics to the universal tendencies of republicanism in all nations and in all ages. History, scientifically considered, thus helped *define* both the nature of the crisis of 1787 for these leaders and their audience, and also determined in large part the "reforms" that, it could be predicted, would end the crisis. To both Adams and Hamilton history proved (so they believed) that sooner or later the American people would have to return to a system of mixed or limited monarchy — so great was the size of the country, so diverse were the interests to be reconciled that no other system could be adequate in securing both liberty and justice. In like manner Patrick Henry's prediction, June 9, 1788, in the Virginia Ratifying Convention, "that one government [i.e., the proposed constitution] cannot reign over so extensive a country as this is, without absolute despotism" was grounded upon a "political axiom" scientifically confirmed, so he believed, by history.

The most creative and philosophical disciple of the Scottish school of science and politics in the Philadelphia Convention was James Madison. His effectiveness as an advocate of a new constitution, and of the particular constitution that was drawn up in Philadelphia in 1787, was certainly based in large part on his personal experience in public life and his personal knowledge of the conditions of America in 1787. But Madison's greatness as a statesman rests in part on his ability quite deliberately to set his limited personal experience in the context of the experience of men in other ages and times, thus giving extra reaches of insight to his political formulations.

His most amazing political prophecy, formally published in the tenth *Federalist,* was that the size of the United States and its variety of interests could be made a guarantee of stability and justice under the new constitution. When Madison made this prophecy the accepted opinion among all sophisticated politicians was exactly the opposite. It is the purpose of the following detailed analysis to show Madison, the scholar-statesman, evolving his novel theory, and not only using the behavioral science techniques of the eighteenth century, but turning to the writings of David Hume himself for some of the suggestions concerning an extended republic.

It was David Hume's speculations on the "Idea of a Perfect Commonwealth," first published in 1752, that most stimulated James Madison's thought on factions.[2] In this essay Hume disclaimed any attempt to substitute a political Utopia for "the common botched and inaccurate governments" which seemed to serve imperfect men so well. Nevertheless, he argued, the idea of a perfect commonwealth "is surely the most worthy curiosity of any the wit of man can possibly devise. And who knows, if this controversy were fixed by the universal consent of the wise and learned, but, in some future age, an opportunity might be afforded of reducing the theory to practice, either by a dissolution of some old government, or by the combination of

scattered historical precedents as to how a projective free enterprise system might work, because nowhere in his mercantilist world was a free enterprise system of the sort he described on paper actually operating.

[2] David Hume, *Essays, Moral, Political, and Literary* (London, 1875). All page references to Hume in this article are to the 1875 edition. Madison apparently used the 1758 edition.

men to form a new one, in some distant part of the world." At the very end of Hume's essay was a discussion that could not help being of interest to Madison. For here the Scot casually demolished the Montesquieu small-republic theory; and it was this part of his essay, contained in a single page, that was to serve Madison in new-modeling a "botched" Confederation "in a distant part of the world." (I, 480–481, 492.)

Hume concluded his "Idea of a Perfect Commonwealth" with some observations on "the falsehood of the common opinion, that no large state, such as France or Great Britain, could ever be modelled into a commonwealth, but that such a form of government can only take place in a city or small territory." The opposite seemed to be true, decided Hume. "Though it is more difficult to form a republican government in an extensive country than in a city; there is more facility, when once it is formed, of preserving it steady and uniform, without tumult and faction."

The formidable problem of first unifying the outlying and various segments of a big area had thrown Montesquieu and like-minded theorists off the track, Hume believed. "It is not easy, for the distant parts of a large state to combine in any plan of free government; but they easily conspire in the esteem and reverence for a single person, who, by means of this popular favour, may seize the power, and forcing the more obstinate to submit, may establish a monarchical government." (I, 492.) Historically, therefore, it is the great leader who has been the symbol and engine of unity in empire building. His characteristic ability to evoke loyalty has made him in the past a mechanism both of solidarity and of exploitation. His leadership enables diverse peoples to work for a common end, but because of the power temptations inherent in his strategic position he usually ends as an absolute monarch.

And yet, Hume argued, this last step is not a rigid social law as Montesquieu would have it. There was always the possibility that some modern leader with the wisdom and ancient virtue of a Solon or of a Lycurgus would suppress his personal ambition and found a free state in a large territory "to secure the peace, happiness, and liberty of future generations." ("Of Parties in General," I, 127.) In 1776 — the year Hume died — a provincial notable named George Washington was starting on the career that was to justify Hume's penetrating analysis of the unifying role of the great man in a large and variegated empire. Hume would have exulted at the discovery that his deductive leap into the future with a scientific prediction was correct: all great men who consolidated empires did not necessarily desire crowns.

Having disposed of the reason why monarchies had usually been set up in big empires and why it still was a matter of free will rather than necessity, Hume then turned to the problem of the easily founded, and unstable, small republic. In contrast to the large state, "a city readily concurs in the same notions of government, the natural equality of property favours liberty,[3] and the nearness of habitation enables the citizens mutually to assist each other. Even under absolute princes, the subordinate government of cities is commonly republican. . . . But these same circumstances, which facilitate the erection of commonwealths in cities, render their constitution more frail and uncertain. Democracies are turbulent. For however the people may be separated or divided into small parties, either in their votes or elections; their near habitation in a city will always make the force of popular tides and currents very sensible. Aristocracies are better adapted for peace and order, and accordingly were most admired by ancient writers; but they are jealous and oppressive." (I, 492.) Here, of course, was the ancient dilemma that Madison knew so well, restated by Hume. In the city where wealth and poverty existed in close proximity, the poor, if given the vote, might very well try to use the power of the government to expropriate the opulent. While the rich, ever a self-conscious minority in a republican state, were constantly driven by fear

[3] Hume seems to be referring to the development in cities of a specialized product, trade, or industrial skill, that gives the small area an equal interest in a specific type of economic activity. All the inhabitants of Sheffield from the lowly artisan to the wealthiest manufacturer had an interest in the iron industry; every dweller in Liverpool had a stake in the prosperity of the slave trade. It was this regional unity of occupation that Hume was speaking of, not equality of income from the occupation, as is shown by the latter part of his analysis.

of danger, even when no danger existed in fact, to take aggressive and oppressive measures to head off the slightest threat to their power, position, and property.

It was Hume's next two sentences that must have electrified Madison as he read them: "In a large government, which is modelled with masterly skill, there is compass and room enough to refine the democracy, from the lower people, who may be admitted into the first elections or first concoction of the commonwealth, to the higher magistrates, who direct all the movements. At the same time, the parts are so distant and remote, that it is very difficult, either by intrigue, prejudice, or passion, to hurry them into any measures against the public interest." (I, 492.) Hume's analysis here had turned the small-territory republic theory upside down: *if* a free state could once be established in a large area, it would be stable and safe from the effects of faction. Madison had found the answer to Montesquieu. He had also found in embryonic form his own theory of the extended federal republic.

Madison could not but feel that the "political aphorisms" which David Hume scattered so lavishly in his essays were worthy of his careful study. He re-examined the sketch of Hume's perfect commonwealth: "a form of government, to which," Hume claimed, "I cannot in theory discover any considerable objection." Hume suggested that Great Britain and Ireland — "or any territory of equal extent" — be divided into a hundred counties, and that each county in turn be divided into one hundred parishes, making in all ten thousand minor districts in the state. The twenty-pound freeholders and five-hundred-pound householders in each parish were to elect annually a representative for the parish. The hundred parish representatives in each county would then elect out of themselves one "senator" and then county "magistrates." There would thus be in "the whole commonwealth, 100 senators, 1100 [*sic*] county magistrates, and 10,000 . . . representatives." Hume would then have vested in the senators the executive power: "the power of peace and war, of giving orders to generals, admirals, and ambassadors, and, in short all the prerogatives of a British King, except his negative." (I, 482–483.) The county magistrates were to have the legislative power; but they were never to assemble as a single legislative body. They were to convene in their own counties, and each county was to have one vote; and although they could initiate legislation, Hume expected the senators normally to make policy. The ten thousand parish representatives were to have the right to a referendum when the other two orders in the state disagreed.

It was all very complicated and cumbersome, but Hume thought that it would allow a government to be based on the consent of the "people" and at the same time obviate the danger of factions. He stated the "political aphorism" which explained his complex system.

> The lower sort of people and small proprietors are good judges enough of one not very distant from them in rank or habitation; and therefore, in their parochial meetings, will probably chuse the best, or nearly the best representative: But they are wholly unfit for county-meetings, and for electing into the higher offices of the republic. Their ignorance gives the grandees an opportunity of deceiving them.[4]

This carefully graded hierarchy of officials therefore carried the system of indirect elections to a logical conclusion.

Madison quite easily traced out the origin of Hume's scheme. He found it in the essay entitled "Of the First Principles of Government." Hume had been led to his idea of fragmentizing election districts by his reading of Roman history and his contemplation of the historically verified evils incident to the direct participation of every citizen in democratical governments. The Scotsman had little use for "a pure republic," that is to say, a direct democracy. "For though the people, collected in a body like the Roman tribes, be quite unfit for government, yet when

[4] *Essays*, I, 487. Hume elaborated his system in great detail, working out a judiciary system, the methods of organizing and controlling the militia, etc. The Scot incidentally acknowledged that his thought and theories on the subject owed much to James Harrington's *Oceana* (London, 1656), "the only valuable model of a [perfect] commonwealth that has yet been offered to the public." For Hume thought that Sir Thomas More's *Utopia* and Plato's *Republic* with all other utopian blueprints were worthless. "All plans of government, which suppose great reformation in the manners of mankind," he noted, "are plainly imaginary." *Ibid.*, 481.

dispersed in small bodies, they are more susceptible both of reason and order; the force of popular currents and tides is, in a great measure, broken; and the public interest may be pursued with some method and constancy." (I, 113.) Hence, Hume's careful attempts to keep the citizens with the suffrage operating in thousands of artificially created electoral districts. And as Madison thought over Hume's theoretic system, he must suddenly have seen that in this instance the troublesome corporate aggressiveness of the thirteen American states could be used to good purpose. There already existed in the United States local governing units to break the force of popular currents. There was no need to invent an artificial system of counties in America. The states themselves could serve as the chief pillars and supports of a new constitution in a large-area commonwealth.

Here in Hume's *Essays* lay the germ for Madison's theory of the extended republic. It is interesting to see how he took these scattered and incomplete fragments and built them into an intellectual and theoretical structure of his own. Madison's first full statement of this hypothesis appeared in his "Notes on the Confederacy" written in April 1787, eight months before the final version of it was published as the tenth *Federalist*.[5] Starting with the proposition that "in republican Government, the majority, however composed, ultimately give the law," Madison then asks what is to restrain an interested majority from unjust violations of the minority's rights? Three motives might be claimed to meliorate the selfishness of the majority: first, "prudent regard for their own good, as involved in the general . . . good"; second, "respect for character"; and finally, religious scruples.[6] After examining each in its turn Madison concludes that they are but a frail bulwark against a ruthless party.

In his discussion of the insufficiency of "respect for character" as a curb on faction, Madison again leans heavily upon Hume. The Scot had stated paradoxically that it is "a just *political* maxim *that every man must be supposed a knave:* Though at the same time, it appears somewhat strange, that a maxim should be true in *politics,* which is false in *fact* . . . men are generally more honest in their private than in their public capacity, and will go greater lengths to serve a party, than when their own private interest is alone concerned. Honour is a great check upon mankind: But where a considerable body of men act together, this check is, in a great measure, removed; since a man is sure to be approved of by his own party . . . and he soon learns to despise the clamours of adversaries."[7] This argument, confirmed by his own experience, seemed to Madison too just and pointed not to use, so under "Respect for character" he set down: "However strong this motive may be in individuals, it is considered as very insufficient to restrain them from injustice. In a multitude its efficacy is diminished in proportion to the number which is to share the praise or the blame. Besides, as it has reference to public opinion, which, within a particular society, is the opinion of the majority, the standard is fixed by those whose conduct is to be measured by it."[8] The young Virginian readily found a concrete example in Rhode Island, where honor had proved to be no check on factious behavior. In a letter to Jefferson explaining the theory of the new constitution, Madison was to repeat his category of inefficacious motives, but in formally presenting his theory to the world in the letters of Publius he deliberately excluded it. There was a certain disadvantage in making derogatory remarks to a majority that must be persuaded to adopt your arguments.

In April 1787, however, when Madison was writing down his first thoughts on the advantage of an extended government, he had still not completely thought through and integrated Hume's system of indirect elections with his

[5] *Federalist,* X, appeared in *The New York Packet,* Friday, Nov. 23, 1787. There are thus three versions of Madison's theoretic formulation of how a properly organized republic in a large area, incorporating within its jurisdiction a multiplicity of interests, will sterilize the class conflict of the rich versus the poor: (1) the "Notes" of Apr. 1787; (2) speeches in the convention during June 1787; and (3) the final polished and elaborated form, in the *Federalist,* Nov. 1787.

[6] James Madison, *Letters and Other Writings,* 4 vols. (Philadelphia, 1867), I, 325–326.

[7] "Of the Independency of Parliament," *Essays,* I, 118–119.

[8] *Letters,* I, 326.

own ideas. The Virginian, nevertheless, had not dismissed the subject from his thoughts. He had taken a subsidiary element of Hume's "Perfect Commonwealth" argument and developed it as the primary factor in his own theorem; but he was also to include Hume's major technique of indirect election as a minor device in the constitution he proposed for the new American state. As the last paragraph of "Notes on the Confederacy" there appears a long sentence that on its surface has little organic relation to Madison's preceding two-page discussion of how "an extensive Republic meliorates the administration of a small Republic."

> An auxiliary desideratum for the melioration of the Republican form is such a process of elections as will most certainly extract from the mass of the society the purest and noblest characters which it contains; such as will at once feel most strongly the proper motives to pursue the end of their appointment, and be most capable to devise the proper means of attaining it.[9]

This final sentence, with its abrupt departure in thought, would be hard to explain were it not for the juxtaposition in Hume of the material on large area and indirect election.

When Madison presented his thesis to the electorate in the tenth *Federalist* as justification for a more perfect union, Hume's *Essays* were to offer one final service. Hume had written a scientific analysis on "Parties in General" as well as on the "Parties of Great Britain." In the first of these essays he took the position independently arrived at by Madison concerning the great variety of factions likely to agitate a republican state. The Virginian, with his characteristic scholarly thoroughness, therefore, turned to Hume again when it came time to parade his arguments in full dress. Hume had made his major contribution to Madison's political philosophy before the Philadelphia Convention. Now he was to help in the final polishing and elaboration of the theory for purposes of public persuasion in print.

Madison had no capacity for slavish imitation; but a borrowed word, a sentence lifted almost in its entirety from the other's essay, and above all, the exactly parallel march of ideas in Hume's "Parties" and Madison's *Federalist,* X, show how congenial he found the Scot's way of thinking, and how invaluable Hume was in the final crystallizing of Madison's own convictions. "Men have such a propensity to divide into personal factions," wrote Hume, "that the smallest appearance of real difference will produce them." (I, 128.) And the Virginian takes up the thread to spin his more elaborate web: "So strong is this propensity of mankind to fall into mutual animosities, that where no substantial occasion presents itself, the most frivolous and fanciful distinctions have been sufficient to kindle their unfriendly passions and excite their most violent conflicts."[10] Hume, in his parallel passage, presents copious examples. He cites the rivalry of the blues and the greens at Constantinople, and recalls the feud between two tribes in Rome, the Pollia and the Papiria, that lasted three hundred years after everyone had forgotten the original cause of the quarrel. "If mankind had not a strong propensity to such divisions, the indifference of the rest of the community must have suppressed this foolish animosity [of the two tribes], that had not any aliment of new benefits and injuries. . . ." (I, 128–129.) The fine Latinity of the word "aliment" apparently caught in some crevice of Madison's mind, soon to reappear in his statement, "Liberty is to faction what air is to fire, an aliment, without which it instantly expires." So far as his writings show, he never used the word again; but in this year of 1787 his head was full of such words and ideas culled from David Hume.

When one examines these two papers in which Hume and Madison summed up the eighteenth century's most profound thought on party, it becomes increasingly clear that the young American used the earlier work in preparing a survey on faction though the ages to introduce his own discussion of faction in America. Hume's work was admirably adapted to this purpose. It was philosophical and scientific in the best tradition of the Enlightenment. The facile damnation of faction had been a

[9] *Letters*, I, 328.

[10] *The Federalist,* ed. Max Beloff (Oxford and New York, 1948), No. X, p. 43.

commonplace in English politics for a hundred years, as Whig and Tory vociferously sought to fasten the label on each other. But the Scot, very little interested as a partisan and very much so as a social scientist, treated the subject therefore in psychological, intellectual, and socioeconomic terms. Throughout all history, he discovered, mankind has been divided into factions based either on personal loyalty to some leader or upon some "sentiment or interest" common to the group as a unit. This latter type he called a "Real" as distinguished from the "Personal" faction. Finally he subdivided the "real factions" into parties based on "interest," upon "principle," or upon "affection." Hume spent well over five pages dissecting these three types; but Madison, while determined to be inclusive, had not the space to go into such minute analysis. Besides, he was more intent now on developing the cure than on describing the malady. He therefore consolidated Hume's two-page treatment of "personal" factions, and his long discussion of parties based on "principle and affection" into a single sentence. The tenth *Federalist* reads: "A zeal for different opinions concerning religion, concerning government, and many other points, as well of speculation as of practice;[11] an attachment to different leaders ambitiously contending for pre-eminence and power;[12] or to persons of other descriptions whose fortunes have been interesting to the human passions,[13] have, in turn, divided mankind into parties, inflamed them with mutual animosity, and rendered them much more disposed to vex and oppress each other than to cooperate for their common good." It is hard to conceive of a more perfect example of the concentration of idea and meaning than Madison achieved in this famous sentence.

It is noteworthy that while James Madison compressed the greater part of Hume's essay on factions into a single sentence, he greatly expanded the quick sketch of the faction from "interest" buried in the middle of the philosopher's analysis. This reference, in Madison's hands, became the climax of his treatment and is the basis of his reputation in some circles as the progenitor of the theory of economic determinism. Hume had written that factions from interest "are the most reasonable, and the most excusable. When two orders of men, such as the

[11] This clause of Madison's refers to Hume's "parties from *principle,* especially abstract speculative principle," in the discussion of which he includes "different political principles" and "principles of priestly government . . . which has . . . been the poison of human society, and the source of the most inveterate factions." Hume, in keeping with his reputation as the great sceptic, feels that while the congregations of persecuting sects must be called "factions of principle," the priests, who are "the prime movers" in religious parties, are factious out of "interest." The word "speculation" that appears in Madison is rendered twice as "speculative" in Hume. (I, 130–132.)

[12] Here is Hume's "Personal" faction, "founded on personal friendship or animosity among such as compose the contending parties." Hume instances the Colonesi and Orsini of modern Rome, the Neri and Bianchi of Florence, the rivalry between the Pollia and Papiria of ancient Rome, and the confused mass of shifting alliances that marked the struggle between Guelfs and Ghibellines. (I, 128–129.)

[13] This phrase, which is quite obscure in the context, making a separate category of a type of party apparently just covered under "contending leaders," refers to the loyal bitter-end Jacobites of 18th-century England. These sentimental irreconcilables of the Squire Western ilk made up Hume's "party from *affection.*" Hume explains: "By parties from affection, I understand those which are founded on the different attachments of men towards particular families and persons, whom they desire to rule over them. These factions are often very violent [Hume was writing only three years before Bonnie Prince Charlie and the clans had frightened all England in '45]; though, I must own, it may seem unaccountable, that men should attach themselves so strongly to persons, with whom they are no wise acquainted, whom perhaps they never saw, and from whom they never received, nor can ever hope for any favour." (I, 133.)

The fact that Madison includes this category in his paper satisfies me that, when he came to write the tenth *Federalist* for publication, he referred directly to Hume's volume as he reworked his introduction into its final polished form. One can account for the other similarities in the discussion of faction as a result of Madison's careful reading of Hume's works and his retentive memory. But the inclusion of this "party from affection" in the Virginian's final scheme where its ambiguity indeed detracts from the force of the argument, puts a strain on the belief that it resulted from memory alone. This odd fourth classification, which on its face is redundant, probably was included because Hume's book was open on the table beside him, and because James Madison would leave no historical stone unturned in his effort to make a definitive scientific summary.

nobles and people, have a distinct authority in a government, not very accurately balanced and modelled, they naturally follow a distinct interest; nor can we reasonably expect a different conduct, considering that degree of selfishness implanted in human nature. It requires great skill in a legislator to prevent such parties; and many philosophers are of opinion, that this secret, like the *grand elixir,* or *perpetual motion,* may amuse men in theory, but can never possibly be reduced to practice." (I, 130.) With this uncomfortable thought Hume dismissed the subject of economic factions as he fell into the congenial task of sticking sharp intellectual pins into priestly parties and bigots who fought over abstract political principles.

Madison, on the contrary, was not satisfied with this cursory treatment. He had his own ideas about the importance of economic forces. All that Hume had to say of personal parties, of parties of principle, and of parties of attachment, was but a prologue to the Virginian's discussion of "the various and unequal distribution of property," throughout recorded history. "Those who hold, and those who are without property, have ever formed distinct interests in society. Those who are creditors, and those who are debtors, fall under a like discrimination. A landed interest, a manufacturing interest, a mercantile interest, a moneyed interest, with many lesser interests, grow up of necessity in civilized nations, and divide them into different classes actuated by different sentiments and views." Here was the pivot of Madison's analysis. Here in this multiplicity of economic factions was "the grand elixir" that transformed the ancient doctrine of the rich against the poor into a situation that a skillful American legislator might model into equilibrium. Compound various economic interests of a large territory with a federal system of thirteen semi-sovereign political units, establish a scheme of indirect elections which will functionally bind the extensive area into a unit while "refining" the voice of the people, and you will have a stable republican state.

This was the glad news that James Madison carried to Philadelphia. This was the theory which he claimed had made obsolete the necessity for the "mixed government" advocated by Hamilton and Adams. This was the message he gave to the world in the first *Federalist* paper he composed. His own scientific reading of history, ancient and modern, his experience with religious factions in Virginia, and above all his knowledge of the scientific axiom regarding man and society in the works of David Hume, ablest British philosopher of his age, had served him and his country well. "Of all men, that distinguish themselves by memorable achievements, the first place of honour seems due to Legislators and founders of states, who transmit a system of laws and institutions to secure the peace, happiness, and liberty of future generations." (I, 127.)

Suggested Further Reading:

There is no recent general history of the period 1776–1789 incorporating the new scholarship in this field. Merrill Jensen's two volumes, *The Articles of Confederation** (1940, reprinted 1959), and *The New Nation* (1950) remain unchallenged except in their interpretation; Jackson T. Main's *The Antifederalists: Critics of the Constitution,* 1781–1788 (1961) is a work of perceptive scholarship sympathetic to Jensen; see also Main's newest work, *The Social Structure of Revolutionary America* (1965). E. James Ferguson has written an excellent study of public finance covering 1776–1790, *The Power of the Purse* (1960). Richard P. McCormick offers a fine account of New Jersey, *Experiment in Independence: New Jersey in the Critical Period, 1783–1789* (1950), as has John A. Munroe for Delaware, *Federalist Delaware, 1775–1815* (1954). The best account of Shays' Rebellion is in Richard B. Morris, "Insurrection in Massachusetts," in Daniel Aaron, ed., *America in Crisis* (1952); this should be read in conjunction with Robert J. Taylor, *Western Massachusetts in the Revolution* (1954) and Marion L. Starkey, *A Little Rebellion* (1955). See also Richard B. Morris, "The Confederation Period and the American Historian," *The William and Mary Quarterly,* 3rd Ser., XIII (1956), 139–156, and Cecilia M. Kenyon, "Men of Little Faith: The Anti-

Federalists on the Nature of Representative Government," *ibid.*, XII (1955), 3–43.

On the Constitution there are two useful general studies, Max Farrand, *The Framing of the Constitution of the United States** (1926), and, more recent, Broadus and Louise Mitchell, *A Biography of the Constitution of the United States** (1964). Justice requires a fair reading of Charles A. Beard, *An Economic Interpretation of the Constitution of the United States** (1913, reprinted last in 1954). The most savage review of Beard is by Robert E. Brown, *Charles Beard and the Constitution* (1956); Brown denies the existence of "propertyless masses" and contends the Constitution was adopted by a society that was fundamentally democratic. Forrest McDonald, in *We the People** (1958) also denies class or sectional motivations but presents much new evidence in discussing the conflicting interests at work. McDonald's recent *E Pluribus Unum* (1965) is a pungent, highly readable account of the emergence of the Constitution, 1776–89. For more on Beard, see Lee Benson, *Turner and Beard: American Historical Writing Reconsidered* (1960). The best study of the historiography of the tenth *Federalist* is Douglass G. Adair, "The Tenth Federalist Revisited," *The William and Mary Quarterly*, 3rd Ser., VIII (1951), 48–67. Perhaps the best collection of essays on the Constitution is in *The Constitution Reconsidered,* ed. Conyers Read (1938).

GENERAL BIBLIOGRAPHY

1. Bibliographical Guides

An extraordinarily useful introduction to colonial sources is *The Harvard Guide to American History,* ed. Oscar Handlin *et al.* (1954). Among other valuable reference works are: Grace Gardner Griffin *et al., Writings on American History,* first issued by the American Historical Association in 1902, and since 1918 published as part of the *Annual Report* of the Association; the Association has also published an *Index to the Writings on American History, 1902–1940* (1956), and its Service Center for Teachers of History has issued Louis B. Wright's *New Interpretations of American Colonial History,* and Edmund S. Morgan's *The American Revolution, A Review of Changing Interpretations* (1958). A unique guide to colonial imprints is Charles Evans, ed., *American Bibliography: A Chronological Dictionary of All Books, Pamphlets and Periodical Publications Printed in the United States . . .* (14 vols., 1903–1959); not as complete as its compiler hoped, this work affords the reader a remarkable barometer of colonial social and political taste. The already considerable value of Evans has been enhanced by Clifford K. Shipton's enterprise in furnishing to universities a microprint edition of all the items listed in Evans which are still extant.

For the English background there are a number of useful guides: see Conyers Read, ed., *Bibliography of British History: Tudor Period, 1485–1603* (1933, rev. ed., 1950); Godfrey Davies, ed., *Bibliography of British History: Stuart Period, 1603–1714* (1928); Stanley Pargellis and D. J. Medley, eds., *Bibliography of British History: Eighteenth Century, 1714–1789* (1951).

Students are also directed to Wood Gray, *et al., Historian's Handbook: A Key to the Study and Writing of History* (1959, rev. ed., 1964).

2. Source Books

There are numerous general anthologies which incorporate documentary materials relating to the broad expanse of American history, but the best — in terms of documentary sources — remains Henry Steele Commager, ed., *Documents of American History* (2 vols., 1963); the best documentary coverage of the colonial period is Merrill Jensen, ed., *American Colonial Documents to 1776* (1955); less recent but still valuable is William MacDonald, ed., *Select Charters and Other Documents Illustrative of American History, 1606–1775* (1899).

J. Franklin Jameson *et al.* edited a different species of source material in their famous *Original Narratives of Early American History* (19 vols., 1906–1917, reprinted 1952). Wilcomb E. Washburn's *The Indian and the White Man* (1964) is a useful documentary survey. A notable examination of Anglo-American sources is supplied by Richard L. Perry in *Sources of Our Liberties: English and American Documents from Magna Carta to the Bill of Rights* (1959; paperback ed., 1964). For further coverage of the English scene, see: Leo F. Stock, *Proceedings and Debates of the British Parliaments Respecting North America* (5 vols., to 1754; 1924–1941); Andrew Browning, ed., *English Historical Documents,* (VIII), *1660–1714* (1953); and W. N. Sainsbury *et al.,* eds., *Calendar of State Papers, Colonial Series, America and West Indies* (1860–96).

3. General Works

A good historian is also a good geographer: the study of the colonial period of American history is greatly assisted by an awareness of historical geography, as furnished by such works as C. L. and B. H. Lord, *Historical Atlas of the United States* (1953), and Ralph H. Brown, *Historical Georgraphy of the United*

States (1948). Also important is an awareness of the more useful reference works in American history: the most accessible are: E. R. A. Seligman *et al.*, eds., *Encyclopedia of the Social Sciences* (15 vols., 1930–1935); Allen Johnson and Dumas Malone, eds., *The Dictionary of American Biography* (20 vols., 1928–1937); Richard B. Morris, *Encyclopedia of American History* (1953, rev. ed., 1961); and Michael Martin and Leonard Gelber, *The New Dictionary of American History* (1952).

If today seems to be the age of the monograph, yesterday was the age of the multivolume general history. It is a testament to yesterday's scholarship that so many of these physically formidable tomes can and should still be used profitably by students of early American history. There are three particularly helpful sets dealing with the colonial period: Herbert L. Osgood's *The American Colonies in the Seventeenth Century* (3 vols., 1904–1907), and *The American Colonies in the Eighteenth Century* (4 vols., 1924–1925); Charles M. Andrews, *The Colonial Period of American History* (4 vols., 1934–1940); and, still in process, Lawrence Henry Gipson's monumental *The British Empire Before The American Revolution* (1936–) — ten volumes are now in print, volumes XI and XII are in press, and XIII is in preparation.

Arthur M. Schlesinger, Sr. and Dixon Ryan Fox edited the first large scale study of American social history, *A History of American Life,* four volumes of which relate to colonial history: H. I. Priestly, *The Coming of the White Man, 1492–1848* (1929); Thomas J. Wertenbaker, *The First Americans, 1607–1690* (1927); James T. Adams, *Provincial Society, 1690–1763* (1928); and Evarts B. Greene, *The Revolutionary Generation, 1763–1790* (1943).

A more recent multivolume series is the University of Chicago's *History of American Civilization,* edited by Daniel J. Boorstin. Thus far in the colonial field there are Howard H. Peckham, *The Colonial Wars, 1689–1762* (1964) and *The War for Independence: A Military History* (1958); the latter work is helpfully accompanied by Edmund S. Morgan's excellent *The Birth of the Republic, 1763–1789* (1956). Richard B. Morris and Henry Steele Commager are the editors of the important *New American Nation Series.* Volumes in this series which deal with various aspects of colonial history include Wallace Notestein, *The English People on the Eve of Colonization, 1603–1630* (1954); Louis B. Wright, *The Cultural Life of the American Colonies, 1607–1763* (1957); Lawrence Henry Gipson, *The Coming of the Revolution, 1763–1775* (1954); and John R. Alden, *The American Revolution, 1775–1783* (1954). David Donald is the general editor of a shorter series, *The Making of America,* in which have appeared Clarence L. Ver Steeg, *The Formative Years, 1607–1763* (1964), and (less successful) Esmond Wright, *Fabric of Freedom, 1763–1800* (1961). All the foregoing volumes include bibliographies that vary in quality from good to excellent; the best are found in the *New American Nation Series.* While obviously regional in complexion, *A History of the South,* edited by Wendell Holmes Stephenson and E. Merton Coulter offers two important volumes for the colonialist: Wesley Frank Craven, *The Southern Colonies in the Seventeenth Century, 1607–1689* (1949), and John R. Alden, *The South in the Revolution, 1763–1789* (1957); Clarence L. Ver Steeg is now completing *The Southern Colonies in the Eighteenth Century.* Finally, attention is directed to the Anson G. Phelps Lectures in Early American History delivered at and published by New York University; among notable contributions in this series are: Leonard W. Labaree, *Conservatism in Early American History* (1948); Thomas J. Wertenbaker, *The Golden Age of Colonial Culture* (1949); Carl Bridenbaugh, *The Colonial Craftsman* (1950); Wesley Frank Craven, *The Legend of the Founding Fathers* (1956); Richard H. Shryock, *Medicine and Society in America, 1660–1860* (1960); and Edmund S. Morgan, *Visible Saints: The History of a Puritan Idea* (1963).

The English have long been devoted to multi-author series, of which the best known are J. H. Rose, A. P. Newton, and E. A. Benians, eds., *The Cambridge History of the British Empire* (7 vols., 1929–1930), and Sir George Clark, ed., *The Oxford History of England* (12 vols., 1934–); in the latter series the relevant volumes are: J. D. Mackie, *The Earlier Tudors, 1485–1558* (1952); J. B. Black, *The Reign of Elizabeth, 1558–1603* (1936, rev.

ed., 1959); Godfrey Davies, *The Early Stuarts, 1603–1660* (1937, rev. ed., 1959); G. N. Clark, *The Later Stuarts, 1660–1714* (1934, rev. ed., 1955); Basil Williams, *The Whig Supremacy, 1714–1760* (1939, rev. ed., 1962); and J. Steven Watson, *The Reign of George III, 1760–1815* (1960).

The present renaissance in colonial studies probably owes much to two developments in the 1940's: the organization of the Institute of Early American History and Culture, and the editorial enterprise of Julian P. Boyd. The Institute publishes the only journal devoted to early American history, *The William and Mary Quarterly*. In addition to monographic publications, the Institute also sponsors a paperback series of *Documentary Problems in Early American History;* see, for example, Edmund S. Morgan, *Prologue to Revolution* (1959), Robert J. Taylor, *Massachusetts, Colony to Commonwealth* (1961), and M. G. Hall and L. H. Leder, *The Glorious Revolution in America* (1964). Yet another series sponsored by the Institute is *Needs and Opportunities for Study,* three volumes of which have appeared to date: Whitfield J. Bell, Jr., *Early American Science* (1955); William N. Fenton, *American Indian and White Relations to 1830* (1957); and Bernard Bailyn, *Education in the Forming of American Society* (1960).

Julian P. Boyd's success contributed to a current editorial vogue: the awesome projects under way for the Founding Fathers. These multivolume editions of private and public papers offer much more than convenient access to vital primary materials; in many cases the editorial commentaries supply unique insight into the culture and politics of eighteenth-century America. Presently in progress are: Julian P. Boyd *et al.*, eds., *The Papers of Thomas Jefferson* (1951–); Leonard W. Labaree *et al.*, eds., *The Papers of Benjamin Franklin* (1959–); William T. Hutchinson and William M. E. Rachal, eds., *The Papers of James Madison* (1962–); Lyman H. Butterfield *et al.*, eds., *The Adams Papers* (1961–); and Harold C. Syrett and Jacob E. Cooke, eds., *The Papers of Alexander Hamilton* (1961–1963). New editions are anticipated for the writings of John Marshall, John Dickinson, and perhaps even George Washington.